Barthes

In memory of my mother, Colombe Samoyault-Verlet

Barthes
A Biography

Tiphaine Samoyault

Translated by
Andrew Brown

polity

First published in French as *Roland Barthes. Biographie*, © Éditions du Seuil, 2015
This English edition © Polity Press, 2017

This book is supported by the Institut français (Royaume-Uni) as part of the Burgess Programme.

ROYAUME-UNI

This work received the French Voices Award for excellence in publication and translation. French Voices is a program created and funded by the French Embassy in the United States and FACE (French American Cultural Exchange).

French Voices Logo designed by Serge Bloch

Polity Press
65 Bridge Street
Cambridge CB2 1UR, UK

Polity Press
350 Main Street
Malden, MA 02148, USA

ISBN-13: 978-1-5095-0565-4

A catalogue record for this book is available from the British Library.

Library of Congress Cataloging-in-Publication Data

Names: Samoyault, Tiphaine, author.
Title: Barthes : a biography / Tiphaine Samoyault.
Other titles: Roland Barthes Biographie English
Description: English edition. | Cambridge ; Malden, MA : Polity Press, [2016]
  | Previously published by Seuil : Paris, France in French as Roland Barthes.
  Biographie, c2015. | Includes bibliographical references and indexes.
Identifiers: LCCN 2016018321 (print) | LCCN 2016027065 (ebook) | ISBN
  9781509505654 (hardcover : alk. paper) | ISBN 1509505652 (hardcover : alk.
  paper) | ISBN 9781509505685 (mobi) | ISBN 9781509505692 (epub)
Subjects: LCSH: Barthes, Roland. | Linguists--France--Biography. |
  Critics--France--Biography.
Classification: LCC P85.B33 S3613 2016 (print) | LCC P85.B33 (ebook) | DDC
  410.92 [B] --dc23
LC record available at https://lccn.loc.gov/2016018321

Typeset in 10.5 on 11.5 pt Times New Roman MT by Servis Filmsetting Ltd, Stockport, Cheshire
Printed and bound in the UK by Clays Ltd, St Ives PLC

For further information on Polity, visit our website: politybooks.com

Contents

Acknowledgements

This book came into being in response to a powerful and persuasive suggestion from Bernard Comment. I owe a great deal to his detailed knowledge of Barthes's work, to his close and generous rereadings, and to his encouragements. May he be, at the threshold of this book, the first to be thanked.

The help and support of Éric Marty and Michel Salzedo have also played a decisive role. This biography would never have seen the light of day without their trust, without the dialogues I enjoyed with them, or without the numerous documents they made available and gave me permission to consult. I am extremely grateful to them. Thanks in particular to Éric Marty for certain very valuable suggestions.

A biography cannot be written in isolation. It draws on information conveyed by both books and word of mouth; it is inscribed within a memory, in both its insights and its omissions. I would like to begin by thanking all those who have talked to me about the Roland Barthes they knew, and granted me interviews: Jean-Claude Bonnet, Antoine Compagnon, Jonathan Culler, Régis Debray, Michel Deguy, Christian Descamps, Pascal Didier, Colette Fellous, Lucette Finas, Françoise Gaillard, Anouk Grinberg, Roland Havas, Julia Kristeva, Mathieu Lindon, Alexandru Matei, Jean-Claude Milner, Maurice Nadeau, Dominique Noguez, Pierre Pachet, Thomas Pavel, Leyla Perrone-Moisés, Georges Raillard, Antoine Rebeyrol, Philippe Sollers and François Wahl.

I would also like to express my gratitude to the critics and scholars whose work has constituted an indispensable and valued basis for my understanding of Barthes's life and work: first and foremost, Louis-Jean Calvet and Marie Gil, who wrote biographies of Barthes before me; also, Cecilia Benaglia, Thomas Clerc, Claude Coste, Alexandre Gefen, Anne Herschberg Pierrot, Diana Knight, Marielle Macé, Patrick Mauriès, Jacques Neefs, Philippe Roger, Susan Sontag and Marie-Jeanne Zenetti.

I would like to thank, in their several institutions, the people who generously helped me with my research: Marie-Odile Germain and

Guillaume Fau in the manuscripts department of the Bibliothèque nationale de France, Nathalie Léger and Sandrine Sanson at the Institut Mémoires de l'Édition contemporaine and all the staff at the Abbaye d'Ardenne who welcomed me on several occasions.

At the Éditions du Seuil, Flore Roumens followed the book as it took shape, with all her talent and enthusiasm; Jean-Claude Baillieul made several essential and detailed corrections. My warmest thanks to both of them.

To all those of my friends who kept me company during my progress on the book, I would also like to express my gratitude, especially: Bertrand Hirsch, Maurice Théron and Damien Zenone, and also Marie Alberto Jeanjacques, Christine Angot, Adrien Cauchie, Charlotte von Essen, Thomas Hirsch, Yann Potin, Zahia Rahmani, Marie-Laure Roussel and Martin Rueff.

Bibliographical note

Quotations from Barthes's works are mainly taken from existing English translations. Where there is no translation published, references are to his complete works in French: *Oeuvres complètes*, new edition by Éric Marty, 5 vols (Paris: Seuil, 2002). These cover Barthes's books, shorter texts and interviews from 1942 to 1961 (vol. I), 1962 to 1967 (vol. II), 1968 to 1971 (vol. III), 1972 to 1976 (vol. IV), and 1977 to 1980 (vol. V). References to the *Oeuvres complètes* follow the format *OC*, volume number (as roman numeral) and page number – e.g.: *OC* V, pp. 634–5.

Archives are quoted in accordance with the French system; i.e. the class number of the Roland Barthes archive in the manuscript department of the Bibliothèque nationale de France (BNF), followed by the number of the dossier consulted – e.g. BNF, NAF 28630. Some documents have the former class number from the IMEC (Institut Mémoires de l'édition contemporaine), where the archives were held until 2012.

The provenance of other unpublished documents is indicated in the notes.

Foreword by Jonathan Culler

In 1979 Wayne Booth called Roland Barthes 'the man who may well be the strongest influence on American criticism today'. Booth did not mean this as a compliment, I hasten to add. He was complaining about the nefarious temptations to which he thought American criticism was succumbing. If Barthes bore the blame, it was because he had done more than anyone else, first, to convey the idea that literary criticism necessarily involves literary theory: conceptions of what a literary work is, how it functions and what readers do with it. And second, with his essays in *Mythologies* on other cultural practices, from wrestling and ads for detergents to the creation of images that become mythic – Einstein's brain or Greta Garbo – he had helped to bring into being what we now call Cultural Studies, in which literary study risked being submerged.

The Barthes who first became known to English and American readers in the 1960s presented himself as a semiologist or analyst of cultural sign systems, in the lively brief essays of *Mythologies*, which are still fun to read today, or in compact essays on works and authors, from La Bruyère to Brecht and Robbe-Grillet, some published in the *Times Literary Supplement* and collected in *Critical Essays*, that discussed literature as a practice designed to upset cultural stereotypes by experimenting with language. (The task of literature, he wrote, is not to 'express the inexpressible' but to 'unexpress the expressible', a tantalizing idea.) As the author of short essays with snappy punchlines, he was the most accessible of those French thinkers, grouped together first as 'structuralists' and then as 'poststructuralists', who were transforming the study of culture. But while thinkers like Michel Foucault, Jacques Lacan and Jacques Derrida pursued ongoing, coherent projects through a series of writings, Barthes was different. He enjoyed announcing the importance of some new mode of investigation or angle of approach, but he was quick to turn his back on the systematic projects he had himself championed – such as semiology or narratology – and write something quite different, in which he often mocked his previous declarations. His most popular books in the US and the UK are his early *Mythologies* and his last book, *Camera Lucida*, reflections on photography centred around a single photograph of his mother. Other unconventional books include *A Lover's Discourse*, which he calls not an analysis but a simulation of the ways a lover thinks and talks about the vexed relation to the beloved, and *The Empire of Signs*, about 'Japan as I imagine it', an alternative to western culture. He is hard to pin down, hard to associate with any particular theory for very long. In some ways, he is both the archetypal structuralist, with his writings on semiology and narratology, and the model poststructuralist, with his rejections of systematizing projects, his love of the fragment and his increasing evocations of the personal and affective dimensions of thought. And the range of interests reflected in his writings is particularly remarkable.

Barthes is a very accessible yet mysterious figure, whose life and projects are splendidly revealed in this magisterial biography, admirably translated by Andrew Brown, himself an authority on Barthes. Tiphaine Samoyault, writer (essayist and novelist) and literary critic, has had access to a lifetime of letters, diaries and notes, and has made good use of them in reconstructing for us the projects, engagements and resistances of this singular figure, whose life always seemed in various ways marginal, until he was elected to a professorship at the Collège de France, the nation's most distinguished institution.

Son of a naval officer, who was killed in action before Roland's first birthday, Barthes was raised by his mother, with whom he lived until her death in 1977. 'His formative problem', he writes of himself, 'was money, not sex', as they scrimped to buy shoes or schoolbooks. Then he contacted tuberculosis, and two lengthy stays in a sanatorium in the Alps prevented him from following normal studies for an academic career and also made him miss being involved in the Second World War, which was formative in different ways for most Frenchmen of his generation. Finally, from 1946 to 1962, Barthes lived by short-term measures with no clear direction or assured job – his time as a cultural affairs officer in Romania, which Samoyault describes in detail for the first time, was probably the most interesting – until eventually he got a position at an academic institution in Paris. One result of these uncertain situations was his readiness to accept almost any sort of writing commission, from prefaces for book club selections to interviews with *Playboy*. This habit continued after the need for these little jobs had vanished, as if, although complaining all the while, he needed the challenge, the intellectual stimulation of an odd commission. In the five volumes of his collected works, the occasional pieces outweigh the published books and reinforce the impression that Barthes was above all a writer – driven by a desire to write in order to, as he once put it, 'construct the intelligibility of our time'. He was above all responsive to the conflicting, often clashing cultural forces of the past and present. 'The full meaning of Barthes's intellectual enterprise', writes Samoyault, 'the full dramaturgy of his career, lies in the way he was always listening to the languages of his period, their difference and the exclusions they impose.'

Tiphaine Samoyault seems to have all Barthes's writing at her fingertips, which is a great boon for readers who might want to follow up this or that intriguing essay. What she gives us is not a biography that places his books in a chronological sequence and summarizes them, but an analysis of his projects in their intellectual context, accompanied by a narrative where no important details are ignored. She begins, in an eloquent and often elegiac Prologue, with the drama – and the puzzle – of Barthes's death (in March 1980, on his way back from a lunch with presidential candidate François Mitterrand, he was hit by a van and suffered injuries first judged not serious but that, given the weakness of his lungs, led to his death). Samoyault rightly judges that a detailed evocation of the man Barthes had become, and his situation in these final weeks, will be particularly engaging, especially since several of his friends wrote about his death in lightly disguised novels. She judiciously sifts through the many writings on Barthes to give us the main assessments of his career, before turning to the life itself and its unusual circumstances. But while providing detailed narratives of key moments in Barthes's life, such as the tense, close-fought contest for election to a chair at the Collège de France, she aims above all to let us see how Barthes develops his projects and negotiates the French intellectual scene, and she chooses to explore his very different relations, some more intellectual, some more personal, with a series of major figures – Gide and Sartre, both important influences – and also his contemporaries – Foucault (who led the campaign to elect him to the Collège de France), Lévi-Strauss (who declined to direct his doctoral thesis), and Sollers (novelist and editor, to whom Barthes was very loyal). Samoyault's biography thus gives us a shrewd, focused and personalized account of forty years of French intellectual life.

One of the mysteries of Barthes is that someone with such broad interests should have found so little joy in life, especially once he had reached a pinnacle of success. Can this be linked to another curious fact, that someone would be attracted to literature who has so little interest in plots and characters (he perversely takes the notational style of the haiku as a model for thinking about novels)? Samoyault allows us to see that what drives him above all is a desire to write that is not connected with imagining scenarios of action, endings, outcomes: when not constrained by a particular commission, he tended to write fragments. I particularly admire her willingness to offer theories and propose explanations without attempting to attribute them to Barthes himself, as biographers so often do ('doubtless he imagined that . . .', or 'he told himself that . . .'). She stresses the radical, transformative character of many of his projects, set against the rather melancholy figure of the man: 'We need to register the violence of the oeuvre, in its striking contrast with the gentleness of the person (all the eye-witness evidence is in complete agreement here) and the relative insignificance of the life.'

This unusual biography explores a whole range of issues and problems that Barthes tackled, and analyses a series of intellectual enterprises and their significance, including his late flirtations with the idea of writing a novel, or at least of thinking and writing about literature *as if* he were going to write a novel. I myself have always been a partisan of the early, structuralist Barthes, who championed the idea of a poetics that would not interpret literary works but would explore the signifying systems and conventions that make them possible, and who offered a host of new ideas about literature; and I have always regretted that he would move on so quickly, abandoning one promising enterprise after another. But Samoyault's probing and illuminating biography convinces me that the affective, often sentimental Barthes, driven above all by a desire to write, who valued writing above its arguments, is not only a figure of great interest but, ultimately, the true Barthes.

Jonathan Culler

Jonathan Culler is the author of *Barthes: A Very Short Introduction*, as well as *Structuralist Poetics*, *On Deconstruction* and *Theory of the Lyric*.

Prologue:
The death of Roland Barthes

Roland Barthes died on 26 March 1980. Lung problems from which he had suffered in his youth flared up again after his accident; in addition, he went down with a iatrogenic infection of the kind that is regularly contracted in hospitals and can prove fatal. This was probably the immediate cause of his death. People tend to remember, however, that he died after being knocked down on a pedestrian crossing in the rue des Écoles, by a dry-cleaner's van coming from Montrouge. This is also true. On 25 February, he was returning from a luncheon organized by Jack Lang: this may or may not have been linked to the presidential elections that were due to be held just over a year later. Lang, the future Minister of Culture, wanted to see François Mitterrand surrounded by significant artists and intellectuals. Or else it was Mitterrand who liked this idea and who entrusted Lang with the task of organizing regular meetings. It was nearly 4 o'clock in the afternoon. Barthes had walked from the rue des Blancs-Manteaux over the Notre-Dame bridge and up the rue de la Montagne-Sainte-Geneviève; he was now in the rue des Écoles, not far from the corner with the rue Monge. He continued down the pavement on the right, almost as far as the Vieux Campeur store that sells hiking equipment. He was just about to cross over to the pavement on the left – he was heading to the Collège de France, not to teach, but to settle the details of his forthcoming seminar on Proust and photography: he would be needing a projector. A car with a Belgian registration number was double-parked, so his visibility was limited. But he stepped into the road and this is when the accident happened. The van was not travelling very fast, but fast enough, and the impact was violent. Barthes lay unconscious on the road. The dry cleaner stopped, the traffic was halted, the ambulance and police (there was a station on the Place Maubert nearby) soon arrived. On the victim they could find no ID, just his membership card for the Collège de France. They went over there to find out more about him. Someone (certain witnesses claimed it was Michel Foucault, but it was actually Robert Mauzi, a professor at the Sorbonne and a longstanding friend of Barthes) confirmed Barthes's identity. Michel Salzedo, his brother, was informed, as were his friends Youssef Baccouche and Jean-Louis Bouttes. They went to La Pitié-Salpêtrière hospital where Barthes had been taken. They found him shaken but lucid. He had sustained several fractures, but apparently nothing serious. They returned home somewhat reassured.

That morning, Barthes had been preparing for his luncheon invitation. As on every other day, he carried out his morning's work at his desk, this time writing a paper that he was to give at a conference in Milan the following week. It was a piece on Stendhal and Italy to which he had given the title 'One Always Fails in Speaking of What One Loves'. His ideas were close to the lectures he had just finished at the Collège de France on the 'preparation of the novel': he was discussing Stendhal's shift from keeping a diary to writing a novel. While Stendhal had been unable to communicate his passion for Italy in his diaries, he succeeding in doing so in *The Charterhouse of Parma*. 'What has happened – what has transpired – between the travel journals and *The Charterhouse*, is writing. Writing – which is what? A power, probable fruit of a long initiation, which annuls the sterile immobility of the amorous image-repertoire and gives its adventure a symbolic generality.'[1] Barthes typed out the first page and the start of the second. Then he got ready, perhaps not entirely sure what had led him to accept this luncheon invitation. His interest in the signs of the social world and people's behaviour in it had already led him to attend a similar luncheon with Valéry Giscard d'Estaing in December 1976, at the home of Edgar and Lucie Faure, and some of his friends had been critical of what they saw as his pandering to right-wing politicians. Now, however, his own leanings and those of his friends and acquaintances made it seem more natural for him to go. But he told Philippe Rebeyrol, then ambassador in Tunisia, that he felt he was being dragooned into Mitterrand's electoral campaign. Who were his fellow guests? Philippe Serre, a former MP for the Popular Front, was not at home, but he had lent his apartment for the occasion, since Mitterrand's place in the rue de Bièvre was too small for this kind of invitation – in any case, it was more Danielle Mitterrand's home than that of the future French President. The composer Pierre Henry, the actor Danièle Delorme, the director of the Paris Opéra Rolf Liebermann, the historians Jacques Berque and Hélène Parmelin, Jack Lang and François Mitterrand himself were all there. There were perhaps other guests whose names have not been recorded. As was to be expected, Mitterrand was a great admirer of *Mythologies*, but he had probably not read anything else by the intellectual who on this occasion was sitting at his table. The meal was a highly entertaining occasion, sprinkled with jokes, pithy comments on the history of France, and witty remarks that roused gusts of laughter. Barthes contributed little to the conversation. The guests went their separate ways at around 3 o'clock. Barthes decided to walk to the Collège de France. He had plenty of time; Rebeyrol had returned from Tunis the previous day, and Barthes and he were due to meet, but not until the end of the afternoon. And it was while he was making his way to the Collège that the accident happened.

Barthes regained consciousness at La Pitié-Salpêtrière hospital. His brother and his friends were there. Agence France Presse issued a first bulletin at 8.58 p.m.: 'The lecturer, essayist and critic Roland Barthes, aged 64, was on Monday afternoon the victim of a traffic accident in the 5th arrondissement, rue des Écoles. Roland Barthes was taken to the hospital of La Pitié-Salpêtrière, as we were informed by the authorities there, though at 8.30 p.m. they had still given no information on the writer's state.' The following day, another bulletin issued at 12.37 p.m. was much more reassuring: 'Roland Barthes is still hospitalized at La Pitié-Salpêtrière, where, we have been told, he is under observation and in a stable condition. His publisher has stated that the writer's state is giving no cause for alarm.' Was this an attempt on François Wahl's part to minimize the gravity of the situation, as Romaric Sulger-Büel has stated, and Philippe Sollers continues to claim?[2] Did the victim's condition deteriorate in a gradual but surprising fashion? The narratives seem to indicate that both elements played a part. Initially, the doctors were not particularly concerned, but it could be that they did not sufficiently take into account the gravity of their patient's lung problems. When he found breathing difficult, he was subjected to intubation. He was then given a tracheotomy, which weakened him further. Sollers gives a more dramatic version of the accident in his novel *Women*, in which, under the name of Werth, Barthes appears just after the accident, bruised and battered, surrounded by all the apparatus of intensive care: 'A tangle of wires . . . Tubes . . . Switches . . . Red and yellow flickers . . . .'[3] For many of those present, there was shock at the brutality of the event, but also a feeling of necessity. It was as if, ever since his mother's death, he had gently been allowing himself to slip away. 'I can still see Werth at the end of his life, just before his accident . . . His mother had died two years before . . . The great love of his life, the only one . . . He let himself drift more and more into complications with boys; that was his penchant, and it suddenly grew more marked . . . He thought of nothing else, though he dreamed all the time about breaking off, abstinence, beginning a new life, the books he ought to write, a fresh start . . . .'[4] He gave the impression that he was at the end of his tether, no longer able to respond to all the requests being made of him. Even his friends and acquaintances who were tactful enough not to refer to his dependence on boys insist on how he felt crushed by the weight of demands, letters, telephone calls. 'He couldn't say no. The more things were a burden to him, the more he felt obliged to do them', is Michel Salzedo's sober view of the matter. The retrospective hypothesis that he gradually let himself die after the traumatic death of his mother has been occasionally put forward: it is either an exaggerated bit of psychologizing, or else the narrative needed to tie up a life's loose ends and give it a definite shape. That the tiredness from which he was suffering was partly the result of his grief and also had all the characteristics of depression is highly likely. But Barthes definitely did not believe in some sort of heaven where he would see his mother again. He was not now deliberately allowing himself to die, even if his intensely poignant gaze, as witnessed by his friend Éric Marty, conveyed such despair 'as if he were the prisoner of death'.[5] Even if you do not give all the external signs of a grim struggle with illness and death, you are not necessarily abandoning yourself to the respite they might bring. As Michel Foucault told Mathieu Lindon when they talked about Barthes's death, people do not realize how much of an effort is necessary to survive in hospital: 'letting yourself die is the neutral state of hospitalization'.[6] You have to fight to survive. 'He added, in support of his interpretation, that people had imagined something quite different for Barthes: a long and happy old age, as for a Chinese sage.' And yet the impression with which he left Julia Kristeva was that he had decided to let himself fade away, as she described it in *The Samurai*, where she depicts herself as Olga and Barthes as Armand Bréhal. And Kristeva still thinks so today. The man with whom she had had such a strong bond, who had admired her so greatly, who had been the president of the jury at her thesis defence, whom she had accompanied on the trip to China in 1974, would no longer talk to her. She thought repeatedly of his voice. His eyes seemed to express abandonment and his gestures farewell. 'There's nothing more convincing than a refusal to go on living when it's conveyed without any hysteria: no asking for love, just a deliberate rejection, not even philosophical, but animal and final, of existence. You feel like a moron for clinging, yourself, to the bustle called life that the other is relinquishing with such indifference. Olga loved Armand too much to understand what made him go with such gentle but unquestionable firmness, but she could only respect his carelessness, his last-ditch nonresistance. But just the same she told him she loved him very much, that she owed her first job in Paris to him, that it was he who had taught her to read, that they'd go on another trip together, to Japan perhaps, or India, or the Atlantic coast, the wind on the island is marvellous for the lungs, and Armand could sit in the garden with the geraniums.'[7] The lack of air, the sense of being sucked into death, is also evoked by Denis Roche in his very fine 'Lettre à Roland Barthes sur la disparition des lucioles' ('Letter to Roland Barthes on the disappearance of the fireflies'), where he writes: '[T]he first thing I hear is that you have fallen onto your face, which is now no more than one big wound; a friend we have in common relates his visits to the hospital and tells me he found intolerable the gesture you had when you waved at the tubes through which life was continuing to reach you, a gesture that seemed to say: "go on then, let's unplug them, it's not worth it any more".[8] Like Franco Fortini at the same time, Denis Roche thought of the death of Pasolini, which Barthes had imagined, a few months earlier, turning into a novel: 'A novel depicting righters of wrongs. The idea of starting it with a sort of ritual murder (exorcising violence "once and for all"): looking for Pasolini's murderer (he's been freed, I think).'[9] Roche cannot fail to think of the Pasolinian dimension of this death, where we are immersed 'in the dark gleam of the *finally discovered* sex of death'. He links it to photography, pointing out that *Camera Lucida* contains only full-face portraits; and he also links it to the appearance-disappearance of the fireflies, one July evening in Tuscany: light-extinction . . . light-extinction . . . light-extinction. . .

In the text he was typing out on the day of the accident, Barthes had described a daydream he had had a little time previously, on the grey, dirty and twilit platform of the Milan railway station. This was in January, barely a month earlier, for an award presented to Michelangelo Antonioni. On 27 January, Dominique Noguez had come to collect Barthes at the railway station and had driven him to the Hotel Carlton ('the brand new, sterile décor of a luxury American hotel, huge and empty: Tati + Antonioni . . . – indeed, this is where Antonioni is staying, too').[10] In his diary, Noguez evoked the 'true lover of cities – of cities at night – already seeking, as it were, to get his bearings, to gauge the favours the cities will bestow on him, to prepare – who knows? – the escapade he will embark upon no sooner than we have left him.' But Barthes had got no further than his dream of setting off on a long journey. He had needed to change trains at Bologna, and had seen a train leaving for the far south, for the Puglia region. On every carriage he had read the inscription 'Milano–Lecce': 'I began dreaming: to take that train, to travel all night and wake up in the warmth, the light, the peace of a faraway town.'[11] This image of a long journey revealing what lay at the end of the tunnel was not just the fantasy of a death. It was also a transition from the greyness of the everyday to the light, figuring the passage from a glum, banal life to a transfigured life, to the *vita nova*, to the life-as-work-of-art. It involved the opposite movement to that of the fireflies: extinction-light . . . extinction-light . . . extinction-light . . . and is thus connected with what Denis Roche says about photography in the homage he wrote for his deceased friend: that it is an interruption in the flow of the single sentence, a little break that means the great caesura of death could be avoided; photos are 'like so many postilions of memory, a

gentle aerial bombardment that precedes each of us in the flow of his
endless sentence, beyond the death of others (Pasolini's death points
to your own, Pound's death to mine, identifying belatedly the date
of another indication on his tomb), a gentle and damp bombardment indefinitely resumed in the open framework of loved faces,
seen full face, obsessed by their mouths superimposed upon others,
the dampness within them, sinking forever into the more general
dampness of the tomb.'[12] You fall on your face, and you can photograph people full face, but it is not so easy to look death in the face.

Barthes died on 26 March 1980, at 1.40 p.m., in La Pitié-
Salpêtrière hospital, next to the Gare d'Austerlitz. The doctors did
not name the accident as the immediate cause of death, which was
brought about by pulmonary complications 'in a patient who was
particularly handicapped by a state of chronic breathing difficulties',
and this is why, on 17 April, the Public Prosecutor's Department
decided not to bring proceedings against the van driver. Barthes had
drawn his last breath. Two days later, his body was placed in a coffin
and shown to a hundred or so friends, students and well-known
figures in a hasty ceremony that took place in the yard behind the
morgue. 'The stunned group which I joined was made up to a large
extent of young people (few of those in their midst were famous;
but I did recognize Foucault's bald cranium). The plaque on that
wing did not have the university denomination "Lecture Theatre",
but said "Salle de reconnaissances" (Mortuary Chamber).'[13] They
did not even feel able to carry out that secular imitation of religious
ritual that consists in reading out texts or uttering emotional and
celebratory homages to the deceased. Some thought that Barthes's
body looked small. Others said a few brief words, such as Michel
Chodkiewicz,[14] who had succeeded Paul Flamand as general director of Éditions du Seuil in 1979. Others present included: Michel
and Rachel Salzedo, Philippe Rebeyrol and Philippe Sollers, Italo
Calvino and Michel Foucault, Algirdas Greimas and Julia Kristeva,
François Wahl and Severo Sarduy, André Téchiné, who had given
Barthes the (minor) role of William Thackeray in his film *The
Brontë Sisters* in 1978, and Violette Morin, together with Barthes's
friends from the rue Nicolas-Houël, where he had spent so many
evenings, just opposite the Gare d'Austerlitz. Some then took the
train to Urt for his burial. One was Éric Marty, who describes the
strange journey of those who took the train because they had
loved this man. 'All I remember of what happened down there was
the pouring, crazy, violent rain and the icy wind that enveloped us,
huddled like a little herd of animals at bay, and the immemorial
sight of the coffin as it was lowered into the grave.'[15]

There were many homages. *Le Monde* published several of them.
A few days after Barthes's death, Susan Sontag's very fine text on
the writer's relation with joy and sadness, and on reading as a form

of happiness, came out in *The New York Review of Books*. The man
whose age you could not really guess had often appeared in the
company of much younger people without trying to pretend he was
young himself: this was appropriate, as 'his life's chronology' was
'askew'. His body seemed to know the meaning of the word 'repose'.
And there was always something a little hidden in his personality,
'always that undercurrent of pathos – now made more acute by his
premature, mortifying death'.[16] As Kristeva would later do, Jean
Roudaut, in *La Nouvelle Revue française*, evoked Barthes's voice,
the rhythm of his phrases, his way of arranging the minims and the
crotchets, and his love of music, a love that was evident in the grain
of his voice. Roudaut described his way of smoking little Partagas
cigars. Above all, he talked about his changing opinions of his own
life and work. 'It was of no importance to him to be well known;
but, through what made him well known, to be *recognized*. And
the aspect of his texts that has the most gravity is the way a lived
experience makes a theory tremble: a voice seeks its body before,
belatedly, it slips into the poignant *I* of the last books. If one writes
in order to be loved, writing has to reflect what one is; there must
be within it a trace of that lack, that place where, even if it is empty,
the appeal to the other is made.'[17] Barthes or the ambiguities: where
was he when he was present? What would his absence mean? Death
reveals to others entire swathes of emptiness or lack that the life
chosen and displayed can no longer conceal. This voice that sought
a body – how would it continue to echo? Several people combined
a homage to Barthes with a review of *Camera Lucida*, notably
Calvino. The immobility of the face is death, hence Barthes's resistance to having his photograph taken. The book became a text full of
premonitions, marked by a longing for death. If this interpretation
appears a little circumstantial, and as such needs to be treated with
caution, it does suggest a truth in which *Camera Lucida* plays a part.
Barthes's inner solitude was indeed at that time echoed by a social
isolation, a sense of being marginalized. The huge sales of *A Lover's
Discourse*, the vogue for his courses at the Collège de France, were
not without negative effects. He was shunned by certain intellectuals, who saw the development of his autobiographical narrative, his
inclination towards the novel and photography, as a compromise
that seemed to some to smack of a desire for worldly success. At
the same time, he had to suffer the distance and even disdain of
many non-academic critics. The book by Burnier and Rambaud,
Le Roland-Barthes sans peine (Roland Barthes Without Tears)[18] did
actually bring him to the edge of tears; the ringing declaration in
his inaugural lecture, 'language is fascist', in 1977, had contributed
to tarnishing his image among philosophers and militant theorists,
who rebuked him for yielding to the siren song of fashion, while
they also denounced him for his political indifference or perhaps,

quite simply, his difference. In particular, his last book, into which he had poured so much of himself and which was the tomb he had designed for his mother, one that he could share with her, met with a lukewarm reception. His remarks on photography were not yet taken seriously. At least, there was felt to be a lack of theoretical clout in them, and people did not dare to tackle the more intimate aspects of the book directly. Indifference as a response to such a display of private feelings is always painful, and any writer may lose the will to live as a result. Even if not all of them actually die, they are all affected.

What did Barthes die of? The question is still, as we can see, an open one, in spite of the apparently definitive clinical diagnosis. Jacques Derrida preferred to emphasize the plurality of the 'deaths of Roland Barthes'. He wrote: 'Death inscribes itself right in the name, but *so as* to immediately disperse itself there, so as to insinuate a strange syntax – in the name of only one to answer as many.'[19] Further on, he described this plural in more detail: 'The deaths of Roland Barthes: *his* deaths, that is, of those close to him, those deaths that must have inhabited him, situating places and solemn moments, orienting tombs in his inner space (ending – and probably even beginning – with his mother's death). His deaths, those he lived in the plural [. . .], this thought of a death that begins, like thought and like death, in the memory of language. While still living, he wrote a death of Roland Barthes by himself. And finally *his* deaths, his texts about death, everything he wrote, with such insistence on displacement, on death, on the theme of Death if you will, if indeed there is such a theme. From the novel to the photograph, from *Writing Degree Zero* (1953) to *Camera Lucida* (1980), a certain thought about death set everything into motion.'[20] This death in life was doubtless there from the start, and it made it difficult to be Barthes's contemporary. Or else it implied living in a different time zone. Derrida, who makes this suggestion, says that he got to know Barthes mainly when they were travelling, sitting opposite one another in the train to Lille or side by side across the aisle in the plane to Baltimore. This heterogeneous contemporaneity could also be read in Proust, in the captions Barthes gave to certain photos or in his last lectures. As he wrote: 'I am only the imaginary contemporary of my own present; contemporary of its languages, its utopias, its systems (i.e., of its fictions), in short, of its mythology or of its philosophy but not of its history, of which I inhabit only the shimmering reflection: the phantasmagoria.'[21] Something of death invaded his life and impelled him to write. Something of the death of the work had found its way into the last moments of the course he was giving. On 23 February 1980, Barthes had resigned himself to abandoning the attempt to make the end of the course coincide with the real publication of the Work whose progress he had been following with his students. 'Alas, as far as I'm concerned, there'll be no question of that: I'm unable to pull any Work out of my hat, and quite obviously certainly not this *Novel*, whose *Preparation* I wanted to analyse.'[22] And he then acknowledged, in notes written in November 1979, that his desire for the world had been so profoundly affected by his mother's death that he was far from sure that he would write any more. Georges Raillard says that, a few days earlier, he had driven Barthes to the École poly-technique to contribute to one of the courses he was teaching at the time. That afternoon, driving Barthes back to the rue Servandoni, he asked him what was, after all, an unexceptional question from one teacher to another: 'What do you plan on teaching next year?' To which Barthes replied: 'I'll show some photos of my mother, and remain silent.'

Almost a year earlier, on 15 January 1979, he had given the sub-title 'Banal and Singular' to one of the entries in his column in *Le Nouvel Observateur*: 'A runaway car crashes against a wall on the eastern ring road round Paris: the fact is (alas) banal. Neither the cause of the accident nor the five occupants of the car, all young, and almost all dead, can be identified: this is singular. Such singular-ity is that of what one might call a perfect death, in that it frustrates twice over what might appease the horror of dying: knowing who and from what. Everything comes down not to nothingness but to something even worse: to *nullity*. This explains the kind of intense chronicling which our society elaborates around death: necrologies, annals, a history, everything that can name and explain, afford a purchase to memory and to meaning. How generous is Dante's *Inferno*, where the dead are called by their names and discussed according to their sins.'[23] Death needs more than a magazine column: it calls out for a narrative.

Death, indeed, is the only event that resists autobiography. It justifies the activity of biography, as it is someone else who writes it. If the statement 'I was born' is autobiographical only in the second degree, because our existence attests to it, because there are such things as identity papers, because we have been told that it occurred, and in such and such a way, it is still possible to say 'I was born': 'I was born in', 'I was born to', 'I was born by'. It is not possible to say 'I died in', 'I died of', 'I died by'. Someone else must say it for us. If 'I was born' is autobiographical only in an oblique or mediated way, 'I died' or 'I am dead' constitutes the impossible limit of all uttering, since death cannot be spoken in the first person. Barthes was fascinated by all the fictions that managed to get round this impossibility, hence his obsession with the Edgar Allan Poe short story 'The Facts in the Case of M. Valdemar', in which the eponymous hero says, at the end, 'I am dead'. Barthes comments: 'The connotation of the phrase (*I am dead*) is of an inexhaustible richness. Of course there exist any number of mythic narratives in which the dead speak; but it is to say: "I am alive". There is here a true *hapax* of narrative grammar, a staging of *speech impossible as speech: I am dead.*'[24] In the case of this death under hypnosis, the voice that makes itself heard is the intimate voice, the profound voice, the voice of the Other.[25] Biographical reason (or unreason) is doubtless here, in the way the Other, the third person, takes over the narrative of death. This is also what fascinated Barthes in Chateaubriand and his *Life of Rancé:* the fact that both of them, the author and the man whose life he was writing, both dwelt on life's withdrawal in its second half, the former because he felt, in the course of his long old age, that life was abandoning him, and the latter because he was deliberately abandoning life: 'for one who voluntarily abandons the world can readily identify himself with one whom the world abandons: the dream, without which there would be no writing, abolishes any distinction between active and passive voices: abandoner and abandoned are here merely the same man, Chateaubriand can be Rancé.'[26] This state of death without oblivion, where one is nothing more than time itself, can be experienced very early on, thanks to two tendencies both of which Barthes himself knew at a very young age: boredom and memory, for memory can offer life a complete system of representations. These tendencies protect from the anguish of death, against which writing tirelessly struggles. Indeed, one fragment from the Urt diary in 1977 is entitled 'The fictitious does not die.' Literature is there to protect you from real death. 'Of any *historical* character (or person), that is, anyone who has really lived, I can immediately see only this: that he is dead, that he has been struck down by real death, and this always seems cruel to me (a feeling that is difficult to express because it is *matt*, a feeling of anxiety at death). Conversely, a fictitious character is one I can always consume with euphoria, precisely because, not having really lived, he cannot really be dead. We must avoid at all costs saying that he is immortal, as immortality remains trapped within the paradigm, it is merely the opposite of death, it does not undo its meaning, the wrench it inflicts; it is better to say: not touched by death.'[27] Sometimes, however, even in literature, the wrench still occurs. These are the moments when the death of a character makes it possible for the most intense love that can exist between two people to be expressed: the death of Prince Bolkonski while talking to his daughter Maria in *War and Peace*; and the death of the Narrator's grandmother in *In Search of Lost Time*. 'Suddenly literature (for it is literature that matters here) coincides absolutely with an emotional landslide, a "cry".'[28] It turns pathos, so often decried, into a force of reading; it expresses the naked truth of that for which it provides consolation.

Death leads to writing and it justifies the narrative of a life. It begins the past over again, it summons new forms and figures into being. It is because someone dies that we can undertake to relate their life. Death recapitulates and reassembles. This is why I have begun this Life with the story of a death. While it breaks away from life, and in a certain way is life's opposite, death is at the same time identical with life as story. Both are the remainder of a person, the remainder that is at the same time a supplement that does not replace anything. 'All those who have loved a dead person survive the wound opened by his death, by keeping him present, alive. Memory then takes the place of an omnipresent time; the cut-off past and the impossible future blur into the intensity of a permanence where I, in remembering, am affirmed in, through and at the expense of the dead person.'[29] These words of Julia Kristeva's were written while she was still in mourning for Barthes, and they express the extent to which this life story is unwarranted: it is not a duty of memory but a constraint of survival. It occupies the place left vacant by the death. In many respects, this limit of all biography is even more of a problem in the case of Barthes. He is the one who discourages the enterprise of biography for reasons that he himself laid down and for others that, while they do indeed depend on him, impose themselves almost in spite of him. For the death of a writer is not part of his life. One dies because one has a body, whereas one has written only in order to suspend the body, to lessen its pressure, to lighten its weight, to mute the unease that it arouses. As Michel Schneider writes, in *Morts imaginaires*: 'So we must read the books that writers have written: this is where their deaths are related. A writer is someone who dies all his life, in long sentences, in little words.'[30] The death of a writer is not really the logical conclusion to his existence. It is not the same as the 'death of the author'. But the death of a writer makes both the life of the author and an examination of the signs of death laid out in his oeuvre possible. This death is neither death-as-sleep, 'where the motionless escapes transmutation', nor death-as-sun, whose revealing virtue 'discloses the style of an existence',[31] as Barthes puts it in his study of Michelet: it is a death that lies at the start of every new entrance.

'Drive more slowly, you might run over Roland Barthes.'

Introduction

The voice

The aspect of Barthes that does not die is his voice. This is a strange phenomenon, since there is nothing more temporary than a voice. You need only listen to recordings from the past to realize this. A voice is soon outmoded, it 'dates' the speaking body. Gide noted this with regard to himself, in his *Journal*: 'The most fragile part of me, and the one that has aged most, is my voice.'[1] But when we hear Barthes expressing himself, we have the very vivid sense of a presence here and now – his voice resists going out of fashion. Listening to the recordings of his courses at the Collège de France, and the several radio and television broadcasts he took part in, the listener finds himself in a familiar environment. The grave, gentle timbre envelops the discourse, giving it a musical inflection. The 'grain of the voice' – and it was no coincidence that Barthes theorized this, as he knew that his own had perceptible properties – bears witness to a past able to act in the present, a continued memory, a recollecting forwards. Thus, what marks most people with the seal of mortality and transience is, in him, the opposite, guaranteeing a form of survival – something that also resides in what he says when he is speaking, of course. His remarks, and not just his voice alone, unite what is general for all with what is true for each person individually, and so continues to touch and persuade us today. This is how the voice counts, by drawing the truth from various and sometimes contradictory sources: intelligence and sensibility, ancient values and contemporary watchwords. This attitude is not without its risks. It often gives the subject a feeling of being an imposter. Barthes felt this all his life: belonging to several times and several places makes you into a person without a place, always in movement. One day, listening to a presenter finishing a broadcast on him with the words 'And now, children, the nineteenth century is over!', Barthes immediately noted down on an index card: 'Yes, I'm from the nineteenth century. And

on this I hang all of my excessive sensibility (which is never visible),
my homology with the novels of that century, my taste for its literary
language. Which means that I am trapped in a cruel paradox: on the
one side "me" (the inner, unexpressed self), the affective imaginary,
the fears, the emotions, the love, the intractable faith in an ethic of
delicacy, of gentleness, of tenderness, the wrenching awareness that
this ethic is insoluble, aporetic (what would it mean to make gentleness "triumph"?), and on the other side the world, politics, fame,
aggressions, pranks, modernity, the 20th century, avant-gardes, my
"oeuvre", in short, and even certain sides, certain practices of my
friends. → condemned to a "hypocritical" oeuvre (theme of imposture) or the scuttling of that oeuvre (hence the desperate tacking
manoeuvres attempted in the last books).'[2] Between two centuries,
between two postulations – the self and the world – Barthes feels
torn; contradictory, like his voice. This is what gives his oeuvre
its powers of prefiguration. The avant-garde and revolt disfigure;
the past refigures and the contemporary age configures. The undecided, paradoxical posture cannot adapt to clear-cut gestures. Quite
the opposite: it arouses a sense of unease, a way of being a misfit that
leads one to seek completely new solutions in order to exist all the
same, to be of one's time in spite of everything. This quest, which
sometimes took a shape so impetuous that Barthes brought upon
himself the charge of opportunism or fickleness, defines the condition of the precursor, the one who runs on ahead. Literally, he goes
ahead of fashions, proposals and movements. More abstractly, he
also opens a path for thinking about a new order of the world and
our knowledge of it. The end of the book, the extension of the sphere
of the biographical, the fragment, the withdrawal from logical argument, the use of hypertext, the new mechanography of memory:
these are some of the questions Barthes explored and that make his
oeuvre a field to explore today. Like all great thinkers, his powers of
anticipation were as great as the mark he left upon his time: if we still
read him today, this is because his criticism took new paths.

   The voice, in Barthes, is a constant biographical feature. It unites
all those who knew him into a unanimous group, all acknowledging the 'beautiful voice' he had. His voice has become his mark,
his monogram. This sign has the advantage that it can bear at once
absence and presence, the body and discourse. It sums up the prolonged resonance of a critical thinking for our time. For Barthes,
indeed, everything is a matter of tact and timbre. It cannot rest
content with being in discord with his age, as this would produce
a dissonance. It is one thing to love the nineteenth century and the
classics, to feel that one is sentimental and romantic; but to be sensitive to contemporary languages, showing that they can no longer,
or barely, tolerate these past effects is quite another thing. The full
meaning of Barthes's intellectual enterprise, the full dramaturgy of

his career, lies in the way he was always listening to the languages of his period, their difference and the exclusions they impose. This does not mean that we have to give up loving what we have loved of the past, either by reactivating the force of its modernity, the life still living within it, or by condemning ourselves to a certain solitude. Always we find the same oscillation between affirmation and withdrawal, aggression and gentleness. On 21 September 1979, looking back over his itinerary, Barthes noted: 'The only problem in my active, intellectual life has been to bring together intellectual invention (its ebullience), the constraint of the Modern, etc., and maternal values that have to be superimposed on this: like anchoring points.'[3] This problem defined his specific place, both participating fully in his own times and yet feeling always somewhat to one side. The paradox of a politically committed solitude also explains how Barthes shook up the institutions of knowledge. This considerable contribution was, for Foucault, what legitimated Barthes's status as a precursor: 'He was definitely the one who most helped us to shake up a certain form of academic knowledge that was non-knowledge. [. . .] I think that he's someone very important when it comes to understanding the dramatic changes that have been taking place over the last ten years. *He was the greatest precursor.*'[4]

'Life'

It is not absolutely necessary to produce a life story in order to shed light on Barthes's intellectual programme and contribution, and people may wonder why there is any need for a new biography. Among the main reasons that make it difficult to relate his life story is the feeling that there is not a great deal to be learned from such a narrative today. The huge effort put into editing Barthes's unpublished work since the early 1990s by Éric Marty and others has considerably increased the autobiographical heft of his oeuvre. With *The Preparation of the Novel*, *Mourning Diary* and *Le Lexique de l'auteur*, many facets of Barthes's life have been illuminated in succession. And if the main biographical reason appears in removing obscurities, discovering what was missing, and laying bare what was hidden, what meaning can there be in doing so for an author who sought increasingly to gain in clarity? Reading the vast number of index cards, taking into account the desk diaries and notebooks, allows us now to say that, for the period in which Barthes was becoming Barthes, every moment of his life is detailed. With an author who himself aimed at clarity, and did so without succumbing to the illusion of synthesis or a continuous narrative, how can we show the lacuna and the fragment, which are there right from the start, as adequate forms? There are three solutions, all equally flawed and disappointing. The first consists in going into ever more detail, correcting the narratives, and rectifying the facts: this is competitive and thus futile. It might show that in certain parts of the oeuvre, the author has turned his life into a legend, while in other places he has concealed great swathes of activity. But this narrative would never win out *against* the narrative put forth in the oeuvre, since life, though it may not always be what one says of it, remains what one does with it. Papering over the cracks, the second solution, is not a satisfactory method either. Biographical prose inserts the glue of continuous duration between fragments made of facts, emotions and texts, thereby denying the intimate truth of life, made up as it often is by juxtaposed moments, and crisscrossed by events, by large or small changes of direction, and by things forgotten. And the third solution, explaining the life by the work, is not viable either. It melds two heterogeneous realities together, forgetting to show how they may be rivals, sometimes clashing and sometimes even destroying one another. While a biographical reading can be justified and may produce significant results, it is of insufficient help when it comes to the sometimes conflictual encounter between living and writing in the existence of a writer and an intellectual.

Of course, I will not be able to manage entirely without these three approaches, and my work will also draw on these methods and will share their failings; but I shall at the same time be attempting to let the clarity proper to the oeuvre shine with its own living light, showing how it comes into bright being and sheds its gleam. The narrative will be conducted under the sign of gaps and omissions, and the argument will attempt to think through differences. We need to register the violence of the oeuvre, in terrible contrast as it is with the gentleness of the person (all the eye-witness evidence is in complete agreement here) and the relative insignificance of the life. For Barthes's life was not an adventure story. It was not even exemplary: it did not have the generality or normality that might give a sociological or cultural value to biography. How can one write a life that was fully occupied in writing alone? What is left over from the traces in the texts and what type of revelation do we have a right to expect? The first revelation is probably this one: a writer's life can be understood from the lacks which underlie it.

One difficulty lies in Barthes's own ambivalence about biography, which he stated forcefully in his prefatory remarks to the interview with Jean Thibaudeau: 'Any biography is a novel which dares not speak its name.'[5] It is not as if he had always despised biography, or as if, like Bourdieu, he had denounced it as an illusion.[6] True, he leaves 'Racine as an individual' out of it, but he treats authors (Michelet, Racine and Sade, for example) as places for experimentation and assemblage. Throughout his texts, he demonstrates a desire for signs of life that largely determine his almost sensual attachment to literature. The notations that, after 1971, in *Sade, Fourier, Loyola*, he called 'biographemes' are those shards of life, of singularity, that point us to the bodies of the subjects mentioned. A person consists in details and in their scattering, 'somewhat like the ashes we strew into the wind after death'.[7] These biographemes define an art of memory linked to an ethic of biography often mentioned by Barthes's commentators: 'Were I a writer, and dead, how I would love it if my life, through the pains of some friendly and detached biographer, were to reduce itself to a few details, a few preferences, a few inflections, let us say: to "biographemes" whose distinction and mobility might go beyond any fate and come to touch, like Epicurean atoms, some future body, destined to the same dispersion.'[8] These famous words provide us with the programme for a life story that is less that of a biography than that of the 'amnesiac' autobiography of *Roland Barthes by Roland Barthes*, where the anamnesis, directly contrasted with biography, is defined as a 'counter-march' or 'counter-descent': '[. . .] a (hostile) challenge to chronology, to the false rationality of the logico-chronological, the *ordo naturalis*: it is an *ordo artificialis* (flash-back).'[9] It is all there, unconnected, unyoked, as a fragment or trace. Polyphonic, opened up to the infinite process of re-composition, it turns any continuous narrative into a form of 'obscenity' (the French word *cochonnerie*, or swinishness, is used in *Sade, Fourier, Loyola* to refer to the *flumen orationis*, the fluvial aspect of continuous discourse) because it fixes an image, because it forgets that the self is forever shifting and inventing itself. By turning Barthes's own self-portrait into a fetish text, many readers see biography as the most anti-Barthesian of gestures.[10]

And yet, what Barthes held up in contrast to continuity was still a quest for unity. On Michelet, he wrote: 'I have sought merely to describe a unity, not to explore its roots in history or in biography'.[11] It is, conversely, by pluralizing Barthes that we will compensate for the spirit of continuity inherent in the life story – not seeking any homology between the life and the work, but including both of them within stories and histories (here, too, in the plural), contexts and relations, and describing different kinds of genesis – the strata of archives, the things which life deposits within the documents of the real, the leitmotifs and refrains of the oeuvre. If biographemes are to biography what photos are to History, as Barthes seems to suggest in *Camera Lucida*,[12] we will complement the biographemes with *legends*, linking them up or binding them together, drawing out the ideas within them. What is left – events, writings and traces – can be appropriated only in writing, in other words in the movement of a thought.

The writer of a biography might have been discouraged by other external reasons, beginning with the amount of work that has been done on the author, during his lifetime and since his death, both

in France and abroad. It is striking that Barthes's own reservations about biography should have entailed a veritable passion,
among critics, commentators and writers, for his life. The term
'Rolandism' has even been coined to describe this drive to view
the author as a character in a novel or to relate his life. In the very
fine lecture he gave at the Collège de France on 19 October 1978,
called 'Longtemps, je me suis couché de bonne heure . . .', Barthes
suggested the name 'Marcelism' for the special interest readers can
take in the life of Marcel Proust, distinct from any liking they might
have for his style or his oeuvre.[13] This loving approach to the author
is made via the *disoriented* narrative he gave of his own life in his
oeuvre. In the same way, we can use the term 'Rolandism' to refer
to this relation with a subject who returns endlessly to his own life
as to a succession of figures. The profound relation between life and
writing that is tirelessly staged in the books, lectures and seminars is
one explanation for the interest many readers take in Barthes's life:
as if there were some magic key there, some spell that would open
up several doors at once, the door of his personal quest and the door
of the desire for writing that everyone harbours. Another reason
for the wish to turn his life into a 'Life' is probably the fact that
Barthes's life is an accumulation of all the gaps one can imagine –
gaps that always cry out to be filled. The initial lack was the father's
death; the parenthesis, the sanatorium; the concealed dimension,
homosexuality; the discontinuous element, fragmentary writing;
while the final lack was the silly road accident. These holes, these
lacunae, require a narrative, a filling, an explanation.

Biographies, eye-witness accounts, critical investigations that
also trace out a life, novels: the books that refer to Barthes's life
are now legion. Thirty-five years after Barthes's death, the present
biography is already the third to be published. In 1990, Louis-Jean
Calvet produced a first complete 'Life' of Barthes.[14] As the book
came out so soon, it could be based on many eye-witness accounts.
Barthes's various milieus – family, intellectual circles, friends – are
described in a detailed, vivid way. Calvet's work is not an intellectual biography as such: while it studies the genesis of the work and
offers explanations for it, that oeuvre is not grasped as a project of
thought and writing. A second biography, by Marie Gil, saw the
light in 2012. In it, the author takes literally the idea of *life as a
text*, one that appeared often in Barthes's seminars and was linked
to the diary.[15] The continuity is not the naive one of a life that can
be unwound like a ribbon, but it appears in the homogeneity that
is suggested between text and factual existence. Within this context,
it is also a matter of highlighting the 'graphy' of a life,[16] placing
writing and life on the same level, and affirming 'the homogeneity
of all the materials [. . .]: facts, thoughts, writings, and that which
is unsaid, the silences'.[17] As well as these biographies, there are

various eye-witness accounts. In 1991, Patrick Mauriès published a collection of memories staging different aspects of the personality of Barthes as a teacher and *maître à penser* for the young.[18] In 2006, Éric Marty published his own work, presented as an essay and gathering texts of argumentative prose that shed a great deal of light on the notion of the 'oeuvre' and the idea of the 'image'.[19] But Barthes's oeuvre is also discussed in terms of its unfolding, its sequence, in order to explain its intellectual genesis. The first part, 'Memory of a Friendship', is an extremely powerful set of memories of Barthes's final years. Marty, who devoted several years to the editing and publication of Barthes's complete works, is also the best transmitter of his life and thought so far. In books of interviews and memories, Tzvetan Todorov and Antoine Compagnon describe at length the Barthes they had known. Gérard Genette also paints his portrait in *Bardadrac*, and Barthes is one of the numerous secondary characters in Mathieu Lindon's book on Foucault, *Ce qu'aimer veut dire* (*What love means*).[20] Colette Fellous, in *La Préparation de la vie* (*Preparation for life*) paints a very loving portrait (full of rare odours – the perfume of Barthes's mother, for example – and of the grain of his voice) of the man who remained her guide in life from the day when, coming out of a seminar (she had followed all of them between 1972 and 1976), he taught her to say 'I', to speak in her own name. 'I follow his voice', she writes, 'and I rediscover the odour of Paris, of the Bonaparte and Balzar cafes, of the rue du Sabot, of the rue Saint-Sulpice, of the little Chinese restaurant in the rue de Tournon. I also rediscover the way his eyes wrinkled when he was trying to find the right words.'[21]

What is perhaps even stranger is the way Barthes has, since his death, become a character in a great many novels.[22] Here too, the explanation lies in a wish to give continuity to his life – to make it continuous and to extend it – but also, no doubt, in the way Barthes set up an interplay between essay, autobiographical fragment and the desire for the novel. The 'burning contact with the Novel' that he presented in the lecture on Proust as the power to express an effective order, the words 'It must all be considered as if spoken by a character in a novel' at the threshold of *Roland Barthes by Roland Barthes*, the oeuvre-as-life, also called a 'third form', the novelistic (*romanesque*) as a way of dividing up the real, as a writing of life: these suggestions comprise an appeal and, at the same time, a puzzle. The eye-witness accounts are extended, and the legend accentuated, in such works as *Women* by Sollers, first published in French in 1983; Renaud Camus's *Roman roi* (*Novel king*), published the same year; Kristeva's *The Samurai*, first published in 1990; *L'Homme qui tua Roland Barthes* (*The man who killed Roland Barthes*) by Thomas Clerc (2010); and *La Fin de la folie* (*The end of madness*) by Jorge Volpi (2003). The same is true of two novelized accounts of Barthes's last days and his first days too, and the account of one of his summers.[23] Some represent Barthes under transparent pseudonyms; others make him a character under his own name, introducing him into the fiction as a historical character rubbing shoulders with the fictitious characters. In every case, these texts cross the borders between novelized biography, historical novel and eye-witness account.

Even critical studies play on the interlacing of thought, life and novel, and often rest on the account of an intellectual career forced to convey the story of a life. As early as 1986, Philippe Roger's *Roland Barthes, roman* showed a certain continuity to Barthes's career by taking a close interest in the early texts and insisting on the omnipresence in Barthes of a great literary project that made any attempt to split his oeuvre into periods futile. In 1991, Bernard Comment's *Roland Barthes, vers le neutre* (*Roland Barthes, towards the neuter*) also saw the unity of the subject as resting upon the coherence of a certain project, this time 'the Neutral, understood not as a compromise, a lessened form, but as an attempt to escape from the obligations and constraints of the logos, of Discourse'.[24] This portrait of an intellectual endeavouring to abolish distinctions was destined to be a landmark.[25] The projective dimension of Barthes's texts, their relation to the fragmentary and to note form, the love of the fleeting and the paradoxical, make this coherence compatible with contradiction, hesitation and even palinode. To base one's authority as a teacher on phantasy is to free oneself from the principle of non-contradiction; it is to draw oneself and others into a whirlpool where it is very difficult to find any foothold. While he never produced any system, any 'strong thought', Barthes shaped his pupils and his readers by showing the need to place different forms of knowledge in tension, to detach oneself, to develop a culture of affects, to encounter the improbable. Finally, whether they put forward the hypothesis of a coherent Barthes whose endeavours follow a guiding principle, as do Philippe Roger, Bernard Comment, Gérard Genette, Claude Costa, Diana Knight, Marielle Macé and Vincent Jouve, or whether they imagine a Barthes cut in two, abandoning the great scientific project of the 1960s so as to enter a time of scepticism and egotism (this is Todorov's point of view), or else of a Barthes of *several* identities, whose itinerary was shared out in successive moments (Annette Lavers, Stephen Heath, Steven Ungar, Patrizia Lombardo), all of them show how complex is that oeuvre inseparable from the life in which it was composed and written.

While seeking to conceptualize the difference between living, thinking and writing, I will in my turn postulate the unity of Barthes's career as lying in the desire to write, which appeals to a potential intellectual project and an erotic dimension (accepting, too, the liking for change). But this unity is based on caesuras and lacks that create breaks and turnabouts. It is also subject to phenomena of discord, which make Barthes the contemporary of several times at once. Preferring to follow the 'otobiographical' project of Jacques Derrida and his dramaturgy of critical listening,[26] I will be pricking up my ears to hear how the grain of Barthes's voice also shaped his writing, but in a fundamentally discontinuous way. By presenting various types of raw material (the immense number of index cards, unpublished manuscripts, letters, notes made in desk diaries), I will make the work tremble under the impact of echoes from the outside world. In turn, the work will regularly displace the life story, shedding light and darkness on it in turn, sometimes giving it a shape, sometimes restoring it to shapelessness. Certain words will act as guiding threads: gentleness, delicacy, the heart-rending . . . and maternal love as the underground guide to the whole journey. On the other side lies the obsession with death, which impels one to write but also frequently inflicts great gashes on life. Among the principles guiding my narrative will be the desire to give the rhythm and movement of writing its vital dynamism, inscribed in breathing, in the body, in the vicissitudes of existence. This involves departing from the logic of books, the logic through which we most often envisage Barthes, so as to enter the time of production of his ideas and texts. Barthes did not give the book as a finite object closed in on itself any great significance, except in that it was still, in his day, an important instrument for the spreading of ideas and the winning of recognition. In one way, Barthes foresaw the book's disappearance; or at least, his relationship to writing prefigured other ways of expressing ideas and spreading texts. Most of his books are collections of articles published in reviews several years earlier and, by the time they were published, Barthes was often haunted by other questions. Situating oneself in the time of writing sometimes allows us to shed new light on the oeuvre, to perceive from within an intellectual history while revealing its power to reflect our age. Thus, my book will follow chronological order; but to make sure it does not try to pass itself off as the natural way of proceeding, I will make the order of years yield at times to other principles. Parallels between Barthes and the decisive companions of his existence allow us, as required, to examine the relevant leitmotifs as and when Barthes encountered certain people, and not just in accordance with the order of years – for themes sometimes bring together texts and facts. Thus, certain years may be discussed twice over, in distinct chapters, but this is always so as to shed a somewhat different light on them, to put them in a different perspective.

I have been granted access to a quite considerable amount of completely new material in writing this biography: a significant portion of the correspondence, all the manuscripts, and above all the index cards which Barthes added to throughout his life, subjecting them to various classifications and re-workings. These index cards, which Barthes began as a student, using them as a bibliographical and then lexicographical resource, gradually became the place where he recorded a great deal of his life. In them, he assembled things he had seen and heard, travel impressions, phrases that he liked, ideas and plans. In the last two years of his life, the index cards became a veritable diary; thus, to designate what in the Fonds Roland Barthes is called the 'Grand fichier', I regularly use the expression *fichier-journal*, or 'index-card diary', which seems to correspond to his own hybrid use, one that he had invented himself. Michel Salzedo, Barthes's brother, opened the doors of Barthes's office in the rue Servandoni to me and authorized me to consult the desk diaries that Barthes used in a strange but persistent way from 1960 until his death. He did not use them in a prospective fashion, to note his meetings and his obligations for the next few days, but as an account book, in which he retrospectively noted the work he had completed, and the people he had met the day before.[27] These volumes, like the index cards, pave the way to an altogether enthralling practice of ordinary, everyday writing. And these documents, almost none of which have been published, provide us with important bases for the story of his life. They can also be burdensome at times: the need to note down one's life can make the labour of biography futile. At the same time, they invite us to seek other things than just facts, and to take account of the many spheres – public, semi-public, and private – in which writing is deployed.

I am not one of Barthes's contemporaries. I was 11 when he died and it was not until six years later that I heard his name for the first time in a philosophy class where I had been asked to read *The Pleasure of the Text*. So I did not attend his lectures and most of his experiences are not known to me. However, Barthes is indeed my contemporary because I know that I owe to him a way of reading literature, the relationship that I am weaving between criticism and truth, and the conviction that thought proceeds from writing. By relating the story of the various paths he followed, existential, intellectual and literary, I am seeking to understand a part of what has shaped me and, at the same time, what made this shaping possible. When he died, Barthes felt that he had reached a turning-point in his life, but he did not think it was almost all over. The imperative of the *vita nova*, so obvious in the last seminars and a consequence of his mother's death, implied less the idea of a downward slope than that of a new inflection to be given to his plans, a last stage of life to be discovered. In his lecture on Proust on 19 October 1978, he reflected on the major breaks that affect the 'middle of life': that of Rancé, who abandons the world after discovering the decapitated body of his mistress and retires to the monastery at La Trappe; and that of Proust, when he lost his own mother. This justifies, in Barthes's lecture, the possibility of a 'Proust and I' bringing together in one and the same event the deaths of mothers: 'A cruel bereavement, a unique and somehow irreducible bereavement can constitute for me that "pinnacle of the particular" Proust spoke of; though belated, this bereavement will be for me the middle of my life; for the "middle of life" is perhaps never anything but the moment when you discover that death is real, and no longer merely dreadful.'[28] I was reading Barthes's *Mourning Diary* on the day in February 2009 when I lost my own mother. I felt that I too was in the middle of the way. This was sign enough for the work to begin.

1

Setting off

Lost in a box of biographical and administrative documents from the Roland Barthes archives in the Bibliothèque nationale are seven sheets of manuscript, torn in half then roughly taped back together: the tranquil written attempt at autobiography, or the still living remembrances of a memory full of holes, a 'fragmentary memory' as the subtitle indicates. They may represent, as Anne Herschberg Pierrot suggested when she published them in *Le Lexique de l'auteur*,[1] a first version of the 'Anamneses' we find in *Roland Barthes by Roland Barthes*.[2] But we can also see them as the opposite and antagonistic form of these 'Anamneses', the only time the author ever tried to set out a continuous biographical account of himself. The anamnesis, which is defined as an operation that tears you apart, marking the division within the subject, does, after all, imply a violent discontinuity. It is excerpted from the narrative, cut out of it, so to speak, and displaced from the chronology of a life.

1915: I am born, they tell me, on 12 November at 9 a.m., in Cherbourg, a mere garrison station for my father, an officer in the Merchant Navy who has been mobilized as a naval ensign.

1916: My father is in command of a trawler (the *Montaigne*) patrolling the North Sea; on 28 October [*sic*], sailing off Cap Gris-Nez, his boat is sunk by the Germans.

1915 [*sic*]–1924: my widowed mother retires to Bayonne, where my grandparents on the Barthes side live (my grandfather, my grandmother and my aunt Alice, a piano teacher); [. . .] With my mother, we live in Marracq, a still quite rural part of Bayonne. Every Sunday we go to lunch at my grandparents': **in the evenings, we come home by tram, and both have dinner together in the bedroom, beside the fire – soup and toast**; a young Basque woman, Marie Latxague, looks after me. I play with the middle-class children from this part of town, Jean and Linette de Lignerolles, the Rime children, Julien Garance, Jacques Brisoux; we wander round the little country districts of Marracq. I have a tricycle. There are some fine summer evenings. In the Protestant church in Bayonne, at Christmas, there's a smell of candles and mandarin oranges; we sing *Mon beau sapin* ['Oh Christmas tree']; the harmonium is played by my godfather, **Joseph Nogaret**; from time to time he gives me **a bag of walnuts and a five-franc piece.**

I go to the nursery school in Marracq and then the lycée in Bayonne nearby; I start in the *dixième* class,[3] with Mme Lafont; she wears a suit, a blouse and a fox fur; she rewards you with a sweet that tastes and looks like a raspberry; she is very popular. In the *neuvième*, the teacher is M. Arouet; he has a rough voice with a drinker's edge; at the end of the year, he sometimes takes his class out into the grounds of the lycée next to the old château de Marracq where Napoleon had some interview or other with a King of Spain, I don't know which one.

Every year, my mother goes to spend a month in Paris and I go with her; we set off in the evening, **in a landau from Darrigrand's** as far as the railway station in Bayonne, after playing Pope Joan while waiting for the train; we arrive in the Gare d'Orsay, which is underground. In Paris we stay in a furnished apartment but we spend a great deal of time at the home of **the pastor Louis Bertrand in the rue de l'Avre, in the La Motte-Picquet area; he is very kind, speaks solemnly, with his eyes closed**: his parish is a mission to the poor, it's a very deprived area. At every meal the Bible is read slowly, so slowly that we risk missing the train if this is the evening we are leaving; the Bible is covered in cloth; so is the tea-pot; there are lodgers: a Swedish lady doctor, Mlle Berghoff, cures migraines by massaging the forehead.[4]

Photos of the white snout of the tram of childhood, the Maison des Allées (since razed), the grandparents and Aunt Alice are reproduced in *Roland Barthes by Roland Barthes*. Another war orphan, born two years before Barthes and brought up in the South of France, turns the tram into one of the main biographemes of childhood. Claude Simon remembers his journeys in the driver's cabin taking travellers from the city to the nearby seaside. The tram transports travellers and memories. Its existence is linked both to ritual and to the sacred, to the movement and permanence of things – 'when, once it had gone past the toll-house, the vehicle entered the city, first going down the long slope that led to the park, along its wall, turning left when it reached the War Memorial and, following the Boulevard du Président-Wilson, gradually slowed down along the allée des Marronniers to come to a stop at the end of its journey, almost in the city centre, opposite the cinema whose entrance was protected by a glass awning with alluring posters that, in gaudy colours, offered potential spectators the gigantic faces of dishevelled women, their heads flung back and their mouths opened in a cry of horror, or demanding a kiss.'[5] It's the same period, the same tram, the same part of the country – the South-West which Barthes turned into his origin, 'the land of my childhood and my teenage holidays',[6] he liked to say. Sometimes, an open wagon was harnessed to the tram; everyone wanted to climb into the wagon: 'Through a rather empty countryside, one enjoyed the view, the movement, the air, all at the same time.'[7] This old tram no longer exists, but it remains as the memory of a pleasure both sensual and luminous. It went from Bayonne to Biarritz and from Biarritz to Bayonne. 'Bayonne, the town where my paternal grandparents lived, played a Proustian role in my past – and a Balzacian role, too, since I heard there, over many visits, the discourse of a certain type of provincial bourgeoisie, which from an early age I found more diverting than oppressive.'[8] Proust was important for the sensations that maintain the connection with our childhood: the two different walks, the pleated dresses and the odour of the houses, the discovery of intimacy; Balzac for the apprenticeship in social codes and codes of class: two aspirations, towards the inside and the outside, and in both cases an obvious attention to signs.

Barthes came from the hereditary petty bourgeoisie, with its rules and its self-awareness, but without its capital, either cultural or economic. 'The social class I belong to is, I would say, the bourgeoisie.'[9] But there is some doubt about this. At a period when the main characteristic of the bourgeoisie was social ascent, Roland Barthes's family was not typical. The impoverishment from which his family suffered on both sides did not inevitably mean they were in social decline, but did place them in the long-term category of people of modest means, at least as far as Barthes and the family he later formed with his mother and his brother were concerned. 'In short, my social origins amount to one quarter landed bourgeoisie, one quarter old nobility and two quarters liberal bourgeoisie, the whole mixed together and unified by a general state of impoverishment: this bourgeoisie was either tight-fisted or poor, a poverty that was sometimes acute; which meant that, being a "war widow", and since I was a "pupil of the state", my mother learned a trade, book-binding, from which we scratched a living in Paris, where we had moved when I was 10.'[10] While his mother's side of the family was much less well endowed with capital, it was also less open and rather uncharitable. The relative indifference with which Madame Barthes and her son were viewed explains why Barthes's account of his origins gives more importance to the distinctive features on his father's side: the provinces, the South, ritual and poverty. When he mentions this family, in texts and interviews, he always emphasizes the imbalance between the prejudices, the reactionary ideology of this class and 'its

economic status (sometimes tragic)'.[11] In the South-West he reads
the paradox of this history that sociological analysis often ignores.

A father dead at sea

The sea was there from the start. At the child's feet. In the place
of birth, Cherbourg, and the place of childhood, Bayonne. It was
also the instrument of the first major break in Barthes's life, since
it was the sea that took away his father. The homophony in French
between '*la mer*' (sea) and '*la mère*' (mother) makes this monosylla-
ble the term of connection and separation at the same time. Barthes
would find it impossible to break the first, primitive attachment
every child has with its mother, and the reason for this lies in the
depths of the sea. Paronomasia takes over from genealogy. The
history of the connection is now to be forged in language.

So, on 12 November 1915, Roland Gérard Barthes was born at
107 rue de la Bucaille in Cherbourg, where his parents had provisionally set up home. They had met on a steamboat sailing to
Canada, on which his father was serving as a lieutenant and his
mother was going out to visit her brother Philippe, who had set off
to try his chances and seek his fortune in a faraway land. Barthes
was born in a town he would not actually know, since, as he told
Jean Thibaudeau, 'I have, literally, never set foot there, being only
two months old when I left'.[12] Barely a year later, while commanding a small fishing vessel converted for war use as a 'patrol boat',
Louis Barthes was attacked by five German destroyers. The single
gun on his boat was soon knocked out of action and he himself
fatally wounded. The *Montaigne* was sunk on 26 October 1916,
in the North Sea, off Cap Gris-Nez, in the Pas-de-Calais. Louis
Barthes died at the age of 33. Roland Barthes was the orphan of a
father who would be mentioned in dispatches and posthumously
made a chevalier de la Légion d'honneur. The child was made a
'pupil of the state' by decree of the civil court of Bayonne on 30
November 1925. The state subsidized part of his living expenses and
all expenses linked to his education, thus indirectly taking over the
heritage of his father by recognizing the debt the country owed him.

There are few surprises in the history of Barthes's father and his
paternal family. Louis Barthes was born on 28 February 1883 in
Marmande, in Lot-et-Garonne. His father, Léon Barthes, was an
inspector for the Chemins de fer du Midi (the Southern French
Railways), a company which, at one period, managed to constitute its very own mythology. It emerged, with five other private
companies, from the thirty or so original railway companies that
each corresponded to a particular line: known as the 'Compagnie
des Chemins de fer du Midi et du canal latéral à la Garonne' (or

the 'Compagnie des Chemins de fer du Midi' or just the 'Midi'),
it was set up in 1852 by the Pereire brothers. It served that part of
South-West France between the Garonne and the Pyrenees and by
the beginning of the twentieth century covered 4,300 kilometres.
In 1934, it merged with the Compagnie du chemin de fer de Paris
à Orléans (PO) and in 1938 was nationalized to become part of
the SNCF (Société nationale des chemins de fer).[13] The history of
the Chemins de fer du Midi brings together several features associated with the story of Roland Barthes: apart from the fact that his
grandfather worked for it, this company was closely linked both to
the South-West area where he spent his first years, and on which he
conferred a genealogical value, and also to a business-oriented bourgeoisie belonging to the religious minorities of France. The brothers
Émile and Isaac Pereire were Jews from Bordeaux, and also close
to Protestant business circles with which they worked.[14] Now the
connection with these two minorities was of some significance, as
we shall show, for the construction of Roland Barthes's identity.
He was Protestant on his mother's side and laterally Jewish through
the father of his brother, whom he saw regularly throughout his
youth, even if he rarely spoke about him publicly. Furthermore, the
Pereire brothers were responsible for the architectural design of a
good part of that region of the Basque coast which was the territory
of Roland's childhood. The railway line, filled with travellers in the
summer but emptier in the winter, had to turn a profit. So the busi-
nessmen decided, after reforesting the forêt des Landes, to build the
winter town of Arcachon. Its clean air would make it a good place
for sufferers of TB (another major feature of Barthes's life) and all
those who lacked sunlight and healthy breezes. With the help of the
architect Paul Regnauld, a picturesque hybrid of a town, protected
and comfortable, quickly came into being. The spa was inaugurated
in the presence of Napoleon III, the Empress Eugénie and their son
in 1865, at a splendid ceremony, which the members of the Barthes
family were in no position to attend; for a while they had formed a
line of notaries, in Mazamet, in the Tarn, but gradually lost their
wealth – it was the steady decline in their condition that had led
Barthes's grandfather to become a humble railway worker.

His grandmother on his father's side, Berthe de Lapalut, although
of noble descent, was from a petty-bourgeois, modest and provincial cultural background; in Roland Barthes's terms, the members
of this family were 'impoverished provincial nobility (from around
Tarbes)'.[15] It was in their house and in their company that Barthes
would spend his early years. They were Catholics but not practising, which explains why it was his mother's Protestant, or Calvinist,
religion (in his own terms) that he acknowledged as his own. What
is certain is that he was not raised in the odour of incense, or in the
secrets of the surplice or the lies of the confessional. This marks his

story out from that of other French intellectuals and writers and brings him closer to Gide.

The Proustian character of his childhood owed a great deal to that grandmother, of whom he writes, in the caption to a photograph in *Roland Barthes by Roland Barthes*, that she was 'steeped in bourgeoisie – not in nobility, from which she was nevertheless descended – she had a lively sense of social narrative, which she served up in a fastidious convent French, safeguarding each imperfect subjunctive; gossip inflamed her with a passion – an amorous passion whose principal object was a certain Mme Leboeuf, the widow of a pharmacist who had made a fortune in coal tar; this woman was a kind of black flower bed, mustached and beringed, who had to be lured to the monthly tea party (the rest in Proust).'[16] The 'rest' was the microcosm of Combray observed from her bedroom by Tante Léonie and her famous lime blossom. 'On the other side, her bed lay by the window, she had the street there before her eyes and on it from morning to night, to divert her melancholy, like the Persian princes, would read the daily but immemorial chronicle of Combray, which she would afterwards commentate with Françoise.'[17] The countless smells of the bedroom seem to be transported from one house to the other, from one text to the other. It is difficult to distinguish between Mme Bouilleboeuf (Proust) and Mme Leboeuf (Barthes). It's the same five-franc coin that is given to a child.

Louis-Jean Calvet, who obtained from the Historical Services of the French Navy the various documents concerning Louis Barthes's periods of service and the report on his death, was the first to reconstitute his brief and modest career.[18] Louis Barthes started out in January 1903 as an apprentice on a long cruise (nearly three months) on the steamer *Amiral Courbet*. Then, he alternated between periods in harbour – Toulon in 1903–04, Bordeaux in 1906, Le Havre in 1909 – and periods at sea, either as a lieutenant or just as a sailor. According to Calvet's calculations, 'from 10 January 1903 to 13 February 1913, a period of ten years and thirty-three days, he spent just over seven years at sea on different steamships (the *Bretagne, Montréal, Québec, Ferdinand de Lesseps, Mexico* . . .)'.[19] In 1909, he went to Martinique, to Fort-de-France, before returning to Le Havre. According to the extract from the Navy register, in 1913 he was appointed 'captain of ocean-going ship first class' and recruited as an 'ensign in the first class reserve'. When war broke out, Louis was a lieutenant in the reserves and reassumed his service at the beginning of 1916 when he took his family with him to the Pas-de-Calais (we do not know the exact town). The battle took place in October: he died on the night of 26 October and not 28 October as Barthes wrote in his autobiographical sketch transcribed at the beginning of this chapter. The *Montaigne* was sunk, and the father's body was dragged down with it and never resurfaced. In a

narrative published in 1927, *Sur les bancs de Flandre*, Paul Chack
gives a lengthy description of the night of 26–27 October during
which twelve German torpedo ships came down from Ostend and
sank the *Montaigne*. Six of them had made for Dover, destroying
several English herring boats and killing many officers and sailors; a
second detachment headed towards Gris-Nez. 'Now in that sector,
a French sector, the trawler *Montaigne* was patrolling, commanded
by Barthes, a naval ensign, and the old fisheries protection ship
Albatros, under Captain Hamon, boatswain. Ensign Barthes had
just arrived in the Vignaux division. He was on his first patrol. And
his last . . . .'[20] At twenty minutes past midnight, he was fatally
wounded. His second in command, boatswain Le Fur, took over,
but the ship sank shortly afterwards off Sangatte. In his report, Le
Fur states that before leaving the boat he lifted Commander Barthes
up and laid his head against the threshold of the port entrance to
the bridge. 'Do you know of a more moving gesture than that of the
young boatswain lifting up the body of the young officer who has
just died at his post and placing him, on the bridge, in the position of
a chief who has died honourably?'[21] Paul Chack's comments show
how deeply he was moved and, together with his account as a whole,
give the death of Barthes's father a historical significance.

   But the mother, and then the son, had to cope with this absence:
the absence of the living body and the absence of the dead body.
There is no doubt that Barthes remembered his father when he
became interested in Pierre Loti and wrote about *Aziyadé*; the fate
of Barthes's father was in many respects similar to that of Loti's
brother Gustave, who was drowned in the straits of Malacca, and
many of the short stories by Pierre Loti, the author of *Mon frère
Yves*, can stand in for the tale of the missing father. Furthermore,
by deciding to go and live with her husband's family, the mother
re-paternalized her son, as it were, inscribing into his childhood the
mark of the father, even if this father was absent. As for the son,
the signs can be sought in his work, in spite of the relative lack of
any explicit discourse on this subject. Three elements seem decisive:
effacement, shipwreck and union with the mother.

   Effacement can be read in the parable of the blackboard in *Roland
Barthes by Roland Barthes*, one that has often been analysed. The
scene takes place in Paris, at the Lycée Louis-le-Grand. M.B., a
teacher in the *troisième* class, 'a socialist, a nationalist', wrote the
names on the blackboard of students' relatives who had 'fallen on
the field of honour': the teenaged Barthes is embarrassed about
being an exception (many pupils can cite an uncle or a cousin, but he
is the only one whose father has been killed) and also embarrassed
by the braying patriotism and the pathetic pride in family values
shown by the teacher. He wishes to remember only the effacement,
the sign that is written down and disappears in almost the same

movement. 'Yet once the blackboard was erased, nothing was left of this proclaimed mourning – except, in real life, which proclaims nothing, which is always silent, the figure of a home socially adrift: no father to kill, no family to hate, no milieu to reject: great Oedipal frustration!'[22] What is missing are the figures of Authority, whether this Authority takes the form of Law or of Meaning. Childhood and adolescence seem, in retrospect, to be marked by the lack of any site of opposition. This is why Françoise Gaillard, who analyses this passage in 'Barthes juge de Roland', shows that his gestures, almost all of them connected to this absence of any reactive utopia, are more a matter of imitation than of opposition. She develops the idea that, unlike most of the intellectuals of his generation, who were essentially on the side of the opposition, deriving their legitimacy from the struggle against the powers that be, Barthes invented the figure of the intellectual as a solvent, a dissident from within rather than one who attacks from without. 'The role in question is that of the person who decomposes legitimacy, following on from the role bequeathed by the Enlightenment, that of the destroyer of dogmas legitimated by the mere exercise of power.'[23] In Gaillard's view, in this little narrative of erasure, Barthes is giving himself the authority to assume this role precisely because he was deprived not just of symbolic fathers but also, as it were, of a private father: to call attention to this, she says, has a legitimating function, implying that emancipation lies behind it. She links the fragment about the blackboard to the one about 'Decompose/destroy', in which Barthes describes 'the intellectual's (or the writer's) historical function, today, [which] is to maintain and to emphasize the *decomposition* of bourgeois consciousness', and distinguishes between destruction, which comes from outside, and decomposition (which 'dismantles' this consciousness, 'weakens' it and 'breaks [it] down on the spot'): decomposition comes from within.[24] Gaillard's comparison of these fragments is all the more justified as, in 'Politics/ethics', Barthes serenely says that 'the only Father I have known (have granted myself) has been the political Father',[25] even if, as we shall see, submission to that authority was itself discreet.

But this theme of effacement can also be given another reading; in the way, for example, it leads, in the family novel of *Roland Barthes by Roland Barthes*, to a form of replacement. The caption to the photograph showing the child at the age of about sixteen months connects him to another genealogy to which we have already referred, a recurrent genealogy, the family novel par excellence: 'Contemporaries? I was beginning to walk, Proust was still alive, and finishing *À la Recherche du temps perdu*.'[26] The operation calls for a certain irony. It also invites us to close the circle. On the day he died, Barthes was scheduled to give his seminar on Proust and photography. From among the images by Paul Nadar he had selected is a photograph of Gabrielle Schwartz as a child, with the same big eyes, looking rather lost and leaning forward a bit, like the photo of young Roland. The justification he gives for this portrait from 19 February 1883 to illustrate the world of Proust's *In Search of Lost Time* is not the connection with Proust, which is 'tenuous': 'I'm showing this photo because I'm very fond of this little girl's face.'[27] Effacement disturbs genre. It also disturbs the social milieu. The mother, as the origin of everything, displaces the solid, ritualized milieu of the father's side of the family. '[I]n reality I had no milieu when I was an adolescent, insofar as I was attached solely to my mother and hers was my only household. [. . .] And so, having no real social milieu, I experienced a certain solitude.'[28] In other words, 'he belonged to no milieu'.[29]

Inheriting a lack does not mean, however, that you lack a heritage. The effacement of the father's figure can also be read from more discreet signs, even slips of the pen that lead him to write that his mother was widowed in 1915, the year of his birth and a year before his father's death. This second wrong date in the 'Biography' is connected to the explicit discourse Barthes held in various interviews and to different interviewers, where he treated the matter with relative casualness. The main thing here is to give himself his own origin, his own territory – to be his own law. Roland Barthes *by* Roland Barthes. Himself by himself. Over time, the father's figure does sometimes reappear, mythologized, admittedly, but accompanied by questions about what he might have been like, or might have thought. On 9 March 1978, attending a lecture at the Institute of Oceanography, Barthes gazes in the lecture hall at 'a huge realist painting' showing sailors busy on the deck of a ship. He notes: 'Fascinated by the clothes (and thus the morphology) of the sailors. 1910. Adolescence of my father. He must have looked like that.'[30] On 1 August, in Urt, while the death of his mother is definitely stirring up memories of his father too, he gives one fragment in his folder-diary the title 'Death of my father', in which he copies Ariel's song from Shakespeare's *Tempest*:

> Full fathom five thy father lies;
>   Of his bones are coral made;
> Those are pearls that were his eyes:
>   Nothing of him that doth fade,
> But doth suffer a sea-change
> Into something rich and strange. (Act I, Scene 2)

Shipwreck may be an exclusively metaphorical theme in Barthes's work, but it was a decisive real event in his life. By being lost at sea, his father deprived him not just of an authority and an opposing force; he left him in a state of unbalance. He left him at sea, with his mother (*en mer, avec sa mère*). He made him pitch and toss, so that he needed his sea legs. Barthes did not treat this as a theme, directly, but these different motifs come together in *W, or the memory of childhood*, by Georges Perec, in which the shipwreck of young Gaspard Winckler is directly linked to the father. In that novel, the last words of chapter 7 are 'the boat sinks' and the first words of chapter 8 are 'I possess one photograph of my father'.[31] In Perec's book, it is the mother who dies, but the terms of shipwreck are linked to the father as much as to the mother. This leads to a kind of coldness about their deaths, which for a long time means it is impossible to come back to the matter or raise questions about it. 'I don't know what my father would have done had he lived. The oddest thing is that his death, and my mother's, too often seems to me to be obvious. It's become a part of the way things are.'[32] In Barthes, we find the same discourse of dryness, a distance that could be seen as indifference. 'My father was a navy officer; he was killed in 1916, during a naval combat in the Pas-de-Calais; I was eleven months old.'[33] In *Roland Barthes by Roland Barthes*, the caption on the photo showing the father is more intimate in tone, even though such terms as silence, and the marks of negation still put everything under the sign of effacement: 'The father, dead very early (in the war), was lodged in no memorial or sacrificial discourse. By maternal intermediary his memory – never an oppressive one – merely touched the surface of childhood with an almost silent bounty.'[34] Not having a father to kill may seem to have its advantages. But it also lies behind a twisted and complex relation to confrontation and subversion. Julia Kristeva says that Barthes's way of always putting himself in the place of the disciple indicates that there was something of his father that he always lacked, and he sometimes connected this lack to language.[35] Instead, there was fear: 'I'm afraid, so I'm alive.'[36] And Barthes links fear to birth, to the deep insecurity felt by the infant, the 'basic fear' or 'underlying threat' that stays within human beings and that they are often afraid to acknowledge.

Shipwreck involves both falling and being swallowed up, vagueness[37] and instability. All these motifs can be found scattered throughout the texts. One fragment in *Roland Barthes by Roland Barthes*, with the title 'A memory of childhood', tells the story of falling into a hole. This happened in Marracq, in the area of Bayonne where Roland spent his childhood. Children were playing on the building sites: 'This neighbourhood was full of houses being built, and the children played in the building sites; huge holes had been dug in the loamy soil for the foundations of the houses, and one day when we had been playing in one of these, all the children climbed out except me – I couldn't make it. From the brink up above, they teased me: lost! alone! spied on! excluded! (to be excluded is not to be outside, it is to be *alone in the hole*, imprisoned under the open sky: *precluded*).' The open grave might well be his father's. The adult also remembers that the child would often perform the shipwreck scene regularly, staging it in different ways. But his mother was not far and her presence made the nightmare of shipwreck less intense: 'Then I saw my mother running up; she pulled me out of there and took me far away from the children – against them.'[38] Hence two fundamental fears: the fear of vagueness and the fear of exclusion. Vagueness is not far removed from flabbiness, and yet it comes with a certain insistence. It exists in certain words, and in an accompaniment of language in which we 'decompose' something rather than destroying it: 'By decomposing, I agree to accompany such decomposition, to decompose myself as well, in the process: I scrape, catch, and drag.'[39] Thus we find shipwreck in writing, in the concrete practice of language. It is the pitching and tossing of structures, of oppositions between much we must not choose. It is also connected to the feeling of being forever detached, excluded from the code and 'forever assigned the place of the *witness*, whose discourse can only be, of course, subject to codes of detachment: either narrative, or explicative, or challenging, or ironic: never *lyrical*, never homogenous with the pathos outside of which he must seek his place.'[40] Shipwreck is the other name for separation; it deprives you from being a native, from having a relation to your native soil. It remains a threat in everyday situations and in the hollows of language, as it places the subject in a permanent position (not always deliberately chosen) of deterritorialization. To resist this basic instability, Barthes proposes to situate himself in the allegory of the ship *Argo*. *Argo* is the anti-*Montaigne*, the opposite of his father's ship: *Argo* is the permanent, the substitutable, the unsinkable. 'A frequent image: that of the ship *Argo* (luminous and white), each piece of which the Argonauts gradually replaced, so that they ended with an entirely new ship, without having to alter either its name or its form.' This vessel contradicts the usual genealogy, as it has emerged from itself alone. It is produced 'by two modest actions (which cannot be caught up in any mystique of creation): *substitution* (one part replaces another, as in a paradigm) and *nomination* (the name is in no way linked to the stability of the parts): by dint of combinations made within one and the same name, nothing is left of the *origin*: *Argo* is an object with no other cause than its name, with no other identity than its form.'[41] If at a certain moment it becomes a metaphor for the book itself, of which each fragment could be gradually changed,[42] this vessel gives birth to a counter-history. The name remains even if the origin is scattered to the winds. It cannot sink, as it is always new. How could the reversal of the signs of absence be any better expressed? Thus the vessel also gives rise to a counter-genealogy, as it defines the very being of genius, which is its own origin.

The mother as replacement father

The absence of any stable anchoring-point and the difficult relationship with any native land do not mean one breaks away entirely from
one's lineage. By deciding to move to South-West France with a son
who could not as yet walk or talk, Henriette Barthes may not have
completely filled the gap, but she did put the four pillars of genealogy, the necessary reference points, on a firm footing. The texts
always present all four of them, both together and yet in contrast.
A remark from the interview with Jean Thibaudeau, detailing the
reference to this in *Roland Barthes by Roland Barthes*, points to the
ambiguity of the construction: 'The social class I belong to is, I would
say, the bourgeoisie. So that you can judge for yourself, I'll list my
four immediate forebears (as the Vichy regime did under the occupation to determine the degree of a person's Jewishness): my paternal
grandfather, a white-collar worker in the *Compagnie des Chemins de
Fer du Midi*, came from a family of lawyers living in a small town in
the Tarn region (Mamazet, I was told); the parents of my paternal
grandmother were impoverished provincial nobility (from around
Tarbes); Captain Binger, my maternal grandfather, from an Alsace
family of master glassmakers, was an explorer – he explored the
Niger region in 1887–89; as for my maternal grandmother, the only
wealthy one in this constellation, her parents came from Lorraine
and had a small foundry in Paris. My father's side was Catholic, my
mother's Protestant; since my father was dead, I was given my mother's Calvinist religion.'[43] Whichever way we turn, from interviews to
published autobiographical texts, via the unpublished writings, we
find the two sides, interrelated and balancing one another, anchored
both genealogically and socially – the bourgeoisie, either poor or
well-off. This recurrent concern with balance, all the more striking
as it does not correspond to the reality, shows how the narrative of
the forebears constitutes the novel. Conversely, the imbalance in the
situation of the parents is very probably the basis on which language
is constituted. The union with the mother *(mère)*, silently celebrated
in the depths of the sea *(mer)*, is the sign of this necessity and this
desire: a novel way of espousing the shape of a lack.

As we have said, the mother is a replacement father, and provides
paternal reference points. And not just because she reinscribes the
child in his father's territory. She also gives him a mother tongue,
being at once father and mother, law and singularity. Even if
Barthes is careful to distinguish between the mother tongue and the
national language, he makes of this language a twofold gift – witness
one of his critical essays on music: 'I believe that the explosion of
the mother tongue into the musical text is an important phenomenon. To remain with Schumann (the man with two wives – two

mothers? – the first of whom sang and the second, Clara, who visibly gave him abundant speech: one hundred lieder in 1840, the year of his marriage), the explosion of the *Muttersprache* in musical writing is really the declared restoration of the body.'[44] This is obviously because language marks out the territory of the umbilical cord, as he writes in *Roland Barthes by Roland Barthes*, but also because it continues to deterritorialize while territorializing. It informs a form of non-belonging that, in Barthes, is on the side of the father-mother. When it comes to this mother tongue, we feel its 'cruel deficiences' and, in it, we recognize its 'threatening division'.[45] The mother is also the future of privation. The pathos that we feel on reading *Camera Lucida* comes from the way the mother has become the little girl and, when Barthes refers to his mother's death, he does so in the terms, and with the sorrow, of parents who have lost their child. 'During her illness, I nursed her, held the bowl of tea she liked because it was easier to drink from than from a cup; she had become my little girl, uniting me with that essential child she was in her first photograph.'[46] This is no longer the successful, reparative substitution of the vessel *Argo*. It reverses the order of things without offering any alternative. It reminds us that an accident, a shipwreck, can suspend the line of descent without destroying it. Only death completely breaks it.

The mother's side of the family also contributes something of the sea. As you will remember, Barthes's parents met on a boat sailing to Canada. Louis-Gustave Binger (1856–1936), the father of Barthes's mother Henriette, was an officer in the naval infantry and enjoyed a colonial career that took him for a long time to Senegal and then to Côte d'Ivoire. Instead of being the place where things are swallowed up, the sea is now presented as the unconditional opening towards adventure, the future, the South. While his position was that of a colonial administrator, Binger experienced this as an adventure, and it was probably as an adventure that he told his grandson about it. He was very keen on geography and in 1887 he mounted a substantial expedition to find definitive proof for the hypothesis, not yet cartographically demonstrated, that there was a distinction between the Niger and Senegal rivers, and that another river, the Volta, also existed. 'I gradually nursed the dream of going to fill in one of the big blank spaces in the map of Africa',[47] as he puts it at the beginning of his work. During his expedition, he met the Malinke chief Samori, who frequently opposed the colonial troops between 1883 and 1898, even though he had signed a treaty placing his states under a French protectorate. Apparently, Binger acted as a mediator between him and the French government, in spite of the deep mistrust his book evinces towards the glorious epic image of Samori and his tyrannical government.

Published in two volumes, the story of his exploration along the

Volta, *Du Niger au golfe de Guinée par le pays de Kong et de Mossi* (*From Niger to the Gulf of Guinea through the land of Kong and Mossi*) is imbued with colonial ideology, paternalistic and explicitly emancipatory. It is a travel story attentive to the countries visited and the people met, and it is also so precise that the text is akin to the discourse of ethnology. As an example of the book's manner, here is what it has to say about the market at Ouolosébougou: 'Today is Friday, the day of the big market in Ouolosébougou. Founé Mamourou, who comes to see me, tells me that my presence here is going to attract a lot of people from the surrounding area. Around eight in the morning, the sellers start to arrive; by eleven, the market is in full swing. As I want to avoid creating a false impression, I won't use expressions such as "important market, commercial centre, big market", and so on, as they are all potentially ambiguous: I'll simply give a complete list, below, of everything there was in this market.'[48] There follows a list of the different products (millet, goats, shea butter – or karate nut butter, for which he later gives the method of extraction – needles, gun flints, calico, etc.) together with their respective quantities and prices. As Claude Auboin puts it in a monograph he wrote to celebrate Binger's travels: 'He methodically drew on his travels for botany, zoology, ethnology, sociology, geography, and geology, taking advantage of the rise of photography.'[49] But he never shed his prejudices against 'Negroes' and barbarian customs, so today's historians tend to relativize the significance of his eye-witness accounts, even though they recognize the pioneering character of his enterprise. For example, they credit him with having, from quite an early date, promoted economic relations with West Africa, to the detriment of purely military actions.[50] His work on topographical profiling, his knowledge of African languages (he published an essay on Bambara) and his close links with various African chiefs are also mentioned favourably.

Louis-Gustave Binger was appointed civil governor of Côte d'Ivoire between 1893 and 1896, but he waited until the arrival (after the birth of his son Philippe in 1891) of his daughter Henriette on 18 July 1893, in Chennevières-sur-Marne, before leaving. He embarked two days later at Bordeaux, and reached Grand-Bassam at the beginning of August. He returned to France regularly for health reasons (he suffered from malaria), but he was viewed as a good administrator, building all the necessary buildings, organizing the school, postal and justice systems. From 1895 onwards, he sought to return to France and decided to retire from the Ministry of Foreign Affairs. But the new Minister for the Colonies, André Lebon, appointed him director of African Affairs, a post that he would occupy until 1907. In 1899, he left on a secret mission to Senegal at the time of the Fashoda Incident, when France and England confronted one another. Separated from his first wife, Roland Barthes's

grandmother, in 1900, he married Marie Hubert and with her had a
son, Jacques, in 1905. In 1900, the capital of Côte d'Ivoire was given
the name Bingerville. In 1934, Abidjan became the new capital, but
Bingerville was not renamed and the city still exists under this name
today. He retired from the Ministry of Colonies in 1907 and entered
the Compagnie de l'Ouest africain français (French West African
Company) of which he was a shareholder. When this company went
bankrupt on the eve of the First World War, he too was almost
ruined. He then retired to L'Isle-Adam until his death in 1936. It
was here, in the large house at 53, rue Saint-Lazare, that Roland
Barthes, when he moved to Paris with his mother, would go to see
his grandfather regularly on a Sunday.

So Louis-Gustave Binger was a famous grandfather. He was made
a Grand Officer in the Légion d'honneur in 1932, and so had the
right to a national funeral. A bust to his memory rises over a square
in L'Isle-Adam. Two postage stamps were issued with his likeness on
them, one showing him next to Félix Houphouët-Boigny (President
of Côte d'Ivoire from 1960 to 1993). Binger was to some extent a
hero of colonization, and his role may have caused some embarrassment to the intellectual Barthes, who was starting to write and make
a name for himself at a time when empires were falling. But there was
more to Binger than that. He was a scientist and a writer, even if his
non-specialist writings play only a very small part in his posthumous
fame.[51] All the experts emphasize his great talent for drawing, as
well as the role he played in promoting the arts in Sudan and Mali.
He was also fascinated by body arts, such as scarifications, which he
described with great precision: he was among the first to recognize
that they involved both a social code and a form of writing.[52] He also
took an interest in the domestic arts and rituals of divination.

Two of the texts in Barthes's *Mythologies* suggest an ambiguous
relationship to this grandfather. The first, of course, is 'Bichon and
the Blacks'.[53] Here, Barthes is reacting to an article published in
Paris-Match in January 1955, written by Georges de Caunes, 'Une
famille française chez les Nègres rouges' ('A French family among
the Red Negroes'), relating the expedition undertaken by Maurice
and Jeannette Fiévet among 'the most primitive tribes in Africa'.
She records, while he draws and paints. A child is born and 'the
cannibals have been swayed by this child's smile. He has become
their idol.' Barthes of course denounces the article's openly racist
character and the pathetic heroism that lies behind this tale of colonial adventures: 'First of all, nothing is more irritating than heroism
without an object. A society is in a serious situation when it under-
takes to develop gratuitously the *forms* of its virtues. If the dangers
incurred by baby Bichon (torrents, wild animals, diseases, etc.) were
real, it was literally stupid to impose them, on the mere pretext of
doing some painting in Africa and satisfying the dubious ambition

of getting on canvas "a debauch of sun and light".'[54] Barthes's remark on drawing may appear as a way of casting aspersions on Binger. But an attentive reading of the text actually suggests that there is, in between the lines, a kind of acknowledgement at work here, too. Not only does Barthes contrast scientific explorations with purely publicity-hungry explorations such as those of the Fiévet family, but he ends his article by drawing a distinction between science and mythology: 'And now, if we will contrast with this general imagery (*Match*: approximately a million readers) the ethnologists' efforts to demystify the Black phenomenon, the rigorous precautions they have long since taken when obliged to employ such ambiguous notions as "Primitives" or "Archaic Societies", the intellectual probity of such men as Mauss, Lévi-Strauss, or Leroi-Gourhan confronting the old racial terms in their various disguises, we will better understand one of our major servitudes: the oppressive divorce of knowledge and mythology. Science proceeds rapidly on its way, but the collective representations do not follow, they are centuries behind, kept stagnant in their errors by power, the press, and the values of order.'[55] The deconstruction of prejudices and unconscious representations undertaken in the *Mythologies* here finds its intellectual and ethical programme: at the same time, slow and patient scientific work needs to be defended against petty-bourgeois myths. And while Binger does not appear in the list of great ethnologists, there is no doubt that Barthes sees his research and observational activities as a real contribution to knowledge.

The second 'mythology' that may shed light on Barthes's relation to Binger is the one he writes on Jules Verne under the title '"Nautilus" and "Bateau ivre"'. The *Nautilus* is neither the *Montaigne* (the boat that has to face a real danger) nor the ship *Argo*, an allegory of replacement. The *Nautilus* is less a symbol of departure and adventure than a metaphor of enclosure and containment. The text refers to the way children love hide-and-seek, tents, things that are underground. 'All the ships in Jules Verne are perfect cubby-holes, and the vastness of their circumnavigation further increases the bliss of their closure, the perfection of their inner humanity. The *Nautilus*, in this regard, is the most desirable of all caves.'[56] Figured as a protective womb, the boat is here the mother's womb, after being the space of the father (the *Montaigne*) or of the son (the *Argo*). Barthes links this *imaginaire* of the boat as womb to that of the mysterious island, 'in which the manchild reinvents the world, fills it, closes it, shuts himself up in it, and crowns this encyclopaedic effort with the bourgeois posture of appropriation: slippers, pipe and fireside, while outside the storm, that is, the infinite, rages in vain'.[57] Apart from the fact that the itinerary refers precisely to Binger's life, it also links up with a whole series of ideas developed by Barthes in the classes he gave in Rabat

in 1969 on Verne's *Mysterious Island*, where he relates this mythological construction to colonization.[58] Here is the place occupied by
the grandfather, linked to Verne[59] and the colonies, a figure both
masculine and feminine in character, on the side of both father and
mother at once – just as, in *Twenty Thousand Leagues Under the
Sea*, a male captain is associated with the protective womb formed
by the vessel.

Barthes's grandmother on his mother's side, Noémie (sometimes
spelled Noémi) Lepet-Révelin, was already separated from her
husband when Barthes knew her as a child. In the texts mentioning
Binger, she appears as a rather superficial woman, taking advantage of her status to organize big parties in the colonial dwellings in
which her husband had lived. She sometimes left her two children
in France to go off and enjoy herself in Côte d'Ivoire. Born in 1872,
Noémie Élise Georgette Lepet came from a wealthy family of indus-
trialists. After the breakdown of her marriage to Binger in 1900,
she went on to marry a professor at the Lycée Sainte-Barbe, Louis
Révelin, who also appears as an important figure in the symbolic
make-up of Roland Barthes. From his years at the École normale
supérieure, Louis Révelin had kept up close political and intellectual
links with Péguy and the *Cahiers de la Quinzaine*, as well as with
Léon Blum. He played a part in the apparatus of the Socialist Party.
With his wife, who was starting to hold a salon and receive poets
and intellectuals (in particular Paul Valéry, but also Paul Langevin,
Henri Focillon, Léon Brunschvicg and Charles Seignobos), Révelin
embodied a form of intellectual avant-garde linked to the École des
hautes études sociales founded by Georges Sorel to pursue similar
work to the Collège libre des sciences sociales.[60] The effervescence
of the Third Republic in the circles that defended Dreyfus, and
whose slogans came directly from the Dreyfus Affair, left a deep
impression on Barthes, if only in his *imaginaire*. Half a century
later, when he entered the École pratique des hautes études, he must
have thought about the man who had preceded him in this place, on
the margins of university life. In 'Lectures d'enfance' ('Childhood
reading'), he notes that the period to which he feels closest is more
the pre-war years than the years of his own childhood. 'In fact, if
I feel any nostalgia, it is more for that period which I never knew
except – and this is a decisive factor – through words. In the analysis
of the institution of the family, I reckon that we underestimate the
imaginary role of grandparents: neither castrators nor strangers, but
veritable mediators of myth.'[61]

One decisive element in this myth may well have been the figure
of Paul Valéry. Barthes met Valéry while still a boy, through his
grandmother, whose salon (in the rue Vauquelin and later at 1,
place du Panthéon) Valéry frequented. Valéry was Barthes's predecessor at the Collège de France. Barthes says that he followed the

earlier writer's lectures, and above all attended his opening lecture at the Collège de France on 10 December 1937; Barthes gave his own inaugural lecture there forty years later, and mentions Valéry in the first lines. But also, even more clearly, Valéry was Barthes's predecessor in the kind of writing and criticism that he produced. With Noémie Révelin, Valéry had what seems to have been a close friendship. This is the view of Michel Jarrety in his biography of Valéry, and the documents he quotes do indeed show that the two were close. For example, Valéry sent her one of his last missives, in July 1945, to offer her his condolences when she lost her last son. This very beautiful woman, whom Barthes always kept at a distance because of her difficult relations with his own mother, was imaginative and cultivated. She contrived to turn her salon into a dazzling and captivating place that philosophers as well as scholars enjoyed frequenting. The talk was of culture and politics. Among the habitués of the salon, Jarrety also mentions André Lebey, Jean Baruzi (to whom Barthes attributes his discovery of Michelet) and René Lalou. 'It was also in this left-wing salon that Valéry met the mathematician Émile Borel, professor at the University of Paris where he held the chair in the calculus of probabilities, and the physicist Jean Perrin who had just been elected to the Académie des Sciences.'[62] But does this mean we should consider Valéry as a model? While he is not one of the writers most frequently referred to by Barthes – as we shall see, Gide played a much more considerable formative role – the texts where he does talk about him suggest that he was quite an influential figure, especially when it came to thinking about the 'self'.[63] *Monsieur Teste* and the fascinated relation with the self that is played out there is presented as an 'absolutely anticonformist book',[64] of extreme marginality. Valéry, says Barthes, is part of his 'earliest memory', that of the readings that shaped his taste and from which he never really detached himself, even if he wrote little about them.[65] He returns to him regularly, especially to certain key themes that he turns into leitmotifs: the idea that we think only through the work of the word and the sentence, the 'sentence-thinker' or the 'sentence-thought'; and the idea that 'in Nature there is no "et cetera"', that only human beings think that we should leave some things unsaid. While seeing Valéry as part of classical rhetoric, Barthes also views his work as developing ideas about language that are very close to those of Saussure and, later, Jakobson. He quotes him regularly when writing on one or other of these latter figures. 'For Valéry too, commerce, language, the currency and the law are defined by the same system, that of reciprocity: they can be maintained only by a social contract, for only a contract can make up for the lack of a fixed standard.'[66] Barthes also regrets the way Valéry had fallen out of favour, something that makes Barthes himself feel out of step with his own times.[67] There is an intellectual heritage here, directly transmitted by his grandparents, forming what Barthes calls 'the *imaginaire* of one's grandparents'. In a late text on Cy Twombly, this is linked to the love of the houses of southern France that he shares with Valéry.[68]

As can be seen, we are a long way away from laconic and infrequent formulae that would flatten out Barthes's family history, turning it into the standard narrative of an impoverished bourgeoisie. The biographical reality was more varied than this and, while Barthes does not lay any direct claim to the heritage it brings, he does preserve traces of it, more or less readable in the texts. Like the rag picker of Walter Benjamin, he plays with the left-overs and rejects of a history that precedes him, from which he is as distant in time as I am from him. That is why it can be interesting to highlight these neglected details: so as to have a new, changing relation with the figures that have preceded us. Barthes was also the product of a lack which he attributes simultaneously to his generation and to history. An abandoned fragment of *Roland Barthes by Roland Barthes* evokes an odd emptiness around the year of his birth: '1915: I really don't like the year of my birth (this year has its importance: we have to give it so many times in the course of our lives; it is bizarrely part of our identity). [. . .] Historically, 1915 is an anodyne year: lost in wartime, undistinguished by any event; nobody well known was born or died that year; and, either because of the demographic shortfall or bad luck, I practically never meet one of my contemporaries who was born the same year as me, as if – the height of paranoia – I was the only person of my age.'[69] This is obviously not true. Barthes has some illustrious contemporaries and, among the people he socialized with, several were born the same year as he was. He turned the death that affected him into a phenomenon of general disappearance in which the year of his birth, 'lost in wartime', shared the fate of his own father, who was also lost in the war.

Louis-Gustave Binger:
'Back from hunting'.

Noémie Binger, Barthes's maternal grandmother.
After her second marriage she became Noémie
Révelin.

The hut of Governor Louis-Gustave Binger
in Assinie, Côte d'Ivoire.

Léon Barthes, the
paternal grandfather.

Berthe Barthes, the paternal
grandmother, with her cat.

Noémie Binger and her two children,
Philippe and Henriette (who was later
to be Barthes's mother), around 1895.

Henriette Binger, around 1903.

Louis Barthes, the future father of
Roland Barthes, around 1912.

Louis Barthes on the deck of a Merchant
Navy vessel. He died in the North Sea on
the night of 26 or 27 October 1916.

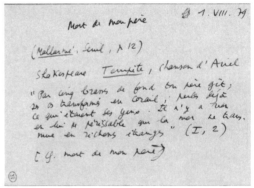

'Death of my father.' Index card
from 1 August 1979.

Roland Barthes and his mother,
Cherbourg, January 1916.

Biographie

(il s'agit ici de souvenirs
d'une mémoire fragmentaire)
v. 1971, III, citer

Régie

1915 – Je nais, dit-on, le 12 Nov à 9h du matin, à Cherbourg (...),
simple halte de garnison pour mon père,
officier de marine marchande mobilisé comme enseigne de vaisseau.   (le Montaigne)

1916 – Mon père commande un chalutier ...
en patrouille dans la Mer du Nord; le
28 Octobre, ... à hauteur du Cap Gris-
Nez, son bateau est coulé par les Allemands.

1915-1924 – Ma mère se retire à Bayonne, ...
mes grands parents Barthes (mon grand père,
ma grand mère et ma tante Alice, pro-
fesseur de piano); ... ils ont une
maison qu'ils louent depuis longtemps dans
un grand jardin, sur Allées Paulmy,
au coin du chemin des Arènes. Avec ma
mère nous habitons à Marracq,
quartier encore en campagne de Bayonne. Nous allons tous les dimanches déjeuner chez mes grands parents ... le soir
on rentre en tramway, " dîner" ... d'
un feu de bois, de bouillon et de pain
grillé; une jeune basquaise, Marie
Lafague s'occupe de moi. Je joue avec
les petits bourgeois du quartier, les Jean et
lenette de lignerolle, les enfants Rémie ...
lulú Jarance, Jacques Brisson, j'ar-
pente la petite campagne de ... Marracq,
j'ai un petit tricycle. Il y a de beaux
jours d'été.

Au temple de Bayonne, protestant,
à Noël, ça sent
la bougie et la
mandarine; on
chante ... bien beau
Sapin; l'harmonium
est tenu par les soeurs
de mon parrain, Freth
Nogaret; de tout en tout
il me donne une idée
de ... ... GF

Manuscript of a sketch for a 'Biography', written in 1972 as
part of the preparation for Roland Barthes by Roland Barthes.
The 'anamneses' were based on this.

2

'Gochokissime'

As a child I made a retreat of my own, a cabin and belvedere, on the top landing of an outside flight of steps, looking
onto the garden: here I would read and write, stick butterflies, make odd things; this was called (Basque + Latin)
'gochokissime'.

'Grand fichier', 1 May 1978

From the seaside . . .

The whole of his childhood was spent not far from the sea. Bayonne
was a small port with a population of less than 30,000: here Barthes
would live from his first year to the age of nine. So this is where all
his earliest years were spent, within this city in the South-West of
France, crossed by the rivers Adour and Nive. Berthe, his grandmother on his father's side, lived with her daughter Alice in the
allées Paulmy, a fine avenue dating back to the eighteenth century,
stretching along Vauban's ramparts and leading down to the quay-
side. This thoroughfare owes its name to Antoine-René Voyer
d'Argenson, Marquis de Paulmy (1722–87): while he was Secretary
of State for War, he authorized Bayonne to create an avenue for
pedestrians opposite Vauban's glacis and to plant trees along it,
which at the time contravened the laws on fortifications.[1] It was
here that, until 1919, Henriette lived with her son after her husband's death. For the child, the years before school were the years
that he could not remember – and this loss itself transformed them
into a paradise. We should note that in the following years, when
Barthes lived alone with his mother and with a young maidservant
in Marracq (1919–24), somewhat outside the city centre, he spent
his Thursdays and his Sundays at the home of his grandmother; he
would sometimes stop off there for a bite to eat after school. All the
values of the *childhood home* are conferred on this house 'with three

gardens' described in *Roland Barthes by Roland Barthes*, which had all the characteristics of a fairy tale, being at once a chalet and a chateau. This perfection was generous. It was attributed to the city as a whole: 'Bayonne, Bayonne, the perfect city: riverain, aerated with sonorous suburbs (Mouserolles, Marrac, Lachepaillet, Beyris), yet immured, fictive: Proust, Balzac, Plassans. Primordial image-hoard of childhood: the province-as-spectacle, History-as-odor, the bourgeoisie-as-discourse.'[2] This love song, which opens the book – where it forms the caption for the second photograph – expresses all the ambiguity of childhood: happiness and boredom, the unlimited possibilities of a time open to the future together with a feeling of confinement. At that time, Bayonne was undergoing considerable transformation. After 1897, the state authorized the city council to gradually tear down some sections of Vauban's ramparts encircling the city, girded with 58 hectares of military terrain for a city of 40 hectares. This authorization had a significant impact on the shape of the city: the military were no longer in control of redevelopment, and the building work sometimes turned urban life into total chaos. The Réduit and the casemates were destroyed between 1905 and 1910, and a park was created in their place, planted with silver limes and maples, able to withstand the strong winds from the west. But then the war broke out and Bayonne again became a fortified place where foreign troops, including the Czech Legion, came to train. Redevelopment and property speculation were temporarily suspended. After the war, work was resumed, but at a slower pace. A section of the old ramparts, situated between the Château-Vieux and the park, was finally razed in 1923, while the other section was listed.[3] The city grew and changed appearance: the roads were widened, the Esplanade was lined with apartment blocks around what are now the rue Jules-Labat, the rue Léon-Bonnat and the allées Paulmy, and led to the War Memorial that was inaugurated on 11 November 1924, the very same month that Barthes and his mother left for Paris. There was talk of the 'new Bayonne', and its centre, between the wars, was near the Feria, the new theatre, the tram station for Biarritz – in short, right next to the allées Paulmy where Barthes's grandmother lived. The big cinema, Le Majestic, opened here in 1926. But the old quarters were not far, and this was a good place for a stroll: the fine villas of Les Arènes, the allées Marines, the banks of the Adour, the tiny streets around the Cathedral Sainte-Marie. A temporary bullring with 7,000 seats had been built very close to the allées Paulmy in 1893 by a company set up by the banker Salzedo and wealthy city traders. The bullring operated until 14 August 1919, when the audience burned it down with a bonfire of chairs to protest about the late arrival of six Portuguese *toros*. Salzedo was ruined and sold his establishment. The young Barthes must have seen the burnt-out building, abandoned for several years, every day. What he recalled from this period was mainly sensations, those that later on would fleetingly restore his past to him: the smell of the Parc de la Poterne, the patisseries and the sugar bought at the 'Bon Goût', the sexuality of the park that 'floated' along the banks of the Adour: these sensations were indestructibly linked to particular places.

The Maison Lanne, the one in the allées Paulmy, with its 'three gardens', remained the metonymy or enclosure of this childhood. Although there was just one garden, it was divided into three areas, distinguished by Barthes as the 'worldly garden', the 'domestic garden' and the 'wild garden'. The first was used to greet visitors and say goodbye to them, 'taking tiny steps, pausing often'; the second was set out like a house, with its alleys, its lawns, its beds of herbs and flowers, 'roses, hydrangeas (that awkward flower of the South-West of France), carpet grass, rhubarb, kitchen herbs in old crates, a big magnolia whose white flowers bloomed on a level with the upstairs bedrooms', and a fig-tree, which is the object of an 'amorous' memory: to gather the highest figs there was 'a long bamboo pole and a tin funnel stamped with rosettes that was fasted to it';[4] the last garden, the 'wild' one, was 'undefined, sometimes fallow, sometimes planted with vegetables that needed no tending'.[5] This tripartite space made it easy to move from one zone to another and adapt to different possible worlds – it is connected by Barthes to the utopias of Jules Verne and Fourier in which the author felt at home – and to the various spheres of social life. It was another way of not having a definite milieu. In this garden, as in his family structure, the child experienced some loneliness and real boredom: he mentions this twice, as being among the irreducible feelings of childhood, with a proneness to attacks of despair and vulnerability. Thus, the memory of an early childhood that was happy and pampered, in which the young boy was the object of the endless attentions of a tiny community of women – was it this memory that fed into the work on the *béguinages* in the seminar on *How to Live Together?* – was also affected by moments of distress that are not just the sign of a melancholy memory. 'I explained that I'd been happy because I was surrounded by affection and that, on this very important level, I had been satisfied. But at the same time I had a difficult childhood and youth.'[6] There is always a darkness cast over the sunny glow of the discourse on childhood, the only shadow shed by the death of his father, and by death as such, which had been there right at the start of his life. But there are bright memories too, almost all associated with the ideal environment this house provided for a child, with its nooks and crannies where he could play and hide. At the end of his life, Barthes remembered that he had built a cabin for himself: 'As a child I made a retreat of my own, a cabin and belvedere, on the top landing of an outside flight of steps, looking onto the garden: here I would read and write, stick butterflies, make odd things; this was called (Basque + Latin) "gochokissime".'[7] His grandmother and his aunt helped him to set it all up, to find the name for his den, drawing on the Basque word for 'sweetness' and thus 'pleasant place.' They, together with his mother, were perfectly kind to him; his memories in this respect are entirely positive. 'Thought that these women, my mother, were extremely kind, good, generous (not mean or jealous, etc.); and then thought, in an odd detour, or "discovered", that basically Freud never focused on the "kindness" of parents. It's all one in his view, being nice or nasty. And yet this kindness can be "decisive".'[8] And it probably was, for Barthes, just as his own kindness was a main quality, according to almost all the people who knew him. The adjective 'kind' (*gentil*) is the one that even today still comes most often to the lips of Michel Salzedo in connection with his brother. And if this adjective sometimes has slightly pejorative connotations, we should here grant it all its force as a constantly benevolent way of behaving: Barthes would later turn this into a value he called 'delicacy'. In 'Some notes on *Maman*' in his *Mourning Diary*, he notes: 'Her delicacy was absolutely atopic (socially): exclusive of classes; without insignia.'[9] He passionately sought for this quality in the people he met, but before that it had cast a great swathe of gentleness around his childhood: this was a period in which Barthes was unacquainted with fear.

Apart from Sundays on the beach and the visits his grandmother received, and sometimes the charity bazaars he mentions in *Sade, Fourier, Loyola*, in which he would gaze at grand *tableaux vivants*, '*Sleeping Beauty*', for example',[10] this was the time when he was starting to learn – language and music simultaneously ('I was composing small pieces long before I could write').[11] Aunt Alice was a piano teacher and gave lessons at her home. The house echoed to the sound of melodies and wrong notes. Immersed in his family's musicality, which was also, in this modest milieu, a source of income, he listened as art and pedagogy mingled, and melody was interwoven with the endless false starts of pupils struggling with the rudiments of music. He mentions this in the last complete text he wrote before his death, 'Piano-souvenir' ('Piano-memory'), whose themes intersect with those mentioned by Pascal Quignard in *Leçons de solfège et de piano*, where he talks about his three great-aunts, Juliette, Marthe and Marguerite, at whose home the young Louis Poirier, the future Julien Gracq, came for his lessons in Ancenis, in a poor house that nonetheless had 'a piano on every floor, string instruments everywhere to play trios, quartets, quintets, on the spot. But apart from that, nothing.'[12] 'From my bedroom', writes Barthes, 'or, more often, coming back home through the garden, I would hear scales, pieces of classical music; and neither my distance nor the often rather tiresome character of music teaching were disagreeable to me, quite the opposite; it was as if the piano were preparing to become a memory; for each time that I hear from afar a piano that someone is practising on, it's my whole childhood, our house in B. and even the light of the South-West that force their way into my sensibility.'[13] Thus, he adds, he does not need any phrase from Vinteuil to activate his memory, he just needs a scale, one of those exercises that for him define the piano, which he would play all his life long, comprising the very rhythm of his existence. In these few phrases are contained several of the qualities of his childhood, those *qualia*: the auditory sensation, which is accompanied by a tactile sensation as Barthes goes on to note that the most incomparable effect is produced by the contact between 'the ivory key and the skin on the fingertip', the metonymic power of the piano that brings back both the house and the light he loved so much. He also points out that music is not, for him, just a melody, but also a text, which is explained by the way he learned how to read and how to play music at the same time: from this, Barthes would keep throughout his life a taste for reading a score, preferring to work from the written notes rather than to play from memory: 'For me, the piano was also a literature. In the "little salon", there was a big filing cabinet with boxes of separate pieces and bound scores.' Here he would find the clear handwriting of his aunt or the freer pencil strokes of the notations made by his grand-mother as a little girl: 'Beethoven, Schumann, these are not just airs or themes, but also a text, in which is written and deposited, in a family, the movement of generations.'[14] In the evening of his life, Barthes could still see in his mind's eye the aunt he called 'Ady', and he would think back with nostalgia 'to her big handwriting on the working notebooks of her piano pupils, to the lesson she gave every week in Castillon, the property of the Lahouche family in Tarnes (they would come to fetch her in a landau), to the books she read at night (she was an insomniac), to her poor life, and all of a sudden it pierces me like a dagger, brings all life to a halt. (What, all of that for *nothing*?).'[15] What profoundly saddens him is the disproportion between what was once everything for the child and of which all that is left is a vague memory, one that cannot be shared, is already almost dead; but also the idea that he cannot make his memory of her exist by writing it down, which would enable her to last for a while, at least for the time of his own celebrity.[16]

Unlike professional artists or musicians who can detach for a while their practice or their art from the context in which they learned them, as he himself would do for writing, Barthes always kept a domestic dimension when it came to the piano – in this sense we need to distinguish between his relation to the piano and its connected objects from his relation to music, whether or not this music was for the piano – a theme to which we shall be returning.

The instrument defines the space of a private practice, corresponding to a lofty version of amateurism, preferring 'wandering, fragmentation, and sensible caprice' to a perfect execution.[17] It also defines a bodily technique: we read a score with our eyes and our fingers; we engage our bodies simultaneously in acts involving both sight and fingers. What we have here is a perfection of reading-writing that constitutes the dream of the writer-critic: the ergonomy involved will require a whole lifetime's work to mature.

In 1919, Roland moved with his mother to what was at that time known as the 'suburbs' of Bayonne, now considered as one of its more 'distinguished' quarters. In Marracq (which Barthes usually spells 'Marrac') there are large properties side by side with rural areas occupied by market gardeners, military zones and allotments. Several hectares of military terrain had just been liberated by the army and the city council had started to divide this into plots, but without doing a great deal to ensure the provision of drinking water and gas. In the early 1920s this work was well under way, but still largely unfinished. Henriette lived close to building sites that were great play areas for children from poor families: even if Barthes still remembered playing with lower middle-class children, Jean and Linette de Lignerolles, the Rime children, Julien Garance and Jacques Brisoux, it is more than probable that his companions, like him, had quite modest lifestyles. After he had moved here, Barthes started attending the nursery school at Marracq, then the Lycée de Bayonne, a primary and secondary school that had opened in Marracq in 1896, just outside the city and so quite close to his home: this proximity was perhaps one of the reasons why Henriette Barthes had moved, the other probably being her desire to free herself from the supervision of her in-laws. Apart from the times spent in the building sites, or riding through the more rural parts of Marracq on his tricycle, the other games Barthes enjoyed as a small boy will have been society games (Pope Joan), walks in the gardens, day-dreaming about the boats leaving the harbour, perhaps teasing the cats . . . On Sundays he would go to the family home for lunch, taking the second line of the tram which passed right in front of the lycée.

One other important aspect of these early years was Barthes's initiation into religion, which occupied a far from negligible place in his childhood and above all in his teens, when he went through real mystical crises. Roland Barthes was baptized into the Calvinist religion in the Protestant Church in Bayonne. This building was on the rue Albert-1er and had been opened on 20 June 1847; its sober façade, decorated simply with an open Bible, followed a design by the architect Boulanger. Barthes's godfather was Joseph Nogaret, whose sister played the harmonium during the services: this godfather sometimes took care of Barthes, gave him Christmas presents, like all godfathers ('a bag of walnuts and a five-franc piece'). The Protestant community in Bayonne, which at the beginning of the century had around 300 members, was very influenced by Joseph Nogaret's father, also called Joseph: he was the pastor in the church for forty years. His son, Barthes's godfather, was a key figure in this community, too, and the author among other works of a short 'history of Protestantism in Bayonne'.[18] The Protestants of Bayonne were in a tiny minority in an episcopal city, which, being close to Spain, was naturally a bastion of Catholicism, and they were even outnumbered four to one by the Jewish community: they had waited 300 years for a church of their own to be built. They felt tolerated, but were imbued with a sense of being an exception, of being different. The Protestants, often of foreign origin – the community initially comprised Lutherans and Calvinists who had come to this port city from Germany, Holland and England for socioeconomic reasons – were often viewed by the rest of the city as non-French: another form of marginalization. Barthes remembered this history less than he remembered the rites and the associated sensations that children enjoy: the smell of smoky candles and the mandarins at Christmas, the hymns . . . He continued to learn the Bible in Paris, where, every summer, he went with his mother to visit her side of the family. In those days, the train journey took fifteen hours. They often stayed with the pastor Louis Bertrand, in the rue de l'Avre, 15th arrondissement, in the La Motte-Picquet district. This evangelist, who was born in 1867 and died in 1941, was well known for the help he gave to the poor and homeless; he led missions to Fresnes prison and local hospitals and had, until 1919, been pastor in Bayonne,[19] which explains his connection with Henriette Barthes: he most probably baptized Roland Barthes. After his wife's death, he took the position at the Grenelle hostel for the most underprivileged.[20] The fact that Henriette Barthes frequented people such as Louis Bertrand and Joseph Nogaret show that she was well integrated into this community, the existence of which was, for Barthes, a second or third home. What Barthes remembered of Louis Bertrand was essentially the slow way he read the Bible. 'The Bible is read so slowly at every meal that we sometimes miss the train if we are leaving that evening.' This slowness of reading would prove a tenacious biographeme. We find it used to describe the way Lucette Finas reads Georges Bataille in a 1977 text by Barthes called, aptly enough, 'Question de tempo': 'The remorseless reading, the sustained insistence, the conjunction of a "mobile vigilance" and a "delay . . . that is almost a fixation" produce an effect of fascination.'[21] We also encounter it in the way he evokes walking, defined as 'the slow and rhythmic penetration of the landscape'[22] as well as in his relation to the piano. He uses syncopation and unusual durations, and refers to his excessively slow speeds, while generalizing this invitation to slow down.[23]

This southern childhood left its traces, and permanently marked the body. It imprinted on Barthes a form of distance that can be seen in a certain accent, a sensitivity to certain curves in the landscape and to a unique kind of light. This was all admirably summed up by Barthes in the text he wrote for *L'Humanité* in 1977, 'The Light of the Sud-Ouest'. Childhood is, first and foremost, a memory of the body, with the smell of chocolate, the squeaking of rope sandals, the taste of Spanish olive oil, 'the congested look of the dark shops and the narrow streets, the flyspecked paper of the books in the municipal library'. It can also be heard from his accent, even if he has by and large lost it: 'I say "socializme" and not "socialissme"', which perhaps means he is some distance from real socialism, as he amusingly suggests, but also, we might add, at an equal distance from *parisianizme* and *familializme* . . . Something from his childhood protects him from ideology: his own domain, separate in space and time, the experience of margins and above all the experience of the difference with which this light of the South-West imbues everything: 'It saves this country from all vulgarity, from all "gregarity" too, making it inapt for facile tourism and revealing its profound aristocracy (not a question of class but of character).'[24] The absence of a father; poverty; religious marginality: all these differences are summed up and subsumed into this light-space, liquid and trenchant, capable of expressing the grain of each thing and the very nature of its difference. This light protects one from uniformity. It writes something specific onto the dark background of childhood: a kind of sensibility, a way of moving one's body and above all a system of signs that writing will seek to discover, between serenity and loss, between slowness and disarray.

This light, both luminously gentle and heartrending at once, should help us to understand Barthes's relation to his mother – in this light, as it were. It should be grasped gently, with her kindness and delicacy being seen in the context of all the sorrow they entail when remembered afterwards, and essentially linked to this light. On 13 August 1979, in a note of what would posthumously become the *Mourning Diary*, we read: 'Leaving Urt, after a difficult stay, in the train near Dax (that South-West sunlight, which has accompanied my life), in desperate straits, tears over *maman*'s death.'[25]

. . . to the heart of Paris

1924 November: My mother decides to move to Paris. The three of us (including Marie L.) arrive one grey November morning. The apartment, rented by correspondence, in the rue de la Glacière, is occupied. We're out on the street, with trunks and suitcases; a dairywoman offers us, at the back of her shop, chocolate and croissants. We move into the rue Jacob (in a dreary hostel for War Widows), rue Bonaparte, no. 20, in an attic room, on mattresses with mice scampering round them, rue Mazarine (no. 42) and rue Jacques-Callot (no. 16). My mother works in a workshop binding art books, for Mlle de Felice, in Courbevoie . . .

1924–25: I enter (in mid-year) the Lycée Montaigne, in the *huitième*. The teacher, M. Lebeau, is really mean; he is always forcing us to do cruel sessions of mental arithmetic, and pulls the pupils' hair. I feel lost and unhappy, struggling to keep up; either because I can't settle down or because my health is fragile (I often have ear-ache), I frequently miss the classes. A bearded doctor is consulted and prescribes that I sniff salt water and, what is more important, says I should stop going to school (this doctor lived in the rue de Rome and his name was Dr Clément; I recently discovered he must have been the same doctor who treated Raymond Roussel). Six months' break: **in the workshop of the rue Mazarine, snuggled into a comfortable armchair, I spend my days reading magazines (especially film magazines: they discuss Cavalcanti's *La Jalousie du Barbouillé*) bought from a woman from Toulouse who ran a small shop in the rue Mazarine (it smelled of the frying potatoes she was still chewing as she came out of her office)**; with Marie L. [. . .], every week I go to the Danton cinema to see silent films in several episodes (*Jean Chouan*) and Charlie Chaplin (*The Gold Rush*).

1926–27: My time in the *sixième* is interrupted. In January 1927, we move to Capbreton, where my brother (my half-brother) Michel is born in April. I am eleven and a half. During these months in the Landes region, I play with the local kids; I go with them looking for pine soles that we sell at 1 franc per bag. In the evenings, by the fireside, I read Sue (*The Wandering Jew*). We spend the summer of 1927 in Hossegor, which is not as yet fashionable: there are only two hotels on the lake, nothing at La Mer Sauvage where nobody ever goes.

1927–30 I return to the *sixième* at the Lycée Montaigne where I am now a 'good pupil' in 'arts' subjects (especially in French and history). **In 4e, the teacher is M. Grandsaignes d'Hauterive. He has a tortoiseshell lorgnon, and smells of pepper; he divides the class into 'camps' and 'rows', each one with its own 'leader'; the whole time is spent in contests.** I also play in the Luxembourg Gardens; our gang has its assembly point in the alley where they play *boules* these days; it's a bench, the 'sacred bench'; we play at skittles, measure the perimeter of the Gardens with a rope, do endurance runs. The park guards tell me off, ask me if I'm not related to Senator Barthes [*sic*], famous for having ensured that a law was passed to give 'warm wine to the soldiers'; sorry, but I'm not. One day, in the distance, I see a pink monument being inaugurated in honour of José Maria de Heredia.

Period of religious fervour: I read the New Testament a lot, I want to be a pastor. Every Sunday morning, I go across the Pont des Arts and attend the service at the Oratoire du Louvre; this is the hive of liberal Protestantism.

For each school holiday, I go to stay with my grandparents in Bayonne . . .

The end of childhood came early, in the break represented by leaving for Paris in 1924. Until then, Paris had been a place for holidays. Now the journeys were the other way round. The geographical change was also a sociological displacement. Arriving in Paris was a radical change from the bourgeois social milieu and a more explicit descent into poverty. It is not entirely clear why Henriette Barthes decided to leave Bayonne. Perhaps it was Pastor Louis Bertrand who found her this job at a bookbinder's. It is also possible that, having made an attempt to have her son recognized as a 'pupil of the nation' (as he was a few months later, in 1925), she thought it would be best if he continued his education on a bursary in a good Paris lycée. Whatever the reason, in November 1924 Barthes was in Paris with his mother and the young Basque maid Marie Latxague, initially in a hostel for war widows, then in transitory lodgings where they could find them, rooms without running water or any comfort in various streets of the 6th arrondissement where they always had a cat to keep them company.

He started the *huitième* class (CM1) at the Lycée Montaigne, behind the Luxembourg Gardens. He remembered the problems he had as a provincial lad having to adapt to Paris, and his feelings of loneliness. In this context, his illness, which was starting to make its presence felt, appeared like a blessing. It paved the way for him to learn about other things, at his own speed, from magazines and cinemas, and serial novels: all the places where children's culture and popular culture come together.: They left their mark on him. He explored the city by bus, and this enforced leisure gave him a new and more familiar feel for the place. He now felt at home here, and the house in Bayonne became his holiday home even though it was still 'his' place. This did not stop him feeling bored, and the absence of his mother weighed on him; she was forced to work in the suburbs, as we read in this biographeme included in *A Lover's Discourse*: 'As a child, I didn't forget: interminable days, abandoned days, when the Mother was working far away; I would go, evenings, to wait for her at the U^{bis} bus stop, Sèvres-Babylone; the buses would pass one after the other, she wasn't in any of them.'[26]

In summer 1925, Henriette met an industrial ceramist by the name of André Salzedo, who became her lover. He was an alluring man, a horse-rider of distinction who frequented the high-society resorts on the Atlantic Coast. The following summer, she became pregnant by him. This was the year Barthes started the *sixième*, entering secondary school. He took a break from school in January so that his mother could spend the rest of her pregnancy in peace at Capbreton in the Landes: this was a small fishing port located 17 kilometres from Bayonne, not far from André Salzedo who lived at Sainte-Martin-de-Hinx with his wife, the artist Maggie Salzedo, and their three children. Although he was married, Salzedo decided to acknowledge his son, who was born on 11 April 1927. Roland Barthes was eleven and a half. This event probably marked the end of his childhood in his own eyes; it led to a confusion in his memory that meant he tended to link it to the period when they had moved to Paris. It also to some extent confirmed the absence of any obstacle on the path of his exclusive feminine love for his mother. Far from posing as a rival, this little brother, born just as Roland was entering adolescence and the period of his sexual life, was a child whose father was not absent, like Roland's own, but so rarely present that he could be forgotten; this new child was symbolically speaking much more the child formed by the mother and her eldest son as a couple, rather than a younger brother who would get in the way of this love. Often left to his own devices, and never finding himself in the company of other children from his own family, Roland Barthes was already very independent by this time. Furthermore, the 'family without familialism' to which he belonged authorized changes of place. His mother was not inclined to be authoritarian and did not seek to endorse the law. 'She never made any observations.' This remark often recurs in the author's personal notes, some of which found their way into the *Mourning Diary*: it is found in several variant forms: 'She has never spoken to me as if to an irresponsible child'; or, for a text he was planning to write about her: 'To begin: "All the time I lived with her – all my life – my mother never made *an observation* about me".'[27] It seems that she trusted him right from the start and based all his upbringing on her love and this trust. This behaviour fostered a precocious sense of independence in the boy, and gave him a sense of responsibility.

By bringing into the world this little boy called Michel, Henriette Barthes, whose upbringing, as we have seen, was quite free and easy, demonstrated her indifference to convention. She was in love with a married man, an artist who led the *vie de Bohème*, and a Jew. The Salzedo family had always been one of the most ancient and most important Jewish families in Bayonne, those who were known as Portuguese in allusion to the role this city played in taking in the Jews of Spain and Portugal when they were persecuted and then expelled from those countries at the end of the fifteen and sixteenth centuries. It was in Bayonne that the biggest Judeo-Portuguese community existed in the eighteenth century (3,000 inhabitants around 1750), mainly gathered in the Saint-Esprit district, which had several establishments and included a number of rural Jewish communities from the Basque country and the Landes.[28] In spite of her regular attendance at church and her manifest belief in Protestantism, Henriette was not held back by any potential prejudices. When she was buried, in October 1977, the pastor apologized in the name of the Protestant community of Bayonne for the fact, not so much that she had been an unmarried mother, but that she had been so with a Jew.[29] It seems also that her own mother, Noémie Révelin, cut off her living allowance after this birth. In fact, in spite of her comfortable social position and her apartment on the Place du Panthéon, where she held a salon, Noémie gave little help to her daughter in her hour of need. Several of Barthes's intimate texts bear the imprint of a reluctance to visit his grandmother to beg for a piece of clothing too big for him that had belonged to her younger son, or a few coins to help get through to the end of the month. Does this show a belated desire to follow the bourgeois conventions on the part of Noémie Révelin, or was she jealous of her daughter? It is difficult to decide what were the social reasons for this distance, and what was the result of social factors. Something that was rumoured in the family, and has been reported by Michel Salzedo, is that Noémie Révelin was jealous of Roland and his excellent results at school, which showed up the poor marks of her youngest son, Étienne, just a few years older than his nephew. All these reasons no doubt played a part; the relation between mother and daughter was fraught, and there was no financial help to be expected on that side. In 1977, Barthes told Bernard-Henri Lévy, in an interview for *Le Nouvel Observateur*: 'There was often no food in the house. [. . .] we had to go and buy a bit of pâté or a few potatoes at a little grocery on the rue de Seine.' He also mentioned the problematic rhythm given to life by the arrival of the deadline for paying the rent, and the little dramas attendant on the start of each new school year: 'I didn't have the necessary uniform. No money when we were supposed to contribute to a collection. Not enough to buy text books.'[30] He justified his later taste for spending money on the basis that they had been at this time constantly short of cash, which had caused acute embarrassment.

Relations with Roland Barthes's family on his father's side also deteriorated. After his brother's birth, the teenaged Barthes went to Bayonne alone, while Henriette rented a house in the Landes, first at Capbreton, at Hossegor, and then on a more regular basis at Biscarrosse; Barthes joined his mother and his brother for a week or two during the summer holidays. Here, Henriette Barthes met up with André Salzedo who also sometimes came to see his son in Paris.[31] Their relationship continued, on an intermittent basis, for many years, but it seems that they did not get on; their son remembers that they quarrelled frequently, even after André Salzedo's divorce in 1931. So anything that might have seemed to suit family life, an idea of the family or some family spirit, was always compromised. Only grandfather Binger carried on receiving his daughter and her two sons, in his home in L'Isle-Adam, almost every Sunday. Without there having been any concerted plan, many events and situations conspired to ensure that those pillars of the bourgeoisie, family and modest comfort, crumbled away. Henriette Barthes and her two sons moved home often, so there was no settled environment. This was perhaps what gave Barthes the feeling of being 'decentred' when he looked back on that Parisian period of his childhood. Only school offered a certain external stability. Barthes continued to be a very good pupil, in spite of the regular interruptions entailed by his illness. When he remembered one of his teachers from the *quatrième*, M. Grandsaignes d'Hauterive, he emphasized the spirit of emulation and competition that this teacher imbued in his pupils. Robert Grandsaignes d'Hauterive, aged about 50 when Barthes had him as a teacher, had not as yet published the works that made his name as a grammarian, his dictionary of Old French and above all his important *Dictionnaire des racines des langues européennes* (*Dictionary of the Roots of European languages*).[32] Only his thesis on the pessimism of La Rochefoucauld had been published, in 1914. But he had passed the competitive *agrégation* exam and was correspondingly erudite: this, together with the fine manners he had inherited, and his noble family name, was bound to impress his pupils.

Barthes spent his leisure time sometimes alone, sometimes in a group. Like his classmates, he would meet his friends in the Luxembourg for games that they usually played in 'gangs'. But he tended to go to the theatre or the cinema, and to concerts, alone, or with Marie Latxague or one or other of his friends. He dates to this period his discovery of the 'cartel of the four' actors, Louis Jouvet, Gatson Baty, Georges Pitoëff and Charles Dullin, who lay behind the creation of a popular theatre. He often went to the Atelier, which Dullin had set up in 1921, as well as the Mathurins, which Pitoëff did not take over until 1934, which shows that Barthes's memories, like the childhood memories of all of us, do not come with dates, even though he himself places his inability to 'date himself' only to his later years. 'I remember my childhood and youth quite well, I know the dates and can point out the landmarks. And after that, strangely enough, I don't remember any more, I can't recall the dates, the dates of my own life. As if I had a memory only at the beginning, as if adolescence formed the exemplary, unique time of memory.'[33] But these dates are themselves unstable and it is more likely that he attended these theatres, as well as the Colonne and Pasdeloup concerts, when he was well into his teens, after he had started at the Lycée Louis-le-Grand. On the other hand, he remembered the precise occasion when he saw, as a very young boy, Buñuel's *Un Chien andalou*, at Studio 28 in the rue Tholozé in Montmartre (the film came out in Paris in 1929). The chronological jumps backwards and forwards that make the narration of this film so unique can be seen as symbolizing the compact ordering of distant memories, sometimes dragged out over time, sometimes muddled or in the wrong sequence.

The end of his time at the Lycée Montaigne marked Barthes's entry into his second adolescence. It was here, in the *quatrième*, that he met Philippe Rebeyrol: the two became friends. This was the time when Barthes freed himself from the yoke of religion. To his first sexual emotions were linked new books that opened other worlds to him. This was the role played by two works: *En Grèce* (*In Greece*), a collection of photos by Antoine Bon with a commentary by Chapouthier, and *Nietzsche en Italie* (*Nietzsche in Italy*) by Pourtalès.[34] They intimated to him that there are things to be learned outside the classroom and that literature can be lived directly. 'This book will have achieved its purpose', wrote Fernand Chapouthier, 'if the reader, taking up his old texts, gave a new frisson to well-known words.' This set out the programme for the next few years, years of long-lasting friendships, first loves, first new homes . . . but also the incorporation of the Ancients through the study of Greek and Latin and the discovery of the theatre. A note from July 1979 suggests all this pell-mell: 'First loves: Jacques G., the young Manterola girls. The room in the rue Gambetta, sexual desire, the Allées marines, the flies, the letter in the post, the evenings . . . '[35]

Roland Barthes at the age of 2.

Roland Barthes around 1930.

The Barthes family house in Bayonne ('the three gardens').

de Bayonne, qui s'y prêtait avec ses recoins.[?15]
→ Pensé qu'enfant je m'étais fait une
retraite à moi, cabane et belvédère, au
palier supérieur d'un escalier extérieur, sur
le jardin : j'y lisais, écrivais, collais
des papillons, bricolais ; cela s'appelait
(basque + latin) "GochoKissime" → Pensée que ma grd mère et ma tante avaient
favorisé cette installation, trouvé le
nom etc — Pensée qu'elles, ma mère, é-
taient profondément "gentilles", "bonnes", gé-
néreux (sans mesquinerie ni jalousie etc) —
→ Et alors pensé, par un détour bizarre —
ou "découvert" qu'en somme Freud ne s'
est jamais occupé de la "gentillesse" des
parents. Tout est égal devant lui
le bon et le méchant. Cependant cette gentillesse
peut être "déterminante"....

'Gochokissime',
Grand fichier,
1 May 1978.

On the beach with his mother and
his brother.

3

His whole life ahead of him

The years of apprenticeship

Barthes now became a student at the Lycée Louis-le-Grand, whose main façade, completely renovated at the end of the nineteenth century, was located at the corner of the rue Saint-Jacques and the rue Cujas. It was a logical progression for him to find himself here: in 1885, the younger pupils in Louis-le-Grand had been transferred to Montaigne, which comprised the annex of the lycée for local boys. Barthes's route to school changed: after the rue Clément, where he picked up the two Blanchard brothers, then the rue Férou and the Luxembourg, he now went down the rue Mazarine, the Rue de l'École-de-Médecine, the boulevard Saint-Michel and the passage Gerson.[1] The classrooms were in the old buildings of the Collège de Clermont, where the Jesuits had taught Molière and Voltaire; Baudelaire had been a more recent pupil. Barthes finished his schooling here, from the *troisième* to his final year, *terminale*, where he took literary subjects (in those days this was known as the *classe de philosophie*); he was always a good student, especially in literary subjects, and his school career was untroubled until it suffered a major interruption with his first stay in a sanatorium, in Bedous in 1934, which meant taking time out of his *terminale*. The rhythm was fixed by the school calendar, and Barthes spent all his holidays in Bayonne, where he enjoyed the happiest days of his teenage life, in the company of his friend Jacques Gilet, busying himself with music – he played the piano, alone or in duets with Jacques or his aunt Alice. The memories recounted in the long autobiographical note would provide almost none of the anamneses used in *Roland Barthes by Roland Barthes*. This was no longer a time of buried memories requiring an effort to be disinterred, a dive into the darkness, into a scattered haze of fragments; rather, it represented the opening up of social time, which shapes people more than they shape it, and binds individuals more tightly to the collective.

1933: I get a mark of distinction in the Latin prose at the *concours général²* (why Latin prose?) and I take my baccalaureate in the *Première*; the subject for the essay is 'the romantic hero' I am [*text torn*] and I manage to get by, as I use the [*text torn*] from the classes that I've learned. – In the summer, in Bayonne, I have a friend, Jacques Gilet, from Bordeaux; I see him every day; we play piano duets between 2 and 8 o'clock, we play everything and anything; I meet up with him in the mornings, on the beach and often in the evenings in Biarritz; one day, my aunt stops while playing the piano and says to me, sternly, '*Don't you think you're overdoing it?*'

1933–34: At Louis-le-Grand, with a few friends, Rebeyrol, Brissaud, Oualid, we make the big mistake of going for M. Millaud's class – he gets a lot of pupils through the exams; he reels off his lessons by heart; he has a ready-made cravat mounted on a little metallic apparatus; sometimes, without his realizing, it springs open and the cravat droops forward like a wilting stem; he talks of Bergson and Théodule Ribot. The history teacher is Mouzet, nicknamed Navet [turnip – Trans. note]; the students play up in his lessons, he enjoys this – so, sadistically, they are sometimes well-behaved: this puts him right off his stride. The class is politicized; there are a lot of fascists (Jeunesses patriotes); it's the year of 6 February; there aren't many left-wing students (Chautemps, Chaudié, Rebeyrol); we form – rather pompously – a group called *Défense Républicaine et Antifasciste* (DRAF), as I've already for some years been a reader of *L'Oeuvre* (the radical newspaper) and Jaurès (Marxism: unknown).

I've been giving private lessons for three years: an honourable intellectual and social chore. I decide to be the permanent tutor of the two sons of Dr G, who lives on the boulevard Saint-Germain, looking over the square (the block where the Banque Nationale de Paris is now); but on 10 May 1934, I have a haemoptysis; I drop my studies at the lycée two months before the bac and take refuge in Bayonne: here the weather is hot and stormy. The family doctor, Dr Croste, treats me with injections of gold salts, Spanish fly on the thorax, and this piece of advice, which I don't understand: *and don't even think about seeing any girls*. However, my friend Jacques Gilet keeps his distance from me.

1934–35: to avoid the sanatorium (though this is a mistake), I spend a year in personalized treatment (with my brother and my mother) in Bedous, a large village in the Vallée d'Aspe, just before you get to Somport; we live in three rooms in the home of Larricq, a draper: he's a handsome man, with distinguished manners, who married an exiled Russian aristocrat whose mother and sister live there, in a single room where they make tapestries for days on end, to earn a living; the sister, a hunchback and a charming woman, gives me German lessons; I manage to hire a piano in Pau from Pétion. Apart from that, I'm bored, and live in an unspeakable state of sexual oppression; but in literary terms, it's Virgilian; there are plenty of lines in Virgil that can be applied to this life in the country.

1935–36: return to Paris, in a new apartment, in the rue Servandoni. Prepare for the exam for Normale Supérieure? Impossible: I wouldn't be able to get up early again, to go to the lycée. I enter the Sorbonne, for a *licence* in classics (probably a mistake: it would have been better to choose philosophy or history); the lessons bore me so much that I spend the days in the almost empty library, gossiping with a group of friends; we also go for coffee at Marcusot's, opposite Gibert's, or in the little Austrian patisserie in the rue de l'École-de-Médecine. We set up an ancient theatre group, which occupies all our time: we rehearse *The Persians*, which is on the syllabus (but in the Greek oral, when I was given Atossa's dream, I didn't know the meaning of a single word).

1936 May: it's the Popular Front and the premiere of the *Persians* in the courtyard of the Sorbonne (I play Darius, make my appearance through the door of the Chapel).

From Bayonne, Barthes corresponded with his friends still in Paris or away on holiday in other places, including Brissaud and Rebeyrol, Sadia Oualid and Jean Huerre. In Paris, he exchanged passionate letters with Jacques Gilet. These correspondences are a source of information about the main lines of Barthes's apprenticeship and the plans for the future that these young men were making. In *troisième*, he was given a prize for a good mark from the hands of the minister plenipotentiary of the King of Romania, the guest of honour who was there to hand out the prizes: Barthes got one first prize, for history and geography, and six distinctions, including one for gymnastics. In *seconde*, he was just as successful. With his friend Philippe Rebeyrol, an even better student, he decided to prepare for the École normale supérieure. They discussed their literary tastes: Mallarmé and Valéry, then Baudelaire and Proust, whose descriptions of provincial life in *The Way by Swann's* Barthes found gripping, even though he would read the rest of the work only two years later. In the summer of his *seconde* year, he enthusiastically read Jaurès on the recommendation of his French teacher. He tried to convert his grandmother to his ideas, but she apparently showed some resistance. On 30 August 1932, he wrote to Philippe Rebeyrol: 'I'd find it difficult not to get really enthusiastic. Until recently, I was a socialist – pretty pompous for a boy of 16 – and partly out of a spirit of contradiction against the whole reactionary, nationalist clan. Now that I've read some Jaurès, it's impossible to be content with lukewarm positions, the *juste milieu* that the French love so much. Jaurès demonstrates such a sweeping attachment to social-ism, so powerful and truthful, so holy, that you can't resist. [. . .] If you look at things more deeply, you see that in Jaurès's work there is less politics than humanity: and this is what is so admirable about him: everything he says is wise, noble, human and above all kindly. His speech to Young people, about Peace, is a masterpiece of eloquence and emotion.' Politically speaking, those years were guided entirely by Barthes's reading. Every time he made some new philosophical or literary discovery, he was filled with the same admiration and a sense of agreement: this was how he lived out his apprenticeship.

At 17, he passed his first bac, in spite of the still difficult material conditions. He earned enough to go to the theatre or to concerts by giving a great number of private lessons. He was always happy to rediscover 'this admirable country with its sunshine and heat',[3] the South-West where he felt at home and among family, and where he divided his time between long bike rides, 'which, since I don't have a lyre, enable me to visit some delightful places',[4] music and literature. Planning to set up a review with his school friends from the lycée – 'though of course it never saw the light of day'[5] – he wrote a pastiche of the *Crito*, or rather a pastiche of a pastiche, based on the pas-tiches of Jules Lemaître, improving the endings of classical works by imitating the style of their authors:[6] here, Barthes gives Socrates a supplementary life, embellished by wine and figs. Published in the review *L'Arc* in 1974, in the special issue devoted to Barthes, this amusing text is a good example of classic schoolboy humour. 'Phaedrus said: ". . . but what about History?" – "History?" said Socrates, "Bah, Plato will fix all that!"', before reaching for another fig off the plate. Barthes comments on the various strata that led to his writing this first text: the most obvious one is the culture fos-tered in the humanities classes at school, which at that time were the 'noble' classes where pupils were taught to write a French far removed from the spoken language, a sort of translation from the ancient languages; this culture transmitted a very circumscribed relationship to Greece, for which the lycée did not arouse any spe-cific desire: 'We had to leave all this behind in order to guess from other sources (a bit of Nietzsche, a bit of statuary, a few photographs from Nauplia or Aegina) that Greece could also be sexuality.'[7] The second stratum is composed of teenage readings: there is no refer-ence to avant-garde works, or to Bataille or surrealism or Artaud, but to 'Gide, just Gide, among a pile of indiscriminate readings, a hodgepodge of Balzac, Dumas, biographies, minor novelists from 1925, etc.' The third stratum was, as ever, childhood and the

South-West, the figs in the family garden in Bayonne, small and
wrinkled, sometimes unripe (and dry), sometimes ripe (and rotten).
In this constantly unripe ripeness, we can see an indirect assessment
of his teenage attempt at writing: on the margins of, but still in thrall
to, school exercises.

On the other hand, Barthes attributed a greater importance to
his first novel. In his year in *première*, Philippe Rebeyrol and he
talked a great deal about their respective plans. Rebeyrol's novel,
which Barthes analyses in a long letter of 14 April 1933 – during
the Easter holidays – presents an ambitious character who goes
through one defeat after another. Promoted to the rank of a literary critic, Barthes advises his fellow student to 'kill off [your] friend
Serge much younger; he can't resist all these successive failures'.
Then he describes his own plan, first specifying that his hero is not
himself, even if many of the details of his novel are taken from his
life as it would have been if he had stayed in Bayonne. He presents
us with a young man from the provinces, Aurélien Page: 'His family
is essentially a bourgeois family, part of the provincial aristocracy,
the world of *comme il faut*. The spirit of this world, this tyrannical,
hypocritical spirit so typical of bourgeois morality, is embodied by
Aurélien's grandmother (not from any personal analogy; far from
it; my grandmother is a spirited woman with none of the feelings or
principles of old Mme Page; but because there needed to be quite
a big age difference between the combatants).' The young man has
revolutionary aspirations that make him stand out from and oppose
his milieu. 'He wants to leave, but he is held back by his mother,
whom he can neither take with him nor leave behind, and the same
family and social laws that make him suffer so greatly, but that he is
not strong enough to break.' He then meets a young woman, Hélène
Manory, who is even more of an obstacle to his breaking out of the
form of society in which he feels condemned to live . . .

The references are perfectly readable, as in Rebeyrol's work:
Balzac, first of all, then the French social novel of the 1920s, a provincial variation on the *Bildungsroman* as it can be read in Robert
Estaunié, Georges Duhamel, Henri Bordeaux and Jacques de
Lacretelle, and, of course, François Mauriac. Indeed, at the end of
his letter Barthes points out that, in order to write the story of this
duel between a young man and society, he drew inspiration from a
novelist he 'really like[s], René Boylsve', who 'showed how shame-
ful was the servile situation in which a "well brought-up girl" was
placed when she got married. I'd like to show that this obligation
is just as inevitable for boys.'[8] As regards the story and the human
relationships it presents us with, the hero's loyalty to his mother
is amusing, as is the conflict that sets him at odds with his grandmother – all rather unexciting in narrative terms. Barthes worked
on this planned novel for several months and finally abandoned

it only the following year, when his own development had taken him too definitively far from his character. On 1 January 1934, he wrote to Philippe: 'Despite being in Bayonne, I'm not thinking at all about my novel; I'm absolutely sure that I won't carry on with it; that's definite; there are several reasons; the first is that my life here, with all the attractions of this house where I'm spoiled like a well-fed priest from Anatole France, is just too pleasant, and so the novel I might write could never be imbued with the same bitterness, the same sour, vengeful bile that I imagined a few months ago. At my age, you can't yet say "I'm growing old"; but in the end, you have to admit that you're developing, and our manly indignation can be aimed at more significant targets than the depravity of a certain social world. I mean, my grandmother's stories, which she tells so wittily, amuse me and disarm my anger. That's the practical reason, I think.' But he adds a more specifically literary reason, showing that the essay-novel is already resembling an investigation into form: 'The theoretical reason is that, personally, if I were ever to write something, that something would always strive to be in the framework, in the "tonality" of Art; but the novel is by definition an anti-artistic genre; form is basically an accessory in it, and psychology inevitably stifles the aesthetic dimension. This isn't a criticism, by the way: everything has its own role to play. It seems to me that I have a certain conception of the work of art in literature that, so far, has not met with much confirmation.' The reasons, as we see, have to do with the genre itself, which seems too narrowly defined to the teenaged Barthes. His investigations would more likely lead him to more aesthetic forms, which he indeed tried out in short plays or musical compositions, a divertimento[9] and even the beginning of a sonata.

The school year 1933–34 was marked by two main events. The first was external and came as the first sign of pressure from history on Barthes's life. The second was personal and constituted the first significant impact of illness on him. Apart from the literary review he was trying to set up with friends, which they called *La Règle organique*, Barthes felt the need to show some political commitment. Many young people were strongly right-wing, in Action française, the Jeunesses patriotes and even, in some cases, the Camelots du roi. Only a few students stated they were firmly on the left. Barthes mentions Rebeyrol, Chaudié and Chautemps, who was related to the prime minister. Hitler had come to power in March 1933 and anti-parliamentary feelings, linked to the discontent aroused by the effects of the Depression, spread through Europe. On 25 December 1933, the manager of the Crédit Municipal pawnshop in Bayonne (a locality that inevitably attracted Barthes's attention), Gustave Tissier, was arrested for fraud and for putting into circulation 25 million francs worth of false bonds. It soon came to light that the fraud had

been organized by the founder of the pawnshop, Serge Alexandre
Stavisky, with the complicity of the deputy mayor of Bayonne,
Dominique-Joseph Garat (who was given a two-year jail sentence),
as well as several other leading figures from the legal profession, the
police and the government. The scandal became public knowledge
and Stavisky was found dead, in a chalet in Chamonix, on 8 January
1934. The press waxed ironical: 'Stavisky commits suicide with a
revolver; the shot was fired at point-blank range.' And: 'Stavisky
committed suicide with a bullet shot from three metres away. He
must have had a really long arm!' Anti-parliamentary feelings
increased as a result of this affair and, in combination with an anti-
Semitism that no longer hesitated to express itself (Stavisky was a
naturalized Ukrainian Jew), led to the 6 February riots that Barthes
viewed as one of the key events of his youth. In the previous few
days, the shouts of far right demonstrators were aimed in particular
at Chautemps and the Garde des Sceaux,[10] Eugène Raynaldy. On
the day a new government was due to be sworn in, in the Chambre
des Députés, the Phalanges universitaires called for a demonstration
on the Place de la Concorde to protest against 'revolutionary organizations' and lead a great national movement that would be ready to
'fight the invader'. The gathering turned into a riot and, that evening,
blazes and clashes with the police led to sixteen deaths and hundreds
of wounded. Many students from Louis-le-Grand responded to the
appeal from the far right leagues, while left-wing students felt they
had a greater need to defend themselves against the rise of fascism
in France. They set up a group called Défense républicaine et antifasciste (DRAF), more influenced by Waldeck-Rousseau and Léon
Blum than by the Groupes de défense antifascistes created by the
Communists in the 1920s. They stated they were ready to defend
freedom by every means, while remaining true democrats. The
political commitment shown here by the teenaged Barthes, with the
heroic figure of Jaurès inspiring him from on high, was somewhat
romantic but far from abstract, and we should not ignore its formative aspect. The fact that he found a political identity based on the
fight against extremism may shed light on his later positions. In
some late notes from his diary files, Barthes returns to these events
that left their mark on his life as a young man: he sees 6 February
1934 as one of the decisive scenes in his education,[11] together with
the DRAF; and he remembers the Stavisky affair in his *Mourning
Diary*: 'Last night, a stupid, gross film, *One Two Two*. It was set in
the period of the Stavisky scandal, which I lived through. On the
whole, it brought nothing back. But all of a sudden, one detail of the
décor overwhelmed me: nothing but a lamp with a pleated shade and
a dangling switch. Maman made such things'.[12] In his correspondence, he also wrote of his desire to have intelligent people around
him, with whom he could talk about politics and literature. 'I'll

only ask one thing of them: to be "non-conformists", companions of David, *Davidsbündler*;[13] his model here was the club founded by the composer Robert Schumann in 1834, made up of real and imaginary persons, with Schumann himself attending in various shapes (Eusebius the dreamer and Florestan the extrovert): the club met at the Kaffeebaum in Leipzig to fight against all forms of bourgeois academicism and conventionalism.

The possibilities for action were limited – and this was even more so after the attack of haemoptysis that he suffered in May 1934: he coughed up blood, and although the diagnosis of pulmonary TB had still not been made, the symptom was alarming enough to lead the doctors to prescribe a treatment involving fresh air and rest. Barthes had to give up the idea of taking his baccalaureate in June, and his plans for the future were now in jeopardy. At the age of 18, an event like this was inevitably a dramatic development. It cut him off from his friends and from his studies, raising the daunting prospect of a long illness and the ultimate possibility of death. This first experience of isolation, before Saint-Hilaire-du-Touvet and Leysin, largely set the pattern of his later life: his marginality, his sense of being an imposter, the escape he found in literature and writing. He left for Bedous, in the Pyrenees, with his mother and his brother Michel. In this village in the Aspe valley, with its spring of sulphur and ferruginous water recommended for many kinds of treatment, doctors first gave him intravenous injections of gold salts. The Barthes stayed in a house belonging to the family of the draper Larricq, looking out over the main road, the *route nationale* from Pau to Saragossa. Life fell into a quiet pattern in this little town with its three doctors, a notary, a chemist, a tax collector, a postmaster and three or four primary school teachers. Michel went to the local school on the village square near the church. They socialized with such people as the pastor of Osse and Madame Best, where they sometimes went for lunch on Sundays and occasionally played the piano. To begin with, Barthes revised for the baccalaureate, including philosophy, science, and Greek and Latin. He played the piano for two hours a day, and decided he would learn to drive. Here is the detailed description of the area he gave in a letter to Philippe Rebeyrol written on 4 December: 'Bedous is a nice little dump, at the entry to Le Vallon. Le Vallon is a sort of widening of the valley of the Aspe, in the shape of a bowl, with a circumference of some 7 to 8 kilometres; the mountains that surround it form the limits of my horizon. The *gave* [mountain stream – Trans. note] of the Aspe, the railway, the *route nationale*, cross it lengthwise, all in parallel. All along Le Vallon are little villages that each overlooks a sort of valley which plunges into the mountainside and is covered with pastures: these are Bedous, Osse, Lès, Athas, Accous, Jouers, Orcun and again Bedous, which is much more important. Arranged in an irregular pattern along Le Vallon in front of or behind the line of the villages are small hills 50–75 feet high called *turons*; these *turons* serve as pastures for the sheep. The mountains that close off the horizon are quite high (1,000–1,500 metres). Towards France (i.e. towards the north), the valley grows narrower and forms a sort of gauze that marks the true start of the valley towards Oloron; you understand how, as you come out from this dreary, narrow corridor into this small valley with its broad, harmonious horizon, its bright and luminous colours, its fine pastures, its rows of poplars, the *gave* and the little clumps of villages arranged from place to place like children's toys (often the smoke rises slowly into a very pure sky) ... well, you understand the impression of joy and peace one feels. Towards Spain, towards the Col du Somport, i.e. towards the south, the valley is closed off by two rocks that almost join, leaving room only for a wild, narrow pass: this is the Forge d'Esquit; behind the jagged edge you can make out the high mountain. I'll send you a drawing of the Vallon separately.' The quality of this description of the landscape, like everything to do with nature and vegetation, is a quite remarkable feature of Barthes's correspondence at this period, but also subsequently; he is forever attentive to all the blossoms, and every little bend and curve in the landscapes he is describing. He developed a pronounced taste for this countryside that he found so admirable, with its clear-washed skies, its snow-covered mountains, in which the horizon seemed to dwarf the onlooker. The topography of the places, where he was here isolated with his mother and his brother, gave this stay all the features of a regressive repose in a state of childhood, in a protected luminous and tranquil spot, the 'gochokissime' of the house in Bayonne. This was also a time where he shared his life with his young brother alone: he saw much less of Michel when he was in the lycée in Paris, often out with his school mates; he would be separated from him for almost the entire war. They would regularly remember this stay together in later years, in the way one remembers happy days and times shared. Thus, in spite of the break it marked in his life, this first ordeal of illness and separation from the world was also an unexpected resurgence of childhood, which made the latter perhaps into a permanent and repeatable horizon rather than nostalgia for a lost land.

Barthes's feelings during his withdrawn existence in Bedous were not always this harmonious. He went to Paris in October to take his baccalaureate, but there was now no chance of his attending the *classes préparatoires* for the École normale supérieure, as the obligatory medical examinations for this institution debarred TB sufferers from attending. Philippe Rebeyrol entered the *hypokhâgne* in Louis-le-Grand to prepare for entry to the ENS, in October 1934, in a class of seventy boys and, quite unusually, several girls. He told Barthes all about his teachers, including Pierre Clarac, Albert Bayet and

Arthur Huby in history: Barthes replied that he was worrying over his own future. For a while he thought about applying to the École des Chartes, but abandoned the idea as this would have meant submitting to regular study and the pressures of a *classe préparatoire*, which his state of health ruled out. He registered as a first-year law student but continued to study Latin intensively thanks to the works that his friends sent him. He read Mauriac, Balzac (*The Peasants*), Julien Green's *Épaves*, which he thought was too long: the author's anguish might have struck a chord with him, but he did not have the same sense of guilt; Green's Catholicism left him cold. He also read *Combat avec l'ange* (*Combat with the angel*), the latest Giraudoux (published in 1934), Montherlant, *The Divine Comedy* and, above all, Gide, whose *Strait Is the Gate* made a lasting impression on him. He loved Katherine Mansfield but said he was disappointed by *The Brothers Karamazov*. He also read Arsène Lupin. Barthes swung between phases of euphoria and discouragement. Thus, on 23 July: 'Since I've been ill, my life has been much more intense, much warmer. If you like, I'm becoming more aware of who I am.' But on 9 August his mood was darker. 'My youth was nothing but a long series of difficulties, of ever more tragic years; I don't know if you would believe me if I told you about them, since it would seem too much like a novel or a drama. I thought that one misfortune would chase away the others, and my illness would mean I was exempted from other torments, or so I hoped up until now. But I need to abandon such hopes; I'm struggling again, and now deprived of physical strength, which in any case is being worn out by this activity. [. . .] There is in my life one very powerful factor, various boring problems, let's say, which explain many of the facts of my psychological and nowadays of my physical life.' As we read his correspondence, we see that this was the period when he developed a tendency to complain that few personal events would later modify or appease. We realize – he realized – that he was starting to develop the psychology of a person who is forever ill, worried about everything, passing his time in observing his symptoms, drawing correlations and making deductions. At that time a great number of TB cases still proved fatal, and this awoke in him a fear of death that only an ability to create something might assuage.

But fatigue, the obligation, at frequent intervals, to remain lying down, and an ill-focused quest made it difficult for him to write. On 6 November 1934, he confided in Rebeyrol, describing the torment into which this unproductive life plunged him: 'Pessimism stems only from my frequent inability to create. I feel full of creations but none of them can see the light; I receive everything with the intention and the need to feel it deeply; but nothing comes out. If you like, I have a perfect artistic receptivity, I can sense it; but if I were so unwise as to try and express it, it would be mediocre, shrunken, ridiculous. So you can't imagine all the novels, all the dramas, all the essays, the poems, the symphonies, the noble feelings, the adventures, that I construct by the day, by the hour, by the place. They are all sketches, "brilliant" in their diversity, but they only ever remain modest outlines, misty, empty signs, the sight of a marvellous land forever retreating. [. . .] my taste for the sensual, and thus the real, and thus the present, and thus the elusive – all of this gets in the way of my creative joys.' Nonetheless, he did make a start on a new novel, an 'Île joyeuse' ('Joyous Island') with a certain Judith de Vere as its heroine. While it is a realistic novel into which he again put a great deal of himself, this work simultaneously set out to be a defence of paganism and an illustration of the ideas of Nietzsche, whose books had overwhelmed him: 'It's absolutely true; it knocks the breath out of me so much that it hurts.' There are three parts in the novel: Julien, Christine and Judith. In December 1934, the plan and the scenario (the sequence of scenes) are ready. The argument sets Christian Goods versus Pagan Goods, though the story abstains from deciding which are the 'True Goods' ('Vrais biens'), the title that he had provisionally chosen. The synopsis shows that Barthes was still heavily influenced by religion, even if he stated he had lost his belief. He continued to find a great deal of beauty in Protestantism in spite of his denial of it – a tendency encouraged by his fascination for Gide, whom he continued to read. He applied to himself this quotation from Duhamel's *Tel qu'en lui-même* (*As into himself*): 'As for us Protestants, d'Argoult used to say, we only ever fall out with God, we don't really break off relations with him. We are escapees, freed slaves, perhaps, but not renegades, not real apostates. I understand our God to be so human that even when we strip him of his universal functions, we keep for him, within us, a place of honour and respect.'

His exile meant that he lived partly vicariously. He dreamt of long journeys, in particular because he was fed up with French conformism and sensed that living abroad would be a great liberation for him; he longed to set off on some great Mediterranean trip; but he could only follow from afar the preparations his friend Philippe was making for his journey to Greece in April 1935. He recommended that Philippe place less trust in his eyes, 'the most disappointing of our senses', than in his skin: this would enable him to 'enjoy his share of the Dionysian joys of the world'. He also asked him to take with him Gérard de Nerval's *Voyage to the Orient*; he told him what a wonderfully exciting book it was. His main problem was that, in Bedous, he rarely got to speak to any young people of his own age with a lycée education. He decided not to finish his year of law studies: he was finding it a struggle to study by himself, and the work was dull. Until October 1935 he remained in Bedous, apart from a few infrequent stays in Bayonne or Paris. His health improved and

the doctors told him he could register at the Sorbonne as a student
for the academic year starting in autumn 1935. He thereupon began
a *licence* in classics, and the family moved to the apartment in the
rue Servandoni. On his last day in Bedous, before he finally left for
Bayonne and then Paris, he wrote: 'I can see now that the grudges
I harboured against this reclusive life will vanish really quickly. All
that will be left is the memory of a happy, peaceful year, not without
a certain poetry. My eyes have opened to colours; my senses have
been really rather spoiled.'[14]

Elective affinities

The dominant feeling in those years of his second adolescence were
without any doubt those of friendship, which Barthes soon turned
into an art: his liking and talent for correspondence, his humour and
his loyalty seemed to foster this type of affection and fellow-feeling.
He had a great number of friends: Rebeyrol, of course, the closest of
them, but also Brissaud, at whose home in Sauveterre he spent his
holidays in August 1934, and in Cazalet in April 1935. There was
also Cyrille de Brunhoff of whom he was very fond; he exchanged
many letters with him (we have not been able to see these). He had
more of a love–hate relation with Sadia Oualid, criticizing him for
his low behaviour, which he attributed to his 'Israelite' origins, and
hating his 'dreary little flirtations and love affairs', in his view a sign
of a young man of mediocre mind. At the same time, it was Barthes
who supported Oualid when he thought he had failed his baccalaureate and he included him in the satirical sketches that he put on with
his closest friends. His most loyal friendship, with Philippe, gave rise
to intense feelings that would shed their light on his whole life. In
December 1935 he wrote: 'In this parity (as they say these days) that
connects us, there is something wonderful, extremely rare in time
and place; it is like an infallible promise of inseparability, eternity,
permanence, and I swear that for me it holds a large and promi-
nent place in my life . . .' That same year, he classified the letters he
had received from Rebeyrol and noted that they formed a total of
seventy-two sheets of the same format: this suggested to him that
their friendship was a great novel, full of twists and turns, dramas,
attacks of conscience, scruples, and intense if muted longings.
    But though the passionate friendship of adolescence rested on a
secure footing, it left room for other desires, more or less directly
expressed. When Barthes questioned his friends about what they
understood by the term 'love of men', he was also demanding the
pleasures of the flesh 'for earliest youth, which is pure by definition,
entire and without restraint. But I'm saying this only to young men
who can view the humble and secret delights of a cinema as akin

to the delights of Capua, though I wouldn't say these are the ones most to be recommended.'[15] He said he liked Racine because of the abnormal, almost monstrous character of the love he depicted on stage, far preferable to the model of the petty bourgeois heterosexual couple which Barthes always talked of in tones of disgust. We have already referred to his crush on Jacques Gilet, who seems to have been his first love. In summer 1933, he spent all his time with him, at the beach or at his grandmother's in Bayonne, playing piano duets. The attachment was so intense that Aunt Alice remarked on it and the teenaged Barthes remembered, years later, that she told him off about it. When his friend seemed to be drifting away from him at the beginning of 1934, he seems to have suffered greatly. And he was still talking about it in 1979, in his preface to Marcel Beaufils's book about Schumann: 'I myself began listening to Beethoven's symphonies only by playing them four hands, with a close friend as enthusiastic about them as I was.'[16] But the uncertainty of all adolescence, with its freight of possibilities, also led him to fall in love with young women. He had a passion for a Spanish dancer called La Theresina whom he saw one evening in the casino in Biarritz. 'As far as dancing goes, I place her among my true gods in music and poetry: Beethoven and Valéry.' And in Bedous he fell madly in love – for a full ten days – with a young woman by the name of Mima. Here is what he wrote to Philippe about her, on Monday, 13 August 1935:

Dear friend,
If I haven't written, it's because I've fallen in love. Madly in love with a charming young girl of 16, called Mima. Mima has very dark skin, hair and eyes. Perhaps it's because I'm blond and have blue eyes. She has a way of doing things that makes people say she's 'comical' or 'funny' or 'amusing', but personally I find it adorable. She's got exactly that indefinite charm of which Corneille speaks. We haven't spoken to each other much as yet, and I don't want to say much more to her. Sometimes I meet her, with her family, at Bousquet the grocer's, and this makes me happy for two days. On Sunday evening there was a public ball on the square and we danced together. She couldn't dance, and neither could I. Never mind: it was absolutely delightful. We definitely made a charming couple. But I can see that I haven't told you enough about her grace; and yet I can't tell you any more; I would need – though what art would suffice? – to describe to you the exact proportion with which lightness is combined in her with harmony, gravity, childishness, her rather coarse voice, that of a girl who is no longer just a girl, her air of mild surprise, etc. etc. (I'm not ashamed of romantic clichés). [. . .]

I have thought of her often, a little heroine à la Musset, 1935-style, who has entered into my life – ah so little, so much! – with a train of such poetic things in her wake: the ball, her hat, the few banal things we said at the pelota game, and when she appeared on the path filled with flowers and sunlight . . . all that furiously romantic imagery – all those little incidents taken from Faust and other adventures and given fresh allure, arousing in me the charm and the suffering distilled by every love. Why am I telling you all this? Is it serious, or literary, or ironic? A bit of all of them. I don't know, I don't know; I am letting myself be swept away by this wave of poetry, this wave of beauty, and this wave of banality too.

In this little love story, the obstacles are all part of the picture. Mima had a pretentious cousin in her entourage, Annie. She also had a cousin, Jean, 'extremely arrogant, haughty, but rather less intelligent than Pascal's man' in whom Barthes recognized all his phobias, his disgusts and his indignations. 'This feeling of revulsion is expressed in the physical itch to give him a slap on the face.' And the young man turned out to be a fervent devotee of the military. At a public conference against fascism, addressed by a Communist teacher, this Jean started to yell out as soon as the orator started to speak. And Barthes ended his letter to Philippe with these words: 'You can also see that it's sad to fall in love with someone from a family like this.' A few days later, it was all over:

23 August 35

Old pal,
Mima is already forgotten; I knew she'd be forgotten pretty quickly, and yet I told you about her as if she was a major event in my life.
    It was a moment – perfect as such – that has passed, as a soap bubble bursts in the air.

The imaginative power of adolescence and its paradoxical logic leave their mark on life in the formula 'and . . . and . . .' rather than 'neither . . . neither . . .': the youngsters writing to each other were simultaneously pupils and students, children and young men. They were still caught up in varying and fleeting desires, often taken to excess. Only the passions they deliberately cultivated endured: literature and, for Barthes, music. One day, in Osse, at the home of the Protestant pastor for the Bedous region, he was asked to conduct two choirs: a Basque group and a Béarnais group. To hold a conductor's baton and command a musical ensemble were something he saw as a dream come true. Music always seized him violently, as he put it himself. He enjoyed the performance aspect. He learned the basics of harmony from his aunt, and composed his first pieces.

He helped her organize concerts in Bayonne. From this time dates his love of Schumann, whom he would never stop playing subsequently. Of the latter's *Six Concert Studies on Caprices by Paganini*: 'I can play the whole piece but not at the right speed', 'I can read the score but I can't play it.' He said the same on the France Musique radio programme: you need to let yourself take your time, leave room for the hesitations and silences too systematically erased by recordings (that he thereupon decides he doesn't enjoy). The feminine universe of the house in Bayonne offered a sort of habitat natural to Schumann: he is the musician of 'the child who has no other link than to the Mother'.[17] In his *lieder*, the presence of the *Muttersprache*, the mother tongue, is clear. And in *Camera Lucida*, Barthes talks about one of the last compositions of the musician who was about to relapse into madness, and describes 'that first *Gesang der Frühe* which accords with both my mother's being and my grief at her death',[18] and comparing it with the photo of her in the Jardin d'hiver. On 15 March 1935, he wrote:

Vanity of everything except music. I don't just feel love for music; it's much more; it's certainty, it's faith. It's as if I had attained the certainty of a world superimposed upon ours, a world whose foundation was level with our ears.
    Thought: uncertain.
    Music: truth, certainty, reality.

Whereupon he set out a 'little philosophy of music', according to François Noudelman, which relies on an 'understanding of the relation between spontaneity and reflexivity'.[19] Barthes, indeed, devoted almost as much energy trying to 'convert' his friend Philippe to music as he had spent trying to proselytize for Jaurès. 'You know that's it a real musical box here and I make music and listen to it as much as I can. Still, my friend, you'll have to be converted sooner or later to the ideas of this muse of the Bachs, Beethovens and Schumanns: take my word for it, she is the equal of the muse of Verlaine and Valéry. I will also recommend the melodies of Henri Duparc on poems by Verlaine, Baudelaire and others that you will certainly like.' Music suited their friendship. It was the elective affinity par excellence, and Barthes would stay loyal to it. 'I love Schumann', he said in a radio broadcast. And when Claude Maupomé asked him, 'How do you hear Schumann?', he declared: 'I hear him as I love him, and perhaps you'll ask me "how do you love him?" and, well, I can't answer that because I'd say that I love him with just that part of myself that is to myself unknown; and I know that I've always loved Schumann and that I'm very sensitive to the fact that, as always when you love someone, I often have the impression that we don't love them the way we should, we don't love them enough, and in particular I have in mind something really cruel: at a certain moment in the history of last century, someone I love, Schumann, was executed by someone I admire, Nietzsche.' In *Beyond Good and Evil*, Nietzsche attacks this chauvinistic, delicate, small-scale music. But Schumann has simplicity and ethical nobility, replies Barthes: his music is untimely, not territorial, and belongs to every country and to every time. If we are to love, these forms of escape towards the unknown must exist, opening up time and territory.

Such an adolescence, open to all possibilities, came to an end without really ending: it had been an essentially protected and quite happy period, in spite of the lack of comfort and the attacks of illness.

'I'm going to plant a few seeds of Petunia Hibrida.'

'Right now, I'm translating Shelley's hymn to intellectual beauty.'

'Our garden is full of roses; in the evening, when it's less hot, I arm myself with a pair of secateurs, and I spend a good while walking up and down the miniature alleys, cutting off the faded flowers; outside in the warm, calm afternoon, we drink China tea and we eat strawberries from the woods.'[20]

At the Lycée Montaigne, in the *classe de quatrième*. Barthes is in the top row, fourth from the left. Philippe Rebeyrol can be seen just below him, fourth from the left. In the front row, the sixth from the left is the teacher Grandsaignes d'Hauterive, mentioned in *Roland Barthes by Roland Barthes*.

At the Lycée Louis-le-Grand, *classe de seconde*. Barthes is in the second row, fourth from the left. On the same row are his friends Rebeyrol, Oualid and Huerre – sixth, seventh and eighth from the left respectively. Barthes had won a distinction for his academic work.

The village of Bedous in the Pyrénées-Atlantiques, around 1930.

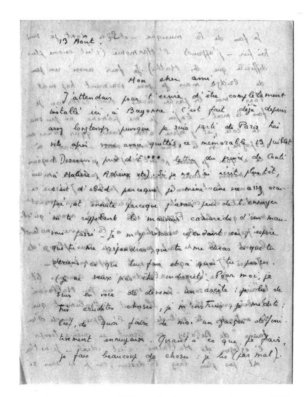

The first letter to Philippe Rebeyrol, 13 August 1932.

Roland Barthes in Paris, around 1935.

Philippe Rebeyrol, around 1935.

4

Barthes and Gide

He was a Protestant. He played the piano. He talked about
desire. He wrote.
                              'Of What Use Is an Intellectual?', p. 261.

Barthes's relation to Gide was more a matter of shared tastes than
of intellectual agreement. It was deeply linked to those formative years in which one's inclinations are sometimes the product
of social milieu and upbringing but are mainly marked by forms
of recognition and identification. As a teenager, Barthes said he
knew no other writer than Gide. In the 1920s, Gide represented
the figure of the writer, the one you went to see when you yourself
had aspirations to become a writer – so much so that the 'Visit to
Gide' could well be the subject of a fascinating anthology[1] – the
man whose social position did not altogether take away his power
of subversion and whose texts, without being avant-garde or
obscure, still held out the prospect of a future filled with change and
renewal. But there was more behind the encounter between Barthes
and Gide: reading Gide was what brought desire into the relation
between Barthes and his apprenticeship, his reading, his writing
and his attraction to boys. The dialogue that thus began was not
just textual, and would not occur between the respective oeuvres
of Barthes and Gide, but it would be existential, and crucial in
every way for laying the foundations of Barthes's personality.
Gide authorized the teenager to do a certain number of things –
including to erase Gide himself. This is probably the explanation
for the fact that, in spite of a first article dedicated to Gide, Barthes
never wrote a book on him, rarely presented him as one of his reference points, and acknowledged how much he owed to him only
belatedly. Although Gide was a 'crucial contemporary', in the well-
known words of André Rouveyre in *Le Reclus et le retors* in 1927,
just as he was for Maurice Sachs and Jean Genet, Barthes could
have said of him what Camus wrote of him: 'Gide later reigned over
my youth and once you have admired someone even just once, how

can you fail to be forever grateful to them for having raised you up to this highest point of the soul! And yet, for all that, he was never for me either a guru or a writing master: I had found others. Gide struck me, rather [. . .] as the model of the artist, the guardian, the king's son, keeping watch over a garden in which I wished to live.'[2] Returning to him over the last years of his life, Barthes would see in him the last great French figure to be both a great intellectual and a great writer.[3]

The beginning and the end

In July 1942, in the review of the association 'Les Étudiants en sanatorium' ('The Sanatorium Students'), *Existences*, Barthes published his notes 'On Gide and His Journal'.[4] This was his second publication after 'Culture and Tragedy', a few pages published in *Les Cahiers de l'étudiant* in the spring of that same year. He left these notes in their fragmentary, spontaneous state, written in the margins of his reading. He is clearly treating Gide as a kind of magnetic pole: in this deliberately shapeless discourse, there is a desire to explain Gide that resembles a quest for the self. The oscillation between Protestantism and paganism, the lure of Greece, the perpetual interrogation of one's self, the indecision between different genres, the relation to the classics: all these are as much a self-portrait as a portrait, and the letters of this period echo this. 'Many entries in the *Journal* will doubtless irritate those who have some prejudice, secret or otherwise, against Gide. These same entries will delight those who have some reason, secret or otherwise, to believe themselves like Gide. This is true of any personality which *compromises itself*.'[5] At this same date, June 1942, Barthes wrote to Philippe Rebeyrol: 'And then you must always compromise yourself, in reality there is no greater pleasure.' Resemblance and compromise were thus at the heart of this relation, which had nothing to do with influence or dialogue. Gide was much more of a model: self-exhibition in his case was not negative; the risk he took was also taken for others, for literature and for ethics. In particular, Barthes focused on two leitmotifs that in his view were most characteristic of the writer and shaped his own relation to literature: fidelity in mobility, and the connection to language. The first lay in a way of exposing different aspects of oneself without ever abandoning their simultaneous existence. The impression of a shimmering mobility is here the mark of a certain authenticity. It cannot be enclosed in a unique form or a single permanent genre. 'Gide explains himself, surrenders himself, delicately retracts or asserts himself bravely enough, but never abuses the reader as to his mutations; Gide puts everything in the *movement* of his thought

and not in its brutal profession.'[6] It is obvious how this characteristic is both a self-presentation on the author's part and an ethical
programme for the future. It is – like the second leitmotif, which
has to do with writing – a personal key to becoming a writer.
Classicism is another.

> As Montesquieu said: 'We do not describe without omitting
> the intermediate notations.' And Gide adds: 'There is no work
> of art without foreshortenings.' This does not occur without
> an initial obscurity, or an extreme simplicity, which makes a
> mediocre mind say that it does not 'understand'. In this sense,
> the Classics are the great masters of the obscure, even of the
> equivocal; i.e., of the preterition of the superfluous (that super-
> fluous of which the vulgar mind is so fond), or, if you prefer,
> masters of the shadow propitious to meditation and to indi-
> vidual discovery. To oblige us to think for ourselves, that is a
> possible definition of classical culture; whereby it is no longer
> the monopoly of a century, but of all rigorous minds, whether
> they are called Racine, Stendhal, Baudelaire or Gide.[7]

In the following years, Gide is mentioned as a reference when it was
a question of defining a classic or illustrating classical language and
grammar, including in *Literature Degree Zero* where he appears
as 'an author without a style', as well as being the representative,
with Valéry and Montherlant, of 'great traditional writing'.[8] But he
is mentioned as it were just in passing, almost always in a list with
other names, and a little out of date. For example, in Barthes's text
on Jean Cayrol from 1952, Gide acts rather as a counter-model:
Barthes sees the enumeration of objects in Cayrol as 'a parody
of Gide's elegies'.[9] Only with the publication of *Roland Barthes
by Roland Barthes* did the reference to Gide find expression; only
then did Barthes acknowledge a debt and the critics started to
take notice: 'And Gide occupied a great place in his early reading:
a diagonal cross-breed of Alsace and Gascony, as Gide was of
Normandy and Languedoc, Protestant, having a taste for "letters"
and fond of playing the piano, without counting the rest [. . .].'
Then, in the table of the 'phases' of his literary career, he related
Gide to the 'desire to write'. Finally, he declared: 'Gide is my original language, my *Ursuppe*, my literary soup.'[10] In a review of this
third-person autobiography in *La Nouvelle Revue française*, Jean
Duvignaud referred to the way Barthes had transformed the primitive *imaginaire* of his life. He compared this with the demystifying
enterprise conducted by Sartre in *Words*, while saying that Barthes
was seeking to introduce a touch of desire into it, the stirrings of the
body. 'A masked desire, a desire that shuffles the cards, emerging,
effacing itself. [. . .] Barthes often talks about Gide. Gide, too, was

adept at prowling around like this, hesitantly but fervently.'[11] In a long interview for Radio Canada, transcribed later in the *Revue d'esthétique*, Barthes did however relativize Gide's importance in terms of influence:

> What influence did Gide, for example, have on you? Don't we find you writing in your book: 'Gide is my original language, my *Ursuppe*, my literary soup'?
> Yes, I said that in this book as I was talking about myself. So I naturally highlighted certain facts about my teens that nobody could have known. So, when I was a teenager, I read a lot of Gide and Gide had a great deal of importance for me. But I have to point out, with a certain malice, that all the same, up until now, nobody had suspected as much; nobody had ever said of me that in what I'd done there was the least little bit of Gidean influence. And now that I've drawn people's attention to this, it seems that everyone is quite naturally finding sorts of hereditary filaments between Gide and my own kind of work: so I have to say that it's a comparison that is, after all, quite artificial. Gide was important for me when I was a teenager, but that doesn't in the least mean that he is there in my work.[12]

It is less a matter of liquidating a predecessor or denying a heritage than putting him in the right place. We need to understand that the debt is elsewhere. It resides, in our view, in the geological strata of a certain upbringing. And there are two reasons why the reference to Gide disappeared in Barthes's maturity and reappeared on the threshold of old age: in the end is the beginning, and the affirmation of the writing of the self with the *Roland Barthes by Roland Barthes* breathes fresh life into the original model. The fact that the fragment that acknowledges the debt has the title '*Abgrund*' is very meaningful: in German, this word refers to what is archeologically deepest, but first and foremost it means the abyss, the precipice.[13] Attempting to find this abyss can be dangerous. What Barthes mainly acknowledges is that he wanted to be himself. He had at the time thought he was someone else, and had reproduced the person he wanted to be. 'The first want (I desire and I pledge myself) establishes a secret system of fantasies which persist from age to age, often independently of the writings of the desired author'. And, a little further on: 'The Gidean *Abgrund*, the Gidean core, unchanging, still forms in my head a stubborn swarm.'[14] The way that he had recognized himself in Gide produced, for the rest of his life, strange forms of stubbornness. In buried form, or as a kind of echo, music was there even though the lines of the composition were not always clearly distinct. Thus, the part played by Gide in Barthes's work was a score for several instruments: in it, a relationship to language, to music and to the body were performed simultaneously.

Music on the large scale and the small

Susan Sontag has highlighted this perfect symmetry: Barthes's first writing was on Gide's *Journal* and, in the last study he published in his own lifetime, he meditated on the journal he himself kept. 'The symmetry, however adventitious, is an utterly appropriate one, for Barthes's writing, with its prodigious variety of subjects, has finally one great subject: writing itself.'[15] This subject bears the imprint of a certain music, a 'little music' as Proust would say, like the refrain of a style, or rather the research into writing carried out whenever one is an assiduous reader. We might almost think that Barthes has made his own the injunction given by Gide in his *Conseils au jeune écrivain* (*Advice to a young writer*) that, although published after his death, brought together the recommendations he had given to all those teenagers who wanted, more than anything else, to write: 'Always write as simply as you can; it is important above all not to deceive yourself; be always on guard against your own self-indulgence and be forever vigilant that you don't become your own dupe.'[16] While he did not always stick to the rule of simplicity, Barthes adopted the principles of vigilance and distance invoked here, correcting, altering, afraid of being neither elusive nor contradictory, nor even of writing in minor forms. So we can agree with Susan Sontag when she adds that Barthes's very language bears the mark of Gideanism: 'Gide supplied Barthes with the patrician model for the writer who is supple, multiple, never strident or vulgarly indignant; generous . . . but also properly egotistical; incapable of being deeply influenced. He notes how little Gide was altered by his immense reading ("so many self-recognitions"), how his "discoveries" were never "denials". And he praises the profusion of Gide's scruples, observing that Gide's "situation at the intersection of great contradictory currents has nothing facile about it".'[17] By turning Gide into the first of the non-stylists, and thereby excluding him from the list of writers such as Hugo, Rimbaud and Char, whose style suspends them over the course of history, Barthes includes himself within another community, imbued with more freedom and even a lightness of touch, as found in their shared relation to politics, where you commit yourself when you have to, but still maintain a certain withdrawal. 'The very type of an author without a style is Gide, whose craftsman-like approach exploits the pleasure the moderns derive from a certain classical ethos.'[18] So he compares Gide not to other writers, but to musicians such as Saint-Saëns, whose work consisted in continuing Bach, and Poulenc, who rewrote Schubert and was

also thus drawn into a relation with a certain history and society.
As Emily Apter emphasizes in an article for *Critique*, it is not sure –
despite the almost mystical reverence with which Barthes treats
style – that he places the non-stylists in inferior zones. 'Barthes
assumes that modern writing has a profoundly citational, predatory
nature. In a context like this, Gide's status changes dramatically: if
the title of "last stylist" is refused him, he is granted the more prestigious rank of the first "non-stylist", and hence becomes a capital
writer in Barthes's sense of the term.'[19]

The strains of Gide's 'little music' that we can also hear in Barthes
are the themes, such as the self as a vocation, and life as a reading
of the self. When his mother died, Barthes regretted that he could
not produce a portrait of her as heartrending as the one Gide produced of his wife Madeleine in *Et nunc manet in te*. Referring to
this work, Barthes was weaving together two leitmotifs: the grief
from which one makes a book (in 1978, what would later form the
Mourning Diary was just a collection of fragmentary notes); and
the unique love one has for a woman, the mother: either because
Madeleine played the role of a vigilant mother towards Gide, as
Frank Lestringant suggests in his biography, quoting in support
these words from Gide's *So Be It*: 'As also, but only in the dream,
the figure of my mother is sometimes, in a subtle and as it were mystical way, replaced by that of my wife, without my being particularly
surprised';[20] or because Barthes had an unconsummated marriage
with his mother, like that between André Gide and Madeleine
Rondeaux. For a long time, Gide was the figure of what is not, and
cannot be, said: a buried secret. In the relationship with him there
was an element of confrontation and an element of subjectivity
linked to their positions and choices, their way of being in the world,
the way they put their bodies and their senses to use, their unusual
tastes. In *A Lover's Discourse* and then in *How to Live Together*,
the course he gave at the Collège de France in 1977, Barthes quoted
the strange expression from Gide's *Judge Not* – '*mon cher grand
fond Malempia*' ('my dear old cave of Malempia') – which Mélanie
Bastian, locked away in her bedroom by her mother for twenty-six
years, applied to the prison bedroom to which she wished to return:
he thus expressed, indirectly, the structure of constraint and desire
characteristic of his relation to Gide. The other dominant themes,
those that can be heard most clearly, concerned the Protestant religion and the piano. The shared Protestant origin was in itself a sign
of the community to which Barthes and Gide had belonged. If we
also add Rousseau, it justified the impulse to write about the self: 'A
Protestant adolescence can provide a certain taste for or a certain
perversion of inwardness, the inner language, the subject's constant
dialogue with himself.'[21] It did not make guilt a central element in
one's consciousness, and the relation to psychology, especially in

the novel, became less intense. When, in 1942, Barthes read Gide's *Journal*, he told Philippe Rebeyrol that it was the only work from which he derived any entertainment, or anything of value. 'I find more consolation in it, it entices my thoughts more than a Bible.' Thus the beloved author and the original religion are merged together, Gide's *Journal* and the Bible, in an image of foundation – and here, the *Journal* and the Bible are practically equivalent.

But Barthes and Gide were also linked by the piano, and both their lives had a musical accompaniment. They both liked their performances to be unhurried. Just as Barthes preferred tempi that were slow and even too slow, Gide said with respect to Chopin that it was important to play him slowly and uncertainly, 'in any case without the intolerable self-assurance of an over-hasty movement. We stroll from one discovery to another, and the performer should not suggest too easily that he knows in advance what he is going to say, nor that it is already all written down.'[22] Like walking, music enables you to enter landscapes that you need to enjoy, while allowing them to preserve the power of the discoveries they harbour. A serene performance of the music enables you to attain more easily a certain form of grace that can resemble a slow motion film. 'We have seen, in the cinema, the surprising grace that a movement made by a human being or an animal can have, when presented in slow motion; this is elusive when the movement is quicker. This does not mean (although it is quite possible) slowing down excessively the tempo of Chopin's music. Rather, it must not be hurried, but allowed to follow its natural movement, as easy as breathing.'[23] So we are closer to the body, thanks to the piano practice that Gide so much enjoys, as he regularly says in his *Journal*: it is far from the somewhat frigid virtuosity Barthes criticizes in concert performances on discs – a virtuosity that takes us far from the body. 'It is because Schumann's music goes much farther than the ear; it goes into the body, into the muscles by the beats of its rhythm, and somehow into the viscera by the voluptuous pleasure of its *melos*: as if on each occasion the piece was written only for one person, the one who plays it; the true Schumannian pianist – *c'est moi.*'[24] And again, in the late diary, in Urt: '11 July 1979. I happen to hear, on France Musique (Blandine Verlet) a "courante" by Bach*(?) that I adore, playing it, in my case, slowly (I have no choice . . .): it is profound, mellow, sensual and tender, very singing. The harpsichordist plays it three or four times faster, so it takes me a while to recognize it; all the features I've just mentioned are lost; a particular little phrase, adorably singing, is no longer even noticeable. – The harpsichordist is well-informed and intelligent, she must be right. But what a shame, what a disappointment! – This points to the problem: someone who can take pleasure only in deformations, in misinterpretations, is torn. And also: the "modern" manner of rejecting, annulling sensuality (the trend for baroque music, the rejection of romantic music).'[25] It takes time to engage one's body. It's an entire movement that goes from hands to head and from head to hands. In this area, Barthes knows that he is a little old-fashioned. But he insists on his need for romanticism, as this is linked to his ethos of the amateur and the pleasure he takes in it.

Unlike performers, composers are less the subject of critical analyses than of amorous discourses, and what we find here is a veritable erotic relationship. Gide talks of Chopin as someone he adores, and Barthes loves Schumann. Originally, Gide's *Notes sur Chopin* were to be called 'Notes sur Schumann et Chopin', but life gradually led him away from the former. For Barthes, the intimate relationship he had with Schumann remained just as intense, even when he felt loving him was out of fashion, and he was doing so alone. But this very fact made his love responsible: 'it inevitably leads the subject who does so and says so to posit himself in his time according to the injunctions of his desire and not according to those of his sociality.'[26] This sort of love is absolutely intimate, and thus inevitably solipsistic.

Homosexuality

It is not always that easy to affirm desire. While he acknowledged the part Gide played in his life, Barthes, while making explicit the relation to religion, writing and the piano, evaded homosexuality, resorting to euphemistic formulae of which the most obliterating is the phrase 'without counting the rest'. It is also buried in the phrase 'a thousand things about him that interested me'.[27] And yet there can be no doubt that Gide represented for Barthes, as for many homosexuals, a kind of crucial revelation. When he read Gide, between 1935 and 1942, he was also having his first experiences of love and sex in the sanatorium at Saint-Hilaire-du-Touvet. The words in Gide's *If It Die . . .* ('in the name of what God or what ideal, do you forbid me to live according to my nature?')[28] find many echoes in Barthes's correspondence of that time. Barthes protested vehemently against any remorse for the pleasures of the flesh. He never felt regret about them – just nostalgia. 'In this sense and as regards this precise point,' he wrote in June 1942 to Philippe Rebeyrol, 'if I related my life to you chronologically, you'd see that I'm already really quite *self-affirmed*. Oh, not enough as yet, perhaps; but then, self-affirmation mustn't become ostentation.' The publication of Gide's *Corydon* in 1924, *If It Die . . .* in 1926 and, to a lesser extent, Proust's *Sodom and Gomorrah* in 1921–22, made open and avowed homosexuality part of contemporary literature. Hence Mauriac's lament, in 1926, that 'many of these sick people who were unaware of their natures are now all too fully aware thanks to Gide and Proust. Many who used to hide will now no longer do so.'[29] Barthes is forever drawing comparisons between Gide and Proust. In *The Preparation of the Novel*, for example, almost every reference to the name of Gide is followed by a long reference to Proust. But only a 1971 article on Proust's *In Search of Lost Time* seems to bring the two authors together in connection with homosexuality, or more precisely what they both call inversion, enabling us to read 'the same body as the super-impression of two absolute contraries, Man and Woman (contraries which Proust defined biologically and not symbolically: a period feature, no doubt; in order to rehabilitate homosexuality, Gide proposes examples of pigeons and dogs); the scene of the hornet, during which the Narrator discovers the Woman in the Baron de Charlus, is theoretically valid for any reading of the interplay of contraries.'[30] Hence the discussion of reversal as a feature of homosexuality: for this, Barthes suggests the neologism 'enantiology' (from the Greek *enantios*, opposite), which also appears as a law of expansion. He notes that, while at the beginning of Proust's *Search* its population, 'heterosexual at the outset, is ultimately discovered in exactly the converse position – i.e., homosexual (like Saint-Loup, the Prince de Guermantes, etc.): there is a pandemia of inversion, of reversal'.[31] But overall, Barthes made very few public pronouncements on this subject, and only with the posthumous publication of the *Incidents*, where the anecdotes belong to the tradition partly opened by the Gide who had narrated his sensual and sexual trips to North Africa, and the 'Evenings in Paris', did we learn more about his own activities. His private language was more explicit: love and friendship often mingled together in it: 'Almost all my friendships with boys have started out as love affairs; admittedly, time almost always clarified them, while leaving them with an aroma which I prize highly. Conversely, on the rare occasions when I have loved a woman (why not admit that, in reality, it's only happened once), it began with what the world calls a friendship.'[32] Barthes came out about his homosexuality to Philippe Rebeyrol in the spring of 1942, when Philippe was visiting him in Saint-Hilaire-du-Touvet, and after that his confidential remarks became more frequent and emphatic. But private writing is different from public writing, and the books and articles he published leave a place for this theme that is not negligible but is still kept concealed.

Even the *Lover's Discourse*, where a devastating biographical experience can easily be read between the lines, does not explicitly describe homosexual love, which Barthes absolutely refused to mark with any radical difference, even if difference, or pluralization, is a way of triumphing over conflict and keeping the duality of the sexes at bay. In his seminar on 'the lover's discourse' that he gave at the École pratique des hautes études between 1974 and 1976, he was sometimes more direct and referred directly to Gide in connection with the latter's North African escapades, especially those on

his honeymoon in Algeria which he related in his *Journal* and again
in *Et nunc manet in te*. The intoxication of bodies to which Gide
yielded with abandon and his absolute hedonism were constrained
only by the gaze of the third party, Madeleine, but this was precisely
the aspect that interested Barthes: Madeleine, witnessing, as a 'frigid
but loving reader, her husband's diffuse desire for the young models
on the piazza di Spagna and the Algerian schoolboys in the train
from Biskra to Algiers.'[33] For Barthes, the constraints were of a different kind. For a long time it was important to protect his mother
from any 'revelation' on the subject, even if certain books referred
to it explicitly, from the self-portrait and fragments on 'The goddess
H.' and the couple of antagonistic adjectives 'Active/passive' in
Roland Barthes by Roland Barthes onwards. After his mother's
death, when he no longer needed to hide, the social awkwardness
of paying for sex, of prostitution, were another reason for him to be
reticent. He is evasive in *Incidents*, thanks to a dense, fragmentary
and, yet again, obliterating style of writing: 'The little Marrakesh
schoolteacher: "I'll do whatever you want", he says, effusively, his
eyes filled with kindness and complicity. Which means: *I'll fuck
you*, and that's all.'[34] From Gide to Barthes, yet again, something
has been reversed; the predatory activity is still predominant, but
sensual lyricism is no longer a possible language. In spite of sexual
liberation, the hint of colonialist exploitation persists. The figures of
westerners, in *Incidents*, are often farcical, phantoms of the French
presence, 'wrecks from the Protectorate', or an old Englishman
who asks to be called 'Daddy': to avoid being seen as one of these
negative characters, Barthes had to disguise himself even more. It
was no longer possible to compromise oneself in the way that Gide
had done.

Journal

Among the planned books listed in *Roland Barthes by Roland Barthes*,
there is indeed the one called *The Discourse of Homosexuality*, which
shows that Barthes did not view this subject as taboo and wondered
how he might say something about it that would be different from
militancy, generalization or affirmation. This idea stayed with him
all his life. He returned to it regularly in the index cards he used for
his journal:

> Not the same homosexuality as Fernendez or Hockenghem
> [*sic*]. It's not the same thing that I have the *duty* to say, to
> express, to write.
>   Unsurpassable, insurmountable banality of porn description
> (R. Camus).

> I would agree to talk about H[omosexuality] only in a
> way that would be not just personal (without generalization,
> without meta H[omosexuality]) but also individual: the pure
> individual that I am, the absolute margins, irreducible to any
> 'science' or parascience.[35]

One important section of the index cards has the entry 'homosexuality' and, as he has not yet found the right form for his thoughts,
Barthes reserves his remarks for ordinary writing, private writing.
This is another characteristic linking him to Gide: the obsession
with day-to-day writing, the note, the reminder. But, unlike Gide,
he does not give this kind of writing any stable place. Although he
was fascinated by Gide's *Journal* and wrote one of his first articles
on it, Barthes could not bring himself to keep a diary on a regular
basis. He did so only on an irregular, because indecisive, basis. It was
not having to write things down everyday that bothered him – he
developed other forms for this – but the continuity that the journal
required on the level of the sentence. The journal (or at least this is
what Gide's journal taught him) bridged the gap between 'ordinary
writing'[36] and 'literary writing'. It is a perpetual questioning of
the link between the public and the private sphere. But for almost
the whole of his life, Barthes had a purely private and, as it were,
domestic practice of everyday writing. He experimented with all possibilities in this area: index cards, travel journals, notebooks, letters,
lists of things to do, desk diaries . . . When he was in a familiar spot,
the apartment in the rue Servandoni, he systematically and thoroughly kept up a desk diary and, at the same time, noted things down
in index cards. When he was travelling or on holiday, he resorted to
other forms, and it was in these circumstances that he tried keeping
a diary. Apart from those he kept in Morocco and China, he started
one in summer 1973, in Urt – this became part of the 'harvest-diary'
preparatory to writing *Roland Barthes by Roland Barthes* – and
another in 1977, of which he published a very short extract in *Tel
Quel* in 1979, and almost none of which has yet been published.

'Am I not justified in considering everything I have written as a
clandestine and stubborn effort to bring to light again, someday,
quite freely, the theme of the Gidean "journal"? At the terminal
horizon, perhaps quite simply the initial text.'[37] Linked to the
mastery of time, to the most elementary workings of the relation
between time, writing and memory, the journal is a companion
before being a horizon. Barthes loves it as an old-fashioned practice,
its structure (that of time going by – even when not much is going
on). He returns to the obsessions of his mode, the weather, the diets
(Éric Marty has shown that these were major points of reference),
inscribing circular effects of time into chronology. Thus, all private
writing will tend to turn itself into a journal. When Barthes devotes

himself actively to drawing, from 1971 to 1976 or thereabouts, he
does so in a way reminiscent of ordinary writing. He dates the first
drawing to 24 June 1971 and, most of the time, it is the date that
works as a title. The whole set of drawings can be 'read' as a journal
without psychological remarks, without any events, a sort of ideal
of the writing of the self.

For Barthes, as probably for Gide (even if for the latter writing a
journal became a 'work' of literature in the full sense of the term),
keeping a diary was also similar to the old family practice of keeping
a '*livre de raison*', a very common habit in the French South-West,
especially in Protestant areas. Between the shop and the household,
this *livre de raison*, initially an accounts book (*liber rationibus*), also
became the book of life in which were noted down births, deaths and
events that affected the family – but also the seasons, money coming
in, departures. *Livres de raison*, which are nowadays very valuable
archives of private life, were especially important for Protestants as,
since they had no civil status, the father of the family had to keep
an account of its members. Furthermore, the book bore witness to
an upbringing in the faith that was lived and transmitted in secret.
When it became more individualized in the shape of the personal
diary, the use of such a book opened an even bigger space for intimacy, even if it left a place otherwise unknown for the trivial, the
insignificant, the incident. 'What is the intimate body, what is the
Intimacy of the surface, that which is Intimate but anodyne? What
we have here is not a reality as such, but a dimension of the subject
that is very close to the writing of a Journal',[38] as Éric Marty has
remarked on André Gide's *Journal* – and this ties in with a question raised by Barthes: there is no room, in day-to-day writing, for
psychological explanation; you note down precisely the things that
cannot be fixed, like a photo without a fixing agent – nothing is
definitive either in interpretation or in memory.

After 1976, Barthes's friendship with Éric Marty was the opportunity for a dialogue on Gide and the genre of the diary. This dialogue
was made public by an exchange of dedications. The extracts from
the Urt diary published by Barthes in *Tel Quel* in 1979 were given 'for
Éric Marty'. In return, the latter's article that appeared in *Poétique*
in 1981 was dedicated 'to R.B. in Memoriam'.[39] After taking
the *agrégation*, Marty, who had already been attending Barthes's
seminar for two years, decided to focus his research on Gide: this
decision fascinated Barthes, who discovered that his young 'disciple' or friend was following in his own footsteps. In 'Deliberation',
which is also based on a re-reading of Kafka's *Diary* ('perhaps
the only one that can be read without irritation'), the question is
less that of defining a genre than distinguishing between a superficial, inconsistent writing, and literary writing. So it is no longer a
matter of 'Should I keep a journal?', since in reality keeping or not

keeping a journal are practically equivalent options, but 'Should I keep a journal *with a view to publication*?', to turn it into a work of literature.[40] Is a journal a kind of writing? By raising it above the ordinary, turning it into a book about oneself and for others, the risk is that one will deprive it of its main attributes: the collection of individual pages, easy to permute and suppress (something that means the journal is not a book, but an album), the absence of sincerity and the dimension of secrecy. This relationship with secrecy is basically what brings Gide and Barthes closest together. Their journals explicitly discuss a homosexuality concealed from a single person: in Gide's case, Madeleine, and in Barthes's, his mother. Thus, Marty writes about Gide in terms that apply perfectly well to Barthes, too: 'What is fascinating here is the fact that the hidden, insofar as it is known to everyone (to the whole World) except to one woman, completely reverses the general laws of the Secret: kept outside the worldly laws of what can and cannot be said, it is more a specific mode of consciousness vis-à-vis an Other than just a matter of being secretive.'[41] Thus the mother's death makes it possible to publish – but does it make this necessary, insofar as the dimension of secrecy then disappears? Furthermore, in Barthes (and this is where he is so different from Gide and his enterprise), the journal takes its place within another system, that of a mobile and non-totalizing system, to which several of his books and plans attempt to give a provisional and partial form. Most of the time, Barthes indexed his journal and put it into index cards, abandoning the temporal structure and adopting instead the structure of the glossary, which meant it was no longer publishable as a diary.

A second risk lies in the way the text can be subjected to manipulation and at the same time find its deep ambitions curtailed. Barthes brings it up to date through an intertextual game. Claiming to be reading his own diary, he quotes from it phrases that irritate him: 'Very soon, continuing my re-perusal, I get tired of these verbless sentences ("Sleepless night. The third in a row," etc.) or sentences whose verb is carelessly condensed ("Passed two girls in the Place St-S.").' But these phrases, as the manuscript indicates, are taken directly from Kafka's *Diaries* and Barthes contents himself with simply transforming Wenceslas Square in Prague, in the original, into the place Saint-Sulpice that he himself crosses every day.[42] An even more serious problem is that the detail without importance cannot invariably be recuperated in writing. The diary is probably of value only if it is kept up without end, without purpose: 'I can rescue the Journal on the one condition that I labor it *to death*, to the end of an extreme exhaustion, like a *virtually* impossible Text'.[43] In this sense, it is indeed a perspective of which Barthes regularly envisages the horizon: the end of the book and its replacement by individual pages whose order can be changed around – these days, the Internet hypertext is one variant of this idea. As a Limbo of the Text, the journal's value lies in its continuing to be a form that has not been fixed.

Barthes's literary memory, he said in 'Lectures de l'enfance' ('Childhood readings'), was composed of three spaces with distinct functions: teenage readings from the relatively recent past, Proust, Gide, Valéry, who gave him the impulse to write; the contemporaries with whom he entered into debate, the present, Sartre, Camus, Brecht; and finally the classics, the distant past, with whom he evolved throughout his life, freely.[44] Like Proust and Valéry, Gide was, for Barthes, a recent past, not nostalgic, an incitement, someone in whom he had recognized himself and to whom he owed a debt of gratitude. What he says in his first text about Gide's relation to his choices and his models can also be applied to this particular debt: 'Gide's predilections indicate not an influence but an identity.'[45] The journal, present at the beginning and end of his work, expresses something of this accompaniment: its roots lie in the ordinary life from which we seek to liberate it.

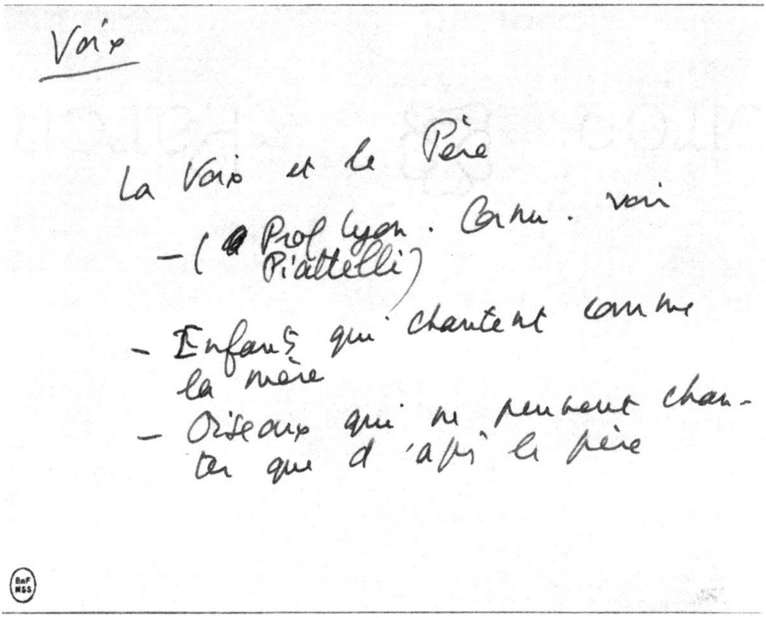

Voix

La Voix et le Père
— (à Prof Lyon. Cornu. voir
Piattelli)

— Enfants qui chantent comme
la mère
— Oiseaux qui ne peuvent chan-
ter que d'après le père

Two of Barthes's index cards on the voice.

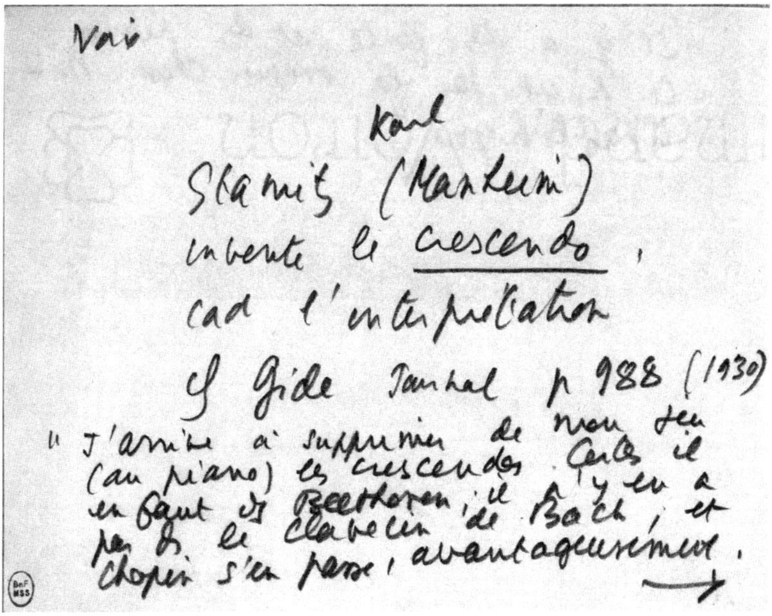

Voix

Karl
Stamitz (Mannheim)
invente le <u>crescendo</u>,
cad l'interprétation

cf Gide Journal p 988 (1930)
" J'arrive à supprimer de mon jeu
(au piano) les crescendos . Certes il
en faut dans Beethoven il n'y en a
pas dans le clavecin de Bach ; et
Chopin s'en passe, avantageusement .
→

Barthes playing the piano, around 1930.

5

His whole life behind him

Time had opened up several possibilities for Barthes in his teens: plans for writing, political commitment, the awakening of the senses; but life soon decided to close these off for him earlier than expected. While for some people war was a time for departure, and for several of them a decisive turning-point, as narrated for example by Daniel Cordier in *Alias Caracalla*,[1] it was for Barthes a time of withdrawal and introversion. From these years onwards, right up to the end, his relationship to the outside world would be in the almost exclusive mode of complaint, a long lament on wasted time and missed opportunities. The years leading up to the outbreak of war were still marked by exciting discoveries, especially the discovery of acting in the theatre, and by formative journeys too – but regret at not being able to complete the studies for which he felt destined cast a shadow over his youth. Barthes knew that he was not cured and that his health was good only when in remission. Compared to the future his friends could look forward to, his own seemed hopelessly limited. The lack of interest he was able to muster in his literary studies at the Sorbonne was probably the consequence of the feeling that he had lost status – a feeling that was persistent and became even more acute at this time. However, just then, as was always the case later on, he managed to find another scene in which he could foster his desire. While suffering because he had not found his right place, he invented other places, set apart or in the margins, which meant that he could be the person he hoped to become.

From Antiquity to Greece

This first scene was literally that of theatre – for this is where Barthes found his greatest satisfactions between 1936 and 1939. With his friend Jacques Veil, he founded the Groupe de théâtre antique de la Sorbonne, based on the model of the Groupe de théâtre médiéval set up by Gustave Cohen and called 'Les Théophiliens' after the performance of Rutebeuf's *Le Miracle de Théophile* in May 1933, in the Salle Louis-Liard. The two alumni of Louis-le-Grand were soon joined by Jacques Chailley, Jean Ritz and Nikita Élisséeff, and it was Maurice Jacquemont, inspired by Jacques Copeau, who put on their repertoire, having directed the Théophiliens between 1933 and 1936. The avowed aim of the Groupe was to perform plays from the Greek and Roman repertoire and make them more popular. It thought of itself as an outside space, in two senses: it was outside the university, even though it was set up within it and under its authority; and outside the professional, legitimate theatre. As with music, Barthes here found an opportunity to indulge his taste for amateur activities to which the theatre could also give a certain patent of nobility. In his 'Lettre au sujet du Groupe de théâtre antique' ('Letter on the subject of the Groupe de théâtre antique'), written in November 1961 and published in the review *L'Arche* in 1962, Barthes claimed to draw on the model of 'autarky', assuming responsibilities both cultural and material. Something that had not been able to take proper shape in the lycée in the form of the political grouping around the review *La Règle organique* here found its space and its contours. Twenty-five years later, the word that came to him when he thought back to the experience of founding the group was the word 'happiness'. 'In the first months, and in any case up until the production of *The Persians*, in May 1936, we were happy, I think one can say, because we were united: our work was really collective, really anonymous; to speak a philosophical language that was unknown at the time, we had in common the same *praxis*.'[2] And he continued by linking this political experience with the Popular Front, which distinguished this period from those preceding and following it: hope at last existed and the imperative to commit oneself politically was less urgent. 'The student could take on a cultural task, invented and sustained by himself alone, without in the least having the feeling that he was being distracted from something more important or more urgent; all of this led to an action both passionate and happy.'

There is not much in the way of documentation on the first years of the Group: statutes, programmes, letters, a few press cuttings as well as a long letter from Jacques Veil written in 1937 as an account of the first two years.[3] It is mainly the programmes that give us an impression of the spirit that drove its members, their aims and the role that each of them played. These programmes opened their columns to students and teachers alike. In the programme for *Amphitryon*, performed in 1937, Gustave Cohen, the lecturer who ran the Groupe de théâtre médiéval, and André Plassart, professor of Greek, mentioned the names and motivations of those who had founded the Groupe the previous year: 'Our young and dear Ancients are the children of the Théophiliens. I still remember the evening of the Rutebeuf Festival at the beginning of January 1936, when Barthes and Veil came looking for us in the Louis-Liard room, among the half-naked celestial and infernal company, to ask me what I would feel about a resurrection of the ancient theatre analogous to the one we had undertaken for the medieval theatre. You can imagine the enthusiasm with which I encouraged them, promising to lend them all our technicians and support them with our experience. As everyone knows, their efforts were crowned with success and we can still see in our mind's eye the admirable performance of *The Persians* in the courtyard of the Sorbonne on 3 May 1936.' The lecturers were in their turn always thanked and the performances linked to the university syllabus. The endeavour thus claimed to be inseparable from a philosophical reflection, and the relation to the texts was marked by an attention to both faithfulness and exegesis. The members of the Groupe strove to be literal, and retranslated some parts of the texts so as to bring them more into line with the way they imagined Antiquity: 'We have taken care to translate the text as literally as possible', they wrote in relation to *The Persians*. And in the programme to *Amphitryon*, it is stated that, 'as for *The Persians*, we ourselves did the research'. They also wrote: 'We have based our work on the articles in the Encyclopaedias of Daremberg and Sagio and Pauly-Wissowa'; and: 'Much of the information provided by the text about costumes, the mise en scène, all the relevant suggestions made during the session [to discuss the play] were gathered and put together in a dossier that later turned out to be extremely useful.'[4] The elements of adaptation were always based on archaeological findings and, as Sylvie Patron emphasizes in her article, we can see a veritable obsession with reconstruction at work, as if the new run always needed to involve rediscoveries and restoration.

But this new run of an old play was also forward-looking. Thus, the desire to bring the play up to date was much in evidence; it was part of the spirit of the age (Giraudoux, Cocteau). It was a matter of getting close to history and the characters in one's sensibility, while demonstrating a political understanding of the play. The Groupe de théâtre antique addressed its audience by playing on the character, both timeless and contemporary, of its repertory: 'May our attempt achieve its purpose and thereby enable the students and the teachers, the profane and the initiated, the artists and the humanists, to appreciate in a now more direct way the eternal beauty of ancient theatre.' With *The Persians*, performed for the first time in 1936 but regularly repeated the following years, and with *Antigone* in 1939, the Groupe focused directly on political events of the day. *The Persians* denounced the pride of the conquerors, with Zeus reminding everyone that they would be crushed. With *Antigone*, the lesson was even clearer and was perceived as such in the accounts written at the time: 'It is she who proclaims in the face of the tyrant the sovereignty of laws whose divinity illumines the conscience of mankind, and it is she too who utters the magnificent cry: "I was born to share, not hatred, but love!"' This declaration, within hearing of the imminent war, touched the spectators to the heart. The mise en scène was meant to transmit this allusion to the present. Faithfulness to the text came at this price: it was not a matter of reconstructing the choreographic figures on Greek vases, but of adopting simple movements that could still in modern times transmit a 'religious and patriotic gravity'. According to Veil, 'Jacques Chailley restored to the choral sections the vesture and support of a melody in complete conformity with the canons of Greek music', but it was the resources of a very contemporary instrument, the ondes Martenot, that suggested 'the song of the wind, the echo of the trumpets or the tears of the sea'.[5] The first performance, on 3 May 1936, was a stunning success. On the following days, the Groupe received from the press index more than 200 newspaper cuttings. After a performance in Provins on 5 July, and two others at the université des Annales, tours were organized in France and Belgium. Georges Duhamel wrote: 'I saw *The Persians* performed at the université des Annales by the pupils of M. Mazon. I came away feeling shaken to the depths of my soul.'[6]

In *The Persians*, Barthes played the role of Darius.[7] Though we cannot tell whether as a cause or a consequence (and it does not really matter), this character meant that he could develop a conception of acting that would be developed in his later thinking. Darius is a father. Darius is a dead man. Darius is the dead father who arises from the kingdom of the shadows to curse his son Xerxes who has been defeated by the Greeks. In two long monologues, he hurls his regrets, his execrations and his curses at the audience. Barthes playing the role of a father returning from the dead was already a way of transforming one particular feature of his biography. But this is not the most important point. It was a role that enabled him to give voice to a certain silence of the body. Darius is not really related to the other characters. Dead, speaking in the mode of prosopopoeia, he adds depth to distance. He sets in motion something that the ancient theatre most intensely activated: a speech that expects no reply, as Blanchot writes, 'a speech from on high, a relation without reciprocity'.[8] Dead, he is at once a body and an absence of body. So he invites the performer to declaim rather than embody him. Playing this character was the experience in which, for Barthes, a gap opened up between speech and presence, between speech and body. As well as helping us to understand Barthes's fascination in the post-war years with Brecht's alienation effect, this experience defined a relation to acting that preferred diction to identification, and that was as far removed as possible from the psychology of acting. From his teenage years onwards, he claimed to prefer Dullin to all other actors because the latter did not embody his roles, 'it was the role that imbued Dullin's breathing, always the same breathing, whatever role he was playing'. It was this same quality that he found in Pitoëff and Jouvet. Barthes was opposed to disguise, metamorphosis, the becoming-other so characteristic of a certain acting style that aimed at verisimilitude in performance. Instead, he preferred the declamation of a higher mode of speech, in action *as* speech that enables us to glimpse something unknown and new, 'a foreign and sovereign language [. . .] whose constitutive quality was neither emotion nor verisimilitude, but merely a sort of passionate clarity'.[9] In *On Racine*, which dates to three years before this 'eye-witness account of theatre' detailing his experience of ancient theatre, he granted the same virtues to Alain Cuny when directed by Jean Vilar. Realizing that one should proceed by focusing on the big picture rather than on details or attitudes, Cuny brought out the 'disproportion between the signified and the signifiers', he underlined the main intention, ridding the piece of a psychology that was now merely marginal. Tragic roles place the characters in relation with the gods. Racine's Theseus is like Aeschylus's Darius, they are chthonian creatures, who have become acquainted with the dead: to perform tragedy, 'it is necessary and sufficient to act as if the gods existed, as if one had seen them, as if they had spoken: but then, what a distance there is between oneself and what one says!'[10]

The gap thus produced in the diction has the consequence of setting the body at a distance, pushing expression into the background. The photo of the performance of *The Persians* reproduced in *Roland Barthes by Roland Barthes* showing Darius, majestically white, slender and wearing a headdress, at the top of the steps in the main courtyard of the Sorbonne, is accompanied by a caption that sheds light on the sense of a cut: 'Darius, a part that always gave me terrible stage fright, had two long declamations in which I was likely to forget my lines: I was fascinated by the temptation of *thinking about something else*. Through the tiny holes in the mask, I could see only very high up, and very far away; while I delivered the dead king's prophecies, my eyes came to rest on inert – free – objects and books, a window, a cornice, a piece of the sky: they, at least, weren't afraid. I excoriated myself for getting caught in this uncomfortable trap – while my voice continued its smooth delivery, resisting the *expressions* I should have given it.'[11] Apart from the historical distance, here accompanied by the distance of irony, we can see how much Barthes always links theatre to a *discrepancy*. Fear leads one to seek vanishing points, to separate oneself, as it were, from one's place and body. It dissociates the voice from the person uttering the sounds. What was initially just a challenging ordeal, making one feel anxious and awkward, later became a quality of the theatre, one of its powers of revelation. It found expression, in life, in the maintaining of a distance perceptible to those around him between the awkwardness in his body's external covering, an awkwardness that could only intensify with age, and an ease in the voice that created a connection with others, which enveloped them better than the body. The power proper to the voice did not arouse fear. In writing, this fear led to a definite taste for divisions, for transversal or oblique slashes, for the different sorts of cuts that make thinking possible. Becoming a writer seems to have been the imaginary resolution of this often painful separation. Becoming a writer would no doubt allow Barthes to unite body and voice, and turn speech into presence. His investigations into this area, which he pursued throughout his whole intellectual life, demonstrated a hesitant emergence from division. Barthes's conviction, gradually affirmed, that basically he did nothing except write, the advance of the neutral, the abandoning of structures – all of this, as we shall see in the course of his career, to some extent corrected the discrepancy, the painful split within himself.

Two difficult and distinct bodies: the covering of flesh, and the social body – or rather the body as it is inscribed socially. It is necessary to compromise with both of them. Another way of doing so involves music, in particular in its vocal dimension that Barthes explored a little later in this period. While he was finishing his degree at the Sorbonne, he decided, with his friend Michel Delacroix, to go and ring the doorbell of the singer he admired the most, Charles Panzéra. As they did not know any other teachers, and were passionate admirers of his voice, with the intrepidity of the young they turned to him, and in return he demonstrated a very great generosity, agreeing to give them lessons for free. And so, until he left for the sanatorium, in 1942, Barthes trained his voice in accordance with the melodies of the beginning of the twentieth century, carrying as far as he could the inflections of a French language that would soon be vanishing. A text from 1977 pays homage to that generous master. And it is interesting to read that, while talking about his voice and his way of speaking, Barthes finds the same qualities that he attributed to Dullin and Cuny, namely a diction stripped of the overemphatic effects of meaning. To do so, he distinguishes between pronunciation, which maintains continuity, legato and line, and articulation, which gives the same phonic intensity to each consonant in accordance with a logic of expressivity – a logic that is 'highly ideological'. According to Barthes: 'in the arts of articulation, language, poorly understood as a theater, a staging of meaning that is slightly kitsch, explodes into the music and deranges it inopportunely, unseasonably: language thrusts itself forward, it is the intruder, the nuisance of music; in the art of pronunciation, on the contrary (Panzéra's), it is music which enters the language and rediscovers there what is musical, what is "amorous".'[12] There is a remarkable continuity here between the denunciation of the petty-bourgeois aesthetic of the Comédie-Française that puts one off the theatre, and a certain art of singing. In this emphasis on the value of voice and language, of the voice *for language* and not *for meaning*, we can detect not just the desire to imply a permanent distance between the saying and the said, between the implicit and the explicit, but also the complex strategy of dissimulation of bourgeois culture. The liking for French melody, for Duparc, Fauré and Debussy, was undeniably the result of an intimate relation with this culture which Barthes was at the same time always concerned to reject, to subvert. Instead of distancing himself radically from this culture, he would often implement a whole series of discursive stratagems to show that it bore *within itself* the ferments of its own subversion. He was thus led to distinguish usages and manners, one of which might be, as it were, an enjoyment without acceptance – his way of appropriating something without agreeing with it. It can also be a means of inte-riorizing the feeling that one has lost status by turning this into a choice, a value. Here, we can see an ambiguity essential to Barthes's character: though he showed a certain conformism in his tastes, in his desires and his objects of choice, he also detached himself from them through the aptness of his critique and his intuitions.

The passion expressed for theatre at this period was subsequently extended in various forms. First in the auditorium, among the spec-tators, and in criticism. Even if his life was in practical terms marked by a gradual move away from the stage to the auditorium and from the auditorium to the exit (in 1965 he acknowledges that he had loved the theatre and yet hardly went there any more),[13] his work remained marked, from beginning to end, by an attention to all the phenomena of theatrical display, to the signs that were produced on stage, to movements in space. 'There is not a single one of his texts, in fact, which fails to deal with a certain theater, and spectacle is the universal category in whose aspect the world is seen.'[14] However, verismo and expressive intention are always condemned by him. Neither theatre costumes nor diction should bear any values other than those of the theatrical action itself, reduced to its essential ges-tures and its main functions:[15] to show, to quote, to repeat – these are the watchwords of theatricality, and they can be implemented in many places, in other forms of engagement. Theatricality becomes, so to speak, the main figure whereby signs are kept at a distance. *Mythologies* begins with texts devoted to theatre or theatricalized forms: all-in wrestling, where Barthes discovers 'a grandiloquence which must have been that of ancient theatres', the photographs of the Harcourt Studio which turn actors into useless gods, and the peplum and its mongrel signs that confuse signs with their signi-fieds. Speech in myth is itself theatrical, and the scene of myth, like the classical theatre, explains nothing. 'I see theater everywhere', Barthes told Bernard-Henri Lévy, 'in writing, in images, etc.'[16] The more the theatricality of the world became apparent, the less the theatre as such became necessary. However, the powerful commitment to the theatre Barthes felt in his youth provided him with some tenacious lines of thought. Thus, the little anthology composed in 2009 by Persida Asllani of all Barthes's 'questions' and consisting of a list of the interrogative sentences in his *Oeuvres complètes*, opens with tragedy ('So what happened in those periods, in those countries, that made it possible and even easy for tragedy to exist there?') and closes with the contemplation of the spectacle of the world: in the 'Soirées de Paris' ('Evenings in Paris'), 'what then would I do when I go out? [. . .] What will the spectacle of my world come to be?'[17] The fact that the first word is also the last is confirmed by an abandoned fragment from the *Lexique de l'auteur* called 'Le premier mot' ('The first word'): 'He wrote, as an epigraph to his master's dissertation (on incantations and evocations in Greek tragedy) Claudel's words on Japanese Noh theatre: "It is not an actor speaking, but a word in action." All the rest (the idea of an efficiency of language) was already in these words, as if it were merely the first inscription of a programme, as if there were a certain genetics of the intellect: the terribly fixed nature of a subject, indicated right from the start by his first word (even if this word comes from another), taken further by him without any other idea than to vary it – not to transform it.'[18] Barthes spots that his ethos of variation stems from a distance from himself in which the word is liberated and creates its own theatre, shaping both his life and his writings. The stage as the place of the world, the world as a stage: from beginning to end, the theatre is the metaphor of a way of being in the world in which he finds himself ever more entangled, though without ever ceasing to be a stranger.

From the Mediterranean to the Atlantic

Those years 1936–40 were marked by instability and a sense of relative inner poverty. Barthes often succumbed to discouragement. Work on his degree was not making quite the progress he would have liked. In June 1936, he failed his certificate in Greek in spite of his assiduous study of Aeschylus: 'In the Greek oral, when I was given Atossa's dream, I didn't know the meaning of a single word.' Although several of his friends passed the competitive exam to enter the École normale supérieure in the rue d'Ulm, Paris, he had the feeling that he was reduced to mediocrity, not through his own fault but through force of circumstances. Among the key scenes of his life that he remembered when he was writing 'Vita Nova', one stood out: 'My tears when Ph[ilippe] R[ebeyrol] passed the exam for Normale.'[19] It was sad to see that their paths were no longer the same; and it was painful to have to bid farewell to an image of his future that he had nursed.

A vacation in the Béarn was no consolation; he said that he was suffocating far from those he loved. However, he decided to continue his degree while giving private lessons, especially to Serge Mainguet whom he helped even during the holidays, spending time with him in Normandy in summer 1936. At the start of the new school year, his maternal grandfather was hospitalized in Val-de-Grâce, where he was kept under observation for a while before returning to L'Isle-Adam where he died on 10 November at the age of 80. He was buried with full honours in the Montparnasse cemetery. The media hype over his death, which many of the newspapers of the day echoed, did not leave Barthes indifferent. He was not yet ashamed of his grandfather and still felt some of the admiration he had felt for him as a child.

The years 1937–38 were marked by two significant journeys. The first, from June to August 1937, took him to Hungary with a group of students, to the University of Debrecen, in the heart of Puszta, not far from the border with Romania. Before it was almost entirely destroyed by the Second World War, the city was prosperous and encouraged tourism thanks to its recreational facilities in a central park (the 'big forest') at the heart of the city. With its Protestant majority (including the university where Barthes gave a few French classes as lector), the town was imbued with an atmosphere of ease and freedom that left their mark on the young man. The following year, he travelled to Greece, a trip that he had dreamed of for so long. He went there with the Groupe de théâtre antique and their itinerary took them from Athens to Mycenae, by way of the islands, Santorini, Delos and Aegina. He was following in the footsteps of Philippe Rebeyrol whose route he had followed in his imagination while he himself was stuck in the Pyrenees: 'At every moment in Greece, I thought of you. You had made this journey. On that tiny rock, Delos, you had passed by. I was very often touched now that I was really making this journey when I had passionately followed you, when I was in Bedous.'[20] He went on to develop an art of travel as an art of outlying areas and borders,[21] in the margins, on the threshold. While admiring the main features, justly celebrated – the monuments, museums and statues – Barthes kept them at a distance, or left them within their own distance. Instead, the 'threshold' art of travel prefers places that have been left out: the rocks that nobody notices. It is characterized by two features: heading off away from the group, which meant that he could visit districts on the edges, far from the centre and the tourist traps; and taking notes, a practice that he started during this trip and that he never subsequently abandoned. The material in these notes later served for composing fragmentary, ambulatory texts, which provide the reader less with a narrative than with a set of sense impressions. 'En Grèce' ('In Greece'), published in *Existences* (the review of the Saint-Hilaire-du-Touvet sanatorium) in July 1944, was the first evidence of what is presented as a combined art of travel and a notation based on the marginal and the minor; an art of writing while walking on the edge or along the crest of the hill. Barthes also explains what the Mediterranean has given him. This included what had struck him in reading Nietzsche, of course, such as the intensity of the light, the beauty of the statues, the thoughts awoken by the ruins, the combination of sun, water and earth; but, even more than that, everything that is small and dark, lurking in the background: 'simple rocks', the 'wretched filth', 'a narrow beach', 'a shabby little boat', the 'tiny cup' from which one drinks milk, the offal of animals – the *acrocolia*, the guts, brain, liver, foetus, sweetbread and udders – which, despite being such humble fare, were ennobled by the fact that the Ancients enjoyed eating them. 'The monuments of Athens are as beautiful as has often been said. There's a squalid district that I really liked; it's at the foot of the Acropolis; it consists simply of market streets, short and narrow, but full of life; I often went for a stroll there.'[22] Everything lies in the juxtaposition of the two propositions, and in the proximity of the two contrasting districts: admiration and beauty on the one side, producing a form of indifference; pleasure and disorder on the other, which lead to participation. We are far from the pantheon promoted by the *Blue Guide* where the emphasis is on picturesque points of view and where 'the human life of a country disappears to the exclusive benefit of its monuments'.[23] The voluptuousness of statues is nothing in comparison with the gentleness with which the merest young barber shaves you, using 'many different and dubious creams, but applied so lightly that this grubby magician calms your fears and revulsions'.[24] Only in these surroundings was it possible to have an adventure. It was here, more than on the bright coasts or indeed the stretches of land where ruins and stones were strewn together, that Barthes could see bodies in movement, allow himself to be attracted by one of them, or to catch another person's eye. The approach to places and to the people who occupied them was already creating a whole subtle palette of colours – what Jean-Pierre Richard so aptly calls Barthes's 'true landscape of emotions'.[25] Among these *qualia* was oil: this would later be mentioned in connection with *tempura* in *Empire of Signs*[26] and then in relation to Réquichot's painting ('Oil is that substance which augments the foodstuff without fragmenting it: which thickens without hardening it'),[27] and finally with regard to mayonnaise in an unpublished fragment of *Roland Barthes by Roland Barthes*.[28] Oil brings together the opposite properties of devouring pitch (maleficent) and the unctuous smoothness (beneficent) that here conquer thanks to the 'glazing' that will be noted and theorized in connection with the 'ornamental cuisine' of the magazine *Elle*.[29] The threshold art of travel and notation thus allow the real landscapes Barthes has traversed to be superimposed onto territories recomposed into images by his desires and personal associations.

On his return from Greece, Barthes spent a week or so near Saint-Gervais at the home of his friend Michel Bauer, in an isolated village, where he enjoyed a certain solitude. During this period, he was shaken by mystical crises that made him long for withdrawal, and where a liking for small communities was demonstrated – a liking that would be discussed in more detail in the course he gave on *How to Live Together*. What touched him when, that summer, he and the Théophiliens visited a Benedictine abbey near Bruges in Belgium was less spirituality than the stability that imbued this place, the efficaciousness of an organization and a rule. We find this phantasy in the session of the course given on 12 January 1977, which Barthes said was an original dream: neither living as a couple, nor a collective living-together, but 'something like solitude with regular interruptions: the paradox, the contradiction, the aporia of bringing distances together'.[30] It was, he said, when he read *L'Été grec* (*The Greek Summer*) by Jacques Lacarrière that this phantasy was spurred into life by a particular word, 'idiorrhythmia', used of monks who are both isolated and linked together within a single structure on Mount Athos. Regularly, even before he entered the sanatorium, Barthes felt that he was more alive in those small autarkic groups, even when they had a monastic character. 'The rule of daily life, a very fine one', he wrote to Philippe Rebeyrol on 1 March 1939 – this was the sign of a perfect and productive stability, something of which Barthes dreamt his whole life long.

The rise of the European crisis did not favour this stability. The personal documents from 1939 show an intense preoccupation with the outside world in which the 'self' was no longer the sole centre. As Barthes wrote in a letter to Rebeyrol: 'With all that's going on in Europe at the moment, it's not just that we fear for our lives and for peace – for our peace, but also and above all for the splits and sufferings within our conscience. It's a terrible malady that the soul feels within itself, all these slaps in the face to justice. I can't tell you how disgusted I am and how intensely I'm suffering morally, I weep inside myself for all the sufferings of the world, for all the terrible crimes committed by different states as the result of a truly impious pride. We are living through times of apocalypse and martyrdom. Every day, our consciences as men are buffeted and we feel surrounded by the leprosy of a permanent dishonour, one that is also threatened by this sea of crimes, boorishness, acts of cannibalism that are all protected and supported by the laws, the press, etc. It's absolutely sickening and, every day, I have a few moments when I feel utterly depressed, ashamed of being a man, and I can dissipate these feelings only out of an instinct of self-preservation just so as to get through the rest of the day in spite of it all.'[31] The style is reminiscent of Victor Hugo (he was reading the latter's *La Légende des siècles*), or perhaps stems from more recent writers, such as Thomas Mann and Oswald Spengler: it expresses an almost metaphysical anguish about the future. His view of the world is less directly political – even though he denounces nationalism – and more the swansong of humanist belief. The phrase 'ashamed of being a man' that Deleuze would later echo in the expression 'the shame of being a man', repeated several times in the *Abécédaire*,[32] evinces a deeply rooted resistance to the oppression inflicted by states, the awareness of belonging to a world that is being destroyed. Language can still carry the emotional charge of the discourse of the universal that the violence of imminent destruction was about to demolish forever. The outbreak of war exposed Barthes to a reality that he had hitherto kept at bay. 'I didn't focus my thoughts on the problems of the world, I didn't understand a thing about it – but now my eyes are gradually opening and I have the impression that I can just see how it's all happening and even how it's all going to happen. And my impotence, my silence, the silence of others, make me suffer cruelly. At times, I really do have the impression that the harsh reality is burning me, and I come to a halt, aghast, on the edge of an abyss.'[33]

From the Atlantic to behind the lines

While most of his friends were mobilized, Barthes himself was exempted by the Conseil de réforme that summoned him in September 1939: for the time being, at least, there was no auxiliary service for those suffering from pulmonary illness. His planned trip to England, where he was to take up a post as lector, was postponed. For the rest of his degree, Barthes could choose whether to complete it, turning it into a teaching degree, or to extend it into a diploma of higher studies, more oriented towards research. But he needed to work so as to share the material burden with which his family had to cope. In November, he was offered a job teaching a *classe de troisième* in the lycée in Biarritz, where his brother was at school: here, Barthes taught French, Latin and Greek. The family occupied a small flat in the rue du Cardinal-Lavigerie, in an apartment block known as 'Les Sirènes', and his mother regularly performed small tasks at the hospital. His first experiences as a teacher were difficult: Barthes was aware of the responsibilities of the profession. He felt he had a certain authority with the pupils, but he was anxious about his image. 'It's a terrible profession,' he wrote to Philippe on 29

November 1939, 'where for every action you have to make an inner choice straight away, and this choice can have terrible circumstances [*sic*]. And this power that you have burns your fingers, and yet you must never drop it.'[34] He was inspected two months later and knew he had made a dreadful mistake about the Greek verb *hekein*, 'to have arrived', but he was deemed to be doing well, as the report of the inspector, Cayroux, attests: 'R. Barthes, *délégué rectoral*, is starting out as a teacher. He still of course lacks the qualities that only experience of the profession can give: flexibility in the way he asks questions, the art of discerning what needs to be said and what can be left out, in short, the ease and self-assurance that give animation and life to the class. But the analysis of the text that he gives in my presence has been prepared with immense care; it is simple, clear, exact, and comes with a host of detailed and extremely useful remarks. [. . .] I think that the inevitable period of settling in and feeling his way will soon be over for him. As soon as he arrived, he produced a good impression at the L. [lycée] of Biarritz; he is very popular with his pupils, who follow his lessons with pleasure, and I am giving a very favourable account of him to support the renewal of his post.'[35] Overall, Barthes too said that he was happy to be teaching and even managed to tell his pupils about his literary passion of the moment, Charles Péguy. Biarritz, with its Belle Époque and Art Deco architecture, its luxuriant gardens and its open, relatively empty beaches, gave him some pleasant times. He went for long walks along the beach, towards the lighthouse (*Itsas argi* in Basque, meaning the light of the sea) on the promontory of Cap Saint-Martin. 'Yesterday, I went up to it on my way home from the cinema;[36] the night was really strange, quite immobile, almost matt and filled with a stagnant warmth. At the edge of a terrace, raised very high above the sea, I moved closer, as just opposite me there was an incredible crescent moon, golden yellow, slender, curved, pointed, a real scythe; and down below, I could sense, in a sort of cosmic fright, that vast immobile movement of the sea in the rocky depths.'[37] Indeed, Biarritz is a small port sheltered by the cliff and beaten by the wind and the waves. While Bayonne extended its commercial activities from the eighteenth century onwards, Biarritz remained a little fishing harbour. The lighthouse, erected as part of the huge programme to set up beacons along the French coasts in the 1820 and 1830s, was completed in February 1834: it is white in colour and sits on a lofty promontory, and was linked to the town by a communal promenade that allowed pedestrians to go up to the parapet to observe and hear the continual movement of the ocean, with the Basque mountains on the one side and the horizon on the other, which was not obstructed by the Barre de Bayonne. One needs to imagine the resonance the roar of the sea would have had for a young man whose eyes were opening to the problems of the world, on that motionless night with the thunder of war in which several of his friends were fighting. In a few weeks the lighthouse would be extinguished and the German Army would be in control of the coasts. Biarritz and the whole of the Basque country were in the occupied zone. Philippe Rebeyrol was taken prisoner.

After the capitulation in June 1940, Barthes, his mother and his brother returned to occupied Paris. Their return meant he could see Michel Delacroix again: he resumed his relationship with him, half friendship, half love, stable and happy. Rebeyrol, who had escaped, moved to Lyon, in the Free Zone, to work towards the *agrégation* in history. Barthes too dreamed of pursuing his studies, but he knew that he would need to work to earn a living. 'The material situation is hard. It's difficult to work because of the cold. I still don't have any work, and I'm broke. Today I've heard about a potential job as an assistant editor at the Beaux-Arts; I'm going to look into it. But this already raises the fearsome problem of choosing between normal studies and earning a living, as I need to. At every moment I'm faced with these dilemmas, and more than ever I'm immersed in inextricable conflicts on all sides – they are spoiling my life, which is already so gloomy and hostile.'[38] All the same, he registered for his diploma in higher studies on rites of passage in Greek tragedy (Sophocles, Aeschylus, Euripides), with Paul Mazon as his thesis director, while also taking up a job as *délégué rectoral* (*surveillant-répétiteur* and assistant teacher) in the Lycée Voltaire (avenue de la République) and the Lycée Carnot (boulevard Malesherbes). The long and frequent commutes made it difficult to do everything at the same time. Things were made harder because several events added suddenly to his woes: Michel Delacroix, a TB sufferer like Barthes, was hospitalized; his paternal grandmother, Berthe Barthes, died in May 1941, the very same day as his philology exam, which meant he had to return to Bayonne and miss the exams in the first session. So he spent the whole summer there, keeping his grieving aunt company; he still played music with her, while studying for the diploma and the certificates that he passed in October.[39] In November, he had another episode of pulmonary tuberculosis. He underwent a pneumothorax (also known as a collapsotherapy), a regular procedure for TB patients right up into the 1950s (and even after antibiotics made an appearance in 1946): the lung was deliberately collapsed so as to make the damaged pleura scar over thanks to the movements of breathing and the creation of tubercular caverns, though this entailed several respiratory complications that sometimes made it necessary to lose the lung. In 1935, a book had been published with the title *Et moi aussi, j'ai eu vingt ans!* (*I too reached my twentieth birthday!*) by François Abgrall,[40] who had died from this illness at the age of 23. In it, he describes this painful, exhausting therapy, which consisted in placing the lung in a state of 'repose', while allowing the air to enter by injecting an oily product between the layers of the pleura, thus detaching the lung from the ribs. This surgical technique has become well known mainly thanks to a famous scene in Thomas Mann's *The Magic Mountain*: having just arrived in the Berghof, Hans Castorp is surprised by the whistling noise made by Hermine Kleefeld, who has undergone a pneumothorax. His cousin Joachim Ziemssen, who has been under treatment for several months, explains: 'If she's been walking rapidly, then she can whistle from inside, and of course she uses it then to startle people, especially newly arrived patients.'[41] In November, after this ordeal, Barthes found a job as a teacher at the Hattemer private school in the rue de Londres, but then immediately had to take steps to enter the students' sanatorium at Saint-Hilaire-du-Touvet, where he was admitted in January 1942.

Here began Roland Barthes's other war, the only war he really experienced, in his entrenched position: the war against illness. For more than four years (1942–46), apart from a few short periods of leave when he could go to Paris or Bayonne, his life would be lived in the paradoxical space of sanatoria, confined even in the fresh air, isolated even within a community. The chronology of these events deserves to be given in full, as it displays the character – both terrible and ordinary – of the stages of the illness. Relapses were frequent, almost normal, but they made a cure seem a distant and uncertain prospect. So Barthes entered Saint-Hilaire-du-Touvet in January 1942. In April, he suffered a grave relapse with a pleural haemorrhage that forced him to be confined to his bed for more than a month. He convalesced in the usual way between August and December and left Saint-Hilaire in January. From January to July 1943, he thought he had recovered and stayed for aftercare in a clinic for students just opened by Dr Daniel Douady in the rue Quatrefages, near the jardin des Plantes in the 5th arrondissement of Paris, to ease cured patients back into ordinary life. In July, while he was staying with his family in the house that his grandmother, Noémie Révelin, owned in Hendaye, he suffered a relapse that brought him back to Saint-Hilaire-du-Touvet. For three months, he suffered the worst period of his internment: this involved the treatment then indicated for patients in his state, namely silence, complete immobility and lying in a reclined position with the head lowered. He stayed there for the whole of 1994 until February 1945, when he was transferred to the Alexandre clinic in the sanatorium at Leysin, in the Vaud canton in Switzerland. He spent three months there, and was then in September again transferred to the university house for aftercare in the rue Quatrefages in Paris. Another relapse took him straight back to Leysin, where he underwent another pneumothorax in October. He stayed there until February 1946, with a brief stay in Paris in December 1945. On leaving Leysin, he went on a short trip round

Switzerland to say goodbye to the friends he had made during his treatment, and returned to Paris on 28 February. But it was not all over yet. As he was trying to settle back into ordinary life, finishing his teaching degree and taking the last certificate he still needed (even though he knew that his illness severely and perhaps even definitively compromised any career in the national education system),[42] he again had to spend the summer months in aftercare at Neufmoutiers-en-Brie, in Seine-et-Marne. Thus it was only in September 1946 that he could move back once and for all to the rue Servandoni.

These were the years in which scientific research finally developed the antibiotics that could cure TB. In 1942, Selman Waksman discovered streptothricin and, in 1943, with his pupil Albert Schatz, streptomycin, which, in 1944, became the first antibiotic to cure a patient severely ill with TB. However, Barthes was treated with methods that had been in practice since the end of the nineteenth century, in the sanatorium, with rest cures and sun cures, and even silence and complete immobilization. His long stay in the sanatorium occurred at the end of this 'golden age' of the sanatorium, which lasted from 1882 (the date when the TB bacillus was identified by Robert Koch) to around 1947. His timetable was marked by having his temperature taken (no less than four times a day), meals and rest cures. Barthes suffered this illness at a time when it was still very deadly: it killed more than 60,000 people in 1938 in France as a whole, and the majority of these were young men[43] – the shadow of death hovered over the summits on which TB institutions were situated. The death of Michel Delacroix on 28 October 1942 was a dramatic reminder. Barthes said that he had never felt 'such a wild grief and I am here, locked away, I have to go on living as if nothing had happened'.[44] After this event, he succumbed to a depression that lasted several months. With his friend, he had nursed all his dreams, and had been encouraged to indulge in his numerous desires (for literature, for music). He remembered that they would follow people in the streets, turning them into fictional characters.[45] With nobody else had Barthes's novel ever been such a real possibility. So the violence of illness, the proximity of death, struck him right to the heart. But tuberculosis was also a myth, in the sense Barthes would give it in 'Myth Today': a social mythology and a literary myth. As Isabelle Grellet and Caroline Kruse wrote, in a book based on a thesis defended in 1978 at the École des hautes études with Roland Barthes himself as a thesis director, 'the dreams and fears of a society find a major means of expression in phthisis'.[46] Barthes already knew this, just as he knew that literature had given a second wind, so to speak, to this infection: he himself now embodied the recognizable type of the intellectual or writer – for this is how he dreamed of himself – occupying an entrenched position far removed from real life and action.

Tuberculosis was incontestably the major event of his life, and it exaggerated certain characteristics of his personality – his sense of being apart, and his tendency to complain – while fostering others, in particular the social affability encouraged by community life and the withdrawal of a man of letters as authorized by relative leisure. The paradoxical nature of the place (creating isolation while at the same time forcing him to share a collective life) pointed to an ambiguity in his social and political behaviour: a strong desire to belong without participating completely, giving people and political causes a somewhat distant support rather than any real commitment.

This point is certainly reinforced by the fact that his medical seclusion occurred during the war, at the time of the Occupation. Barthes was, in every respect, remote. At that time, he took part in only vague activities intended to improve his state and fill his days as best as possible. His comrades were mobilized and taken prisoner, and some of them were forced into exile or joined the Resistance, and in July 1944 he learned of the death of his friend Jacques Veil who was a Resistance fighter:[47] he himself, meanwhile, was absent from the event. From the vantage point of Saint-Hilaire, the Liberation looked rather like a 'village fete'. The main choices and commitments of his generation, those for which everyone would later claim responsibility and that would form the basis of the political and intellectual lines of force in the following decades, did not concern him. At a key moment in his life, his own history became separated from History as such. The event of illness cut him off from events. The feeling that he sometimes had of being lower in status than others, or on the margins, found expression in actuality. He was away from it all.

In fact, he was at a height of 1,200 metres in a centre opened in 1933 with Daniel Douady as its director. After the war, Douady would be Director of Health in the Ministry of National Education: his centre was meant to enable students suffering from TB to pursue their studies as well as they could, while making the most of the fresh air, in summer as in winter. The establishment faced south-east and was protected from the winds of the north and the north-west by the Dent de Crolles. Between the centre and this mountain peak, a pine forest enabled patients to stroll in the verdure and benefit from the pure air: this then seemed one of the best possible treatments for their illness. It was reached by a funicular that led from Les Eymes to the Petites Roches plateau in twenty minutes. Perhaps when Barthes arrived, he thought of the resonances of the very name of Saint-Hilaire and the role it plays in Proust (whom Barthes had only recently read), 'its steeple [. . .] inscribing its unforgettable form on the horizon where Combray had not yet appeared [. . .] there was a spot where the narrow road emerged suddenly on an immense plateau closed at the horizon by jagged forests above which rose only the delicate tip of the steeple of Saint-Hilaire, but so thin, so pink, that it seemed merely scratched on the sky by a fingernail which wanted to give this landscape, this exclusively natural picture, that little mark of art, that indication of human presence.'[48] There is no church in Saint-Hilaire-du-Touvet, but the powerful memory of his reading of Proust endowed this place with an aesthetic quality.

The sanatorium was associated with the University of Grenoble and lecturers came from there to give classes. In 1942, a director of studies was appointed. The day was arranged around an inflexible timetable, as everyone's memory of the place bears witness: breakfast at 8 a.m., washing, rest cure from 9 to 11, meal at noon (in the dining room for those who were not immobilized), cure of silence from 2 p.m. until 4 p.m., a walk or reading, another rest cure at the end of the afternoon, dinner at 7 p.m., lights out at 9 p.m. The doctor went on his rounds in the morning, accompanied once a week by the chief doctor. During periods of immobilization, which Barthes underwent in June–July 1942 and then from August to October 1943, the meals were brought into the bedrooms on trays and the patients had a table fixed to the head of the bed that could also be used to read and write on. They relied entirely on the nurses for their physical needs. During the reclining cure, which he was given in 1943, Barthes had to lie at an angle to the horizontal for eighteen hours out of twenty-four, his lower limbs raised above the level of his thorax and his head, which made it difficult even to read. There are two texts which show how uncomfortable this treatment was. One is Benoîte Groult's novel, *Les Trois Quarts du temps* (*Three-Quarters of the Time*), which involves a young medical student, a member of the French Resistance, undergoing treatment from September 1943 onwards in the sanatorium of the plateau d'Assy. His stay there coincides exactly with that of Barthes, and he too undergoes a pneumothorax and the reclining cure: 'It stops me writing, especially as you have to lie on the side where you are ill – in my case, the right side. You can hardly read. In short, I am condemned to absolute immobility. And I am amazed at my absolute lack of reaction.'[49] And the memories of Jean Rousselot relate to the same period, but this time in Saint-Hilaire-du-Touvet. He describes in minute detail the timetable, the treatments, and ordinary everyday life. He also evokes the way everything was suspended: 'The snow seems to have settled for all eternity upon us as upon all things. Our roots are lengthening, warm under this endless sheet of snow, but where are our branches, our leaves? Where are the asperities that still kept us attached to the world of men? We are no longer from here, or from anywhere; we neither regret nor hope for anything: we just are [. . .] The bird itself no longer knows whether it has ever flown, ever sung . . . .'[50] Absence from time and history is echoed by nature. The summits, the clarity of the air, the whiteness of the mountain peaks, the whiteness of everything in winter: all give nature an inviolate character. Nothing, not even life – provisional in these places and indeed provisional *tout court* – as led by these young women and young men placed in different buildings ('Savoie' for the women and 'Dauphiné' for the men), interrupts the teaching of a class or changes the order of things. In *Un Homme de passage*, Serge Doubrovsky also relates his time in Saint-Hilaire-du-Touvet, though this was after the war, 'unable to grasp time as it passes, to measure it by any other means than the pumping up of the pneumo every week, immobilized day after day in a bedroom for three'.[51] This mountain was certainly not 'magic', except insofar as its coordinates were not those of the different space–times of the world; but it did not metamorphose or cast its magic spell on anything at all, because it merely delayed life and allowed the world to go on without its inmates. Barthes no longer needed to set himself deliberately apart, to dream of autarky or to find other stages on which to live his life. He was, in practical terms, held in suspense, at a distance. Living 'behind the lines' was the current metaphor for those protected from war. Objectively, it was something of a misnomer: after all, he was ill and had no choice but to undergo isolation and treatment. But it did chime in with his subjective disposition. Events had made the decision for him. Without any direct connection to things, without having been able to make a commitment when he should have done so, he would henceforth need others if he were to find a place for himself.

With the Ancient Theatre Group of the Sorbonne after a rehearsal of Aeschylus' *The Persians* (Barthes is in the middle), in 1936.

The Ancient Theatre Group during rehearsals for Plautus's *Amphitryon*. Barthes is sitting on the left, 1936.

Roland Barthes in 1938.

Trip to Greece with the Ancient Theatre Group, summer 1938.

The students' sanatorium at Saint-Hilaire-du-Touvet, where Barthes lived from 1942 to 1945.

Postcard to Philippe Rebeyrol, June 1941.

6

New vistas

The previous chapter presented the chronology of the sanatorium years, from 1942 to 1946, marked by relapses, moves from one place of treatment to another, the slow progress of a cure of which Barthes could not, at the end of a certain time, be sure. We now need to go over the details of that period, which was so decisive for Barthes's thought and his writing, for the development of the methods that he would later make his own. The time spent away in the sanatorium gave a particular density to existence: not much happened there, but the experience of isolation and withdrawal fostered autarkic practices of the relation to the self and to books that led him to give a special attention to signs. The sanatorium was also the place of an alternative social life, neither a family nor a collective: it was a little community in which people lived together in a society cut off from the rest of the world. These were also the years in which Barthes published his first texts in reviews. It is not without significance that his official entry into writing took place here: it marked publication, as well as the thoughts that led up to it, with a distinctive sense of separateness; it immediately defined a form of atopia, an absence of a fixed place that defined his work and its surprising novelty.

The body and its illness

Until he entered the sanatorium, Barthes had a long, slim body. Barthes imagined it would last forever like that, permanent and indifferent. 'I had the morphology of someone *super-slim* for my entire youth, and in fact I wasn't accepted for military service because I wasn't the right weight. And at that time I always lived with the idea that I'd be slim, for ever and ever.'[1] It was at Leysin, after his second pneumothorax, that, he says, he completely altered shape, 'changing (or appearing to change) from slender to plump'.[2] This transformation was disturbing for more than one reason: it modified his self-image and forced him to 'take care'. Throughout his life, Barthes would control his body, weighing himself and going on diets. So his diaries note for every day, during the times he was restricting his food intake, the number of calories consumed, the number of grams gained or lost. A diet is a strict measuring system in which everything is counted. But it is also a rule, as in religious orders: 'It's a religious phenomenon, it's a "religious neurosis". Embarking on a diet has all the distinctive features of a conversion. With the same problems of a relapse followed by a return to conversion. With some books that are treated as gospel truth, etc. A diet mobilizes an acute sense of guilt – it threatens you, it's there at every moment in the day.'[3] It involves turning one's body into an object for analysis, reading it like a text. At the beginning of the illness, the body becomes a set of signs. It is examined, weighed, measured, X-rayed, opened, segmented. In 1902, a specialist in tuberculosis, Dr Béraud, described the obsession with all this measuring: 'There is something eccentric and sometimes amusing about this meticulous, almost religious focus on self-obser- vation. The patients themselves trace the curve of their fever, wait for the time to "take their temperature", eager to see whether it has risen or fallen, is stationary or making progress [. . .] Next to temperature, weighing oneself is a major psychological factor for the TB patient in the sanatorium. For him, it is a second thermometer, which represents the aim of a week or fortnight of efforts, and its decrees are awaited with anxious impatience.'[4] The caption to the illustration reproduc- ing the temperature chart entitled 'Recurrent tuberculosis' in *Roland Barthes by Roland Barthes* waxes ironical in a parenthesis on this way of inscribing one's body and unrolling it in the way you would with a parchment: 'Every month, a new sheet was pasted on the bottom of the old one; at the end, there were yards of them: a farcical way of writing one's body within time.'[5] While temperature as the main way of giving a rhythm to one's days is a theme in most narratives of sanatorium life – its strict observance is linked, in Thomas Mann, to a good integration into the life of the sanatorium, where it becomes the main metaphor for time[6] – it is noteworthy that Barthes immedi- ately pushes the analogy between text and body even further. Noting down figures was not, for him, just a way of marking the drawn-out, circular and monotonous time of a life lived in isolation; it was a sign, a way of exhibiting oneself, fragmenting oneself, and enduring. It highlighted the history-body and the text-body. The first text on Michelet, published in 1951 in the review *Esprit* and based on the attentive readings of Michelet's work undertaken by Barthes in the sanatorium, develops a way of looking at history that is imbued with succession and a sense of being dragged out – with the concomitant idea of wasting away, an idea that becomes more acute with illness. 'Getting worse is, for Michelet, so much a sign of the historical that his History saw the inert as the place of a disintegration, and thus of a signification.'[7] His own history, for Barthes, was expressed through his different maladies: 'He was always complaining of a headache, feeling sick, a cold, a sore throat', as one of his friends recalls.[8] Thus, the immobilized body is the one that offers itself to the most attentive reading: it is not disturbed by anything flowing in from the outside or that might clash with it, and it becomes a pure place of observation for the movement that leads from life to death. It is a 'certain body', as Arab scholars say of the text if we are to believe *The Pleasure of the Text*, which enjoys quoting this 'admirable expression': neither the body of the anatomists, as described by science; nor the erotic body, which follows its own ideas; but the body readable in its different cross-sections, exchanging its properties with the text which is an 'anagram of the body'.[9] Thus, the attention to signs demonstrated in the different medical centres where Barthes spent some five years of his youth and where he pursued part of his education, had two main consequences for his thinking about the body: in the first place, the body is no longer *one* body. It is segmented into a number of distinct bodies that partly determine the analogy between body and text. 'So there are several bodies.'[10] And: 'Which body? We have several.'[11] In *Roland Barthes by Roland Barthes*, the entry 'The rib chop' presents us with a fable of this dispersion, this fragmentation of the body into several pieces. Referring to the ablation of a small part of his rib during his second pneumothorax, carried out in Leysin in 1945, he goes on to reflect on his relation to the relic, one that is simultaneously distanced, ironic – as we would expect from his Protestant upbringing – and vaguely anxious. Put away, with other 'precious' objects, into a drawer, the bone ends up being chucked over the balcony overlooking the rue Servandoni: the description itself hesitates between the image of a romantic scattering of ashes and the image of a bone thrown to the dogs. The fragment of the body is at once the object of a pious devotion and a surplus, a piece of waste; too much and too little. The fable also tells us – and this is the second revelation of thinking about the body – that the body is pure externality: the signs that are visible in or from the outside occupy more than the sick interior. For instance, it is striking that Barthes does not consider the lung to be an important organ. Discussing its role in singing, he later described it as a 'stupid organ (lights for cats!)', which 'swells but gets no erection'. He also rejects the idea that singing is an art of the breath.[12] Finally, the body is the place of a fantasy, and the other reason for the analogy stems from this. It was something that Michelet had realized when he endeavoured to resurrect past bodies and to turn History into a huge anthropology. To situate oneself here, i.e. in the place of the fantasy, means both refusing to occupy the place of the Father, 'always dead, as we know',[13] and to enter a mobile, variable, living space. The constrained body is thus the instrument of a considerable opening up of the body. Scattered, dispersed, segmented in space, it is also prolonged in the historical time, contemporary with the body of Hans Castorp when he enters the sanatorium of the *Magic Mountain* and contemporary with the young bodies of the present: capable of being cut up, and thus modular.

Thus, the sick body is the first object of investigation, and encourages the self-portrait. While pondering his *Lexique de l'auteur*, Barthes at one point thinks of an entry on 'Medicines' where he imagines that he could reconstruct someone's portrait from their pharmacopoeia, from the medicines to which they had remained faithful. The result of this projection of the body into everything that is supposed to cure it takes the form of a painting by Arcimboldo, 'he paints himself entirely in medicines, his head as an aspirin tablet, his stomach as a packet of bicarbonate, his nose as a spray, etc.'.[14] Such a self-portrait, composed of things meant to cure you, also emphasizes things that poison you. Here we can read the paradox of illness, which brings you closer to the body while inflicting considerable violence on it, a violence that both emancipates and constrains it. While theatre had relegated the body and favoured the voice, illness brought back the body while inflicting other wounds: the scattered, fragmented body is admittedly readable, but it thereby becomes monstrous. Thus it leads to a certain closing up of the self, linked to the obsession with death that an attention to signs and the breaking apart of one's own body entail. 'Death = they all think about it, but it's taboo'; 'Illness, the slow, contemplative approach of Death'.[15] In this way, *The Magic Mountain* becomes not just the fiction of a positive experience, but a book that falls into the category of the 'Heart-rending', as Barthes puts it in the second session introducing the course on *How to Live Together*: 'I described my relationship to this book in the inaugural lecture: *a.* projective (because: "that's exactly it"), *b.* disorientating, but in a chronological sense. 1907/1942/the present moment, because it means my body is historically closer to 1907 than to the present day. I'm the historical witness for a work of fiction. A book I find very poignant, depressing, almost intolerable: a very palpable investment in human relationships + death. Belongs to the category of the Heart-rending. → I felt out of sorts on the days I spent reading it – or rather rereading it (I'd read it before my illness but had only a vague recollection of it).'[16] The experience of separation, so splendidly represented in Thomas Mann's novel, is as vivid for the person who really goes through it as it is difficult to fit in with the time at the 'foot' of the mountain or of ordinary social life. Hence the difficulty Barthes had in communicating to his correspondents anything at all about this experience, which was, he says, so dreary for those in good health. 'Ah, what a gulf there is between those who are well and those who are ill', he wrote to his friend Robert David on 16 January 1946. Hence his feeling of being lost to the world, half-alive. 'All sorrows here arise from the sense of being more or less separated from something.'[17] The adjective 'heart-rending' (*déchirant*) often occurs in his correspondence, in particular when Barthes is talking about 'Maman'. For example: 'her letter is full of hope that I will come. It's heart-rending.'[18] Later on, this adjective (one of the key words in the work) describes the relationship to literature: 'By practicing to the bitter end an antiquated form of writing, do I not say that I love literature, that I love it in a harrowing fashion, at the very moment when it is dying?'[19] Thus, from the mother to literature, from the sanatorium to the interminable convalescence that followed the death of Henriette Barthes, we find inscribed the mark of two heart-rending loves, which are perhaps the same and perhaps different: these two 'heart-rending loves' and their encounter are in any case the two most powerful signs ordering the continuity of Barthes's existence.

The present of the sanatorium could, in spite of everything, be rich and intense, so long as one put oneself in a condition of perfect openness. 'You have to abolish inner memories, those obsessions of the soul that comprise the continuity of a human being. You have to suppress every point of comparison between the past – home, mother, friends, the streets of Paris, the living world where everything is possible – and the present – the present of those people with whom you are going to be living for a long time, with no connection to them other than that of an illness which, indeed, has very different shades and intensities.'[20] The propensity to reverie and a literary sensitivity are powerfully magnified as a result; in particular in the periods of total immobilization that bring the past back to life in such a clear and spontaneous way that they give the sensation of literally 'living' Proust. Max Blecher was another habitué of sanatoriums: he suffered from Pott's disease, a tuberculosis of the bones that meant he had to spend a great deal of his brief life lying down – he spent several years in Berck and then Leysin: he wrote that illness and seclusion in one's room led to a crack in the thin partition between the certainties of the reality of the world and all its uncertainties. 'Things were seized by a veritable frenzy for freedom; they proved their independence from one another, an independence that was not just isolation, but exaltation, ecstasy. [. . .] At the supreme moment, the crisis came to a head like this: I was floating outside the world – a state both pleasant and painful. If I heard footsteps, the room immediately reassumed its former aspect.'[21]

Roland Barthes does not evoke the parallel worlds that arise when one has to keep to one's bed, alone, in these terms. But there is no doubt that, when he says he has the impression he is 'living' Proust, he is not referring solely to involuntary memory but to the sensations felt in intermediate states, such as that of the order of worlds one holds around oneself while asleep, or that of the bedroom changing shape and position as you wake up. Thus, for a long time, the bedroom becomes a space in itself, a place of great significance. 'Indeed, the luxury of the bedroom derives from its freedom: a structure protected from all norms, all powers; as a structure – an exorbitant paradox: it's unique.'[22] Even when reduced to a bed and an adjoining table, as in the sanatorium, and as at Aunt Léonie's in Proust's *In Search of Lost Time*, even when subjected to the metaphor of bareness,[23] the bedroom is the secret place (the site of the primitive scene) and the place of secrets, where you hide away your treasures. It easily becomes the space of introspection and, beyond separation, the forging of new links. When the room is shared, as in Saint-Hilaire, it fosters and reinforces connections; when it is a single room, as sometimes in Leysin, it offers a protective refuge propitious to meditation. Already attentive to 'proxemics', to the attention one pays the relationship between a being and its immediate environment, and to the arranging of a framework for one's most common gestures, Barthes set out his objects with great care: 'I live between my two tables', he wrote to Robert David in November 1945, with 'my bag, my Michelet, my watch, my box of index cards',[24] all those elements that organize space and give time its rhythm. Thus, the bedroom was the framework for a good life inside a bad life, one that guaranteed a certain independence, giving order to those activities that freed one from idleness: reading, writing letters, writing *tout court*.

'At the sanatorium, I was happy'

In spite of being isolated and confined, in spite of the illness which cut him off from the world and from his future, the sanatorium years also had a positive and luminous aspect. 'At the sanatorium, apart from towards the end, when I felt saturated, overcome by the system, I was happy: I read, and I spent a great deal of time and energy on my friendships.'[25] The word 'happiness' often occurs in his letters, especially in connection with his reading, or with a sense of fullness in his self-awareness: '*Happiness* is perhaps what I understand best in the world.'[26] Medical centres provided an alternative to the social life, one which Barthes grew used to and reflected upon: 'and while other diseases desocialize, tuberculosis projected you into a minor ethnographic society, part tribe, part monastery, part phalanstery: rites, constraints, protections'.[27] His early thoughts on living together, as yet unformulated at this time, were starting to emerge in his letters. It was very difficult to be separated from his family for a boy who was so close to his mother and was now far away from her – the Occupation made it difficult for Henriette to travel to visit her son. They wrote to each other almost every day, but letters did not make up for their absence. Barthes referred, in this respect, to a lost unity. But in the sanatorium there was a certain conviviality which allowed other connections to develop, especially with the medical staff, Mme Lardanchey, Drs Klein, Cohen, Douady and Brissaud (who followed him to Paris). There were discussions between friends about the merits of different doctors, especially with Georges Canetti who was himself a doctor. In spite of the somewhat forced character of this conviviality, as described by Pierre Guillaume ('in the sanatorium, cheerfulness is a collective imperative, a group display'),[28] the many distractions provided by the place were experienced as quite positive, even if Barthes contrived to mark his difference, especially in the matter of dress,[29] as well as in his reading matter and his ability to hold his own in arguments. He played a full part in group activities. He went to film showings on Saturdays and he listened to the radio. In July 1943 he was elected to the Association of Sanatorium Students – more specifically, as library rep. He enjoyed communal meals, which would be subjected to close analysis of 'eating together' – conviviality in the strict sense of the word – in his 1977 classes on small communities. If the doctrine consisting of overfeeding TB patients had been rendered obsolete in the 1920s, and the sumptuous meals of the sanatorium-hotel of Davos were no longer served, especially in the context of war,[30] the dining room fostered new encounters. 'Eating together is a crypto-erotic scene where things happen', things linked to the changing of one's place and the overdetermination of pleasures. It can be the sign of a rebirth, a *vita nova*. Every improvement in one's health is measured by a gain in weight ('I haven't had any bacilli for two months and I am regularly putting on weight');[31] according to the analysis in *How to Live Together*, the patients in *The Magic Mountain* are given huge helpings so as to be born anew on the other side of illness, 'stuffed with food in the hope it will turn them into new human beings'.[32] This regeneration forms the storyline of many narratives, starting with *Siloé*, by Paul Gadenne (1941): his character Simon turns the sanatorium's position, both above and outside the rest of the world, into a dramatic space for change and for the dawning of his self-awareness. It was a regeneration which Barthes also experienced. In May 1943, after just a few months in the Grésivaudan, he described that particular state, a mixture of heightened perception, reminiscence and sensuous plenitude: 'I looked towards the valley where I knew of other men, where I sensed the miracle of bodies and glances. How can I describe to you that powdery substance, that ponderous light that shed its blue sunshine on the flat level of the valley? As I've told you, it was warm; a mild wind with an undercurrent as fresh as silk intoxicated you and brought back to your soul all the summers of bygone days, those when I was a child, scraping gravel at the foot of the clumps of hydrangeas in the garden in Bayonne, the summers when I was a young man, my throat parched with love, absolutely, body and soul, up to my neck in an adventure (a word I fill with the most dreadful seriousness). Behind my bedroom a quartet was playing gently. [. . .] I don't know if the living – I mean those who are not ill, since now I'm only half-alive – can feel life this way, all naked, all atremble if you like, without there being any need of action or love to sharpen its contours, to display it. An armchair, a window, a valley, music – and this was happiness, life entered me from all sides, without my making a movement: my motionless senses were enough. And it seems that, forced to lurk in hiding, because of the illness, my senses were less likely to scare life away and life could approach them trustingly, with all its train, its pomp, the intimate beauty of its essence, perhaps invisible for those who are less frail, more robust, those who make an effort to grasp it.'[33] Seclusion and separation find their compensation in the more vivid awareness they grant you of things, and this can be a reassurance, a consolation, implying a form of consent to life.

In this way, Barthes's two main experiences in the sanatorium were friendship and reading. 'The first experience was one of friendship – you live for years with people your age and you often share a room with one or two others. You see one another every day and the deep emotional ties which develop in that milieu – with its joys, its problems and its whole novelistic aspect – give you enormous support.'[34] He made the acquaintance of François Ricci, Georges Canetti and above all Robert David, who would be such an important figure for him. At Saint-Hilaire, he shared room 18 with André Lepeuple, a medical student, and Dang Khoc Khan, a student at Sciences Po. In Switzerland, he would become friends with André Mosser, Rosèle Hatzfeld, Georges Fournié and the Sigg family, who regularly welcomed him at weekends and with whom he had a somewhat distant relationship based mainly on money. Robert David, whom he met in Saint-Hilaire in 1943, regularly came to see him during these years: he underwent a first period of aftercare in December 1944 and then joined Barthes in 1945 in Leysin, shortly after Barthes had been transferred there. On 17 September 1945, he left Switzerland for Neufmoutiers where he too underwent aftercare. His friendship for this young man, eight years younger than he was – David had only just turned 21 when Barthes met him – quite soon developed into love and came to occupy, in his heart, the place that the death of Michel Delacroix had left wounded and vacant.[35] Barthes asked him fairly soon to be his room-mate and told him about his favourite authors and the music he liked. The times when they were separated and the end of their treatment gave rise to an intense correspondence that showed that Barthes's passion for David was intact even if the latter did not respond to his passion as Barthes would have wished. 'I don't think you love me enough to accept my love; this will consume itself idly away. I'm not happy, my dear; I chose you, I attached myself to you, you hold the key to my happiness . . .'[36] One of the recurrent themes in his letters is his regret that such intense friendships as those which he feels for a few people cannot find any sexual or social expression. 'Please understand and forgive what I'm about to tell you,' he wrote in November 1943 to Philippe Rebeyrol, thinking of him but also of Robert David, 'but I did regret then, in the midst of a pure emotion, that such a fine and intense friendship between two young men such as us, by the commandments of God, Nature or society, can never be raised to the dignity of a love that would free us from having to wander around seeking something else in life, as it is the height of what one can desire and that for which we have been placed on earth. There are such heavy impossibilities in my destiny that I no longer live except for one or two affections such as yours. Without these bonds, only the mere mechanism would make me live, and always in the middle of such ravages that one day it would end up breaking prematurely.'

The correspondence with Robert David was very different from the one with Rebeyrol: in it, Barthes talked much less about art and literature but, in almost daily letters of several pages, poured forth the purity and power of his feelings. 'The more I now, the more I feel that I love you without any pretence, the more I sense that my salvation lies in this feeling.'[37] He was soon contrasting a 'daytime David', who kept him at bay, with a 'night-time David' who could understand him and offer some response more sensitive to his love. 'And if the night-time David penetrates me with such an impulse of friendship that I wish he would let me put myself in his hands for the rest of our days, completely, with all that there is within me, I can understand that the daytime David, who has made me suffer, has also gained my esteem and my love, and I hand myself over to the two of them – if the two of them will have me.'[38] More than a real dialogue, the whole correspondence comprises a sort of long monologue, albeit one aimed at the man who gave meaning to his diminished life. 'Life has a meaning for me, it's worth living; there is a goal, and this goal demands an effort. [. . .] First, to will to get better. Then, to prepare for this return, i.e. for example to work relentlessly to have something to offer you from my brain. [. . .] Michelet will dash along at full tilt, the work will be intensified by life in bed, disdain for others and the love of one person.'[39] With a few other young men, Barthes did however have initially more carnal relations. Around him there developed a little *cénacle* – with Fédoroff, a 42-year-old musicologist, Frémiot, a student at the Conservatoire, Deschoux, studying for the *agrégation* in philosophy, and Picquemal, a student at the École normale supérieure – whose passionate debates focused on literature and music but also triggered the expression of personal feelings. The slender distinction between love and friendship meant that passionate feelings preceded the formation of a more intellectual bond. The pleasure of seduction and the desire for subservience were the main features of his quest. The unbridled sexuality attributed to TB patients had long been a theme in medical treatises, with what was called, at the beginning of the twentieth century, the theory of feverishness bringing out the impetuosity of sexual desire in these patients: 'Dorsal decubitus', wrote Dr Delprat in 1924, 'leads to a congestion of the slanting organs, in particular the prostate, and this congestion entails an erection.'[40] It had been popularized by a novel by Michel Corday, with the apt title *Les Embrasés* (*The Feverish*), in 1902. While the complex procedures aiming at getting men and women together (as described by Gadenne in *Siloé* at the sanatorium of the Crêt d'Armenaz, where the two sexes were separated as at Saint-Hilaire) were a dramatic device that did not concern Barthes, the latter said how very preoccupied he was by young men. His emotions were in turmoil and he was tormented by desire. In this sense, the sanatorium, far from stifling his aspirations in this area, sharpened and focused them. The explanation lay, to some degree, in the fact that he was far away from his family, especially his mother: first because, deprived of his strongest affection, he expected even more from friendship; second because, in his seclusion, he no longer needed to hide his desires or his behaviour from himself. What we find here, perhaps, is one of the mainsprings of his concealment of his homosexuality, at least from his mother; it was expressed, for such a long time, in almost 'reserved' places, in a kind of dark night – a theme which, with the theme of silence, pervades the letters that Barthes wrote to Robert David when they were separated.

All this happened during the Occupation. Until November 1942, the almost unpassable line between the free zone and the occupied zone cut him off from the world, from his friends and his family. Events came to knock only feebly at the doors of the sanatorium, even if there were children hidden at Saint-Hilaire: Yvette Heilbronn and Marcel Müller, for example. It was difficult to travel. Michel Salzedo, his younger brother, never made the trip to Isère. Philippe Rebeyrol came to see Barthes at the end of December 1943, but this was a parenthesis which opened only to close all the more firmly afterwards. Barthes's mother came to see him twice, and stayed at the foot of the funicular, in Crolles. She brought him soap, brown shoe polish, shoe laces and music manuscript paper. He managed to see his family again in rare intervening periods when he was not confined, from January to July 1943 when he was in aftercare in the rue Quatrefages, and in July 1943 in Hendaye. He found them suffering from the strains of the situation, and often saw his mother wearing herself out doing a variety of jobs and doing her utmost to ensure their survival. Michel was not as hardworking as his brother and his future was a source of worry for Henriette Barthes. After the war ended, and Barthes was transferred to Switzerland, it was easier to travel and, in September 1945, his mother and his brother stayed with him in Leysin. But overall, the separation was real and painful. 'For four years, I've been in dismal cheap joints, separated from my loved ones; I want to live with Maman for a while.'[41] The few moments when they could be together again left, in their brevity, a sense of being torn away, 'an image of being torn apart that I had sworn to erase as soon as possible'.[42] This image intensified his anxiety about the situation and the future, and reinforced the sense of uselessness. Though, at the beginning of 1944, he thought about studying medicine – an understandable and common ambition among young people caught up in the melancholy of hospital life, whose existence was entirely medicalized – he said he had abandoned the idea because of the lengthy studies that would force his mother to remain poor, something that made him feel guilty. He was especially worried when his family was worried, and as his health was thus reflected in the anxiety of others, he was trapped in an incapacitating solipsism.

Barthes had not initially registered for a diploma, but still attended a number of lectures and in 1944 registered for a preparatory certificate in medicine. Social life at Saint-Hilaire was centred on one's studies and he took advantage of all the resources lavished by this establishment, which was an educational trailblazer: theatre, music, a library and a film club, concerts in which he took part as a player or as a musical critic. He also regularly took English lessons 'with the adorable Grünwald, an excellent teacher, full of enthusiasm and tact [. . .]. For the past month I've been making progress that I'm pretty pleased with.'[43] Between March and June 1943, he attended the lectures of André François-Poncet (just before the latter was arrested by the Gestapo in August 1943), the professor of dramatic art Béatrix Dussane, the theologian and member of the resistance Fr Henri de Lubac, Maurice Denis, and the philosopher Jean Lacroix, who gave a presentation on 'friendship'. When it came to entertainment, the students even had the right to a recital by Maurice Chevalier and several concerts of classical music. Music continued to hold a major place in Barthes's life. He had several pianos he could practise on, including the piano reserved for concerts; he attended the lectures of his friends Fédoroff and Frémiot on Mozart; from October 1943 onwards, he offered a technical seminar on music, mainly focusing on harmony. The library of Saint-Hilaire-du-Touvet, with which he was involved at that period, was very well stocked: before the war, it received twenty-three Paris dailies, thirteen provincial dailies, twenty French weekly papers, and forty-seven reviews and periodicals. Regularly, the journal *Existences* drew up a list of the books and reviews received, which was an opportunity to thank the publishers for sending them – something that was highly valued given the war. Barthes read a great deal, which was obviously nothing new, as he had also read during his free time as a teenager. What changed was the way he read, which had an impact on the way he wrote. What he had embarked on in the course of his travels he continued, now that he could not travel, in the margins of the books he was reading, taking notes and starting to use index cards – a practice he would refine throughout his life. The first shock, in 1942, was Dostoyevsky, whose world seemed to echo his own. *The Idiot*, in particular, both the novel as a whole and the personality of its protagonist, seemed to encapsulate him fully. He recommended this book to all his friends, as well as *The Thistles of the Bărăgan* by Panait Istrati. Then came Gide, on whose *Journal* he wrote a few notes in spite of the fact that he found it difficult to grasp and express it. 'Soon after we arrived in the sanatorium,' relates André Lepeuple, 'Barthes abandoned his Bible and plunged into a new book. He told me this was André Gide's *Journal*. [. . .] He devoted to the reading of this book (which was quite unknown to me) all the rest periods that were called "treatments" and seemed so absorbed that I didn't dare bother him to find out more about the object of his interest. During the "inter-treatments", periods of relative freedom, he would settle down at the table in our room, open a notebook of the kind used for rough work, like those we used when we were children, at primary school, picked up an ordinary school penholder, dipped it in a bottle of Waterman ink and started to blacken page after page in perfectly regular handwriting, without the least crossing out.'[44] But his main reading matter, a prolonged, active, exhaustive reading that he continued throughout those years in the sanatorium, an obsessive reading, sometimes enthusiastic and sometimes despairing, was his reading of Michelet. As he was starting to get fully into Michelet's work, he referred to the 'really fruitful method of reading'[45] that he had embarked on at the beginning of his illness, and that consisted of annotating what he was reading.

To Georges Canetti, he wrote that he took 'more interest in the method, the regularity, the progression' of his reading 'than in its content'.[46] His psychological state could be measured by the ups and downs of this practice. In 1944, in a moment of intense discouragement, he said he had given up any system of making notes and keeping a diary. But, a while later, he recovered his zest and pursued his readings. His decision was partly a matter of chance, linked to the presence in the students' library at Saint-Hilaire of series of complete works, but also his predilection for excess, for an intelligence of the senses, indeed a sensual and even visionary intelligence. Michelet's distant Protestant origins, the way he migrated across disciplines, his interrupted public career, the relation he established between a literary style of writing and history, and his distanced stance vis-à-vis his own century, were also reasons for Barthes to feel akin to him. In return, the nosographic attention Barthes devoted to Michelet's book *Le Peuple* (*The People*), even though Michelet himself rejected the 'medical, physiological fatalism' of his period, obviously stemmed from the conditions under which Barthes had discovered his work. In several places in his letters, Barthes mentioned the pathological state in which reading Michelet placed him: 'I am trying terribly hard to work, but when faced with Michelet, I'm like someone who feels sick but is being forced to eat.'[47] The programme announced by the quotation from Michelet's letter to Eugène Noël, 'Men of letters always suffer, and live no less for that',[48] the opening discussions of Michelet's migraines, are thus, in reality, almost autobiographical. The multiple lives of which the historian is capable, in spite of his successive 'deaths', have the force of an encouragement.

He was also reading Steinbeck and Hemingway, while another novel, decisive for his subsequent career, would be Camus's *The Stranger* (also translated as *The Outsider*; published in French as *L'Étranger* in 1942). Barthes read this in 1944 and also wrote an article on it, 'Réflexion sur le style de *L'Étranger*', then a book, *Writing Degree Zero*, in which he developed the hypothesis of a 'neutral style', a 'blank voice', the 'zero degree'. What Barthes discovered was thus not so much a matter of interesting books per se, but rather his own ability to produce ideas, to write on the basis of what he had read. The practice of using index cards originated in these years of confinement when he also started to consign his thoughts to them. In January 1946, he wrote to Robert David that he had already assembled a thousand index cards on Michelet! He was developing a form of writing based directly on his reading. It really did arise from an invention – maybe Barthes's main invention – which consisted in making the reading of a book emerge straight from the book: the reading arises from the book in order to study the world, its signs, its little phrases, its images, its mythologies . . . It also arises from the book in order to become a form of writing, and to bring the world back into writing once more.

The first texts

Existences, founded in October 1934 as a quarterly bulletin for the association of 'Sanatorium Students', was, by its third issue in April 1935, a veritable publication, with articles, editorials, reviews and a regular column.[49] During the war, it was forced to return to being typed and mimeographed as when it first began, but it continued to be a proper literary review; it emphasized this aspect even more.

In issue 26, of May 1942, an editor's note presents the choice they had been forced to make: 'Either more or less completely abandon the external public, giving the review the intimate character of a sanatorium chronicle (an exhaustive account of the festivities and the activities of the various disciplines) [. . .]. Or else we could sacrifice to the external public, by reducing, in particular, the chronicle of sanatorium life and giving the whole thing a literary and artistic feel, to make it as accessible as possible to the majority of readers. In this way, while remaining "young", the review would become more serious without becoming too pedantic.'[50] The same editorial says that it wishes to reserve a place in every issue for medicine and fundamental articles on TB treatments. It was at this time and within this context that Barthes published his first texts. And in the first issue (straight after the one containing this editorial), in which he wrote his article on Gide's *Journal*, there was a short text by Paul Hertzog on the advantages of the treatment of TB by complete immobilization in the case of patients suffering only a moderate form of the illness.[51]

The first text published by Roland Barthes dated back to his pre-sanatorium days, however. It was a contribution to the ephemeral *Cahiers de l'étudiant*, 'written by students for students'. The editor-in-chief was the novelist Robert Mallet, born the same year as Barthes: his first novel, *La Poursuite amoureuse, 1932–1940* (*The Amorous Pursuit, 1932–1940*) was published in 1943 by Mercure de France. As well as Barthes himself, René Marill Albérès and Paul-Louis Mignon would also be well-known critics after the war. The title of the issue was 'Essai sur la culture' ('Essay on culture') and Barthes's contribution was, logically enough, called 'Culture et tragédie' ('Culture and tragedy'). Here he contrasted tragedy, the mark of eras and places that bring together a style of life and a style of art, a genre immersed in pure human suffering, with the drama, which is the representation of a present, historical suffering. There is no doubt that he was thinking of contemporary events when he wrote; of his own period, he concluded: 'It is certainly painful, and even dramatic. But nothing as yet proves that it is tragic. Drama is something you bow to, but tragedy is something you deserve, like everything that is great.'[52] The review announced that 'the next *Cahiers de l'étudiant* will not appear until October 1942 due to the summer vacation. The focus will be on the following problem: the student and social life.' As circumstances would have it, this issue never materialized and this promising issue was not followed by any other.

In July 1942, then, Barthes published his 'On Gide and His Journal' in *Existences*; here, for the first time, he imposed a fragmentary form on his critical thinking, a form directly derived from his practice of reading and, more indirectly, from his piano playing: the art of the fragment was an art of attack, of the 'strike'.[53] He did not use his notes as a whole, but corrected only minimally the ones meant for publication and merely reordered the fragments. The year 1943, spent half in Paris and half in reclining treatment, was less prolific. He published two reviews in *Existences*. One was on Robert Bresson's *Angels of Sin*, which came out on 23 June 1943 and was immediately shown at Saint-Hilaire: this film struck Barthes with its sobriety and its vibrant subject-matter. The other was on the 1943 issue of the review *Confluences* devoted to the 'Problems of the novel' – an issue that was to be a historical milestone, though at the time Barthes could see only its faults: he found it prolix, repetitive and muddled. It is interesting that his final judgement compares the misguided ways of literary criticism to a certain medical charlatanism: the references still belong to his own world. 'When I see seven-and-fifty authors all giving their opinions about the Novel without consulting their neighbour, I feel I'm watching the quarrel of the seven-and-fifty doctors around a patient in Molière. But the novel, like every patient in Molière, is not actually moribund.'[54] His distanced appreciation applies both to the review and to the genre of the novel itself, here suspected of inauthenticity. Here we recognize an ambiguous relation to fiction, together with a complicated relation to himself; the TB patient too is very often not actually moribund. He is a singular case, unapproachable because of his very difference, one of the living even though he is in a world apart.

Two of the first articles published in *Existences* discuss writers who suffered from the same lung infection.[55] Though Gide and Camus did not go into a sanatorium, they also saw their existential itineraries significantly affected by the signs of TB when they were in their teens. Gide went off to Tunisia to try and regain his health: here he made the definitive discovery of his homosexuality. Camus learned that he had TB in December 1930 at the age of 17; he was hospitalized in the Mustapha hospital in Algiers and underwent the cycle of X-rays, consultations, insufflations and pneumothorax that blocked his future prospects and radically transformed his relationship to life. His experience was very similar to Barthes's: he was forced to break off his studies, to give up football (this was a real sacrifice for him), could no longer envisage taking the competitive exam for the École normale supérieure and his planned career as a philosophy teacher, was dispensed from army service even though he wanted to sign up in 1939 and, above all, he felt death's approach even though he felt he was only starting out on life. As for Barthes, Camus's posture as an intellectual was at odds with that of his contemporaries, who followed more institutional paths. This difference partly explains Camus's relationship to Sartre, even though this was played out in terms different from Barthes's relationship to Sartre. While there is no allusion to this common biographical point in the two articles devoted respectively to Gide and Camus in

Existences, in 'On André Gide and His Journal', Barthes does refer to suffering as a major theme in Gide's novellas, and his *Notebooks of André Walter*. He also introduced the theme of the new life, to which he would regularly return. Two years later, in July 1944, in his 'Réflexion sur le style de *L'Étranger*', he concluded his analysis by saying that Camus's style was the product of a break, the language of an absence – and these were all questions that came directly from his own experience of isolation.

If we undertake a joint reading of all the texts written in this period, other themes seem to create lines of force: two adjectives, 'classic' and 'neutral', and two proper names, 'Greece' and 'Michelet', to which we can add 'Orpheus', an allusion of a more subterranean but emergent kind. They are all important because they lay the ground for the first books. The adjective 'classic' is the most powerful subject. It appears regularly in the text on Gide, defining an art of evasion, understatement, equivocation, the short-cut, 'the shadow propitious to meditation and individual discovery'.[56] But it is the main object of investigation for the following text, 'Plaisir aux Classiques' ('Pleasure in the Classics'), published in the April 1944 issue. The text is presented as a rather discursive argument, not without its moments of banality ('You cannot write well unless you think well', and 'Boredom is something they do not always avoid, but is it not compensated by a great number of beauties and considerable vivacity?'). He makes a veritable apologia for the classical style based on economy, decency, clarity and brevity. The subjective adoption of the stylistic characters of classical works becomes the yardstick by which most products are judged. So it comes as no surprise to read, in the text on *The Stranger* published a few months later, that 'Camus has created a work of art which has the same musical simplicity as *Bérénice*'.[57] But the appropriation of the term also allows for new connections to be made: for the first time, Barthes can move smoothly from the 'classic' to the 'neutral'. The 'silence of style', the 'indifferent' style we find in Camus in this text, in Barthes's view, are to some extent an extension of classicism, preserving its 'attention to form' and relying on 'the habitual devices of classical rhetoric'; but they also give a sense of strangeness linked to its complete absence of grandiloquence – the *repoussoir* word that is also used of theatre and song – and to its invisibility. As a critic, Barthes uses for the first time the expressions 'blank voice' and 'neutral', which, as we know, would be developed in his later work, though as yet they did not have the meaning they would have in *Writing Degree Zero*. The style of *The Stranger* 'is a sort of neutral substance, albeit quite dizzying in its monotony, sometimes crossed by flashes of lightning but mainly subjected to the submarine presence of unmoving sand banks that bind this style together and give it its colour'.[58] There is something

'discreetly attentive' about it, 'the sort of familiar tenderness of
everyday things'.

The myth of Orpheus, another important factor on which *Writing
Degree Zero* draws, makes its discreet appearance in 'Plaisir aux
Classiques' ('to renew the myth of Orpheus and bind recalcitrant
objects and men to speech') and in a letter to Robert David. The
other lines of force are: Greece, evoked sensually in 'In Greece',
published in the review for sanatorium students in July 1944, and
described philosophically in the article on Gide, which discusses
Hellenism and the 'Dorian side' of the author of *Corydon*; and in particular Michelet, an underground but growing influence throughout
those years. In articles that cite a huge number of names, Michelet is
present with his phrases, and we can see that Barthes was so imbued
with Michelet at this time that he could use him for every purpose.
So the study of these early texts is exciting both for the echoes with
Barthes's own life that they arouse (we see the same discussion of
pride, for example, in the private correspondence and in the article
on Gide) and for the premonitions of his future work.

On 26 January 1946, Barthes wrote from Leysin to Robert David:
'This morning I've received a message from Maman saying that
Dr Brissaud agrees to me going back. This is a big piece of news.'
The day before, a local earthquake had thoroughly shaken him: 'I
was really scared, filled with profound panic, thinking of Maman
and you.'[59] Though the concomitance of these two events does not
need to be interpreted, it had great resonance. While it was desired,
Barthes's return also represented an intense disturbance. Barthes
had no material means of support and no institutional post that
could constitute a refuge for him. He was being thrown 'down
there', 'into the valley' – it is these terms taken from *The Magic
Mountain* that he uses in his letters – almost without any safety net.
Five years of isolation had made him a stranger, a silent man, almost
neutral as far as the external world was concerned. 'I see the world
passing me by, it is so rich and I am nothing in it.'[60] While he hated
Switzerland, with its feudalism, he did not see France as a political
ground he could rely on. In a tone markedly inspired by Michelet,
he wrote to Philippe Rebeyrol: 'The French newspapers I read appal
me; they have no critical distance, they can't see a thing. It's terrible.
Is France really a lost cause? If so, we will need to be Jews, so to
speak, wandering around everywhere, swarming, spreading the salt;
the day France died, it would still have its messianic role; but I'm
perhaps wrong about this, too; perhaps the drama lies in the very
fact that the world is going to shrink, and will no longer wish for any
Messiah from the past.'[61] He could of course count on the love of his
family, but his years in the sanatorium had led him to dream of a life
other than that in an apartment shared with his mother and brother.
What often appears as a powerful feature in Barthes's biography,

the fact that he always lived with his mother, needs to be relativized. Not only did he live without her for the entire duration of the war: in the sanatorium, he forged friendships that made him hope for a life shared with other people. During his last period in Leysin, he suffered from the distance Robert David imposed on their relationship, he was jealous of the women that David frequented (Rosèle Hatzfeld) or was in love with (Françoise), and jealous of the boys he saw. 'So it's difficult, you say, to be affectionate with me because I have certain ideas? You sometimes come up against feelings of an affection you find it difficult to put up with? I understand what you mean, my dear, but how cruel you are! Those words hurt me, and I struggle to reply. [. . .] I love badly because I love too much.'[62] He was all the more sad as he had formed the crazy plan of living with David on his return. 'I envisage this common life in the fullest and completest sense that we gave it here, which is still the happiness without which I no longer wish to live.'[63] In a very distressing letter in which Barthes asked this of his friend, he knew at the same time that it would not be possible and, by way of compensation, asked for at least four fully shared days in the same apartment.

The pains of love, and anxieties about the future, made him postpone his return. With the money lent by the Sigg and Chesseix families to whom he went to say goodbye, he bought some clothes and offered his mother a dream stay in a top-notch hotel in Lugano, the Federale. He returned to Paris on 28 February 1946: this marked the beginning of his aftercare, which would not be over until the end of the summer, with a stay in Neufmoutiers-en-Brie, where he was luckily accompanied by Robert David once more. Here he continued his reading of Michelet and examined in depth the previous conditions of his inner life, postponing the plunge into material life for a few more months.

In May 1947, just over a year after leaving Leysin, Barthes produced 'Esquisse d'une société sanatoriale' ('Social life in the sanatorium'), which appeared as his first essay in social critique. The text reveals that the sanatorium years, in spite of the occasional joys to which they gave rise, were difficult ones. The description Barthes gives of the artificial order created in this place was harsh. He described how there was a rigid hierarchy in place, and everything was arranged to deprive the patient of his awareness, even of the sense of being in exile. The sanatorium was a replacement world, open only to its members. Even friendship was forbidden there, 'because sanatorium society is scandalized by the idea that you can be happy outside it'.[64] This is a society that prefers to foster association as against friendship, and community as against society. 'Paternalist, feudal or liberal, bourgeois sanatorium society, through its various feints, always tends to go back to the irresponsibility of childhood.' But it is far removed from the protective maternal cocoon of real childhood; rather, the sanatorium illustrates what Barthes would later call the 'myth of childhood', a separate, ordered and fictitious world. Although in actual fact Barthes made real friends in Saint-Hilaire and Leysin, was able to develop his own abilities and even find happiness there, his negative experience of collective life left its mark on him forever. It explains his reluctance about political organizations and bolstered his decision to live an autarkic life with his mother.

Roland Barthes in the
library of the sanatorium
at Saint-Hilaire-du-Touvet.

Robert David, the
friend Barthes made
in Saint-Hilaire-du-
Touvet.

EXISTENCES

REVUE TRIMESTRIELLE DE L'ASSOCIATION
" LES ÉTUDIANTS AU SANATORIUM "

SAINT-HILAIRE-DU-TOUVET (Isère)

N° 29. — Année 1943

Sommaire

Imp. Plancher, Bonneville (Haute-Savoie)   Le Gérant BEAUDEGUIN.

A. Q. I. N° 2087 du 3 août 1943.

Contents page of the review of the sanatorium at Saint-Hilaire-du-Touvet, *Existences*. Above, issue from August 1943; right, issue from July 1944.

EXISTENCES
A. E. S.

Sommaire

N° 33

The main table of the Leysin clinic in Switzerland where
Barthes lived between 1945 and 1946.

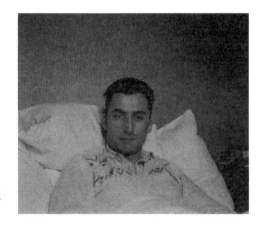

Roland Barthes confined
to bed in Leysin, 1946.

7

Sorties

Far from the sanatorium

Between leaving the sanatoriums and aftercare institutions in the autumn of 1946 and the publication of his first book in March 1953, Barthes came to the end of adolescence, looking forward to a future that would not be so different from what he had envisaged as a teenager. He was 31 in November 1946. He endeavoured to make up for wasted time even as he was trying to find a place for himself, in Paris or the world. He needed to implement a certain number of strategies – personal, social and philosophical – that would enable him to become part of the intellectual landscape of his generation, affirm his own voice, *become* someone. The first of these strategies – a term that we need to take in the most neutral way possible, in the sense Bourdieu gives it, to refer to the set of practices and postures aiming at legitimation – was Marxism. 'After the armistice,' he told Jean Thibaudeau in the 1970 interview, 'I was a Sartrian and a Marxist.'[1] This double conviction, at least the second part of it, had been acquired at the sanatorium, during prolonged discussions with friends who were, as he was, isolated, but who had been brought into contact with other necessities and other commitments by their previous experience. This was especially true of Georges Fournié (generally known by his name in the French Resistance: Philip), whose TB had not been detected in his adolescence, but seems to have been contracted in Buchenwald. Fournié talked persuasively to Barthes about Marxism; he was 'an ex-typographer, a Trotskyist militant returning from deportation'.[2] Later on, Barthes saw the moral freedom, the serenity, the elegant distance of Georges Fournié as one of the reasons for which Marxism had proved seductive to him. His friend did not, as he did, come from the impoverished middle classes but from a working-class background; he had fought alongside the Republicans in the Spanish Civil War, and had joined the French Resistance, which gave him an undeniable aura; and on top

of all that, he was a Trotskyist, which placed him in the margins of
the dominant discourse: 'Thus, the chances of life brought Barthes
into the presence of a singular and singularly seductive embodiment
of Marxism: in the complicity of illness, under the triple sign of the
working class, the epic, and heterodoxy.'³ Barthes claimed that what
had seemed particularly attractive was the force of dialectical thinking, which provided him with a framework, a structure, for textual
analyses. The letters of that period are full of a lyrical proselytizing
on this question and its possible concrete deployment in French
politics. To Rebeyrol, he wrote: 'Politically, I can now hardly think
in any way other than Marxistically, since their description of the
real world seems to me to be correct; and then, together with them,
I have the hope of a society that would be, as it were, virgin pure,
where in a way everything will finally be spiritually possible; for in a
sense, I feel deeply that there will not be any true inner freedom until
we have a really socialist society; it seems to me that man will not be
able to philosophize until that time.'⁴ Barthes even went so far as to
distance himself from existentialism, which can have meaning and
be of use only after 'that time'; and he really raised the question of
the place and role that intellectuals could have in this revolution. If,
in concrete terms, Marxism could have be politically effective, its
philosophical scope was more indistinct and problematic. He often
said that reading Marx bored him, especially *The Holy Family* – he
read this in Neufmoutiers-en-Brie and thought it was insipid and
childish. So the personal documents of that period suggest that we
should play down somewhat his commitments in the immediate
post-war period, seeing them as a quest rather than a profound conviction (a quest that would find its form in *Mythologies*), a strategic
protocol with many different facets rather than full and complete
support – especially as he strongly disliked any form of government
communism. To Robert David he wrote: 'Communism cannot be
a hope. Marxism yes, perhaps, but neither Russia nor the French
Communist Party are really Marxist.'⁵ The words he used of the
French Communist Party were very harsh: 'contemptible', 'boring',
'terribly overblown'. In a more lyrical tone, we find the same critique
extended to the whole of the Communist International, in the article
published in *Combat* on the *Description du marxisme* by Roger
Caillois: 'For several dissidents, whose individual destinies Marxism
continues to fertilize, Muscovite dogmatism is not a scandal: it is
a tragedy, in the midst of which they try to maintain nonetheless,
like the ancient chorus, the awareness of misfortune, the taste for
hope and the will to understand.'⁶ So his ambition for France was
not just to struggle against communism in the name of the true
Revolution ('there are other means of not being bourgeois') but also
to help towards 'the Jacobinization of socialism', the creation of a
pure socialist force within the nation. While Robert David was very

taken by his reading of the Marxist economists, Barthes reminded him of 'man in "the current life of the world" (an apt expression of Michelet's)'; and 'even if socialism is imperfect, if it lacks men for the time being, this is still where we need to go, you as well as me, David'. While socialism strikes him as a non-bourgeois position, the only one able to implement Marxist thought, his rejection of tactical engagements and the communism of party politics still marked a limit to his desire for concrete involvement in Marxism and his conviction concerning its possible application to the national and political areas. He too emphasized the importance of heterodoxy and, using a word that would reappear regularly in his publications in this period, 'dissidence'.

In autumn 1946, Barthes wore himself out trying to find work. He was tired by the little editing jobs and the private lessons that gave him inadequate status and income. Philippe Rebeyrol had taken up a job as director of the French Institute in Bucharest and, in November, Barthes expressed the wish to join him there, with the permission of Dr Brissaud who thought that he was sufficiently well to lead the life of an expat.[7] He wanted his friend, who had already given him so much – encouragement, support, money – to find him a job as lector at the University or the Institute. He wished if possible to take his mother to Romania with him and needed a salary that would be big enough for him to live on and to support her, and decent accommodation. Philippe managed to find him a teaching job that he could take up at the start of the next academic year, but in March 1947 this pedagogic position was turned into a post as librarian of the Institute, which really delighted Barthes, who felt less able to teach now that he was fully embarked on a thesis. In fact, in October he had registered for the *troisième cycle* at the Sorbonne, with René Pintard as his thesis director. Pintard had suggested two possible subjects, one on Vico and Michelet, the other on the techniques of history in Michelet, which Barthes finally decided on. He was already thinking in terms of an informal essay on that work, but he also enjoyed immersing himself in the particular work of documentation and type of argumentation that are both features of a thesis. His thesis director, born in 1903 (he died in 2002) was a specialist in the seventeenth century, but also took on subjects relating to other periods so long as the studies proposed focused on the 'mentality' ('*conscience*') of an era. Pintard's thesis, published in 1943 by Boivin, was called *Le Libertinage érudit dans la première moitié du XVIIe siècle* (*Scholarly freethinking in the first half of the 17th century*) – a movement of thought and a kind of intellectual sociability that both sought to free themselves from the orders of religion. Very attentive and generous to students – the evidence on this point is unanimous – he was particularly interested in Barthes's proposal, and met him on several occasions in the course of the academic year 1946–47. Thus, in February, Barthes wrote to Philippe: 'The interview with Pintard was a great success; he completely accepted my proposals, commented on them with a great deal of intelligence, without any qualifications, and even with a certain enthusiasm, which really fired me up; apart from all the usual proprieties of the subject, he thinks it could be a new kind of work that would express a new direction in (academic) criticism; nothing could give me greater pleasure, you know that I attach a methodological importance to this research, and the general nature of a modern criticism will, I think, need to be that it describes more and explains less, is more phenomenological than logical, and is more closely attached to the work of art itself, its organic constitution, the permanent lineaments of the spiritual universe that it reveals, rather than to its sources and its contexts, whether sociological or literary.'[8] The exciting programme of an immanent critique, partly inherited from Baudelaire but brought up to date, was already emerging in this period. His director demanded the scientific seriousness which the exercise required, but allowed him to deploy freely a descriptive method that was gradually being put in place, giving all the space to the texts and keeping context at bay. The box of index cards was starting to fill up, with thematic entries such as 'Migraine', 'Body', 'Walking', 'France' and 'Unity'. Some of these would serve as section titles for Barthes's *Michelet*.

In spite of his academic activities, Barthes did not abandon his desire to pursue literary criticism in reviews, of the kind he had started to practise in *Existences*. He was soon given an opportunity to do so when he met Maurice Nadeau in June 1947. He saw him for the first time at the home of his friend Fournié, whose TB was not fully cured when he left Leysin so he was obliged to live in the countryside. With his wife Jacqueline, Fournié rented a house in Soisy-sous-Montmorency, where he hosted his Trotskyist and other friends. The meeting was not unplanned. Fournié had talked with great enthusiasm to Nadeau about Barthes's originality and his profoundly literary temperament. At that time, Nadeau ran the books page in *Combat* with Camus and Pascal Pia. Jacqueline, who had gone to Leysin with her husband, also succumbed to the charm of Barthes's intelligence.[9] That day, they mainly talked about Michelet, and Nadeau suggested that Barthes write an article. Immersed in his thesis, Barthes reserved Michelet for research and preferred to pursue his investigation into contemporary literature, something he had embarked upon with his thoughts on *The Stranger*. On Fournié's advice, he sent Nadeau at an earlier date, and in any case before they met, an article on blank writing and the ethics of form that Nadeau felt was too difficult for his paper; he did not publish it and in fact lost it.[10] This time, Barthes suggested 'Writing degree zero', which was published on 1 August, shortly before he left for Romania. This piece was followed by several others, mainly republished in the 1953 book, with the exception of 'Faut-il tuer la grammaire?' ('Should we kill grammar?'), a reply to the criticisms that readers had made of his August article, and a few reviews.[11]

'Nadeau, to whom I owe that capital thing, a debut . . .'[12]

As he would do for many others subsequently, Maurice Nadeau played for Barthes the decisive role of establishing him in the literary world. He gave him access to the journalist milieu that had emerged from the Resistance, thus making him part of a lively, committed space of which his years of isolation had deprived him. The newspaper *Combat*, based since 1944 in the premises of *L'Intransigeant*, at 100 rue Réamur, wanted to remain a locus of resistance even after the end of the war. Its main organizers, Camus, Pascal Pia and, after 1947, Claude Bourdet, were opposed to party politics and wanted to sustain a non-communist Marxism, so they shared the opinion Barthes had expressed in his personal capacity. Since 1945, Nadeau, who had been introduced to Pascal Pia by Paul Bodin, wrote two little columns on books every Friday, defending Sartre's *The Reprieve*, and works by Jean-Louis Bory, Valery Larbaud, Aimé Césaire, René Char, Jacques Prévert, Henry Miller and Claude Simon. His stances, his emotions, his definite likes and dislikes soon made his name, and with the lifting of the restrictions on paper in June 1946, and the growth of the newspaper to four pages, it was suggested to him that he build up a real books page. 'Between the provocative phrase, the passionate enthusiasms and the sober critiques, written honestly but without getting too hot under the collar, Maurice Nadeau battled forcefully against the placatory conformism that emerged from the Liberation.'[13] He saw it as his task to demonstrate his ability – which would become legendary over the next half century – to spot promising writers and individual voices. It was with this in mind that he recommended to his readers André Frédérique and above all Claude Simon, whose first novel, *Le Tricheur* (*The Cheat*) he compared to *The Stranger*. It was also with this aim that he introduced Barthes to potential readers.

Even if Barthes himself sometimes felt a sense of illegitimacy at this sudden accolade – a feeling that he never stopped expressing when his books came out[14] – he knew also how to take advantage of it by shifting the struggle onto the field of writing, which he immediately turned into a 'combat sport'. Nadeau did not merely give him a platform and introduce him to people – he accompanied his gesture with a formal accolade. He put a lead at the top of Barthes's first article, praising the piece and suggesting that its author's ideas had a bright future ahead of them: 'Roland Barthes is unknown.

He's young, he has never published anything, not even an article. A few conversations with him have convinced us that this man, fanatical about language (for two years he has focused exclusively on this question) had something new to say. He gave us the following article which is far from being a newspaper article, as it is so densely thought through, without any picturesque adornment. We think that the readers of *Combat* will not mind that we have still gone ahead and published it.'[15] Nadeau expresses his praise in distanced terms so as better to point out the piece's distinction: it is not journalism, but something even better. He also twists the truth ('he has never published anything not even an article') to highlight his own role as a discoverer of talent. By his own admission, he was really worried about the reception the text might meet with, as some people could have seen it as an attack on Camus. He reiterated his praise in even more fulsome terms when Barthes's first book came out, publishing a very long article on it in *Les Lettres nouvelles* of June 1953, and celebrating yet again 'a body of work whose debut we must hail. It is a remarkable beginning. It announces an essayist who currently stands out from all the others.'[16]

For Barthes, who was so sensitive to the question of beginning, 'Liking to find, to write *beginnings*',[17] whose 'debut in life' had been postponed for so long and who so explicitly marked it by calling his 'first' article in a Paris review, as well as his first book, 'degree zero', these signs were particularly powerful. A bond of friendship grew between him and Nadeau, made up of trust and loyalty, but not of real closeness. They were so very similar: of the same generation – Nadeau was four years older – and both from the South-West, and they were also both pupils of the nation. So they very soon dropped the formalities and invited each other out for meals. Thus, Nadeau remembered being invited to the apartment of Noémie Révelin, in the place du Panthéon, when Henriette and her sons moved there shortly after Noémie's death. He describes Barthes's mother, 'simple, cultivated, friendly', and quotes letters he received, full of warmth, that speak of a 'definitive trust – if this word doesn't shock you too much, coming from me who have done next to nothing, to you who have already done a great deal'; after Nadeau left *Combat* in 1951, Barthes wrote that he would like to 'be able to work for you and with you, again'.[18] And Nadeau did indeed get Barthes to write for *L'Observateur* and *Les Lettres nouvelles*. But the communities formed during the war and the Resistance were not that easy to get into. While Nadeau, Fournié and the others had drawn from this experience the spirit of the collective intellectual, Barthes remained more individual, somewhat on the outside, withdrawn from any form of organization. Although he was very grateful for the attention Nadeau paid him, and respected and admired him, he kept him at a distance, as the following detail shows: in spring 1952, he was still spelling his name 'Nadaud' in a letter to Rebeyrol. For his part, Nadeau attributed this growing distance to the increasingly heavy tasks with which they both burdened themselves. 'Life is there and it places us, with our gifts and our merits, in different little areas, subject to obligations that make us gravitate around worlds of which we become prisoners without realizing.'[19] But the question of politics was equally decisive. Barthes's refusal to sign the 'Manifesto of the 121' on the 'right of insubordination' in the Algerian War, and what Nadeau called his 'defection' in 1968, were causes that in his view explained why they drifted apart. In Nadeau's book of memories, his evocation of Barthes eventually turns ironic and indeed quite evidently critical. We can also attribute this increasing distance to Nadeau's difficulties in sustaining his friendships over time. His role as publisher and editor of a review involved not letting himself being swamped by his relation with authors, maintaining an asymmetry that would guarantee his own authority by maintaining theirs. This was also what made him a great editor – he could keep a politic distance from others, even those closest to him, by creating forms of organization everywhere.

However, the thirty years that followed this early collaboration were punctuated by several meetings: Barthes and Nadeau even wrote, as joint authors, an article for *L'Observateur* in January 1953, 'Oui, il existe bien une literature de gauche' ('Yes, there really is a left-wing literature'), the synthesis of a survey on literature and the left to which Barthes had given his own reply two months before. If, in the 1950s, Barthes sometimes said he was pulled in opposite directions by *Esprit* and *Les Lettres nouvelles*, he sent his texts to both reviews in about equal numbers. When Maurice Nadeau and François Erval founded *La Quinzaine littéraire* in 1966, he at one time considered drafting Barthes onto the editorial committee. He knew Barthes was very busy and so abandoned the idea, but he regularly asked him for articles, on Benveniste, on George Painter's biography of Proust, on Severo Sarduy, Julia Kristeva, Jean Louis Schefer, and Gérard Genette; about two per year, sometimes three, until 1975 when the demand peaked and came to an end with the piece 'Barthes puissance trois' ('Barthes to the power of three'; it was Nadeau who provided the French title), which was an article by Roland Barthes on *Roland Barthes on Roland Barthes*. There was another lead by Nadeau, another weighty encomium (Barthes was compared to Gide, to Alain, to Valéry), but still somewhat at a distance: Nadeau acknowledged Barthes's ability to step back from a position, something that was fascinating when it had to do with the world of opinions and stereotypes, to everything that ties you down or freezes you, but Nadeau also pointed out that, more ambiguously, Barthes did not bother with 'what this constant "drift" meant to him'.[20]

On 13 March 1974, Barthes and Nadeau were both invited to take part in the radio programme 'Dialogues' chaired by Roger Pillaudin on France Culture. 'I was just there to make Barthes look good, and I was perfectly happy to play that role', Nadeau remembers.[21] This was not entirely true. Admittedly, Barthes called the shots, affirming the social and ideological character of the idea of literature and literary language, Nadeau initially defending a more standard position of the different status of the language of literature, which resembles no other. But they adopted a friendly and informal tone in their radio debate and though Nadeau managed to pick up the excessive nature of some of Barthes's remarks – for example about the necessary 'perversion' of literature – he was more prolix when it came to contemporary literature, with which Barthes was less familiar.[22] Apart from an interview with Renaud Camus, the partial reproduction of a dialogue on France Culture published on 1 May 1975, i.e. two months after his article on *Roland Barthes by Roland Barthes*, Barthes no longer wrote anything for *La Quinzaine littéraire*, although he did make a present of several of his drawings for the great auction that Nadeau organized in 1975 to save his review. Their distance brought out their different positions. Barthes was a professor at the Collège de France, while Nadeau was on the other side of the cultural field, working as he did in publishing and journalistic criticism. He expressed the desire to publish Barthes's inaugural lecture at the Collège de France. In his memoirs, he reproduced a letter in which Barthes promised him that he could. But then Barthes told him that it could only be published by Seuil: Nadeau was wounded. Apart from the small political divergences and the technical misunderstandings, their distance became a social distance. And yet, when Barthes died, it was Nadeau in person who paid homage to him in his journal, hailing 'one of the finest minds of our time', the teacher and the writer 'who had succeeded in sharing his sensual taste of language'; he also recalled 'the friendship he had shown for our *Quinzaine* and its staff'.[23] The brutal nature of Barthes's death meant that his tribute was heartfelt but, a few years later, the last pages of Nadeau's *Grâces leur soient rendues*, picking up on the homage he had written in 1980 and adding a few more episodes to it, related the separation between the two men.

Far from Paris (1). Bucharest

Barthes alternated between studious periods during which he pursued work on his thesis, and periods of psychological and professional instability. He felt he was going mad, swinging between moments of depression and forgetfulness and spectacular recoveries. He had a very great ability to identify fully with whatever was new, to make every occasion into the possible springboard for a new destiny. This was the case for a few months with his planned medical studies, and again in June 1947 with a training session in a vocational guidance centre in Versailles that made him want to work in the social services. He was very aware of the inconsistency of the solutions proposed for social problems and, if it had not been for the handicap of his illness, he said that he could have thought quite seriously about moving into this area. Meanwhile, in the previous months, he had enjoyed a complete period of tranquillity in Rebeyrol's house in Roquebrune, on the heights above Menton. His brother Michel had left for England, and he serenely headed south with his mother, to enjoy a delightful spring. 'Now we have heaps of violet irises, lilacs, in other places lavender and this floral spring, although quite sombre, is extremely beautiful. In other parts of the country, the landscape strikes me as misinterpreted, in the sense of culture, prettiness, a facile euphoria, the warming of one's old bones. But here it's really pure, wild, rather tragic as the South always is. I'm in really good health. Thanks to your big table, I've got into the habit of not working in bed anymore and it suits me really well, I get more done.'[24] The company of flowers and the material organization of the space (around the rectangle of the table and the light of the lamp) defined the conditions favourable to writing, a kind of autarky. The liking for withdrawn places, where you 'live on the installation' in the same way you can live 'on an estate' corresponded to a phantasy that could be realized, especially each time he was in the countryside: '[T]he countryside (a house) is more self-sufficient than an apartment, thanks to its "reserves" (the store cupboard, the wine cellar): garden + store cupboard + tools = autarky → not going out for days on end → creation of a stable microsystem, like that of a boat.'[25] And Barthes continued this session of his course on *The Preparation of the Novel* by referring to the importance of the work table on which the writer's existence really depends. He mentions Kafka's refusal to go on holiday with Max Brod because this would mean leaving behind his work table, even if only for a few days. The table is a structure, a functional space, centralizing relations with other micro-functions (stationery, order/disorder . . .); it defines a relation between the subject and writing.

In November 1947, Barthes started to get ready for Romania, after spending one part of the vacation in Bayonne, another in the Nièvre, in Pougues, at the home of his friend Jacqueline Robin where he had already stayed the summer before, in the company of her two sons. But he was at the disposal of the French Foreign Ministry and it was not until 12 January 1950 that he received his official appointment for the beginning of 1948: 'M. BARTHES Roland, professor with a *licencié-ès-lettres*, is incorporated into the metropolitan service from 1 January 1948 as teaching associate and retroactively placed at the disposal of the Minister of Foreign Affairs for a period extending from 1 January 1948 to 30 September 1949 so as to perform the duties of a professor at the French Institute of Bucharest (Romania).'[26] He organized his journey, making arrangements to rent out the Paris apartment to Robert David who would keep Michel Salzedo company when he came to Paris, while Barthes himself happily set off with his mother. He had difficulty obtaining visas: these had been officially requested in autumn 1947 for Barthes Roland and for Barthes Henriette, 'his wife ([. . .] who is accompanying her husband'[27] – an amusing slip. Still, Barthes finally managed to obtain visas for both of them: they needed several, as the journey – by train, made necessary by his state of health – took them through Switzerland, Italy, Yugoslavia and Bulgaria. He arrived in Bucharest to take up his job as librarian straightaway, while Philippe Rebeyrol was still director of the Institute. This Institut français des hautes études roumaines (IFHER – French Institute for Higher Romanian Studies) had been set up in the 1920s on the model of the École française d'Athènes, in the euphoria that followed the formation of Greater Romania and with the aim of reinforcing Franco-Romanian links. Under the decisive influence of Mario Roques, director of the Institut de philologie roumaine at the Sorbonne, and Henri Focillon, whose interest in Romania had sprung from his close friendship with Georges Opresco, it has been inaugurated on 29 May 1924 in the presence of King Carol II, in an apartment block belonging to the Union française on Lahovary Square. In 1934 it moved to the building where it is still located today, at 77 boulevard Dacia.[28] Directed by Paul Henry from 1925 to 1932, by Alphonse Dupront from 1932 to 1940 and then by Jean Mouton during the war, it had developed very significant cultural and pedagogic activities, coordinating French teaching establishments throughout Romania, enriching the libraries, and setting up cultural events in Bucharest as well as Cluj, Brașov, Iași, Sibiu, etc.

Philippe Rebeyrol was appointed there on 2 August 1946 at the age of 28. He embodied the sense of renewal not just because of his youthful age, but thanks to the aura he had acquired by escaping from German captivity and fighting with the Free French forces. At the same time, he arrived at an impossible time: the Communist revolution was striving simultaneously to purge the Romanian universities and to Sovietize culture. Before the new regime came to power, and before the proclamation of the Constitution of March 1948 that made the Great National Assembly the 'supreme organ of state authority', he managed to maintain a significant level of activity and to keep all his personnel in post. It was a matter of diplomatic will-power and symbolic links. The privileged relations that had long been maintained with France lost their intensity only slowly, in spite of repeated snubs. Pressure was brought to bear on pupils to stop attending the Institute; a lecture by Pierre Emmanuel scheduled for Braşov on 7 November 1947 was banned; and there was a widespread trend towards the boycotting of French culture. From March 1948 onwards, the director of the Lycée français was forced to agree to include in his pupils' curriculum a 'cultural educational element' controlled by a Romanian educational councillor: this was neither more nor less than a propaganda course. So it was in this difficult context that Barthes started his job as a librarian, replacing Germaine Lebel who had been appointed to Algiers but would not leave for another six months. André Godin, author of a work on the history of the IFHER, says – doubtless with some exaggeration – that Barthes's Marxist culture gained him the trust of his communist interlocutors;[29] still, at this time he had published only two articles in *Combat* and was not a member of any party. But he had other assets, including his talents as a lecturer and his competence in the domain of music, and he would be able to make the most of these during his two-year stay.

The French libraries – Bucharest, Cluj, Iaşi and Timişoara – were surviving quite well in spite of the censorship, which Rebeyrol tried tactically to bypass. He noted, in his report to annual congress in 1948: 'I felt I could ask teachers to limit purges to what was strictly necessary, i.e. to censor just books and not authors (for example: to remove Gide's *Back from the USSR* or some of the volumes of the *Men of Good Will* by Jules Romains, but otherwise to leave their oeuvre alone).' In this context, Barthes took two initiatives that successfully enabled them to prolong their activity. In the weeks following his arrival, he first suggested creating two separate libraries, one for the sciences, the other for lending. The 'scientific library', essentially medical and technical, was open until 9 p.m. and could be used every day by doctors and engineers, most of them students. Barthes also wanted to develop the social sciences sector, which had far fewer books. The second library, open in the mornings, allowed all readers who wished to read books in French to borrow them. It was heavily used and more than 1,200 books circulated every month. His second initiative consisted in continuing the lectures on music on Saturday afternoons, a tradition of the Institute that he undertook to revivify by giving most of the lectures himself under the title 'A few problems in musical language'. There were big audiences for these sessions on French music, which were given in the hall at 77 boulevard Dacia. He talked about French song, about Ravel, Gluck and *Pelléas et Mélisande*, but also about the French *chanson* (including Édith Piaf and Charles Trenet). He played records and commented on them: the Fauré *Requiem*, Ravel's *L'Enfant et les sortilèges*, and *Jeanne d'Arc au bûcher* by Honegger and Claudel. There were sometimes recitals. Some lectures were such a success that he had to deliver them three times over so that everyone could

hear. Indeed, at the height of the crisis, just as the French government was deciding it had no other solution than to repatriate all of
its staff, Barthes felt anxious at his growing success: 'There is an
overflowing audience in the hall, and I think this success is really not
wise. I'm going to resort to a system of invitations. I'm a bit worried
about this; the crowds of listeners are making us vulnerable.'[30]

In spite of these difficulties, life was organized successfully.
Barthes and his mother occupied an apartment above the library.
There was a swimming pool in the establishment. He learned to
drive so that he could get around the country, and he bought a
car. Freed of economic constraints, even if he was not yet being
paid his full salary, he spent money with abandon. Indeed, his
mother was sometimes obliged to tell him to be more sensible (so,
for example, in a letter that Henriette Barthes herself addressed to
Robert David, she mentioned her own 'meanness' and reasons for
economizing which are 'those which Roland can't understand!'[31]).
He made friends with several French teachers, such as Jean Sirinelli,
a Hellenist, who had been a fellow student of Philippe Rebeyrol at
the École normale supérieure in the rue d'Ulm, but after him as he
was born in 1921 (he was lector at the University until 1948, when
he returned to Paris and became *chargé de mission* at the Ministry
of Foreign Affairs). Another friend was Pierre Guiraud, a language
teacher, who, after several jobs abroad and the delayed defence of
his thesis on Valéry, would produce an important body of work in
linguistics; his pioneering work in textual statistics at the University
of Nice would influence Étienne Brunet and Louis-Jean Calvet,
Barthes's first biographer (in the early 1950s, after his return from
Alexandria, Barthes regularly visited him in Copenhagen where he
had taken up a post). There was also Charles Singevin, a philosopher, a great friend of the poet André Frénaud, who directed studies
at the Institute (in 1948 he was appointed to a post in Alexandria,
where Barthes joined him in 1949). Thus, a small community of
intellectuals and teachers came into existence. Rebeyrol gave a
course on contemporary French painting; Singevin a course on
'Cartesianism in the history of French thought'; Jean Sirelli and
Yves Régnier a course on Molière and another on French literature.
Among the teachers, there were also several local recruits, as it was
common at that time for Romanians to be bilingual in Romanian
and French.

Barthes made friends with Petre Sirin, another French teacher,
born in 1926 and a future documentarist of distinction. They were
brought together by their liking for music and their homosexuality. Sirin, born in Chişinău to a Polish father from Odessa and a
Ukrainian mother from Kiev – his real name was Petre Hrşanovschi,
but took his father's pseudonym, Sirin, and was called Pierre – had
a complicated family life and had derived, from his transnational

childhood, an attitude to life at once enlightened and eccentric. He could speak several languages and was at ease in every milieu. He was quite open about his homosexuality, and was unabashed about it both with his family and his friends. He was for a while Barthes's lover and introduced him to homosexual circles, presenting him to young men with whom he had affairs, witness a letter to Barthes of 3 February 1949.[32] This was what he related in his personal papers (diary and correspondence), posthumously published in 2013 (Sirin died in 2003) as *Castele în Spania*.[33] In his letters, Barthes admitted that he was more clearly attached to this part of the world because of the close friendships he had formed there. On 16 March 1949, he spoke with Philippe about this 'special bond which, as subsequent developments have unfortunately shown, was not to be taken lightly'. In Leysin, he had told Philippe where his desire as a whole was leading him. But he remained discreet on the matter, as his friend had asked him not to talk about them. He was also obliged to maintain his discretion by circumstances. Since the end of 1948, foreigners had been under close surveillance and the new regime viewed homosexuality as deviant behaviour. On 31 August, he wrote: 'In the afternoons, I go to the club where I can do my own work in peace. I spend all my evenings with a friend whom I love dearly, but for some time I've been worried that my private life is being watched or used, and this is the essential reason why I *absolutely need* to leave, get away from a country where this year has tied me down in terms of affection, by the greatest of boons and the greatest of misfortunes.' However, he did not like everything and everyone in Romania. He complained about the food, which was too rich and too copious, he wished he could make more progress with his thesis on Michelet, he thought the circles of French expatriates were inclined to silliness, he longed for Paris, in spite the frequent excitement he felt when he remembered that he was living abroad. Above all, he complained about not getting the satisfactions of popularity and recognition that teaching would give him – official teaching rather than the free public expression of opinion that lectures would have afforded him, but for which he felt he did not have enough brio. This distinction between two sorts of transmission was one he would continue to draw subsequently, contrasting the concentration of the seminar, for example, with the circus of courses given at the Collège de France. He saw his personality gradually becoming more brittle and mistrustful. 'I have to admit,' he wrote to Robert David, 'that my sociable character is increasingly becoming sombre and harsh. I think I'm now very far away from the kind of general charity, the other side of the desire to be loved at any cost, that had turned my first stay in Saint-Hilaire into a period of popularity around myself.'[34] He told David that he enjoyed considerable intellectual prestige at the Institute, but he thought it was less his knowledge or his argumentative abilities that were responsible for this than his '*clarity* (!) which is found impressive'. If, in this letter, he emphasizes this word 'clarity', both underlining it and giving it an exclamation mark, this is because, two years previously, he had made it the unique characteristic of his personality, the essence of his nature, declaring his kinship with a Mediterranean, African-Roman family that had sprung from a shared quality, the sun, 'and I will say, almost without metaphor, that this Roman sun flooding man like a total knowledge, refusing to allow him any refuge in a flabby and obscure imposture, forces him to a kind of hard-edged happiness, a desperate happiness, a rage for lucidity that can place man only in the desert.' Further on, he speaks of a 'rage for clarity', an 'inability to tolerate obscurity'; 'I go into everything, I will not allow any mystery to ripen, I prefer to suffer than not to know.'[35] This analysis, written during the great crisis in his love life that took place in the winter of 1946, can be read not just as a complaint but as a plea; it emphasizes the contrasting characters of David and himself and highlights the distance and obscurity that make him suffer when he is staying at his friend's. But this analysis also draws attention to a significant feature in the man and the writer, for whom most gestures, both intellectual and material, from cataloguing on index cards everything he saw, heard, read or experienced to the minutely detailed interpretation of texts, aimed at explaining both himself and literature as well as one through the prism of the other.

This was a period in which he continued to read widely. His index cards show that, while he continued to read Marx, Sartre and Merleau-Ponty, he also took a close interest in history (tangentially to Michelet), especially the historians of the Annales school such as Marc Bloch and Lucien Febvre, whose book on Michelet was published in Lausanne in 1946 – Barthes was pleased to see that Febvre focused on structures and sensibilities. This was, furthermore, a time when he began reading around in the field of linguistics: contrary to what is often said, it was not Greimas who first initiated him into this subject in Alexandria. In Bucharest, Barthes was already discovering Viggo Brøndal's *Essais de linguistique générale* (*Essays in General Linguistics*), which had been written in French and published in Copenhagen in 1943. Other works on linguistics that Barthes read were: *Des mots à la pensée, essai de grammaire de langue française* (*From words to thought, an essay on the grammar of the French language*) by Jacques Damourette and Édouard Pichon, and the *Histoire de la clarté française* (*History of French Clarity*) by Daniel Mornet, a great specialist in the French eighteenth century and the author of manuals for students of literature that were very widely read in the French-speaking higher education world of the 1930s and 1940s. Thanks to these works, Barthes embarked on a long investigation into certain myths about language, such as clarity – an investigation that he would continue in the following years.

Barthes did have some reasons to complain, however: the situation for French people in Romania was becoming more difficult by the day, even if it was easier than that of the Romanians themselves who, in the intellectual sphere, experienced censorship, unremitting surveillance and, at the least sign of dissidence, deportation and internment. Thus the Securitate, one of the most important political police organizations in the Soviet bloc, recruited a considerable number of civil informers and, once it had been set up in 1948, started to track down all 'class enemies' and to obstruct any links between Romanians and foreigners.[36] Annie Guénard, the author of a study on the progressive suppression of French culture in the popular democracies, indicates that Romania, a sort of laboratory for the exercise of Soviet power, was the first to 'put an end, in an extremely rapid, brutal and almost total way, to the presence on its territory of the cultural agents of France and to demand the closure of all the places on which that power could intervene in the cultural sphere'.[37] On 20 November 1948, the Franco-Romanian cultural accord was denounced and most French bodies, including the Institute, were forced to close. Everywhere, the new authorities condemned 'western cosmopolitanism' and Paris was described as the 'intellectual capital of the cosmopolitanism denounced by Moscow'.

Shortly before leaving, Barthes produced a study deconstructing the foundations on which were built the new Romanian science that rejected North American and West European research and affirmed the pre-eminence of Soviet science. Barthes emphasized in particular the 'nominalism of all Stalinist writing': 'The history of the words *nationalism* and *cosmopolitanism* is exemplary; these two words, both pejorative, are reserved for "western" sentiments; when these same sentiments become "Eastern", they change name, are endowed with a euphemic meaning and become: *patriotism* and *internationalism*. Thus, every word constitutes a breach of trust since it is the vehicle of a deliberate equivocation aimed at muddying the water for any critical reaction.'[38] The analysis is conducted with subtlety and deploys a method for deciphering formal principles that forms a bridge between *Mythologies* and *S/Z*.

Philippe Rebeyrol left in March 1949, accompanied by a large number of French civil servants. Some of these forced departures constituted human dramas which Barthes echoed in his letters, at a time when he was still trying to sort out 'the problem of Romanian husbands left behind'. The only ones who were kept in post were Barthes himself, who was to be appointed as cultural attaché, Paule Prié, the ex-headmistress of the École primaire française (French Primary School), Pierre Dillan, a former secretary, Mmes Rassiat and Hagi-Hédouin, secretaries who shared the job of looking after the library, drawing up a list of books and material to be repatriated. Barthes tried to find a solution that would ensure that the 45,000 volumes in the French libraries of Romania did not completely disappear. In all, 12,000 would stay put (though it was quite natural to be anxious about their future), some would be sent back, and he gave others to people he could trust, leaving it up to them whether they lent them, in a personal capacity, to students. One of these was the professor of French philology at the University of Iaşi and dean of the faculty, Ion Popa, with whom Barthes entered a correspondence on this subject that is kept in the archives of the Institute. A letter from Popa written on 11 March 1949 thanked Barthes for sending his 'fine French books' and congratulated him on his appointment as cultural attaché, saying that he did not doubt that he would be able to continue the cultural collaboration between their two countries, 'inspired by our shared progressive ideology'. In a letter of 3 June 1949, Barthes insisted on the conditions in which these books were being gifted: 'You would be able to do with them entirely as you wished, on condition that you enabled some of your students to benefit from them, in a private capacity, each time that this is possible, and later on to send them back to the French department when the general situation makes this possible.' In July, Popa thanked him for sending ninety-six volumes and said he was still hoping that Barthes might be able to stay on in Romania. But the situation for Barthes and his mother had been growing worse for several months. Like all the diplomats and the personnel in the legation, he no longer had the right to travel in the country, except to Predeál and Sinaia, between Bucharest and Braşov (after August, he would no longer even be able to go to those places). He fought hard to obtain identity cards for the personnel, in other words to have them recognized as proper officials in the legation, which would enable them to travel. He also found it extremely difficult to obtain food cards and was worried he might not be given a return visa for the vacation. The previous year, he had been able to go home for the summer, but now he seriously doubted whether this would be possible, even though he was homesick and the gardener had not even been growing roses in the garden. He felt like a prisoner, and dreamed of other destinations. Rome was mentioned, and struck him as a far more spacious city. Alexandria was also a possible, and desirable, horizon.

Part of his work consisted in protecting the deserted centre, 'less from Romanian requisitioning than from the cloud of French locusts (a colony lying in wait for this alluring prey of empty rooms, chairs, tables, beds, etc.)'[39] and organizing the repatriation of material: books, three grand pianos, silverware, linen, cinema apparatus, records . . . . There were also the paintings lent to the Institute by the

Mobilier national: a Vlaminck and a Bonnard, among others. All of this took up practically the whole of his summer. 'It's a death agony that is being prolonged mainly so as to hand over one's responsibilities to death.'[40] On 21 July, the note of definitive expulsion finally arrived even though people were no longer expecting it. Strangely, Barthes's name was not on it, with the possible implication that the Romanian government was keeping him on as cultural attaché. He saw no drawbacks to this since his life was more than tolerable, in spite of the circumstances: he had his mother with him, his love life was going well and he had close friends. But this respite was apparently short-lived. He was still being refused his food cards and his travel permit. His departure took place in September. He made the arrangements for his appointment to Alexandria. He came home by car; his brother met him in Vienna to help him with the driving. Before he left, he bid farewell to the audience at the last concert. 'Today is the last time, for the foreseeable future, that I am addressing you, as the Romanian government has asked all the officials of the Legation who were members of the Institut français to leave, including the cultural attaché and six of his colleagues. They left last week; I myself will be leaving Romania in a few days.' The library was handed over to Margareta Petrescu, in whom he had full confidence, and the Institute to other Romanian officials who would not perhaps be so zealous in maintaining its spirit. Less than a year later, in March 1950, repression and censorship would also be brought to bear on the Romanian personnel, especially the lectors. About twenty of them were arrested for collaboration with the enemy.

This all leaves the question of whether this experience may have led Barthes to shift his Marxist position. Barthes, for the time being, remained silent on this point.

Far from Paris (2). Alexandria

After this turbulent and at times painful episode (one of his close friends, Dan, committed suicide in the spring of 1949), Barthes had little wish to stop for long in Paris. He wished at all costs to remain in the system of French expatriates, a system that appeared in his eyes to provide him with considerable material security and social stability. It was not particularly prestigious posts that were being offered to him, but, in comparison with what they would be in France, they gave him an appreciable degree of recognition; his expat's bonus gave him a more than expected purchasing power, especially in countries that were economically less well-off, such as Romania and Egypt; the fact of belonging, even marginally, to the diplomatic corps meant that he could frequent culturally privileged circles on both national and local levels. In short, Barthes was

counting on Rebeyrol and his new relations in this world to give him
a hand up. Two months later, he flew to Egypt, this time without his
mother, who stayed with Michel Salzedo in Paris, and moved to a
place near the house of Charles and Anna Singevin, occupying two
rooms in a family home and going for all his meals to the home of
these friends whom he had met in Romania.

In 1949, French was really flourishing in Egypt, even if the
Egyptians were gradually trying to assume control of French
schools and the language was starting to come up against stiff
competition from English. Jean-Claude Chevalier has found the
following figures in the archives of the French Foreign Ministry;
they were sent by Ambassador Arvengas on 17 April 1948: 'There
are 34,887 pupils in the French educational system, including 4,746
in secondary schools, 1,090 in technical schools, 2,051 in vocational
schools, 14,000 in primary schools and 13,000 for kindergartens. In
comparison, in the Egyptian system, in 1948, there are 48,000 pupils
in secondary schools and 44,000 preparing for competitive exams.'[41]
Education was destined mainly for Egyptians, especially for the
Jews and Greeks who were numerous in Alexandria, but also for the
French who were living there. Barthes mostly taught the language,
but, together with Charles Singevin and Greimas, he also managed
to get books into Egypt for the students. The archives contain a
letter of 8 June 1959 requesting the Ministry to send some 100 or
so contemporary works (novels, but also Piaget's *Treatise on Logic*)
and, a year later, Maurice Couve de Murville, ambassador between
1950 and 1954, requested that a French library be set up in Egypt.
The situation was fragile, as in Romania, but for other reasons: it
left those involved a great deal of room for parallel initiatives, for
flexibility, for encounters, for circumstances. It offered people a different way of fostering ideas from what they would have found in
academia back in France. And, like his companions, Barthes made
the most of this floating world.

His life unfolded in a way very different from what he had known
in Bucharest. He was freer to move around as he wished and he had
far less of a technical and administrative burden. In November, he
went to see the Pyramids, and in February he went to Aswan and
Upper Egypt: later, he would say this was his happiest memory
of his stay in this country. He told Philippe Rebeyrol, who had
been appointed to a post at the Institut français in London, that
he was feeling well: 'I now have quite a comfortable apartment, in
a peaceful district, with gardens; I have a domestic help and some
free time: nine hours' lessons per week, which do not require any
preparation; in fact, language teaching here takes priority over
any literature; it suppresses worrying questions about ideology'.[42]
While he had written very little during his years in Romania, caught
up in the novelty of the situation and the changing circumstances,

and busied with various practical annoyances and writing reports that were as interminable as they were necessary, in Alexandria he could find the peace of mind necessary for pursuing his work on Michelet and writing new articles. It was here that he wrote, in particular, a few reviews but, more importantly, his first major article on Michelet, published in *Esprit* in April 1951, 'Michelet, l'Histoire et la mort' ('Michelet, History and death'), and finished the series of articles in *Combat* on writing that would form the subject-matter of *Writing Degree Zero*, for which the idea came to him at just this time. In autumn 1950, he started writing his article on Cayrol. He tried to reproduce his experience in Bucharest by giving a lecture on music, but it was perceived as much too intellectual and not artistic enough: this very much hurt his feelings and made him feel that he had not been properly understood. However, he liked the warm air and the gardens and had the impression he was living a kind of dream. He said that he was feeling nostalgic for Romania and the friends he had left back there, but he adapted. Alexandria reminded him of Biarritz. 'Against the somewhat melting evanescence of the setting, my sorrows, my problems and my questions regain something of a tragic edge, because I have what is the essential condition of the tragic: solitude. I'm not far from *understanding* a certain tragic materialism – which perhaps, in my maturity, will be the position that synthesizes my two periods of youth.'[43] He did have one worry: he had been turned down by the Egyptian medical commission because of his TB, and it was more or less impossible to get round this decision in a country that took rules and regulations seriously. Though it was decided not to repatriate him straightaway, it was still likely that he would be unable to extend his teaching post for another year. It was difficult for him to imagine what the future would bring. He took refuge in the present, with nocturnal, contingent encounters made possible in special places indicated to him. He had long philosophical conversations with Charles Singevin who was at this time profoundly Marxist and would later publish several essays on Plato and on the philosophy of language;[44] he also played the piano with Anna. In particular, in this city where nothing of the mythical library remained, he formed with various other people a group for reflection and discussion that had a profound intellectual influence on each of its members.

Indeed, in Alexandria Barthes had one of the decisive meetings of his life, in the shape of Algirdas Julien Greimas. It was the first time that equality had been operating on so many levels at once: equality of generation, of marginality, of a liking for theory. This was an encounter rooted neither in the companionship of adolescence nor in the sociability of the sanatorium; it was due both to circumstances and to choice; the previous itinerary of the two protagonists immediately gave them many reasons for becoming close friends.

Greimas was one of a group of researchers who had gathered in
Paris just after the war; they called themselves the 'group of non-
agrégés' (those who had not passed the *agrégation*), all more or less
centred on Charles Bruneau, who held the chair in French language
at the Sorbonne. In comparison with the '*agrégés*', the 'non-*agrégés*'
all shared a certain number of features that meant Barthes could
join the club. First, they held a first degree but had not been able
to take the *agrégation* as they were foreigners or had been ill; they
were pursuing a doctorate despite suffering severely from a lack of
resources, which had forced them to seek jobs abroad. This was the
case of Michel Butor at the same period. 'They had only a mediocre capital, in all the senses of the term. At least they had a lot of
fellow-feeling and often spent their holidays together.'[45] The second
characteristic of this group was the fact that they were united by
their choice of subject, often less demanding than those given to
agrégés, and often involving research into vocabulary. Finally,
they had very variegated careers. Born in 1917 in Russia, but of
Lithuanian nationality, Greimas had taken a *licence* in Grenoble
before the war, and during the war returned to his country, studying as well as he could in Kaunas. After the war, he registered to do
a thesis on lexicography with Bruneau, and made a fairly wretched
living working with his wife on the General Inventory of the French
Language by Mario Roques, for which they created lexicographical index cards. When Barthes met Greimas, the latter had been a
lecturer at the Faculty of Letters in Alexandria since 1949 – and he
would remain here until 1958. At the age of 31, he had just defended
his thesis at the Sorbonne. His thesis director was Charles Bruneau,
and the title of his work was *La Mode en 1830. Essai de description
du vocabulaire vestimentaire d'après les journaux de mode de l'époque*
(*Fashion in 1830. An attempt to describe vestimentary vocabulary
on the basis of the fashion magazines of the period*). In it, he applied
the lexicological method of Georges Matoré, whom he had known
in Lithuania in quite dreadful circumstances, and with whom,
that same year, he published *La Méthode en lexicologie, à propos
de quelques thèses récentes* (*Method in Lexicology: on a few recent
theses*) and then, in 1950, *La Méthode en lexicologie, II* (*Method in
Lexicology II*).[46] There is no doubt that Barthes remembered these
works when he started doing his own research in this area at the
beginning of the 1960s. Greimas's strong Lithuanian accent did not
let you forget his origins – and in any case he did not seek to conceal
them: his status as a foreigner everywhere and his marginalized
discourse allowed him to hold fast within the non-place of generality that would be of decisive importance for theoretical research.
Barthes and he had long conversations on literature and Greimas
made Barthes read linguistics: mainly Saussure and Hjelmslev[47]
(Barthes preferred Brøndal to the latter), but also Merleau-Ponty

(who struck Greimas 'in many ways – bearing in mind the author's personal tone and multiple convergences of ideas – as an extension of Saussurean thought)[48] and Lévi-Strauss. Greimas's influence on Barthes, and Barthes's influence on Greimas, were both real. Greimas refers to this in an article of the *Bulletin du Groupe de recherches sémio-linguistiques*[49] and in his final remarks to the colloque de Cerisy devoted to his work, in 1983. 'I think I may say', he wrote, 'that he was a friend.' In his first article on 'L'actualité du saussurisme' ('The importance of Saussureanism today'), published in 1953, he refers to *Writing Degree Zero* and literary metalanguage as a possible programme for semiotics.

Based on these men and their friendship, but also in the orbit of Charles Singevin who seemed to be the philosophical authority here, there formed an animated discussion group that met every week at the home of Dr Salama, who had followed Heidegger's classes, as Greimas told Pierre Encrevé and Jean-Claude Chevalier.[50] It was 'a sort of philosophical club: there were sociologists, psychologists and philosophers. There was only one possible theme, shared by all, and this was epistemology, the conditions of knowledge. For seven years, every week or almost, we did epistemology Alexandria-style.'[51] They were joined by Jean Margot-Duclos, a pupil of Mauss, Bernard Clergerie, a philosopher, and François Neel who went on to pursue a career as a cultural adviser. They read Jakobson, the Danish linguists, Lévi-Strauss and, a little later, Lacan. When Barthes showed Greimas his article on Michelet and mentioned his thesis, Greimas retorted: 'What about Saussure?' Reading Saussure, which Barthes now did with books lent to him by Greimas, was a crucial factor structuring the years of writing that would follow. The community that had come into being provided such a firm basis for Barthes's plans and ideas as he struggled with methodological problems – he lacked books and could not manage to yoke together the historical method and the structural method – that he glimpsed a solution in linguistics. On 1 April 1950, he wrote to Rebeyrol: 'A young Lithuanian who is teaching here, Greimas, who has a doctorate, insists that I convert – it shouldn't be a problem he says – my thesis into a piece of lexicological research under the aegis of which I could carry out all the research I wanted, but would ensure I pretty quickly got a professorship in France, as there is a drastic shortage of candidates in the philological disciplines. On a deeper level, this would entail finally finding an order of positive research, a non-hypothetical way of doing sociology through language . . . an old nostalgia. I'm discussing all this with him a great deal.' For his part, Greimas relates: 'I told him: "Literature is twaddle, it won't wash." I started to sell linguistics to him. In Alexandria, we were both pretty isolated. The French were a colony of people from Vichy who came over during the war when the French fleet had taken refuge in

Alexandria. They claimed they'd become Marxists, Communists. Barthes came from Romania where the Communists had closed down the Institute; the Egyptians had detected traces of TB in him; checks were needed; he left after a year. After, we stayed together for twenty years or so.'[52] Barthes was full of determination and wanted to teach in higher education; he had no wish to continue wandering 'from one fascist country to another, deprived of all material for a piece of critical investigation that would be worth the effort of a life that has already a considerable part of its course'.[53] So he would need to find the right strategies: the one that Greimas had suggested seemed quite astute, even if it had not provided Greimas himself with a real job.

So this year 1949–50 in Alexandria was important for the period that followed, for institutional choices as well as scholarly results. Not only had Barthes long since realized that it would not be easy for him to find a university position, but he had come across people who were in the same position as him, who were all fighting to make a living in spite of the difficulties, to turn their marginality into a source of strength. Thus, Alexandria gave him a community base despite his status as a lone wolf. More specifically, the bonds he formed with Greimas led to a great number of decisions: on the academic level, Barthes decided to abandon the thesis he had begun with Pintard as his director and turned instead towards linguistics; and on the level of writing, he decided to exercise his critical intelligence within the materiality of language, to seek ideology in the rhythmic patterns of words and sentences. The people he met in Egypt did not merely represent the linguistic turn in Barthes's thinking; they also gave his writing a more philosophical cast. What was affirmed and displayed was a structured, abstract thinking, a constructive method.

Modes of writing: the Ministry and 'Degree Zero'

Barthes returned to Paris, having failed to gain an extension to his post in Alexandria because of his health problems. He was given a job as an editor in the Direction générale des relations culturelles, the cultural relations wing of the French Ministry for Foreign Affairs. He was put in charge of pedagogic missions for French as a foreign language, an issue of which his two sojourns outside France had made him particularly aware. His working days were all spent in the premises of the Ministry on the Quai d'Orsay and he had office hours that left him but little time for writing. Being as it were a humble clerk, as office workers used to be considered, did not always make it easy to carry out work of one's one. Even if he did not find his occupation especially irksome, he was torn between the need to have a way of earning a living and the desire to find a position that would suit him better, symbolically and intellectually. This made him somewhat indecisive. He dreamt of a less cramped job, one that would give him the maximum time and enable him to immerse himself into an ascetic life for the three years he would need to finish his thesis. He applied for a job in Cambridge for the academic year 1951–52, and in June was accepted, but he eventually turned it down, to the great disappointment of Robert David, who had been hoping to take over his job in the Ministry. He felt that now was the time for him to make his name in France: later, it would be too late. It was probably pointless to try and find a geographical solution by fleeing the country: the solution, if there was one, was essentially psychological. A little later, in December 1951, a new post as a lector seemed a possible option, this time in Bologna, but it did not work out. In 1952, his application for a UNESCO pedagogic post in Lebanon, for one year or two, extremely well paid and attractive, also failed: 'I was the candidate supported by the directors (it was their idea) and I had the blessing and the support of everyone (Joxe, Baillon, Lucte, Abraham and Bizot), but the Lebanon delegate, a really hypocritical priest (Mgr Maroun) chose another candidate.'[54] Barthes was overwhelmed by the sense of his inability to create, and it was easier for him to attribute the cause to his administrative job as he could see his friends finding new directions in life, and not suffering from a lack of fulfilment as he was. On a visit to Paris, Greimas – who, since Barthes's return, had stayed with his wife in a hotel in the rue Servandoni when on holiday in the capital – introduced Barthes to Georges Matoré with whom he had been collaborating for a long time. It was indeed thanks to Matoré that Greimas had obtained his post at the Inventaire of Mario Roques, and with whom he was writing what would later be more than just a textbook: *La Méthode en lexicologie*, published by Didier in 1950. There were many atypical career paths among the members of this group whom Barthes had met abroad and who consisted mainly of non-*agrégés*, but Matoré's was doubtless the most spectacularly unusual. He was an autodidact like his parents – his father was a recognized violinist and portrait painter – and he did not attend a lycée, but instead registered at the École Boulle before becoming a set designer. Military service took him to North Africa, where he learned the local Arabic dialect, and continued to study the language on his return at the Langues O' (School of Oriental Languages), specializing in classical Arabic. Before the war, he did a *licence* while at the same time acting as secretary for the Concerts Lamoureux. In 1938, he was sent as an envoy to Lithuania where he met Greimas. At the start of the war he spent several months in prison, on the arrival of the Soviet troops, while continuing to extend his knowledge of languages. As a lector at the University of Vilnius, he was then considered as a subversive element by the Gestapo, and arrested. Upon his release, he returned to Paris where he wrote his two theses (the main thesis and the complementary theses), which he defended in 1946: his thesis director was Charles Bruneau. He was appointed to a job at Besançon, where he was Dean until 1952, and then to the Sorbonne, and he was very frequently invited to lecture abroad. Though he is somewhat forgotten these days, he was a crucial figure for a long time in the areas of linguistics and even philosophy – his essay on *L'Espace humain* (*Human Space*)[55] had found a place as a model for philosophy classes in lycées – and published several works, on Proust, on dictionaries, and several critical editions including the complete works of Molière. He was living proof that it was possible to have a prestigious academic career even if one had not followed the conventional route – a possibility that, paradoxically, was more frequently made available by the mandarin academia of those days than it is today.

Barthes was counting on Matoré for a post as assistant in his laboratory for structural lexicology, where his job would be to work his way through a huge number of works to establish a great manual database, with the aim of ensuring that structuralism was separated neither from meaning nor from history. It was a militant programme that opposed certain abstract and even mechanistic tendencies in structural linguistics, and Matoré set out his project in the preface to *La Méthode en lexicologie*.[56] But while Barthes had expected an answer by June 1951, he was still without news in October. Luckily, the news of the bursary for this project finally arrived in November ('the best thing that I could have hoped for over the past two years'),[57] which freed up his time for personal work and allowed him to think he might be able to finish a thesis in three years. Then, Matoré advised him to register with Charles Bruneau too, an eminent specialist in dialects who had continued the *Histoire de la langue française* (*History of the French Language*) by Ferdinand Brunot. The subject, close to that of Greimas in methods and in the period it focused on, was *Le Vocabulaire des rapports entre l'État, les patrons et les ouvriers de 1827 à 1834, d'après les textes législatifs, administratifs et académiques* (*The vocabulary of the relations between the state, managers and workers from 1827 to 1834, as found in the legislative, administrative and academic texts*). The following year, Barthes assiduously frequented the Bibliothèque nationale in the rue de Richelieu to work through studies on nineteenth-century working-class history. The archives still bear the traces of this tenacious labour. Barthes was looking for an alternative method that would save him from this boring analysis of text after text that turns research into such drudgery. He used index cards of onion-pink paper or yellow paper cut into four. The top of the card generally includes the name of the author and the date on the left. At the bottom of the card there is, where relevant, the catalogue number of the work in the Bibliothèque nationale. He also listed 'value words', things to 'keep an eye on', such as: '1) Highlighted words (starting with sensitivity, routine, ladies) / 2) The diptych (life, psychology, / propriety) / 3) Cliché-couples (hovel ≠ palace) / 4) Notional areas / 5) The social profile of a word / Technical profile of the word (factory, manufacture) / 6) The different types of language (legal, moral) / 7) Shifts from proper meaning to figurative meaning / 8) Neologisms . . .' He wonders how one can make up for the absence of a word, and ponders the need for a word. He indexed Fourier and Saint-Simon, but also works by and on Béranger, Blanqui, Blondin, Babeuf, Cabet, Armand Carrel, Considérant, etc. He also analysed a considerable number of newspapers as well as parliamentary archives.[58]

On certain index cards, the ambition of his work becomes clear, and shows that his indexing was not just an aide-memoire of concepts of bibliographical details, as was often the case with people writing a thesis before the digital age, but also extended to expressing contents: 'The whole meaning of the thesis should be something new as compared to etymology and semantics: words do not proliferate through their compounds and derivatives but through their complements. [. . .] It is the states, the *fields* of the word that change.' And then there is an index card that clearly expresses the intellectual scope of the thesis and its consequences for the way we think about language: 'My phraseological repertoire – if it were exhaustive – should make it possible to see the degree of mobility of the articulation of the lexicon. We could measure exactly the power of connection of each word. One word would be numerically richer in possible situations than another. We could thus produce a sort of classification of words in terms of their flexibility, their elasticity, their electricity, their valency content. These consequences would be incalculable, as it would point to an extensive dynamics of the words, each viewed in context. It would involve countering an essentialist, associationist idea of language, where each unit is usually considered as able to be brought into ideally countless combinations, which is false, as the existence of a word is included within certain possible limits of situations. This is the problem of man and mankind. Words are not free; there is a spatial death of words.' The energy Barthes deployed here was considerable, even if this preparatory labour did not tend towards the production of a continuous discourse. There was already a perceptible reluctance to engage in argument in this method. However, Barthes's two supervisors said they were very pleased with the progress he was making. The career dossier of the CNRS includes very positive reports from Bruneau and Matoré. For example, Matoré writes: 'I have been able to appreciate the considerable interest of the work of M. Barthes, who has so far analysed a

considerable number of newspapers, and administrative and legislative texts, as well as authors of the time, whether novelists, historians
or political writers. M. Barthes's studies use texts of which we know
the dates; they are based on the concrete details of words, following
an objective method that most French lexicologists use nowadays. It
is certain that M. Barthes, thanks to a tried and tested method, and
thanks above all to his intelligence and his wide culture which I have
often been able to appreciate, will make a contribution of the highest
order to this period, in the course of which most modern ideas about
society were born.'[59]

In spite of the time he was spending on his thesis, Barthes was
able to divide his energy almost equally between writing articles
for reviews, working on his books, and documentation. The intellectual's timetable was henceforth stabilized. This did not prevent
him from suffering from regular periods of depression. The one he
underwent in 1951–52 had a certain intensity to it. At the age of 37,
he could sense the middle of his life approaching, a recurrent motif
that started to sound like a constant refrain. 'The diffuse – and
admittedly rather commonplace – "mid-life" crisis, but, alas, this
mezzo del cammin di nostra vita is even more of a wasteland: I have
still not achieved anything. I am arriving at the heart of maturity
with an imperfectly fulfilled youth. To tell you the truth, it is not
ageing that bothers me; it's ageing before I have exhausted the
social rites of each age.'[60] In spite of his various plans, the increasing throng of requests for articles, the books due to be published,
he still could not discern the programme for a *vita nova*. If his life
was to change, it would probably be necessary, at this moment
in his life, for other people to change. The almost necessary link
between intellectuals and communism was a terrible headache for
him. He wanted to see new people, make new acquaintances. His
best friends, Rebeyrol and Greimas, were abroad and he could see
them only for brief periods. Robert David was being a little distant.
Sirinelli was in Paris again, but his religious conversion led him
into making political analyses that Barthes found quasi-fascist, and
he moved away from him. He did not know what to do with his
evenings, where to spend them, who to see. He watched the all-in
wrestling at the Élysée-Montmartre, where the Torturer of Béthune
took on the White Angel; he went to films, a few concerts, plays.
The night welcomed him but could not hold on to him. Travel was a
source of interesting changes of scene. His trips abroad freed up his
life and indeed his whole being. In July 1951, he spent three weeks in
Denmark and, in the spring of 1952, he went to see Pierre Guiraud,
who was working at Groningen in Holland. He took advantage of
this to embark on a real tourist trip that took him from Amsterdam
to The Hague, from the Rijksmuseum to the Mauritshuis, where he
fell in love with Dutch painting: this inspired him with the idea of a

form of art criticism based on subject-matter and not on painters or schools. When he was abroad, he felt lighter, and no longer needed to protect his mother or his position. He made friends, went out a great deal in the evenings, managed to 'live freely', as he euphemistically put it in his letters.

The last decisive encounter he made in those years – of which there had been many – was with Jean Cayrol, whose acquaintance he owed to Albert Béguin,[61] following Barthes's review of *Lazare parmi nous* that was published in the 21 September 1950 issue of *Combat*. Cayrol at this time was an important figure in the literary domain. While, before the war, he had published only poetry, after his return from the camp at Mauthausen, where he had been deported for his activities with the Resistance, he wrote stories and essays. Approached by Paul Flamand in 1949, he started working for Éditions du Seuil. With them, in 1956, he founded a review, *Écrire*, completely dedicated to the publication of the first texts of young authors, which gave it the appearance of a collection (which it became, in 1965). In December 1956, Philippe Sollers, under his name Philippe Joyaux, wrote a letter to Cayrol saying that he hoped he could be published in this series.[62] Many future members of the review's editorial committee published their first texts here: Sollers, Jean-Pierre Faye and Marcelin Pleynet in 1957, Fernand du Boisrouvray and Jacques Coudol in 1959, and Denis Roche in 1962. Cayrol produced a very sombre portrait of contemporary literature: he wanted to discover new authors while forcing them to face up to the climate of general anaesthesia in which they were caught and the need to escape from it. Cayrol's position was at the crossroads of several tendencies in this milieu: existentialism, which he rubbed shoulders with in the person of Camus; Christian personalism, which was very influential at Éditions du Seuil, and the avant-garde as embodied by the young writers whose work he commissioned for *Écrire*. Éditions du Seuil had been founded by Henri Söjberg as a forum for young Catholics who shared a desire to engage in society. The company, which was joined by Paul Flamand and Jean Bardet, published mainly for young people and for the Scouts movement until the Occupation. Lacking symbolic and economic capital, young publishers needed to attract authors of importance who might occupy a significant place in post-war France. They sought to gather the progressive Catholic networks of the Resistance who would be in a position to bring other former members of the Resistance along with them. Éditions du Seuil therefore approached the Swiss publishing house of La Baconnière, run during the war by Albert Béguin, who had published Resistance poets and was at this time professor at the University of Basel. He moved to Paris in 1946 and Éditions du Seuil offered him a place on their editorial committee, which also meant they had a link with the review *Esprit* which Béguin now directed. In 1947, Jean Cayrol's book *Je Vivrai l'amour des autres* (*I will live the love of others*), co-published by La Baconnière and Seuil, won the Prix Renaudot, and the author thereupon joined the committee himself. The strategy also consisted in not getting trapped in a confessional and religious image, and diversifying the image of Seuil among the critics and the general public: it was with this aim in mind that the company republished Maurice Nadeau's *History of Surrealism* in 1945, Pierre Klossowski's *Sade my Neighbour* in 1948, and *La Signification humaine du rire* (*The human meaning of laughter*) by Francis Jeanson in 1951.[63] In 1951, the money generated by the extraordinary success of Giovanni Guareschi's *Little World of Don Camillo* – 1.2 million copies in French translation – was invested in various collections that might make a profit but would above all ensure a place in the intellectual and literary field. So it was in a young publishing house that was in rude health and keen to promote the avant-garde that Barthes signed his first contract, in 1952, on Cayrol's initiative.

This encounter was decisive for three reasons. First, it brought Barthes to a publishing house to which he would belong through-out his life, Éditions du Seuil, at the very same time as Raymond Queneau, at Gallimard, turned down *Writing Degree Zero*.[64] Second, it freed up his essayistic writing and gave him material to think about and encouraged him to take up a particular position. And finally, it enabled him to forge new connections, making him part of a literary milieu that was neither that of the Trotskyists, opened by Nadeau, nor that of academia. Barthes started to publish in various different places. Thanks to his encounter with Albert Béguin, who in October 1950 asked him to contribute something following the publication of his article on 'the degree zero'[65], he offered his major article on Michelet to *Esprit* and the editorial committee immediately invited him to take part in an unusual collaboration. From 1952 onwards, he was to publish his first 'mythologies' before giving them to *Les Lettres nouvelles* for publication. When we read the article today, we can see what impressed the readers of 'Michelet, l'Histoire et la mort'. In a society that had discovered mass crime, the thoughts developed in the article suited that time of ruin. In this article, there are passages that anticipate the 1954 book and would indeed be repeated in it: on the vegetal, the tableau, the various types of bodiliness that we find in Michelet's text, the fertile tension between narrative and tableau. While the pages on post-history, a post-revolutionary time, without any true temporal dimension, may have contradicted Marxist hope, they did correspond closely to the sense of the collapse of culture that was prevalent at the end of the Second World War. In this sense, this article can also be understood in the terms of Cayrol, with Cayrol's own reflections on the possibility of survival in the context of the con-centration camps. The common point between the images associated with Lazarus in Cayrol's work and Barthes's account of Michelet's history was a capacity to live through death, to assume, in thought and writing, the weight of 'the carnal death of millions of people.' In Cayrol, as in Michelet, from this direct encounter with death comes the possibility of a resurrection. But just as, in Cayrol, rebirth is not total, literature bears the trace of the disaster, the memory of the injury and the stigmata of the 'great fear',[66] Michelet's aim 'is not a complete resurrection that would still allow life to continue with its confrontation with death'.[67]

Barthes's remarks in the article on Michelet are sometimes akin to those made by Lucien Febvre in his lectures at the Collège de France during the war: in front of his audience, Febvre would turn his seminars into veritable lessons in resistance. For example, he would say that by 'creating' the history of France wholesale, Michelet had freed it from race; he invited his audience to react against 'this great liquidation, this great demolition of a material but also a spiritual and moral world', and to free themselves from death.[68] It is possible that Barthes attended some of the lectures in the 1943 course on 'Michelet, the Renaissance', as he was in aftercare in the rue Quatrefages between January and July 1943, and, during the daytime, he was allowed to go out to work on his *certificat de licence*. Already immersed in his reading of Michelet, and doubtless aware of the lectures being given at the Collège de France, right next door to the Sorbonne, it is possible that he set foot in the auditorium on more than one occasion. We have no information to prove this, and Barthes did not mention Febvre in his own inaugural *Lecture* at the Collège de France in 1977, but the historian was for him a major and recurrent historical reference point, which makes this a credible hypothesis. There is one rather disturbing coincidence. When Febvre reviewed Barthes's *Michelet* for *Combat* in 1954, he began with a reference to Lazarus: 'Living history . . . But surely the most living of all histories is, first and foremost, the history of men who were given the precious gift of resurrection? *Lazare, veni foras* – and Lazarus rises, comes out and walks.'[69] It would be difficult to find a better illustration of their profound affinity.

There were several characteristics that Barthes shared with Cayrol. Like Barthes, Cayrol lived with his mother, in the village of Saint-Chéron, in the Essonne, where Paul Flamand also had a house. From his experience of the concentration camp, Cayrol had pondered on the different ways of escaping one's situation in which Barthes recognized himself more than he did in the behaviour of a committed intellectual in whom struggle and armed resistance led to an unbridled will to change the world. Without reducing the deportation camp to a kind of sanatorium, which would be scandalously trivializing (the way humans and individuals are treated in the two institutions are at polar opposites), Barthes discovered in Cayrol a way of transcending the trials of exclusion and confinement. Defining the literature of the time on the basis of the notion of the 'novel of Lazarus', Cayrol, the author of *Lazare parmi nous*, made captivity into the crucial experience of our time. Indeed, he was – together with Jean Rousset – one of the first to envisage literature as able to transform itself under the impact of the camps. Barthes was well aware of this in the complex study he began writing in 1951 and published in the March 1952 issue of *Esprit*: 'Cayrol's whole novel tends to show that there is an order of existences – perhaps those of people who survived the camps – in which the power to assume a human suffering formed within our own personal histories constitutes a state heavy and rich with humanity, a very elaborate triumph coming after times of unbelievable poverty.'[70] In his work, moving beyond disaster involves two figures: the witness denouncing a certain state of humanity and the world; and the idea of reversal, in which the passage through death leads to the emergence of something new. Barthes made Cayrol, alongside Camus, into one of his main contemporary reference points at this period, and picked up on essentially two lines of force in his reading of their work. One was Orpheus, the mythological version of the Christian story of Lazarus (the two share a great number of features – they are figures of metamorphosis in which a limit is displaced, and figures of renewal); the other was blank writing. Though this means overlooking some of the historical and ethical dimensions of Cayrol's thought, Barthes managed gradually to draw out of Cayrol's suggestions certain aesthetic themes close to his own. In his introduction to *Writing Degree Zero*, Barthes turns Cayrol into one of his examples of blank writing, together with Blanchot and Camus. Rather than setting these texts back in the theoretical and historical orbit of *Lazare parmi nous*, Barthes appropriates Cayrol's work and uses it in the service of his own definition of writing, non-literary and atonal. He gradually draws a veil over the spiritual dimension in Cayrol and the reference – albeit a crucial one – to the concentration camps, thereby displaying his habit of, as it were, confiscating the texts he loves – something that he would subsequently turn into a guiding principle.[71]

During this period, Barthes wrote or revised the articles of *Degree Zero*: he reread them, crossing out a lot, then typed and reread, deleted and replaced. In the introduction, for example, the words: 'Classical writing therefore disintegrated, and the whole of Literature, from Flaubert to the present day, became the problematics of language' were followed, in the manuscript, by: 'an unresolved problematic, of course, for History is still alienated and consciences torn: the annihilation of forms of writing is still impossible.'[72] These corrections aimed not just to lighten the proselytism of the Marxist discourse, but also to purge the style, to reduce the images, perhaps to bring his own writing closer to the kinds of writing he was discussing. The work was published in March 1953 in the 'Pierres vives' collection created in 1945 by Paul Flamand, though at this stage edited by Claude-Edmonde Magny (who had also published with the Éditions de la Baconnière just after the war and still wrote for the review *Esprit*). The book came with an extremely programmatic review slip, albeit one that modestly presented the text as a hypothesis. This hypothesis itself had a poetic dimension – it was obsessed by the idea of a non-style or a purely spoken style, in short a 'degree zero of literary writing' – and a historical dimension, too, since Barthes traced this distance between the writer and a separated language back to the nineteenth century. It was a short book, which in its brevity was a response to an anxiety that had dominated the previous years: a fear that both time and courage might be missing. 'Why not deliberately produce a short literature?' he asked Rebeyrol in December 1951. If this brevity corresponded both to a constraint and a desire, it led him to feel nervous about how the critics would react. The leap of publication made Barthes vulnerable. Now he had 'come out' of the dark years and was finally exposed, in that literary world from which he expected so much but where he continued to feel a misfit, and always somewhat stifled.

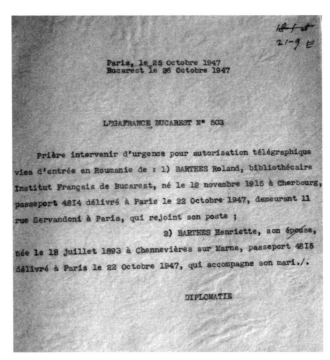

Visa request 'for Roland Barthes and his wife' (*sic*).

The Romanian French Institute, boulevard Dacia.

With a group of women students and his mother (who is in the front row, second from the right) in Bucharest, in 1949.

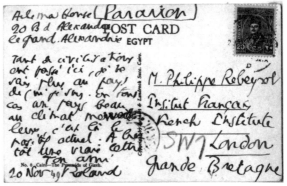

Postcard of the Pyramids
sent to Philippe Rebeyrol,
November 1949.

In Egypt, in 1950.

8

Barthes and Sartre

Barthes had already gained a foothold in the intellectual sphere, and now sought to define his role, his critical position, his political discourse. In 1953, he had just published his first book, but he was still pondering the social and political scope of writing. It was within the context of this quest that he inevitably encountered the figure of Jean-Paul Sartre.

The parallel between Barthes and Sartre depends less on a biographical narrative in the strict sense of the term – their paths barely crossed and they had no direct personal links – than on the need to grasp a *historical life*, in other words a life caught up in its period, a life that could at the same time give a certain representation of that period. This was the essential issue for both of these men who, with their similarly sounding names, turned thought into an art (and 'art' lies at the very heart of their two surnames): Sartre, Barthes – these monosyllables mark the boundaries of a historical period. French twentieth-century thought includes both of them in its pantheon, and their decisions, like their works, stem from the way they view their time, from within or without. However, were they really contemporaries? ('Who are my contemporaries? Who do I live with?' Barthes asked in his first lectures at the Collège de France. 'It's no use asking the calendar.')[1] Did they share a history and a vision of history? Does a retrospective glance at their crossed paths place them in the same movement? Obviously not. When, just after the war, Sartre appeared as the crucial reference point for modernity, Barthes had no intention of defining himself in the terms of such an injunction; and when, later, Barthes became the champion of the avant-garde with the *nouvelle critique*, Sartre advocated a return to humanism which now seemed outdated. Sartre's active commitment contrasted with Barthes's oscillation between a committed and a non-committal stance, an oscillation that was as regular as the beating of a clock. From the outside, they thus presented the double face of the French intellectual, the one always directly plugged into the world, the other in a movement of attachment and detachment that gave freedom and dynamism to his thought. However, we cannot limit a double portrait of the two men to one of mere contrast. There were also many points, albeit more secret and internal, at which they were similar, and this encounter – more readable in their texts than in anecdotes from their lives – explains why we need both of them, today, to understand what was at stake in the history of cultures at that moment, in France and in the French language: they embodied a completely new connection between literature, politics and philosophy that gave an unparalleled critical and cognitive power to literature, endowing it with every capacity – for transformation, revolution and understanding. This connection has since then been severed, and this power blunted; but if we now trace the history of this connection, and understand what it entailed, we will be able both to remember its restorative role after the disaster of the two world wars and the inconceivable horror of the extermination of the Jews, and to affirm that criticism can have a social impact, for example when it draws on literature and becomes literature itself – partly, no doubt, for this very reason.

Pausing in our chronological narrative will enable us to survey a few important aspects of Barthes's career. First, we can measure the degree to which Sartre was a decisive factor enabling Barthes to affirm himself, to lose his fear of his powers of affirmation. Second, we can understand the varied and sometimes divergent relations between the critical intellectual and the modern world. And finally, we can grasp a relationship between sexuality and mastery (or non-mastery) that partly defines separate intellectual positions.

The argument about responsibilities

Thus there are several reasons why we can compare Barthes and Sartre and relate the story of their connections. People have often commented on the way *Camera Lucida* is dedicated 'in homage to Sartre's *The Imaginary*', on the difference between their political commitments, on the authority they respectively exercised in the cultural and intellectual field, on their ambiguous relation to systems and on their almost simultaneous deaths. A special issue of the *Revue d'esthétique*, in 1991, associated their names in a single celebration: not to compare them in any systematic way, but to place their two figures face to face and on the same level – to mark their equality in the history of thought. And yet, Sartre was the senior figure. Not only was he ten years older, but he made his debut in literature when still quite young, while Barthes was a late starter – after a gap of some fifteen years. So Sartre was already a reference point for Barthes as the latter made his entry into intellectual life. Barthes agreed about this in his interview with Normand Biron for

Radio Canada, in which he told Biron that he felt in the position of a reader vis-à-vis Sartre: 'I embarked on intellectual life straight after the Liberation of Paris, just when the writer everyone was reading, the one showing us the way, the one teaching us the new language, was Sartre. Now one of Sartre's most important actions was precisely the way he demystified literature in its institutional, reactionary and sacral aspect, as it were; this was one of his main endeavours.'[2] Barthes added that he had, in his own way, played a part in this operation, first performing tasks of ideological demystification (for example in *Mythologies*) and only subsequently focusing again on literature. At the same time, in *Roland Barthes by Roland Barthes*, he stated that 'his [i.e. Barthes's] way of writing was formed at a moment when the writing of the essay sought a renewal by the combination of political intentions, philosophical notions, and true rhetorical figures (Sartre is full of them)'.[3] In this way, he reconstructed his intellectual autobiography on several occasions in the 1970s, always hammering the message home, acknowledging a direct influence, an insistent impact.[4] But can we take these reconstructions literally? Nothing could be less certain. What we have is a – complex – history of a 'long series of gestures of filiation and de-filiation'[5] that can be read in the way Sartre's name appears in Barthes's writings, and then again is sometimes erased.

Admittedly, as Barthes's relation to Gide became more concealed, his relation to Sartre – which likewise involved an element of comparison and contrast – intensified. Gide died in 1951, just before Barthes had really started to publish, and gradually this new influence became apparent. Unlike Gide, this was not a matter of a concordance or connivance of temperaments, but rather a sort of more or less conscious rivalry, expressed more or less clearly. To claim that one is an intellectual of significance, to have a voice – a voice that counted – implied that Barthes was both like Sartre and yet different from him. Thus, their positions quite often diverged, but their existential choices, just like the details of their biographies, also made them akin. 'Both of them were politically committed. Not in the same way: Sartre alone was sometimes prepared to go down into the arena, and he did sometimes go down, even if he never left his desk. But they were both writers first and foremost, and it was as such that they committed themselves.'[6] Susan Sontag (who wrote the preface to the English translation of *Writing Degree Zero*) saw commitment as the place in which a difference between their characters found expression: 'Sartre has an intellectually brutal, *bon enfant* view of the world, a view that wills simplicity, resolution, transparence; Barthes's view is irrevocably complex, self-conscious, refined, irresolute.'[7] The one writer sought confrontation, the other shunned it; the one was directly political, while the other had a more elusive relation to politics.

In a highly strategic manner – it was, with Marxism, the second visible strategy he had displayed in his career so far – Barthes positioned his *Combat* articles and his first book in a dialogue with Sartre. This was a clear statement of his desire to play a part in the intellectual debates of the time; it was also, perhaps on a more secret level, a way of drawing a line under the years of retrenchment when he had not been present to history. Barthes never quoted Sartre's words in *Writing Degree Zero*, but the latter's name appears three times in the book and some of Barthes's suggestions are direct replies to questions raised in Sartre's 1947 work, *What is Literature?* Barthes also voices objections to some of Sartre's ideas. It is also striking to see how a whole tranche of Barthes's efforts, as we can see in the manuscripts, consisted in removing any explicit reference to Sartre, any mention of his name, from Barthes's own books. He did not include the first article in *Combat* (on the 'Responsibility of grammar') in *Writing Degree Zero*, even though he there praised the solutions found by the author of *The Reprieve* to the problem of the impasse of style; likewise, Barthes considerably modified the last article, reworked as 'The utopia of language', partly removing the reference to Sartre, while paying him quite a direct homage by using the term 'utopia', present at the end of 'Who does one write for?' (the title of the *Combat* article had been 'The tragic sense of writing'). In the second manuscript version of *Mythologies*, there is another example, perhaps even more striking: there are nine notes on Sartre, referring to his work as a whole;[8] in the final, published version, they are reduced to a single note, on Sartre's *Saint Genet*. If Sartre did indeed constitute a model – and a counter-model – this was not something to be disclosed to all and sundry, as this would have been a way of placing him above Barthes himself. Barthes took care to mark the relation, the difference, the need to measure himself against the notion of commitment, to take part in the debate on the responsibility of literature – but he wanted his own voice to be heard, without assimilating his words to an external framework or context.

One aspect of Sartre's conception of literature appears as self-evident in *Writing Degree Zero*: the link between literature and prose, but also the ethical character of the literary imperative. But while Sartre constructed an ethics of ends, a functional view of literature – 'by speaking, I reveal the situation by my very intention of changing it; I reveal it to myself and to others in order to change it. [. . .] at present I dispose of it; with every word I utter, I involve myself a little more in the world, and by the same token I emerge from it a little more, since I go beyond it toward the future'[9] – Barthes prefers an ethic of form that opens up literature considerably. 'Placed at the centre of the problematics of literature, which cannot exist prior to it, writing is thus essentially the morality of form, the choice of that social area within which the writer elects

to situate the Nature of his language.'[10] Sartre oscillates between
a sacralization of literature (it is 'everything') and a disdain for its
playfulness and irresponsibility. As for Barthes, he hesitates between
the death of literature and the assumption of writing; he essential-
izes form in a way that seems to contradict the disappearance we
mentioned above. Instead of the question 'What is literature?',
Barthes, at the beginning of his book, prefers to ask the parallel
question 'What is writing?', which is both a symmetrical question
and an answer to Sartre's question. In Barthes's view, the true writer
is the one who escapes from literature, a writer without literature,
producing a blank writing, a 'degree zero' – he uses the formula of
Viggo Brøndal (whose *Essais de linguistique générale* he had read
in Romania, as we have seen), and also takes up the latter's term
'neutral'[11] – before becoming a metaphor that can be aptly used to
express several different things (there are a good fifty or so occur-
rences in his work as a whole). For example, young people are the
'degree zero of social class',[12] the Eiffel Tower is the 'degree zero of
the monument',[13] Racine is the 'degree zero of the critical object',[14]
or the École pratique des hautes études, described in an unpublished
fragment of *Roland Barthes by Roland Barthes* as the 'degree zero of
any teaching institution'.[15] The formula 'degree zero' has enjoyed a
considerable degree of success and can be used by anyone. And yet
this degree zero of writing was viewed by Barthes as a tragic sign,
since it led to a dead end. 'However hard [the writer] tries to create
a free language, it comes back to him fabricated, for luxury is never
innocent: and it is this stale language, closed by the immense pressure of all the men who do not speak it, which he must continue to
use. Writing therefore is a blind alley, and it is because society itself
is a blind alley. The writers of today feel this; for them, the search
for a non-style or an oral style, for a zero level or a spoken level of

writing is, all things considered, the anticipation of a homogeneous
social state; most of them understand that there can be no universal
language outside a concrete, and no longer a mystical or merely
nominal, universality of society.'[16] This almost conclusive moment
in *Writing Degree Zero* helps us to read the three strata of discourse
that subtend Barthes's language in this text (it is the mixing of the
three strata that create its complexity). First, there is the *existen-
tialist discourse* of freedom, of impulse, of humanity; second, as
in Sartre, but in a perhaps even more emphatic form, we have the
Marxist discourse of classless society as the ultimate aim; and third,
the *discourse of linguistics* is present here through the expression
'degree zero', and everywhere else in the distinction drawn between
language, style and writing. This intermingling, which sometimes
borders on a fusion of the terms, is one way of marking his distance
from Sartre, of going further than him, perhaps,[17] to take up a different position in the way he wrote essays.

Barthes's procedure, in this first of his books to be published, was thus revelatory of what would later be a distinguishing feature of his thought: he was both assertive and elusive or reserved, seeking a way of making his mark in writing while rejecting labels. Thus, the words 'we know that' with which the first article begins, and the other peremptory phrases of the kind, coexist with more sinuous expressions such as 'the search for a non-style or an oral style, for a zero level or a spoken level of writing',[18] in which old descriptions no longer fit and writing becomes a quest that does not hesitate to lose itself in uncertain equivalences or even in blatant contradictions.

If *Writing Degree Zero* can be considered to mark an essential date in Barthes's vocation as a critical intellectual, this is partly because of his way of occupying a certain position in the field of thought (of which Sartre was, for Barthes as for many other left-wing intellectuals, the main figure) and partly because of the way he built up his very own style, attaching himself to and detaching himself from the words of others. It is easy to see just how many writers Barthes had read; they lurk in the background of the text: but we can also see how Barthes appropriated them and mixed them together so as to create 'his' thought, 'his' style. He was so caught up in his reading, in such an existential and emotional way, that when he recognized an image or a thought in another author, he could make it entirely his own. In the fragment of *Roland Barthes by Roland Barthes* called 'What is influence?', he distinguishes between the authors on whom one writes, who are the object of an analysis, and with whom one has a clearly stated relation, and the authors one reads. What comes from the latter writers is 'A kind of music, a pensive sonority, a more or less dense play of anagrams'.[19] Between these two poles, the writer one loves on the one hand, the one whom reading has transported and who continues to live on in one's memory and one's heart, and, on the other, the public figure of the intellectual one admires, who irritates you by his presence and some of his commitments, reside, in all probability, the complexity and force of Barthes's relation to Sartre. It is clear that Barthes was, right from the start, laying claim to a place in the intellectual field. This involved having a certain idea of history, but also clearly stated positions. It is interesting to note that if Barthes's book, compared to the articles in *Combat*, seeks to camouflage the reference to Sartre and some of the admiration that Barthes felt for him, Barthes also added two completely new unpublished texts that showed a striking sense of involvement with Sartre's field of action, in particular as regards his analyses of the 'Situation of the writer in 1947': in the first part, the chapter entitled 'Political modes of writing' picks up on certain aspects of the report Barthes wrote in Romania on Stalinist language and introduces a new type, the 'scriptor', made necessary by the expansion of the political sphere into the field of letters: the scriptor is 'halfway between the party member and the writer, deriving from the former an ideal image of committed man, and from the latter the notion that a written work is an act'.[20] Thus, the writing found in *Esprit* and the writing found in *Les Temps modernes* join hands in a common defence and illustration of a shared aim that has now become an institution: the aim of 'presence'. Both these types of writing 'are therefore in a complete blind alley', concludes Barthes with some violence, 'they can lead only to complicity or impotence, which means, in either case, to alienation'.[21] In the second part, the additional chapter is called 'Writing and revolution'. It is a loaded critique, extremely polemical and ironic, on French-style socialist realism, as illustrated for example by André Stil – a conventional form of writing that bears all the signs of bourgeois literature, 'mechanizing without restraint all the intentional signs of art'.[22] If he excepts Aragon from his harsh verdict, because the latter managed to combine realism with the colours of the eighteenth century, we can see what strategic directions Barthes is leading his book in – towards a notably Marxist position, but one strictly separate from communism, as he had previously said was his intention when discussing the matter with his private interlocutors; and also towards the outlining of a clear distinction from committed writing as implemented by Sartre in his essays and his review. And this was indeed how Sartre himself took it, for, in the context of an extremely favourable reception to Barthes's first book (with the eight-page article by Nadeau, highly favourable reviews by Dominique Arban in *Le Monde* and Roger Nimier in *Carrefour*), the text devoted to the work in *Les Temps modernes* by J. B. Pontalis was decidedly more critical. While he hailed the birth of a writer, he also rebuked him for a 'somewhat irritating self-assurance in his tone', a 'confused set of ideas', and a certain schematicism.[23]

This parallel and yet overlapping itinerary followed by these two figures would continue in the same mode of distanced proximity, and almost always in the same pattern, with Sartre being set up as a model and anti-model by Barthes. When Sartre was holding positions he asserted strongly, and was a powerful presence on the public scene, Barthes ignored or underplayed his influence: this was true of the 1950s and 1960s when he refused to take part in Sartre's commitments, signing neither the 'Manifesto of the 121'[24] nor the text of 10 May 1968 published in *Le Monde* and expressing solidarity with the student movement – at these times, Barthes referred to him relatively rarely. But when Sartre was attacked or weakened, Barthes came to his aid and took up his defence. This happened with Sartre's play *Nekrassov* in 1955: we will be returning to this in the next chapter. Here, Barthes – alone against almost everyone – vigorously defended Sartre against the mass of his detractors. It also happened in the 1970s, when the older man was losing his

authority as his physical strength abandoned him. In 1974–75, after
Sartre had already suffered two strokes, the second of which had
left him almost blind, Barthes clearly stated the influence the senior
figure had had on him. This particular psychological configuration,
in which a sense of dependency was concealed while attacks from
outside were withstood, formed the basis of a relationship of *filiation*. The relative lack of contemporaneity of the two men rested
on this influence, an influence from which a certain detachment was
necessary if one was to have one's own identity, but from which
there also stemmed a heritage, an emotional bond whose transmission was worth ensuring. A relationship of filiation is not the same
as a relationship with a master; when it has been deliberately chosen,
and is not just a generational effect, it is much more malleable and
can lead in a variety of directions. This was often the way Barthes
allowed other people to leave their mark on him. He was less of a
disciple – being too free and too marginal for that – than he was a
son, a brother or a friend, and the three roles could be conceived
together, a form of attachment and detachment, in a space that the
father's absence had left completely free.

Childhood and history

The absence of a father was a shared element in the biographies
of Barthes and Sartre, and it was not without its influence on their
respective words and deeds, on their relation to history and the narrative of their lives. There were several similar factual details in their
lives: their fathers, both of whom served in the Navy, died when
their sons were aged 1. They were brought up in partly Protestant
circles, by their grandparents (maternal in Sartre's case, paternal
in that of Barthes), and in their families they both had powerful
grandfather figures, Charles Schweitzer and Louis-Gustave Binger
respectively, both from Alsace, both of whom opted for France in
1871, even if the first constituted more of a paternal figure than the
second in the final version of the narrative composed by the two
writers. Their solitary childhoods encouraged them to seek shelter
in long hours of reading widely and learning to play the piano. Like
Barthes, Sartre was at one time a pupil at the Lycée Montaigne and
then went to the Lycée Henri-IV, near Louis-le-Grand. Both aimed
for literary careers, and Sartre was able to follow the path all the
way to the École normale supérieure and the *agrégation*. But the
most significant of these shared experiences was, of course, the death
of their fathers: the lack of a superego was expressed in almost the
same terms by both men. As Barthes put it, he had 'no father to kill,
no family to hate, no milieu to reject: great Oedipal frustration!';[25]
this was echoed, in Sartre, by the idea of a 'very incomplete Oedipus

complex': 'Against whom or what could I have rebelled? No one else's whim ever claimed to be my law.'[26] And, before that: 'I left behind me a dead young man who did not have time to be my father and who could, today, be my son. Was it a good or a bad thing? I do not know; but I am happy to subscribe to the judgement of an eminent psychoanalyst: I have no Super-Ego.'[27] In both cases, the ambiguous freedom, based on a lack and on the absence of any definition imposed by the law, led to a sense of harmony and gentleness: 'My mother was mine and no one challenged my quiet possession. I knew nothing of violence and hatred and I was spared the harsh apprenticeship of jealousy; I did not bump myself on its corners, so I distinguished reality at first only by its cheerful inconsistency.'[28] In a less analytical, but equally explicit way in Barthes, the 'demand for love' was addressed solely to the mother and the father's existence was barely perceptible: 'By maternal intermediary his memory – never an oppressive one – merely touched the surface of childhood with an almost silent bounty'.[29] They derived from this a sense of being left in suspense, which Sartre would translate as 'contingency' and Barthes as a 'being *pour rien*',[30] which smooths away obstacles, extends the territory of the possible and, for Barthes, frees one from the question of reproduction.

This freedom, which could sometimes be experienced as a misfortune, explains the propensity we find in these two authors to contradiction, to reorientation, to correction – not the result of any weakness, but of a singular force of their thought. By taking the opposite view, by sometimes thinking against themselves, they continued to assert their non-determinism, their atopia. In *Éloge de l'apostat* (*In Praise of Apostasy*), Jean-Pierre Martin has shown the extent to which these shifty or renegade lives, marked by changes of tack, by metamorphosis and displacement, could also, against all expectation, be faithful lives. His chapter on Sartre indicates how the fractures – in his commitments and his oeuvre – are also related to a form of amnesia, an absence of retraction, a sense of faithfulness to one's self in which there is 'a strange relationship to the past and, more generally, a strange relationship to time that could be summed up in the phrase [. . .]: "I have no temporal continuity with myself"'.[31] In Barthes, the twists and turns in the timeline are less of a break and more a matter of successive turns, sudden interruptions, backtrackings, displacements and contiguities that demonstrate his rejection of a continuous pattern of evolution. This aspect of things has compared several critics to count the different 'Barthes', to distinguish a first, a second, a third Barthes; this has become a veritable topos, and some of them, like Antoine Compagnon, ask 'Which is the true one?'[32] In *Ghosts in the Mirror*, Robbe-Grillet makes what seem a rather pejorative comparison between Barthes and an eel, but he chooses to see this as the very essence of Barthes's thinking:

'"messages" that change, branch off, veer in other directions – this is what he teaches'.[33] He depicts a non-dogmatic thinker who wants to be anything but a *maître à penser*, who prefers to allow his reader to be free. Robbe-Grillet then draws a parallel with Sartre who found himself compelled to leave everything unfinished, as the very idea of freedom had undermined all his endeavours from within: 'Though he wanted to be the last philosopher, the last thinker of totality, he will have been, in the final analysis, part of the avant-garde of the new structures of thought: uncertainty, the shift, the sideslip.'[34]

Before Barthes imposed upon himself the imperative of the *vita nova*, with the appearance of the 'conversion' theme, he veered off course, formulated second thoughts, 'expressed with a sense of nuance and casualness, it is true, alternating between a technical modification and a pirouette, a palinode and a swerve, but these *pentimenti* do, when laid out in a line, comprise what is ultimately a fairly consistent apostasy towards the "theoretical super-ego"'.[35] This predisposition to change doubtless sprang from a tenuous relation to the law of the father but it was also a way of escaping from repetition and fighting boredom – that boredom, all-pervasive and ontological in character, that eventually comprised the main feature of his personality and contaminated everything – though these things were doubtless linked, with boredom stemming perhaps from the tranquil state, the absence of any conflict at the origin. In writing, the reaction to boredom took the form of a phobia for repetition: 'Repetition is a baleful theme for me – stereotype, the same old thing, naturalness as repetition.'[36] He contrasts it with 'cruising' for sexual partners, which implies a temporality that emphasizes the encounter, the first time. By allowing this first time to arise anew again and again, cruising, though it is repeated, frees repetition from itself.

Thus, the tendency to change is also a libidinal disposition. The fact that neither Barthes nor Sartre had to measure themselves against a father meant in consequence that they gave themselves no masters. They did not recognize themselves in any epigonal relationship – but this was not expressed in the same attitude towards mastery. Sartre's active attitude led him to seek forms of power, dwelling on objects for long periods. It was still gauged by a sexuality attuned to possession and capture. But he also took pains to demystify any posture of mastery, rejecting the Nobel Prize and destroying, from within, a certain intellectual leadership.[37] Barthes's more passive attitude made him more flexible vis-à-vis his objects and his positions. He preferred short forms, never tarried for long over his subjects, and while his sexuality was marked by the quest, and even the chase, the pleasure of seduction was never followed in his case by a will for possession. His freedom from any idea of mastery brought him definitively under the sway of desire and curiosity, as we see in the way he viewed the seminar as a kind of phalanstery: taking a fantasy as the basis for his courses ensured the circulation of language and emotion. It was his life and his activity that Barthes was thus proposing as models, rather than structures of principles to be applied.[38]

If we are to grasp the particular configuration of the relation between Barthes and otherness, including his relation to Sartre as a model, we need to link his skills as a reader – with his faculties for empathy, identification and appropriation – and his creativity as an author, all a matter of displacements and delicacy. Taking up someone else's words, or 'reprise', is always a way of bearing memory forwards; in so doing, it is a way of freeing oneself both from one's models and from one's self. Reprise opens up a cycle of absorption and rejection that prevents any fixation, any narcissistic contemplation in writing. It makes it possible to develop a dynamic of *reprise/déprise*, taking up and letting go as a way of skirting mastery. The subject evolves in accordance with the readings and encounters that act as travelling companions, in a process that requires the 'uncertain quotation marks', the 'floating parentheses'.[39] The movement of *reprise/déprise* here comes up against another theme that Sartre also explored in *Words*, that of inauthenticity, linked to an absence of homogeneity with one's self, to the fact that writing fails to express its author entirely. On the threshold of *Roland Barthes by Roland Barthes* we find an acquiescence in this realization: 'Once I produce, once I write, it is the Text itself which (fortunately) dispossesses me of my narrative continuity.'[40] Thus it is that, throughout his life, Barthes brought Sartre back, without necessarily realizing so with any degree of clarity: Sartre's 'Explication de *L'Étranger*' ('An analysis of *The Stranger*)', which Barthes read in the sanatorium, in the *Cahiers du Sud*, provided ample material for Barthes's own reflections on Camus, containing as it did a discussion of the theme of silence and a formulation of the neutral, here called the 'absurd': 'His hero was neither good nor bad, neither moral nor immoral. These categories don't fit: he is the member of a very singular species, for which the author uses the name "absurd".'[41] The expression 'empire of signs' comes from Sartre's *What is Literature?*[42] Later on, Barthes could draw on the Sartre's texts on Genet and Baudelaire as the model of essays that lay at the crossroads of knowledge and fiction. *Camera Lucida* takes so many ideas from Sartre's *The Psychology of Imagination* that it would be tedious to enumerate them all. In short, Barthes incorporated Sartre.

What was assimilated, admired, adopted was a style of discourse. Sartre's power, for Barthes, lay in the invention of a new style of essay, 'which has left a mark in the history of French intellectuality'.[43] This style is direct and suggestive, it mingles thought with literary form. It has the same quality that Barthes too wished to give everything he did: it was seductive. 'No sooner has Sartre suggested an idea that this idea seduces, at any rate seduces *me*.'[44] By pulling philosophy away from its academic language and, as it were, secularizing thought, Sartre placed it back in the *polis* which it should never have left.

An invitation to the imaginary

As with Gide, then, it was only belatedly that Barthes could acknowledge the role played by Sartre, at a time when it could be expressed in terms of affect. 'I like Sartre', he stated in his self-portrait. In January 1977, he announced to his audience at the Collège de France a forthcoming seminar on Sartre.[45] While there may have been a skilful covering up of Sartre's influence in certain texts, we cannot say, as certain critics have claimed, that there was a betrayal here. It then becomes much more interesting to understand the closeness of the two men than to point out the way they occasionally differed. There is much too widespread a tendency, for example, to contrast the way they wrote their autobiographies, the one in a constructivist, narrative, totalizing way, the other more dilapidated and fragmentary. This is to forget how Sartre made a radical innovation in the genre of autobiography, and to dismiss a little too easily the text's intensely critical and demystificatory character. *Words* was a moment of quest and inquest, and aimed to be not merely a reflexive self-examination, but the search for a completely new fusion of the philosophical and the narrative. It still involved working against codes and genres – a process that Barthes appreciated and which authorized him to try something similar. The vacancy left by the absence of a super-ego was a powerful invitation to the imaginary, understood as projection and as certainty. The affirmation of a subjectivity becomes more important than any peremptory assertion, and this evolution involves Sartre. The gap between Barthes and Sartre was bridged with the dedication of Barthes's 1980 *Camera Lucida* to Sartre's *The Imaginary*, which at that time Barthes viewed as a magnificent book. So, at the end, Barthes encountered the Sartre of the beginnings who had been active in phenomenology, where 'I sense', 'I feel' is more important than 'I think', or at least precedes it. 'I see, I feel, hence I notice, I observe, and I think.'[46] Even if Barthes's phenomenology was vague and even, as he claimed, casual, the relations between the subject and the world were again extremely mobile and it was the singularity of experience that counted above all else. Thought, the scientific project, had really and truly taken refuge in the imaginary. They corresponded to the project of a *mathesis singularis*, a science of singularities as set out in *Roland Barthes by Roland Barthes* and above all in *Lecture*: all sciences are present in literature, but in a shifting, unstable form: '[L]iterature, in this truly encyclopedic respect, displaces the various kinds of knowledge, does not fix or fetishize any of them; it gives them an indirect place, and this indirection is precious.'[47] The encyclopaedic dream was, in Barthes, based on movement – and for this dream he would seek forms throughout his life: an encyclopaedia that was forever relaunching the interplay of different kinds of knowledge, placing them within 'the machinery of infinite reflexivity'[48] and staging them in writing.

Here too we find a closeness to Sartre. In this singular project for an encyclopaedia, Barthes owed a great deal to the Roquentin of *Nausea* and his desire to see things clearly, to say, as he did, 'how I see this table, this street, the people, my packet of tobacco' (this reminds us of the oranges of Werther or the tobacco of Michelet); he shares the autodidact's mania for classification, always going over and rearranging things. Like him, he set out his knowledge in alphabetical order, the order of the library – but he turns it into a 'farce', like the encyclopaedia of Flaubert's *Bouvard and Pécuchet*. Here, language achieves autonomy, resisting the intimidation of natural language by becoming matter and savour. Hence the family resemblance that brings together Proust, Sartre and Barthes. Proust: 'Words present us with clear and familiar little pictures of things, like the pictures hung on the walls of schools'.[49] Sartre: '[E]ach word has its own physiognomy [...] the physiognomy of the word becomes representative of that of the object.'[50] Barthes: 'I have a disease; I *see* language.'[51] What Barthes mainly owes to Roquentin is the sense, both disturbing and exultant, of floating, of no longer coinciding with himself. And to the Poulou of *Words* he owed the unpleasant impression of wearing masks. Thus, *Camera Lucida*, which quotes Sartre at length, and with proper quotation marks, appears as a synthesis of all that Barthes owed Sartre and that enabled him to assume his own positions.

It then becomes possible to maintain that Barthes extended a path that Sartre had opened up in the relation between literature and thought. By dint of thinking along the lines of literature, they invented a form of essay halfway between the novel and the treatise, in which writing, instead of fixing the argument, opens it up to a world as huge, as utopian, even, as the world of novels. Thus they reinvented the essay by turning it into the site of a dreamy, enthused, personal language, 'where writing and analysis compete'. Far from philological modesty, from the stiffness of academic language that not only advances wearing a mask but is protected by all kinds of scholarly and rhetorical armour, this third form, often disdained by academia, did however have two merits: it liberated rationality, and it affirmed the force of literature for the operations of thought.

In tandem with philosophical discourse, but in a form and a procedure that were completely the opposite, the discourse of the novel (always in the process of being made, always being written) proposed another language, much more unstable than that of theory but possessing a truth that the times needed: Barthes and Sartre had realized that a place had to be given to the fleeting, to the neutral, to what undermines systems and large-scale oppositions (and may correspond to a certain idea of the novel). The opening gesture of *Nausea* thus appears as an absolute stroke of genius, since nausea is almost exactly the novel, its formless form. Everything that falls away, no longer holds, is transformed and liquefies, the taste of ashes on a Sunday, the colours that twist and turn, the vague movements, everything that from moment to moment dilutes or crumbles, is the sign of contingency and the ephemeral character of states of being. 'It flows through me, more or less quickly, and I don't fix anything, I just let it go. Most of the time, because of their failure to fasten on to words, my thoughts remain misty and nebulous. They assume vague, amusing shapes and are then swallowed up: I promptly forget them.'[52] *Nausea* is the story of this shift from the positive discourse of theory to the negative, privative discourse of the novel.

From this, Barthes took the idea of the incident, the fantasy of an immediate but ephemeral relation to the real, to the being-there of things, which writing can convey without any connotation: a sort of obviousness of the real that seizes the person writing and, without transition, fetches up in the text. The remarks on the haiku in *The Preparation of the Novel*, following the suggestions he had made about them in *Empire of Signs*, make the haiku the exemplary way of noting the present. In the haiku, the weather 'brings the subject's *feeling-being* into play, the pure and mysterious sensation of life'.[53] There is a present of sensation, of the sense of being in the world, of the passing of time and the weather, of history and meteorology, that 'unsticks' the pieces and helps to turn form into something unformed.

Thus his reading of Sartre was an important stage on Barthes's path towards the Neutral, one that he followed throughout his career.[54] The degree zero of the neutral was not the neither/nor, the flabby in-between of the petty bourgeois golden mean, it was a Janus-faced term, able to destabilize the doxa and bring about the advent of a new type of meaning that registers all that is indeterminate. The Neutral can be reached thanks to a certain form of availability and openness to the world granted by intermediate states, hypnagogic states that favour co-presence without stabilizing meaning: nausea in Sartre, going to sleep in Proust, the *hupar* or gentle ecstasy in Barthes, the subtle intoxication, the 'great clear-eyed dream' that allows one to experience variations of intensity. In all cases, there is a yearning movement towards something elusive or impossible, a pursuit of something that one immediately sees vanishing.

A singular equation of intelligence and sensibility brought Barthes close to Sartre and even today means that there are similarities between their oeuvres. This encounter, an intellectual encounter, was of historic importance. It gave rise to two major changes in the history of thought: a profound change in the modes of interpretation, which Barthes would take up and develop as the result of an initial dialogue with Sartre; and a new form of critical activity thanks to its shift towards writing, what Todorov has called the 'bridge between prose and criticism', the corollary of which is a conception of theory as fiction. The 'transformation of discursive writing' which brings the critic closer to being a writer, as Barthes wrote in *Criticism and Truth*,[55] marks the beginning of a period in which a real social significance is granted to critical thinking informed by literature, to critical thinking as literature. The philosophical fiction proposed by Sartre, the various kinds of writing that he deployed, opened the way. As Barthes said, looking back: 'To some extent, theory is also a fiction and it was always in this guise that it tempted me: theory is, as it were, the novel that people enjoyed writing over the last ten years.'[56] Theory, like the novel, opens up possible worlds.

Letter from Roland Barthes
to Jean-Paul Sartre,
7 December 1955.

In the office.

Grand fichier, index card from
19 July 1979.

9

Scenes

The second half of the 1950s saw Barthes deploying his energy across several scenes. First there was, of course, the concrete scene of the theatre, which he no longer experienced as an actor, but as a spectator and a critic. Then there was the literary scene on which his role was extending and becoming more established, with the result that he was turning into a major interlocutor. Finally, there was the scene of a struggle in and with language, at a time when he was engaged on several fronts, sometimes using his own words as weapons, able to be directed against language in their turn.

Barthes analysed the terms 'scene' or 'stage' on several occasions: in every case, he was referring less to the space of theatrical representation than to the war between languages. His mistrust and indeed fear of language became apparent. 'If scenes have such a repercussion for him, it is because they lay bare the cancer of language. Language is impotent to close language – that is what the scene says.'[1] This remark is linked to the hatred of language demonstrated by the avant-gardes, according to Jean Paulhan's 1936 work *Les Fleurs de Tarbes* (*The Flowers of Tarbes*) (though it is not certain that Barthes read this).[2] Theatre forces the scene to come to an end, and thereby inflicts a salutary violence on the violence of language itself: this was perhaps a reason for the passion that Barthes felt for theatre at this time; theatre was in some degree a response to language itself. This was the topic of the first seminar at the Collège de France, 'Tenir un discours' ('Holding a discourse'), in 1977, in which Barthes analysed the discourse of the Baron de Charlus in *The Guermantes Way*: the words of the other unleash a wave of emotion that makes the dialogue border on insult: words are like the lashes of a whip.[3] At the same period, in his discussion of the 'scene' as a lovers' quarrel in *A Lover's Discourse*, Barthes developed a link between scene and mastery. The desire to have the last word, the will to conclude, are ways of hammering meaning out: '[I]n the space of speech, the one who comes last occupies a sovereign position, held, according to an established privilege, by professors, presidents, judges, confessors: every language combat (the *machia* of the Sophists, the *disputatio* of the Scholastics) seeks to gain possession of this position; by the last word, I will disorganize, "liquidate" the adversary, inflicting upon him a (narcissistically) mortal wound, cornering him in silence, castrating him of all speech.'[4] Conversely, the person who does not wish at all costs to conclude imposes an anti-heroic ethic on himself or herself: this is the ethic of Abraham, consenting to sacrifice without uttering a word; it is the ethic of the Zen master who, faced with the question, 'What is Buddha?', replies by taking off his sandal, placing it on his head and walking away; it is the ethic of all those who prefer non-mastery to mastery. This position, to which Barthes tended all his life long, was, however, one that was still not being clearly affirmed in the 1950s. His critical and political commitments, as we shall see, sometimes led him to seek confrontation, to get involved in quarrels and to experience the violence of language directly.

Liquidations

With the publication of his *Michelet* in the collection 'Écrivains de toujours' of Éditions du Seuil, Barthes brought to an end his years of solitary companionship with that historian, and thus liquidated his past as an anonymous and isolated figure. The work had been commissioned from him by Francis Jeanson when the article in *Esprit* had been published in April 1951: in the light of what were his current interests, the book could now appear a 'belated' work,[5] as Éric Marty puts it, a text from a previous era in his life, and its insistence on the closure of Michelet's work echoes the context in which Barthes had read and thought about it. Later, he would say at the colloque de Cerisy that *Michelet* was 'the book of mine that I can put up with most easily and that people discuss the least';[6] it thus comes across as the synthesis and end product of several elements of what had been set in place in the course of the previous years, both in terms of Barthes's ambitions and in terms of interpretation and methods. Barthes's attachment to this encyclopaedic oeuvre was of benefit to him on four levels. The first thing he drew from it was that it enabled him to cross disciplines. Michelet's oeuvre made it possible for him to emerge from the exclusive terrain of literature and open up to the full range of the human sciences. By publishing *Writing Degree Zero* and *Michelet* within just a few months of each other, Barthes presented an image of himself as a non-specialist, something he viewed as a distinct advantage. In notes that he made with a view to a later rereading, he acknowledged that this was something he owed to Michelet: 'Just as an ethnologist doing field work must, as he starts to study a particular community, turn himself into an archaeologist, a linguist, a botanist, a geographer, an aesthetician, etc., likewise with Michelet, faced with the world, history, the body, you have to become everything all at once.'[7] The fact that he had been immersed in the work of a historian for several years favoured this intellectual openness, while convincing Barthes that problems always needed to be connected to history. Thus it was Michelet, with his desire to write a history of the labouring classes, those without a voice, who led Barthes to Marx (initially to his analyses of the French Revolution) and to historical materialism: this meant that Michelet continued to exert his influence during this period.

The second thing Barthes drew from his reading of Michelet was a certain kind of critical writing. By giving sustained attention to the sensual aspects of the work, readable in the titles given to the fragments – 'Michelet provided me with a mine, a prodigious quantity of *sensual objects*: flint, fish, swan, pebble, goat, camellia, ogive, hole, heart, flame, etc. In fact, it was *essentially* this that I saw and loved in him' – by emphasizing the categories of the sensory world (the dry, the smooth, the acrid and the sopitive, the warm), he worked out a thematic and effective critique for which Michelet himself had provided the template. 'In Michelet's work, there is a critical reality independent of the idea, of the influence, and of the image: it is the theme.'[8] These themes (words or images brought together in a network) imply a specific reading grid based on lists, and on the highlighting of a system of values. This programme for a thematic critique was indeed greeted warmly on the book's publication. Albert Béguin and Jean Starobinski were enthusiastic, and Gaston Bachelard, the most illustrious representative of this type of criticism at the time, sent Barthes some flattering comments. Barthes had probably read Bachelard's analysis of Michelet's *La Mer* (*The Sea*) in his *Water and Dreams*, first published in French (as *L'Eau et les rêves*) by José Corti in 1942. 'In your work,' wrote Bachelard, 'the Detail becomes Depth. Your technique of creating illumination in bursts of light penetrates into the depths of being. You do not need the thread of history to maintain the continuity of being. The themes are so aptly chosen that the relief reveals the intimate ideas. You have just serenely written a great book. I am telling you this just as serenely.'[9] Starobinski wrote: 'This, indeed, is the way that criticism needs to proceed. [. . .] Don't give up thematic research!'[10] It is a subjective form of criticism, though Barthes did not project himself into it entirely. As in every gesture of appropriation, there were obviously thematic hooks, such as the 'migraines' with which the work began, drawing the critic and his subject together in their relations with the body, but there was also the recognition of critical writing as a stylistics of the gap: the nerviness, the exacerbated sensibility of Michelet did not coincide with

Barthes's own quest for neutrality. In fact, for that very reason, the migraines could become the place to draw a distinction: 'So different from Michelet's migraines, "amalgams of bewilderment and nausea," my migraines are matte. To have a (never very strong) headache is for me a way of rendering my body opaque, stubborn, thick, *fallen*, which is to say, ultimately (back to the major theme) *neutral*.'[11] This retrospective differentiation was not just a way of reducing their shared space. It was a way of stating that the self-knowledge granted by the literature of ideas is not the product of a parasitical activity but of the grasping of a difference. There is perhaps another reference to *Nausea* here and to the character of Anny, built up out of the illustrated edition of Michelet's *History of France*. The consistency sought in the figure of Michelet, in a refusal to separate his strictly historical works and his other writings as is generally done, does of course involve this critical appropriation in which self-interpretation and the interpretation of the other overlap.[12] But very early on, Barthes had transformed into theory certain existential observations that might possibly link him to Michelet via Sartre. An intimate reflection on mood, in his letters to Robert David, was expressed in philosophical and psychological terms. These observations, inspired by his reading of Sartre's *The Age of Reason*, in 1945 in Leysin, see mood as 'the contemporary form of ancient fate' which makes tomorrow different from today, with one night being enough 'to make something that had been built in enthusiasm collapse into nausea'.[13] It contrasts with the passion of the classical view and is presented as the 'driving force of the philosophies of the hour, of the novels of Sartre, of the days lived by Barthes'. The countless variations it entails, which create moments of opacity, lines of convergence, but also illuminations, need to be read in the texts of others, but also encourage us to read each person as a text. It is 'the *total* inner being, belly and brain, moving *totally* through time.'[14] This is how the book was written, in a two-way journey between text and body, in an effort to theorize his intimate life while situating himself at the very heart of the text. In this respect, it prefigures the works of the 1970s and links the beginning of Barthes's career to its end.

   Michelet's third contribution was methodological. The collection 'Écrivains de toujours' gave room, as its format dictated, to a large number of texts by Michelet. Thus, each chapter is based on alternating quotation and analysis, which correspond almost term by term with subtle variants. The anthological nature of this and other works was far from being a constraint for Barthes. It removed his fear of having to compose long texts and allowed him to apply the index card method, both fragmentary and theatrical, to the book. The flexible and non-authoritarian nature of the fragment was echoed by the pinpointing of a feature or an image in the form of a tableau or a scene. 'Bloodletting', 'Woman humiliated', 'Marriage of skin and silk', 'The hair of a woman': each entry is the caption to a painting or the subtitle to a display. This method makes literature very lively and visual. It can be connected to Barthes's need to have photographic aids when he was working. As early as 1945, he was asking Robert David to send him a photograph of Michelet and he was extremely touched to receive his portrait by Nadar; he immediately placed it on his desk, where he could see Michelet, his hand thrust into his frock coat, watching over his work with an air at once benevolent and haughty.[15]

The last of Michelet's contributions was stylistic. In this book, Barthes cultivates assertion: the syntactic order subject-verb, the indicative mode, the phrase 'it is' (*c'est*), an emphatic assertion modalized by adverbial phrases, such as 'in other words', 'evidently', 'in short', the binary structure that saturates the space ('both/and', 'neither/nor', 'either/or') . . . The discourse stages and frames itself. For example, the fragment entitled 'Michelet the walker' begins: 'How does Michelet eat History? He "grazes" on it; i.e., he passes over it and at the same time he swallows it.'[16] All the elements of a discourse of knowledge are present: question, answer, assertion, development, understanding. We can also see how Barthes stages this discourse of knowledge. First, he uses a capital letter, which really is the trade mark of style in this text, as Jean-Claude Milner has noted: Barthes does not use the conceptual capital letter proper to philosophical discourse (as when he writes History with a capital), but he brings these concepts into relation with ordinary sensations that are also subjected to a capital letter: '[. . .] the Wet, the Dry, etc., so that the more usual capital letters (Woman, France, Robespierre) were affected by this and in turn inflicted with the mark of an uncanny strangeness.'[17] Thus he offsets assertion with a use of figurative language: the animalization of Michelet's relation to history is suggested by the verb 'to graze', itself placed in quotation marks, which is a way of underlining it and at the same time distancing oneself from it. And so we can see that what is being produced is a highly characteristic kind of writing, one that is apparently extremely authoritarian until you look more closely, when you discover that it is very mistrustful of expressions of truth, and displays a gap, preferring images, fantasies and reverie: a kind of writing that is endeavouring to be different from what it seems to be. By struggling against the authority of language itself, Barthes sometimes adds an extra dimension of stiffness to his expression. But – and we will have occasion to come back to this, so great is his desire to mark all of his writings with the wish to bend the arrogance of the assertive mode – he always contrasts this to figures of withdrawal, of delicacy.

Proceeding by means of a collage of fragments in *Michelet*, Barthes is already introducing a 'weakness' within the discourse that

is meant to reduce the affirmation of a particular thesis. The way he
wrote in the manuscript version, lightening the discourse as he went,
shows the same desire. He wrote on skin paper or on the reverse
side of ministerial forms (expenditure memos, a form for foreigners
residing in France, purchase orders and so on). Here is an example
of stylistic reduction: for the first paragraph, the manuscript has:
'*I need to inform* the reader *in all honesty*, he will find neither a
history of Michelet's thought nor a history of his life – still less an
explanation of the former by the latter, *and in short, nothing about
his "psychology"*.'[18] The beginning and the end (italicized here) are
suppressed in the final version.[19] This makes the remarks firmer,
but also more uncertain and more veiled. The book erases any hint
of pedagogy. It prefers to insist on the organic power of Michelet's
work, its materiality, its sensuality, the way it sticks closely to
material things. The omnipresence of the body reminds us of the circumstances in which Barthes read Michelet's complete works in the
sanatorium. All of this creates an intensely vivid and poetic portrait
of the historian, but does not sum him up in a few easily understandable key words. This may be why the work met with a chilly
reception in the literary reviews when it came out. Robert Coiplet,
in *Le Monde*, and Robert Kemp, in *Le Figaro*, openly mocked
Barthes's method. But friends came to his aid. Bernard Dort forcefully pointed out the strengths of *Michelet* in *Critique*.[20] And Albert
Béguin defended Barthes against his detractors in issue 215 of
Esprit: 'Barthes's originality appears only to an attentive reading,
and seems to have eluded those whom his book has scandalized as a
profanation or a piece of indiscreet curiosity.'[21] Far from it, he continued: this method, which the author modestly calls 'pre-criticism',
is an innovative kind of inquiry, well suited to showing what historical discourse usually conceals: moods, reiterations, fantasies. The
private letters to Barthes were also very positive, even if his method
sometimes caused surprise. Michel Vinaver concluded his words of
praise with a few ambiguous remarks: 'You've done too much for
him [Michelet] to escape. This is a book that I read the way you
watch a battle. It was really exciting.' But Jean Genet, whom he had
met at the home of Marguerite Duras, wrote to him in a clearer,
albeit equally lyric style, that he had felt, as he read the book, as if he
had been 'swimming back upstream not just through the moods and
the blood of Michelet but also through the moods and the blood
of history'. In particular, Barthes won the recognition of historians
thanks to the article by Lucien Febvre in *Combat*: though Febvre
very gently rebuked him for not having devoted sufficient attention
to Gabriel Monod's book on Michelet, and had reservations about
the idea of Michelet's 'lesbianism', his praise was very warm: 'How
well he puts things, and sees things clearly! How well he has been
nourished, well nourished, on the best of Michelet. How he judges

from within, and no longer from without! How he loves and understands the life in Michelet, and Michelet through life!'[22]

The years 1953–54 were also marked by several deaths: that of
Dr Brissaud who had taken such good care of him throughout
the time he was suffering from TB, a death that Barthes felt more
deeply than he might have expected; and, something that had more
of a material impact on him, the death of his maternal grandmother
Noémie Révelin, who passed away in August 1953 at the age of
81. At the time, Barthes was again in Holland, staying with Pierre
Guiraud, where this time he had gone with his mother. The news
brought him hurrying back to Paris and forced him to tie up his
grandmother's affairs – money, and movable and immovable assets.
His grandmother's last years had been overshadowed by the death
in 1945 of her youngest son, Étienne, whom she had had with her
second husband and who was just a few years older than Roland.
Even though Barthes was not particularly fond of her, he did see
her on a regular basis, and in particular her difficulties and her
health problems, at the end of her life, had been a major worry for
Henriette Barthes. The inheritance was a complicated matter. His
mother and his uncle, Philippe Binger, who lived in Canada, inherited the family foundry in Lorraine, as well as the house in Hendaye.
The apartment in the place du Panthéon in Paris did not belong
to the Révelins but they hoped to buy it as a good investment.
With this in mind, they moved into the apartment in October, 'so as
to increase the chances of having this apartment, which would be a
magnificent bargaining counter'.[23] It was here that Barthes put the
final touches to the manuscript of *Michelet*, a number of the pages
of which have the heading of his grandmother's address: 1, place du
Panthéon (Paris, Ve).

The inheritance was the promise of a better life, freed from the
money worries in which Barthes had felt entangled ever since he had
left the sanatorium. His bursary from the CNRS was not enough to
ensure the rent and to feed three people. He agreed to teach a course
on French civilization for foreign students at the Sorbonne, and was
given several allowances by the journals to which he contributed,
but not enough to free him completely. So his grandmother's death
was a significant turning-point in his personal life, giving him a
wider margin for expenses, less guilt towards his mother, and less to
complain about. 'The sole aim', he wrote in September to Philippe
Rebeyrol, 'is of course to ensure that Maman can have a comfortable life, without getting tired. So the first thing we want to do is to
increase the size of our accommodation.' After some highly complex
procedures, which the letters to Philippe show (it was Philippe's
uncle, Pierre Rebeyrol, who executed the will), the foundry was
sold, the apartment in the place du Panthéon was leased out, and
the Barthes could now buy the fifth-floor apartment in the rue

Servandoni as well as an attic room on the top floor. For the first time in Paris, Barthes now had a separate office (which he always just called his 'room'), in which he could receive guests and lead a freer life. Later on, once Michel Salzedo had married Rachel and after they had been living together all this time in a somewhat difficult but overall happy period, Barthes would rent a second-floor apartment into which he moved with his mother in 1976 when the latter started to succumb to illness. In October 1960, he had a trapdoor made which enabled his office to communicate with his mother's apartment (in 1964, Guy Le Clec'h was already turning this way of organizing things into a little legend in *Le Figaro littéraire*: 'He raises a trapdoor made in the floor of his room. He goes down a few steps, comes back with his coat, and we leave the cabin in which some of the most captivating ideas of the last few years are being developed').[24] While Barthes often had lunch with his mother, he went out almost every evening, to the theatre or to dine with friends, and his possession of a separate place ensured the harmonious functioning of this protocol. He placed his desk up against the wall, at right angles to one of the two windows, and set on it his stationery, the books he was using at the particular moment of his work, photographs, reproductions of paintings, and post cards. 'This space is the same everywhere, patiently adapted to the pleasure of painting, writing, sorting.'[25] There was a certain accumulation of things, but no mess: the obsession with having everything in the right place was tangible. His schedule was organized in line with urgent tasks, but also followed a division into four sectors which he used as shown in *The Preparation of the Novel*: '(1) The part for Basic Needs: eating, sleeping, washing (already cultural!). (2) Part for creative Labor: the book (the Course? yes, but it's already less creative than the real writing, that of the book). (3) Part for Administration: letter-writing, manuscripts, *writings*, the inevitable interviews, proof corrections, shopping (hairdresser's!), private views and friends' films. (4) Sociality, Conviviality, Friendship. All that, as reduced, as restricted, as one could make it. Over 24 hours: ten hours given over to Basic Needs, four to conviviality (for example, the evenings), five to creative work, five to administration.'[26] In the 1950s, the time devoted to management was less occupied by replying to requests entailed by his own fame than by the activities made necessary by having to earn a living and long letters to and from friends, but the actual way these activities were divided up stayed more or less the same.

So Barthes worked on an increasing number of projects. Following the publication of *Writing Degree Zero*, which met with what was, for a first book, considerable critical attention, he was invited to Britain for a series of lectures in London, Manchester and Edinburgh. He set off with two different papers to deliver, one on the language of literature and the other on theatre. He recycled some of his articles in them. He was already saying he felt awkward at the 'false genre of the lecture',[27] which would become a leitmotif right up to the caption to one of the photos in his self-portrait: 'Distress: lecturing'.[28] But it gave him a chance to travel, which was a major compensation, as he always felt in good spirits when abroad, surrounded by languages that he did not understand or only half-understood, but whose music he could hear, the rustle – other signs than those of language. He travelled a great deal in the course of those years. In May 1953, he had been to Spain with Cayrol, to an old fort transformed into a comfortable place to stay in Pasajes on the Basque coast; then he had been to Holland with his mother and now, finally, to Britain. In the following years, he travelled in France, to the home of Michel Vinaver on the shores of the Lac d'Annecy, to Avignon (for the festival) and several times to Italy. He started to make intellectual connections there that would assume great importance in the following period. He went back to England to take part in BBC broadcasts in the spring of 1954, living with Jean-Pierre Richard and his wife Lucie (the younger daughter of Lucien Febvre), who at the time had a position in London and had been introduced to Barthes by Sirinelli. He very often stayed in Hendaye in the house bequeathed to him by his grandmother, the Villa Etchetoa, which now struck him as a pleasant place. It has to be said that this imposing house, built in the 1930s by the architect Edmond Durandeau, was not without a certain allure, with its external balcony running along the two sides most open to the outside, and overlooking the sea.

He enjoyed intense friendships. Apart from those he struck up in relation to theatre, one of the most significant at this period was his friendship with Violette Morin. This intelligent, eccentric woman, two years his junior, had preserved from her native region, the Dordogne (she was born Violette Chapellaubeau in 1917 in Hautefort), a strong South-Western accent, which made her not just a contemporary of Barthes, but a fellow-countrywoman. She was studying philosophy in Toulouse when Jankélévitch, whose classes she was following with admiration, was banned from teaching by the Vichy regime in 1940. She organized a demonstration in the streets and it was on this occasion that shed met Edgar Nahoum, later known as Edgar Morin, alongside whom she became an active communist and then joined the Resistance network of the Mouvement national des prisonniers de guerre et déportés (MNPGD; National Movement of Prisoners of War and Deportees). After the Liberation, they married and for a while lived at the home of Marguerite Duras, Robert Antelme and Dionys Mascolo in the rue Saint-Benoît in Paris, where, according to the biographer of Edgar Morin, Barthes first met them at the end of the 1940s.[29] He grew close to them; they were both involved with projects in the sociology of communication. In 1954, Barthes read Edgar Morin's *L'Homme et la mort* (*Man and Death*) and wrote to him from Hendaye on 12 August 1954 to tell him how much he admired the work. But it was actually Violette to whom he felt most attuned: with her he had a sustained and deep friendship. Although her career had been more traditional than his (she had passed the *agrégation* in philosophy), her personality meant that she did not just follow the usual well-worn paths. Her passion for Jankévélitch was contagious and, as the latter had also come to Paris after the Liberation, she took Barthes to his apartment on the Quai aux Fleurs where they could share their love of music and the piano (even if Jankélévitch no longer listened to German music, so that they could not talk about Schumann or romantic music). She was interested in two subjects that were marginal and innovative for that period: eroticism, on which she would publish a book in 1965,[30] and humour and jokes, in which she would become a real specialist, working in particular on the functions of the comic in mass communications.[31] Barthes introduced her to Greimas, whose schema of the 'semiotic square' she would apply to funny stories. In her turn, she encouraged Barthes in his plan to write 'mythologies': she had views that converged with his when it came to the way the death of Édith Piaf and other subjects were treated. They shared a liking for neologism and writing, that could also be read in her texts – she invented, in an article on humorous drawings published in *Communications*, the verb '*disjoncter*' ('to disjunct'), which went on to enjoy great success. They would remain close until the end of their lives, and went to the cinema together at least once a week throughout the 1960s. When she separated from her husband, Barthes often visited her in her apartment in the rue Soufflot, where she lived with her daughters, Véronique and Irène. His engagement diaries for 1962–63 often have the note 'Irène lesson', indicating that he gave the younger daughter a hand with her work.

Violette Morin and Barthes, together with Edgar Morin, were involved in many of the new projects of that period. They took part in the venture of *Arguments*, a review founded by Edgar Morin in 1956 at the Éditions de Minuit with a 'post-Marxist' outlook (which was necessary after the terrible shock of the Hungarian crisis), including a heterodox set of ideas and clearly marking the new importance of the social sciences. They exchanged views with Franco Fortini, Jean Duvignaud, Colette Audry, François Fejtö and Dionys Mascolo. In the first issue there was an article by Fortini on Auerbach's *Mimesis*, another by Greimas (brought in by Barthes) on the book by Marcel Cohen, a great specialist in Semitic and Hamito-Semitic languages called *Pour une sociologie du langage* (*For a sociology of language*). Barthes's piece was on the 'tasks of Brechtean criticism', with a programme at the crossroads between sociology, ideology, semiology and ethics.[32] The history of this review, designed to be a free space for intellectuals who, apart from Barthes,[33] had all been supporters of communism and had now left the movement, also proves the existence of links between personal life and thought. The review was presented as a bulletin and stayed, right up to the end, a very home-made enterprise to which everyone gave a hand; '*Arguments* affirmed itself as a group-in-fusion both in its rapid and friendly formation and in its lucid and brutal dispersion. So it comes as no surprise that it lived by the sword – a double-edged sword, as is usual with this kind of group: a great communion of thought, of action, of situation, but also a muddled exaltation that smoothed over antagonisms and admitted that it had been vanquished by the heaviness of institutions',[34] which finally brought the endeavour to a close in 1962. But the venture proves that, at this time, Barthes managed to live his intellectual and political positions collectively, even if only for brief periods.

Finally, in the extremely interventionist if somewhat uncertain activities of those years, Barthes also took part in the creation of CECMAS, the Centre d'études des communications de masse (Centre for Studying Mass Communication) at the École pratique de hautes études, directed by Georges Friedmann.[35] Barthes, already associated with the work of the Centre d'études sociologiques since 1956 (witness a report of the management committee),[36] contributed regularly to the work of CECMAS throughout the 1960s, attending seminars and meetings, and was also close to Olivier Burgelin. Violette Morin remembered that time and the part Barthes played in it with precision; she narrates it in a text written as a homage upon the death of Friedmann: 'It was in 1959, on a sunny June morning. Gathered on the terrace of his apartment, shaken and transfixed by that optimistic clear-sighted attitude that sometimes gave him, slipping from under his heavy eyelid, the prying laugh of a teenager, there were four of us listening to him as he laid out the sociological scope of our future work: Paul Lazarsfeld, Roland Barthes, Edgar Morin and me. It is with some emotion that, hearing his voice, I bring together again those four people, all "present", whose names he liked to chant rhythmically, as a memory that had survived battles, a memory from a forest clearing. He enjoined us, there and then, not to leave it all to the Americans when it came to assessing the significance of audio-visual media and to refine those well-known analyses of content of which the school of Berelson had provided the first models. That morning, everything was promised as already a fait accompli.'[37] Finally, Barthes also played a role in setting up the review *Communications* in 1961, as well as the plan for an 'international review' under the aegis of Blanchot, to which we shall return.

As Barthes had not completed the lexicological project on which he had embarked, the CNRS did not renew his bursary in 1954. So he thought seriously about abandoning this work on vocabulary that he had started with Georges Matoré, with whom his relationship had grown distinctly chillier in 1954 – 'something has gone wrong since my book which visibly got on his nerves; he thought it was really badly written, while I find it increasingly difficult to believe in the pallid aspect of his sociology, which pretends to be innovative but actually goes back more or less to that Théodule Ribot whose ideas were set out for us by the sinister and criminal Milhaud (criminal because he taught us philosophy so poorly).'[38] And he toyed with the idea of registering yet a third subject for a thesis, on theatre or fashion. He made contact with André Martinet; yet again, it was Greimas who organized the encounter. Many years later, having distanced himself from Martinet, Greimas narrated this first encounter. Barthes wanted to work on fashion and asked the linguist what the most significant aspect would be. Martinet apparently said 'the legs', while Barthes thought, no doubt correctly, that 'the scarf' expressed much more meaning.[39] The semiotics that the two friends from Alexandria wished to promote was here already coming up against a programme that had little room for literature. It was finally in Friedmann's sociology laboratory, which left more room for his method and his demystifying way of looking at objects, that Barthes would seek to register his new subject of research, fashion writing; and a new bursary was granted him the following year. Meanwhile, he needed to find a means of subsistence and Robert Voisin, the director of Éditions de l'Arche, offered him a position as literary adviser for his publishing house on the rue Saint-André-des-Arts, which he accepted, and not just for financial reasons: this job perfectly suited his activities in drama criticism.

Now that he was a recognized critic, Barthes was in great demand from journals and reviews, especially after the publication of the first 'mythologies': the one on all-in wrestling, in *Esprit* in October 1952 made him extremely well known and earned him several letters of admiration. As well as *France Observateur*, where he was given a monthly drama column, the *Lettres nouvelles* that Nadeau had just set up and to which Barthes sent his subsequent 'mythologies' for publication, under the title 'little mythology of the month', and *Esprit* to which he continued to work on a regular basis, he was asked to write for *Les Temps modernes* and *La Nouvelle Revue française*. When Paulhan told him in 1953 that it would be very good if his 'name could appear frequently, next year, on the contents page of the *NRF*'[40] and offered him a rate of 2,000 francs per page, Barthes sent him nothing; when Marcel Arland pressed him the following year to provide articles for *La Nouvelle NRF*, he was obliged to reply that, as long as his situation at the CNRS was not clear and his membership of the sociology section was not definite, he could not take on any new tasks. The rough draft of this letter bears these words, later crossed out: 'I set my wish to embark on a real sociological work before any other task and *I will not feel free towards literature before I have exhausted all possibilities of gaining the support of the CNRS, which at present makes sacrifices of time necessary.*'[41] This obviously shows a desire for social recognition, but also the feeling that the shaping of a real work involves length and duration, something that the brevity and immediacy of most of his productions contradict. This was also the time of the venture represented by *Théâtre populaire*, which both ate into his time and was very exciting: this would occupy most of his time between 1954 and 1960.

Theatre

'At the crossroads of the entire oeuvre, perhaps the Theater.'[42]

Barthes's involvement in theatre life was admittedly the extension of a passion that went back to his teenage years, but it was also the characteristic of a whole era and his desire to play a role in it. We need to remember the importance of the theatre in those years, the extraordinary ferment of the dramas that were staged, and the privileged relationship between art and politics in the theatre. While the memory of the 'cartel' of actors (Louis Jouvet, Charles Dullin, Gaston Baty and Georges Pitoëff) was still vivid, and some of its members still active, more important was the innovative movement headed by Jean Vilar at the Palais de Chaillot, where he was appointed in 1951 and to which he gave the name Théâtre national populaire (TNP), and in Avignon where he had been director of the festival since 1948. At that time, theatre played a social role that is difficult to imagine these days: in twelve years, Chaillot sold 5,193,895 seats, i.e. an average of 2,336 spectators per performance! Thus, Barthes acknowledged 'the sociological scope' of Vilar's activity; 'thanks to Vilar's experiment, theatre is tending to become a great popular leisure activity, just like cinema and football'.[43] But he credited him with even more than that: Vilar had brought about a complete aesthetic transformation. 'Today, when people talk about the Vilar saga', writes the dramaturg Brigitte Jaques-Wajeman, 'they mainly insist on the social revolution that his theatre entailed. They forget about the aesthetic revolution he achieved, which made all the rest possible: a new perception of the crucial issues and perhaps even the function of the theatre. Vilar lays bare the space of the stage, and in Barthes's view this was a new basis: he empties it, he strips it of all decoration, of everything that *glues* things together, *clagging* the gaze and the mind of the spectator. [. . .] Once the decor has been abolished, the space finally opens up and Barthes applauds "the birth of a clear space in which everything can finally be understood outside a blind patch in which everything is still ambiguous."[44] So Barthes found in the theatre what he would later find in the novels of Robbe-Grillet, namely, a veritable critical space, a form able to show the social sphere and to transform it, a politically committed form that presented itself to the intellectual of that time as a real place for his own activity.

It was within this context that the review *Théâtre populaire* was founded to support Vilar's efforts, but also to promote the invention of a drama criticism that would be on the same high level as these efforts, fearing neither to impose difficult texts (the publication of complete texts of French or foreign works, such as Maturin and Büchner, were examples of this) nor to arouse displeasure by voicing sharp criticism that could be intransigent and at times unjust. The editorial committee brought together first Morvan Lebesque, Guy Dumur and Roland Barthes (for the first issue), all chosen by Robert Voisin on the basis of their atypical careers and their public commitment to the TNP,[45] as demonstrated by Barthes in *Les Lettres nouvelles* on the occasion of Vilar's production of *Prince Friedrich of Homburg*. For the second issue, they were joined by Jean Paris, Jean Duvignaud and Bernard Dort, with whom Barthes struck up a friendship. In May 1953, the editorial of the first issue, mainly composed by Morvan Lebesque and Barthes, attacked the established theatre, or what they called the 'bourgeois theatre', albeit without any precise ideological tendency. The review's stated vocation was thus to 'shed on works the light that suits them: in short, to inform, to provide the explanation that Art bears within itself but does not express, since there is between it and us a difference of language'. At that time, their ambition as review writers was as critical and aesthetic as it was political. Jean Duvignaud remembers that it was at that time that there appeared in their discussions the term 'theatricality', echoing the intuitions of Artaud in *The Theatre and its Double*. 'This theatricality', says Duvignaud, 'was something that we saw as immersed in the social and the public. To the dazzling postulations of the poet we gave a root in those audiences that we did not really know at that time and to which, sometimes, with a certain naivety, we gave the same conscious innocence that the Law gives to the "jury".'[46] Their political commitment led them to take an interest in new forms of stage writing, such as Roger Blin, Jean-Marie Serreau, Roger Planchon, the 'Théâtre des Nations' led by Claude Planson at the Théâtre Sarah-Bernhardt, which presented foreign troupes of actors, and, in particular, the works of those who had gone into exile from Weimar to America and now returned

(Piscator, Brecht). This is where the theoretical and political idea defended by Barthes, one that lay at the basis of the creation of the review, involving a theatre placed at the service of social critique, found its real illustration. The ideological issues were more clearly stated and the combat was aimed at the indifferent – those who did not like the theatre or did not go to the theatre needed to be told that it was the political and civic art of the time – and at the 'consumers' of theatre as mere entertainment.

The story of Barthes's involvement with the review *Théâtre populaire* was his clearest experience of belonging to a certain generation, with the idea that art can intervene in history and that this intervention needs to be made as part of a community, on the one hand, and in conflict with one's elders on the other. It was necessary to envisage a solidary, reconciled society able to appreciate a purification of the theatre capable of attaining a bareness, a 'degree zero', which the plays of Adamov, Beckett and Ionesco seemed to achieve, getting rid of psychology and denuding the space of the stage. The members of the review generally agreed, but not on all aspects of the theatre, and there was no lack of internal conflicts. Marco Consolini, in his thoroughly well-documented book on *Théâtre populaire*, narrates these divergences amongst collaborators on the review who did not meet regularly, and were content just to read each other's work.[47] Dumur liked Giraudoux, whom Barthes loathed; he was interested in Jules Roy, whom Barthes said he mistrusted 'because all that Boy Scout war stuff always leads finally to fascism';[48] and they were equally ambiguous about Claudel. On the other hand, Dort took the same editorial line as Barthes in his much more committed positions against theatre spectators who influenced a market aimed mainly at 'consumption'. His article 'Un théâtre sans public, des publics sans théâtre' ('A theatre without audience, audiences without a theatre'), published in issue 3 of the review in December 1953, shifted the line to a directly political tendency, necessitating what Barthes, in *Les Lettres nouvelles* of 1953, called a 'total critique'.[49] This radicalization was even more evident in the editorial of issue 5, January–February 1955, this time written by Barthes, where he attacks bourgeois theatre with considerable violence: 'The general complacency towards bourgeois theatre at present is so great that our task can initially only be destructive. We cannot define the Théâtre Populaire except as a theatre purified of bourgeois structures, de-alienated from money and its masks. So it is our opposition that needs to be highlighted first and foremost. This opposition has great ambitions and will not get bogged down in nuances.'[50] The vehemence of this diatribe led to Guy Dumur distancing himself, and Morvan Lebesque even more so: his disagreement with Barthes came to a head shortly after on the occasion of the Barthes–Camus polemic.

Gradually, Voisin, Barthes and Dort managed to make themselves the sole leaders and it was their positions that were defended. This did not fail to create ripples in their milieu. It has to be said that they represented a hard-line stance and their attacks were scathing. Gérard Philipe, who at first had met with their approval, was lambasted for his stereotypical depiction of the role of Richard II: 'Behind the *embourgeoisement* of Philipe, a whole party is lying in wait, that of mediocrity and illusion. These are vast forces that need only the tiniest crack to force their gangrene in.'[51] This slating did admittedly appear in *Les Lettres nouvelles*, but it was revelatory of the passionate and polemical tone that Barthes employed when discussing theatre, where every detail caught his attention: costumes and curtains, actors and critics, the repertoire and the young actors. There was of course a strategy at stake here, in the massive occupation of a space in which he could ensure his own visibility, but there was also an intense conviction, at the crossroads of the aesthetic and the political, that made this time in his life particularly dynamic: his Marxist views lost no opportunity for finding expression, and he was decidedly pleased to find himself taking part in the ruckus.

From 1954 to 1963, Barthes wrote eighty articles or reviews of plays that he published in twenty-two different journals, including some fifty or so in *Théâtre populaire* and *France Observateur*. Most of these articles were written before 1960 and discussed almost all of Jean Vilar's productions (*Richard II*, *Ruy Blas*, *Macbeth*, *Le Triomphe de l'amour*, *Le Faiseur*). Not all of these were lauded to the skies. Other productions discussed were those of Roger Planchon, Jean-Louis Barrault (he, too, was not always defended by *Théâtre populaire*), and Raymond Hermantier. Barthes's pieces were almost always written in the tone of social critique advocated by the review, even when they were published in other journals. These very numerous interventions were marked by the reiteration of his passion for Brecht, every time an opportunity arose.

The discovery of Brecht was, of course, 'capital', as it replaced the Sartrian model with a new way of describing the relation between literature and political commitment. It allowed Barthes to affirm two powerful trends in his thinking: Marxism, through the idea of a responsibility of form; and structuralism, through an investigation on the distancing effect of signs. If the performance of *Mother Courage* in June 1954 had 'set him on fire', as he told Jean-José Marchand in the 1970 television interview, and as he again stated to Jean-Jacques Brochier in 1975,[52] this was the result of an alliance between responsibility and pleasure in which he recognized the thought: 'His exemplarity, in my eyes, derives in truth neither from his Marxism nor from his aesthetics (even though both have great importance), but from the conjunction of the two: i.e. from the conjunction of a Marxist reasoning and a semantic form of thinking: he was a Marxist who had reflected on the *effects of the sign*: and this is rare.'[53] This 'bedazzlement' (a word taken from his *Michelet* and used again in 'Théâtre capital') was a conversion that was simultaneously individual and collective. Barthes appreciated the extreme clarity of Brecht's endeavour: he found reasons in it for which the theatre was the true art of the time, and also the reasons for a combat. For *Théâtre populaire*, this 1954 production would be, as it were, the most important performance right until the end. 'The review finally found its real identity in it. The whole team experienced this performance as a revelation and this shock led to a black-out as regards the rest of the Festival.'[54] In 1957, Barthes again insisted on this extraordinary clarity: 'When I saw the Berliner Ensemble production of *Mutter Courage*, in 1954, I realized clearly (with a clarity that did not, of course, exclude a vivid impression of beauty and, in a word, a profound emotion), I realized that there was a responsibility of dramatic forms.'[55] The play also presents the figure of a heroic mother, which added a strong, private resonance to the encounter.

The first article, on the visit of the Berliner Ensemble to Paris and the performances of *Mutter Courage*, was published in *France Observateur*, where Nadeau, who had run the literary supplement since leaving *Combat*, had given Barthes a drama column. This article, called 'Théâtre capital', was published on 8 July 1954 and ascribed to Brecht four major revolutionary qualities: his was a theatre of liberation, a political theatre, a justified theatre and a disorientating theatre. Barthes contrasted it with retrograde theatre, in other places called 'fat theatre', which consecrates the existing order with complicity and insistence; but he also contrasted it with a certain progressive theatre, which displayed its thesis too explicitly without allowing the spectator's consciousness to free itself. By detaching the spectator from the play, by placing objects at a distance, the play effectively prepares him or her for the operation of demystification. A fortnight later, on 22 July, Barthes published a new article on Brecht, this time on the acting style and the dramaturgy of distance. In the meanwhile, he had read Brecht's critical texts and assimilated the importance for Brecht of what he had learned from the codifications of the oriental theatre, far removed from any ontology. He knew he had followed the master class given by Mei Lanfang in Moscow in 1935, in the company of Eisenstein and Stanislavski, and had at the same time discovered Shklovski's principle of defamiliarization (*ostranenie*), to which the theory of the alienation effect owed a great deal. Barthes referred to the Noh theatre of Japan to convey the abstraction necessary to the actor.

In 1955, finally, an article for *Tribune étudiante* mentioned the three lessons to be remembered from Brecht. First, the art of theatre is not addressed solely to the senses, but needs to be thought intellectually. Second, the political needs to elicit its own dramatic form. And finally, commitment in the theatre must be total. So Brecht is inviting us to de-alienate both the repertory and the technique of theatre. The articles that followed discussed French productions of Brecht, including that of *Man for Man* by Jean-Marie Serreau at the Théâtre de l'Oeuvre, whose efforts Barthes praised though he criticized the 'climate of approximation', incompatible in his view with the rigour that Brecht's theatre required, and Roger Planchon's production of *Fear and Misery of the Third Reich* at the Théâtre de Lyon. Barthes also wrote about every appearance made by the Berliner Ensemble on French soil. He produced no fewer than twelve articles on Brecht in three years: this was an enterprise of general monitoring. By publishing work on Brecht in very different journals, he extended both Brecht's terrain and his own. By stating that this was a veritably political theatre, the one that was in a position to forge a link back to Greek tragedy and its force for intervention in history, he was also affirming himself as a political critic.

At the same time, as literary director of the Éditions de l'Arche, Barthes published in several volumes an edition of Brecht's *Complete Theatre*. The publishing house had agreed to do so via Gérard Philipe who wanted to put on plays by young authors and not just the repertory, to publish all the texts of productions from Vilar to Chaillot. This represented a great contribution to spreading Brecht's work, with Barthes's help. Robert Voisin and Barthes decided to implement an editorial campaign of both advertising and propaganda. They published the texts in the form of small volumes, including three plays, each volume being led by a 'catalyst' play such as *Mother Courage, The Caucasian Chalk Circle, The Life of Galileo, Mr Puntila and his Man Matti*, etc. At the same time, L'Arche published, in its collection 'Les Grands Dramaturges', Geneviève Serreau's essay on Brecht, and *Théâtre populaire* devoted the whole of its issue number 11 to it, discussing Brecht's break with the past in revolutionary terms, a break with twenty-four centuries of Aristotelian theatre being viewed as 'natural'. The editorial was not signed, but it was largely written by Barthes and aroused significant negative reactions in theatrical circles as well in the group that ran the review, causing Jean Paris and then Jean Duvignaud to leave. Shortly afterwards, in 1956, Morvan Lebesque settled the score in *Carrefour*, using his review of Ionesco's *L'Impromptu de l'Alma* to write a kind of pamphlet against *Théâtre populaire*, in which he presented himself under his own name, assailed by three doctors, Bartolomeus I, II and III, who try to get him to write an acceptable theatre – the two first dictating the gospel of Brecht to him and the third the good news of boulevard theatre. Lebesque wrote: '*Théâtre populaire* is a review which, originally, was simply meant to respond to the curiosities of a public of theatre-goers, enthusiastic for the work of Vilar. Two young Marxist doctors, MM. Roland Barthes and Bernard Dort, turned it into the instrument of a particular doctrine [. . .]. The group became a sect, and before long a Church: *Outside Brecht, no salvation*. Rites, excommunications, liturgical formulae (the social *gestus*, *theatricality, demystification, historicity* . . .), it was all there.'[56] As we can see, the disagreements were intense and were expressed openly in an arena where every verbal position adopted was a joust and every stance a combat.

Dogmatism was, of course, a feature of those years: both a generational posture and an engine able to drive a review forward. Indeed, Barthes had written, in the editorial of issue 9 in September 1954, that 'our "dogmatism" simply means that we judge our task to be clear and our aim evident [. . .] To struggle on every front and view contemporary bourgeois theatre as the object of a total investigation. And if this investigation sometimes assumes a somewhat over-dogmatic form in the eyes of some people, may they forgive us, but understand us too: the bourgeois theatre is well defended, one cannot fight it with half measures.'[57] It can be interesting to try and see more precisely what Barthes's attitude and behaviour in the meetings of the review may have been. Since this was one of his most intense generational experiences, the most significant since his adolescence, this makes it possible to say something about his relation to the collective. Michel Vinaver refers to his anti-establishment spirit, his sense of the festive: 'There was an iconoclastic attitude due, in my opinion, to Barthes's personality. Barthes rejoiced in that violence that was the source of intellectual energy; this was part of the perpetual festival represented by the review.'[58] Other eye-witness accounts insist on Barthes's firm, tranquil authority and his non-hysterical way of imposing his point of view. Relating to Marco Consolini the way committee meetings went, Pierre Trotignon referred to Bernard Dort with his trenchant positions and his sense of persuasion, contrasting these with Barthes's much more reserved posture: 'He would stand next to the radiator, for example, by the window, with a somewhat Buddha-like smile, listening to the arguments, and then he would intervene with a gentle voice, very gently . . . He was very cunning, as he would let Dort speak, let him go on, and then at the last minute, when the others couldn't agree . . . Vannier for example wouldn't agree . . . he would intervene in a few quite gentle phrases, rubbing his hands, uttering two or three opinions that finally settled the matter.'[59] The game the two men, Barthes and Dort, played was certainly very well honed, given the friendship between the two men, and it explains how they managed to dominate the editorial committee for several years.

For those years of theatre were very productive of friendships. They marked, indeed, the start of Barthes's relations with younger men, an inclination he would maintain subsequently. He intensified his strong relations with certain people, especially Bernard Dort and Michel Vinaver. The first, Bernard Dort, had been born in 1929 to a family of junior school teachers and went to Paris in 1945. He lost his mother at the age of 10 and, during his years at boarding school at the lycée in Auch, he read omnivorously and fostered several passions – for theatre, opera, cinema and literature. While studying law in Paris, he started to write for journals such as the *Cahiers du Sud* and *Les Temps modernes* in which he defended the same authors as Barthes (especially Cayrol and Camus), and which appreciated his encyclopaedic knowledge as well as his anti-establishment intelligence, capable of strokes of brilliance, wild enthusiasms and real revelations. Indeed, it was he who first enabled Barthes to discover Robbe-Grillet for the first time: Dort published two articles on the latter's *The Erasers* in 1954, before Barthes published his own piece in *Critique*. The following year, they both went on to publish an article on *The Voyeur*. Dort passed the competitive exam to enter the École nationale d'administration in 1951 and became an administrator at the Ministry of Health in 1953, while continuing to write about literature, opera and cinema. But his real passion was theatre, of which he was one of the best critics of his day (he stayed at *Théâtre populaire* until it closed in 1964 and, in its wake, founded the review *Travail théâtral*), which enabled him to quit his job in the Ministry in 1962, after defending a thesis on Brecht, and to take up teaching posts at the Institut d'études théâtrales and then at the Conservatoire. He made such an impact on this milieu for forty years that he is still a major reference point in it. He was extremely hard-working, and wrote for countless journals and reviews, while publishing important books, such as *Lecture de Brecht. Pédagogie et forme épique* (*Reading Brecht. Pedagogy and epic form*)[60] and *Théâtre réel* (*Real theatre*).[61] Barthes and he met at *France Observateur* for which they were both writing, and they were already friends when they went to the performance of *Mother Courage* in 1954. They both attended the full dress rehearsals of plays and when, after the show, they went to have dinner and smoke a cigar, they were usually in agreement. Their homosexuality was another point in common, as they had no family obligations.

Dort's extrovert and fiery personality, always drawn to the avant-garde, identifying it almost before it actually existed, made a good match for Barthes's more reserved but sharp mind, his desire to play his part in history and not miss out on his time. Their intelligences were similar in that they mistrusted ready-made ideas, acquired positions. They preferred the fragility of nascent structures and movements – Dort would also be a fervent supporter of the Nouvelle Vague when it started – to anything more established, of whatever kind. Dort, a singular intellectual, as his biographer describes him,[62] chose to devote himself resolutely to the spreading and transmission of ideas, while Barthes, who wished to experiment with ideas in varied territories, would always keep more time for his own thinking. They grew apart when Barthes stopped going to the theatre and practically gave up intervening in that area, but continued to follow each other's work, meeting up from time to time to dine together, roughly once or twice a year in the 1960s. However, we can here see the first inklings of a characteristic feature in Barthes's relation with his male friends. His friendships were marked by rapid and intense enthusiasms that enjoyed a phase of exaltation in which it sometimes happened that he would see his friend every day, as was the case with Dort in 1954–55. Then, other urgent demands on his time came along and the relationship grew more distant, which was sometimes felt as a real blow by Barthes's friend. Dort said that he felt some resentment at his treatment by Barthes, or at least a sense of nostalgia. Nonetheless, the friendship was not broken and it was a particular trait in Barthes that he could make enthusiasm compatible with loyalty, even if things sometimes changed over time. So even if we can give several intellectual reasons for Barthes's gradual disaffection with theatre, there is still a more psychological reason that was his need for discovery, for change, his fear of repetition and boredom, that made him regularly shift his ground.

At this time, it was his encounter with Michel Foucault that seemed to stir things up. When they were together in Paris, which was rare (Foucault was then pursuing a career abroad, in Sweden, Poland and Germany), they met up every other evening; they would go to watch the all-in wrestling matches, and have a drink, often with other friends, such as Robert Mauzi who had met Foucault at the Fondation Thiers and introduced him to Barthes, and especially Louis Lepage. Between 1955 and 1965, if we are to believe Foucault, who was talking to Jacques Chancel for the 'Radioscopie' programme in 1975, they were very important for one another, both as friends and on the intellectual level, 'at a time when he was alone too', according to Foucault, in other words in a context where their theoretical propositions were not yet unanimously accepted.[63]

With Michel Vinaver, born in 1927, Barthes developed a very different friendship, made up less of companionship and evenings out together than of mutual admiration and trust. Vinaver had been born in Paris to Russian parents, with the name Michel Grinberg. He volunteered at a very young age in the Second World War, went to the United States for the first part of his higher education, and then came to France where Albert Camus published his first novel *Lataume*, with the Éditions Gallimard. His itinerary was altogether unusual in that he would produce a literary oeuvre while pursuing a very brilliant career as a businessman. He found a job with the Gillette company, whose CEO he became after barely ten years,

while also producing a considerable amount of writing, almost all
of it for the theatre, from 1955. His meeting with Barthes, at the
very beginning of the 1950s, had a decisive impact on this development. Barthes had already asked him to join *Théâtre populaire* when
Vinaver, who had published a few articles for the review, was doing
a course in amateur drama at Annecy during the summer of 1955
under the direction of Gabriel Monnet. The latter suggested that
he write a play for him. This was to be *Aujourd'hui, ou les Coréens*
(*Today, or the Koreans*), later just called *Les Coréens*: Barthes followed its composition and it owed a great deal to their discussion
on the creation of a political theatre that would not be a theatre of
propaganda.[64] The play was certainly politically committed: barely
three years after the Korean War, it brought together on stage two
antagonistic discourses, that of a group of French volunteers and
that of a small peasant community from North Korea. Produced at
the height of the Algerian War by Roger Planchon in Lyon in 1956
and then by Jean-Marie Serreau in Paris in 1957, it aroused considerable interest, both from the supporters of independence and from
those on the other side (Gabriel Monnet was not given permission
to put it on during his summer course in Annecy as it was judged
to be so subversive). It also caused debate within the journal, with
Barthes involved in a direct polemic with André Gisselbrecht. While
the latter felt that Brecht's lesson had not been sufficiently learned,
Barthes celebrated the freshness of its language and its powers of
demystification, comparing it with Chaplin.[65] Vinaver went on
to write a new play in 1957, *Les Huissiers* (*The Bailiffs*), on the
Algerian War: this mixed the hollow language of political discourse
with dramatic episodes from the war. Here too, Barthes followed
his work attentively, giving him advice while he was writing it, for
example on how to 'find some means of creating the impression of
the Algerian gaol [. . .] without swelling it in phraseological terms'.[66]
Later, Vinaver would state that this proximity in work, the fact that
he had Barthes as his first reader, had been decisive. In Vinaver,
Barthes found a true intellectual interlocutor and, in his work, 'the
elements of a truly new form of criticism'.[67] Vinaver admired in
Barthes an unfailing sense of adventure that always drove him to
take his work further. When *S/Z* was published, Vinaver described
to Barthes what seemed to comprise the heart of the bond between
them: 'What happens here is an emergence. The recognition of a
continuity of the adventure (in your work), deployed beyond what
I might have imagined, and also of a continuity (between you and
me) in what arouses interest, with the same shudder and the same
laughter, or smile.'[68] Their correspondence is also proof of a friendship that remained strong and true, but the halting of the venture
of *Théâtre populaire* brought their close collaboration to an end. As
with Dort, a very intense bond was brutally stretched (and this was

Barthes's doing). Michel Vinaver was saddened by what he felt to be a form of abandonment.

Barthes turned the theatre into the main space for political commitment, the focus for a total critique. The shift away from the Sartre he had drawn on in *Writing Degree Zero*, from the writer's responsibility to the responsibility of form, did not, therefore, have any direct impact on his own behaviour as a man who stated positions clearly, who defended tooth and nail what he recognized to be right and just in political and ethical terms, deploying an unparalleled energy to change the behaviour of the audience and even what was being written, both in the area of criticism and in that of dramaturgy. Apart from the fact that it demanded a great deal of time and involvement, this position was the corollary of a conviction and of a desire: art could have an impact in the social field, and nowhere better than in the theatre did it express this impact in those years. That is why, among all the explanations that have been put forward for his disaffection – Brecht had 'swept everything else away', different personal commitments had supplanted this particular one, the Algerian War intervened – the most interesting seems to be the one suggested by Philippe Roger: de Gaulle and Malraux had recuperated alternative theatre and used it in the service of state policy.[69] In his last 'little mythology', published in *Les Lettres nouvelles* in April 1959 after *Mythologies* had come out as a book, Barthes waxed ironical about Malraux's reform that espoused the language of revolution while relying on 'a specious causality [. . .]: we want things to change, and that is why we won't be changing anything'.[70] There was admittedly an element of social project at work in the reform, but it addressed a contemporary myth, that of Youth, instead of concerning the world and its potential transformation. The second thing Barthes took from those years marked by his passion for theatre was a stylistic feature that might be called a tendency to 'pin things down' in the double sense of defining them and exhibiting them for critical inspection. This was the opposite of 'sticking things up' like a poster, a piece of advertising, a sign displayed: it was necessary to use incisive language that would militate against 'common sense'.

Barthes's militant stance is evident in the language he uses, in a threefold capacity to spot something, seize it in a witty turn of phrase and hold it up for all to see. One example: 'Three concurrent obligations [. . .]: a mass audience, a high-cultural repertoire, and an avant-garde dramaturgy.'[71] Or: 'The broadening of the theatre audience should at no time be the fruit of charity; quite the opposite – it needs to be the sign of a democracy without fraud.'[72] On Maria Casarès: 'One needs to commit one's face, one's whole face, to the theatrical venture.'[73] On the critic Jean-Jacques Gautier, whom he detested: 'That man isn't a critic, he's an automatic barrier: enter, don't enter; the choice has been dictated right from the start and nothing can change it.'[74] Whether Barthes's critical remarks are positive or negative, they are clear, assertive and well defined; he is pinning something down so as to state his position. As well as pinning things down, he is also pinning them up – cutting them out, exhibiting them, sticking them on the wall like a picture or a piece of paper. It is interesting in this respect to emphasize that part of Barthes's interest in the theatre shifted to photography – the two interests overlap in *Mythologies*. The last article he wrote on Brecht focused on the photos taken by Pic of the second performance of *Mother Courage* by the Berliner Ensemble in 1957. Barthes noted that the most valuable aspect of this series, and of photography in general, was that photography reveals 'exactly what is swept away by the performance', namely the detail.[75] It was on this detail that his attention as a semiologist would fasten, but it was as a militant that he had uncovered the detail itself. The other shift, from theatre to photography, marked a movement from duration to the instant, from history to intimacy, but this journey would take a good ten years or so to accomplish in full. Let us just say that we can here see the first phase of this movement.

One last strength of the years of Barthes's engagement with theatre lies in its expression of the collective. Barthes was involved in every endeavour and his influence spread across the whole intellectual field: in several areas, it seemed that he was an indispensable presence. His contribution involved a full if nuanced participation, an affirmation without violence in spite of the high stakes involved in the arguments of the day and the polemics that brought criticism alive. This can be illustrated by his highly enlightening interpretation of the concept of the *Verfremdungseffekt*, the 'alienation effect' that he called '*distancement*' or 'distancing', and that acted as a slogan, drawing a distinction between rival sects, between 'crusaders and heretics', as Geneviève Serreau recalls.[76] For Barthes, 'to distance something is to perform it', an idea that doubtless came to him from his intense feeling of inner distance from everything. This was also evident in his relation to the cinema of the following decade, for example the *Chronique d'un été* of Rouch and Morin, the making of which Barthes followed. Barthes was now at home in his period, in the *Zeitgeist*: he did not follow it in every respect, but he did reveal it, from a distance.

The year 1955

The 1950s were not just a time when Barthes saw the most stage performances. They were also those when he 'staged' himself, where he saw the literary scene as a great theatre. The year 1955 was exemplary from this point of view: he was at the heart of three debates in which he unhesitatingly played a part, performing a role as a fully engaged actor. In the course of that extremely prolific and active year – he published no fewer than forty critical articles – there was, first of all, in January, the very negative article he wrote on *The Plague* that led to a polemic with Camus; then, in the spring, the lively exchange with Jean Guérin (alias Jean Paulhan); finally, in the autumn, the passionate defence of *Nekrassov* against its detractors. These three episodes are significant and need to be interpreted correctly. They are not, as is often claimed, evidence just of the versatility or opportunism of the main role Barthes played in them, but bear witness to a complex inner debate touching on his philosophical relation to Marxism and, at the same time, the way he thought about literature.

As we have seen, in those years Barthes believed that political action in the theatre was legitimate. He had more doubts about the effectiveness of literature in its other forms and he doggedly tried to think how this might come about. The article against Camus needs to be read with this idea in mind. *Writing Degree Zero* had already evinced a hesitation, uneasy and sometimes obscure (being sometimes contradictory) between responsible literature and impossible literature. Since that time, he had seen Camus as the spokesman for the only type of literature possible, namely a literature that was not reconciled with the world and its languages: at that time, Barthes relied on stylistic analysis alone, using it as a means of revealing formal features. In 1954, he showed that Camus's *The Stranger* could be read in a different way. In *Club*, he published an article with the title '*L'Étranger*, roman solaire' ('*The Stranger*, a solar novel'). This time, he insisted on the text's lyricism and linked it to a solar myth that provided it not only with an ethic, but a 'humour' or basic mood too (he was here using the same vocabulary as Michelet). Where, in his 1944 article, Barthes had mainly perceived the silence in the novel, he could now describe its symbolism: this, in his view, explained why the novel was already a classic.

In 1955, everything changed again. Barthes criticized *The Plague* for its symbolism, though he had praised precisely this feature in 1954 in his second look at *The Stranger*: this had been a time when he seemed to be defending it from Sartre and the work's other detractors on *Les Temps modernes* after the extremely painful breach between Sartre and Camus in 1952. When Barthes wrote that he could see in the work 'a lyricism that would probably have been criticized less in Camus's later works if it had been at least glimpsed it in his first novel',[77] he was not addressing this criticism to himself but to those who had slated *The Plague* two years earlier. But how, then, are we to interpret the article on *The Plague* that was published in the same journal, *Club*, less than a year later? Was this, as is sometimes claimed, a U-turn? Should it be seen as a need to go with the flow and join all those who were 'liquidating' Camus? It is true that, at this date, Barthes felt closer to Sartre than to Camus. Furthermore, a discussion of *The Plague* in 1955 was not exactly anything new (the novel had been published in 1947) – unless, yet again, Barthes wished to contribute to the polemic at *Les Temps modernes*. So we can see it as a pretext. And this pretext, for Barthes, marked a desire to understand the posture of an intellectual rather than to attack a book. True, Barthes as a critic rebukes Camus for rejecting both history and tragedy; he thinks that Camus's symbolism debars engagement with real struggles and prevents him from supplying a 'reflective political content' that alone would be able to combat historical injustices. But he also acknowledges the book's beauty and states that the effects of generalization induced by the symbol make the text even more emotionally powerful.

In actual fact, Barthes is arguing with himself in this text: he finds a certain grandeur in Camus's withdrawal, even though he thinks that forms of commitment are necessary. When he reduces his judgement of the book to a judgement of Camus as a person, it is easy to see that Barthes, who was so involved with these debates at the time, defending – thanks to theatre – the intellectual's need to explain history, is asserting his own position as against that of Camus. '*The Plague* has opened up for its author a career of solitude; the work may be born from an awareness of History but it does not seek its evidence from History and prefers to turn lucidity into a moral lesson; it is the same impetus that has led its author, the foremost witness of our present History, to an ultimate rejection of the compromises – but also the solidarity – of his combat.'[78] The formulation here is ambiguous. True, Barthes's choice is clear: he wants to encourage solidarity. But Camus's posture is understandable ('rejection of the compromises') and his solitude is perhaps desirable. So there is no U-turn here. Barthes is attempting to solve an aesthetic problem – what can literature do these days? what form must it take? – and he will soon find answers in Robbe-Grillet, realizing that Camus had brought the novel to a theoretical dead-end. He is also trying to solve the moral problem of the roles of writer and critic in the social arena and of his avowed support for Marxist principles. Here too, Camus's solution did not strike Barthes as the correct one. Nonetheless, he was tactful enough to address his criticism to Camus before publishing it and the journal printed Camus's reply (dated by the latter 11 January 1955) in the same issue as the article, with Barthes's agreement. In a letter of 13 January 1955, Camus expressed his gratitude: '[M. Carlier] has told me that you are in agreement and I would like to thank you for being so generous – experience has taught me that this is something one doesn't often come across.'[79]

The other positions Barthes adopted in 1955 were of the same tenor: he was asserting his intellectual commitments, but again with more intense conviction. Camus's reply was astute and picked on the 'contradictions' in Barthes's article. On the aesthetic level, Camus did not understand how what had been a strength in *The Stranger* was being criticized in *The Plague*, when he had merely moved towards a greater sense of the collective and of solidarity; as for symbolism, his reply was that he did not believe in realism in art. On the political level, he swept away with a stroke of his pen the criticism that his work was ahistorical, and asked Barthes to say in the name of what superior ethic he was rejecting what Camus thought was the perfectly explicit ethic set forth in his novel. Barthes's reply to Camus's reply, which was published in *Club*'s April issue at the explicit request of Camus, stated his 'solutions' more clearly: he was defending a 'literal literature' (recalling Sartre's view that 'the function of a writer is to call a spade a spade'[80]) and expressing, for once literally, his Marxism. 'You ask me to say in the name of what do I find the ethic of *The Plague* inadequate. I make no secret of the fact, it is in the name of historical materialism: in my view, an ethic of explanation is more complete than an ethic of expression.'[81] And he added an argument that was meant to justify him but in fact turned his commitment into a method of analysis more than an allegiance: 'I would have said as much earlier if I was not always afraid of being extremely pretentious by claiming to draw on a method that demands a great deal from its supporters.'

This episode, in which Barthes affirmed his Marxism, encountered another. In the same month, April 1955, Jean Guérin, in *La Nouvelle NRF*, attacked the 'little mythologies of the month'. He referred to four of them and commented on them in his column devoted to reviews and journals, querying Barthes's definition of myth – 'But maybe Barthes will tell us, one day, what is *not* a myth?'[82] – and finally asks the following question, to which Barthes felt he needed to reply in the July–August 1955 issue of *Les Lettres nouvelles*: 'But after all, perhaps M. Roland Barthes is quite simply a Marxist. Why does he not say so?' Barthes took this opportunity to say again that Marxism is above all a method and that it is in this sense that he applies it. But he does so more scathingly, accusing Guérin-Paulhan of McCarthyism and expressing his disdain for labels as being both over-hasty and reductive. Does the literary institution want to pigeon-hole writers so as to grant itself more superiority and freedom? Much good may this do it – but it will not replace the effectiveness of reading. Barthes concluded: 'Thus, I have only to read *La Nouvelle NRF* to recognize its perfectly reactionary character; I do not need any declaration about the matter.'[83]

The third occasion on which Barthes presented himself as a polemical Marxist followed this episode almost immediately.

The new theatrical season was marked by an intense opposition to Sartre's play *Nekrassov* on the part of almost all drama critics, with the exception of Morvan Lebesque (who was in this case on Barthes's side even though he had criticized the latter's attitude to Camus a few months earlier in *Théâtre populaire*) and Henri Magnan in *Combat*. The play was a barely disguised transposition of the Victor Kravchenko affair that had caused a huge stir in the press a few years before, and assumed the characteristics of a fist fight between Communists and anti-Communists. The former viewed Kravchenko as an imposter, while the latter brandished his memoir *I Chose Freedom* as a weapon against Stalinism. Seen with the benefit of hindsight, the debate clearly suggests that the Communists and a great number of French intellectuals were wrong, but in 1955 memories were still vivid of how Kravchenko had successfully sued *Les Lettres françaises* for libel, and there were many reasons for doubt if not for complete certainty: *I Chose Freedom* had been partly written by an American author and we now know that the CIA took advantage of the trial to set up an anti-Communist war machine in France. But Kravchenko's detractors were not shaken in their views by the evidence of Margarete Buber-Neumann, deported by the Stalinist regime to Kazakhstan before being handed over to the Nazis (she was the first, on this occasion, to draw a parallel between the camps of Stalin and Hitler): this suggests a certain blindness of their part. However, in spite of the ruling in Kravchenko's favour, the French Communists gathered a great deal of support for their views.

For Sartre, who had become close to the French Communist Party in 1952, after the arrest of Jacques Duclos,[84] the subject had symbolic significance. He seemed to side with the Communists in his satire against crude anti-Communism, in which the personality of Kravchenko is mentioned in some of the characters' speeches. Be this as it may, the episode was somewhat murky; the fact that Barthes took sides and supported the play suggests clearly that he had something to defend that went beyond his avowed aims. What he was initially opposed to was a conventional, refined and polite conception of 'literature' as 'fine writing'. What he liked in the play – or what he wished to defend in it against its detractors – were its lapses of taste, its badly brought-up feel, and the black-and-white Marxist view of things (which he justified as plausible): yet again, what really made him angry was the bourgeois conception of literature, including its finicky psychological considerations. By launching an attack on the serried ranks of the press and its representatives, criticized by name, from Françoise Giroud to Thierry Maulnier, Barthes was again defending the conception of a criticism that did not place itself at the service of institutions. But behind this, there was above all a reply to Camus (who was himself rebuked in the article) and his rejection of realism: Barthes's view was that bourgeois morality wanted psychology, where politics chose the realism of a general reality, so as to lay bare, for example, the reality of a world in which the government and the mainstream press were in cahoots. The text was militant and unconcerned with subtleties: Barthes was defending a political camp.

And yet it was not altogether *his* camp. Barthes never wanted to be identified with the Communists, or even subjected to the label of being a 'Marxist'. His Marxism was first and foremost a method of reading, a principle of demystification. If he continued to see historical materialism as a guide, a framework for analysis, this was because, like many of his contemporaries, he believed that it was a necessary and unsurpassable horizon. French society was perceived as ossified and the Fourth Republic appeared unable to carry out any profound transformations, bogged down as it was in its colonial policies and by the imbalance within its institutions. Barthes did not like the France in which he was living, and this was also the reason why he intervened. And behind all these commitments lay the burning question: what does it mean to be an intellectual these days? Through the quest for a correct position, the obsession of all those years, we can detect the desire to find an alternative to indoctrination, to Sartre's change of heart and to the isolation of Camus. Although he mistrusted the avant-garde, which could always be recuperated, he still believed in 'the profound revolution of languages and myths', as he defined it in another well-known text from 1955, 'La vaccine de l'avant-garde'.[85] He would prove his conviction in three ways, which together indicate the positive and active direction that Barthes wished to imprint on his interventions: to discover contemporary literature; to denounce colonization; and to pin down the French as they were in his day.

Theatricality

Camus's literary solution had turned out to be a dead end. So Barthes would continue to seek out from contemporary work whatever deserved to be recognized as real literature, in other words as a conscious production capable of meeting the political and aesthetic demands of a society. In the theatre, he found this literature in Beckett, Adamov and Ionesco, who contributed to reflect on the transformations of the stage arts in stripped-down pieces that deployed a new language. For the novel, things were more difficult as, ever since Proust, the most powerful works had always been aimed against themselves, criticizing the programme they had fixed for themselves – the novel as such. In an important article with the title 'Pré-romans' ('Pre-novels'), Barthes indicated for the first time how he envisaged authentic creation in the field of the novel. In Cayrol, Robbe-Grillet and Duvignaud, he could see that the traditional novel had been shattered along with its myth of profundity: psychology and metaphysics had been ousted. Here, Barthes saw that a potential literature lay in a new accommodation of the gaze able to explore surfaces. A few weeks later, he again discussed Cayrol's *L'Espace d'une nuit* (*The Space of a Night*) in *Esprit*: he maintained and reinforced the idea of a novel always yet to come, guided by 'a language which attempts tragically to become a novel'. In Barthes's words: 'Like all of Cayrol's other works, *L'Espace d'une nuit* is a pre-novel, or, if you prefer, a language caught between the image and the rejection of the novel, so that the reader is drawn along after Cayrol in a march along the novel, or towards it, but never within it.'[86] Barthes formulated a highly personal and precise conception of the novel, one in which the novel and criticism were inseparable: this conception would henceforth guide his critical endeavours and his plans for writing. This idea of a literature that always presented itself on the horizon of writing, a literature that was always yet to come, was certainly inspired by Barthes's reading of Blanchot in the early 1950s, when the latter was publishing his major articles in the *NRF* and in *Critique*. It was an idea that definitively separated Barthes from Sartre.

The second way in which Barthes could forcefully state his positions was in his opposition to colonialism. The explicit criticisms he could formulate in the reviews enabled him to be clear, especially in the 'mythologies' published in *Les Lettres nouvelles*: in 'La croisière du Batory' he compared Soviet totalitarianism with colonial totalitarianism; in 'L'usager de la grève' he criticized the way reserve soldiers were called up (and at the same time, in his private life, he gave moral support to Dort who declared that, if he were called up, he would desert); in 'Grammaire africaine', he presented a dense analysis of the 'official vocabulary of African affairs', deciphering the ideology concealed behind the phraseology where such terms as 'war' were used as if metaphorically to hide the fact that a real war was being pursued, or the word 'population', 'a cherished word in bourgeois vocabulary', and an antidote to the term 'class', which was too politicized: the term 'population' was used in the plural, as in 'Muslim populations', which suggested a disparate plurality that needed to be gathered together under France's unifying imperial aegis. After the publication of *Mythologies* in 1958 and 1959, he became even more openly critical. He used an article on Jean Vilar's production of *Ubu* to mock the government's ridiculous protests about the 'pacification in Algeria'. In a new 'mythology', he scathingly denounced the interventions of General Massu's wife and her so-called 'Knitting at home' initiative aimed at Algerian women: here, the critique becomes a powerful, and justified, denunciation,

for 'to claim, in a Moslem country, to liberate its women is surrepti-
tiously to transform the colonial responsibility into an Islamic one,
for it suggests that the Moslem Woman is retarded because she is
subject to a religion it is well known she subserves'.[87] He continued
his deciphering of language by inspecting the phrase 'Algeria is
French' or in his denunciation of the heroic rhetoric of de Gaulle.
Replying to a questionnaire on the regime of General de Gaulle
in 1959, and the need for intellectuals to denounce an authoritarian power, he replied, as always, by resorting to the technique of
demystification, and even suggested opening 'a sort of Bureau
for Mythological Information', [to] replace ethical protests with
analyses of content, of whatever form'.[88]

As we can see, Barthes's commitment was direct and unambigu-
ous. What made it different from the commitments of many of his
contemporaries was the way that it took less the form of a collective
militancy than that of an intensely focused work upon and against
languages. Theatricality appeared on the stage of language. Barthes
extended his programme of denunciation of the bourgeois order to
the doxa as a whole. He thus gradually found the right space for his
own intervention in what he called mythology, in other words in a
deconstruction of myths. This explains why, in comparison with
other commitments of the age, his has remained effective. For while
he denounces surfaces and objects, he simultaneously lays bare the
fundamental operations of language that turn it into a major instrument for power that fosters sclerosis, mendacity and reification.
While *Mythologies* is still Barthes's best-read book these days, this
is not because of the objects it discusses – most of which are now
museum pieces – or at least not solely for these, but for his acute way
of holding them up for inspection, the power of the critique which,
as we have seen, played such an active part in the denunciation of
the Algerian War. Tracking down things that seem natural (but are
not), Barthes hunted down traces, and went beyond merely producing a picture of the life of the French in the 1950s as is often claimed.
(The illustrated edition of the book maybe reduces it a little bit too
much to this aspect.[89]) Instead, he carried out in full the programme
of a critical thinking. Against naturalness, against common sense,
against the way History is forgotten, he sets the intelligibility of
signs.

The enemy is the doxa, the ready-made discourse, the stereotype. The doxa is a key concept in *Mythologies* and refers to the
opinions and prejudices on which everyday communication is
based. By building knowledge on the recognition of what it already
knows, the doxa prevents us from seeing the very same reality that
it carves out of the world in the shape of myth: 'One of our main
sources of servitude: the appalling divorce between mythology and
knowledge. Science follows its path swiftly and surely; but collective

representations do not follow, they are centuries behind, maintained in their stagnant form by power, the media and the values of
order.'[90] The notion of myth is thus the other fundamental concept
of *Mythologies*. The myth is a sign. Its signified is a fragment of
ideology, its signifier can be absolutely anything: 'Every object in
the world can move from a closed, mute existence to an oral state
where it is open to appropriation by society.'[91] The myth converts
the cultural into the natural, history into essence. Barthes finds this
conversion intolerable: 'I suffered from the way, at every moment,
Nature and History became muddled together in our contemporary
narrative, and I wanted to lay bare, in the decorative exposition of
what goes without saying, the ideological misuse that, in my view, lies
concealed within it.'[92] And again, in 'The myth today': 'The world
enters language as a dialectical relation of activities, of human acts:
it emerges from myth as a harmonious display of essences.'[93]

Against the view that things are 'self-evident' – the only real
form of violence, according to the fragment in *Roland Barthes by
Roland Barthes* entitled 'Violence, evidence, Nature' – he presents a
theoretical project combining a Marxist-inspired critique of ideology, a reading of symbols and sensuous qualities (a reading that
he inherited from Bachelard and was already at work in Barthes's
Michelet), and Saussurean semiology. And thus, perhaps more
than the Citroën DS, the Dominici affair, the Tour de France,
the floods along the Seine, Minou Drouet and the evangelist Billy
Graham, more than Poujade, the recipes in *Elle* and the *Blue
Guide*, what counts is Barthes's ability to pin down what is most
material in matter: what is smooth and layered, what is sticky and
pitchy – all those attributes of the doxa that are contradicted by the
discontinuous, astute freedoms of thoughtful writing. The strength
of this method was the result of extensive work. It includes many
cross-references between the articles he wrote on theatre and the
Mythologies. Thus, the text on Maria Casarès refers to the portraits
of the Harcourt studios; 'The world of wrestling' is read through
Greek tragedy, while the 1953 article on the 'Pouvoirs de la tragédie
antique' ('Powers of ancient tragedy') alludes to all-in wrestling. In
particular, the power of Barthes's critique stems from the fact that,
in spite of the violence of his opposition to the doxa, he does not
just condemn it outright. He was a pioneer in media analysis, and
investigated the mass communications that were fostering the new
mechanisms of conformism. He anticipated the coming of the era
of visual communication by showing how powerfully seductive
images could be. He did not set himself up as a superior judge: he
recognized the attraction of myths, their magical effect. But he also
believed in the critical capacity of the spectator, one that counter-
balanced the hypnotizing effect of the mass media. He said as much
in an extremely lucid article in *Communications*, on contemporary

stars such as Soraya, Jackie Kennedy, Brigitte Bardot and Marilyn Monroe. When people claimed that 'an analysis of the press (a structural-type analysis) is infinitely more urgent than interviews for an audience', this was because they feared they might realize that 'turning people into stars is a process that can arouse resistance'; all those people who succumb to the lure of the stars also have an 'acute awareness of the phenomenon, "held at arm's length" by the subject, even when the latter still yields to the charm, in accordance with the best rules of the critical spirit'.[94]

This volume included only texts that had already been published in reviews: it came out in 1957 in the 'Pierres vives' collection, with an advertising strip featuring some of the myths studied in the book. This greatly boosted sales. Jean-Claude Milner was attracted to the book thanks to the portrait of Garbo as Queen Christine on its cover. As for Antoine Compagnon, he said he had bought the book for its picture of the Citroën DS.[95] Barthes made a few changes from the versions published as articles in *Les Lettres nouvelles*, leaving out some things and adding others, but nothing major. He was mainly concerned to free the texts from their circumstantial origins based on a complicity with the reader and the immediate link between mythology and current affairs as conveyed by the ephemeral media of the day (a press article, a photo in a magazine, an exhibition, a film). The most substantial changes were made to the piece on 'Toys' that had been originally called 'L'enfance et ses jouets' ('Childhood and its toys'): he suppressed the somewhat moralizing discourse on adults.[96] More generally, he was not just removing references to the original context, but creating a greater density and generality. The mythologist was talking less about things that really existed than he was uncovering the oblivion on which the myth rested. Just as anyone who drank red wine needed to remember that what he was drinking was also the product of an expropriation (in particular a colonial expropriation), likewise, the critical, demystifying reader needed to de-alienate reality by pulling it out of the amnesia to which it had been relegated, rediscovering history to re-politicize it. In this way, pinning down the myth was also a way of laying it bare in true Enlightenment fashion: Montesquieu pointed out that the people could eat sugar in Europe because of the enslavement of the negroes. The main example in Barthes was also directly political, yet again: in the image of the 'negro saluting the French flag', the myth existed as soon as the French imperial mission appeared 'natural'; if it was recognized or laid bare as an alibi of colonialism, it would destroy itself. The method was extremely effective, presenting the two discourses at the same time, giving the reader the feeling that he was playing a part in the process of elucidation. In this sense, there was indeed a certain theatricality in *Mythologies*, both magnificently comic and at the same time pedagogic – 'It's really a book about spectacles such as Theatre, Posters and Signs', he noted in his index cards.[97] The critic was inviting the reader to see reality in a new way, to scrutinize its culture, its daily habits, the language with which it surrounded him: this would encourage him to mistrust these things, to laugh at them, to keep them at arm's length, to cease being their dupe. He was not denouncing so much as showing, holding something out for inspection, hence the highly successful balance between prescription and description, moral discourse and literature, which makes Barthes akin to the classical moralists and shows that there can be a social and, one might almost say, popular effectiveness in the essay. Thus, by practising writing in the way a theatre producer puts on a play, Barthes gave a political response to the question of the responsibility of form that he had raised in *Writing Degree Zero*. He sold almost 30,000 copies of the book in its first edition, then more than 300,000 when it was reissued in 1970: he had the same impact as Vilar with the theatre, and with this book managed to reach two audiences – and this had a significant effect on the place the human sciences would occupy in the following years.

Barthes became part of the intellectual constellation of the 1950s – and his success was twofold. He became a permanent part of the intellectual scene, where his heterodox but politically committed language gained a significant hearing; he was also already recognized outside this limited milieu. On 29 May 1957, he recorded with Pierre Desgraupes the television programme 'Lecture pour tous' ('Reading for all'), on *Mythologies*, which the interviewer presented as a book accessible to everyone, at least in its first part. Barthes started to get invitations abroad: in summer 1958, he went to the United States as a visiting professor at Middlebury College in Vermont. He travelled by sea, and took advantage of his trip to go to New York and meet Richard Howard, at whose home he would reside regularly thereafter.[98] In particular, the way Barthes placed his intelligence at the service of a quest for the right stance, engaging in many different activities and intervening in various forums, eventually provided him with firm positions to defend, as well as a style. He was now able to put forward a method, to give it a name (semiology), to place it within a paradigm (structuralism) and to ensure that his action was passed on to others.

Introduction:

Michelet mangeur d'Histoire

> "Les hommes de lettres souffrent toujours et n'en vivent pas moins" (M. à Eugène Noël)

Migraines — La maladie de Michelet, c'est la migraine, ce mixte d'éblouissement et de nausée. Tout lui est migraine: le froid, l'orage, le printemps, le vent, l'Histoire qu'il raconte. Cet homme qui a laissé une oeuvre encyclopédique faite d'un discours ininterrompu de soixante volumes, se déclare à tout instant "ébloui, souffrant, faible, vide." Il m'écrit toujours (pendant survivant le six ans de sa vie adulte), et pourtant jamais dans un effarement total. Grands événements dans cette vie: un orage qui oppresse, une pluie qui délivre, l'automne qui revient. Le corps tué par un souffle mal venu, Michelet ne cessa de le déplacer: dès qu'il peut, il voyage, change de pays, se tient à l'affût des conditions de vent et de soleil, s'installe cent fois, déménage autant. Mourant toujours, et le croyant pour de bon, il renaît d'autant plus délicieusement; voyez le à quarante quatre ans: il se sent entrer dans "ce corps supplicié, la vieillesse"; mais retrouvez le six ans plus tard, à cinquante ans: il est en train d'épouser une jeune fille de vingt et commence allègrement une troisième vie. Ce n'est pas tout: après la Femme, les éléments; Michelet connaît encore trois grandes renaissances: la Terre (bains de boue à Acqui près de Turin), l'eau (son

Michelet: manuscript (first page).

Michelet: manuscript (list of Michelet's main themes).

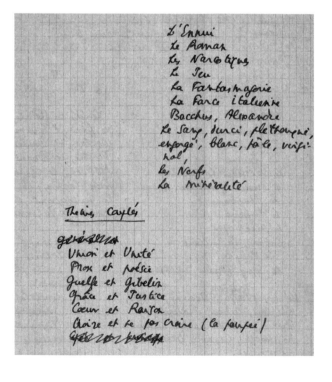

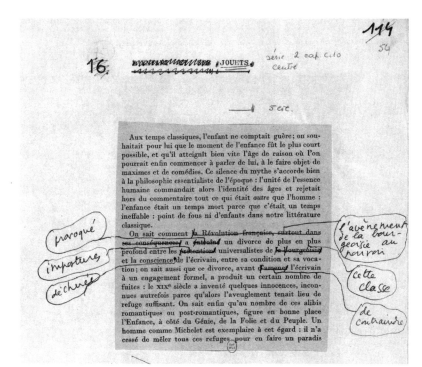

Mythologies: corrections to proofs

Mythologies: corrections to proofs ('Toys').

Villa Etchetoa in Hendaye.

In Middlebury,
Vermont, in 1958.

10

Structures

After the dispersal of the previous period, with its many interventions in very different contexts, and the abundance of short forms used by Barthes, he now seemed to wish for a more stable posture, to settle down into a long piece of work, a work of scholarship. The years 1955–65 marked a period of anticolonialist commitment; they also witnessed the emergence of the notion of structure, which brought together a large number of his intellectual endeavours. Barthes's increasingly secure harbour in the École pratique des hautes études favoured his scientific self-affirmation; a more comfortable material existence provided him with a refuge that fostered his writing.

In an article commissioned by the Yugoslavian review *Politica* in 1959, Barthes made a distinction between two types of literary criticism: 'the criticism of the launchpad', as found in newspapers and reviews (essentially an evaluative criticism or criticism of judgement); and 'the criticism of structure', which connected the work of art with something beyond itself, had a cognitive dimension and was in itself 'a true questioning of literature.'[1] There is no doubt that what he had in mind at the time was to create a critique of structure, to produce a work of scholarship. By the mid-1950s, he was expressing this desire for research leading to a long piece of work: 'I really would like to be shot of all that', he wrote as he was assembling his texts for the volume *Mythologies*; 'to stop being, at least for a while, too much of the intellectual, but just a researcher instead.'[2] And he gave a negative answer to the overwhelming number of requests made of him – for example, Sartre's invitation, after the *Nekrassov* affair, to write a regular column in *Les Temps modernes*: 'I have since been appointed as an attaché at the CNRS (at least for this year) and this, for both administrative and material reasons, means I cannot undertake any new tasks outside of Research.'[3] And so, apart from the period in 1954–55 when Barthes earned a living working for L'Arche, he was an intern at the CNRS from 1952 to 1954, in the lexicology department, then

attaché in the sociology department between 1955 and 1959 (when
he again lost his bursary before being 'picked up' by Fernand
Braudel at the EPHE). The various projects and reports that he
drew up throughout those years in order to present his research led
him to shift his method of studying vocabulary to semiology and
to change the objects of his study, from political language to social
language (fashion first and foremost, but food as well). His mastery
of linguistic tools provided his analyses with a solid framework,
and these were the foundations of what he was striving to turn into
a systematic way of thinking.

So the desire for science was no longer motivated solely by the
search for an institutional base, but rather by the quest for an intellectual order. The conversations with Foucault, who had embarked
on his path-breaking researches into madness (and who, significantly, made Barthes read Dumézil), as well as with Robert Mauzi
(who was writing his thesis on the idea of happiness in nineteenth-
century French literature and thought), with Edgar and Violette
Morin and Georges Friedmann, and his continuing dialogue with
Greimas, all confirmed his desire to tackle a large, complex theme.
This filled him with a degree of anxiety, as he knew he found it
difficult to produce a continuous argument, but it also filled him
with happiness: the temptation to undertake a long piece of work
had been with him all his life, from the first novels he wrote as a
teenager to the Proustian dream of his last years.[4] Looking back,
Barthes refused to see this period and its productions in terms of
crisis; it was a time of confidence and enthusiasm that put him on
the same wavelength as the thought of his age: 'I lived through a
(euphoric) dream of scientificity (of which *The Language of Fashion*
and *Elements of Semiology* are the residue).'[5] We need to take these
two works into account if we are to understand those years (even if
they were published at a later date), as they were being worked on
and brought into being in that period, and bear witness to Barthes's
great structuralist work in progress.

The sign

In this itinerary towards scholarly recognition, the first main achievement was 'Myth Today', the essay that concludes *Mythologies*.
Barthes wrote it in 1956 – mainly in the summer, in his house in
Hendaye – with the aim of making the work less tied down to its
original journalistic circumstances, and to give it a general dimension so it could contribute to the contemporary discussion on
myth. The text has a functional definition – a response to the initial
question 'What is a myth?' – and a programmatic function explaining the type of reading and analysis it will deploy. Certain of the

reference points are literary (Valéry, Sartre), but most are linguistic: Saussure first and foremost, even if, as for Sartre, Barthes tended to systematically cut out the direct references to his authors from one manuscript version to another. Thus, five notes on Saussure are dropped between the second manuscript version (which still bore the title 'Sketch for a mythology') and the published text. Of the sixty-nine notes of this intermediary version, only thirty survived into the final version.[6] All the same, the model of intelligibility was still Saussure's description of the sign, defining semiology as the postulation of a relation between two terms of different orders, a signifier and a signified, placed in a relation not of equality but of equivalence, and situated in a three-dimensional schema whose third term was the sign.

Barthes hypothesized that myth was a second-order semiological system that created the same schema a second time, on the basis of the third linguistic term. This semiology – which could be called structural as it was based upon the thought of language as a set of systematic relations – rested on three principles. First, the examination of *connotations*, of all those second-order signifiers that are added to the first or literal meaning, for which Barthes took the programme explicitly from Saussure and in a more covert way from Hjelmslev.[7] Second, the idea of a *three-term structure* (and not one with two terms, as a certain structuralist doxa claims), which brought him closer to the semiotics of Charles Sanders Peirce, even though Barthes had not yet read him (his name did not appear in any of Barthes's bibliographies until the *Elements of Semiology*, in 1964). And third, a combination of formalism and history in order to understand how ideology is inscribed and by what operations myth naturalizes itself. These three principles together led to a hybrid method, neither hermeneutic nor formal, which seemed to suit the myth as defined by Barthes, but was apparently difficult to generalize. Its hybrid nature, which is evident from certain textual obscurities – Barthes states right from the start that mythology as a new science is entirely part of semiology and then presents the discipline as 'a part both of semiology inasmuch as it is a formal science, and of ideology inasmuch as it is an historical science'[8] – created several misunderstandings, but also indicated some of the directions that his later work would take. Critics not uncommonly complain that this scientific venture of Barthes was an ill-judged excursion into an area not his own, and that an attentive examination of these texts will enable us to see how vulnerable they are – victims of an absence of rigour on the part of their author and of the coating of subjectivity he gives them. Or else we read that, in the alternative between ideologizing and poeticizing posed by the text – 'It seems that this is a difficulty pertaining to our times: there is as yet only one possible choice, and this choice can bear only on two equally extreme methods: either to posit a reality which is entirely permeable to history, and ideologize; or, conversely, to posit a reality which is ultimately impenetrable, irreducible and, in this case, poetize'[9] – an alternative to which there cannot be a synthesis, Barthes ultimately chose poetry. For other critics, conversely, Barthes placed his project within the context of science, while actually taking it down unusual paths: on this reading, his work still deserves to be discussed scientifically, on the basis of its theoretical presuppositions. After all, was not Barthes almost the most important representative of that semiology which he had started to define in 'Myth Today' and which led to the creation of a chair in that discipline at the Collège de France that he occupied from 1977 onwards? If we examine the main stages of a career as a continuous process, as autobiography allows us to, it is clear that there is nothing imaginary about this. Whenever Barthes found himself at a dead end, up against his own contradictions, he tried to shift his method, resorting to new interpretations, with new interlocutors – this was the role that Lévi-Strauss would play for him in the early 1960s – while continuing to take an interest in the same kind of objects: those which concentrated the greatest number of 'social' elements within themselves, crystallizing the greatest ideological charge or else endowed with an intense symbolic density.

Following straight on from his little mythologies, Barthes allowed himself to be imbued with the material objects of everyday life so as to move ahead with his research. In this area, all objects were good objects; the more they engaged the body and the senses, the better: thus, his interest in clothing did not come solely from the research conducted by Greimas and at his suggestion, but from Barthes's own liking for clothes (he took great care over his clothes, which he bought twice a year at Old England or, later, when he had more money, from Lanvin) and his awareness of what his contemporaries wore. Food, too, was not just raw material for sociology, but the object of a close attention he paid to what was on his plate, to his likes and dislikes: to this, too, he added a critical dimension. These 'contemporary systems of signification', which formed the basis of his first courses at the École pratique, were an intimate interweaving of life and theory. This could create the feeling that he was too close to his objects to have the requisite distance from them that a true science needs. Myth often appears to be a weightier matter when it is analysed on the basis of a corpus distant in space and time than when it is found in immediate everyday life (which cannot be seen in isolation from its historical dimension). But Barthes's work brought together, inseparably, a desiring impulse and an ethnographical ambition that he hoped would converge. His impulse led him to always connect desire with critique: thus, the *Mythologies* are not always purely acts of denunciation. Their force stems also from the

fact that not everything is semiological or the object of an ideological critique; the power of desire also plays a part, whether it be for
wrestlers, for Garbo, or for wooden toys.

So fantasy counts for a great deal. It unleashes writing. This is so
evident, in hindsight, that Barthes would later place the phantasm
at the point of departure of his method, reflection and teaching: he
defined it as 'a scenario in which the subject situates himself in terms
of his desire',[10] an origin, a figure that was imprinted upon science.
Circumstances also played their part. He saw the film *Le Beau
Serge* in 1959 and initially devoted a 'mythology' to it in *Les Lettres
nouvelles*, in which he expressed his immediate feelings: tenderness
for certain scenes ('the children's football match in the street') and
exasperation for the aimless realism that he claimed was that of
the director.[11] The following year, the same film was used as an
example for a structural systematization of the 'problem of meaning
in cinema'.[12] He saw *Goldfinger* with Violette Morin in 1965, and
immediately dashed off, in the heat of the moment (witness the
notes in his desk diary for the following days), a study whose main
points he summarized more coolly in the 'Introduction to the
Structural Analysis of Narratives', published in *Communications* in
November 1966. When he was asked to write something about the
Encyclopédie, he rushed to the Sorbonne the next day to consult
its many volumes – and used them to write an article, published in
1964 as the introduction to a separate edition of the plates, with the
title 'Image, reason, unreason'. At first glance, this article is a pure
application of the methods of structural semiology to an iconographic system. But if we read it attentively, we realize that Barthes
has managed to detect within the system of its signs a rationality
that spills out beyond its own borders, threatening any totalizing
enterprise and allowing desire to appear. We find the same duality
of perspective and narrative as is conveyed in the objects he is studying: 'if you read the plate from bottom to top, you obtain in a sense
an experiential reading, you relive the object's epic trajectory, its
flowering in the complex world of consumers; you proceed from
nature to sociality; but if you read the image from top to bottom,
starting from the vignette, it is the progress of the analytic mind that
you are reproducing; the world gives you the usual, the evident (the
scene); with the Encylopedist, you descend gradually to causes, to
substances, to primary elements, *you proceed from the experiential
to the causal, you intellectualize the object.*'[13] The control imposed
by explanation is a form of appropriation, but it does not mean that
the desiring gaze that was there from the start vanishes completely.

Barthes combines fantasy with an ethnographic ambition: his
description of daily life also spills out over the borders of his pur-
ported project. It corresponds to a liking for what is close at hand,
for the apparently insignificant event, for the habitual – together

with an interest in the way men occupy their environment by giving meaning to it. Anticipating on the analyses of Michel de Certeau in *The Practice of Everyday Life*, Barthes indicated how much 'the observation of the evidence' endows scientific research with a 'salutary anxiety'.[14] Details of clothing, for example, are not just interesting signs to observe, they reveal an 'everyday life' aspect, and thus subvert the relation between what is meaningful and what is not. This quest was certainly influenced by Barthes's reading of Henri Lefebvre, whose *Critique of Everyday Life* had been published in 1947 (the second volume, with the title *Foundations for a Sociology of the Everyday*, came out in 1961). Lefebvre and Barthes became friends in 1948, having first met in the circles of Blanchot and Mascolo.[15] They were both from South-West France: in the summer, Barthes often went to see Lefebvre in his house in Navarrenx and Lefebvre regularly visited Barthes in Urt. Barthes also recognized his own positions in the resolutely anti-communist Marxism of Lefebvre after 1958. Even if they were not always in complete agreement (Lefebvre signed the 'Manifesto of the 121' and was at the forefront of the events in May 1968), they both recognized the need to lay the bases for a true ethnology of everyday life. The ever-increasing number of objects, the rise of a consumer society, played a great role in the importance they attributed to this programme. However, more than products or usages, the two writers were interested in their residues, their remnants. In a text on Lefebvre, Blanchot noted that 'the everyday' is 'what is most difficult to discover'. And this same 'everyday' also 'belongs to insignificance; the insignificant being what is without truth, without reality, and without secret, but also perhaps the site of all possible signification'.[16] It lies concealed behind events, ideologies, everything we are used to viewing as important; it lies in what Perec – who was deeply influenced by Lefebvre, whom he had read, and by Barthes, whose courses he had followed – would later call the 'infraordinary': 'what's really going on, what we're experiencing, the rest, all the rest.'[17]

So what Barthes invented was a situated science, relative to its own age and even ephemeral, involving a dual grasp of problems and objects – a grasp that was both sensual and intellectual. The dual structure of the *Mythologies* promoted this method in an exemplary way. This did not prevent him from taking pains to be accurate, to provide relevant analyses, as we see right up to *The Language of Fashion*. Two factors make his structuralism flexible. One is the third term, neither *a* nor *b*, the famous zero degree or neutral that is always there between the lines, even when Barthes yields to the binarism of structures. The second is the element of play or interplay. From mythology, 'which may well make sarcasm the condition of truth',[18] to the fashion utterances set out at the beginning of each chapter in *The Language of Fashion* – 'for a lunch-time party in Deauville, a soft canezou',[19] for example – Barthes manipulates irony, observes from a distance. In comparison with the structuralism of Lévi-Strauss, conceived as 'a general theory of relations', which uncovers laws on the basis of the organization of series of variants, structural semiology continues to harbour a demystifying ambition as it attacks dominant opinions, the doxa, and ultimately language itself. This entails admitting to a mistrust of method. The mythologist should be susceptible to being treated as the object of a mythological analysis just as 'there is, there will one day be, inevitably, a semiology of semiologists'.[20] Not only does 'the semiological project give the analyst the formal means to incorporate himself into the system that he is reconstructing',[21] but it makes him aware of the risks of a fake distance. This metacritical lucidity, ubiquitous in all the texts of this period, is also a way of taking the programme of science in another direction and showing, in the final analysis, the melancholy of the mythologist, who constantly runs 'the risk of causing the reality, which he purports to protect, to disappear',[22] or 'who expresses his future death in the very terms in which he has named and understood the world'.[23] But this is also how he does not exempt himself from history and can once again be part of his time.

The École

Barthes's first academic consecration took place when he entered the École pratique des hautes études (EPHE), in the 6th section (which was to become the EHESS or École des hautes études en sciences sociales in 1975), at that time directed by Fernand Braudel. Barthes was appointed *chef de travaux* in 1960, then director of studies in 1962, with forty-two votes out of sixty (his official appointment was dated 1 July 1962): this authorized him to teach. The institution was admittedly peripheral when compared with the Sorbonne, but it was far from being marginal. Ever since it had been created in 1868 by Victor Duruy at a suggestion from Renan, who found German intellectual life much richer and more productive than its equivalent in France, it was simultaneously complementary to and an alternative to the University. It was complementary in that it provided training, erudition and research in disciplines that the traditional university system largely ignored; and it was alternative in that it placed greater emphasis on the pedagogy of seminars than on formal lectures, and took 'no account of the academic qualifications of its teachers (who could be recruited without having come from the academic world and were called "directors of studies"), nor, to some extent, of its students' qualifications either'[24] (students were viewed as 'auditors' rather than pupils). The titles of chairs were not fixed and depended on recruitment. The courses were open to the public, with subjects and timetables announced by posters. The EPHE contributed greatly to the rise of the social sciences, and the rapidity of their development meant that new initiatives could be undertaken – we have already mentioned the creation of the CECMAS by Georges Friedmann – and the credits allocated increased. In this establishment, Barthes was fully able to transform himself from being an intellectual expressing his views in various opinion columns to a scholar engaged in long-term research that was the product of mature reflection, designed to be transmitted to others.

This metamorphosis deserves a moment's scrutiny. As we have said, Barthes wanted to embark on a long-term project, something that would count. There was also his desire to obtain a job that give him a better social standing than piecework for various newspapers. But there is one point that still seems obscure: why did he choose sociology when literature and theatre had been the main objects of his analysis, of his inclinations and his interests? The impact of the *Mythologies* is one explanation, and his liking for the analysis of everyday life. Another reason lies, perhaps, in his ideas about the irreducibility of literary language, which makes it a fundamentally discontinuous and aloof entity, not easy to envisage as the site of an interpretation and of a form of knowledge that can be shared. As he writes in *Criticism and Truth*: 'The ambiguities of practical language are nothing compared with those of literary language. The former are in fact reducible by virtue of the situation in which they appear: something outside the most ambiguous sentence – a context, a gesture, a memory – tells us how to understand it if we want to make practical use of the information it has the task of conveying: circumstances create a clear meaning.'[25] As the work of literature is not part of any situation, and is characterized by its absence of context, it is difficult to give it a meaning, to subject it to a grid or transmit it as an object of knowledge. Of course, Barthes would try to do so, gradually applying the structural programme to literature (in *On Racine* and various articles from this period). But it certainly seemed easier to him, as he set out, to stick to practical language. One final reason probably stems from the political situation. The coming to power of General de Gaulle in 1958 reduced to a considerable degree the conditions of possibility of a left-wing critique. The colonial question that had preoccupied Barthes so much in the 1950s was about to be settled – by the Right. Barthes's response to the disquiet voiced in the questionnaire of Blanchot and Mascolo about the anti-democratic nature of the regime that came to power on 13 May 1958 was clear: the event changed the scope of intellectual opposition. It was not now a matter of denouncing a form of fascism, but of understanding the alibis, the organization of values of this power, on every level. It was no longer possible to be content with a merely superficial opposition, a militant opposition; it was necessary to abandon the repertoire of gestures drawn from the revolutionary arsenal in order to undertake a longer-term work that would make it possible to struggle against the ideological regression occasioned by the advent of Gaullism.

A few months later, Barthes published in *France Observateur* an extremely hard-hitting and committed article attacking the *Memoirs* of de Gaulle, in which he tried to provide evidence for his conviction: since, with de Gaulle, all criticism was suddenly rendered impotent, there was a need to try to continue the struggle by understanding the very reasons that had led to this disarray. And one of these was the way the political dimension had drawn on literature, giving the hero a sacred aura, and raising history into the metaphysical realm. 'The French have always viewed their writers (I won't say the same of their intellectuals) as "nice" people. In the almost unanimous admiration of the critics for the General who is also a Writer, there is a sense of security, the assurance that, fundamentally, nothing bad, nothing damaging, can come from a man who takes the trouble to write good French.'[26] Literature as value or exorcism put paid both to the suspicion of fascism and the possibility of any criticism. Faced with this realization, people needed to keep to themselves, like a secret, another conception of literature, less reducible to ideology, and to align with intellectuals rather than writers. But since, yet again, intellectual life itself was being completely transformed, it is easy to understand why Barthes muted his public, journalistic voice, restricted the forums in which he intervened and withdrew into research – all decisions dictated by the current situation.

This is also probably the context in which we need to interpret the episode of Barthes's refusal to sign the 'Manifesto of the 121'. He is so often criticized for this, and yet it was perfectly logical when seen as part of the evolution of the function of the intellectual, a topic to which he was devoting much thought. Blanchot and Mascolo, who were involved in many initiatives against the nascent Fifth Republic, composed a text on the protests against the Algerian War. This text was to go through various versions – Blanchot referred to the series of 'countless, almost daily meetings'.[27] Observing that control over the colonies was collapsing, the manifesto highlighted the army's political role in the conflict, and denounced the practice of torture, which went 'against democratic institutions'. The 'Declaration on the Right of Insubordination' ended with three propositions on which there was no consensus, not even among the signatories: 'We respect and deem justified the refusal to take up arms against the Algerian people. We respect and deem justified the behaviour of the French who feel that it is their duty to bring aid and protection to the oppressed Algerians in the name of the French people. The cause of the Algerian people, who are contributing decisively to destroy the colonial system, is the cause of all free men.' The call to insubordination had a deep impact and explains why this text became such a historic phenomenon, among the countless other initiatives undertaken against the war at that time.

When, over the summer, Mascolo, Schuster, Nadeau, Pouillon, Péju and Leiris turned to writers and intellectuals to gather signatures, some of the people they canvassed agonized over the question of illegality. Barthes had long discussions with Morin on the subject, and at meetings of the *Arguments* committee it was the main topic of debate. Claude Lefort, Jean Duvignaud and Edgar Morin thereupon decided to compose their own 'Appeal to Public Opinion', which would come out one month after the Manifesto (which itself was published on 6 September 1960 in the magazine *Vérité-Liberté*) in the monthly periodical of the FEN (Fédération de l'éducation nationale). This text was fully committed to pacifism and opposed to military power, and demanded an immediate negotiated peace in Algeria. It was signed by dozens of intellectuals, as well as everyone on the *Arguments* committee: Étiemble, Maurice Merleau-Ponty, Jacques Le Goff, Paul Ricoeur, Jacques Prévert, Jean-Marie Domenach, and others. The intellectuals who supported the FLN (Front de libération nationale)[28] criticized this initiative, which did not seem hard-line enough. But the second petition brought together those who refused to countenance anything illegal while still agreeing on the need for protest. Barthes's position, as well as reflecting the social circles in which he moved at the time (he was closer in terms of friendship to Edgar Morin than to Mascolo or Nadeau), was guided by a deeper conviction that revolutionary militancy was no longer meaningful in contemporary society. He did not believe in the para-political arms of protest, as he said clearly in 'Sur le régime de Général de Gaulle'; on a more hidden level, perhaps his status as 'pupil of the nation' prevented him from adopting an awkward, disobedient attitude towards the Republic. In any case, we cannot deny that he again strove to be as fair as he could be, at the risk, as happened this time, of falling foul of several of his friends and of history itself. For, these days, people remember only the 'Manifesto of the 121' and its exceptional, aggressive courage, which even led to some of its signatories being gaoled for several days and having their apartments searched from top to bottom. The context suggests we can exonerate Barthes from the accusation of not showing sufficient commitment. If he preferred the appeal put forward by Lefort and Morin, this was not because he felt lukewarm about the matter or was docilely submitting to the state; it was more that he had an acute awareness of the gestures of protest and their ideological implications. He returned regularly to his distrust of heroic attitudes, which transform an action into a posture, always marked by a form of mendacity.[29] The episode reveals his doubts about the possibility for critical intellectuals to express themselves, and helps to explain his withdrawal into the ethos of the scholar.

When faced with the Algerian War, and given his opposition to the regime of de Gaulle, Barthes remained convinced that writers needed to unite, to find some potential communal action. When Blanchot expressed the desire to pursue the endeavour beyond the Manifesto, by creating an international review, Barthes unhesitatingly gave the idea his support. He was forever on the alert to intellectual initiatives and aware, on this occasion, that a profound change had occurred that required a new response – and in this he was in complete agreement with Blanchot, even if he expressed matters in less dramatic terms: he was probably less convinced that a communism of thought could really exist. Blanchot wrote, in a text setting out guidelines for the review: '[W]e are approaching an extreme movement in our time [. . .] we need to try to answer the grave riddle posed by the move from one time to another';[30] Barthes, for his part, was more interested in wielding the concrete tools of denunciation and ideological demystification. To this extent, he was doubtless less philosophically political, even if he was convinced that the Gaullist state was clearly responsible for the ruin of all intellectual life in France.[31]

Blanchot first contacted Sartre, who refused to commit, whereupon Blanchot endeavoured to set up a tripartite committee that brought together, in France, Antelme, Blanchot, Duras, Butor, Des Forêts, Leiris, Mascolo and Nadeau; in Italy, Calvino, Vittorini and Pasolini; and in Germany, Bachmann, Enzensberger, Grass, Walser and Uwe Johnson. Enzensberger's exile in Norway after the building of the Berlin Wall on 13 August 1961 upset the balance, and the Germans marked their frequent disagreements by regularly threatening to withdraw. It was in May 1962 that Blanchot contacted Barthes to suggest he join the project, which he did, with enthusiasm and a real desire to contribute. 'I was delighted that you agreed to play a part in editing and developing the planned review. As the German and Italian editorial teams are ready to begin work, we need to be prepared to make a start on ours, and we have decided, at least until we have our own separate premises, to meet every Wednesday at 2 p.m. at the home of Dionys Mascolo (5 rue Saint-Benoît, third on the left).'[32] Barthes attended these meetings on a very regular basis and was one of the members who took part in a collective gathering in Zurich to try and find a solution to the German impasse. He flew out on the morning of 18 January 1963 with Des Forêts, Blanchot and Mascolo, but their collective energy was not enough to answer the objections and overcome the ideological oppositions that were raised at every suggestion. A few days later, Blanchot wrote to Uwe Johnson, in a letter that shows the tensions and grievances that had arisen: 'We have been denounced as philosophically guilty of abstraction, guilty of ignoring the "concrete", wallowing in "sublime intellectual heroism" and turning away from the carnal side of things. [. . .] The truth of the matter is that I have been struck by the way the reproach laid at our door is exactly the same as the one that, in France, people on the Right lay at the door of left-wing intellectuals, i.e. that we are people of principle, with a tendency to split hairs and capable only of a poor, longwinded investigation that holds out no certainty of truth. In France, right-wingers unanimously denounce philosophy because they are afraid of the challenges and the questioning that "philosophy" is, essentially, for us, and because, on the pretext of praising the concrete and praising an empiricism without principles, they are basically sticking to the social status quo, to sociological comfort.'[33]

The Italians, Vittorini in particular, resisted concepts that seemed too mystical to them; they quibbled over terms and attacked the 'ontologism' of the French. On a trip to Italy in February, Barthes met some of the Italian group; they expressed their anxieties to him. 'We had a bit of a chat with Barthes on the Italian situation', Vittorini wrote to Blanchot in March 1963. 'We (Leonetti and I) told him that certain "notions" (the notion of silence, the notion of absence) that have a certain meaning for you have a very different and unpleasant meaning for us because of the fact they were introduced into Italy and developed by a school of Christian mystics (the "Ermetici", poets and essayists between 1935 and 1945).'[34] In short, they could not agree on any definition of the demands of literature. However much Blanchot called for more tolerance and openness, the different groups, the national committees, found it difficult to come together on authors they could all agree on, or even decide a title. There was clearly a translation problem between them, even though they had some very interesting exploratory thoughts on the subject;[35] any international consensus was hard to find given the polemics. It has to be said that German and Italian literary milieus were very different from those in France. In those relatively uncentralized countries, writers lived in often distant cities and did not form a close society. The only issue of the review to be published was in Italian, with the title *Gulliver*, as part of the periodical *Il Menabò* published by Einaudi, to which Barthes contributed three short fragments, one on modern performances of Sophocles' *Oedipus*, another on dialogue and a third on the notion of form.[36] The planned attempt to escape from the intellectual solitude everyone felt in their own country led to nothing. But that an aloof writer such as Blanchot should have been brave enough to embark on this public commitment, involving a great deal of diplomacy and technical details, certainly struck Barthes forcefully, and meant that their positions converged on at least one point: the conviction that political community was based on friendship. Indeed, he discussed this with a great deal of feeling in the interview on reviews that he gave in 1979 to Maria-Teresa Padova: 'It really interested me to see someone like Blanchot dramatically confronting those problems. There were many preparatory meetings and they were all affected – in fact, it was a wonderful sight and rather awe-inspiring – by a sort of . . . negative destiny or *fatum*, which came from . . . Blanchot; in other words, basically, I would say at a second degree, the fate, the necessity of the endeavour, was that it should not succeed.'[37] In all other respects, the two differed on many questions.

A few years later, when Blanchot again asked Barthes to comment on and sign another text expressing resistance to the Gaullist regime, Barthes declined, as he had for the declaration on the right to insubordination, and with arguments similar to those he had used in 1959 in his reply to the survey carried out for *14 Juillet*. The text proposed for him to read and perhaps emend was an extremely violent indictment. While denouncing a 'strangely regressive regime', regressive in both social and political terms, brought to power by a military coup and year by year becoming more authoritarian, it asked 'all thinking men, writers, scholars and journalists' to break off from any form of alliance with the regime, refusing to make any 'contribution to services, organizations, institutions or platforms controlled by the government and having no true autonomy, such as the ORTF [French Broadcasting Company], and to forbid it to use their words, their writings, their works, or their names.'[38] Barthes gave three reasons for his refusal. The first was ideological. If it was necessary to struggle against this regime – and in his view, it was – it was by analysing the regime's nature as accurately as possible, and not by seeing it as a dictatorship (which it was not, properly speaking), and thus succumbing to the stereotype. And 'if the analysis is not accurate, it will inevitably force people to make false gestures'. The second reason was political and placed the field of struggle on the international and not just the national level, with Barthes claiming that everything 'needed already to be related to the future war between the United States and China'. The last reason was ethical: the writer cannot use his name and his work as a capital that gives him extra-literary advantages and means of exerting pressure. Apart from pointing out the paradox that would be involved in signing a text about the very refusal to participate or sign, he questioned an intellectual gesture that made the writer's work a justification, 'a capital that ballasts extra-literary decisions'. He continued: 'How can one sign a text in the name of a work of literature, at the very same moment that we are attacking on all sides the idea that a work can be signed?'[39] This makes it easier to understand why Barthes should have so energetically published work in reviews that did not claim to be detached from the functions of literature. The experience of the international review also showed that Barthes had not moved away from literary circles even though he had now taken on a position as a researcher. His scholarly work drew on his work for newspapers; his institutional basis gave weight to his commitments to public life. He often wrote longer, widely discussed articles in reviews read by the whole intellectual class of the time: *Critique*, *Arguments*, *Communications*, *Annales*, and so on. In the decade 1958–68, he occupied, discreetly but confidently, the whole field. The twofold recognition, public and scholarly, that he earned at this period was the direct effect of that extended presence.

His courses also reflected the way he had a foot in both camps. In fact, the audience of his first years was mainly composed of friends. 'There were only two or three of us "normal" students', remembers Jean-Claude Milner. 'There was Violette Morin, the daughter of Maurice Leenhardt, Robert David, a whole small group of friends.'[40] Among the first members of the audience, apart from Jean-Claude Milner, there was Jean Baudrillard, who would derive from the courses the idea for his *System of Objects* (he drew a great deal from Barthes's teaching and from his articles in *Communications*), Lucille Baudrillard, Jean's first wife, Yvonne Bernard, Luc Boltanski, Jacques Bouzerand, Olivier Burgelin and Jacques-Alain Miller: these were, from the end of the first year onwards, 'titular students'. Barthes's chair had the title 'Sociology of signs, symbols and representations', and he devoted the first two years of the seminar to an 'inventory of contemporary systems of meaning: systems of objects (clothes, food, housing)'.[41] He provided the theoretical framework of the semiological method in relation mainly to Saussure, but also to Hjelmslev, Jakobson and Martinet, and he noted the ways in which it could be useful to other disciplines, psychology, sociology, history, economy, anthropology and logic. The seminar, indeed, defines the 'elements of semiology' on the basis of the concepts of structural linguistics, the couples language/speech, signifier/signified, syntagm/system, denotation/connotation. What modifications do these concepts undergo when they are applied to extra-linguistic realities? This was the question he asked of the audience, and he requested them to make index cards on the objects of everyday life. Jean-Claude Chevalier remembers making two of these, one on the homology between the traditional meal *à la française* (entrée, main course, dessert) and the morphology of language (prefix, root, suffix), and the other on the relative correspondence of the colours given to types of meat (white, red or black) and their real colours. Echoes of this are found in 'Elements of semiology'. The restaurant 'menu' thus serves to explain the axes of language, realizing two levels: 'The horizontal reading of the entrées, for instance, corresponds to the system, the vertical reading of the menu corresponds to the syntagm.'[42] Barthes also invited outside lecturers. In the first year, Greimas gave a paper on 'The notion of system in Saussure'; Jean-Paul Aron took stock of 'Historical research on representations of the idea of nobility'; and Jean-Louis Ferrier, a pupil of Pierre Francastel and art critic on *Les Temps modernes*, spoke to the students about 'Painting and meaning'.

In the second year, Barthes's course focused on 'substances other than articulated sound [such as] image, [. . .] music and [gesture]'.[43] In particular, he was interested in the image in advertising messages, and drew a distinction between three types of message: a literal iconic message, a linguistic message and a connoted iconic message. The outside speakers were Robert Linhart, talking about Sartre's *The Psychology of Imagination*, and Christian Metz, on the semiology of the cinema. Barthes drew some important articles from the substance of his courses: 'Le message publicitaire', published in 1963 in *Les Cahiers de la publicité*, in which he re-examined the distinction between the different types of message present in advertising images; 'Rhetoric of the image', a more detailed version of the previous article, was published in issue 4 of *Communications* in November 1964, at the same time as the 'Elements of semiology';[44] in 'La cuisine du sens', he popularized his method, applying it to clothes, to cars, to cooked meals, to film, to music, and to the advertising image (the whole programme of his course, in fact) for the readers of *Le Nouvel Observateur*. He also took the material for his lectures abroad directly from his courses: for example, 'Sémantique de l'objet', at the Cini Foundation in Venice, as part of a conference on 'Art and culture in contemporary civilization' which he attended in September 1966, and 'Sémiologie et urbanisme', at the Institute of History and Architecture of the University of Naples in 1967. It is another feature of Barthes's practice that he made a wide and varied use of materials from his own work. He also drew a great part of his fame in France and abroad from the large-scale impact of his research.

'Elements of semiology', the text published in *Communications* in 1964 (and subsequently by Denoël in 1965, at the request of Nadeau, who had just joined the company), also came directly from the first two years of his course. It is a major overview: it is worth examining it in detail, since it sums up Barthes's method and outlines its scope. The four parts are made up of four couples or rubrics of structural linguistics and, after a quick reminder of the definitions of linguistics and the possible variants found in different authors (Peirce for example is cited in the section on signifier/signified), Barthes measures the sociological impact on four areas: written fashion, which is the one most often referred to, as Barthes had a great amount of material in this area; food; furniture; and architecture. In the first chapter, 'Language and speech', he notes the way Hjelmslev modified Saussure to grasp the difference between language and speech (Hjelmslev drew a distinction between schema, norm and usage) and applies it to fashion and food. He shows, for example, that the *language* of food is constituted by rules of exclusion, oppositions (such as bitter/sweet), rules of association, and usages, while the *speech* of food includes all the personal variants in preparation. But he also states that the most interesting systems for study are complex systems in which the elements of speech and language cannot be demarcated a priori: these include cinema, television and advertising. The second chapter, 'Signified and signifier', distinguishes between the semiological sign and the linguistic sign. 'The semiological sign is also, like its model, compounded of a signifier and a signified (the colour of a light, for instance, is an order to move on, in the Highway Code), but it differs from it at the level of its substances. Many semiological systems (objects, gestures, pictorial images) have a substance of expression whose essence is not to signify; often, they are objects of everyday use, used by society in a derivative way, to signify something.'[45] Food is used to nourish us, clothes to protect us, houses to lodge us . . . Barthes suggests that we call these 'sign-functions'. The third chapter, 'Syntagm and system' uses the two Saussurean axes, the syntagmatic (the varied combination of recurrent signs) and the paradigmatic (the internal arrangement of the terms in an associative field corresponding here to the system), whose facts are the object of study: opposition and neutralization. Finally, the fourth chapter examines the couple 'Denotation and connotation', the second of these being precisely the object of study of semiology. At the end of his book, Barthes even calls for 'a linguistics of connotation, for society continually develops, from the first system which human language supplies to it, second-order significant systems, and this elaboration, now proclaimed and now disguised, is very close to a real historical anthropology'.[46]

While drawing on the main information in Barthes's course, 'Elements of semiology' makes several cuts (the many excursions and examples, the pauses, the alternating rhythms produced by orality and the situation of interlocution and dialogue). It can be read as the founding text of the new science of semiology, and this is doubtless how Barthes conceived it, endeavouring to make it part of a contemporary community of research (citing, for example, Lacan and Lévi-Strauss). He clearly placed this science within the structuralism that he tried to define in a certain number of articles that he published in the same period. In 'The Structuralist Activity', published in *Les Lettres nouvelles* in 1963, he sought to define the shared space of these research activities as a whole and to characterize 'structural man' as one who creates meaning. By selecting and rearranging his elements, he produces the '*simulacrum* of the object' that is able to bring out something within it that had hitherto remained invisible 'or, if one prefers, unintelligible in the natural object'.[47] Barthes thus indicated the context that presided over this activity in the work of thinkers such as Lévi-Strauss, Dumézil and Troubetzkoy: in every case it was a formalism, but a creative formalism (in the manner of Mondrian, Boulez or Butor) that could help us read unnoticed meanings in the objects of the world.

The course took place in the premises of the EPHE on the second floor of staircase E, in the old Sorbonne. Jacques-Alain Miller remembers the 'dark oval table' around which gathered, to begin with, some 20 or so people; he also remembers how happy he was to learn 'that everything has meaning, not insofar as everything is a twinkling in the eye of Being, but because everything hangs together as a system, is articulated; nothing human was foreign to Barthes, because in his eyes the human was structured like language in Saussure. He took this postulate seriously, and drew the ultimate consequences. This was a powerful, corrosive operation, enough to shake the being-in-the-world of a philosophy student.'[48] For the young normaliens of the time, this openness to new disciplines, to the human sciences that were not taught at the Sorbonne, was a powerful move encouraged by the teachers at the École normale. If we are to believe Jacques-Alain Miller, Jean Hyppolite did not particularly make philosophy into a positive choice, and, above all, Althusser was suggesting that something important was happening around structuralism. Believing in the development of a Marxism that was not a matter of repetition but of renewal, he invited his pupils to explore this new interdisciplinary realm. Before transferring Lacan's teaching to the ENS as an offshoot of an EPHE set up with the support of Fernand Braudel, he had offered Foucault, who had been following Lacan's seminar at Sainte-Anne since 1953, a post as lecturer in psychology. Thus it was that many normaliens of that period, destined to make a name for themselves as intellectuals, were led to Barthes via psychoanalysis (Jacques-Alain Miller) or linguistics. The latter was a second-year student at the ENS when he followed Barthes's seminar, from the second session onwards. He was an assiduous attender until the third year. He remembers his amazement at the way Barthes thought aloud. 'It was a very special moment that I witnessed, where nothing could be taken for granted. The word "semiology" was completely unfamiliar; it carried promises but uncertainties too. Indeed, when it reached its final form in "Elements of semiology" and *The Language of Fashion*, it became ossified. But at the time, in his courses, we had the impression that we were entering another world.'[49] In hindsight, Milner reads this in political terms. The awareness that the Left was on the verge of disappearing was a trauma that led to the collapse of the posture of the critical intellectual. Barthes realized that it was no longer possible to think in terms of surface and depth. To choose structures meant relying on surfaces and permutations of surfaces. Meaning was no longer a mystery to be interpreted: rather, it was constructed in the shifting movement of signs.

Barthes felt free and happy at the École pratique des hautes études. He took a keen emotional and intellectual pleasure in his seminars, where relations of work, friendship and esteem could be cultivated. Even if people very soon started flocking to his seminars in such numbers that he was obliged to distinguish between two seminars, the 'big' seminar, with a large audience to which he lectured, and the 'small' seminar, where, together with a few choice students, he worked collectively, he loved this society, which seemed to be outside the state apparatus and was akin to 'a society of free spirits (students and teachers combined), to what in the eighteenth century would have been called an *academy* (of knowledge and language)'.[50] Even if, with a certain prescience, he saw that this school, like others, would inevitably be incorporated into the institution, caught as it was between two powers, 'that of government technocracy and that of demands of protest or promotion', he took advantage (while he could) of its open structure, one propitious to the establishment of working communities, foregrounding the importance of listening and given value by that listening. This remarkably lucid note shows what a provisional miracle the Sixth Section of the EPHE was for research in social sciences. Barthes was keenly aware of the transferential value of the teaching relation, in which every attitude is a productive one. As he later explained to Jean Thibaudeau, who questioned him about the dedication of his book *S/Z* to the students, listeners and friends 'who took part in this seminar': 'Liberation does not consist in giving the student the right of speech (a minimal measure), but in attempting to modify the circuit of speech – not its physical circuit (speaking up) but its topological circuit (referring here, of course, to psychoanalysis).'[51] He struck up a friendship with some of his listeners, often seeing them in cafés in the early evening, following a ritual that started to develop at this time. He would leave home in the late afternoon for various successive rendezvous late into the night. Far from being experienced as a disturbance to his schedule or a distraction from his work, teaching was perfectly well integrated into his personal life, acting as a basis for his work and providing him with intellectual satisfactions and fulfilling friendships.

Structure

Structuralism was simultaneously a prestigious brand label, supported by a whole number of publishing initiatives as well as by literary journalism, and a scholarly programme to which all the participants brought their own individuality. It was doubtless the last 'ism' of the twentieth century to subsume many different trends and ideas, with its supporters and its detractors (subsequently, post-modernism was to have fewer supporters and more detractors).[52] The history of structuralism has been written several times already, starting with the time when it was still a new, spreading movement. Even before François Wahl's collective volume *Qu'est-ce que le structuralisme?* was published, there was *Clefs pour le structuralisme* by Jean-Marie Auzias (1967) and *Comprendre le structuralisme* by Jean-Baptiste Fagès (also 1967), and Jean Piaget's volume on structuralism in the 'Que sais-je?' series (1968).[53] Later on, the vast panoramic survey by François Dosse enabled participants in the movement to speak for themselves and endeavoured to provide a comparative study of the variant forms of structuralism. The field has also been investigated from a variety of different points of view: linguistics (*Le Périple structural* by Jean-Claude Milner), sociology (*Homo academicus* by Pierre Bourdieu),[54] literary history (the study of the reception of the Russian formalists in France) and psycho-analysis (*Résistances de la psychanalyse* by Jacques Derrida).[55] In this history, the usual opinion is that Barthes gradually moved away from structuralism – a view that follows that of Barthes himself, who referred to a major shift at the end of the 1960s, when he started to cast some discredit on his work in this area, preferring to highlight a practice more focused on the problems of writing. For example, he said that *The Language of Fashion* was more a piece of do-it-yourself improvisation in which he had enjoyed cobbling a system together, and less a book properly speaking, constructed as such. He also said that he was no longer 'motivated' to produce a linguistic discourse. 'In any case,' he added, 'I was never more than an amateur in linguistics.'[56] Even if we bear in mind the positive con-notations he gave to this term 'amateur', we cannot fail to sense the deprecatory tone in which he is using it here. Anna Boschetti refers to an 'aggiornamento', a renunciation of scientificity; this picks up on François Dosse's remarks on the splits and breaks that showed how structuralism had succumbed to 'exhaustion'.[57]

What is the fact of the matter? Can we really fix definitive labels on Barthes's texts, and are the periods in his work quite so distinct and clear-cut? Did Barthes, aware of the extremely rapid changes in intellectual life, take advantage of the ferment characteristic of all beginnings in order to test out his creative mettle, or did he really believe that the semiological programme could be truly produc-tive? And was it simply the desire to enjoy writing, and to dwell in the pleasure of the text, that led to him turning away from this programme, or were more circumstantial reasons at work? If we are to answer these questions, we first need to understand *in what ways* Barthes was a structuralist. True, there was more to structuralism than semiology but – like the other branches and programmes that developed under the same name – it was based on the Saussurean linguistics that was in vogue at the time thanks to Roman Jakobson; it believed in the possibility that one could create a system of objects and relationships, based on the dominant presupposition that all the human sciences could be as scientific as the sciences that are these days known as the 'hard' sciences, though at that time these latter were in fact the *only* sciences: physics, mathematics and biology. Now, Barthes more than anyone wished to embrace the greatest possible number of objects within his discipline – perceptible objects in particular. But he realized rather quickly that, while the description was correct and the method both applicable and transmissible, it was not, intellectually speaking, all that productive. It did not enable one to understand things as a whole beyond the system of objects described. He soon decided that it was a limited science, as shown by his distant, rather ironic relation to *The Language of Fashion*. His path led him from sociology to literature for reasons that were partly circumstantial, linked to requests made of him, of course – Barthes generally wrote on demand – but also because, like Genette and Todorov, with the help of the Russian formalists who were being introduced into France at that time, and whom he discovered thanks to Kristeva and Todorov, he hoped that there would be more of a future in literary structuralism than in sociological semiology. But we need to go back to a somewhat previous period and describe Barthes's fraught relation with Lévi-Strauss, a relation that was biographically decisive for an understanding of Barthes's path in and through structuralism – and that seems to have been the first disappointment he met with in those years.

In 1960, Barthes asked Lévi-Strauss for a meeting; he was hoping that Lévi-Strauss would agree to supervise his thesis on fashion. He had recently abandoned Matoré's lexicology and, at the prompting of Greimas, he decided to pursue the work on fashion that the latter had started in his own thesis. As we have seen, Barthes's meeting with Martinet had not led to anything and Barthes now decided to turn to anthropology, reflecting that his ideas about myth might arouse the interest of Lévi-Strauss. At the beginning of 1960, Barthes wrote to Lévi-Strauss, who said he would be happy to talk with him and asked him to visit him at home on 16 January, at 6 p.m.[58] This encounter was disappointing: Lévi-Strauss said he did not want to supervise Barthes's thesis; but it was also decisive, for at least two reasons. First, Lévi-Strauss suggested that Barthes read Vladimir Propp's *Morphology of the Folktale*,[59] and second, Barthes now decided to radically change the direction of his work on fashion. We do not know exactly why Lévi-Strauss refused to supervise the thesis. The reason, in any case, is not the one claimed by François Dosse, who says: 'Their disagreement had to do with the limited breadth of the project, since, for Lévi-Strauss, Barthes's work only dealt with a written system of style and not with a general system. Barthes, on the other hand, believed that nothing significant existed beyond the realm of the written.'[60] It was the complete opposite that actually took place: Barthes turned up with the idea of writing about clothes, and it was Lévi-Strauss who suggested that he limit himself to the discourse on fashion; this changed the direction of his ideas and represented an important stage in the definition of his structuralist method. Barthes referred to this turning point several times: 'I had in mind initially to develop a serious sociosemiology of clothing, of all clothing (I'd even begun some practical research), but then, as a result of a private comment made by Lévi-Strauss, I decided to homogenize the corpus and confine myself to *written* clothing (i.e., as described by the fashion magazines)'.[61] As we can see, Barthes immediately went along with Lévi-Strauss's suggestion, and started to work his way systematically through fashion magazines such as *Elle* and *Le Jardin des modes*, and it is more likely that Lévi-Strauss's refusal stemmed from different reasons. He disagreed with Barthes over two major issues: myth and structure. Without things being explicitly formulated at this first meeting, it is not difficult to see that the considerable extension Barthes gave to the notion of myth, with its sociological and ideological dimension (ideology was merely *one* aspect of the social totality for Lévi-Strauss), aroused a certain mistrust in Lévi-Strauss, who was then composing the great *summa* that was his *Mythologiques* (English translation: *Introduction to a Science of Mythology*); the first volume of this appeared in 1964 (published by Plon). Even if they agreed in their critical attitude to the narratives put about by explorers in the mass media that concealed the processes of history (the lectures in 'Connaissance du monde', in Lévi-Strauss's case, and the reports in *Paris-Match* for Barthes), and even if Barthes's 'Myth Today' gave a definition of myth as metalanguage that was in line with Lévi-Strauss's *Structural Anthropology*, in the view of the latter Barthes's analyses still seemed to give too big a place to sociological and stylistic factors that Lévi-Strauss himself was playing down at the time. As well as this scholarly difference, symbolic rivalry probably also played a part. Ever since the success of *Tristes tropiques* in 1955, it had been Lévi-Strauss's ambition to create a literary, and not just a scientific, body of work. Barthes's occupation of the two fields, literary and scientific, may have seemed threatening to him, or arrogant – and their subsequent relationship would confirm this sense of rivalry.

The other disagreement concerned the notion of structure: while both of them drew on linguistic usage, they did not give it altogether the same function. While Lévi-Strauss's attitude to observed data 'always favour[ed] the membership of the data in a system, the present state of that system (rather than its genealogy), and its internal coherence',[62] always placing the greatest emphasis on the inductive method, Barthes was above all interested in the varia- tions (highlighted in *The Language of Fashion* through the notion of 'shifter' taken from Jakobson) and the element of difference they could entail – something that Barthes would later celebrate as 'the *vagueness of distance*', in the fragment from *Roland Barthes by Roland Barthes* called 'The shifter as utopia'.[63] It is clear that Lévi- Strauss and Barthes had a different view of the scientific project that the notion of structure was meant to serve. Lévi-Strauss worked on several versions of the same myth to smooth out the differences; he sought universals where Barthes was interested in the signs and codes present in discourse. The former believed in the power of science, while the latter always gave his work a playful aspect and favoured a language that produced uncertainty and difference, sudden shifts and contradictions. Vincent Debaene has given a good summary of the difference in the way the two men used the term 'structure'; he says that, for Barthes, it was a way of organ- izing meaning, while for Lévi-Strauss it was a set of rules making it possible to move from one given to another. 'We are also dealing with a difference in the very projects of these two figures: for Barthes it is a matter of unveiling and discovery, and for Lévi-Strauss a matter of reconstructing the conditions for the practice of symbolic thought. There is a difference of method, as well: in Barthes we see the dismantling of a stack of significations, and in Lévi-Strauss we encounter the study of rules of transformation. Finally, there is a difference of object: for the former, it is the study of a given utterance – *Sarrasine*, *Goldfinger*, or a fashion catalogue; for the latter, it is the study of different versions of the same story that have been unmoored from their linguistic foundations.'[64] Furthermore, there were academic consequences for Lévi-Strauss in this scientific project. Throughout his career, he did not hesitate to play down the impact of his influences (in particular Mauss and Durkheim) and to attempt to liquidate those of his contemporaries whom he viewed as enemies. He would have many other differences of opinion, with Foucault and Derrida for example, and the consequence was that he was soon in sole command of the structuralist field.[65]

Lévi-Strauss adopted a somewhat superior attitude to Barthes right from the start. He saw the latter as one of the modish struc- turalists rather than as a serious scholar. As he later told Didier Éribon: 'I never felt close to him, and this feeling was confirmed by his later development. Late in life Barthes went completely against what he had done before, which, I'm convinced, was far from his true nature.'[66] He largely kept his reservations to himself, as Barthes was useful in gaining recognition for him; Barthes wrote two articles about him in prestigious journals. The first and most important,

'Sociology and socio-logic',[67] came out in 1962 in the newly launched review *Information sur les sciences sociales*, and was reprinted in a 1979 volume on Lévi-Strauss in the 'Idées' series published by Gallimard. It discussed *The Savage Mind* and *Totemism*, and pondered the possible application of structural analysis to the objects of modern society. The second article, 'Les sciences humaines et l'oeuvre de Lévi-Strauss', is simply the presentation of a special issue on Lévi-Strauss published in *Annales* at the end of 1964, and stated that his main work involved a reconfiguration of the human sciences as a whole. But the first article showed that, while Barthes was a great admirer of Lévi-Strauss, and set him up (albeit not for long) as a father figure, this did not mean that he fawned on him. Indeed, it is striking that 'Sociology and socio-logic' brings everything down to a comparison between their two objects and their two methods (and Barthes actually refers more to fashion than to the examples taken from the anthropologist). By distinguishing between an ethnographic society and a sociological society, he implicitly justifies the existence of several structuralisms. In addition, he questions the universality of the binary logic put forward by Lévi-Strauss, suggesting that the latter himself had recognized the value of the neutral, especially in connection with mana as a zero symbolic value. 'We may speculate (though this is merely an idea, not even a hypothesis) whether in fact, as opposed to ethnological societies whose logic is binary (even when they practice a zero degree of the sign), sociological societies do not tend to develop more complex logics (or quite simply, less affirmed ones), either because they multiply the recourse to terms derived from the matrix-opposition, or because they have the power to imagine *series* of terms, i.e., intensive paradigms in which language introduces an entirely relative discontinuity.'[68] The objection to the totalizing project was a significant one, and the importance of structural semiology for an understanding of contemporary societies was reaffirmed. So Barthes's article was far from being an uncritical homage to the master, and it is doubtful whether the latter really liked it. Barthes's greatness, evident from 'Myth Today' onwards, is that he overcame the contrast between anthropology and history, and endeavoured to bring them together. Nothing escapes the historical dimension – not even the body. 'It is strange: is not the human body, belonging as it does to anthropological time, immutable? In no way: morphology is subject to History just as much as to geography.'[69] The reference to history, just as much as the science of signs, may be a tactic against the immobility of all doxa, including that of myth.

Lévi-Strauss had nothing against the ethnography of contemporary life, even if he found it rather trivial in comparison with his own more universal project. On the other hand, when he was given an opportunity to comment on the products of literary structuralism, in which he quite rapidly came to include Barthes, he said it was of little interest: these works were at best a matter of intoning the same old thing, or 'deliriums', even if they were 'coherent deliriums' that revealed 'the mythology of our time'.[70] In 1966, Lévi-Strauss sent Barthes a very harsh private letter: Barthes had sent him a copy of the recently published *Criticism and Truth*. The letter is worth quoting, as it expresses how distant Lévi-Strauss felt from Barthes: 'To be frank, I am not at all sure I completely agree with you. Firstly because, defending the *nouvelle critique* in general, you seem to be including a great number of things that in my view hardly deserve it. Then there is an eclecticism that comes across in the excessive liking you show for subjectivity, for feelings, and, not to put too fine a point on it, a certain mysticism vis-à-vis literature. For me, the work of art is not open (a conception that paves the way to the worst kind of philosophy: that of metaphysical desire, of the subject properly denied but hypostasized in metaphor, etc.); the work of art is closed, and it is precisely this closure that means we can study it objectively. In other words, I do not separate the work from its intelligibility: on the contrary, structural analysis consists in bringing intelligibility to bear on the work. And unless we are to relapse into a hermeneutics à la Ricoeur, it seems to me that we need to distinguish more radically than you do between symbolic forms that are completely and objectively definable (these alone interest me) from the insignificant contents that men and the centuries can pour into them.'[71] Subjectivity, feelings, mysticism: this is a full-frontal attack. It shows that even Lévi-Strauss's work on variants does not look at historical variables but at formal variables. This is the price of scientific objectivity. It is likely that Barthes's article 'From Science to Literature', published the following year, was a kind of reply to this personal letter and this critique. Taking up the distinction between *écrivain* and *écrivant* popularized by his *Critical Essays*, he distinguished between language as an instrument subject to the scientific material and language as 'the very *being* of literature': for, 'though science needs language, it is not, like literature, *within* language; science is taught, i.e., it makes itself known; literature fulfils more than it transmits itself (only its history is taught).'[72] And he then appealed to a shifting of structuralism towards literary writing, which was not in the least contradictory with his previous considerations on metalanguage, considerations that already went beyond the opposition between language and metalanguage; one day, it would be necessary to create a mythology of the mythologist or a semiology of the semiologist. 'It remains therefore for the structuralist to transform himself into a "writer", not in order to profess or practice "style", but in order to recognize the crucial problems of any speech-act, once it is no longer swathed in the kindly cloud of strictly *realist* illusions which make language the simple medium of thought.'[73] In saying this, Barthes was making a logical move based on the acknowledgement of the limits of scientific objectivity in the human sciences and the need to see how closely they were involved in language and writing. This was less an abandonment of structuralism than a reduction of the distance between subject and object.

Derrida was making a similar point at this time, and Lévi-Strauss was embarking on a polemic with Foucault on the very definition of structuralism. Their acknowledgement of the limits of objective science and the discourse of formal rationality makes of them better precursors than Lévi-Strauss, who was confined to his method (for all its indisputable strengths and the very great concrete results he obtained from it). It is curious that this article by Barthes came out in the same year as *The Language of Fashion*, his most structuralist book. But, like *Writing Degree Zero* in its time, *The Language of Fashion* was one of those 'belated books' that he had finished long before they were published. He worked on it every summer from 1959 to 1963 and wrote the final full stop on 25 August 1963, in Urt: 'Ended *Fashion* (apart from the bibliography I need to do in Paris).'[74] François Wahl, who found it a little heavy-going, was in no hurry to publish it, first because the book might come as a surprise to Barthes's usual readers and second because *Criticism and Truth* – a book written for rapid publication, in response to Picard – now needed to be fitted at the last minute into the publishing schedule. In his foreword, Barthes acknowledged that this was an 'already dated'[75] adventure, not just in his own personal career but also in the development of semiology. Indeed, he here drew on a strictly Saussurean linguistics to which Chomsky, Jakobson and Benveniste had already added their own angles. In the interviews he gave to newspapers and reviews when the book came out, Barthes acknowledged his debt to Lévi-Strauss when it came to his focus on written fashion. But this was also an opportunity for him to insist on the fact that he was working on a kind of writing (even if it was a coded and stereotyped writing) and that nothing had meaning outside of language. He also noted that his main subject was literature and that, for this reason, even if he thought it was interesting to try out scientific methods, his aim was not science itself and he could not end his works 'with a typically scientific pronouncement, because literary science may in no case and in no way have the last word on literature'.[76] In regard to structuralism, he stated that 'the moment of separation is approaching'.[77] Different branches of research in this area had initially agreed that man was no longer at the centre of structures, but they now started to diverge, each having its own distinct relation to writing itself. If there was a new direction being taken here, Barthes felt that it involved *all* the promoters of the structural method and not just his own productions.

Subsequently, relations between Barthes and Lévi-Strauss remained distant. They sent each other their books, and thanked each other for them, but only Barthes continued to express his admiration and to see the other as a guiding light in his own development. When *S/Z* came out, Lévi-Strauss sent him a structural analysis of kinship in *Sarrasine* that was apparently an addendum to Barthes's text, a vibrant homage to the book that, at the beginning of his letter, he called 'dazzling'. The text is published in the 'Idées Gallimard' volume devoted to Lévi-Strauss, with the permission of both men.[78] But, less than ten years later, Lévi-Strauss told Didier Éribon that he 'wrote it as a joke. I didn't like *S/Z*. His comments seemed to me far too much like those of Professor Libellule in Muller and Reboux's *Just Like Racine*. So, a bit sarcastically and to avoid awkwardness I sent him these few pages in which I "overdid it", in place of the compliments I felt incapable of making. He took it seriously. I was asked to publish it. Why not?'[79] All rather cruel.

To conclude my analysis of this relationship (which seems altogether to have been a missed opportunity) on a less negative note, it is worth saying that on 5 April 1970, one week after the letter on *Sarrasine*, Lévi-Strauss sent a new letter to Barthes in which, while returning to *S/Z* to add a few remarks to his previous reading, he talked mainly about *Empire of Signs*, which he had just read. He said how much the book had touched him, especially as, 'transformed at the age of six by the gift of a print by Hiroshige – I was already a fan of Japanese art – I spent the whole of my childhood and adolescence pretending to be a little collector, so much so that I almost became an expert; and perhaps it is so that I could preserve Japan as a myth that I was never able to make up my mind to go there. So I am delighted to visit it with you as a guide, when you proclaim, in your very first pages, that you intend to treat Japan as a myth.'[80] This reference to a childhood memory – something not often found in Lévi-Strauss – shows that he was able to consent to fantasy and desire when it was a matter of art, and could even take the word 'myth' in another sense from the one he usually gave it. In 1975, when Barthes was visiting members of the Collège de France as he canvassed opinions on the possibility of his being elected to this body, Lévi-Strauss expressed a few reservations about Barthes's method, reservations that Foucault endeavoured to overcome – but he still promised to vote for Barthes.

The asymmetrical relationship between Barthes and Lévi-Strauss exemplifies the division within structuralism, between those who wished to make a fully fledged science of it and those who viewed it as a field for methodological experimentation. It also tells us that at no moment did Barthes, even in his most formal investigations, ever postulate a transparent and purely objective use of language. Language is not the mere instrument of thought because it needs to be constantly thought itself. So the role of literature is to contest the dominance of codes and languages, including those of science itself.

The house

By 1960, the villa in Hendaye, though pleasant enough, had turned out to be much too close to the bustle of tourists in the summer to be a real retreat; the family now started to look for an alternative near Bayonne. It was not that Barthes had been unable to work in the previous dwelling – he had written 'Myth Today' there, as well as almost all of *The Language of Fashion* – but Etchetoa was located between the beach and the road to Saint-Jean-de-Luz, and it was noisy in the summer. Apparently, his mother was not entirely comfortable there either, as is shown by the last note in the *Mourning Diary*: 'Hendaye / Not very happy / it was an *inheritance*.'[81] Though Barthes enjoyed going to the beach from time to time, in Biarritz or Hossegor, to listen to the sea and watch people, he could not take time off to do this every day. At best, the beach was a place for meditation when there was nobody about, early in the morning, or a place for observation when it was crowded. It was also a space in the process of transformation, one that created a difference between previous times and the present. For example, one of the pages in Barthes's diary refers to this passage of time, with its existential and sociological resonances: 'Yesterday, on the beach at Hossegor, the weather was gorgeous, a lot of people (it was Sunday, too). Uneasy feelings, as far as I was concerned: this adolescent place that I have known deserted, uninhabited, aristocratic – it used to be called "the wild sea", these days little hotels, krapfen, balloons, doughnuts, the densely crowded beach thronged with people, cars, etc.; an image that sums up France: neither aristocratic, nor even middle class, nor even "working class", just *full of people*. What I am most struck by is the way the French now have clean feet, whereas in my past, ordinary people had dirty feet; even when they were washed, they were caked with filth, horribly soiled.'[82] Rather than the instructive but aggressive and distracting seaside, Barthes preferred the countryside, which provided a counterpart to the city. The choice of the Barthes family fell on Urt, a village of some 2,000 residents on the banks of the Adour, in the borderland between the Basque Country and the Landes. Here, they settled on a house called Carboué, which they bought in March 1961. The villa Etchetoa was finally sold in September 1963. In 1960, Barthes was already spending a great part of his summer in what was still a rented property, charmed by the peace and quiet of the place, which reminded him closely of his childhood. The house, a massive white cube built on a bend of the village road, looked out on all four sides: on one, there was a modest garden that had the advantage of being largely out of sight of passers-by. The road that led to and past it was, in Barthes's comparison, like a tranquil river heading off to 'irrigate a whole outlying district of the village'.[83] You sometimes heard a tractor or moped passing by, but these noises merely accentuated the peaceful, rural character of the spot. 'It's a lovely house,' Barthes wrote to Philippe Rebeyrol in July 1961, 'and Maman and I really like it.'[84] From now on, he spent all his summers there, sometimes for two or three months, with short periods in Paris and a few trips abroad. He would drive down there with his mother at the end of June, in a regular transhumance reminiscent of the (aristocratic) rhythms of spending winter in Paris and summer on your estate. He was also usually there for Christmas and the traditional Easter or spring holidays. He enjoyed driving and was not bothered by the eleven or twelve hours he had to spend travelling between his two residences. He had inherited the nice old Panhard from his grandmother Noémie; he liked to knock about Paris in this, but it soon turned out to be inadequate for long journeys (it would always remain his 'mythological' car). At the beginning of the 1960s he bought a Volkswagen Beetle; his brother Michel, who also sometimes took their mother down to the South-West, drove a Porsche.

As in Paris, his life in the countryside followed a regular pattern, but was much less social. When he went out, it was to do the shopping in Bayonne; he could take any of four different roads, which he mentions in 'The Light of the Sud-Ouest'. There was the *route départementale* 261, taken when time was short, picking up someone from the station or driving them back there, or taking his aunt out for the day; there were two cross-country roads; and then there was his favourite road, the one that went along the right bank of the Adour and always gave him a sense of security, with its farms and its attractive houses, a mixture of 'nobility and familiarity': '[T]his is still a real *route*, not just a functional means of communication but a sort of complex *experience* in which occur simultaneously a continuous spectacle (the Adour is a very beautiful, unappreciated river) and the memory of an ancestral practice, that of walking, of the slow and rhythmic penetration of the landscape, which then assumes different proportions.'[85] There were also times when his friends came to stay; first, Violette Morin, François Wahl and Severo Sarduy, Jean Girodon, his old friend from Leysin, François Braunschweig, Marthe Robert and Michel de M'Uzan. The house was welcoming, and all the friends who visited it during Barthes's lifetime remember the warm and solicitous hospitality offered by Henriette Barthes, the mistress of the house, as well as the pleasure of the conversation, and Barthes's enthusiasm for showing them round his area. But it was mainly a matter of family life there, with two, three or four people, as Michel Salzedo spent long periods there with

Rachel, while also taking short trips with her to Spain and long trips to Israel, where his wife's family lived. As Barthes's mother looked after everything, he had few material worries and, when he left Urt, it was to go into town for entertainment, the cinema or a concert in Bayonne or Biarritz, to buy cigarettes or stationery. He had set up his office, which, here too, he also called his 'room', exactly the same way as in Paris, arranging the table and the piano in the same places, reproducing his physical environment in an identical fashion. He was so satisfied with this set-up that he managed to take it with him wherever he went. 'No sooner haver I arrived in a new house that I reconstitute my "structure" in it (people would mock this term less if they knew how much desire it carried); the nature of the objects (the terms) is of little account; the only thing that functions is the form of the space, the relationship between the tools and the decors. This gives rise to an intense DIY activity; it's a perverse force: like the fetishist who turns a plait or a foot into the instrument of his pleasure, I enthusiastically use two chairs for a table – so long as the surface created is horizontal – a cardboard box for a desk – so long as I can attach useless pieces of paper to it: this is a triumph of homology over analogy.'[86] This first version of one of the pieces in *Roland Barthes by Roland Barthes*, written in the house of Daniel Cordier in Juan-les-Pins in August 1974, clearly demonstrates the lucid satisfaction that Barthes derived from his obsessional temperament, visible both in spatial structures (the spaces of work) and in temporal structures (a very regular schedule). Picking up this idea in his 1975 self-portrait, he limits homology to two contrary and yet similar places (the city/the countryside): nothing is ever transported and yet the rooms are identical. 'Why? Because the arrangement of tools (paper, pens, desks, clocks, calendars) is the same: it is the structure of the space which constitutes its identity. This private phenomenon would suffice to shed some light on structuralism: the system prevails over the very being of objects.'[87]

Barthes highlights, twice over, the connection between the rule of life and intellectual method: structures correspond to a mode of life before they become a tool for analysis. They are attractive because they are reassuring: they ward off the anguish of abandonment and death, and thereby set him free.

Temporal organization was equally structured. From Paris to Urt, it was regularity that was transported rather than any strict timetable, as is shown by the desk diaries in which each sequence is marked by an initial letter or an abbreviation. Days in the city are divided into morning (*matin* – m), lunch (*déjeuner* – dej), afternoon (*après-midi* – am), diner (*dîner* – d) and evening (*soirée* – s). Lunches and dinners were often, in Paris, times spent away from the home, occasions for professional meetings (especially lunches) and for seeing friends; when Barthes stayed in, which was rarely, the 'dej' or 'd' are simply followed by the note '*maison*' (home). But most of the time, it is the names of people he met or places he went to that are noted. In Urt, as meals were always family occasions, there was no point in noting them every day. Morning was devoted to work and correspondence, both in Paris and in the countryside. Afternoons in Paris were occupied alternately by classes, visits, or the preparation of his seminars, while in Urt they were also given over to work, to the continuation of tasks he had begun in the morning, or to reading. In addition to these occupations, in the two spaces, there was the nap after lunch, drawing, painting that preceded the resumption of work, writing books, and piano before dinner. The fundamental work, the writing of books, the assembling of data, was done in Urt in the peace and quiet granted by the beneficent coolness of the house when the weather was very hot; he could spend long hours on his work without being interrupted, without any obligations other than those he owed to himself – no visits or meetings outside the home.

In this house, Barthes gathered his things and his thoughts. He gathered ideas, bibliographies, texts and record cards with which to write or imagine books. He gathered his thoughts by limiting the satisfaction of desires (his sexual desires in especial), allowing the outside world to intrude to a minimum degree, and yielding almost entirely to fantasy, the driving force behind all that he wrote. In this way, he could write, in a fragment that would appear somewhat edited in *Roland Barthes by Roland Barthes*: 'The pleasure of those mornings in U.: the sun, the house, silence, music, odours, coffee, work, nonsexual quiescence, holiday from aggressions . . .'[88] He appreciated the almost insignificant monotony of the days that he scrupulously described in the fragment 'Schedule': 'During vacation I get up at seven, go downstairs, and open the house, make myself some tea, break up some bread for the birds waiting in the garden, wash, dust my desk, empty its ashtrays, cut a rose, listen to the seven-thirty news. At eight, my mother comes downstairs too; I take breakfast with her: two softboiled eggs, a slice of toast and black coffee, no sugar.'[89] And so it went on until the evening, regular and trivial occupations, those that made him happy. Several personal documents dwell on the plenitude he derived from the rural, maternal retreat in a region with which Barthes had developed a deep, physical, deliberate relation. Here, the return to childhood was happy and productive. It provided Barthes with what he needed: sensuous qualities such as the sounds of voices, the noise of insects, the perfumes of flowers, the smell of indoors. This was why he preferred inland to the coast: there were more nooks and crannies in which those sensitive, fragile existences that played such a crucial part in triggering writing could be deployed and preserved. Barthes constructed this part of the country that he had largely chosen precisely because it could be a landscape of memory. He was attentive to its movement, its rise and fall; onto it, he could project his memories and desires. '*I like* [. . .] the bend of the Adour seen from Dr L.'s house.'[90] He imagined it as a body. There was nothing completely negative in it, neither in its landscape nor in its climate. In 'The Light of the Sud-Ouest' he writes: '[A]re there never disagreeable moments in this Sud-Ouest weather? Of course, but for me these are not the (quite frequent) moments of rain or storm; not even the times when the sky is overcast; the accidents of light, here, seem to engender no spleen; they do not affect the "soul," only the body, sometimes sticky with humidity, intoxicated with chlorophyll, or languid, exhausted by the wind from Spain.'[91] In his attempt at a diary, at the end of the summer, he wrote: 'In the morning. daybreak is late and still very dark, it's raining (but always, when I open my window, the metonymic power of the odour of the countryside: all of the past, all of literature, etc.). Getting up early, when I do so, gives me as much pleasure as a nice evening in Paris (though it's rather like Marie-Antoinette playing at being a milkmaid). This all means that I'm happy here and that, basically, I enjoy myself as much as I do in Paris.' With the requisite distance (the ironic, unflattering parenthesis), Barthes expresses the nature of this plenitude: it replaces, exactly, the satisfaction found in a relation with other bodies. It fills the senses.

The sociability of village life was not intrusive as it, too, led back to childhood. You had soon met all the people there were to meet in Urt, but they were usually superficial relations, warm and coded. Rather as in Bedous, Barthes went to play music at neighbours' houses, and his mother received a few visitors. His aunt Alice came very often to spend a few days. In particular, there was Dr Michel Lepoivre (the 'Dr L.' in the self-portrait), a GP in Urt between 1963 and 1994; Barthes liked going to his house, where life was cheerful, full of the cries and laughter of his three daughters. Dr Lepoivre was a good violinist and played duets with Barthes – Mozart sonatas, Schubert sonatinas, and so on. He remembers Barthes, dressed in blue overalls in the summer and in the winter wearing a red scarf that a woman friend had knitted for him. 'I think he liked being here, as there was a very different atmosphere from that of the literary coteries of Paris. He could pick up the perfume of the provincial bourgeoisie that, basically, he liked: the father of the family, the mother, three young daughters, everything he didn't have . . .'[92] Barthes loved the protective simplicity of this bourgeoisie, and could excuse its conventional and sometimes frivolous character: 'Conversations at the Lepoivres': on music, life, medicine, serious and choice banalities. It's as if they insisted on being superficial out of a sense of decency, as if depth meant something obscene.'[93]

To begin with, the Barthes family also had a dog, Lux (another 'light' of the South-West!), who contributed to providing protection and serenity. He died on 15 April 1964 when the family was in Urt for the Easter holidays; Barthes, who liked to play with him or have him at his feet while he was reading, was upset. An unpublished fragment from *Roland Barthes by Roland Barthes* shifts this affection into a series of thoughts about the animal's bravery: Barthes has just expressed his hatred of heroic gestures; 'and yet a sort of admiration, for our dog, when he died. This naked death (a death which could not even choose to be silent since a dog can't talk) touched me; all the longwinded Stoic speechifying from my Latin translation exercises came back to me in relation to this dog; purified, at last, of all grandiloquence and, so to speak, of all language, they became *credible*.' The experience with the animal became something philosophical. It corresponded to the specific happiness of the countryside (even if the dog was also with them in Paris, where Michel had found him): a mixture of calm, silence and immutability. It was also a response, a radically different response, to the violence of languages. Just as the dog was a peaceful presence, in the countryside it was possible to be at peace from opinion and discourse.

These years of rootedness in the land of childhood, where Barthes could settle down in two strongly differing places (the Paris apartment and the country house) were, paradoxically, also those of a certain nomadism marked by several trips abroad. Maybe this is not actually a paradox: when you know you belong to certain places, you can move away from them without suffering any anxiety. From 1958 onwards – when he first stayed in the United States – Barthes accepted several invitations and also travelled for pleasure. We can distinguish between three kinds of travel: professional trips, to attend a conference, go on a lecture tour or respond to a specific invitation from one or other institution; trips for pleasure, during the holidays, to explore a region or visit friends, something that Barthes did frequently in Spain, where he went to see Jean-Pierre Richard and his wife Lucie, and in Italy, at La Spezia on the coast of Liguria where the Morins had a house, and Naples at the home of Charles Singevin; and finally, sexual tourism, something in which Barthes indulged, in Morocco, from 1963 onwards and that he made regular habit of in the 1960s.

It is interesting to give an idea of this wide diversity of trips, by drawing up a chronology of his travels over a period of several years. The year 1961 began with a long stay (three weeks) in North America that took him first to Montreal, where he gave a lecture on the *fait divers* and worked with the film director Michel Brault on a film about wrestling, then to Quebec. He travelled on to New York, then returned to Montreal to continue the film. In February, he went to London for a lecture at the French Institute. In July, he went to Italy with Violette Morin for a congress on visual information in Milan, then to Venice for a congress on censorship and from

there to Naples, Florence and La Spezia, transforming the professional trip into a holiday. In October, he went on a lecture tour in
Scandinavia that took him to Hamburg, Copenhagen, Göteborg,
Oslo, Uppsala and Stockholm. In January 1962, he again went to
Italy to stay with the Morins, but he also attended a symposium on
ethnographic film. In March, he went to Brussels at the invitation
of Michel Vinaver and gave a paper on theatre and meaning. His
summer holidays began in June with a trip to La Spezia, Naples
and Sicily, before ending up in Urt. In October, he returned to
Hamburg to give a lecture. In January 1963 he went to Zurich for
the *Revue internationale* gathering; in February, he was in Italy for
lectures in Rome, Palermo and Milan. In April, he gave lectures
at the French Institute in Madrid, went to Barcelona and Madrid
(again) and finally to Lisbon and Coimbra where he again gave a
paper, on literature and meaning. In June, he returned to Madrid
and Lisbon for a holiday. He met up with José, whom he had met
on his previous trip, and travelled with him to Sintra and Estoril.
He then spent three weeks in Urt, before travelling with Michel
Foucault and Robert Mauzi to Marrakesh (where they stayed in the
celebrated Hotel Mamounia) and Tangier. He was in Hamburg for
professional reasons in October, and in Italy for personal reasons in
December. In 1964, he went to Holland with his mother and brother,
and then to Frankfurt. In May, he went back to stay with Ian Boon
in Amsterdam, then went to a conference on Lucien Goldmann in
Brussels. He went to Algeria at the end of the same month, then
spent almost the whole of July in Morocco, in Tangier, Casablanca
and Marrakesh, where he was joined by Robert Mauzi. He went to
Italy in August (holidays) and in September (to teach). At the beginning of 1965, he went on a lecture tour in Italy; at Easter, he went to
Basel and Munich, for pleasure. On 21 May he was in Cologne for
a sociology conference. In June, he went on holiday to Florence. On
27 August, he flew to Warsaw with Jakobson for a semiology conference. In November, he returned to Marrakesh, but he also gave
a seminar in Rabat; in December, he was again in Italy, in Bologna
and Florence. In 1966, he went to Japan for the first time, from 2
May to 2 June, after two trips to the Netherlands and Italy and
before a stay in Morocco in August and a conference in Baltimore in
October (this 1966 conference was to become celebrated). In 1967,
he went back to Japan and Morocco before spending three months
in the United States at the invitation of Johns Hopkins University,
where his mother and his brother joined him in November. He finished 1967 in Japan, travelling directly from the United States.

This inventory may look tedious but it does show that, on
average, Barthes travelled abroad five times a year, almost always in
response to an invitation, even if the initial reasons for the journey
sometimes changed en route. For example, the trip to Japan turned

out to be very rewarding when it came to making friends – and finding sexual partners – even though it had originally been planned as a series of scholarly and academic talks. Conversely, Barthes was sometimes invited to give lectures in Rabat even though his trips to Morocco were mainly motivated by the desire to meet boys. There were several significant features in his art of travelling. First of all, he was never in the least bothered by having to travel, to undertake long trips by car or plane. He could easily fly from Urt to Paris for a stay of just two days. He sometimes drove to Tangier, via Madrid or Malaga, where he picked up the boat. The first time he went to Japan, in 1966, he stopped over in Athens, then spent three days in Bangkok before going to Hong Kong and then Tokyo. When he spent a month in Japan the following year, his plane took the route over the North Pole and the trip took only a day. He sometimes travelled two or three times in the same month. This mobility, typical of the contemporary *homo academicus*, spread his influence in foreign countries, and this resulted in more invitations. He sometimes got tired of always having to set off, but overall the fact he found it so easy to come and go between countries was connected to the high degree of freedom he felt while abroad. He allowed himself to be affected by everything he saw, and he felt as if everything was possible. The intense freedom of travel was the result, first and foremost, of hotels, those often impersonal spaces where life is, as it were, free-floating, irresponsible, open. You rarely feel self-conscious or awkward in them. It is a kind of temporal parenthesis in which we can experience difference and discontinuity. This freedom can be increased by a foreign language – not being able to understand it is a boon rather than a burden. Elias Canetti wrote in *The Voices of Marrakesh* that he was fascinated by the images and sounds whose meaning he could not grasp at first, and dreamed of 'a man who unlearns the world's languages until nowhere on earth does he understand what people are saying'.[94] Likewise, in *Empire of Signs*, Barthes reflected on the powerful attraction of foreign languages: 'The dream: to know a foreign (alien) language and yet not to understand it: to perceive the difference in it without that difference ever being recuperated by the superficial sociality of discourse, communication or vulgarity.'[95] This experience was similar to what he had felt at the death of Lux – it stimulated him to think about the very limits of language. The paternal language, with its grandiloquence and its laws, was forced to bow down before the untranslatable; the real shifted its ground and you could gain access to another imagination of the sign. This is why, for Barthes, love was often associated with a foreign language: if he loved to find love abroad, with foreigners, this was not just because of the freedom he could enjoy now that he was far from home, but also because he could be emancipated from the weight of prejudice and stereotype,

and even from his body, thanks to the gap between languages and the discoveries that this gap made possible. His ideas about 'the rustle of language' stemmed from this experience: he formulated this phrase with reference to a scene in Antonioni's film on China where, in a village street, some children are all reading aloud, from different books: so what we hear is tension, application, breathing, the rhythms of an almost hallucinatory perception in which the 'auditory scene' is imprinted with an intense delight or 'jouissance'.[96]

What Barthes liked about travel – and this was true right from the very first trip to Greece in his teens – was less the cultural high spots of a certain place, its tourist sites, and more the way people lived there, everyday objects, the way in which bodies moved through space, the working-class and out-of-the-way areas. His ethnographic gaze was captured by small differences rather than by the remains of former greatness or the obvious characteristics of the modern society. His travelling companions on the trip to China noticed this. He stayed in the bus when they were being taken on a tour down the sacred avenue of the Ming tombs, but took a close interest in hairstyles, clothes, the way children were looked after. For example, he immediately decided how nice it would be to have a Mao suit made for him. Conferences were an opportunity to get to know his colleagues: boring. When he was invited to give a lecture, he was taken under the wing of the French department of Foreign Affairs, the French Embassy or the French Institute, and invited to cocktail parties and dinners. He still sometimes travelled with his family: in this period, he went to Amsterdam and New York with his mother and his brother – and the fact that, well into adulthood, he continued to travel with the two of them is highly characteristic of the indestructible bond that united them. It was important for him to be able to escape, to find his own spaces that would enable him to enjoy the liberty that he sought when he was travelling and that his travels gave him. He found this in anonymous places where his imagination and his desires were more easily stimulated.

Nonetheless, Barthes would also to some extent see his travels come to an end. At the end of the two decades between 1960 and 1980, two events would slow him down. The first, at the end of the 1960s, was the resumption of his long periods spent living abroad, in particular, a year and a half in Morocco between 1969 and 1971, when he was professor at the University of Rabat. The second was the death of his mother. In 1978, having several times postponed a visit to Tunis where he was supposed to be staying with Philippe Rebeyrol, who had been appointed ambassador to Tunisia, Barthes wrote to tell him that only friendship could still justify a journey that, in fact, he would not now be making: 'I wanted to come and see *you*, since now, and this is quite puzzling, ever since the death of Maman, I have a great resistance to travel "as such".'[97] This remark,

and other like it, confirm that, for Barthes, mobility and structure
were connected. It was because he was rooted in the home, and
entirely structured by his mother's love, that the world belonged
to him and he could travel through it without difficulty. Once his
mother was no longer there, he could no longer live *anywhere* – not
in the apartment in the rue Servandoni, not in the house in Urt, not
in the world as a whole. This loss literally demobilized him. The
penultimate fragment in his self-portrait relates a telephone conversation in which someone just back from a holiday tells Barthes
about his travels without asking him about his own: 'I do not regard
this as indifference; rather the demonstration of a defence: *where I
wasn't present, the world has remained motionless*: great security.'[98]
Throughout almost all his life, this security had been his own.

Roland Barthes in 1959.

The house in Urt.

11

Literature

The celebrated distinction that Barthes drew in 1960, in the review *Arguments*, between '*écrivains*' and '*écrivants*' provided him with the framework for a twofold view of language. Public language of the latter transmitted ideas about the world – the language of academia, politics and research. And the tautological language of the former 'absorbs the world's *why* in a *how to write*':[1] the language of literature. But it was the hybrid figure resulting from a mixture of the two that defined the position Barthes wanted to occupy: 'Everyone today moves more or less openly between the two postulations, the author's and the writer's; it is doubtless the responsibility of history which has brought us into the world too late to be complacent authors and too soon (?) to be heeded writers.'[2] This definition of the intellectual he felt himself to be at the start of the 1960s, when he showed himself to be aware of the place he occupied in history, also demonstrates that, even while focusing intensely on research of an academic kind, Barthes never abandoned literature, as a corpus, a production and a project: literature continued to frame his work in sociology and semiology. While his path took him from science to literature, his main endeavour was to think of language in all its forms.

The deliberate and productive quest for methods on which Barthes embarked between 1958 and 1966 can be subsumed under the idea of interpretation – especially the close reading of texts, which Barthes tried out on different types of language: advertising, fashion writing, cinema and literature. To do so, he had to transform and renew old styles of interpretation. An article with the title 'Oeuvres de masse et explication de texte' ('Mass culture and textual interpretation') that he published in issue 2 of *Communications*, in March 1963, shows the interest of the method as a critique of language, but suggested that it needed to be modified in order to get a handle on a certain number of contemporary objects (commercial cinema, the hit parade, the photo-novel) that might not be properly understood if the usual rules of interpretation were applied to them:

'We will, for example, need to revise critical notions such as that of
originality. We will also need to accept the notion of aesthetic "relevance", i.e. a formal logic within a great collective structure, even
if the latter is extremely "commercial".'[3] This critique enables us to
analyse the major articles of mass consumption as languages (in the
surveys that he carried out for Publicis, for instance), but also to
read literature in a new way. So these were also the years in which
Barthes formed his very powerful theory of the text, as evidenced in
Critical Essays and *On Racine*, where he set out the broad lines that
would lead to his great texts on reading as a model of freedom and
creativity, *S/Z* and *The Pleasure of the Text*, in the early 1970s.

Encounters

If we pay careful attention to the chronology of Barthes's writings,
we will see that it is a simplification to classify his productions into
clearly demarcated periods. During the 1960s when, as we saw in
the previous chapter, he was intensely preoccupied with interpreting
the everyday world, from food to cars via holiday villages and the
rivalry between Chanel and Courrèges, he continued to read and
study literature, to write book reviews in the newspapers ('using
criticism to launch books'), while at the same time actively seeking a
new method for an in-depth interpretation of texts that might contribute to academic structuralism.

His friendships and his encounters fostered this movement.
Barthes met Jean-Pierre Richard in London thanks to Charles
Singevin; Richard had published *Littérature et sensation* in 1954
and was part of a trend that included critics from the Geneva School
such as Georges Poulet, Jean Starobinski and Albert Béguin, whom
he had met right at the beginning of the 1950s. Richard practised
a thematic critique influenced by Bachelard, one attentive to the
material world and its sensations, and Barthes had followed a very
similar approach since his book on Michelet. At the beginning of the
1960s, Richard was working on his major study of Mallarmé and he
may have talked to Barthes about *La Dernière Mode*, the magazine
that the poet had created to discuss fashion, knick-knacks, and
everything that was futile, empty and insignificant (Barthes referred
to it in *The Language of Fashion*, saying that he had dreamed of
doing the same thing). The reference to Mallarmé enabled Barthes
to detect a third level, after the useful and the useless, namely the
level on which fashion became abstract and poetic: this was an
important idea, as it meant one could see how 'men make meaning
out of nothing' and revealed a historical passion for meaning.[4]
Richard introduced Barthes to Gérard Genette in 1956; Genette
was to become a very important colleague and friend in the 1960s,

both in the *Tel Quel* circle (Genette published seven highly influential essays in this journal, including: 'Mallarmé's Happiness?', 'Proust Palimpsest' and 'Fixed Vertigo', on Robbe-Grillet) and at the École pratique, where Barthes helped him to get a position in 1967. Genette was, like Barthes, convinced that criticism could be a kind of literature, and we find in them a shared sense of the inseparable nature of these two kinds of discourse. In 1963, Genette drew up a questionnaire for *Tel Quel* to which he asked Barthes to reply; Genette himself predicted the coming of an era in which criticism would have become truly literary: 'Literature is even more interested in criticism than criticism is interested in literature, and we could, without too much of a risk, predict a time when criticism will no longer have literature as its object, since literature will have taken criticism as its own object.'[5] In the same issue, Barthes, who did not go that far, did nonetheless suggest that 'language has become at once a problem and a model, and the moment may be approaching when these two "roles" can communicate'.[6] There was a real community of views between them. Another significant encounter was with Marthe Robert: Barthes read her book on Kafka at the beginning of 1960 and reviewed it straightaway for *France Observateur*;[7] she very soon became a close friend. Together with her husband, the psychoanalyst Michel de M'Uzan (who also played a major part on the 'rise' of psychoanalytical concepts in Barthes's discourse), the three met regularly, paying visits to other's holiday homes in Hendaye and then in Urt and Antibes. Barthes's friendship with Robert was not quite as close as with Violette Morin, but their correspondence bears witness to a lively intimacy and affection as well as to endless discussions on literature. In particular, it was thanks to Robert that Barthes read Kafka's work closely, especially the *Diaries*, which had an influence on his own diary keeping.

At the École pratique des hautes études, Barthes met Lucien Goldmann, who also played a great role in the development of his ideas about literature: Goldmann spoke at Barthes's seminar in December 1960, where he gave a paper on La Rochefoucauld, and his book on Pascal and Racine, *The Hidden God*, published in 1955, had a decisive impact on Barthes's *On Racine*. At this time, Goldmann was definitely at the centre of what Barthes called 'interpretive criticism', in opposition to the positivist academic criticism, which had more influence. People flocked to his seminars, and his non-mechanistic Marxism, which owed a great deal to Lukács's *History and Class Consciousness*, made him a *maître à penser* for an entire generation who sought to have him as their thesis supervisor: Todorov, Kristeva, Jacques Leenhardt and many others. Barthes said of Goldmann's criticism that 'it is among the most flexible and the most ingenious forms of criticism to take social and political history as its point of departure'.[8] In May 1964, Barthes took part in the Brussels conference on Goldmann's work, giving a paper on rhetoric. Their paths diverged in 1968 and afterwards, but there was a significant period during which Barthes and Goldmann shared the same kind of theoretical Marxism. And they could both, for certain students (such as Kristeva) be charismatic teachers.

Those years of great intellectual productivity were also filled with friends and acquaintances, especially in the literary world. We can distinguish between several circles of sociability that did not necessarily overlap and gave rise to different types of activity. Many of the first circles were defined by the world of publishing and the editorial committees of reviews to which Barthes belonged or to which he was close. He had met Jean Cayrol at Éditions du Seuil, and another decisive encounter there was with François Wahl, who had joined the company in 1957 and been put in charge of literature (especially Italian literature) before moving to the social sciences division in the mid-1960s. Wahl was ten years younger than Barthes, and he had followed a completely different path. As a teenager during the Second World War, he had managed to evade Nazi persecution (though his father died in Auschwitz in 1943) and joined the Resistance. After the war, he studied philosophy, taking a particular interest in psychoanalysis and, between 1954 and 1960, he went into analysis with Lacan, whose friend he became. Barthes and Wahl soon became very close and remained so for the rest of their lives. Their personalities, both reflective and bold, were very similar. Wahl was open about his homosexuality; he lived with the Cuban writer Severo Sarduy, who had been in exile in France since 1961; this too made it easy to strike up a friendship, and fostered an intimacy in which they could share details of their private lives.

At the review *Arguments*, Barthes's friends were the Morins, Kostas Axelos, Franco Fortini (a friend of Edgar Morin, who founded the parallel review *Ragionamenti*)[9] and Jean Duvignaud. At *Critique*, Barthes met Michel Deguy, Jean Piel (who regularly invited Barthes to dinner at his home), Klossowski, Paule Thévenin, Claude Simon and Jacques Derrida. At the *Revue internationale*, he was in close contact with Blanchot, Mascolo and Duras. And at *Tel Quel*, finally, he knew Jean Thibaudeau and Jean-Pierre Faye, but in particular Philippe Sollers, with whom he soon became friends. There was also the circle of his students: Georges Perec attended his classes in 1964; Abdelkhébir Khatibi was also his student that same year; and Barthes made friends with Todorov and then Kristeva while they were attending his seminar. A second tier was formed of friends from his teens, or from the sanatorium, people he saw regularly and whose families he knew. They included Robert David, Philippe Rebeyrol and Jean Girodon; he was firm friends with them and saw them regularly for the rest of his life. There were also his friends abroad, temporary expatriates such as Jean-Pierre Richard in London and then Naples, Maurice Pinguet in Tokyo, Georges Raillard in Barcelona, Josette Pacaly and Jean-Claude Bonnet in Rabat; and also his foreign friends, many of them in Morocco and Italy.

Barthes's social activities and friendships were dictated by the highly ritualized nature of his timetable. There were the friends that he saw alone, or with a couple of others, for a drink or for dinner: François Wahl and Severo Sarduy; Philippe Sollers and, from 1966 onwards, Julia Kristeva; Gérard Genette and his wife Raymonde Debray-Genette. There were those who invited him to dinner, and who offered a more worldly kind of social life: Paule Thévenin, at whose home he met a great number of people (notably Jean Genet and Jacques Derrida), the Dumayets, Klossowski and his wife Denise Morin, with whom Barthes played piano duets. He also met Michel Butor there and sometimes his friend Georges Perros, who also came to play the piano with Denise.[10] Though Barthes sometimes claimed to be bored at meetings of this kind, he nevertheless enjoyed the milieu of creativity and stimulating anti-conformism that they offered. There were also friends he would travel to conferences with, such as Todorov, Derrida and Deguy; and those he spent family holidays with, such as Butor, Marthe Robert and Violette Morin – at her home he also regularly met Pierre Naville, whom she married in 1970 – and Raymond Queneau. Finally, there were the friends he spent whole evenings with, sometimes going out with them after dinner to Paris's homosexual night clubs in Saint-Germain or Montmartre. With Foucault, Mauzi and Louis Lepage, François Braunschweig and Bruno Vercier, Barthes sometimes went to the Fiacre, in the rue du Cherche-Midi, the Apollinaire, the Speakeasy in the rue des Canettes, and then, later on, the Pimm's and the Sept, opened by Fabrice Emaer in the rue Sainte-Anne, in 1964 and 1968 respectively. Barthes also sometimes went alone.

The main encounter of those years was indisputably with François Braunschweig, to whom he dedicated his *Critical Essays* when they first came out in 1964. While Barthes often had his heart broken by unrequited love for heterosexual men or men who did not love him, with Braunschweig he was to enjoy a stable loving friendship until the day he died. While he usually lived out his sexuality in a somewhat surreptitious fashion, in places set apart, with Braunschweig he had a more overt social relationship. He met him in November 1963, in the *Tel Quel* circle. Thirty years younger than Barthes, Braunschweig (born in 1946) studied law while attempting to gain a foothold in the literary world, as he had started to write. In December, the two men set off for Italy – to Venice and then Naples, Capri, Pompeii and Rome, where they saw in the New Year. In 1964, they met up almost every evening, and spent their holidays together; Barthes even sometimes managed to work in

Braunschweig's company in the afternoons. They both went to the celebrated 'improvised lecture' given by Francis Ponge, organized by *Tel Quel* on 13 March 1964, in the premises of Georges Bataille's former Collège de sociologie. They were invited to the homes of common friends – Paule Thévenin, the Genettes, the Klossowskis. They often met up with Wahl and Sarduy. Even when they agreed to see rather less of each other at the end of 1964, they still spent a great deal of time together throughout 1965. They went to Germany in April and Italy in July. Their shared life was significant enough for Barthes's desk diary to have this entry for 8 November 1965: 'At F's, 2nd anniversary of meeting.' In 1966, their relationship became one of friends rather than lovers: they very frequently went out or had dinner together and, during the summer, François went to Urt for a few days with his parents. It is easy to imagine that Henriette Barthes was perfectly aware of the nature of her son's affection for this young man, even if Barthes, faithful to his vow of silence with regard to his mother, maintained the greatest discretion in front of her. They always expressed their mutual love and respect for one another by saying nothing. But, apart from this, Barthes made no secret of his relationship. Many of his friends knew about it, and the dedication of *Critical Essays* was a powerful gesture of public recognition.

That same year, 1964, Barthes wrote an article on some texts that François had asked him to read before publication (in fact, they never were published). This essay, unveiled for the first time in 1984 in *The Rustle of Language*, was soberly and mysteriously titled 'F.B.'; it came with a discreet note by François Wahl: 'Unpublished, this text was written as a footnote to fragments by a young writer who seems not to have pursued a literary vocation and who published nothing.'[11] This extreme reticence on the part of someone who knew perfectly well who François Braunschweig was shows a desire for concealment that seems perhaps no longer suitable today – especially as Barthes himself did absolutely nothing to conceal it. But Wahl, who knew exactly what was at stake, also added: 'A marginal text, then, intended for the person whose enterprise it examines. Here tone and address are distinctly ludic, which does not prevent this text – quite the contrary – from constituting a system of acute propositions on a new type of fictive writing. We can here recognize *in nucleo*, as early as 1964, certain features of Barthes's final manner.'[12] And it is true that Barthes talks a great deal about himself in this text, written at the height of his love for Braunschweig, without fear of any mirror effects, and probably even seeking them. He insists on the way a kind of fragmentary writing is achieved in texts that are neither sketches, nor notes, nor diary entries, but 'splinters of language'. He gives them a name that he had already reserved for his own practice of writing: 'incidents'; they are 'things that *fall*, without a jolt yet with a movement which is not infinite: the discontinuous infinity of the snowflake'. For, in these incidents, there 'reigns the fundamental tense of free literatures, language's last conquest (according to its prehistory): the *indicative*'.[13] Certain remarks on speed, and on the novel-like quality of the fragment, prefigure those of the last course at the Collège de France, on the haiku. Above all, this is a text that talks about desire: not just the 'desire for boys' that is never, writes Barthes, culturalized, but is a desire conveyed by writing: 'In F.B.'s texts, there is never any *undesirable* object. Thus, the author creates a vast metonymy of desire: a *contagious* writing which transfers to its reader the very desire out of which it has formed things.'[14] It is pleasing to read such a remark, filled with the emotion generated by meeting, the pleasure of writing on and for the other, the complicity of reading oneself through the other. Until Barthes's death, he and Braunschweig would continue to meet up often, to dine together or with Hugues Autexier, Braunschweig's new partner, with whom he opened a gallery for French photography and art books, the Texbraun Gallery. This started as a little shop at the Puces de Clignancourt, and then moved to the rue Mazarine: it was soon well known among lovers of photography for its well-chosen displays.[15] It is likely that Barthes drew some of his information about the history of photography from his friendship with these men.

Literary criticism

During the 1960s, Barthes did not simply spend time with friends in literary circles: he was actively pursuing his work as a literary analyst and discovering more about literature, in three time-frames: the classics (the past), contemporary literature (the present) and the avant-garde (the future). He was simultaneously researching various methods of reading and interpretation that would give him a significant role in the establishment of literary structuralism or what is sometimes called literary semiology.

The first area in which Barthes was active concerned contemporary work, which he continued to review for various journals. He reported on several important works of literary criticism and pioneering essays that presented a new picture of what literature could be, such as Marthe Robert's *Kafka*, Foucault's *History of Madness*, Painter's biography of Proust, the first volume of Benveniste's *Problems in General Linguistics*, and so on. He remained loyal to the authors he had known over the previous decade. These included Queneau, to whom he devoted an influential article in *Critique* when *Zazie in the Metro* came out in 1959, seeing it as a monument of anti-literature, a concerted destruction of the myth of literature;

Cayrol, to whose *Corps étrangers* he wrote an afterword when it was republished as a paperback in 1964; and Bataille, whose *Story of the Eye* he reviewed in 1963. A common feature of these readings is that Barthes paid a sustained attention to superficial effects, to the voices that skim the surface. As he wrote in connection with Cayrol, 'like the caress, language here remains on the surface of things; the surface is its realm'.[16] Even if he distinguished between Robbe-Grillet's art of exhaustively describing surfaces and Cayrol's need to stay at ground level, Barthes was keen to relate this work to the theoretical debates of the avant-garde. He did the same with Bataille. On the *Story of the Eye*, he wrote that everything was given on the surface, without any hierarchy. This deployment of the world without any underside or depth requires us to explain it rather than interpret it – to explain it by gradually unfolding its surface, unpicking its textual fabric.

Barthes's relation to Maurice Blanchot sheds a great deal of light on his relation to contemporary literature in general. As we have seen, there was a deep connection between them, one that was real, active and political all at once. It involved an attempt to understand and define the space of literature and writing; and the connection went back a long way, since it was in the sanatorium that Barthes had read Blanchot's first articles in *Les Temps modernes* and *Critique*; he may even have read Blanchot's literary column in the *Journal des débats*, where he might have come across the definition of the essay that Blanchot gave in connection with Jean Grenier, a definition in which Barthes might easily have recognized (or imagined) himself: 'An experience in which the writer, sometimes, indirectly, not only commits himself, but argues with himself, sets himself up as a problem, leads his ideas so far that he is rejected by them, draws from his own personal ordeals a sense that can be accepted by everyone, in a word, turns himself into the hero of an adventure whose meaning transcends him.'[17] Right from the start, Blanchot encouraged Barthes to think about the limits and impossibilities of writing. When Barthes emerged from the sanatorium, where he had been confronted in many ways by death, this idea that literature was disappearance, an ordeal of silence, chimed in with a personal experience that recognizes itself in anxiety and nothingness. Thus, *Writing Degree Zero* engages in dialogue not just with Sartre, but also, explicitly, at least as much with Blanchot, who in turn engaged with Barthes as a major presence in *The Book to Come*.[18] In Barthes, Blanchot's name occurs in a list where, from Flaubert to Camus, writers raise the question of literature by writing literature itself, and the text 'Writing and Silence' takes from Blanchot the figure of Orpheus as the very impossibility of literature, which can write itself only by destroying itself: Orpheus 'can save what he loves only by renouncing it, and who, just the same, cannot resist glancing round

a little; it is Literature brought to the gates of the Promised Land: a
world without Literature, but one to which writers would nevertheless have to bear witness.'[19] To turn round on language is at once
a duty (Moses) and a transgression (Orpheus): an act that implies
both vigilance and destruction. Barthes recognizes the impossibility of a literature that gets stripped of its dangerous, edgy power to
question, once it exists socially *as literature*; but he also perceives
the danger of remaining trapped within this very impossibility.
Where Blanchot evokes an incandescent retreat, Barthes continues
to insist on an 'and yet', 'in spite of everything'; he writes possibility
into the impossible – and this, perhaps, is his Gidean side, one that
re-emerges at regular intervals. While acknowledging that Blanchot
had produced a major, inalienable discourse on literature, Barthes
deploys all possible means to escape from his nihilism. His decision
to defend Robbe-Grillet can be read as a way of imagining a happy
Orpheus, an Orpheus who does not look back. (This was also what
Barthes would find fascinating in Sollers.)

The first way of warding off Blanchot was to isolate him. Barthes
produced lists of names where Blanchot's presence emphasized the
radical nature of his enterprise, but also kept him at bay, as someone
who could not be appropriated. For example, in 'There is No
Robbe-Grillet School', Barthes contrasts the absolute negativity of
Blanchot and Mallarmé, '*oeuvres* [. . .] which have been or which are,
deliberately, the glorious residue of the impossible',[20] and a negation
that in the case of Robbe-Grillet is restricted to the technical level.
In *Criticism and Truth*, he picks up this link between Blanchot and
Mallarmé and discusses works that speak of the conditions of their
absence, contrasting them with Proust's novel, which expresses the
conditions of its birth. In his 1963 answer to the questionnaire in *Tel
Quel* about criticism, he explicitly remarked on his own resistance
to the project, while continuing to state how much he admired it:
'To "annihilate" meaning is a desperate project in proportion to its
impossibility. Why? because what is "outside meaning" is infallibly
absorbed (at a certain moment which the work has the power only
to delay) into *non-meaning* which itself is of course a meaning (under
the name of the *absurd*).'[21] Thus, Blanchot's disquieting force, his
singularity, lies in the way he always stays on this side of meaning,
where he is the first to speak. This is the reason behind his remarkable isolation, which means that only negative categories can be
assigned to him. In the significant interview with Raymond Bellour
that followed the publication of *The Language of Fashion*, Barthes
went so far as to say: 'Blanchot belongs to the incomparable, the
inimitable, and the inapplicable. He is *in* writing, he is in that transgression of knowledge which constitutes literature.'[22] Furthermore,
Blanchot was systematically placed in the tradition of writers, not
of thinkers or critics. He could not be used as a store of phrases

or tools. In spite of Blanchot's public statements of commitment in the 1960s, Barthes never considered him as an intellectual, but as a writer, a superior writer, a real master. Indeed, apart from his course on 'The neutral', where Barthes quoted Blanchot at length, he hardly ever referred to him literally, apart from his analysis of Ulysses and the sirens in *The Book to Come*, quoted on two occasions, in 'Listening', the article he wrote in collaboration with Roland Havas in 1977,[23] and in *Camera Lucida*.[24] For several years, Barthes even seems to have forgotten Blanchot: witness the strange denial in the television interview with Jean Thibaudeau, where he says that he had not read Blanchot when he wrote *Writing Degree Zero*, although he actually mentions him twice in this work.[25] In an important article on the different stages of the relationship between the two men, Éric Marty suggests that, between 1968 and 1977, Blanchot ceased to be a contemporary for Barthes, who placed his fellow writer in the immemorial, among the great dead. 'By reducing to zero the living connection with Blanchot, Barthes gives him a place, a no doubt terrible place but perhaps the only one that can be assigned to him: the place of the dead man who now exists only between Proust and Kafka, the dead man who, from that silent, distant region, appears as a fellow criminal who really shares the furtive desire to write.'[26] Of course, there are several ways of understanding this effacement – the name of Blanchot does not appear in *The Pleasure of the Text*, nor in *Roland Barthes by Roland Barthes*. Perhaps Barthes was wary of Blanchot's 'nihilism'; for instance, he constructed a jubilant image of Sade as against Blanchot's Sade of negation. But, in this perhaps 'impossible' friendship based on anachronism (Blanchot, like Proust, acted on Barthes as a trigger, a memorial power, not as an interlocutor or contemporary), we touch on the truth of this very special relationship. These writers were in fact important for each other because they stimulated each other, led each other to writing. First came the friendly conversation, the dialogue, characterized by various kinds of exchange (including an exchange of letters), but mainly by the two articles Blanchot wrote, one on *Writing Degree Zero* (partly used in *The Book to Come*) and one on *Mythologies*.[27] This initial phase was followed by the 'infinite conversation', as Blanchot called it, that writing entailed. Twice over, Barthes appropriated the words of Roger Laporte: 'Reading Proust, Blanchot, Kafka and Artaud didn't make me want to write *about* those authors (not even, I might add, *like* them), but just to *write*.'[28]

One final explanation for Barthes's drift away from Blanchot is partly related to his struggle against negation, and lies in his intense effort to keep at bay the fear of death during the 1960s. This helps us to understand why Camus and Cayrol, whose works Barthes had passionately made his own in the period 1945–55, were sidelined in favour of Robbe-Grillet and Butor: the analysis of surfaces, and all the games in which meaning was kept at a distance, were preferred to a more or less overt spirituality and the need to confront death in all its forms. We might also suggest that Barthes's focus on the avant-garde, as well as his deliberate practice of keeping daily notes from 1960 onwards, and his ritual timetable, were all strategies of evasion, in which the decision in favour of activity and life is made *against* silence and death. It is interesting that the 1964 article on Cayrol is called 'Cayrol and Erasure', whereas it is more a matter of scratches, of notches made on the surface of things, rather than of erasure as such (and the word is not used apart from the title). What could be a better expression of a form of effacement? It probably springs from the force of the semiological shift carried out in those years, marking the end of any solidarity between man and objects. The relation between signifier and signified now bars the presence of the referent.

The fact that the name 'Blanchot' made a huge return from 1977 onwards (there are nineteen references to Blanchot in the course on 'The neutral'), at the time when his mother was falling ill, confirms this suggestion. Barthes swung between seeing the neutral as a suppression of the link between the sign and the referent, and the neutral as silence (involving a certain negativity, as in Blanchot, and indeed a confrontation with death). In *A Lover's Discourse* (1975), an allusion to Blanchot links him to fatigue: 'I had to wait for Blanchot for someone to tell me about fatigue' and a note states: 'BLANCHOT: Conversation (long ago).'[29] In the course he gave at the Collège de France in 1977–78, which began after the death of Henriette Barthes, this hint is developed at length. In the very first session, fatigue is treated as an unclassifiable place, without specific location, and socially untenable: 'whence Blanchot's (weary!) cry: "I don't ask that weariness be done away with. I ask to be led back to a region where it might be possible to be weary".'[30] Barthes again quotes Blanchot in the next session, when he turns fatigue – a certain form of absence of sociability, and thus a kind of neutrality – into the very condition of his life. At the same time, he remembers the aging Gide who, one year before his death, felt like 'a tire that deflates' and was an example of trying to '"play one's fatigue" by turning it into discourse'.[31] This explicit lineage doubtless shows the extent to which, like Gide, the many-layered Blanchot was situated on the crucial terrain of the immemorial.

So, at the end of the 1950s and in the early 1960s, the avant-garde was a strategy to combat the potentially devastating nature of modern literature when it becomes a confrontation with death. It was also a means of reconciling sociological demystification with literature; it proposed a method whereby texts and objects could be read together. Robbe-Grillet's work was the main testing ground for this approach, and we can immediately see the link that Barthes drew between literature and the concrete object in the articles he wrote on the novelist. The first, 'Objective Literature', was written just as Barthes was discovering Brecht, and can be read as the manifesto for a literature of the surface, a mythologist's literature that is also an ethnography of daily life. In it, Barthes notes the presence of elements from the urban setting and manufactured objects ('reading glasses, light switches, erasers, percolators, dress-maker's dummies, packaged sandwiches')[32] that are exhausted by their description. Without function or substance, they reveal their mystificatory character and at the same time draw the reader into a sensory experience of matter. Torn away from their traditional space, they show themselves in their pure dimension of time. The following year, 'Literal Literature' consolidated the impact of the first article, this time in a review of Robbe-Grillet's *The Voyeur*, which takes this liquidation even further by getting rid of the story itself: 'The plot recedes, diminishes, dies away under the weight of objects.'[33] By renouncing the soul, the idea of the writer as confessor, doctor or demiurge, Robbe-Grillet strips the novel of any essentialism and sets it on the path of a radical formalism that would partly determine Barthes's own methodical formalism over the next few years. These first, well-known articles on Robbe-Grillet, written at the same time as the *Mythologies*, indicate both Barthes's current preoccupations (the nature of objects and metalanguage) and the formal, structuralist framework provided by linguistics. Barthes was also thinking of literature itself as mythology, and focusing on all those texts that put literature on trial or give it an essentially interrogative function.

There was a spectacular about-turn in 1962, when Barthes, in a preface to Bruce Morrissette's book on Robbe-Grillet, seemed rather weakly to acquiesce in Morrissette's more humanistic, less 'superficial' vision of the novelist, while noting that his own conception brought with it a salutary emancipation from the codes of realist literature and a turn to 'a reflective treatment of reality'.[34] But while he stayed loyal to what he called the 'first Robbe-Grillet', he was more lukewarm about the second, the one who produced *Marienbad* and *In the Labyrinth*. This was somewhat surprising. To begin with, it is rather unusual to write a foreword to a book with which you are in such obvious disagreement; furthermore, Barthes seems to be withdrawing support from an author to whose success he had made such a large contribution. *Critical Essays* expresses this relative distance between them – relative, as the two men remained in many ways close: Barthes's preface to Michelet's book on witches, *La Sorcière*, was decisive for Robbe-Grillet's screenplay for *Successive Slidings of Pleasure* (loosely inspired by Michelet's book), and Robbe-Grillet paid powerful homage to Barthes at the colloque de Cerisy in 1977; his remarks were later published as a separate small volume.[35] But there was also a distance between them, stemming both from questions of affinity and from political reasons. Barthes was less close to Robbe-Grillet than to Michel Butor, whom he met at Middlebury College and who soon became a close friend. The correspondence between Barthes and Butor bears witness to a bond of strong affection: they both worried about the health of the other's relations, with Butor asking Barthes for news of his mother and his brother and informing him of the successive births of his three daughters and the health of his wife Marie-Jo Butor. Barthes played something of the same role for Butor as he had played earlier for Vinaver, acting as a literary adviser, and a major source of help in the creation of work in progress.[36] When, in 1962, Barthes wrote about Butor's *Mobile*, this book, a kind of collage presentation of the United States, seemed to correspond more closely, in his view, to the permanent questioning of the unquestioned forms of literature than Robbe-Grillet's latest works. Barthes praised the way Butor had struck a blow against the idea of the book as a sequence, a development, a flow: these ideas announced his views on the 'album' in *The Preparation of the Novel*. He compared Butor's procedures to those of Lévi-Strauss in *The Savage Mind*: both were involved in an intense quest: 'It is by trying fragments of events together that meaning is generated, it is by tirelessly transforming these events into functions that the structure is erected.'[37]

So Barthes's personal friendships could sometimes lead to him showing a more sustained interest in one work than in another. But he also expressed political reservations about the labels used to pigeonhole people: such labels subsumed works that were of quite different types. Without directly attacking Robbe-Grillet's *For a New Novel*, he demurred at the way a whole variety of work was being brought under the umbrella of a slogan that, in his view, was mainly a strategic manoeuvre. In *France Observateur*, in 1964, he told Renaud Matignon that he had never defended the 'New Novel'. He had used it as part of a sociological 'montage' rather seeing it as a doctrinal matter. Barthes was, as it were, raining on Robbe-Grillet's parade. The latter realized this, and when Sollers attacked *For a New Novel* in *Tel Quel* in 1964 (having written an important article on Robbe-Grillet's work in an earlier issue), Robbe-Grillet wrote to him: 'I just happen to have read your little piece on *For a New Novel*. Well, well . . . ! I'm being dropped! People are following dear old Roland Barthes! They're forgetting what was said about *In the Labyrinth* and *The Immortal* [. . .] and even about the main essays contained in this collection! Too bad. We've kept each other company for a while – all that's left for me to do is to wish you *bon voyage* . . .'[38] (Barthes had in fact criticized both *In the Labyrinth* and *The Immortal*.) In the interview he gave Guy Le Clec'h about his own *Critical Essays*, for *Le Figaro littéraire*, Barthes expressed his reservations directly: 'On his work I had no influence. Perhaps I provided him with a few elements that helped him formulate his theoretical views. But since the publication of Bruce Morrissette's study of Robbe-Grillet's novels, his work has concerned me less. We see him being tempted to replace the mere description of objects with feelings, fragments of symbols.'[39]

Critical Essays, which came out in 1964, was structured around the two avant-gardes that Barthes had noted in the 1950s – Brecht and Robbe-Grillet – and then sketched out the path that had led from the *Mythologies* to *The Structural Analysis of Narrative*: he shows how the primacy of the signifier over the signified, and the need to explain surface effects, lead to an idea of criticism in which the reader is left to construct a great deal of the meaning. The real is abandoned and the implicit thoughts contained within language itself are laid bare. In this sense, it is a major book, and generations of students and readers would view it as such. The writers who knew Barthes personally told him how grateful they were for what he had to say about writing. One of these was Claude Simon, who sent him a letter from Salses on 9 March 1964, hailing the great significance of Barthes's analyses. The book included no new texts apart from the preface, but the chronological ordering of the essays gave the whole volume a force and complexity and a definite itinerary, and made certain definite choices, such as excluding the articles on Cayrol (as we have seen, Barthes could be unpredictable . . .). In the essays, the idea of 'theme and variation' is deployed: certain works persist, and return in different forms at regular intervals. We can gauge the force with which Barthes promotes some works and rejects others. Finally, we become aware of the intensity of contradiction for Barthes: it is a life force that, in his preface, he assigns to criticism itself. For critical language is inevitably assertive, and yet longs to be indirect. Hence the infidelity and anachronism that are evident in the book as a whole, and stop us reading it in a teleological fashion, as the 1971 foreword indicates. The present of writing is already past, the past of the anterior is very distant, and yet it is in the present that this past needs to be kept alive.

In the 1964 preface, the main ambiguity lies in the way that nouns such as 'writer' and 'writing', and the verb 'to write', are treated. It is never clear whether Barthes is using them to refer to the authors he is discussing, or to talk about himself. When he writes that 'writing is never anything but a language' or when he describes the writer's 'infidelity',[40] we are left to wonder. However, things become clearer at the end of the text, which, for the first time, explicitly sets out his relation to Proust: the writer is the person whose writing is always a future, who is about to write – and thus the writer can equally be the critic who places his or her writing in suspense. The critic is in search of his 'I', and his horizon is the novel itself: 'The critic is the man who is going to write and who, like the Proustian narrator, satisfies this expectation with a supplementary work, who creates himself by seeking himself and whose function is to accomplish his project of writing even while eluding it.'[41] So, within the general range of strategies, literary criticism has its own role in which the author makes himself a writer-to-be. In 1974, rereading himself while composing his self-portrait, he found his ideas on writing to be muddled and murky, 'an empty, somewhat obsessive rambling: it's often much less intelligent than for the rest – and this is exactly what I love, "my" area, my brand image! Well, maybe that's just the thing: maybe it's the field of my *jouissance* that makes me stupid?'[42] He also recognized the space that belonged to him, his privileged territory, as well as the 'hard and indivisible kernel' of stupidity, the 'primitive'[43] element that was also part of the fantasy depicted in *Roland Barthes by Roland Barthes*. This dual temporality, always directed towards the future and inscribed in the most distant past, gave to the present the stumbling gait of variation and endless repetition.

Critical Essays was first published in French in Seuil's new 'Tel Quel' collection and not as one of their 'Pierres vives' books as Barthes's previous texts had been – another clear indication that they were viewed as a nod to the avant-garde. Barthes had initially been very sceptical about Sollers's review. He felt that the 'Declaration' set at the beginning of the first issue turned literature into a dogma or a mythology – exactly what his own work was endeavouring to denounce. And when Jean-Edern Hallier sent him, on behalf of the review, the questionnaire 'Do you think you have any gifts as a writer?', Barthes roundly told him to go and ask General de Gaulle instead![44] But he did agree, the following year, to reply to the survey on 'Literature today', and he gradually grew closer to Sollers and the *Tel Quel* group as a whole. Apart from the friendship he struck up with Sollers – to which I will be returning in a later chapter – this was a decision that benefited everybody: in 1964, Barthes was a well-known, successful figure, and this boosted the image of the review, which at that time was trapped in endless meandering polemics and finicky hesitations about which line to adopt. His faithful support meant that *Tel Quel* followed a clearly formalist direction, and the exchange of ideas between his seminar and the work then being published intensified. The anthology of Russian formalists edited by Todorov under the title *Théorie de la littérature* came out in the 'Tel Quel' collection just after Todorov had given a paper at Barthes's seminar. Conversely, the group's dynamism gave a high profile to some of Barthes's suggestions, especially his positions on literature and some of the research he was engaged in, which now gained a polemical impact when his influence might otherwise have been confined to more academic publications. Also, *Tel Quel* provided

Barthes with vociferous – and heart-warming – public support at the time of his quarrel with Raymond Picard.

Barthes explains himself

Between his complicated relation to modernity and his deliberate promotion of the avant-garde, Barthes created a third term, thanks to his interpretation of classical works. *Critical Essays* includes several texts on canonical authors, such as Voltaire, Baudelaire, Michelet and La Bruyère, who were also authors he liked, sometimes corresponding to works he had read long ago, sometimes linked to his loyalty to the great centuries of French writing. Here, he thought, one could find the notion of a literature and a language that was subsequently lost sight of; here, signs were exhibited clearly – something of an ideal for writing. Barthes never abandoned the works that he had grown up with. Even authors that might seem problematic (such as Stendhal, Zola and Maupassant) were the subjects of influential articles. Ever since 'Plaisir aux classiques', the article in *Existences*, Barthes had also seen the works of the so-called 'classical' century as the very future of literature: their clarity came with a certain incompleteness, and this kept them open – hence the interest one could still take in them. 'The force of the classics rests on this distinction; the Classics were clear, with a terrible clarity; but they were so clear that, in this transparency, we can sense disquieting gaps. And these gaps are so skilfully managed that we do not know whether the authors in question placed them there on purpose, or simply left them there.'[45] Barthes's close and necessary relation to the fragment is here shown most consummately. The fragment was an open form (La Bruyère), or sometimes closed in a non-totalitarian way, in the spirit of the *pointe* (La Rochefoucauld). And it was also connected to 'notation', as is evident in his preface to La Bruyère's *Characters* – something that continued to preoccupy him right up until the final seminar: 'what has changed, from La Bruyère's world to ours, is what is notable: we no longer *note* the world the way La Bruyère did',[46] since the scope of what we mean by 'the real' had grown to such an extent that a reflection on literature was no longer enough to contain it; specialized sciences had now assumed the task of breaking it down and describing it. Written at the same time, *On Racine*, the preface to the *Characters* of La Rochefoucauld and the preface to La Rochefoucauld's *Maxims* brought out clearly Barthes's twofold relation to the classics. The terms 'classical' and 'classicism' are used in an uncertain, ambiguous way in his work. They are pejorative when they refer to 'classical institutions', seen as guilty of having mutilated the language, or to 'classical criticism', stigmatized in *Criticism and Truth*, Barthes's reply to Picard (classicism was seen as too much of an institution). But they are given a more positive meaning when they characterize works that are open to different meanings, leaving the reader free to imagine everything, offering a wonderful area for exploration. Racine, all by himself, encompasses the two poles: he is the most academic of authors, 'the point of convergence for a host of taboos which I think should be dispelled',[47] but he is also a truly great writer, '[i]f literature is essentially, as I believe, a meaning advanced and at the same time a meaning withdrawn'.[48] Likewise, the classical maxim can convey an essentialist view of human nature and even have a terrorist arrogance, while at the same time being the model for a demystificatory kind of writing. Barthes's frontal opposition to the academic doxa was the first in a long series of such attacks, and it would have important consequences.

As we can see, there is no point in contrasting the classical with the modern in Barthes, since classicism is the bearer of a positive value only if it assumes the characteristics of modernity (silence, incompleteness, uncertainty and openness) or can be used by modern writers. Although La Bruyère does not really strike us as all that novel, reading him in 1963 becomes meaningful in that it allows us to gauge the distance between his own world and ours, to take in 'the modern meaning of his work'.[49] Likewise, Racine should be understood as a thoroughly contemporary writer: 'Let us test on Racine, by virtue of his very silence, all the languages our century suggests.'[50] The point is to explain and, at the same time, to arouse disquiet: the same task is assigned to both the classics and the moderns. This modernity of classicism was, of course, something Barthes had inherited from Gide during his time in the sanatorium. Then, Gide had made Barthes want to 'read the classics', as 'Bossuet, Fénelon, Montesquieu never seem as good as when they are quoted by Gide'[51] – but this modernity was also part of a coherent critical project, entailed not by anachronism as such, but by the recognition of the anachronism that comprised *any* major work of literature, as Barthes wrote in his brilliant essay on Chateaubriand's *Vie de Rancé* in 1965 ('the word read is *anachronic*, and this anachronism is the crucial question it puts to the critic'[52]). Such anachronism made all historical reconstruction pointless.

The project was also an endeavour to join forces with the critical renewal that had recently begun. The preface to *On Racine* is extremely clear on this last point: 'There is good reason for talking about Racine today; in the last ten or twelve years his work has been involved in every critical effort of some importance made in France: sociological with Lucien Goldmann; psychoanalytical with Charles Mauron; biographical with Jean Pommier and Raymond Picard; phenomenological with Georges Poulet and Jean Starobinski.'[53] The fact that Racine's work lent itself to modern criticism was the very sign of literature, in Barthes's view. Literature should never be reduced to an institution; institutions never ask the fundamental question 'What is literature?', as they are too busy attesting to literature's mere existence. In the last essay in *On Racine*, called 'History or Literature?', Barthes, who was explicitly trying to free the author from the educational system and the academic establishment, directly attacked certain historians of literature (including Raymond Picard), claiming instead that a work of literature usually floats free of its own age. In place of this factual, philological and chronological history, Barthes praised the approach of Lucien Febvre: Barthes's essay appeared in *Annales* and he was clearly following Febvre's lead, as he had done already in his first article on Michelet. Febvre's book on Rabelais had highlighted the importance of a study of the milieu in which a work of literature comes into being, of its audience and the intellectual formation of that audience. Barthes even went further than Febvre in accepting the anachronism that Febvre had denied – in Febvre's view, a work is always more or less part of its time. Like Rancé in Chateaubriand's biography of him, the literary work, especially when it continues to be brought into the present, is always more than just a matter of time.

While this, the last essay in the volume, could quite justifiably provoke the wrath of academics, it was mainly the first essay, 'Racinian Man', by far the longest (it was written as a preface to an edition of Racine's dramas),[54] that was most vehemently attacked by Barthes's enemies. Althusser perceived the work's subversive dimension as soon as he read it: 'at last, there's someone who says that the dear old Racinian "psychology" everyone talks about, and the dear old Racinian passions, so violent and pure and wild, *just don't exist!* Someone who says that it's literature first and foremost . . .'[55] We need to reconstruct the drama of Barthes's polemic with Picard in detail, as it is never narrated in its successive acts. Everyone remembers that Picard attacked *On Racine* in *New Criticism or New Imposture*, and that Barthes replied in *Criticism and Truth*. This is to forget rather too quickly that *On Racine* was published in April 1963 and Picard's text came out in autumn 1965, two and a half years later. While the essay on Racine had been met with disapproval by a good number of specialists, these showed their traditional reserve and did not express their opinions. The publication of *Critical Essays*, in 1964, however, was the last straw: the article on 'The Two Criticisms', which contrasted academic criticism and its positivist method (inherited from Lanson) with the new criticism embodied by Bachelard, Goldmann, Poulet, Starobinski, Weber, Richard and Girard, led to an initial reaction from Picard in *Le Monde*, 14 March 1964: 'Academia as such never deigns to reply, but perhaps people will understand if just one academic reacts, in his own name, to attacks that will eventually become dangerous by dint of being repeated, even if they lack substance or even relevance.'[56] The article is rather general and expresses regret at this polarized conception of criticism, which, it claims, is unfair to academia; Picard refrains from embarking upon a polemic, in spite of what he sees as Barthes's unconvincing interpretations of Racine. He then published a long article in the *Revue des sciences humaines* that went into more detail over his reasons for criticizing Barthes's book: this time, given the readership of this type of review, his arguments were addressed to academics alone.[57] By expanding this article, turning it into a little book for a bigger audience, Picard was triggering a debate in the general intellectual field. He listed his objections, such as the way Barthes reduced characters to functions essentially impelled by a spirit of transgression. Above all, he accused Barthes of subjecting the text to anachronistic psychoanalytical categories, thus leading to symbolic characterizations that ignored the literal meaning and the historical relevance of the plays. Some of Picard's objections are silly, as when he reduces criticism to questions of decency and taste, and criticizes Barthes for being obsessed with sex; others are relevant, such as the risk of relativism run by all functional criticism, and Barthes's use of psychoanalytical categories (Picard found this rather slipshod, a point that Barthes acknowledged: 'Its language is somewhat psychoanalytical, though not its treatment.'[58])

These attacks were belated, and came as a surprise to Barthes. It was the almost simultaneous publication of *On Racine* and *Critical Essays* that seemed intolerable: the split between the Sorbonne and more marginal institutions was just starting to make itself felt, and Barthes's influence on students was growing. Todorov relates how, when he arrived in Paris in the spring of 1963, he went to see the director of the department of literature armed with a reference from the Dean of the University of Sofia, and asked what literary theory courses were on offer: 'He looked at me as if I had come from another planet and told me: "There's no such thing, literature needs to be studied from the historical and national perspective".'[59] Likewise, Élisabeth Roudinesco describes how dissatisfied she was by the way she was taught when she began her studies in 1964: 'When you studied literature, the line of demarcation was: have you read the latest Barthes? There were two camps.'[60] If Barthes had started to have an impact on students' minds, and at the very heart of the academic system, then it was time to fight back. While Barthes's activities were confined to the field of contemporary literature, his experiments could do no harm; after all, the Sorbonne did not teach any author who was actually still alive. But now he had laid his hands on works of literature that were a national monument, part of the tradition, a well-established subject for the specialists – Racine: 'Keep Out! Private Land!'. Even worse, Barthes undermined the positivist conception of literary history that had reigned since the nineteenth century (studying the individual Racine is not the same as doing literary history). Now the academics felt obliged to defend their positions.

We need to understand that, while they were personally committed to their views, the two adversaries, Barthes and Picard, each represented a certain camp, albeit at times unwillingly. They were led to harden their respective positions in line with the two groups from which they had emerged, and they ended up embodying two opposite poles of the intellectual and academic field. Thus, this conflict was seen as of exemplary importance for many historians and sociologists – especially Pierre Bourdieu in *Homo academicus*[61] – while the split was actually not so cut and dried. First, they could both be considered as academics, even if Barthes belonged to an institution that was more marginal than Picard's. And second, Picard was far from being the paragon of a musty positivist kind of criticism, entirely devoted to university research. He had published a novel in 1947.[62] In *La Carrière de Jean Racine*, the book on Racine's career based on his thesis, Picard applied to the dramatist a kind of criticism that owed a great deal to sociology, and his preface to Racine's *Oeuvres* in the 'Pléiade' edition even contained attacks on the type of academic criticism that attempted to link every line in the work to the author's life. So he was not a practitioner of biographical criticism in the negative sense that Barthes understood it. Nor was this altogether a Quarrel of the Ancients and the Moderns, even if, looking back, after the decentralization of the Sorbonne that followed May 1968, it is tempting to read things this way and to see this intellectual battle as something of a harbinger of the events of that year and their consequences. To reduce Picard's text,[63] published in September 1965, to a mere pamphlet (echoing the derogatory term '*libelle*' that Barthes systematically used to refer to it) was one of the strategies deployed by the opposition as it grew more entrenched. Some of Picard's criticisms of Barthes hit home, especially those that noted the assertiveness of his language: 'One of the most irritating features of this book,' he wrote, 'is the intellectual assuredness of its author: he decides, he opines, he intrepidly sets forth his views. Mystery itself is, for him, lacking in mystery.'[64] It is true that Barthes can always get swept away by his liking for the neat phrase and his taste for generalizations ('all [Racine's] characters', for example). But, as we have already said, he never employs assertion alone. It is always followed by a slight shift or a qualification that adds a nuance or even a contradiction – something that Picard fails to acknowledge. However, some of Picard's other criticisms reveal a terrible philological narrowness on his part. For example, the way he understands the verb 'respirer' ('to breathe'): this word becomes the stage on which the contrast between 'old' and 'new' criticism is played out. Picard rebukes Barthes for understanding it in its physiological sense, whereas in the seventeenth century its most common meaning was 'to find respite, to rest after an ordeal'. Barthes replied to his critic, who had gently advised him to go and consult a few dictionaries and lexicons, that even in the classical era the physiological meaning had been present; above all, he emphasized how the beauty of Racine's language lay in the fact that, as it crossed the centuries, it accrued new meanings and new ideas. In the first pages of *Criticism and Truth*, Barthes quoted Proust to point out how idiotic Picard's objection was: 'On this point, [. . .] I shall pray Proust to reply, recalling what he wrote to Paul Souday, who had accused him of using incorrect French: "My book may reveal an absence of talent; but at least it presupposes, it implies enough general education for there to be no intellectual likelihood of my making such gross errors as those which you have pointed out".'[65]

While Barthes liked playing certain kinds of game, he was very ill at ease in quarrels, and if truth be told he did not really understand the reason behind Picard's attacks, nor the way they were picked up by the press, which pounced on this opportunity not to support academia, but to display its own anti-intellectualism. This is how rival camps form, with sometimes unexpected alliances being made. The papers had previously praised Barthes's talent, but now lined up almost entirely on Picard's side (even Duvignaud and *Le Nouvel Observateur*) and followed his lead in denouncing the 'intellectual swindle', the 'jargon' and the 'verbal delirium' of Barthes and his like. In *Criticism and Truth*, Barthes took pleasure in noting how *Le Monde*, *Pariscope*, *L'Orient*, *La Croix*, *Carrefour* and *La Revue parlementaire* congratulated Picard on the 'jolly good thrashing' they had administered to him, the blows he had 'unerringly landed', his 'fatal skewering' of Barthes's pretensions. Only Jean-Jacques Brochier, in *Les Temps modernes*, and Pierre Lepape, in *Paris-Normandie*, took Barthes's side. Barthes was deeply affected by the attacks: it was mainly the world 'imposture' that wounded him, as this was a sore point: he had a constant fear of being an imposter – and this even applied to the episode of his election to the Collège de France, as we shall see. So he sought the support of his own camp. He gave a few interviews, for instance to Guy Le Clec'h, who gave him a platform in *Le Figaro littéraire* at the beginning of October and, on 22 October, he attended a meeting at Éditions du Seuil, with Sollers, Wahl, Genette and Cayrol, at which they decided how to respond to Picard. In issue 24 of *Tel Quel*, Sollers took Picard's book to pieces, showing how ideological it was: 'It would be an understatement to say that this discourse is reactionary. It seems to embody the entire moral order itself.'[66] To balance Duvignaud's article, *Le Nouvel Observateur* invited Barthes to reply in its pages, which he did in an article published on 10 October 1965, under the title 'Si ce n'est toi . . .', in which he denounced the proportions assumed by the critical op-eds that had begun almost two years earlier with the article in *Le Monde*: 'We've now reached the stage of the scurrilous pamphlet, in which I still occupy 60 per cent. Tomorrow it will be a whole book . . .'[67] On 18 November, Genette submitted to Barthes the text of a reply to Picard that was not published but that gave Barthes the idea of writing a book in which he would not simply take up arms against his enemy, but prove that his conception of criticism was justifiable. He immediately set to work on what would become *Criticism and Truth*, though all the time he was writing it, it bore the initial title 'Comment parler d'un livre' ('How to talk about a book'). He spent the entire Christmas vacation working on it, in Urt; it was a difficult, anxious time, and he continued through the whole of January. On 3 January: 'Just about to drop it, then I decide to carry on. It's taking up all my time. Anxious about finishing.' On 8 February: 'Finished CPL [Comment parler d'un livre] though the very beginning probably needs redoing (on stupidity).'[68] The book came out in March, barely six months after Picard's, with an alluring advertising strip: 'Must we burn Barthes?' Barthes was wise enough not to address himself to Picard alone, but to draw a contrast between, on the one hand, a traditional criticism that clung to such vague ideas as 'verisimilitude' and 'common sense' and limited the way other kinds of knowledge could be applied to the interpretation of texts, and, on the other, a new criticism that had decided to follow a twofold programme. First, it aimed to turn literature into one of the key elements in a general anthropology (accompanied by disciplines such as history, sociology, linguistics and psychoanalysis). This meant that the force of the work of art, its openness to other approaches, could be gauged by its ability to play a part in the innovative movement of the sciences. Second, it sought to assert the critic's own sovereignty: his approach made him akin to a writer, and this was another way of extending the territory of literary studies, by suppressing the distinction between different modes of writing. So *Criticism and Truth* was not purely defensive: it presented itself as a programmatic text, at once collective (for criticism as a whole, a group activity) and personal (in that it involved the quest for one's own place, marked by the inseparability of different kinds of writing). As Barthes put it: 'If new criticism has any reality, it is there: not in the unity of its methods and even less in the snobbery which, it is so comfortably asserted, supports it, but in the solitude of the act of criticism, which is now declared to be a complete act of writing, far removed from the excuses of science or institutions. Formerly separated by the worn-out myth of the "*superb creator and the humble servant, both necessary, each in his place,* etc.", the writer and the critic come together, working on the same difficult tasks and faced with the same object: language.'[69]

On Racine had already demonstrated that Barthes wished to bring personal and critical forms of writing together, as the expression of a project and a subjectivity. Claude Coste sees an 'On Barthes' hidden in the *On Racine*: in his view, 'by selecting and piecing together fragments of thought, Barthes puts forward a personal set of ideas on the notion of the subject, thereby displaying a subjectivity to which the text of *On Racine* gives material shape in its irreducible (and intractable) subjectivity'.[70] This was indeed probably how Barthes himself envisaged it, as we see from the personal notes in which it becomes clear that the theme of Love-Alienation stems from his own experience. 'On Racine: a book on the *Authority relation* (and not the loving relation, described as subsequent to that); in fact, the whole Love-Alienation part comes from me (me and O^2); this (biographical) origin encountered Love-Passion not in Racine, but in the Racinian *Doxa*. Indeed, this Love-Passion came to me from my cultural knowledge *about* Racine (and not from reading and rereading Racine, whose work I had read but little). This was the way I was in love, because I was familiar with the image of this kind of love in the image of Racine (and not in accordance with Racine as such).'[71] Literature then becomes more than just a programme: it was an explanation of life itself.

The publication of *Criticism and Truth* brought in a good deal of friendly notices and support for Barthes: these went some way to repairing the wound inflicted by the polemic and the type of exposure it had led to. On 17 March 1966, Butor wrote to Barthes: 'When people respond to attacks, it is very difficult not to descend to the same level as their enemies; you have succeeded very well in turning Picard into a mere pretext, one mini-beast among so many others swimming around in the murky waters of the Parisian microcosm. [. . .] People will really regret that they didn't spring to your defence. They will see what a worthwhile cause it would have been, and what nobility and intelligence they could have shown! Too bad for them.' The same day, Louis-René Des Forêts congratulated Barthes on the courage of the truth he had demonstrated, directing the greatest seriousness against the most frivolous polemic. On 12 April, Lacan wrote to say that 'it had been necessary to reply, and this was how to do it'; on 19 April, J.M.G. Le Clézio lauded the subtlety and nuanced tone of the book and added that 'it is no longer possible these days to ignore the profundity of literature, it is no longer possible to stay with cosy, complacent comfort when there have been Rimbaud, Mallarmé and Lautréamont'; on 6 May, Deleuze hailed the book as a model of rigour and, on 16 May, Starobinski wrote Barthes a long letter in which he entirely sided with him in his rejection of 'criticism as a gag', though he expressed some anxieties about the second part in which Barthes had reflected on the 'emptiness of the subject'. In connection with this subject, always outside itself, alienated in speech, Starobinski glimpsed the neutral (neither objective nor subjective) that linked Barthes with Blanchot.[72] Heartened by all these expressions of solidarity, and relieved at having been able to respond, Barthes managed to put the episode behind him – in spite of the feeling of being an imposter that it had intensified.

The year 1966

The year 1966, in which the writing of *Criticism and Truth* was immediately followed by its publication, was a decisive year for Barthes. It involved, of course, a powerful affirmation that while Barthes was now working on the sociology of objects, he had not abandoned literature – far from it. The course on rhetoric that he had started giving at the beginning of the academic year 1964–65 continued, and was an opportunity for him to set out a system of language as *'techné'*. He saw rhetoric as a 'huge, centuries-old effort to struggle against aphasia, based on the idea that language is not "natural" or easy'.[73] The course was framed, he noted in the very first session, by the idea of an anthropology of speech and 'the person who wishes to speak, who is going to write'. The first year was spent exploring the discourse of rhetoricians, from Gorgias to classical rhetoric by way of Plato, Aristotle, the sophistic and the medieval trivium. While writing his lectures, he read Abbé Batteux, and Dumarsais's *Traité des tropes*; he also drew on *La Rhétorique ou l'art de parler* by Bernard Lamy (1675), which he had already quoted in *On Racine*. He was influenced by Curtius's *European Literature and the Latin Middle Ages*, which had been translated into French in 1956. Barthes's bibliography, as presented at the beginning of the long article he published in *Communications* in 1970, 'Ancient Rhetoric' (entirely derived from his lectures), is quite classical: apart from Curtius and the 'fundamental work' by Charles Baldwin, *Ancient Rhetoric and Poetic*, as well as *Medieval Rhetoric and Poetic*, both published in 1959 (Barthes read them in English), the works referred to include: *La Formation de la doctrine classique en France*, by René Bray, *Histoire de la langue française* by Ferdinand Brunot, and *Dictionnaire de poétique et de rhétorique* by Henri Morier.[74] In this same year, he started discussing rhetoric with Marc Fumaroli, whom he met through Robert Mauzi. Fumaroli was still a bursar at the Fondation Thiers and was starting his *thèse d'État* on rhetoric in Corneille – one of history's ironies, since when Fumaroli was given a position as senior lecturer at the Sorbonne in 1976, he was the successor of none other than . . . Raymond Picard!

More than the history of rhetoric or the way it was used by this or that author, what fascinated Barthes were the problems of

classification on which his own intellectual and personal organization depended so much. He was also seeking to verify a hypothesis
according to which, thought of in structural terms, there probably exists a single *form* of rhetoric, shared, for instance, by both
literature and the image. In 1965–66, he grew interested in the disappearance of the system of rhetoric from the Renaissance to the
nineteenth century and wondered what had replaced it. His corpus
was that of contemporary literature, from Flaubert to Butor. That
autumn, Sollers gave a presentation on Mallarmé, called 'Créer un
monde total, neuf, étranger dans la langue' ('To create a total, new,
foreign world in language'), and published a written version of it in
Writing and the Experience of Limits; Oswald Ducrot talked about
Hjlemslev, Marthe Robert about Kafka, Jean Dubois about distri-
butional grammar, and Nicolas Ruwet about Chomsky. Students
who spoke included Genette, Todorov and André Glucksmann.

In February 1966, Julia Kristeva attended Barthes's class for
the first time. She recalls: 'A few days after I arrived in France, in
December 1965 – General de Gaulle gave scholarships to young
people who could speak French, and even if the Bulgarians generally
awarded them to old folks who couldn't speak the language, I eventually got one – I saw Todorov who sent me to Lucien Goldmann
but not to Barthes. I went to see Goldmann at the Collège de France,
and he talked about Lukács, but I also went to hear Barthes talk.
At the first class I attended, there was Marthe Robert, talking about
Kafka.'[75] In 'Mémoire' (published in the first issue of *L'Infini*) and
The Samurai, Kristeva relates the impression of intellectual vitality she encountered in Paris, attending Goldmann's classes; with
him, she abandoned the thesis she had initially planned to write on
the New Novel, whose recent developments she had followed from
Bulgaria, turning instead to a different thesis, on the genesis of the
form of the novel based on a fifteenth-century text, *Jehan de Saintré*
by Antoine de La Sale, which she had been told about by Aragon.
On the basis of this work, she developed the distinction between
pheno-text (the text as it presents itself to reading) and geno-text
(the set of elements that play a part in the writing and genesis of a
text). It was through Genette, whom she met at Barthes's seminar,
that she was taken to the offices of *Tel Quel* where she met Philippe
Sollers and fell immediately and deeply in love with him. This love
story, still going on today, henceforth played an important role in
Barthes's life, as a friend and as a fellow intellectual.

On 3 March 1966, Barthes wrote in his desk diary: 'Meeting
Bulgarian student.' On 4 March: 'Bulgarian woman's questionnaire about criticism.' Kristeva had not as yet given up her work on
the New Novel and wanted to subject a certain number of writers
and critics to a questionnaire. At this first meeting, Barthes was
fascinated not just by the intelligence of this 20-year-old woman,

but also by her energy; she could move mountains (he regularly called her a 'bulldozer') and by the contribution that her expertise in both linguistics and Marxism could, when combined, make to the structural method. Above all, it was she who 'passed' Bakhtin on to Barthes – a crucial moment in the development of his own thinking. By the end of 1966, Kristeva was already giving at paper on Bakhtin at Barthes's seminar; the quality and importance of this paper struck many listeners, including Barthes himself. Kristeva spoke a new language: she was a woman, a foreigner, she was interested in movements rather than structures, she introduced new concepts ('intertextuality', 'paragram'), and she was political. Bakhtin had gone beyond formalism in his work; Barthes soon seized on this as a potential way of giving fresh life to his own system. Bakhtin's idea that a text is not closed in on itself, but contains many languages and discourses, made it possible to think of the literary text in a new way and to read the connections between the text and the other discourses that it transforms and criticizes with considerable critical and political effectiveness. When it came to Saussure, Kristeva was less interested in the *Course on General Linguistics* than in his work on 'Anagrams', which Jean Starobinski published for the first time in *Le Mercure de France* in 1964, and then, a few years later, in *Tel Quel*.[76] Kristeva drew on this work to develop the notion of the paragram, which expresses the relation of perpetual transformation between the units of a text – in her view, this is the only mode of textual production. She thus exploded the notion of the sign as a twofold unit, and put forward the concept of 'gramme', considered as the assembly of all the meanings that a phonetic group can assume.

This new conception of the text, the very word 'text' taken in this dynamic sense, had significant consequences on Barthes's thinking: we can see this from the distance travelled between the 'Introduction to the Structural Analysis of Narratives' (1966) and *S/Z*, in which it was no longer a matter of dwelling on large structures but of observing 'the migration of meanings, the outcropping of codes, the passage of citations'.[77] Kristeva's contribution was a sense of displacement, as Barthes showed in the very fine review of her *Semeiotike* that he wrote for *La Quinzaine littéraire* in May 1970, with the title 'L'étrangère' ('The foreign woman'):[78] in it, he expressed all that he had owed Kristeva right from the start, her subversive force, her way of kick-starting things that had become paralysed into new life. He demonstrated an authentic grasp for what was at stake in her book, and sang her praises: 'Julia Kristeva changes the place of things.'[79] That she was a woman and a foreigner doubtless played a major role in this process. As a woman, she had a powerful bond with the law of the father, and this permitted every transgression. Barthes does not say this explicitly, but it is very likely that the lack of a father in his own life, which ruled out any frontal transgression on his part, led to him being authentically fascinated by her attitude. And the fact that she was a foreigner is something that he *does* state clearly: her work shook up 'the petty nationalism of the French intelligentsia' by opening it up to the other language, 'the one spoken from a politically and ideologically uninhabitable place: an interstitial site, oblique, on the edge – the verge – of irregular action: a *cavalier* site, since it traverses, straddles, panoramizes, and offends. The woman to whom we owe a new knowledge, from the East and from the Far East [. . .] teaches us to work *in difference*, i.e., above the differences in whose name we are forbidden to conjugate writing and science, History and form, the science of signs and the destruction of the sign.'[80] This argument in favour of the foreign was rare but recurrent in Barthes's writings, and a way of expressing his own displacement, in the year in which he published, almost simultaneously, *S/Z* and *Empire of Signs*.

Barthes met Derrida in *Tel Quel* circles, but also saw him, from 1964 onwards, on the committee of the review *Critique*, and became aware of the work Derrida was doing on writing (in *Of Grammatology*) and his undermining of the ideological presuppositions on which the theory of the sign rested. Derrida played a role that was perhaps a little less direct but no less important than Kristeva's when it came to the idea of difference. At the end of 1966, Barthes and Derrida (with Todorov and Nicolas Ruwet) flew together to the conference at Johns Hopkins in Baltimore, for which Barthes had said he would be giving a paper on rhetoric, based on the course he gave. He showed how the final disappearance of rhetoric in the nineteenth century had separated literature from a reflection on language. This was a historical explanation for the interest one might take in a method that endeavoured to bring the two back together again. Under the title 'The Languages of Criticism and the Sciences of Man', the conference, organized by Richard Macksey (who had recently founded the Humanities Center at Johns Hopkins), and Eugenio Donato (who had, the previous year, defended a PhD supervised by René Girard), was financed by the Ford Foundation. It was an attempt to combine critical thinking with the human sciences, or rather to give literary criticism a clear position *as* one of the human sciences.[81] While Barthes's paper, like Lacan's,[82] was one of the best attended and made quite an impact, showing as it did a move away from the idea of structure, it was indisputably, as all the witnesses agree, Derrida's paper that stole the show. While this conference was the first to be explicitly devoted to structuralism in North America, Derrida announced why this very same structuralism now needed to be overcome. By deconstructing certain presuppositions in the work of Lévi-Strauss, and the western essentialism of linguistics (in particular the fundamentally theological character of the term 'sign') that structuralism had unquestionably drawn on, Derrida appeared to North American academics (Paul De Man and Hillis Miller in particular, both of whom would very quickly go on to radicalize this process as 'deconstruction') as a critic of structuralism. Pietro Pucci, Professor of Classics at Cornell, who was the 'respondent' of Jean-Pierre Vernant at this conference, recalls how shocked the audience was to hear, at a conference supposedly establishing the bases for a critical structuralism in American universities, that *another* interpretive voice needed to be heard: one that followed, not Saussure and Lévi-Strauss, but Nietzsche, Freud and Heidegger.[83]

Obviously, we need to give due weight to the disciplinary factors that always lead to a hardening of positions in this kind of context. In a very strategic way, Derrida was seeking to stake a claim for philosophy as against the so-called human sciences. He said this clearly: 'It ought not to be *one of the sciences of man*, because it asks first, as its characteristic question, the question of the *name of man*.'[84] Likewise Barthes, who disliked labels and absolutely did not want to appear as the spokesman of a movement or a group, muddied the waters by putting forward the idea of textual productivity as against the fixity of a structure. This marked one first point shared by Barthes and Derrida: they reacted against anything that stabilized and confined meaning, even if Barthes tended towards pluralization while Derrida emphasized the need for a perpetual slippage (not quite the same thing). Although their work was based on completely different presuppositions and corpuses, they were both always in advance of their own thinking, always overleaping themselves. And even if, for mainly institutional reasons, they still did not say this in 1966, they agreed that the most important thing was to get away from the idea that the book was an open-and-shut argument, a totality. So Barthes had no desire to fix his texts by publishing them as volumes. His books were almost always the result of a commission, a request or a circumstance. He greatly preferred the temporary and up-to-date character of the journal, which allowed his ideas to join in a dialogue with others, invited others to pick them up and develop them, and did not freeze his words into a statue. Umberto Eco tells us that Barthes had no intention of publishing the 'Elements of Semiology' as a volume after they had come out in issue 4 of *Communications*. 'He viewed them as a rough draft, a dossier of notes for use in his seminars.' So he asked Barthes if they could be translated (by Andrea Bonomi) for the review *Marcatre*, and Barthes agreed precisely because the text could be presented as it appeared to him, as a set of working materials. When Vittorini died, the staff at Einaudi told Eco that it had been the writer's wish to publish the 'Elements of Semiology' as a volume for the collection 'Nuovo Politecnico'. 'This request acted as a kind of sentimental blackmail both on Barthes and on myself: I made over Bonomi's translation and Barthes agreed for the volume to be published.'[85] Often, as a matter of convenience, people come to Barthes through his books: but this can create a false impression. If we re-establish the true chronology of his thought by following its production in reviews and journals, thereby turning his books into accidents rather than deliberate acts of creation, we can see a figure much less assertive and definitive than may sometimes seem the case. This gives us a new way of reading the time of thought: moments of opportunity, of research, of experiments and essays, 'definitively provisional', as Queneau would put it, always a work in progress.

Barthes's first visit to Japan, from 2 May to 2 June, was another significant moment in 1966. As he said of his meeting with Kristeva, this discovery radically displaced him. He found himself faced with a language and culture whose codes were all unfamiliar to him. His work on the process of meaning unfolded with all the more freedom, and Barthes finally discovered the language of the edge, of the interstice – a language you can live in, a language in which all games can be played. He was greeted by Maurice Pinguet, at the time Director of the Franco-Japanese Institute in Tokyo, who had been living in Japan since 1958. Pinguet was unlike the usual expatriate diplomat. He had learned the language and knew many subtleties of Eastern culture. The book on voluntary death that he published upon his return to France[86] discussed the tradition of seppuku within the wider context of Japanese culture, and showed his very acute understanding of the country, one that viewed it from the inside, rather than from the western standpoint. Barthes and he immediately struck up a friendship and Pinguet played the role of a veritable guide, somewhat like Virgil for Dante in *The Divine Comedy* – in 1970, Barthes dedicated *Empire of Signs* to him. The comparison with Dante is justifiable, as Japan came as a shock to Barthes, in the full sense of the term. This culture, which celebrates opacity, silence and the refusal of meaning, struck him as the very raison d'être for his work on meaning. He also discovered something that resisted him and whetted his appetite to understand. He went to Japan to give two lectures, one on literary criticism and the other on mythologies, and he delivered these in turn in the universities to which he was invited: Todai in Tokyo, Nagoya, Kyoto, Osaka. At weekends, he sometimes stayed in Pinguet's country house in Hamaya, to which Pinguet also invited other guests. They talked endlessly about the country they were in, but also about all their shared interests. Michaël Ferrier has published, for the first time, the texts that Pinguet wrote about his experience. His portrait of Barthes (as of Foucault and Lacan, whom he also hosted at the Institute) contains several remarks that show how Barthes had hit the spot when it came to understanding a country where human relations are not always easy. 'In Japan, right from the start, Roland Barthes was sensitive to the sobriety of the individual: it suited his own reserve and his horror of drapery.'[87] Barthes derived an aesthetic pleasure and an ethical satisfaction from this. Formalism is not an impoverishment, but a purification. The fantasy that he projected on Japan, a fantasy that he would express powerfully in his *Empire of Signs* through his practice of drawing, was the dream of a major culture in some sense based on the primitive.

On his return, Barthes was eager to go back to this country where he had been so happy. He told Pinguet that he had felt depressed ever since his return. He asked him to try and find him a job in Japanese academia for two or three years so that he could really settle there. And he had already come up with the idea of writing about the country. On Thursday 9 June, he wrote: 'Ah yes, I knew it would happen, I'm in mourning for Japan, this feeling of separation from what you love, basically so close to pure exis-tentiality, so much so that certain languages, such as Romanian and Portuguese, use one and the same word ("fado") to express the idea of a nostalgic separation and that of destiny (*fatum*).' He added that the objects he had brought back were a great help: 'Some of them spread intense pleasure all around me; the others are gradually being integrated into my room; I have in front of me the Samurai photo of the handsome actor Kazuo Funaki (remem-ber my enlargement, little shop in Yurakucho) and I start to put together, slowly, the idea of writing a text about the Japanese face – i.e., one that would gradually turn out to be about Japan.'[88] What he missed was not just – as often when he was abroad – a free-floating sense of freedom in which he could live his sexuality unhampered and let a breath of fresh air sweep into a life that was otherwise extremely well ordered and caparisoned, but the culture as a whole, a different way of regulating (or deregulating) his life. A few days later, he again wrote to Pinguet, telling him how bored he was in Paris; the weight of the tasks he had to perform was too much to bear. 'Japan, yet again, merely crystallized this need for *another* dimension in daily work, the need to balance intellectual hypertrophy with a veritable art of living.'[89] The proof of his total commitment lies in the way he started to learn Japanese on his return to France. The archives preserve meticulous notebooks with long lists of words indicating that he was not just learning how to make small talk; he also practised calligraphy with a student who acted as his teacher. The next two trips to Japan, from 4 March 1967 to 5 April 1967, and from 17 December 1967 to 10 January 1968, strengthened the bond he felt for Japan and added to his understanding of the country. They dictated the materials for one

of the few books in his life that were a response to an inner impulse
rather than to an external request (even if he was in fact asked to
write it by Albert Skira): *Empire of Signs*.

In other respects, the rest of the year was also made up of many
things that lie outside the official record . . . and form the fabric of
a full and active life. Barthes played a part in the genesis of Maurice
Nadeau's *La Quinzaine littéraire*, launched at a cocktail party at
the La Hune bookshop in Saint-Germain-des-Prés on 14 March,
for which he wrote an article on Benveniste. It was Kristeva who
had made him realize how important the work of this linguist was;
she organized a meeting between the two, in December of that same
year. Barthes immersed himself in the first volume of Benveniste's
Problems in General Linguistics that had just been published by
Gallimard, and did not merely emphasize the 'impeccable scholarship', the clarity and richness of a book that was a major addition
to the understanding of culture, which 'establishes linguistically,
i.e., scientifically, the identity of subject and language'; he also
celebrated the book's extraordinary beauty, a style of thought that
gave it 'that *inexhaustible clarity* which also goes into the making
of great literary works'.[90] The year 1966 also saw a further deepening of his relations with Italian writers and intellectuals. These
were not just personal relations, but key moments in intercultural
history. When, in April 1966, he went to Italy for the publication
of the Italian translation of his *Critical Essays*, he had dinner with
Sanguineti – on whom he wrote a text for Feltrinelli the following
year – in Turin. He also met Umberto Eco, who had prefaced the
volume, in Milan, and the writer Lalla Romano. In Rome, he saw
Italo Calvino, Moravia and Manganelli. All these contacts demonstrated that he was a central figure in intellectual life, not just
in France but also in Italy. In the following years, Calvino spent
two years in Paris attending Barthes's seminar on *Sarrasine*; and
when it came to combinatorial writing, Barthes's contribution
was at least as decisive for Calvino as was the influence of Perec
and Queneau. Calvino said this in the text he wrote in homage to
Barthes.[91] As for Umberto Eco, he was a close friend of Barthes:
he was fascinated by the latter's way of combining a scholarly
project with powerful literary writing. In his view, the *Mythologies*
were not just exercises in demystification, but proper little works
of art, part of an ambitious attempt to create a general epistemology.[92] He played an important role in the Italian definition of
semiology and structuralism: this trend was rapidly absorbed into
an academic context, and it had less of a subversive feel than in
France. Barthes's importance in Italy could also be gauged from
the force of the oppositions that emerged there. Cesare Segre and
Maria Corti sought to define Italian semiology as keeping faith
with the philological and historical approach that constituted the

strength of their tradition of reading texts. The disagreement concerned mainly the function of criticism, which in their view ought
to preserve its specificity as commentary, something distinct from
the work of literature as such. The blurring of boundaries and the
ambiguity of the roles of critic and writer seemed, in their view, to
contradict the need to give criticism a scientific status and make it
independent from other practices of writing.[93]
   This was also the year in which Barthes finished his major survey
of cars for Publicis, a commission he had been given by the Renault
company. The interaction between the social world and the intellectual world were now at their height. The articles that Barthes wrote
on media stars, on cars (he saw them as forming a general mythology that extended beyond the Citroën DS), and advertising (hence
his participation in the *Cahiers de la publicité*) in the early 1960s,
his work on mass communications with Georges Friedmann and
Violette Morin, together with the success of his *Mythologies*, drew
to his seminar important industry figures and not just students and
academics. For example, Georges Péninou, director of the Publicis
research department since 1961 (this company was in the forefront
of creating effective adverts), joined Barthes's seminar in 1963 and
under his supervision embarked on a thesis on 'the semiology of
advertising' (he would publish it in 1972).[94] On 12 June 1964, he
invited Barthes to give a lecture on the mutual influence of semiology and advertising in front of the group's leading figures at the
main offices of Publicis in the Place de l'Étoile, Paris, and asked
him to produce analyses of messages that were pragmatically aimed
at improving product diffusion. These analyses had the advantage
that they were very well paid and would give Barthes's research a
higher profile. But the research they required also ate considerably
into his time. In August 1966, Barthes noted in his desk diary that
the text on cars, for Péninou, had taken him nineteen whole days
to complete. The Renault archives have preserved this unpublished
work. On 7 September 1966, Barthes sent his final report in to
Péninou. In the accompanying letter, he expressed some reservations about the validity of the survey: 'I've done my best, and yet
the result is short. This is because I preferred not to drag out what
I had to say, and what I had to say depended on car adverts themselves. Now – this at least is what I've learned from my work – these
adverts are really very poor. [. . .] For my part, I'm convinced that
other products are better suited to a more "nuanced" semantic
analysis; with cars, we haven't had much luck (but this is something
we couldn't know beforehand): we've come up against an object
that is semantically "matt".'[95] Though Barthes did not continue his
work as a consultant, he continued to intervene on an ad hoc basis
at the IREP (Institut de recherches et d'études publicitaires) as an
expert on images.

Thinking the image

For Barthes lived with images. Placing a fantasy at the threshold of every reading, every object choice, was one way of expressing the superior power of the image. One of the most important texts for his whole oeuvre was the first of the *Critical Essays*, which was not about literature but about Dutch painting. It was a sort of programmatic text in which all the themes developed by Barthes were present, woven together: the bourgeoisie, the catalogue of objects, usage, certain concrete qualities (the velvety, the sheen), the body, the absence of style. From the advertising image to cinema, from electoral iconography to photography, it was the whole gamut of iconic representations that Barthes took an interest in. He went to the cinema several times a week in the 1960s, and his tastes were wide-ranging: he liked Godard, Resnais and Baratier, but he also went to see popular French films and American genre films. In 1964, he told the review *Image et son*: 'I saw [Philippe de Broca's] *That Man from Rio* and Bergman's *The Silence* one right after the other.'[96] In 1965, he was enthusiastic about Jean Cayrol's *Le Coup de grâce* and raved to his friend about it.[97] Barthes even had a one-off experience of film-making in Montreal, when he worked on a documentary about boxing with Michel Brault. The latter relates that Barthes's comments played a crucial role in the way the film was made. Barthes first went with him to the Centre Paul-Sauvé to attend a wrestling match. Apparently, Barthes was very keen to dissuade Brault from criticizing the artificial aspect of the spectacle. 'You're mad. It's as if you wanted to take apart the mechanisms of theatre,' he told him.[98] Displaying the real rather than seeking to demonstrate its illusory aspect: for Barthes, the preoccupation with images was not just ideological, but erotic. Even when he demystified certain characteristics, certain codes (the fringe worn by film actors in sword-and-toga movies, the gestures of actors in detective films, the way electoral candidates posed, and so on), he was always involved in a relation of desire with them. This was the case with photography, too. From the 'mythologies' devoted to the Harcourt actor, to shock photos and 'photography and electoral appeal', to the essay entitled 'The civilization of the image' published in the second issue of *Communications*, Barthes demonstrated a passion for the 'literal real', the pure denotation of photography. At the same time, it was because visibility and legibility went together, with these signs being read and translated into words, that they could be studied by semiology. 'The very intense feeling that we now have of a "rising tide" of images means that we forget that, in this civilization of the image, the image itself is never, so to speak, deprived of words (the photo with its rubric, the advert with its voice-over, the talkies in cinema, *fumetti*); it is enough to make us think that the study of this modern world of the image – a study that has not yet really been undertaken – risks getting off on the wrong foot unless we work immediately on an original object, which is neither image nor language, but this image doubled by language: what might be called logo-iconic communication.'[99] This doubling of the visible by the legible explains how advertising constituted a particularly interesting stock of images for analysis. After the essays 'Soap-powders and Detergents', on advertising images, the essay 'Rhetoric of the Image', and a text published in Italian, 'Società, immaginazione, pubblicità', Barthes distinguished between two registers of language (the visual and the verbal) and discussed the way language was an 'anchorage' for the word: it was the word that enabled advertising to constitute a universe of symbols that Barthes called 'imagery'.

Barthes's expertise in images, together with the pleasure that he took in analysing them, resulted in his being asked more and more often to write for catalogues of exhibitions or the work of artists. The most representative text of this type of intervention was the one that he wrote to accompany André Martin's photos of the Eiffel Tower. The images emphasized the light and airy material of the Tower, its harmonious composition and the interweaving pattern of the girders and rivets, the arabesques that opened up so many different prospects and perspectives. The monument's power seems to stem from the difficulty we have in framing it: we need to multiply the viewpoints to grasp something of its architecture, but without ever having the feeling that we can dominate it. Barthes's text starts from the observation of photos, but is far from being a mere commentary on them. It is the Eiffel Tower as image and symbol that would need to be deciphered. The English translation, which makes this essay one mythology among others, mainly captures what is indeed Barthes's demystificatory purpose here. The Tower is a total sign, in which everyone is free to place whatever meaning they wish; it is a pure sign – what human beings wish to see it as. So it can provide a basis for all stereotypes; to talk about it is immediately to lose oneself in metaphors, in received ideas. To outplay this superficial discourse – one that the monument itself encourages – Barthes resorts, in rapid succession, to all kinds of knowledge: literary, linguistic, architectural, scientific. These, like Martin's photos, produce a variety of different perspectives that finally make the Tower very elusive.

Barthes's text is also a powerful discussion of images. The Tower, slender and pointed, has nothing circular about it apart from the figures that characterize it: the full circle (it is seen and it watches) and reversibility or completeness (inside and outside, neither full nor empty). In particular, the Tower is an image and it arouses an entire personal imaginary system, the 'for me' on which every discourse is built, even the discourse of knowledge. So Barthes links the Eiffel Tower to everything that most attracts him about it: the panorama, its raised position that makes of it the modern version of Notre-Dame de Paris[100] and its malleability, which opens it to every interpretation. 'At the moment I begin writing these lines about it, the Tower is there, in front of me, framed by my window.'[101] The Eiffel Tower was indeed visible from Barthes's room in the rue Servandoni; its friendly wave each day indicated to the spectator where he was situated in the cityscape. To express the particularity of the monument most effectively, Barthes invented a very striking, albeit somewhat alarming image: unlike other monuments, in which you enclose yourself, into which you burrow (these monuments are all rather like caves), in the Tower you slide along its emptiness, you become to some extent its parasite. Faced with the urban hustle and bustle that it dominates and the ants' nest of visitors that it welcomes, the Tower sets its own solitude and singularity, its ver-ticality and immobility. To respond to this difference is to multiply the representations of the object – hence Barthes's fascination with miniature reproductions of the Tower: 'By gaining possession of a *reduction* of this monument, the purchaser of a souvenir is again amazed to find that he can *hold* the Tower in his hand, on his table; its real value, namely the marvel of its size, is thus to some degree at his disposal and he can bring a strange, inaccessible, unappropri-able object into his everyday décor.'[102] Seeking to find a gift for a Japanese friend after one of his trips, Barthes can ultimately find nothing better than a little brass replica of the Eiffel Tower.

The importance of the 1960s, leading to the events of 1968, can be seen in the *excess* constituted by literature and the image, an excess that goes beyond the structuralist project, while providing it with many more objects for study. Fascinated by the infinite openness of writing, and the power that images have to give it a new impetus, Barthes gradually shifted his form of criticism, moving it further away from its pretext, turning it into the personal adventure of his own thought and the quest for an autonomous writing. This writing involved the boundless new extension of the powers granted to reading.

SR # 165

Toute la théorie critique du SR est dans ceci : assumer le départ systématique de toute critique.
Thème de la franchise des systèmes — c-a-d protestation du renversement de l'arbitraire en Nature, en Ça-va-de-soi

SR : un livre d'une grande sagesse, d'un grand bon sens — qui ne pourrait être déclaré fou que par un fou.

SR # 18

Idée que l'ordre tragique est seulement l'ordre du langage

Green folder: *On Racine*.

Relisant le livre, je suis stupéfait de ce qu'on ait pu le trouver insolite, bizarre, matière à lazzi, provoquant pamphlet et campagne de presse.

C'est si sage, si tenu

Principes:

1) Immanence : ni Histoire, ni Biographie.

2) Les critiques comme des langages, à essayer

3) Création d'un objet intellectuel (l'Homme rac. / la Tragédie rac.)

4) Fascination héraclitéenne : tout change (Racine n'existe que comme disponibilité), les critiques passent, aucune n'est vraie.

Green folder: *On Racine.*

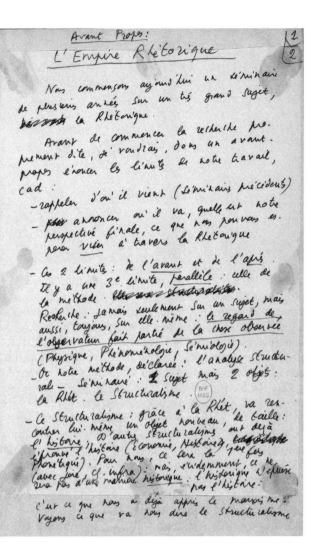

Seminar on rhetoric.

The round table.

12

Events

Barthes was not in France very much in 1967. He went back to Japan for a month at the beginning of spring; he went to Italy twice, once to Morocco and, from September to December, he was in the United States. After the Johns Hopkins conference, he was invited to teach in Baltimore for a semester. For a week, Barthes lived not far from the university, in the Broadview residential hotel, but he spent almost all his weekends in New York where he had several friends, Richard Howard in particular. He recycled his seminar on rhetoric, and used the opportunity to give lectures pretty much throughout the United States: Philadelphia, Boston, San Francisco, Santa Barbara, Indianapolis and Chicago, among other places. This was the year that *The Language of Fashion* was published; but the texts and questions that now occupied him were quite different. Structuralism still seemed a good method (preferable to hermeneutics), but his interest in dissemination and the plurality of meaning led his research in other directions.

Barthes found out more about Japan, continuing to learn the language and reading several important works, such as *Zen in the Art of Archery*, as well as Alan Watts's book on Zen and D. T. Suzuki's work, to which his attention was perhaps drawn by Georges Bataille's *On Nietzsche*, which quotes it at length.[1] He also took an interest in haiku and read translations of Basho and Issa as well as the four volumes of Blyth on haikai. At the same time, he fell in love with Balzac's novella *Sarrasine*: the idea had been given him by an article by the psychoanalyst Jean Reboul published in 1967 in *Cahiers pour l'analyse*, 'Sarrasine ou la castration personnifiée' ('Sarrasine, or castration personified'). Barthes devoted his seminar at the EPHE to *Sarrasine* and started to think about writing a text on it, in homage to Lévi-Strauss.[2] In particular, he wrote about Loyola, using the great number of index cards he had amassed on his work. It is interesting to read these three works together (*S/Z, Empire of Signs*, and *Sade, Fourier, Loyola*), given their close contemporaneity. If at first view they appear quite unrelated – *S/Z* accomplishing

Barthes's scientific programme and *Empire of Signs* picking up on his literary and more personal ambitions – we can also discover the many links between them, the interwoven dialogues: this approach has the advantage that it does not rely on a hard-and-fast distinction between one kind of Barthes and another, but instead enables us to grasp the coherent project he was always following, whatever kind of writing he adopted. So we find index cards on 'Japan' in the 1968 seminar on *Sarrasine*, and references to the Zen masters being used to describe the teaching relation. And the sort of machinery imagined to describe the way Ignatius de Loyola manufactured his writing, the way he cut things up into units, is reminiscent of Barthes's method for reading Balzac's text.[3] The great revolution of this period lay in the way Barthes's attention shifted from writing to reading, which brought to an end the subversion of the codes of academic textual interpretation applied to the classics and suggested that meaning was now infinitely dispersed, in all directions.

Absences

Barthes has often been criticized for his relative indifference to the events of May 1968. While it is true that he was not in the forefront of the protests, they still preoccupied his thoughts. He held steadfast to the behaviour he had adopted ever since General de Gaulle had come to power: no hysterical gestures, no blackmail by the spoken word – 'the spoken word is blackmail' he said in the first session when his seminar resumed after being interrupted by the May events[4] – but no silent acquiescence, either; rather, an acute awareness of the role and duties of critical thought.

The sequence of years 1967–70 comprised a significant unit in his biography, and amounted to something of a crisis (though this is not quite the right term). The shift that resulted was neither a revelation nor a new direction, as has often been claimed, but a deepening of the theme of absence – a theme that involved both an ethos and a certain anxiety. The readings that dominated this period, and formed as it were the background to his daily life in those years, were crucial, as both causes and consequences of this movement. Because Barthes rejected the fixed points imposed by norms, the violence of language, death, he was haunted by the figures of fragmentation, of lack, of emptiness. The texts to which he was drawn (*Sarrasine*, 'The Facts in the Case of M. Valdemar', *In Search of Lost Time*) provided him with networks of meaning, figures with which he could try to understand such apparently elastic notions as dispersion, the remainder, the leftover. The strange fascination exerted on Barthes by *Sarrasine* was continually in evidence – so much so that Balzac's text seems to have been the template or 'pattern', in the sense the term has in couture, of all the texts Barthes wrote in that period. Barthes's work on Balzac crossed paths, in a sometimes unexpected but always interesting way, with his exploration of Zen Buddhism, the practice of the Dao or the kōan. Castration in Balzac's novella is a painful, disturbing lack, whose violence is softened by the emptiness advocated by Japanese culture. The figure of death haunts *Sarrasine*; and Barthes finds another form of absence in the empty subject of classical Chinese thought. He contrasts the *wishing to grasp* or the *wishing to impress* of the full subject, the master of the spoken word (the person who *takes* the floor or grabs the microphone in big public meetings), with the Zen master – a model to which Barthes sought increasingly to conform, especially in his classes – who sets up the ideal of a *not-wishing-to-grasp* inspired by Lao Tse: 'He does not exhibit himself and will shine. He does not assert himself and will impose himself.'[5] In 1968, Barthes's political behaviour followed this programme.

   The famous text on 'The Death of the Author', written in 1967, opens with a reference to *Sarrasine*: 'In his tale "Sarrasine", Balzac, speaking of a castrato disguised as a woman, writes this sentence: "She was Woman, with her sudden fears, her inexplicable whims, her instinctive fears, her meaningless bravado, her defiance, and her delicious delicacy of feeling." Who speaks in this way? Is it the hero of the tale, who would prefer not to recognize the castrato hidden beneath the "woman"? Is it Balzac the man, whose personal experience has provided him with a philosophy of Woman? Is it Balzac the author, professing certain "literary" ideas about femininity? Is it universal wisdom? Romantic psychology? We can never know, for the good reason that writing is the destruction of every voice, every origin. Writing is that neuter, that composite, that obliquity into which our subject flees, the black-and-white where all identity is lost, beginning with the very identity of the body that writes.'[6] The course on *Sarrasine*, which began shortly afterwards, on 8 February 1968, began with a lecture in which the death of the author was already the precondition for working on the text: 'The resurrection of the text implies the death of the author, linked to a foregrounding of reading.'[7] A little later: 'the narrative is a predicative fabric without a subject, or with a migrant, evanescent subject. What speaks is neither the author, nor the character (so it is not the "subject"), but meaning.'[8] It is easy to see how Kristeva's ideas influenced this way the notion of system was adjusted, adding to *structure* the now fundamental question of the *plurality of voices*. The notion of paragram, which turns the text into a network of shifting relations, was used right from the start; and Bakhtin was drawn on for his ideas on polyphony and the dialogue of voices. In the 'Structural Analysis of Narratives', issue 8 of *Communications* on narrative, which Barthes coordinated in 1966, Propp and the

Russian formalists were all considered to be familiar names to the
students – the lecturer explained them only briefly. What was newer,
on the other hand, were the notions of dissemination and efflores-
cence that led theoretical reflection towards intertextuality (even
if the word did not appear as yet): 'Every text is constructed as a
mosaic of quotations, every text is the absorption and transformation of another text', in the celebrated formula that Kristeva put
forward in 1969 *Semeiotike*.[9] In Barthes's 1968 seminar, the text was
already referring only to itself, or to other texts, *ad infinitum*.

The idea of the 'death of the author' expressed the following
abstraction: that of the text as a broken constellation of fragments
of voices, of codes, of quotations that writing weaves together
without ever bringing them together as any kind of unity. In an
intellectual context, where the very idea of subject was being
undermined, where the authority of the power contained within
the spoken word was under attack on all sides,[10] this was a rather
striking formulation: it seemed to destroy the real author, though in
fact it was simply attacking the unifying function the author seemed
to fulfil. In Barthes's view, the author was 'improper', not able to
convey the multiplicity of codes and meanings in the text because
of the unifying and symbolic power the notion of author exercised
over the text. But putting the author to death was also a symbolic
act that displayed a paradoxical authority of its own, given the
supposed dispersal of all functions. Here we recognize the assertive
power, and the art of formula, that characterize Barthes's writing –
though we also note the nod and wink given to Foucault at the end
of *The Order of Things*. But we cannot fail to see, too, the contagious force of Balzac's story in which Sarrasine, the main character,
is murdered.[11] Death accomplishes its work. Admittedly, the reader
and the critic pick up a great deal of the role that the author had,
reluctantly, been forced to yield. But the naturally plural nature
and anonymity of the reader-critic reduce the risk of illegitimate
authority.

The reversal of roles was part of the process of institutional
transformation that May '68 called for. It was the completion of a
protocol that Barthes in his courses had long since drawn up; it can
also be seen in the way the assertive voice in his texts was muted.
Many other people had been experimenting with such alternative
teaching spaces, a different relation to mastery and knowledge,
throughout the 1960s. Louis Althusser's teaching at the École
normale supérieure in the rue d'Ulm, Paris, especially the year in
which he read Marx's *Capital* in 1964–65, and Lacan's seminar
on the foundations of psychoanalysis (now also being held in the
same building) had a considerable influence. The publication, with
the encouragement of François Wahl, of Lacan's *Écrits* in 1966
(the first chapter was an analysis of Poe's 'The Purloined Letter'),

and the collective work *Reading 'Capital'*, with contributions from Althusser, Étienne Balibar, Roger Establet, Pierre Macherey and Jacques Rancière, revealed that attention had shifted from the author to the reader, and that the priority now lay with analysing and interpreting. The crucial thing at this point was the spotlight on new data, non-positivist, non-referential: structures, for instance, or symptoms. In this sense, the changing positions of master and pupil, or Barthes's promotion of the new figure of the reader-author, were already apparent before 1968. It was even the existence of these different propositions that gave an added impetus to the more general need for *transformation*.

Barthes was definitely one of the precursors of the movement in academia, suggesting that another relation to knowledge and another way of viewing the spoken word were possible. In November 1968, one section of the course on *Sarrasine* performed an archaeology of the pedagogical institutions that had led to a hierarchical practice based on the authority of the spoken word. Barthes went on to propose a radical questioning of certain practices of language. The opposition between the spoken and the written word was reframed as a distinction between the monological nature of the spoken word and the polyphony of the written, and more simply as the difference between the oral and the written. To marginalize the authority of the spoken word, Barthes appealed to Japanese culture. Zen allowed the pupil to take the initiative in establishing a relation with the master, and thereby imposed two principles: there was nothing to teach, and the master did not help the pupil. His mastery was first and foremost a mastery of forms to which the pupil, by imitation and continual groping attempts, could sometimes gain access. Sometimes, indeed, it was precisely insofar as he did not understand that the pupil could become the master.[12] If the seminar could be transformed into a space where a certain form could be learned, then writing could replace the spoken word, or least respond to the way 'research is bogged down by the spoken word' by offering 'the spectre or the fantasy of writing'.[13]

So how are we to explain the fact that Barthes did not feel really concerned by May '68, even though he was so much a part of the trend that led to the events? After all, he did join the demonstration outside the Cinémathèque in February to protest against the sacking of Henri Langlois.[14] And his discourse on literature, images and media had such a powerful impact on academic arguments that he was, at this time, a real *maître à penser* and an indirect source of encouragement for the uprising. There are several possible reasons behind his distance, his feeling that he was out of synch with events. He was 52 years old and no longer had the energy that had driven him during the great period of activity in the 1950s. The demonstrators were very young, and he felt excluded; his mistrust of

revolutionary theatricality debarred him from playing a role or striking an attitude – even of the kind he did actually embody, such as
that of the ignorant teacher. In addition, 1968 was the year in which
he fell ill again. On 27 April, while spending the evening with Robert
Mauzi, he fainted in the street. He was taken to the hôpital Laennec,
where he was kept under observation for a few hours after being
given a few stitches over his eyebrow. On 6 May, three days after the
start of the student movement, he went to the avenue Victor-Hugo
for an electroencephalogram; at the same time, eight students from
Nanterre, including Cohn-Bendit, had been summoned to a disciplinary hearing: Henri Lefebvre, Alain Touraine, Guy Michaud and
Paul Ricoeur went with them to show their support. On 7 May, as
major student demonstrations and violent protests against the police
were taking place, Barthes had bleeding in the larynx and went to
Dr Jeanguyot for a check-up. His rhythm of work slowed down. On
10 May, barricades went up in the Latin Quarter; the same day, he
received the results of the EEG, which were not good, to his dismay.
Only on 18 May did he manage to see a neurologist at the Pitié-
Salpêtrière hospital: as he waited, he tried as best he could to deal
with work (his correspondence, theses to be read, student work to
mark, the text on Bunraku he had agreed to write for Sollers, and so
on), while following the unfolding events. He wandered round the
Sorbonne, which had been reopened on 14 May and transformed
into a huge podium open to all; people put forward their views and
spent days and nights arguing about them. On 16 May, he took part
in a lively discussion on what had been taking place: very critical
remarks were directed to him (was this the day of the celebrated
phrase 'Structures do not take to the streets'? Some people say that
he took this personally . . .). That evening, he went to the Odéon with
Wahl and Sarduy to listen to the debates that had brought together
students, trade unionists, high school pupils, locals and the merely
curious. After the huge unified demonstration of 13 May, a general
strike had begun, gradually bringing the city and the whole country
to a standstill; on 18 May, he managed to get to a meeting in spite
of the strike. 'Almost complete relief', he wrote in his desk diary,
though it is unclear whether he was referring to the results of his
check-up or the fact he had made it across the city without difficulty.
The thesis vivas he had been scheduled to attend at the Sorbonne
were cancelled. On 22 May, he spent three hours in a clinic in the rue
Solférino where he was made to undergo hyperglycaemia treatment
so that tests could be made. He watched De Gaulle's speech on television on 24 May, and heard the noise from the demonstrations on
the boulevard Saint-Michel; these were even more violent than usual
and had the feel of a veritable uprising. Barthes no longer described
them as 'demonstrations', but as 'riots'. On 25 May, he was invited
to an enlarged assembly of the 6th section of the École.

This brief collage of the events of collective history and individual existence is not an attempt to let Barthes off the hook for taking only a small part in the events; it is, rather, an attempt to show how one's everyday life can sometimes come into collision with the turmoil of current affairs, whatever the differences in scale. Barthes gradually started writing again, devoting part of his time to the text on bunraku and another to the text on Fourier. The Japanese puppets that he described were part of the show that he had seen at the Odéon theatre on 2 May in the company of his mother and Michel Salzedo. His account of this would be presented, with several changes, in *Empire of Signs*; like his piece on Fourier, it contained several allusions to the May events. By praising the non-theatrical nature of puppet theatre, he was emphasizing the value of limiting the powers of the voice and the suppression of hysteria. The philosophical scope of bunraku appeared to him to lie in the vanishing of the antithesis between inside and outside, between the animate and the inanimate. Antithesis, a privileged figure of western culture, 'converts every name into a slogan opposed to its antonym (creativity against intelligence, spontaneity against reflection, truth against appearance, etc.)'.[15] This riposte to the slogans and chants of May '68 could hardly be more explicit. Of the values promoted by '68 – autonomy, self-realization, community and self-management – the only one that seemed essential to him, the only one he could make his own, was the toppling of the master's authority. The others struck him as too theatrical to be anything other than a form of hysteria. Barthes's critique of this form of revolt appeared in the texts written during the events – though the latter appear only indirectly (in the text on Fourier, for instance, he writes: 'Fourier wants to decipher the world in order to remake it')[16] – and in his correspondence. In his letters to Maurice Pinguet, Barthes referred to his health problems; on 9 June, on learning that Pinguet would be taking up a job at the Sorbonne on his return from Japan, Barthes mentioned 'this terrible strike, which in any case is coming to such a bad end'. He then presented a clearly worried analysis of the situation and a warning addressed to his friend: 'Like all of us, you will need a great deal of courage to confront the resumption of academic life – if it ever happens; you can't imagine the way it has turned people's ideas and languages upside down, all against the background of an absent institution. I don't think that anyone at present can predict what dialectic might unite the Maoist university that is being proclaimed and the Gaullist institution, if it is re-established. For my part, I have to say that, for the time being, I can't see what place I'll have in all this. There have been painful times, with people displaying malevolence and animosity and settling accounts during this huge upheaval; and there is still a great deal of anxiety, on every level. – Of course my travel plans have now become very uncertain.'[17]

Throughout June, as academic activities, like everything else, slowly started up again, he was still worried that he might be attacked and undermined as he had been at the Sorbonne. He attended the big meetings that were organized, but without conviction. The trips he had to take out to Nanterre, for vivas that he conducted with Greimas and Lefebvre, caused him anxiety; he was sure that his role and his lack of involvement would be harshly questioned (the notorious and aggressive questions addressed to teachers at the time included 'From what position do you speak?' and 'What are your concepts?'), while he felt solidarity for at least one thing: the virtue of a transformation of the teaching relationship. Barthes felt that the attacks made on him, in particular in *L'Express* at the very beginning of June, were unfair, and he felt obliged to reply to the latter. In the second of its exceptional supplements, the magazine devoted a long article to French academia and to the 'bankruptcy of the *maîtres à penser*', stating: 'M. Louis Althusser, who has reinterpreted Marx in the light of structuralism, is in hospital: clinical depression. M. Michel Foucault, hailed two years ago as the philosopher of the future, is quietly continuing to teach at the University of Tunis [. . .] M. Roland Barthes, director of research at the École pratique des hautes études, was scheduled to give 56 hours' worth of classes per year. His pupils were advanced students, an elite, in theory, devoted to research. Since classes started, he had being using them to collate marriage announcements in the "Chasseur français" so as to contribute to his linguistic studies. He is thinking of handing in his notice and leaving teaching.'[18] Luckily, continued the writer Gérard Bonnot, Barthes was an exception: most teachers had decided to play along and fundamentally reform their teaching methods. Barthes immediately sent in a correction, which was published in the first issue after the return to normality, on 17 June: 'For one thing, I have never given any seminar on the subject that your writer attributes to me, and I have never "used my students" to collate anything at all for my own work. For another, I have no intention of handing in my notice as director of studies.'[19] There were rumours going round that Barthes was guilty of being detached from events; he had been caught off his stride.

Politically, Barthes no longer knew which position to adopt, or rather he could not see where his position placed him. He did not share the strategic choice that the *Tel Quel* group had made to side with the French Communist Party; in their view, a revolution could only be Marxist-Leninist. Nor did he play a part in the creation of the Comité d'action étudiants-écrivains révolutionnaire (CAEE-R: Students' and writers' revolutionary action committee) that Jean-Pierre Faye created with Michel Butor, Jacques Roubaud, Marguerite Duras, Maurice Nadeau, Maurice Blanchot and Nathalie Sarraute. He did not sign the manifesto in issue 34 of *Tel Quel* with the title 'Revolution, Here and Now', and even if he very occasionally attended the meetings of the Groupe d'études théoriques, on Wednesday evenings in the rue de Rennes, he spoke only once. All this agitation bored him and wearied him and he did not share the feeling of many of his colleagues that history had responded to the summons of the text. He felt that his critical and oppositional role was being undermined. This was perhaps a situation that, sooner or later, every true precursor needs to confront: what he has predicted or set in place is recuperated and assumes a definite shape, so that he finds that his position has become mainstream or even passé. Barthes himself had long since described the fate of the avant-garde in terms of the celebrated metaphor of the 'vaccine': 'A bit of progress [. . .] is injected into the tradition, and tradition is thereby inoculated against progress: a few avant-garde *signs* are enough to castrate the real avant-garde.'[20] This was how the bourgeoisie delegated to a few people the tasks of subversion and protest, with the aim of purifying society of them. Even if this economy could be read only on the scale of long-term history (when the avant-garde could be experienced by its actual creators as a total liberation), the fact could not be ignored that one day, the social order would recuperate this radical creative experience. But, according to Barthes, it was the fundamental political structure of society that needed to be attacked – something which, simply because of the way it operated, this bourgeois society ruled out.

This was to some extent Barthes's own drama: his creative spirit drove him forwards, towards questions being raised by the historical avant-gardes (in particular the link between theory, creation and revolution), but his historical and critical intelligence convinced him that this movement was futile. So he was led towards *Tel Quel* while being persuaded that the group and the review would suffer the same reversal. Barthes probably felt this recuperation all the more painfully in 1968. His subversive force was recognized but institutionalized (more than Vaneigem's *Treatise* or Debord's *The Society of the Spectacle* – for certain margins can keep their subversive power longer than others). It was new avant-gardes of protest and creation that were starting to predominate, leaving him behind. This ambiguity was also evident in the role he was invited to play, one that he was happy to assume: to give advice on the reforms, especially the reform of academic life. He was asked by Edgar Faure to advise about the creation of the new University of Vincennes (one of the positive outcomes of 1968) – he attended meetings on the organization of studies (together with Gérard Genette, Jean-Pierre Richard and others) – and about bringing in people to teach in it. His brother, indeed, was given a teaching post as assistant in the department of Hebrew. Barthes, well aware of the experimental and promising character of the enterprise, was convinced of the need to open the university system up to new methods and other disciplines, and to make teaching available to those who had not passed their baccalaureate. But though he did all this conscientiously enough, it was without the enthusiasm characteristic of that time, when, for many other people, everything seemed to be capable of renewal.

So it was not indifference as such that lay behind his relationship with May '68, but a painful re-examination of his place in the world, as at the time when the discovery of his illness had led to a first set of crises. Barthes felt out of step, ill at ease in his very marginalization. What he wrote and did in the period that followed echoed this disquiet on several levels: first and foremost, because he sometimes attempted to stay very close to the crisis and to produce an acceptable discourse about it. Barthes contributed to the famous issue 34 of *Tel Quel* in summer 1968 with his article on bunraku and, in July, he started to write a text on the May events that was published in the November number of *Communications*: 'Writing the Event'. In it, he drew a logical distinction between the spoken and the written word, insisting on the way in which the revolt could be read as a 'taking of speech' – in the same way that we speak of the 'taking of the Bastille' – but without stating explicitly the extent to which this new authority was, in his view, illegitimate and regressive. The critique was only implicit (one needs to be aware of the other texts he wrote in this period to notice it). Likewise, when his course at the EPHE resumed in November 1968, Barthes proposed his interpretation of the events at a time when almost all the teachers at the École were feeling the need to offer theirs, either because they were responding to student demands, or because they thought that their method was capable of taking the protests in hand. Edgar Morin wrote on the phenomenology of May and explanatory systems, while Michel de Certeau wrote on the difficulties of interpreting the phenomenon. Barthes also played along by emphasizing the 'decentred dissemination, with its outplayed origin'.[21] There was an element of demagoguery in his discourse: his listeners were not working under his supervision, but with him 'at [his] side'; he said he mistrusted all institutional norms. There was already an obvious sense of discomfort in the way he was actively seeking students, defending his own programme of reading as a response to this transformation. This was true, for example, of the 'decoding' of signs: '[T]his is not easy, it requires the sort of continuous labor begun in various quarters, it must be recalled, some years ago.'[22] In the interview with Pierre Daix for *Les Lettres françaises* that he gave in Urt in July 1968, he repeatedly emphasized the merits of semiology and teaching at the École pratique des hautes études as a way of living up to the events. 'We should not need to reinvent the wheel each time', he said. This was a case of special pleading, rare in Barthes when he was sure of his positions, and it marked a definite anxiety about his current role.

On two not insignificant points, however, his analysis was original and politically lucid, at least seen with the benefit of hindsight. The first concerns the immediate nature of discourse and event that gave a completely new power to the spoken word and the taking of power by the spoken word. In this sense, May '68 was the historical consummation of a process of mass communication based both on the media and the immediate, on the message and the ephemeral, on unreflective imagination and the need for mastery. Barthes was merely denouncing an anti-intellectualism that he had rejected ever since the polemics around *On Racine* that that did indeed threaten any possible cultural critique. 'There is an intellectual Poujadism that is always possible: a brutal mistrust of language, a dismissal of forms that are always considered to be sophistical, the accusation of "jargon", the rejection of writing, etc.'[23] In saying this, he was repeating his position against the arrogance of the spoken word of which the *assemblées générales* comprised the theatre. His disaffection for theatre, earlier in the 1960s, was already evidence of a similar difficulty with the spoken word that was always, when it was imposed and violent, on the side of the law. Yet again, he contrasted it with the polysemia of writing, where everything always needs to be invented: writing alone can be the site of a real revolution. This is a leitmotif in Barthes's work: it expresses his disdain for the spontaneity of events and his conviction that a written text – not as transcription of the spoken word, but as a reflection of the plurality of meaning – could bring together the cultural and the political. 'We will regard as suspect any eviction of writing, any systematic primacy of speech, because, whatever the revolutionary alibi, both tend to *preserve* the old symbolic system and refuse to link its revolution to that of society.'[24] As cultural capitalism has merely strengthened its grip since Barthes wrote these lines, we can simply point out how acute his analysis was, coming as it did several years before his friend Michel Deguy's analysis of the same subject.[25]

The other point on which Barthes proved to be a real visionary was the advent of technocracy as a moment in capitalism less concerned with human labour than with the profitability of science. In his lecture of 21 November 1968, he said: 'The present day is certainly a turning point or at least a significant new emphasis. How are we to define it? The conjunction or confluence of an ideology and a politics: an ideology, that of the human sciences, and a technocratic politics. The objective alliance between the human sciences and technology risks invading our schools, with its technological demands (research, specialization, qualification) shared by the bodies and assemblies set up in May (the document of the reform committee: '*Cutting-edge or very specialized sectors*' etc.).'[26] Elsewhere, he pointed out how the slogans of '68 on the university system would, if they were assembled like the pieces of a jigsaw puzzle, form an image which 'resembles the contemporary American university'.[27] This denunciation of everything that sacrificed culture to efficiency is such an accurate projection of the university system as we find it now that we cannot accuse Barthes of having adopted a reactionary attitude in 1968. It was always in the name of the same principles that he established his line of behaviour. While his relation to writing included the possibility of contradiction, in the name of the plurality and the fragmentation of meaning, his political behaviour and the reasons for his rejections or his denunciations did not alter.

The book on May: 'Sade, Fourier, Loyola'

In his text on hippy culture, Barthes wondered whether it might be possible to find a truly political critique of culture: it was only in Fourier that he saw the image of an unconstrained art of life that could bring together both a politics and a culture. The turning point of May '68 led to new plans, new directions for writing. In interviews at the time, Barthes insisted on the need not to make a hollow slogan of 'things will never be the same', for this would simply pander to the desire for everything to return to the status quo.[28] As Barthes told Pierre Daix, it was necessary to 'take advantage of every event to "make" the past' that is, 'to make everything we had been thinking fall back into the past' and try to develop it in a way that involved completely rethinking it.[29] Fourier, and Sade as well, constituted those new spaces in which we can think the event and say what this event might ideally have been. One first commentary on Sade (in the book, this would become 'Sade I') had already been published at the end of 1967 in issue 27 of *Tel Quel*, while the long analysis of Fourier and the other text on Sade were written in the heat of 1968 and its aftermath. ('Loyola' had been written just before the events, though was still part of the spirit of the time.) Fourier turned out to shed a great deal of light on the way that forms of a de-alienated life could be thought in political terms – what, in Barthes's view, a successful version of May '68 might be. This is how he put it in the interview with *Lettres françaises*: 'I would like to describe (i.e. to deduct from writing) some of these domestic utopias, some of these imaginary arts of living. I think I can take them from two great classifiers, both of them implacable enemies of "civilization": Sade and Fourier. I think that the analysis of utopia will allow us yet again not merely to prolong a critique of our culture, but also to give a detailed picture of the way we imagine pleasure, which I feel ought to be present in what is being sought and achieved at present.'[30] As far as the utopian aspects of the injunction to 'change life' and liberate sexuality were concerned, these two authors had, in Barthes's view, found a real version of what the slogans of the 1968 protests had demanded without managing to implement it. After all, utopia could be more effectively created in everyday life, insignificant details and events, than in great spectacular upheavals. Thus his reflection on 'biographemes' stemmed directly from the question of politics. While this question was raised as such in the book, as it would be later in the workshop 'on biographical theatricality' that he gave with Patrick Mauriès in 1973 and, in 1974, with the working group devoted to 'collective biographemes with the Women's Movement', this was part of a desire to compensate for all that History with a capital H tended to forget: Barthes and his colleagues were seeking to rehabilitate minor, non-authoritarian figures. This was akin to Foucault's projected collection of the lives of 'infamous men', defined as 'an anthology of individual existences. Lives that occupy a few lines or a few pages, lives of countless mishaps and adventures, gathered up in a handful of words.'[31]

We can thus see Barthes's *Sade, Fourier, Loyola*, published in 1971, as one of the major texts on what happened in 1968, for Barthes himself, of course, but not just for him.[32] Few others have depicted the truth of what happened at that time as a fantasy, a utopia, a desire: the events of 1968 rapidly became bogged down in a doxa, dragooned into shape by ideological demands. One example: Jean Thibaudeau's *Mai 1968 en France* was published in the series 'Tel Quel' by Seuil in 1970, with a preface by Philippe Sollers entitled 'Printemps rouge' ('Red Spring'). If we compare this with *Sade, Fourier, Loyola*, which came out in the same series a year later, we can see how very different the first book, a kind of mirror of the events, was from the second, which was more a book of ideas. It is true that Thibaudeau drew on the interweaving of many voices, and thereby managed to convey something of the spontaneous creativity and the upwelling of the spoken word that took place at that time, but he adhered too closely to the events, turning them into a past for which people were already nostalgic. By opening the text up to a revolutionary future, Sollers was merely tying it down a little bit more to its ideological origins. Conversely, *Sade, Fourier, Loyola* gave a future to revolt. It criticized, as ever, militancy – in this sense, the book was also a critique of May '68 – but at the same time it opened up a new dimension to revolution. For example, in one passage of 'Sade II', we read: 'The ultimate subversion (contra-censorship) does not necessarily consist in saying what shocks public opinion, morality, the law, the police, but in inventing a paradoxical (pure of any doxa) discourse: invention (and not provocation) is a revolutionary act: it cannot be accomplished other than in setting up a new language. Sade's greatness lies not in having celebrated crime, perversion, nor in having employed in this celebration a radical language; it is in having invented a vast discourse founded in its own repetitions (and not those of others), paid out in details, surprises, voyages, menus, portraits, configurations, proper nouns, etc.: in short, contra-censorship, from the forbidden, becomes the novelistic.'[33] Unlike real censorship, which grips, stifles and clogs its victims, the invention of a language clearly appears as a way of outplaying illegitimate forms of closure – including the ones we do not see as closure because we imagine that they are some kind of transgression.

The text on Fourier did pick up on the injunction of May '68 to 'remake the world', but in radical new ways that seemed to escape the rigid grip of theology and teleology. Combination and classification replaced hierarchical order. Desire replaced Need, as the Domestic took over from the Political. Here the connection – both a relation to '68 and an opposition to it – was clearly established: 'Can a utopia ever be political? isn't politics: *every language less one*, that of Desire? In May 1968, there was a proposal to one of the groups that were spontaneously formed at the Sorbonne to study *Domestic Utopia* – they were obviously thinking of Fourier; to which the reply was made that the expression was too "studied," *ergo* "bourgeois"; politics is what forecloses desire, save to achieve it in the form of neurosis: political neurosis or, more exactly: the neurosis of politicizing.'[34] Barthes's language kept the dominant discourse of '68 at a definite distance, describing it as a speech without a subject (using the impersonal 'one' as a third-person pronoun, and saying 'it was replied' rather than 's/he replied'), in other words as an unattached, purely ideological discourse. But can utopia exist without desire? Barthes criticized revolutionary discourse directly: such a discourse was almost always paradoxical, as, by seeking to reduce its utopian dimension, it also ended up extinguishing any desire for it. Fourier, on the other hand, made it possible to propose other forms of radical change that could act as alternatives (Marxism and Fourierism are regularly seen as two sides of the same coin in this text).

The three writers, Sade, Fourier and Loyola, built a repressive ideological edifice, but at the same time they destroyed it, thanks to an excess that Barthes called 'writing': this disseminated their power into the details. Attention to these tenuous signs was a way for Barthes to submit them to his own *imaginaire* (clothes, the weather, travel, illnesses, flowers) and to bring language up against silence. Great authors can play on the multiple variation of languages, and this leaves readers free to choose the one they prefer, to make certain details echo their own inner lives. An opening up of emotion, and the dissolution that may well attend on this, was preferable to the closed worlds and the grip of languages that confined the universe to an understanding that could only be illusory. 'For if, through a twisted dialectic, the Text, destroyer of all subject, contains a subject to love, that subject is dispersed, somewhat like the ashes we strew into the wind after death (the theme of the *urn* and the *stone*, strong closed objects, instructors of fate, will be contrasted with the bursts of memory, the erosion that leaves nothing but a few furrows of past life).'[35] The biographeme, the detail that will end up being dispersed, is to biography what a memory was to a monument, stone or stele: a fragile but open memory that could set fantasy free and give birth to new work.

When Barthes dealt with these three authors, he was also discovering a new meaning to his experience of the sanatorium. 'They drew up, as it were, a set of instructions for a retreat: for Sade, this was confinement, for Fourier the phalanstery, for Loyola the place of the retreat. Each time, it was a matter of cutting the new language away, materially – cutting it away from the world that might disturb the new meaning. In this way, they create a pure space, a semantic space.'[36] Might what had previously appeared as something of a delaying tactic, imposing limits, not turn out to be in one sense beneficial? This was doubtless what Barthes felt after May '68: secession, distance, a chosen solitude might all allow us to haul ourselves out of the quagmire of the spoken word, the doxa, and lead to writing in the full, boundlessly open sense of the term that he gave it. The fact that he took an interest in different or separate lifestyles, as he did with the three authors in *Sade, Fourier, Loyola*, invites us to think about his own life. The force of the biographical dimension as a critical space was an important factor in Barthes's work and it took shape just as previous spaces appeared to him to be relegated to the past. Weaving together his biographemes – the sanatorium, a certain relation to money and expenditure, the quartier Saint-Sulpice – with those of the authors he wrote about, he kept the 'I' of the social world at bay, bringing it within the infinite movement of the text, which can be read without the inscription of the Father[37] and thus appeared as the complete opposite of political discourse. At the same time, he was composing a fragile art of memory – the art that he would try to establish for himself in the following years.

Changes

The crisis of May 1968 was thus an invitation to travel. This was one of the main themes in his text on Sade and the opening line in his book: 'We travel a great deal in some of Sade's novels.'[38] Barthes lamented to Pinguet that he would not be able to return to Japan in the immediate future: Michel Salzedo had left for a long stay in Israel and he did not want to leave his mother alone while he travelled far away. On 25 July, he decided to leave for Tangiers, where he was joined by Robert Mauzi, François Wahl and Severo Sarduy. He was there again in November and also spent the end of the year there.

This was a place that enabled him to satisfy his desires without any but financial constraints; at the same time, Barthes was creating firm connections within literary and academic circles. He saw Abdelkébir Khatibi, who had attended his seminar in 1964 and become a friend; at the start of his text on Fourier, indeed, Barthes reproduced a long letter on how to make *rancid butter* in certain types of couscous that Khatibi had sent him![39] And in 1979, in a fine homage that would be used as an afterword to Khatibi's book *La Mémoire trouée*, Barthes listed all the things that united them, such as images, and a liking for traces and letters.[40] Another acquaintance was the poet Zaghloul Morsy, whom he had met in Rabat in 1965 through Khatibi, and who was his companion on several adventures in Morocco. Barthes rarely discussed poetry books, but in *Le Nouvel Observateur* he did produce a review of Morsy's collection published by Grasset in 1969, taking up the theme of the 'second language', albeit it literally this time: 'The poem thus shows us how the *other* language (ours) is heard, handled on the other side: this time, we are the ones who are opposite: *we are opposite our own language.*'[41] It was with Morsy, in Tangiers, in the 'Grottes d'Hercule', that Barthes spent the transition from 1968 to 1969, promising that he would come back to this country soon, and take up the invitation of his friend who had been for ten years the director of the department of French literature and civilization at Rabat.[42]

While getting ready for his trip, Barthes spent the first part of 1969 finishing his text on *Sarrasine*, which had not yet been given the title *S/Z*. But his daily life was turning out to be increasingly difficult and gloomy. The health problems that had recurred in 1968 caused considerable physical distress. He often felt tired and even depressed. He was forced to cancel a trip to Belgium at the beginning of 1969, as well as papers he was due to present in Bordeaux and Angers. He did go to England in February, but without much enthusiasm. He passed his time there agreeably enough by going to Oxford and buying a large selection of books on the East. The year 1969 was the one in which he published the least: true, he was completing both *S/Z* and *Empire of Signs* and so we need to see this low level of productivity in that context – but it is notable that he was accepting fewer invitations to write for reviews, exhibitions and newspapers: a significant development.

He signed a three-year contract with the French Ministry of Education to be sent to the University of Rabat as professor of 'French literature' from 1 September 1970. In the meantime, he took part – after much hesitation – at the colloque de Cerisy on the teaching of literature: here, he gave a paper on the classic textbook known as the 'Lagarde and Michard', in which he suggested a counter-history of literature, which would be, first and foremost, the history of its acts of censorship.[43] Rather than remaining in Cerisy for the full colloquium, he made the return journey in a single day, 24 July. Anyone familiar with the difficulties of reaching the château de Cerisy will know that this is quite a feat, and it also indicates that he did not want to take part in a collective debate: at this time, he was ill at ease with this type of academic sociability. In mid-August, he went to the superb Villa Serbelloni in Bellagio, where the Rockefeller Foundation sponsored conferences – in this case, on style in literature. He gave a paper on 'Style and its image' in which he presented style as a succession of transformations of collective or ideolectal formulations. He gave a very personal version of the way that the effects of intertextuality extended to the reader's own life: '[H]aving worked for some time on a tale by Balzac, I often catch myself spontaneously carrying over into the circumstances of daily life fragments of sentences, formulations taken from the Balzacian text [. . .] I am *writing* daily life (it is true, in my head) through these formulas inherited from an anterior writing; or again, more precisely, life is the very thing which comes *already* constituted as a literary writing: *nascent* writing is a *past* writing.'[44] The principle of rewriting no longer concerned literature alone, but the entire way that we wove our lives. This remark confirms how much *Sarrasine* had an impact on this period when life was starting to merge with text – writing was the main theme in both. Balzac's text also formed the basis for an article on 'Action sequences' in which he presented one of the codes analysed in *S/Z*, the 'proairetic' code, which forces one to choose between two terms of an alternative: just as the narrative chooses the term that ensures its survival as narrative, a person seems to choose his future or his own destiny.[45] Here too, text and life come together and join forces.

The concrete desire to make writing into the very meaning of life appeared as soon as Barthes arrived in Morocco, where he stared to keep a diary. This was to go beyond the keeping of notes, a practice he had inherited from the *livre de raison*, with its Protestant origins, and immediately turned the writing of the day's events into a text. As was his habit, he did not take his desk diary on his travels with him, but wrote down his impressions in a separate notebook. It was from these more or less lengthy and detailed notes that the *Incidents* were drawn. Contrary to what is often said, the text did not emerge entirely from the long stay in Morocco in 1969–70. Various previous journeys had already started Barthes's practice of spotting a 'scene' and noting it down. Indeed, by July 1969, before he left, he had already produced a clean version of his notebook, called 'Incidents': the project bearing this title existed and had already found shape. Several mentions in his desk diary prove as much, and he had consigned impressions and things he had seen to the *grand fichier* since 1968, with the same title. This fact also enables us to establish a continuity between the long stay in Morocco and the short periods he spent there roughly twice a year from the early 1960s onwards and then again, frequently, until 1973 (before resuming the habit in 1977). People often contrast – as Barthes himself did – the short, jubilant and luminous times he spent in Morocco seeking pleasure, and his long, wearisome, boring residence there. But things were not quite as clear-cut as all that. Admittedly, that year, Barthes had several administrative and teaching tasks that in some ways made his life in Morocco similar to the one he led in Paris. In addition, his stay happened before the new, ultra-authoritarian direction pursued by the regime of Hassan II (which became explicitly paranoid after the Kenitra coup attempt of 1972); 1970 was marked by large-scale revolts on the part of young people. These severely disrupted academic life and Barthes could not ignore them. Prevented from teaching, he found himself placed in exactly the same situation he had found himself in in Paris two years earlier. His desire for peace and quiet, far from political upheavals, was not to be granted. However, he did not give up the life of pleasure that this country offered him, satisfying his taste for observation, seduction and many different bodies. On his arrival in Tangiers, he noted: 'Saturday 27 September 69: Arrived around 12.30 p.m. Sunshine, warm wind. Hotel, slept, read the paper at the Petit Socco. Relaxed. Renewed zest for this city, a chosen city. It turns cloudy, the wind becomes stormy, it's overcast. I get bored here: absolute solitude, with no relief. Café on the Place de France. Passages. Bought a few things (I can't resist buying things here). Walked back to the hotel. Slept. Terrace bar at the top of the hotel: attractive thematically. Went to M's, dazzling (five!). Called in at the Petit Socco (nothing), a light dinner at the Café de Paris. Isba, found Kiki and the eternal Abdulah. Blow up.[46] Kili, drunk or crazy, bugs me and hassles me; he wants to be my "slave". At the festival, first with Abdulah, then picked up by a certain Ahmed d'Oudja. Came back upstairs at 2, read a bit more Jules Verne.' The alternating pattern of euphoria and consternation is evident throughout Barthes's travel impressions, and gives his writing its momentum. The distress palpable in *Incidents* cannot be attributed solely to the constraints of a long stay. It was also linked to the phase of deflation that follows arousal, to the vicissitudes of desire and to the fact that writing always follows enjoyment (*jouissance*), but is not exactly related to it.

In 'One Always Fails in Speaking of What One Loves', his last article, on Stendhal, Barthes gives a very definite edge to the way he describes his Moroccan sojourns; he sets out what he would like to have found in these periods of exile – a real break, and a sense of emotional liberty: 'Italy is the country where Stendhal, being neither entirely a traveler (a tourist) nor entirely a native, is voluptuously delivered from the responsibility of the citizen; if Stendhal were an Italian citizen, he would die "poisoned by melancholy": whereas, a

Milanese by affection rather than civil status, he need merely harvest the brilliant effects of a civilisation for which he is not responsible. I have been able to experience the convenience of this devious dialectic myself: I used to love Morocco, I often visited the country as a tourist, even spending rather long vacations there; therefore, it occurred to me to spend a year there as a professor: the magic vanished; confronted by administrative and professional problems, I plunged into the ungrateful world of causes and allegiances, I surrendered Festivity for Duty.'[47] Unlike Stendhal, Barthes was unable to shake off his responsibilities and find an adoptive land which he could simply enjoy, where he could be himself without being attached to any collectivity. He was placed in an ambiguous situation, exposed to an ethical dilemma that he referred to indirectly in a text that he started writing in Morocco in August 1970. This was the preface to an Italian edition of Pierre Loti's *Aziyadé*, something that Barthes's friend Franco Maria Ricci had asked him to write. Into this preface Barthes transposed the main themes of his current life: he compared Marrakesh with the Stamboul of Loti's novel, and evoked Loti's drifting, akin to the feeling of rootlessness that he himself experienced in Morocco. He felt that his own situation was like that of the traveller Loti. 'A hundred years later, i.e., in our day, what would have been Lieutenant Loti's Oriental fantasy? No doubt some Arab country, Egypt or Morocco'[48] – two countries in which Barthes himself had lived. All of this indicates a direct, explicit transposition. More obliquely, the passages on homosexuality and on debauchery evoke a different but equally striking parallel.

Aesthetically, Barthes also identified Loti with his own way of proceeding, rather than the other way round. The definition of the incident as a slight fold, a zero degree of what is worth noting, as well as the distinction between Loti as character and Loti as author, Loti I and Loti II (looking forward to *Roland Barthes by Roland Barthes*) all highlighted Barthes's own *ars poetica*. The identification even led him into mistakes and slips of the pen, as when he twice over referred to Loti's famous house as his 'house in Hendaye', when it was in fact in his house in Rochefort that Loti had himself photographed amid all his exotic souvenirs.[49] This was a significant slip, showing that Barthes connected Loti with his own paternal and maternal origins. Loti, a naval officer like Barthes's father, embodied and narrated an unrealized possibility of his own history; for Loti was an explorer and adventurer like Barthes's maternal grandfather, and had himself photographed in a special house, surrounded by his trophies (Binger was photographed in his house in Ville-d'Avray, but Hendaye meant for him his own maternal ancestors). In particular, this text was a first attempt to deal with the themes of residence and dwelling, in a way that was more nuanced than his later attempt in 1980. Here, Barthes mentioned the three possible stages of feeling *uprooted*: travel, residence in a foreign place, and naturalization. Loti was sometimes a tourist, sometimes a resident, sometimes a national (as an officer in the Turkish Army). Though Barthes did not himself experience the third of these, when he wrote this text, he was familiar with the transition from the first uprooting (travel) to the second (residence). He thereupon developed a subtle definition of the difficulty inherent in a 'stay' abroad, where the subject no longer has the 'ethical irresponsibility of the tourist' nor the responsibility of the citizen. This intermediate status provided him with the possibility of becoming a paradoxical, unclassifiable person. This was precisely the state that, elsewhere, Barthes would sometimes describe as neutral, an ever-repeated state that threatened to become fixed. In the space of residence, 'the subject can *dive*: that is, sink, hide, slip away, intoxicate himself, vanish, absent himself, die to everything which is not his desire'.[50]

This ideal side of the long-term stay abroad (as set out in the article on Loti, one which Althusser recognized as a 'luminous' text when he discovered it in the *New Critical Essays*, in 1972),[51] the untrammelled retreat away from it all which Barthes so eagerly sought, where he need feel no fear, was disturbed by another dimension: after all, you cannot always shrug off your responsibilities so easily. Barthes had prepared his classes (on Proust, Verne and Poe) with considerable care before leaving for Morocco, but he needed to adapt to a new audience, very different from the advanced students of the EPHE. In Rabat, it was mainly students doing a first degree whom he was teaching, or older students in his seminars. In February, strikes meant that the classes could not be given. The situation was even tenser after July, when there was a failed coup attempt on Hassan II's summer palace in Skhirat. The Maoist demands voiced by most of the students – supported by many Moroccan lecturers and French *coopérants* – marked a new triumph of the spoken word, something that had caused Barthes so many problems in May 1968. The presence of a dozen Chinese students in the arts faculty in 1969–70 meant that here was a certain rivalry between distinct political groups linked to foreign cultural centres. Thus the Soviet centre and the orange-tree district where the Chinese students happened to live were the main meeting places for members of the Union of Moroccan Students, and the heart of the protests. The cinémathèques of the Soviet and French cultural centres also provided a site for political and ideological debate.[52]

Barthes's difficulty in making the most of the country of his choice, in a way that Stendhal had managed, was probably more an effect of historical transformations than of individual factors. But Barthes's melancholy was not just a result of his dependent status and the tasks he had to carry out: it was also the pressure exerted by death on his character. It turned disengagement, not into a selfish desire to give one's individuality its due, but into a suspension of interest in the outside world, into sadness and boredom. *Incidents*, constituted of what falls under one's gaze, was thus infected from beginning to end by stains: 'a sky-blue sweater with a fine orange stain on the front', 'always a stain on these milk-white garments', 'a stain, a faint smear of something, maybe pigeon shit, on his immaculate hood', the finally annoying fly, 'the dust of the flea-market'; but it was also filled with the colour of djellabas, the 'wild roses in the piles of mint' in the souk in Marrakesh. Some of Barthes's notes remark on the circumstantial details of his short stays in Morocco with friends such as Robert Mauzi, François Wahl and Severo Sarduy, and were probably written before 1969. One, for example, reads: 'At Ito, looking out over a huge, noble landscape, one of us jokingly gives a picture of a naked woman (from some *Playboy* or other) to young Moha, who sells semiprecious stones: smiles, reserve, seriousness, remoteness on the boy's part.'[53] Others instead refer to his teaching responsibilities in Morocco, and mention the students and the French professors. But most of the time, the short scenes he describes are important less for the circumstances they evoke than for what might be called their *punctuality*, a very precise moment or point in the real: exactly what, in *Camera Lucida*, Barthes describes as the *punctum* of photography: 'for *punctum* is also: sting, speck, cut, little hole – and also a cast of the dice. A photograph's *punctum* is that accident which pricks me (but also bruises me, is poignant to me).'[54] That on which you fix your gaze and which sends its arrow back into your heart: dirt, poverty, distress, interest, everything that seizes and grabs you (sexuality). The *Incidents* are snapshots insofar as something in them endures, as in photography. This something is the complete opposite of *jouissance*. It is a leftover, a moment in which the real is derealized, and becomes generalized. In this world of possibilities that Morocco opened up, in which a great number of young men were available (for money, of course), Barthes was led to a veritable frenzy of physical contact. The moment of writing, of 'notes' as one boy says to him ('are you taking notes?'),[55] corresponds to a moment of calm, where all that is left is the clear, obvious, sometimes rather painful fact of what has been.

In Rabat, Barthes lived in an apartment he rented near the railway station. His mother and brother joined him in January 1970. Michel Salzedo wanted to take advantage of this opportunity to add Arabic to his Hebrew, and Barthes introduced him to a professor of Arabic at the university. They used their leisure time to tour Morocco: Barthes took his mother to see the basketwork being made in Salé, and his brother joined them on trips to Tangiers, Asilah and Fez. Michel went back to Paris at the beginning of February and Barthes, who had been freed from his teaching because of the strikes, spent a brief time in Paris for the launch of *S/Z* and the – many – interviews that

followed its publication (in *L'Express*, *Les Nouvelles littéraires* and
on various radio broadcasts). He returned to Morocco alone on 20
February; he was invited to give lectures 'open to the public', more
in tune with the protest movement than closed seminars or classes
for degree students alone. He had already told the dean of the university that he did not wish to serve out his contract to the end. He
felt that his legitimacy and his function were again in question. He
wanted to leave. In particular, his lectures on Proust did not interest
the students, who saw this author as the paragon of the dominant
classical French culture. One of their ideological demands was that
a knowledge of the French language should be separated from a
colonial cultural imposition. In an interview with Guy Scarpetta in
the magazine *Promesse*, in 1971, Barthes came back to this question, expressing a very great distance from this demand: 'In certain
countries still encumbered by a former colonial language (French),
there currently prevails the *reactionary* idea that one can separate
language from "literature", that one can teach French (as a foreign
language) and repudiate French literature (as "bourgeois").'[56] But
some of the students thought Barthes's seminars were really good.
One of them was Abdellah Bounfour: although he was convinced of
the need to highlight the literature of Morocco – he is now a very
distinguished specialist in Berber literature and professor at Inalco,
the Institut national des langues et cultures orientales – he benefited
greatly from Barthes's teaching and analyses.

At the end of February, Barthes embarked on an enjoyable trip to
the south of Morocco with a group of friends. They went to Erfoud,
Merzouga, Ouarzazate and the Todgha Gorge, with the spring of
the sacred fish, and he visited the canyons as well as the palm groves
of Tinghir. On his return, he immediately left for Paris, for the publication of what was, barely a month after *S/Z*, his second book that
year: *Empire of Signs*. He did not return to Morocco until 6 April,
but it was still not possible to teach under normal circumstances. So
he took advantage of the disruption to travel again, alone this time,
to another region, playing the tourist even though he was actually
a resident in the country. He visited Taroudant, Goulimine, the
camel souk, and then went back to Essaouira, where he stayed in a
bungalow hotel. Various French friends came to see him: Tzvetan
Todorov in May, Severo Sarduy and François Wahl in July.
Henriette Barthes and Michel Salzedo had been with him again
since June. Apart from the Moroccans he had known for some
time, he socialized with expatriates who were teaching in Morocco
or had diplomatic jobs there. These included Josette Pacaly, head
of the department of French at the Université Mohammed-V, and
Claude Palazzoli, professor at the faculty of law, who a few years
later wrote a book on *Le Maroc politique*;[57] he often invited Barthes
to parties. There was also Jean-Claude Bonnet, a young *coopérant*

in Morocco, with whom Barthes stayed in the summer of 1970 (the latter had left his apartment in Rabat before taking a new apartment at the start of the academic year for his mother and himself in the rue d'Aumale in Casablanca); and Bernard Sichère, who arrived in the autumn of 1970, also as a *coopérant*. Barthes met Claude Ollier, too, who would stay in the country for extended periods in the years to come, but was already a frequent visitor. Ollier had already published two books set in Morocco: *La Mise en scène* in 1958, and *Le Maintien de l'ordre* in 1961. In his book *Marrakch Medine* (1976), Ollier draws on the encounter between the Arabic, French and Berber languages to invigorate his writing. When he described his encounter with Barthes on two occasions in Rabat, he criticizes him for having not paid enough attention to the country and in particular to its language.[58] It is true that Barthes showed less interest in Arabic than he did in Japanese, and made no effort to learn it. However, Ollier's judgement is a little unfair, and there is some evidence against it, such as the texts he wrote on Moroccan writers (mentioned above) and *Incidents*, as well as the seminar Barthes gave on polysemy where he demonstrated a sustained attention to Arabic culture and even language. The analytical method that he had devised for *S/Z* and also applied to Edgar Allan Poe meant that he focused very closely on texts, and was interested in phenomena of pluralization that always opened texts up to more meanings. His seminar on polysemy made fascinating use of the work of Jacques Berque and Jean-Paul Charnay, *L'Ambivalence dans la culture arabe*. 'Thus, polysemy is successively envisaged in its French context and in its Arabic context.'[59] There are, for instance, homonyms with opposite meanings (the *ad'adâd*, in Arabic, which Barthes called 'enantiosemes') such as the word 'hôte' in French, which can mean both 'guest' and 'host'. They create many possible meanings and do not follow the norms of stability and causality – which is something of a problem for a culture of the written word that rests on the principle of an immutable text. Barthes analyses *azrun* (strength, weakness), *baht'nun* (sea, land), *jawnun* (black, white), and *jarun* (patron, client) as examples of this phenomenon. Derrida found similar ambiguous words in Greek: *pharmakon* (remedy, poison); Barthes saw them as a way of working against an argumentative, rational logic fixated on the truth. They could extend the range of possible meanings. As in Derrida, textual analysis, resting on the unfolding and difference of potential senses, was another, decentred way of bringing a set of ideas to light. It was yet another principle of delicacy, overcoming stark alternatives, making meaning fuzzy, delaying its emergence. Barthes found this same opening in the play of sexuality: '[T]he sexual interdiction is completely lifted, not to the advantage of a mythical "liberty" (a concept only good enough to satisfy the timid phantasms of so-called mass society), but to the advantage of empty codes, which exonerates sexuality from the falsehood of spontaneity.'[60] Oppositions are broken down by these bipolarities, these ambiguities: this is also the case in cookery which provides an entire range of examples. 'many skilful and ambiguous combinations', the 'cuisine of Fez (urbanity): *bstalla*, chicken with sugar; *mrouzia* (a dish for Eid al-Kabir), mutton with honey; *majun*, narcotic and aphrodisiac . . .'[61]

Long before the question of bilingualism became an obvious issue for postcolonial literature, Barthes highlighted the force of a French language written from the standpoint of another language, one that could decentre the European subject. Hence the beauty that he found in the 'Letter from Jilali', reproduced in *Roland Barthes by Roland Barthes*, whose language 'speaks *at the same time* truth and desire';[62] hence, too, the list of linguistic anomalies in *Incidents*, which are a way of making signs slip and slide – something that fascinated him. 'I enjoy Amidou's vocabulary: *dream* and *burst* for *get an erection* and *have an orgasm. Burst* is vegetal, scattering, disseminating, not moralistic, narcissistic, closed off like *having an orgasm.*'[63] And: 'Selam, a veteran from Tangiers, roars with laughter because he has met three Italians who were of no use to him: "They thought I was feminine!".'[64] It also led him into a reverie on Arabic names, something so tangible in this text that seemed to caress everything so gently: Najib, Lahoucine, 'Abdessalam, a boarder at Tétouan', 'Mohammed with soft hands', 'Azemmour' . . . These are sounds, rhythms, phrases that are not as yet sentences; they lead back to the linguistic utopia dreamed of in *Empire of Signs* and *The Pleasure of Text*, when Barthes evoked the stereophony of a Tangiers square. This attention to signs and languages was the proof that Barthes was not indifferent to this country: quite the contrary – he was grateful to recognize its difference, and learn from it.

But what he most liked about Morocco was probably its houses. The Mediterranean house was a common place, but he turned it into a purely individual fantasy. When he was in Morocco, for the brief stays leading up to his year's residence, he regularly went to rest and recuperate in Mehioula, south of Casablanca, with the cliff of Azemmour, not far from the sea, where his friend Alain Benchaya went almost every weekend.[65] Barthes later evoked the house-hotel run by a French woman, 'where light came from petrol lamps and where, in winter, it was freezing cold'.[66] And in *Incidents* he described his enjoyment: 'Happiness at Mehiula: the huge kitchen, at night, the storm outside, the simmering harrira, the big butane lamps, the whole ballet of little visits, the warmth, the djellaba, and reading Lacan! (Lacan defeated by this trivial comfort.)'[67] This is a pure image of serenity, which the ironic sally on Lacan transforms into a place of wish fulfilment and desire. The same desire was expressed in *Camera Lucida* in connection

with a photograph by Charles Clifford: 'An old house, a shadowy
porch, tiles, a crumbling Arab decoration, a man sitting against
the wall, a deserted street, a Mediterranean tree (Charles Clifford's
"Alhambra"): this old photograph (1854) touches me: it is quite
simply *there* that I should like to live.'[68] The desire for a dwelling
transports Barthes towards those utopian places from another time
where the immemorial world of childhood merges into a fantasized
future. This was always within a Mediterranean setting, also mentioned in *How to Live Together*, in connection with Mount Athos:
'Basically, it's a landscape. I can picture myself there, standing on
the edge of a terrace, the sea in the distance, the coarse white plaster
on the walls, with two rooms for my own use and two more close
by for a few friends.'[69] To be in the company of one's friends and
books, in a place that combined solitude and conviviality, distance
and beauty, was a way of finding an equivalent to the mother's
body. Barthes recognized this, logically enough, in *Camera Lucida*:
'Looking at these landscapes of predilection, it is as if I were certain
of having been there or of going there. Now Freud says of the
maternal body that "there is no other place of which one can say
with so much certainty that one has already been there." Such then
would be the essence of the landscape (chosen by desire): *heimlich*,
awakening in me the Mother (and never the disturbing Mother).'[70]
This was also certainly one of the reasons for the happiness Barthes
experienced in Morocco, in spite of all the difficulties: he felt a
profound kinship with this place, where he was surrounded by
close friends, especially Alain Benchaya and above all 'Joël' Lévy-
Corcos, his most important link to Morocco, who attended his
seminar in Rabat and with whom he spent a good deal of his time.
Later on, Lévy-Corcos settled in Israel; this was one reason why
Barthes then spent less time in Morocco. Amongst his friends, in
the big house, he found reconciliation: a peaceable form of speech,
where nobody judged you, intimidated you, or defended some
great cause. He liked the atmosphere and the sense of suspended
animation created by *kif*, as he related in a text where one might
not expect such an intimate disclosure: 'Writers, Intellectuals,
Teachers'. While he himself was unable to inhale the smoke owing
to his lung problems, he loved 'the general *good will* which impreg-
nates certain places, abroad, where *kif* is smoked. The gestures, the
(infrequent) words, the whole relation of bodies (though a relation
that is motionless and remote) is relaxed, disarmed.'[71] Into this
serene fantasy, a few biographemes also penetrated: the cuisine, the
lamps, and the djellaba. This garment is ubiquitous in *Incidents*:
Barthes regularly wore one in the evenings, as he liked its comfort,
its colour, its freedom and its ambiguity.[72] And then there was the
group, in which he played an active part but from which he always
felt somewhat separate.

Cut-ups

The need for decentring was also evidenced by the two books published in 1970, *S/Z* and *Empire of Signs*. They were finished before Barthes left for Morocco,[73] but he received the proofs there. In spite of the tangible differences between the two books, they are both presented in a cut-up form. *S/Z* is a series of syntagms or lexias, comparable to 'the divisions of the sonic flow into measures'.[74] And *Empire of Signs* quickly drew on the notion in its description of Japanese cuisine: 'the only operation they have actually undergone', he writes of the foodstuffs, 'is to be cut up.'[75] In both cases, division does not separate or disperse: rather, it brings out the coherence of the whole. The unease we may feel at the idea of cutting up as something hostile, or as a bar of separation, usually comes from the fact that we divide things up in different ways. Through a sort of contagion of castration that lies at the heart of Balzac's novella, Barthes breaks open the totality to bring things back to a fragmentation that is closer to the truth. He was very attentive about this point in his seminar on *Sarrasine*: objects and words are already cut-ups. We need to get into the habit of thinking in a new way, contemplating the text differently, seeing the real as a text. And we need to cut up in accordance with different principles: 'the procedure followed by all those who seek something tiny and fleeting in a vast homogenous space'[76] – the augur, for example, the archaeologist or the gold-digger. So these two books represent, in Barthes's work, a veritable transformation, and their power – still active even today – lies to a considerable degree in the way they overturn the western signified by decentring the relation between the subject and meaning, renouncing the symbol and rejecting the notion of depth. Dismissing the idea of a model transcending several texts, *S/Z* takes as its main theoretical proposition the idea that every text is its own model and needs to be treated in its difference, right down to the smallest vibration that makes it into its own event. Like *satori* in Zen,[77] or what Barthes called the 'incident', a zone in the text may, as a result of the laws of plate tectonics, shake up all the meaning that the text seemed to hold.

Of this transformation, *S/Z* represents the theoretical and methodological aspect, and *Empire of Signs* the ethical aspect. Barthes acknowledges that the theoretical shift accomplished in *S/Z* stemmed from his rejection of a general structure that could be used to generate the analysis of absolutely any text – something that he had postulated in the 'Introduction to the Structural Analysis of Narratives'. This transformation came from his very approach. By changing the way the object was envisaged, and proceeding more slowly, he had transformed the object itself: 'In going step by step over a text, I changed the object, and in that way was led to a change in theory.'[78]

Barthes recognized that this transformation had also come from his reading of others: 'It's because I was surrounded by "formulators," writers like Derrida, Sollers, Kristeva (always the same names, of course), who taught me things, persuaded me, opened my eyes.'[79] We have already stated what he owed to Kristeva: the idea of the pluralization of the text and the abandoning of any reductionism to a unitary principle. It is important that we dwell for a while on what he owed to Derrida or rather on what made them both simultaneously inventors of new methods. Their parallel course rested on two operations: deconstruction – unfolding, cutting up – and analysis. And above all, when Derrida questioned the concepts of metaphysics, or Barthes probed the western mechanisms of meaning, they had both used a mode of *reading* to gain these ends. They read and reread everything in order to remake it, to forge new connections that went beyond educational or cultural conditioning. Reading and writing were no longer thought of as separate activities but were redefined in tandem, and thus played a part in the reform of meaning. The conviction that reading and writing were not two separate activities gave rise to magnificent passages on reading, rereading, and the rhythms at which one reads; depending on whether one reads quickly or slowly, things that might have appeared opaque can become dazzlingly clear. It is striking to see that, at a time when Barthes was more obviously at ease with his classical tastes and his indifference to the avant-garde, he showed considerable originality in his new ideas about reading. The power he attributed to Pierre Guyotat's *Éden, Éden, Éden* was linked to the fact that the novel undermined our linear habits of reading, habits that discouraged rereading. And the force of his critical method was that it led to a different way of writing: 'To read is to find meanings, and to find meanings is to name them; but these named meanings are swept toward other names; names call to each other, reassemble, and their grouping calls for further naming: I name, I unname, I rename.'[80] Analysis is the name of this interminable operation – so long as it is imagined without the closure of synthesis, as a mode of slippage, forever changing: what Derrida calls *différance*. In Derrida too, reading includes writing. What characterizes writing is *textuality*, which is both the closure and the non-closure of the text: 'We cannot think the closure of what has no end. The closure is the circular limit within which the repetition of *différance* is indefinitely repeated. In other words, its space of play. This movement is the movement of the world as game.'[81] It is noteworthy, too, that self-assertion as a writer, or at least the public expression of a desire to write, should play a part just as the method of textual analysis was setting him up as a critic and a reader. The notion of the *writerly* text expressed and resolved this paradox, since it made the reader into a producer of the text. To work in the signifier was, quite simply, to give oneself the possibility of writing.

The coup represented by *S/Z* was that it comprised the first dive into the murky and unexplored world of reading, an activity which institutions had always endeavoured to channel. '*In the text, only the reader speaks.*'[82] Yet again, Barthes seized on a classic text, one that – like Racine – had been recuperated by the educational system and academia, and completely subverted its codes. He destabilized Balzac's text, showing that it did not just follow the classic law of representation or verisimilitude. He turned it into a free territory, open to every appropriation and every desire. The form of texts was neither architectural nor unitary: it melted into movement, into infinite inflections that alluded to things that had already been read, seen, done or experienced. In this way, every code was one of the forces that could grasp the text, show its variations, its plurality, its 'glistening texture'. Reading helped to undo the origin of utterances and discourses. 'The best way to conceive the classical plural is then to listen to the text as an iridescent exchange carried on by multiple voices, on different wavelengths and subject from time to time to a sudden *dissolve*, leaving a gap which enables the utterance to shift from one point of view to another, without warning: the writing is set up across this tonal instability (which in the modern text becomes atonality), which makes it a glistening texture of ephemeral origins.'[83]

The text's first readers understood the originality of the suggestion: and in the letters they wrote to Barthes, they often added their own readings to his, pursuing the movement engaged upon by the text itself. Lévi-Strauss presented a reading of the 'Sarrasins' (Saracens), while Paule Thévenin wrote a long letter with commentaries on 'sarrasin' (black wheat) and on 'Zambinella' (a little ham, or Hamlet).[84] On 4 August 1969, the very first reader, Barthes's publisher and friend François Wahl, immediately declared himself to be 'jealous' of the extraordinary theoretical advance made in this book: 'You have succeeded: a) in ensuring that, once the infinite number of lexias and codes has been opened, we want even more [. . .] b) in drawing the reader, your reader, into a process of analysis, a conjugation of the infinite chain of meanings with the invincibility of a progress: here, castration, gradually (or rather, having-been-castrated as a state) undermines everything, and the reader (the other reader: RB) finds the opportunity for a golden song.' The rest of the letter put forward several judicious suggestions, though Barthes apparently did not take them into account when he reread his work, if we are to believe the corrections he made to the first proofs. Wahl concluded: 'What makes such an impression when one reads you is the way the writerly is set up, stretching as far as the eye can see, with such systematic endurance: it involves the fabric, the voices and levels of the musical score, and the progressive interweavings . . .; but more than

anything else, when you get to the end of the buttress, through the
sign, the fading of the voices, the pseudo-empirical nature of the
action sequences, the superimposing of the portrait, the signified-
conclusion, the inoperable, the proper name, the masterpiece, the
stage (a sublime analysis) and the suspension: all of the things we
would so like to have finished with ages ago, and you just flick them
away.' He handed the manuscript on to Sollers, the second reader,
who was also filled with admiration. He measured its 'absolutely
crucial subversive impact' and realized that Barthes, in rewriting
'Sarrasine', had produced a masterpiece from a work that had not
been one before he rewrote it. It comes as no surprise that, when
the book was published, in February, Derrida was completely in
agreement. On 22 March 1970, he wrote to Barthes: 'Dear friend, I
wish to tell you quite simply of my gratitude and my admiration for
S/Z. And that with no other text do I at present feel so *absolutely*
in agreement, committed. The way S/Z is staged, in its layout on
the page, should constitute what would have been called, in the old
code, a model, or a method or an exemplary point of reference. In
any case, I am sure that what S/Z is doing, and will do for a long
time, is to draw, multiply, "liberate" a new space for reading and
writing.' Deleuze also praised the radically 'new method' of the
book and its power, recognizing in it, in the vocabulary that he had
by now made his own, 'a new machine'. Jacqueline Risset, meanwhile, realized that the work had been set up in such a way that
the reader would be confronted with 'his own desire for fiction'.
Michel Leiris apologized for the lateness of his reply, justifying it
by saying that, with this book, he was learning to read ('and this –
exciting – apprenticeship naturally takes rather a long time!').[85] The
psychoanalyst Jean Reboul, to whom Barthes acknowledged his
debt at the start of the book, as it was Reboul's article on Balzac's
novella (which he had selected following a suggestion from Georges
Bataille) that had drawn his attention to this text,[86] also expressed
his great interest in the analysis.

As far as Balzac specialists were concerned, however, they were
rattled, and sometimes frankly hostile. The quarrel over *On Racine*
did not repeat itself, but some of the ripostes were very violent. In
Le Monde, Pierre Citron severely criticized a method 'that emphasizes the subjective side of all reading'; and Pierre Barbéris, a
Marxist critic, published an out-and-out denunciation of the book
in *L'Année balzacienne* – a fact that may give the impression that
the whole world of Balzac scholars lined up in his support. The
first criticism concerned Barthes's choice of a marginal novella,
which eclipsed the rest of Balzac's world; the second criticism was
of a methodological nature and attacked Barthes's impression-
istic reading; and the third main objection was Barthes's neglect
of history (in particular the sociopolitical dimension of a novella

written just after the 1830 Revolution).[87] However, with the exception of the specialists, intellectuals as a whole were in favour of the book, as it had invented a new reader, representing its own readers as authors in their own right. Barthes acknowledged that the twofold reception of *S/Z*, in the habitual organs of criticism and in the many letters that he received, including from unknown readers, 'multiplying the meanings I had found and finding others', had been the true justification for his work.[88]

Empire of Signs appeared as the ethical aspect of this new relation to meaning. And Japan was thus another object for Barthes to read and write. In this sense, the book was almost as original as *S/Z*, and radically altered the genre of the travel book. By basing his book more on fantasy than on experience or knowledge, Barthes subjected the country to the laws of his own *imaginaire* and his own desire. Because Barthes turned Japan into a space for the primitive, for emptiness, for the exemption from meaning, it seemed to be a writerly text and constituted an effective antidote to the intimidating spoken word, a way of finishing with the religion of meaning and the terrorism of assertive speech. Japan is a sign, but an empty, elusive sign that splits apart our beliefs and our symbols. It cannot be thought on the basis of an interplay of subject, world and meaning: it needs to be read in its slack materiality. It hardly matters whether Barthes really understood the concepts of Zen and its intimate echoes in the Japan he was discovering. What is important is understanding how Japan helped him to justify his own critical positions, morally and emotionally. The predominance of the visual could have echoed the feelings of every visitor (or tourist) who visits a country that he does not know: you look at things and you photograph them in order to capture what you do not understand. Barthes knew that, and refused to let his gaze merely dwell on the sights. Instead, he agreed to be photographed or seized by the real that surrounded him, and modified by it. Radically reducing the elements of reflex recuperation that might lie in his observations, he allowed things, movements, and places – chopsticks, shops, Japanese characters, stationery – to come to him, and refused to interpret them. It so happened that these were things that he personally liked: his love of stationery, different types of ink, notebooks and pens was not just a random element but something crucial to his biography; it defined the way he lived, the way he worked. He had been intensely fond of gardens ever since childhood. He focused on calligraphy, noting what was a trait, a slit or gash in it rather than a gaze or a soul. In this respect, he was very close to what Lacan called the 'Japanese characteristic': a specific mode of *jouissance* linked to the calligraphic functioning of writing and illustrated by a simple horizontal line that Lacan called the 'littoral', found between knowledge and *jouissance*.[89] This single line is referred to twice over in *Empire of Signs*: in connection with Pachinko, a reproduction, in the mechanical domain, of the 'principle of painting *alla prima*, which insists that the line be drawn in a single movement, once and for all'; and in connection with the eyelid, traced out with a single line, as if by a calligraphic anatomist, 'as it must be in painting *alla prima*', 'with a rapid turn of his hand'.[90]

Barthes's book presented itself as a collection of images, which alternated iconographical documents (in line with the format of the 'Sentiers de la création' series published by Éditions Skira) with prose fragments that often resembled the prose poem as conceived by Baudelaire, at once an astonished reaction to a particular scene and a little parable. But it also contained several important theoretical ideas that followed straight on from his current preoccupations: writing, of course, which had now moved into the entire space of the real and enabled it to be unfolded before our eyes like a huge printed fabric; the body, notably the actor's body, which confirmed suggestions about the absence of exaggeration and need for an overt display of codes that Barthes had long ago developed in connection with Brecht (who had himself, it is worth recalling, learned from the acting style of Chinese theatre); and the foreign language as a necessary displacement, which bolstered – in a more radical form – the feeling Barthes had in Morocco that decentring was important in order to escape from the full meaning.[91] In this way, Barthes could affirm the importance of a model of thinking and acting that was neither paranoid (rationality), nor hysterical (romanticism), but freed, exempted from meaning. By refusing to be caught up in one of the four propositions of the paradigm (A – not-A – neither A nor not-A (zero degree) – A and not-A (complex degree)), Zen breaks the mechanism of language to preserve the value of event in every thought, not dragging it into the infinite spiral of metaphor or symbol. But more than these theoretical formulations, it was the expression of a desire and the inscription of the body – his own, that of the Japanese – that give the book the charm and subtlety that still work on many readers today.

Empire of Signs corresponds to the ordering and shaping of the notes that Barthes habitually took when travelling, in notebooks (his journey to China), or on index cards (his various trips to Morocco and Japan).[92] The book's fragmentary nature also stems from a form of writing that was always close to the diary: the notebook entries, like the index cards, are mostly dated and written very soon after the event (generally the same evening or the next day). But Barthes usually went back over his notes and index cards in order to emend them or reclassify them. In this way he could free them from their initial circumstances before, as in the case of Japan, publishing them. *Empire of Signs* gathered notes written in the course of the three successive trips he took to that country, but

it was the first of these, from 2 May to 2 June 1966, that provided
all the basic material that the following journeys simply refined
or confirmed. The evocation of the floating market in Bangkok,[93]
for example, stems from an observation he made during his first
journey, as this was the only occasion on which he had a three-day
stopover in that city. Likewise, the little lexicon for arranging meet-
ups, and the sketches enabling him to find his way around Tokyo,
were provided by Maurice Pinguet on his first journey. Most of
the work was in fact rewritten during his stay in Baltimore in the
autumn of 1967, which explains the recurrent comparisons with the
United States.[94] *Empire of Signs* was thus a book composed on the
basis of an intimate practice of writing, one that usually remained
private. The other books that drew on the same practice (*Incidents*,
Mourning Diary, *Travels in China*) would be published only posthumously. So this was a book that rested entirely on a certain desire
– first, because Japan filled him with the urge to write and enabled
him to find the novelistic without the novel that Barthes had for
some time called the 'incident'; and second because while in Japan
he felt perfectly attuned to his desire. Here he experienced a veritable art of living, to which he felt adapted and which contrasted with
the impression of being awkward and out of step that he always felt
in France. He dreamt – literally – of the two countries being able to
join up. 'No sooner had I arrived than I had the following dream: my
bedroom in the rue Servandoni, perched up high, as you know, was
directly linked – in the jumbled way natural to dreams – via a vertical staircase with that little alley in Shibuya where the PAL bar is
located.'[95] He loved the simplicity of the relations he could strike up
with people – including for sex – and some of his nostalgia stemmed
from his memory of moments of perfect harmony. 'You know how
I think of this country, of its boys – and also how sometimes I force
myself not to think of it so as not to be immersed in nostalgia', he
wrote to Maurice Pinguet after his second stay in Japan.[96] And on
15 January 1968, after his third stay, he told Pinguet that he felt he
had left Japan only in the most material sense: 'I replace every street
spectacle, every episode in the day, with its Japanese equivalent and
I long for it, with deep nostalgia.'[97] As ever with the things he loved
most in the world (his mother, literature), he thought Japan was
'heartrending'. On 23 May 1967, he wrote: 'I always have a crazy,
heartrending longing to return to Japan, this summer in fact'; and
on 15 January the following year: 'I have moments of desolation
when I think, for example, of young Tanaka, when he came to the
airport, the tie he was wearing and the way he shyly fled: all of this
makes me feel indescribably tender and is rather heartrending.' And
Empire of Signs includes an entire subtext, visible and legible, that
between the lines recounts the adventures of his desire, his liberated
relationship with the body. First there is the lexicon for meeting

up, reproduced in its handwritten form, and thus setting out all the words with which he could communicate with his lovers: 'this evening: komban', 'what time?: nan ji ni', 'tired: tsukareta'.[98] Then there is the small plan sketched out on the back of a visiting card and, as has been noticed, reproducing the route to the 'Pinocchio', a place for homosexual encounters. But it is mainly the images that display his desire. The photos of the face of the actor Kazuo Funaki, the one at the beginning of the book and the other at the end (this last one has an additional smile) belonged to Barthes, as were the photos of Sumo wrestlers in the middle of the book, and the picture of the Kabuki actor with his two sons. It is unquestionable that Barthes devoted the greatest care to the illustrations for his book – witness the fact that he drew on the help of several people. One was Daniel Cordier (who authorized him to reproduce two documents from his personal collection and who was acknowledged on the page of photo credits). Another was a keeper from the Musée Guimet; and a third was Albert Skira himself, who provided access to the holdings in Swiss collections (especially that of Nicolas Bouvier, who provided several of the images for the book).[99] However, it is striking that all the photos of young men were taken by Barthes himself. They show an exchange of glances, or a moment of withdrawal (as with the photo of the wrestler who is helping himself to food and shows only the line of his shoulders and his right thigh),[100] a relation in which Barthes is himself caught up, photographed as much as photographing. This could lead to a form of becoming-Japanese that Barthes showed when, a little further on, he displayed another document: a portrait of himself in the daily paper *Kobé Shinbun* that gave him an almost oriental face, 'eyes elongated, pupils blackened by Nipponese typography'.[101]

Becoming oriental was a desirable state: it led back to the theme of the non-full subject that we have identified as the main quest in this period. Redefining meaning involved apprehending a lack that Barthes staged in a much more violent way in *S/Z*, in the theme of castration. For castration deprives Zambinella of the possibility of orgasm and, as castration is contagious, it also deprives Sarrasine of his desire (which is not true of the emptiness of Japan). S[arrasine] is barred / by Z[ambinella]: the loss of the letter Z in his name, which ought logically to be written Sarrazine, turns Z into the letter of castration, the missing letter, the bad letter. This was a recurrent motif in the texts of that period. In *S/Z*, of course, where it 'stings like a chastising lash', it 'cuts, slashes, or, as we say in French, *zebras*'; it 'becomes the letter of deviation', 'the wound of deficiency'.[102] In *Sade, Fourier, Loyola*, where it is stated that Sade's name came from the village of Saze (*Sazo*): 'In attaining the accursed name, brilliantly formulated (it has engendered a common noun), the letter that, as we say in French, *zebras*, fustigates, the *z*, has given way to the softest of dentals.'[103] But also in the text on Erté's 'Letter-Women', where Barthes views the Z as the opposite of the S, an effervescent, smooth body: 'is not Z an inverted and angulated S, an S *belied*? For Erté, Z is a melancholy, crepuscular, veiled letter in which Woman inscribes both her submission and her supplication (for Balzac, too, Z was a "bad" letter, as he explains in his tale *Z. Marcas*).'[104] But this negativity of the letter also has positive effects insofar as it destroys all plenitude: sex is abolished, language stops and sculptor's art becomes impossible: 'This Replete Literature, readerly literature, can no longer be written.'[105] We here enter a different order of thought – one which Deleuze had also invited us to explore in *Logic of Sense*, published a few months earlier, in 1969. In the form of the celebrated 'body without organs', he too saw castration as a crack in thought, a passage to a new relationship with being.

On the path that led Barthes to reject binary oppositions and dichotomies, *S/Z* was the most consummate stage, as (with Balzac) it managed to overcome the distinction between feminine and masculine, in the name of Sarrasine and in the very being of Zambinella. This muting of the conflict via a process of analysis that literally exhausted the text might indicate two important ways in which we can interpret this period in Barthes's life and suggest how the two books of 1970 concluded it. The first was presented in the form of a riddle, written between the lines: it is a plea for homosexuality and the utopia it makes possible, that of a reunion without opposition. Long before the existence of Gender Studies, Barthes separated the concepts of sex and gender and showed that the binary institutional structure of the sexes was unsatisfactory: this was already what he was saying in his first article in homage to Lévi-Strauss: 'Masculin, féminin, neutre'. It is impossible to resort to a morphological neutral (if only because of the constraints of French, where nouns have to be masculine or feminine), but Balzac's text makes both masculine and feminine tremble.[106] The second way in which *S/Z* helps grasp this period of Barthes's life lies in its reflection of the events of May '68 on him: seeking solutions to get beyond the great disputes orchestrated by the written word, Barthes turned to writing and the displacements of the letter that kept it forever in infinite movement, impossible to appropriate in any definitive way.

Barthes in Morocco in 1969.

Desk diary 1969. In
Morocco.

°

La gardienne du marabout est une vieille femme édentée
qui initie les garçons du village pour cinquante francs l'un.
   (Le tombeau est près d'un cube en torchis du n° 61,qui
est la chambre où on lave les morts; le tombeau est ouvert :
quelques nattes par terre,des étoffes pendues en don au cer-
cueil de bois peint en vert,sous une photo fade de l'ancien
sultan,une paire de sandales traîne sur une natte.)

°

M.,malade,tapi dans un coin ~~sur une natte~~,cachait ses
pieds nus et brûlants sous sa djellaba brune.

°

Le grand escogriffe édenté (pressant et constant) me dit
à voix basse,d'un ton convaincu et passionné,de la plus plate
des marques de cigarettes : "Pour moi,Marquise,c'est comme
du kif !"

°

Le petit I. m'apporte des fleurs,un vrai bouquet champêtre:
quelques têtes de géranium,une branche d'églantines rouges,
deux roses,quatre brins de jasmin. Ce mouvement qu'il a eu,c'
est à la suite d'un grand plaisir que je lui ai fait : écrire
son nom de plusieurs façons à la machine,sur un papier que je
lui ai donné (des fleurs contre l'écriture).

29

ncidents: typescript (1 page).

In Mehioula.

S/*Z*: manuscript (p. 14).

13

Barthes and Sollers

In 1971, as ideological battles raged, *Tel Quel* devoted its issue 47 to Roland Barthes. May '68 had divided opinion, and Sollers's review decided to emphasize the separations and conflicts this entailed. *Tel Quel* was marked by a number of dramatic changes of direction, both theoretical and political, and aroused violent opposition, anger and exasperation. Its implicit programme had, right from the start, aimed at stirring things up, and this dynamism tended to stoke argument. So Barthes's unfailing support seems contradictory, or at least eccentric: after all, as we have seen, he hated noisy polemics and interpersonal conflicts. While he did not take up a front-line stance, he seemed to back, at least implicitly, all of Sollers's decisions, even what was probably the most controversial from his own point of view, when Sollers joined the French Communist Party in May. When Jean-Pierre Faye and the CAEE took over the Hôtel Massa on 23 May, the *telqueliens* denounced these leftist deviations and emphasized the need to stand alongside the Communists, with the prospect of a proletarian revolution raising its head: as such a revolution now looked like being on the cards, unity was a priority; but they split off from the Union of Writers. After the suppression of the Prague uprising, Faye and the Union clearly expressed their solidarity with the Czechoslovak people, whereas the members of *Tel Quel* reacted with a silence which they later explained as arising from their disdain for their opponents, who were 'liquidators' using the event to shield themselves from the revolution.[1] Admittedly, Barthes did not sign the manifesto, 'The Revolution, Here and Now', which was published by the review in the autumn of '68, issue 34. Even though he gave a short talk in November 1970 to the Groupe d'études théoriques, when he put forward the analysis of a text by Freud, he followed their activities from something of a distance (in any case, he was at the time in Morocco). His hostility to the Communist Party was still total, and he was fairly constant in his political beliefs. But he accepted the fact that his friends had different opinions from his,

and Sollers made a convincing case for the reasons for the strategy
he had adopted.

In 1971, although the change in *Tel Quel*'s direction was made
public in the issue that was purportedly a homage to him, Barthes
did not officially voice his support for the 'Movement of June 71'.
Having never supported the French Communist Party, he had no
reason to fly into a rage at its revisionism. Likewise, he did not voice
his public support for Maoism and it was only from a distance that
he seemed to follow the activities of the group and the review. On
the other hand, in the theoretical conflicts stirring the intellectual
field, Barthes definitely took sides, as individual people were here
involved. When the journal *Change* was created – its very name
seeming to cock snooks at *Tel Quel*, whose name in French implies
'things as they are' – the quarrel (which may seem really trivial from
today's point of view) assumed considerable importance for the
precise reason that it was fought within Éditions du Seuil, which
published both journals. Faye accused *Tel Quel* of Stalinism and
Sollers waxed ironical over the generalized desire for transformation advocated by *Change*. Mallarmé and Artaud now became
names around which opposite poles crystallized. Jacques Roubaud
denounced the pseudo-scientific nature of Kristeva's ideas and
Sollers accused *Change* of being a 'fake *Tel Quel*'. Faye went so far as
to claim in an interview with Jean Ristat in the *Gazette de Lausanne*
that, in 1960, the nascent group associated with Sollers had been in
favour of keeping Algeria French. In 1970, *La Quinzaine littéraire*
published a polemic between Pierre Bourgeade and Sollers that was
spectacular in the intensity of its verbal violence.[2] In all these conflicts, Barthes supported his friend Sollers. In issue 34, he expressed
his full agreement with the latter on the political texts published in
the review, and, at the height of the polemic, he always presented
himself as an ally. In a letter addressed to Sollers, but written with
the intention of protecting Sollers against the management of Seuil
in the person of Paul Flamand, Barthes clearly stated his solidarity:
'I do not want any kind of silence (*although in one sense it might
be justified by the pusillanimity and vulgarity of the attacks directed
periodically against your review*) to conceal the operation of defamation which *Tel Quel* has suffered from Faye.' He added: 'There
is always something jinxed about defamation, and thus, *however
great one's desire for silence and work*, it needs to be excised.'[3] Only
with the greatest reluctance did Barthes emerge from his reserve
and his silence: the rhetoric of the parentheses and incidental
remarks is clear on this point. But he felt obliged to do so, for two
reasons. The first was an emotional and ethical reason (it was his
duty to defend his friends), and Barthes remembered how quickly
Sollers had come to his defence during the Picard affair. The second
was a theoretical reason: Barthes was convinced that the research

defended by *Tel Quel* was crucial for philosophy, for literature and for his own work. He said as much in his letter: 'My conviction that your review is right now irreplaceable (and so has no competitors, apart from those who wish to sow confusion for their own ends), the sometimes anxious feeling that if you were not there, something vital would be extinguished for some of us, all of this is well known.' These remarks were neither a strategy, in the negative sense of the term, nor a piece of flattery. Their sincerity can be gauged from the fierce and desperate quest Barthes led to reconcile an increasingly individual, intractable relationship with writing and a social life that might foster its expression. In other terms, Barthes wanted to reconcile the private and the political. He was really convinced that *Tel Quel* was a place where this could happen. Round the review, he formed a network of significant friendships. And he never sought to retreat into an ivory tower: he was always engaged in current events.

Literature, for him as for Sollers, had meaning only if it was resolutely modern, even if he sometimes located this modernity more often in bygone periods than in his own, and his personal tastes ultimately led him to the work of Schumann or Chateaubriand rather than to Messiaen or Robbe-Grillet. If we are to understand Barthes, we need to understand two postulations that are only apparently contradictory, but that create a great number of misunderstandings and even accusations of imposture. *To love literature* is to love its modernity, its way of stating the world in a new way, its power of expression, deflagration and change, in whatever period it might appear: Racine as much as Michelet, Baudelaire as much as Cayrol, Proust as much as Sollers. Second, *to defend literature* in the present is not just to remind people of how much the ancients were once modern, but to defend all the attempts made to get literature to go further, elsewhere, changing the world of finding a new way of depicting it. Experimentation does not always turn out to be as productive as might have been hoped – as Barthes discovered rather quickly in the case of Robbe-Grillet – but it needs to be recognized when it occurs. If Barthes's taste inclined him more towards Proust, he did not want to laud his work *against* contemporary literature. If literature still has meaning in the modern world, it needs to be envisaged in its virtual ability to impose the same revelation as the one that inspired *In Search of Lost Time*. So there is no historical conflict between Ancients and Moderns, in Barthes, and no switching, in his positions, from the avant-garde to the rear guard: this is  exactly what he meant when he said 'I am in the rear guard of the avant-garde' – the position of the modern, which is not a place, nor an ideology, but the conviction of literature's ability to pursue its action upon the world. It is easy enough to see why this ultra-rigorous position, which probably defines the political stance of

Barthes's criticism, could not fail to involve inner turmoil and external conflict in the image other people may have had of him.

Friendship

Barthes's obstinate and unconditional relation to literature was
close to that of Sollers. In the 1960s and 1970s, Sollers expressed this
relation in a different vocabulary, much more radical, dominated by
such ideas as a revolution in language, and the emancipatory virtues
of texts and of madness. In their respective 'pantheons', however,
the only writer they had in common was Sade – and this was not for
the same reasons. But they both shared a taste for assertion, and the
same kind of intelligence, capable of abstraction and synthesis on
the one side and sensibility and sensuality on the other. In principle,
their temperaments seemed completely opposite. On the one side
was the discreet homosexual, the pusillanimous intellectual, the solitary without a superego; on the other, the flamboyant heterosexual,
the ringleader, the murderer of fathers. Although Sollers was a good
twenty years younger (he was born in 1936), they did not have a
father–son relationship, and the generation gap mattered little to
them; nothing in Barthes's attitude made him into a father figure – if
this *had* been the case, Sollers would probably have opposed him.
As for the other parallels I have suggested above, the configuration is different: the other was neither the elder who acts as a model
during the years of initiation (Gide), nor the crucial contemporary,
with whom you are always in a relation, albeit distant, of dialogue,
with its element of implicit rivalry (Sartre). Instead, Sollers was a
friendly contemporary with whom Barthes shared views on what
was the essential area for him, indeed for the two of them: literature. Easily bored, especially in social life, Barthes also appreciated
Sollers's brilliant conversation, his very wide reading, his combative
stance able to face any trial. Even Sollers's spirit of intrigue amused
him. Sollers, for his part, admired Barthes for his independence,
his detachment, his lucidity. In the dinners they had together regularly from 1965 onwards, about once a month, sometimes twice,
without a break right up to 1980, at La Coupole or the Falstaff in
Montparnasse, at Le Flore or La Palette in Saint-Germain, they
discussed their reading and their work in progress. So it would
be unfair to think or say that the bond between them was merely
an alliance, a strategy: it would mean ignoring the deep affection
between them, which is confirmed by several details to which I
shall return. Admittedly, friendship in some contexts may well have
moments of alliance, and the path they trod together did not fail to
bring such moments into being; but they do not contradict the real
affection that they both held for one another until the end. They

both had roots in the South-West of France, and often talked about this fact, to emphasize their distance or their difference from Paris, or explain their closeness to one another: it acted as a solid base for their friendship, on which it shed so much light. 'We were at once in the same region and shared the same horizon: the Enlightenment [*les Lumières*]. This was one of the fixed points we shared.'[4]

They met for the first time in the premises of Éditions du Seuil, 27 rue Jacob, in 1963. *Tel Quel* had a small office there, which was the stage for many ardent battles, successive evictions, strategic decisions and enthronements. Barthes had finally agreed to reply to a questionnaire from the review, after twice stating that he was not really keen. This was the survey on 'Literature today', published in issue 7 in 1961. But it was when he responded to Genette's questions on criticism in a significant essay called 'Literature and Signification', published in issue 16, 1963, that his real period of being a fellow-traveller of *Tel Quel* began, without there ever being a question of his actually joining the committee.[5] Sollers could see what benefit his movement and his review might derive from publishing Barthes in the new 'Tel Quel' collection. The essayist's celebrity could only add weight to their activities. Barthes, for his part, did not want to be trapped in sociology and the scientific programme that he had set out for himself at the École pratique des hautes études. If he could join these adventurous young people, he was bound to feel a sense of openness and renewal; in particular, being associated with a publishing endeavour gave him a place in the literature that was being written, which was a far from negligible benefit.

In 1965, the collaboration between Barthes and Sollers was put on an official footing at the same time as they became truly good friends. Barthes was bowled over by *Drame*, Sollers's third novel. He wrote a long and powerful analysis of it, which he published in *Critique* under the title 'Drame, poème, roman' – a text that its author viewed as decisive enough to be published three times in his lifetime: once in a review, second in a version accompanied by annotations in the collective work devised by Sollers, the *Théorie d'ensemble* of 1968, and a third time in *Sollers Writer*, in 1979.[6] He linked the book to the birth of the spoken word, a time when 'words and things [. . .] circulate on the same level', thus joining the myth of 'the world as book, of words inscribed in the earth itself'.[7] Thus, *Drame* is a return to 'the golden age, that of the coming to awareness, that of speech. The time it evokes is that of the body waking up, still new and neutral, untouched by meaning and by the act of remembrance. It gives us the Adamic dream of a total body, marked at the dawn of our modernity by Kierkegaard's cry: "*But give me a body!*".'[8] As a pure narrator, the subject vanishes, as does the story which becomes the quest for a story. Barthes here discovered a new and decisive experiment in modern literature: meaning and depth are dismissed in favour of a logic of axes and functions that are for the critic to reconstitute, over and above the resistance of reading. The utopia of an incessant productivity corresponded closely to the theory of the text that Barthes was establishing. His defence of a literature that gave a crucial importance to the decoding carried out by an alert, lucid reader comes as no surprise. This defence justifies the critic as well as detecting where exactly the avant-garde is situated. In the literary field, the distance *Tel Quel* now adopted towards Robbe-Grillet, and the attribution to Sollers of qualities that had been recognized in Robbe-Grillet a few years earlier, were clear signs. Literature had migrated over to Sollers and the adventure of writing was now to be found in *Tel Quel*. Barthes had moved on from an exaltation of pure referentiality, from the being-there of objects, to a *semiosis* of literature in which signs refer solely to themselves. A few months later, Sollers sprang to Barthes's defence in the quarrel of the new criticism, with all the polemical verve one associates with him. So the friendship between the two men was now sealed by an alliance, and over the next fifteen years each man would defend the other if he was attacked.

Barthes would have occasion to do this openly on two occasions, both over literary questions; he did not intervene publicly when it came to his friend's political stances. The first time was in 1973, in connection with Sollers's book *H*: Barthes published an article that was both an analysis of the book and a lively riposte to the attacks it had been subjected to in the press. Barthes reacted to the accusations of 'fake novelty', 'formalism' and 'sophistication', reproaching his enemies, as he had formerly criticized Picard, for creating an 'amalgam' – though he himself did rather the same. He instead promoted a critical method that renounced the general idea to produce a fragmentary commentary in the margins of a book that took commentary to its very limits. 'Although I have been enjoying him for a long time,' he wrote of Sollers's work, 'on each occasion I get on to his work while it is still moving. These fragments are the steps which that movement takes. It is what a "fellow-traveller" does.'[9] This is a surprising image: first, because it sounds like a sort of slogan, referring to a political party to which Barthes had never pledged his allegiance (far from it); and second, because this article came out only four months before the trip to China when Barthes and Sollers would be travelling companions in the literal sense of the term. The image here used by Barthes (probably a *hapax legomenon* in his work) is a close mixture of literary practice and political commitment and suggests a certain ambiguity. The second occasion of support for Sollers came in 1978. Sollers had been deeply wounded by the publication of a separate small volume, *Why I Love Barthes*, the talk Robbe-Grillet had given at Cerisy the previous year. Robbe-Grillet, the author of *For a New Novel*, discussed at length the dead end he thought Sollers had run into with his work *Paradis*. Sollers, he suggested, was forced to publish it in serial form in *Tel Quel* because he was aware that, with this work, he had lost the interest of his readers: literature, especially the novel, was now going down a quite different path. When these remarks were confined to a conference and the proceedings to which it gave rise, this might have been relatively harmless; but now that the public display of a bond of affection with Barthes involved an attack on his own work, Sollers felt that it was all too much: he already felt very isolated, as *Tel Quel* had lost a great number of readers over the last few years. Something of a rescue operation was launched. Warned by François Wahl that Sollers had been angered by Robbe-Grillet's text (published by Christian Bourgois), Barthes cancelled a short trip to Cannes to talk things over on 19 November. Together, they composed a statement of gratitude and support; Barthes was happy to express his feelings immediately. It was at the request of Sollers that Barthes organized a two-stage defence: in a column in *Le Nouvel Observateur* on 6 January 1979, he published a dialogue with an imaginary partner, which we might consider to be a kind of 'Why I love Sollers' or 'Why I am defending Sollers'. It was a brave move to state his unconditional support so publicly, given the very wide readership of *Le Nouvel Observateur*. At almost the same time, Barthes brought together all the pieces he had written on Sollers since 1965 and published them in a single volume, together with an extract from the seminar on 'The neutral' entitled 'Oscillation'. All this happened very quickly and the book was in the press by the end of January.

Here too, we still often read or hear that Barthes allowed his hand to be forced, that he was leaned on or blackmailed by a tyrannical, jumpy Sollers; and it is true that the latter was very insistent that Barthes publish this volume. But the argument that Barthes was so far removed from Sollers and *Tel Quel* at that time that, in aesthetic matters, he could not really support him is not entirely fair. The two men continued to be allies, developing in tandem, although not exactly the same direction: this time, the difference in their two ages played a part. While *A Lover's Discourse* was very different from *Paradis*, both writers were convinced that the avant-garde was behind them, that this was no longer where literature was going. They discussed Chateaubriand (important for Barthes) and Saint-Simon (for Sollers) and they both longed to write a big readable work: 'Vita Nova' for Barthes, which would never get off the drawing-board, and *Women* for Sollers, which he published in 1983 and became a bestseller. In 'Soirées de Paris', Barthes describes a meeting at La Rotonde: 'Philippe and I talk about Chateaubriand, about French literature, then about Éditions du Seuil. With him, I always feel euphoric, full of ideas, confidence, and excitement about

work.'[10] The last text that Barthes published in *Tel Quel*, extracts
from his diaries together with his commentary, provided him with
an opportunity to make some very personal remarks about the directions that writing can take: such a text would have been unthinkable
in the review a few years earlier.[11] Here, Barthes seems to be liberated from all theoretical, political or formal constraints. In any
case, Barthes always justified his support for Sollers by referring to
his affection for him. He did not hesitate to side with the minority
in defending him. In 1973, in *Critique*, he even used friendship as
the criterion for the correctness of his way of reading. 'When will
the critic have the right to talk about a book with affection without
being suspected of favouritism? When shall we be free enough (freed
from a false idea of objectivity) to include in the reading of a text
the knowledge that we might have of its author? Why – in the name
of what, by fear of whom – should I cut off the reading of a book
by Sollers from the friendship which I might have for him?'[12] In his
article in *Le Nouvel Observateur*, in January 1979, his reaction to
Robbe-Grillet's sarcasms involved creating an intimate image of
Sollers to hold up against the social image of him in circulation. 'I
see Sollers shrunk to the size of a Jivaro head. All he is now is "the
man who has changed his ideas" (he's nevertheless not the only one,
as far as I know). Well, I think that a time comes when social images
have to be *called back to order*.'[13] And this image was composed of
isolation and grandeur. While Sollers was under attack on all sides,
including at Seuil where his position was precarious and the review
itself under threat, Barthes's attitude was both resolute and support-
ive. It saw friendship as more important than any anxieties about
self-image. A few days later, Sollers wrote to Michel Chodkiewicz,
who was asking whether the adventure of *Tel Quel* needed to be
continued: 'So the question you asked yesterday was "What is the
use of *Tel Quel*?". On reflection it seems to me that I owe you a
more personal answer (and thus one which, if you like, can remain
between the two of us). It's the following – and I'm weighing my
words here: "So as not to die of despair in a world of ignorance and
perversion".'[14] It is clear that questions of strategy overlapped to a
considerable extent with emotional ties. The relationship between
Sollers and Barthes was based on both of these factors: they were
well-known figures, in the public eye; but also, they gave each other
moral support.

   Sollers was just as loyal to his friend. As he told *Art Press* in
1982: 'Barthes was the person whose death upset me the most.
Friendship.' A bit further on, he mentioned Foucault: 'A prickly,
jealous temperament. Indeed, at that time it seemed that you had
to be either friends with him or with Barthes . . . I loved Barthes,
I might meet up with Foucault again . . .'[15] In his memoirs, *Un
Vrai Roman*, he wrote: 'Barthes continued to be a very dear friend

until his accidental death, which was one of the great sorrows of my life.'[16] Like Barthes in 'Soirées de Paris', Sollers, in *Women*, described their regular evenings out in Montparnasse, their cigars ready for after the meal, a Barthes-Werth who was 'elegant, sober, happy to see someone who loved him and whom he loved'. They talked about what they were writing, discussed everyday events and the main things they were reading. 'A common liking for the voice, singing, the abbreviations of Chinese poetry, notebooks, exercise books, pens, calligraphy, the piano . . .'[17] For Philippe Forest, this friendship was 'the longest and firmest, apart from the *Tel Quel* committee, which Sollers ever had with another writer'.[18] We might say the same thing about Barthes: apart from his friendships as a teenager and young man, and his bond to François Wahl, which was just as intense, long and regular, his relation with Sollers was the most faithful and constant he ever experienced. Renaud Camus, who knew Barthes, sketched his portrait in a few biographemes: one of them reads 'He could not stand the least criticism of, or joke about, Philippe Sollers.'[19] Éric Marty remembers a dinner at '7', Fabrice Emaer's restaurant, where Barthes held forth at length about his friendship for the person he called simply 'Philippe': there was in all this, of course, an intense devotion to his writing and, in the solitude of a writer's life, the importance of showing solidarity with the literary milieu. But with Sollers, more was involved, Barthes explained: 'adventure, the absence of repose'. Marty was touched to see that, in Barthes's universe, there were 'foreign planets (or at least one): force, violence, radicalness, the desire for a new beginning, the rejection of heritage, courage, laughter, a vitality without despair'.[20]

Sollers too showed generosity of spirit to Barthes and played a part in contributing to what he was. For example, it was he who, in 1971, 'invented' 'R.B.': not Roland Barthes, but the man who had placed himself some way behind those initials, who became 'R.B.', pronounced in French the same as 'Herbé' (a bit like 'grassy') – a figure. In the special issue on Barthes in *Tel Quel* – in which Julia Kristeva wrote about writing, Marcelin Pleynet contributed two poems, François Wahl discussed Buddhism, Severo Sarduy described Tangiers where he had been with Barthes ('young Socco' and 'stereophony'), Marc Buffat presented some ideas on teaching and Annette Lavers on translation[21] – the portrait of 'R.B.' by Sollers was a sensation: not just because it was an unconditional homage to his work as a whole, from *Michelet* and the texts on Brecht to *Empire of Signs* and his theory of the plural text, but also because it introduced biographical and personal themes that prefigured Barthes's 1975 self-portrait: his Protestantism, which Sollers said was 'emptied, Japanized', and his elegance: 'He arrives on time, is able to transform his weight quite quickly, easily gets bored, never looks as if he's having too much of a good time, and remembers things.'[22] Of course, the text was also pursuing a strategy – denouncing the whole intellectual milieu, those intellectual commercial travellers, those 'rotative and caricatural figures of cosined scholars', the 'dogmatico-revisionists' and the 'cultural notariate' – against whom 'R.B.' appears as the complete opposite, the remedy – but it was at that time the most attractive portrait ever sketched of Barthes. Sollers insisted on the absence of hysteria in Barthes, on the not-wishing-to-grasp that would become the obsession of his later years. And Sollers came up with an image that acted as a counterpart to that of the 'travelling companion' that Barthes had used in 1973 in his text on Sollers: 'We are here,' wrote Sollers, 'on the path which leads from *Mythologies* to *Empire of Signs*: from "Frenchness" to the haiku. In other words, for R.B., the history of a long impatience, of a long and angry march across the overloaded and sated decadence of our culture.'[23] Here again, with the image of the 'long march', the political is singularly emphasized – as the horizon of the journey to China.

So Sollers invented 'R.B.': Barthes would acknowledge this at the colloque de Cerisy when he traced the genealogy of this figure.[24] But this was not Sollers's only intervention. He seems to have been the one who suggested that Barthes give his book about Balzac's novella the title *S/Z* (Sollers, the author of *H*, does seem to have liked initials). This is not improbable: until he had finished writing his text, Barthes always spoke of it as 'Sarrasine'.[25] But discussions with Sollers were decisive for two other projects. The first was what would become the 'Soirées de Paris'. On 24 August 1979, Barthes noted: 'At a suggestion from Sollers, the idea of narrating one of my evenings. Wrote yesterday evening.'[26] The day before, indeed, Sollers had written Barthes a letter saying how much he had enjoyed the second part of 'Deliberation', with its evocation of an evening in Paris. This gave Barthes an idea that might find a place in the great plans for a major work that was harassing him at the time: fragments of this would be published in *Incidents*: 'What if I tried to narrate my evenings in this way? In a "subtly" platitudinous way, without underlining their meaning? Would not a reader derive a truthful depiction of the period from it?'[27] The other suggestion led to a plan that might occupy the two men together. They discovered that they were both very enthusiastic about Chateaubriand ('we discover that we are both mad about Chateaubriand'), Sollers imagined that they might write a 'history of literature by way of desire', one that would emphasize the anti-bourgeois powers of literature. They would not have time to realize this programme, but it haunted Barthes over the following months, as we can see from his card indexes: he imagined a *wild* history of French literature, one in which *sensibility* would play a major part; above all, he imagined that he could combine his literary project, the 'Vita Nova', with this personal history, as in both cases he was attempting to join literature. As for Sollers, he has said that, with *La Guerre du gout*, and *Éloge de l'infini*, he to some extent carried on with this shared plan, albeit alone. Over time, they had started reading the authors that were the other's favourites. In this way Barthes, who had only read Sade and Voltaire from the eighteenth century, started to read Diderot at his friend's suggestion. Thus, Sollers was his guide in the circles of Dante and the fantastic territories of Maldoror, in Lautréamont's book. While their tastes and the history of their relation to writing initially led them to quite different authors, it is noteworthy that, ultimately, they both wrote about Voltaire, Artaud, Bataille, Twombly and others.

But ultimately, the 'friends of my friends' are not just the occupants of the bookshelves or the authors of the past; they are also my contemporaries, the people I meet in varying degrees of proximity. One of the reasons for the continued bond between Barthes and Sollers lay in the triangle that they formed with Kristeva. From 1967 onwards (this was the year when Sollers and Kristeva married), the three of them would very often meet up in the bars and restaurants of the Left Bank, or at each other's homes. With Kristeva, while the relation did open up new intellectual perspectives, things also assumed a more personal aspect and the young woman soon became an essential link. After Kristeva's defence of her first thesis (on Jehan de Saintré, with Goldmann as her supervisor), on 3 July 1968, they all three celebrated her success together. After the defence of her second thesis, at Vincennes in 1973, when Barthes was the chair of the jury, they had a long conversation on the future of literature: that same day, Barthes had declared in public that Kristeva's theoretical inventiveness corresponded exactly, in his view, with what the novel should be doing. Sollers had found this very disturbing. 'She's the cleverest woman I've ever met,'[28] Sollers said of Kristeva, and Barthes certainly agreed, as we have seen from his article on her *Semeiotike*: Kristeva always disrupted one's prejudices. Her conversation was animated; every idea she had pushed her towards some experiment or some discovery. She passed on her interest in Bakhtin, but then she immediately discovered Benveniste and extolled him in turn. She followed Barthes's seminars, but also attended Lacan's; his teaching overwhelmed her and forced her to develop her own ideas. When the three of them were together, they talked about the same things as when there were just two of them. However, the fact that Kristeva was a woman and that she and Sollers were in love was significant too. Barthes was fascinated by the eroticism that imbued this couple, by the overlap of sexuality and theoretical productivity in them (this was common at that time). They were free; they were not afraid of their desire. When he was with them, Barthes was led to a reflection on homosexuality as a vision of the world that continued to preoccupy him. He would try, in a fragmentary fashion, to analyse it in greater depth. They did not impose the burden of heterosexual normativity that so often stifled him and which he fled as much as he could. So this relation, marked by a difference in upbringing, temperament and behaviour, was based on two similar and no doubt interconnected themes: liberty and their work. There was always something driving them on, in a relative indifference to moral norms when these were merely moralizing. Ethics can go together with certain forms of immorality, which often correspond to a rejection of prohibition and repetition. This was the conclusion that Barthes drew from their journey to China, noting the reasons for his disappointment in the plane home: 'So it would be necessary to pay for the Revolution with everything I love: "free" discourse exempt from all repetition, and immorality.'[29]

At the end of his life, Barthes noted the importance of his friends now that all his external sources of protection had melted away: he then wrote down the names of Jean-Louis Bottes and Philippe Sollers, together with this commentary, that in the final analysis expresses the element of trust that comes with friendship: '(I've been on the trapeze without any safety net, ever since I've no longer had the nets of structuralism, semiology or Marxism); the Friend is the one who stands below, looks on with affection, attention, anxiety and trust, and holds the rope of the Trapeze.'[30]

Everyone's off to China

A central moment in this friendship, albeit perhaps not the best, was the journey to China in 1974. There had already been shared enterprises or, rather, times when, in spite of the divergences in their points of view, Sollers had managed to drag Barthes into some rather extreme activities: in 1968, this had been the *Théorie d'ensemble*, the theoretical manifesto that had been placed under the dual aegis of Mallarmé and Marx, where a space was defined, concepts were deployed, a history was unfolded and, above all, a politics was expounded: all part of a construction of a link between writing and historical materialism. Barthes contributed, alongside Foucault, Derrida (with his famous article on '*différance*'), Kristeva, Pleynet, Goux and Denis Roche; in Barthes's case, the piece in question was his article on Sollers's *Drame*, here published for the second time. Against the many detractors of the review, he systematically refused to envisage his approach in the terms of theoretical terrorism: he viewed it as a demystification of liberalism and as a form of radical behaviour – 'and its radical edge probably derives from the energy of the theoretical reflection found in *Tel Quel*, which is highly important and is generally rather underestimated in the

attacks made on this group'.[31] In 1970, Barthes allowed himself to
be swept along into stating his support for Pierre Guyotat's *Éden,
Éden, Éden*; he was happy to do so, as he really admired the kind
of writing he found in this book: he thought it showed the importance that he attributed to the sentence. But the other aspects of
his commentary, the constellation in which he placed Guyotat's
work ('from Sade to Genet, from Mallarmé to Artaud'), were quite
telquelien.[32] During those years, Barthes also wrote for reviews close
to *Tel Quel*: *Manteia*, with the article on 'The Death of the Author',
and *Promesse*, to which he gave a long interview. In 1971, the 'June
71 Movement', a monumental piece of propagandistic arrogance,
declared in an issue devoted to Barthes that it was endeavouring to promote an 'irreversible propagation of the revolutionary
theory and practice of our time: Mao Zedong thought'. Now, the
thoughts of the Great Helmsman were plastered over the walls of
the offices of *Tel Quel* as they were on the first pages of the review.
It was not just the support for what was happening in China that
was so spectacular, but the radical nature of the reversal: 'In spite
of certain positive practical and theoretical results, *Tel Quel* has
made too many sacrifices to an opportunist right-wing line that
aimed to consolidate revisionism.'[33] Of course, Barthes was not a
member of the editorial committee and was not obliged de facto to
endorse the recantations of his allies. But there are three points that
are still unclear. One is the way his own constant political positions
may have mirrored these successive changes of line. Another is the
absence of any reaction on his part to the extremism of some of
Sollers's positions (as, for example when Sollers spoke out in favour
of the Black September group in Munich,[34] an event that had deeply
shocked Barthes, particularly because of the links between his
family and Israel).[35] And the last surprising fact is that he allowed
himself to be duped by what appears to have been a veritable 'myth'
about China, several of the characteristics of which seemed to be
fundamentally at odds with his own critical spirit.

The June 71 Movement was formed after the banning of any sales
or publicity for the book by Maria-Antonietta Macciocchi, *De la
Chine*, at the festival of *L'Humanité* in April. This book had just
been published in French translation by Seuil, and some people read
it as a justification for the Cultural Revolution, while for others it
was simply an instrument in the struggle against Stalinist communism. Macciocchi was an activist in the Italian Communist Party;
she had first been to China in 1954, a visit that had filled her with
enthusiasm. She had not been able to return until 1970, after the
fifteen years of a thaw in the relations between the Soviet Union and
China. She was for a long time in charge of the foreign section of the
newspaper *L'Unità*; she was expelled from the Italian Communist
Party (PCI) after publishing *Lettres de l'intérieur du parti* addressed

to Althusser, in which she expressed her disagreement with certain of the directions being followed by the PCI, and *De la Chine*, where she showed her complete support for Mao.[36] This latter book, which she published on her return from China, where her paper had sent her for a series of reports, is so naively enthusiastic that the reader is disarmed. It is doubtless its starry-eyed, innocent tone, in a narrative where every story is more edifying than the last, that drew some readers to share its vision. The narration is an eye-witness account of the everyday life of Chinese men and women whose lives were being transformed thanks to the wonderful policies of Chairman Mao. Macciocchi produced no political analysis, she did not question any political leaders or officials, she placed an entire trust in her guides and interpreters. She reported what she saw and expressed herself in the mode of a soothing reportage, deploying all the hallowed clichés. Here is her conclusion, coming after a 570-page panegyric: 'What I can say, sixteen years later, is that China has made a leap forward that has no precedent in history.'[37] She shows, for example, how relations between teachers and pupils have been transformed; she defends unreservedly the '7 May schools' for the re-education of cadres: 'I look around. So what creates this strange fraternity, this unknown humanity, and imbues this school? There has been a radical upheaval in values, though without any radical violence, that has affected everyone in the same way.'[38] She believed in the new type of human being. If Barthes read the book – and he most likely did read it, or at least flicked through it, given the place Sollers gave it in issue 47 – he will not have failed to pick up the almost constant use its author makes of stereotypes. But while he kept his distance, and accepted neither the label nor the commitment of Maoism for himself, he consented without uttering a word.

The idea of *Tel Quel* and other French intellectuals taking a journey to China came from Macciocchi, who had been very grateful for the support given to her by Sollers and the review. 'Lacan was quite taken with it all', according to Élisabeth Roudinesco: 'he found the lady "stupefying" and immediately decided to resume Chinese lessons. Sollers took care of the formalities.'[39] Lacan would ultimately pull out at the last minute. Macciocchi herself was not granted a visa by the Chinese authorities. So the group was reduced to five: three *telqueliens* – Sollers, self-proclaimed leader of the group, Kristeva and Pleynet – and two sympathizers, Barthes and Wahl. The trip was organized at a time when the review had been plunged into crisis. Thibaudeau and Ricardou had been forced to resign; Goux and Derrida, neither of whom displayed any enthusiasm for China, withdrew. Sollers was grateful for Barthes's support: he needed it. And Barthes felt sufficiently detached to go along without endorsing all the ideological and political implications of the journey. His readings in Buddhism had stayed with him, and he was interested in the Chinese substrate of the language and culture of Japan. Thanks to *Tel Quel*, he discovered the extraordinary work by Joseph Needham, *Science and Civilization in China*, and – together with Marcel Granet – Needham's name was an indisputable scholarly recommendation. *Tel Quel* issue 49, in the spring of 1972, paid a heartfelt homage to those two figures, and suggested some important studies on Chinese poetry and writing. On the return of the *telqueliens* from China, issue 59 published a fascinating interview with Needham. This deep interest in the ancient civilization of China was perfectly real, and needs to be seen as one of the benefits the travellers derived from their journey there. Like Lacan, Kristeva learned some Chinese, and Sollers took a close interest in ideogrammatic writing, which he put to singular use in his novel *Nombres*. An intellectual and perhaps even spiritual quest can be detected here: though it did not justify the group's political infatuations, it gave them something of a twist. In 'Pourquoi j'ai été chinois?' ('Why was I Chinese?'), the self-criticism that Sollers published in March 1981, in issue 88 of *Tel Quel*, he insisted on the fact that their enterprise had seemed to open up a new future for thought: 'In addition, there was the great discovery around 66–67 [. . .] of Joseph Needham, who produced that wonderful encyclopaedic work, *Science and Civilization in China*. And at that moment, something completely new revealed itself to us, as we sensed that this was the dawn of a sort of new model in knowledge. Needham thought – as he tells us – that China's entry into the history of knowledge was now going to play a role that was absolutely comparable to the model that Greece had been for the Western Renaissance.'[40] It is quite possible that Sollers's enthusiasm, as much as investigations of the Taoist tradition, finally managed to convince Barthes on this point too: he shared the idea that China was a storeroom of potential ideas and images.

However, in the whole episode of this journey to China, Barthes did feel that he was being recruited into the ranks somewhat against his will. Sollers himself recognized the fact: 'Poor Barthes! He was 59 years old and I rather forced his hand to go on this trip, he was in an Epicurean and Gidean phase, he'd enjoyed his freedom in Japan, and here he was being plunged into the fray, the complete opposite of any nuance.'[41] At the time, Barthes was in the middle of canvassing for election to the Collège de France (his first attempts to enter started in 1974) and there were several very close friends who made him incline to stay in Paris. On 4 April, he mentioned in his desk diary: 'struggling to get out of the China trip'; and on 6 April, when he learned that the visas had arrived at the embassy, he noted: 'fed up'. However, he prepared himself for the journey: he bought the Nagle Guide, and he watched Antonioni's film. This film would arouse considerable dislike among his Chinese interlocutors a few weeks later; Barthes would compare it with his own impressions.[42] Between January and March he met several specialists, or supposed specialists, on China: Maria-Antonietta Macciocchi on 26 January; Viviane Alleton, professor of Chinese grammar, who had published a small volume in the encyclopaedic 'Que Sais-Je?' series on Chinese writing; and, on 7 February, several members of the Chinese embassy. At the home of Sollers, he met three Chinese students; on 18 March, he met Charles Bettelheim, an economist and Barthes's colleague at the EPHE, an ardent defender of Mao's transformation of industrial organization. But this intense preparation proved burdensome to Barthes, and he started to feel weary of it all. Everything was being too deliberately planned; he was also worried by the prospect of travelling in a group, the absence of solitude, the break in his schedule and the interruption of his writing.

The five French travellers flew to Beijing on 11 April. Barthes's apprehensions already started to make themselves felt on board the plane: the hostess, the disgusting food, the other passengers all cooped up like animals. Throughout the three-week journey, he was obviously on edge. His relation with Sollers in particular was fraught. In his *Travels in China*, Barthes made several irritated references to him; Sollers's enthusiasm and his habit of proselytizing got on Barthes's nerves. 'Ph. S. is completely blind to the leftist rivalry. All of it quite egocentric: all the press is viewed on the basis of the way it rejects *Tel Quel*.'[43] And Sollers's rhetoric seemed similar to the exhausting propaganda churned out by their Chinese interlocutors: 'Ph. S., too, proceeds by *campaigns* – and is tiring: from one period to the next, he always bangs away at the same old theme, with variations of examples in support, jokes, etc.: at present it's Lacan as a henchman of religion, idealist, etc.'[44] On their countless trips in the 'minibus', Sollers always wanted to strike up revolutionary songs, the *Internationale* and so on. Admittedly, there were moments when the two friends shared experiences, as when, in the Xi'an museum, 'we speak admiringly of Melville, with Ph. S.',[45] but his know-it-all airs and his desire to dominate made the journey sometimes wearisome. In short: 'The only one for whom I'll have needed to show patience will have been Ph. S.'[46]

Barthes never shook off the fatigue with which he had set out on the journey. He was the oldest in the group, which may have meant he was less able to adapt. He noted as much, with a certain irony: '"I'm always the last (in the line)." – Because you're old, the amiable guide with the correct phrases tells me.'[47] He had terrible migraines almost every day.[48] He frequently felt sick. It seems that the only things he really noticed were the constraints under which the group had to operate. These were, indeed, very strict. The group was taken entirely under the wing of the Luxingshe Agency, known simply as the Agency, which set out a timetable and the travel details on an hour-by-hour basis, provided the translators and interpreters and chose who the group would be able to talk to. There was hardly time to draw breath. By 9 a.m., the group was generally already out visiting somewhere – a printing works, a hospital, a university, a museum, a dockyard – and this was an opportunity for endless harangues on the benefits brought by Mao's reforms, or the dark misdeeds of the right-wing group of the Party headed by Lin Piao. Indeed, the campaign that was being waged simultaneously against him and Confucius meant that any questions on Ancient China were deemed to be reactionary and were batted away. The visitors were taken from Beijing to Shanghai, where they took the train to Nanjing; then they went to Luo-Yang in Henan Province, then to Xi'an in the Saanxi, and spent their final days in Beijing, where they met Alain Bouc, the correspondent for *Le Monde*, and Christian Tual, the cultural attaché. They had to take notes – an unremitting chore. Barthes was quite aware of the slightly comical aspect of their tour, which sometimes seemed like *Tintin in the Land of the Soviets* – as some of Barthes's ironic comments point out: '*Tel Quel* and its friends are applauded in the factories of China.'[49] All these constraints made it impossible to gain any real understanding of the country: 'It's the continual presence, smooth as a tablecloth, of Agency officials that blocks, forbids, censors, rules out the possibility of the Surprise, the Incident, the Haiku.'[50] For the first time, no doubt, even if this had sometimes happened on other journeys, such as to the United States (but not so drastically), travel was not a way of freeing him from the burden of everyday life. It did not provide him with the reservoir of things he could write about which the fascinated observation of foreignness could comprise. The weight of ready-made phrases, of a fossilized discourse, of what Barthes called the 'bricks' of ideological discourse,[51] literally wall up Being, life, the gaze. The only escape, where possible, lies in day-dreaming, in drifting thoughts, in the pencil as it sketches, and in desire when it fleetingly awakens. Usually, when he was travelling, Barthes was most captivated by chance encounters, by the places where his desire led him. In China, he suffered from never being in contact with other people's bodies. 'And what can you know about a people, if you don't know their sex?'[52] The claustrophobia lay in a huge repression of sexuality, one that he found frustrating and incomprehensible. On his return, he opened up to his students about this experience: 'The body does not seem to be thinking about itself, projecting itself, deciding that it is this or that; there is no *role* for the body, no hysteria.'[53] This sense of closure could only be overcome if the usual hermeneutics was turned upside down: bodies, perhaps, were not there to signify anything, nor were differences meant to appear. In the absence of the main signifier (the religious) and of the direct signifier (Eros), the absence of any point of contact and the silence of meaning led to a purely phenomenological reading of what he saw. Since it was not possible to interpret things, he needed to be content with noting behaviour, little rituals, surface appearances.

In spite of this, there are a few fragile moments of escape in the *Travels* that set it apart from the notorious report in which Barthes tried to impose some form on his impressions, 'Alors, la Chine?'. These are moments when individual impulses make themselves known, when the traveller stands out from the group, when his own thoughts are freed from mere ideas. There are sallies of wit that interrupt the boredom; Barthes sometimes senses the resistance of the Chinese to the prevailing uniformity (in a hairstyle, a demeanour); there are times when you would like to see something if you do not succeed – for Barthes was desperately seeking signifiers, but he found only a few, and those he did find (such as children) soon turned out to be devoid of interest ('I had initially classified the children among the few signifiers, but they now strike me as a real bore.')[54] Fashion is more or less completely absent, as is any colour, and the tea is insipid. Only the ideograms and the food attract his attention; and the poppies of Luo-Yang, and the tigers in the Nanjing Zoo. He loves the profusion of dishes, their spices, the way they are set out, the cutting up of the meat and filleting of the fish. He loves listing what he has eaten: 'Dinner: hors d'oeuvre in the shape of a fish coloured red and blue, very delicately. Various alcoholic drinks, beer. Warm shrimps, finely chopped with a little salad. Sichuan dish. Meat. Chilli. Pine kernels. Wonderful. Very hot! Sauté of chicken, bamboo shoots. Little fritters of duck liver. (All delicious.) Big fish in sauce, breaded with pine kernels.'[55] While he is aghast at the socialist realist paintings the group is shown (children writing a *dazibao* on a brick wall, a teacher giving a writing lesson), he loves the calligraphy and procures several specimens. In Beijing, he stocks up on brushes, fine quality paper, and rubber stamps for his own work. Indeed, as he contemplates a piece of calligraphy by Mao, he compares it with his own painting: 'utterly elegant (grassy calligraphy), cursive, impatient, and spacious. Reflections on the "frame"; my paintings: also calligraphic blocks; it's not a scene cut out, it's a block moving forward.'[56] His purchases corresponded to the few times when he grew enthusiastic. On their arrival in China, he suggested to his friends that they buy Mao suits, which they had tailor made, and in which they would appear in Paris. In his travel diary, Marcelin Pleynet hailed 'RB's excellent idea, encouraging everyone to buy Chinese suits'.[57] The rest of the time, he was overwhelmed by fatigue and indifference – 'Sometimes, I enjoy not being interested'[58] – when it is not pure distress, a rejection of the whole country or the sense of being at a loss that affected his system and mode of expression: 'All these notes will probably attest to the failure, in this country, of my writing (in comparison

with Japan). In fact, I can't find anything to note down, to enumerate, to classify.'[59] Pleynet referred several times in his travel notes
to the position adopted by Barthes, always a bit aloof. On the day
they visited the Ming tombs, 'RB stayed in the bus'; in the train
to Nanjing, 'RB sits apart and reads *Bouvard and Pécuchet*, JK is
working on her Chinese, Ph S is playing xiangqi (Chinese chess)
with our guide'; and, during a debate between ideologues: 'RB who
seems to be following this discussion rather distantly stares at us
like a fish staring at an apple.'[60] His relief, when they left Beijing on
4 May, was as great as the burden from which he at last felt free.
'Ouf!' he said in François Wahl's ear as the plane started to taxi.[61]

All the travellers discussed their journey to China once they were
back in France. *Le Monde* published Barthes's article on 24 May
1974, and then a two-part report by François Wahl on 15 and 19
June. Issue 59 of *Tel Quel* was yet again devoted entirely to China,
and Sollers, Kristeva and Pleynet all gave their views. Kristeva published *About Chinese Women* that same year, with the Éditions des
Femmes; she included photos from the trip. She based her remarks
on what she had found of most interest in China: the daily lives of
women, their relationship to marriage, to divorce, to children, to
weaning, etc. She returned to her more personal impressions in her
novel *The Samurai*. The most intimate documents were published
only after some delay: Pleynet's diary came out in 1980 and Barthes's
Travels was first published in French in 2009. These two last documents give us many concrete details, but also have the problem
that they are not critical. Pleynet noted the way he felt that 'we are
being gently kept away from what is actually happening here'[62]
and Barthes questioned the stereotypical and edifying nature of the
language used by the Chinese, some of the mythological inventions
they deployed – he quite justifiably queried the official account of the
death of Lin Piao, for example – but their accounts strike us today by
their blindness. Prevented from seeing the true state of affairs by their
extremely dogmatic ideological convictions, the members of *Tel Quel*
remained enthusiastic and one-sided observers: this is understandable, but not entirely excusable. However, what *is* more surprising
is the absence of any critical spirit in Barthes. 'Alors, la Chine?' did
not paint an accurate picture of the China of those years, any more
than did the 1975 afterword added when the article was published as
a separate slim volume.[63] The word 'peaceful', which Barthes used
twice over to describe China, was a form of naivety. Only Wahl was
highly critical, especially of two things. He saw China as a continuation of the Soviet model, and this was not the right thing to say in
those days, in Maoist circles. And he deplored the way China was
breaking away so violently from its past.[64] This lucid language was
intolerable in the eyes of Philippe Sollers, who replied vehemently in
issue 59, contradicting Wahl point by point ('Never has China had

the strength it now has to discuss its own past')[65] and taunting him for his bad faith.

It may seem too facile to criticize the positions of these travellers from today's perspective, now that the crimes of that period are known: many people have criticized them before us.[66] In those days, intellectuals took up such radical and sharply defined positions that people were often reduced to 'choosing their camp' instead of reflecting on the problems in a more nuanced way. However, it was possible to have more qualified positions, as some of them demonstrated. The truth about the Cultural Revolution had already been partly disclosed, and there were many accounts that could have alerted Barthes or led him to seek another truth. In 1971, Simon Leys had already published *The Chairman's New Clothes*, in which he spoke of the hundreds of thousands of deaths caused by the Cultural Revolution. Alain Bouc, whom Barthes later met in Beijing, had replied in *Le Monde*, where he summarily dismissed this account, accusing its author of being a CIA agent, while Michelle Loi shamefully revealed his identity and sided with Macciocchi. But these various controversies could act as a warning. One issue of *La Nouvelle Critique* in November 1971 had picked out all the mistakes in her *De la Chine*. This admittedly stemmed from an intense ideological opposition, but there was enough in the list to shake people's confidence in the work. In Barthes's texts, in spite of his reservations, no threat was seen to be hanging over the country, there was no death to be deplored. 'Another word comes to mind, a more accurate one: China is *peaceful*.'[67] Barthes followed a position he had thought about at length and chose assent to the country rather than distance or critique. This was an ethical choice, but in this case it did not suit an overall political situation in which China and its people were alienated. Barthes seemed to wish to subject his words to a positive value even if this did not go as far as complete support. Assent, Barthes explained to his students, 'responds positively to a demand for recognition and perhaps even to a demand for love, and this is perhaps what I was most sensitive to in China (I'd already sketched out the theory behind this in connection with a play by Vinaver: *Les Coréens*, around 1957).'[68] What should we do with 'Alors, la Chine?' and Barthes's travel notes? How should we read these texts? This moment of direct confrontation with history was, yet again, a missed opportunity for Barthes. There was something dark and irreparable in it all; it can be seen as a major turning point in his life story.

Four years previously, Barthes had written about a play based on Segalen's novel *René Leys*, called *La Fuite en Chine* (*The Flight to China*). He had noted how blind and deaf the characters were, bogged down in miscognition; his critique applies with strange aptness to his own way of viewing China while he was there. He wrote: 'This interpretive situation is indeed tragic: a place where we can listen to the divided messages which seem to come together only on this side of the curtain, where we are. But where we are is still the stage, the last wall of the theatre: language does not stop at that black hole where we are hunkered down in safety, so as more easily to spy on "what's happening" in the light of the theatre projectors.'[69]

Barthes and Sollers at Cerisy, with Édith Heurgon, July 1972.

François Wahl, Julia Kristeva, Marcelin Pleynet, Roland Barthes, with two officials from the Agency on Tiananmen Square.

coureurs peuvent en par-
ler à leur façon (L.S.
Granet etc). Mais pour les
F C n'a qu'un seul
posé d'une façon peu
crédible _ leurs papiers.
Mais ce plumeil même
est de notre côté, saut
de l'intellect _ le plumeil
à l'eau.

- 400 visas viennent d'
être refusés *¹ L'hôtesse S¹
l'avant de notre voyage : elle
dit : vous êtes tranchés !
*¹ à cause du film de
Janne.

Arrivée Pékin

~ "Alors, la Chine ?..."

- Les Jeunes soldats : l'imprimé
de rien sous leur tunique.
Sourires

- Salon aéroport : soleil autérieur
Cuirs . Suisse il y a 50 ans

- Un grand rectangle rouge *²
support surface
*² 2 arbustes verts devant

- Chemin de l'aéroport.
route droite badgé de saules
On croise un chien un
jeune européen faisant la
course en short

- L'interprète : il fait "fres
quet

- Objet fétiche : le grand thermos
d'eau grande pour le thé _
fleuri de décalcomanie, que
des jeunes filles, des garçons
ont à la main

Samedi 14 Avril
(Pékin)

- Tps voilé _ Mal dormi,
oreiller trop haut et dur -
Migraine

- Hier soir : réunion avec les
Guides. Petit salon de l'Hôtel.
Gros fauteuils, appui-coude
en crochets

- La "politesse" et les cameras.

- L'austérité : linge non
repassé.

Travels in China.

Le Bonaparte.
Philippe Sollers is fifth from the left and Roland Barthes is third from the right.

14

The body

This word has gradually appeared in his work; at first it was masked by the instance of Truth (that of history), then by that of Validity (that of systems and structures); now it blossoms, it flourishes; this word-as-mana is the word 'body'.

Roland Barthes by Roland Barthes

In the course of the 1970s, Barthes turned the body into the major signifier that could occupy the place of any signified. It was a vector word, a mana word (he borrowed this term from Mauss, not without paradox, as mana, the principle of spiritual power, is transmitted by ghosts and spirits), a word of many meanings that he used for all kinds of purpose. The mana word is not a cherished word, that is to say, not one that can become a fetish: instead, it is a word that replaces everything for which it is difficult to find a name, such as atopia, supplement and drift. The word 'body' therefore needs to be understood as at a certain distance from one's own body. It makes it possible to keep the subject at bay, in a scattered form; the ego is no longer a centre or the seat of any truth. So we need to approach Barthes's personal writing from the point of view of the mobility and difference of the body. It does not correspond to an autobiographical turning point or the grasping of some 'full' subject (subjectivity was a question that remained quite outside Barthes's work); instead, it was connected to a deliberate shift within writing towards the investments of desire, which are all ways of projecting the body.

This was a period when Barthes refocused his interests: he was moving away from the political and was less interested in theory. To start out from the self and move out towards the world and other people now presented itself as a new phase that was more attuned to the desire to write. Barthes focused increasingly on the manifestations of the individual: his 1970–71 course was devoted to the notion of idiolect, which can help us to grasp the style of a writer in its singularity. The questions that preoccupied him were those linked to writing, the relation between one's own language and the language of the group, and the production of one's work: admittedly, these had always been his questions, but he gently shifted them so as to define his place and his role in new ways. The first of these shifts was made possible by a move into the realm of practice. In several areas, Barthes displaced theory towards practice, showed a liking for doing things, for experience, concrete life and matter – a definite change in some of his habits and concerns. Thus, his interest in calligraphy and painting – on which he was writing ever more important articles – came with an intense period of drawing and experimenting with colour. From 1971 onwards, his schedule now included, almost every afternoon, a time for painting. 'Relief (repose) at being able to create something not directly caught in the trap of language, in the responsibility of every sentence: a sort of innocence, in short, from which writing excludes me.' The modest word 'liking' (le goût), and the verb associated with it (goûter – to have a taste for something, to like something) now became, along with 'pleasure', key elements in his vocabulary – they referred not just to the pleasures of the table, but also of the text: 'Thus, what I enjoy in a narrative is not directly its content or even its structure, but rather the abrasions I impose upon the fine surface: I read on, I skip, I look up, I dip in again' [. . .] not to devour, to gobble, but to graze, to browse scrupulously, to rediscover – in order to read today's writers – the leisure of bygone readings.'[1] Here again, the verb 'to graze', previously applied to Michelet, expresses the movement of minute satisfaction, along the surface, discreet and at the same time out of step. This was the period when Barthes started saying 'I like/I don't like' more often, a period associated with the paintings of Arcimboldo and the voice of Panzéra, the choice of expressions that were tentative but still represented another way of conveying forms of cultural resistance. The general reason for this was the fact that the radical developments in theory and politics which the post-1968 years had endorsed had become exhausted. A more individual reason was that Barthes felt authorized to write this way by his age, his legitimacy, the recognition he had achieved. While still pursuing the same quest, Barthes did not abstain from 'taking his pleasure'. This was what drove him most in the 1970s; in this respect, he was close to the imperatives of the time, still marked by growth and sexual liberation. Without altogether adopting the post-'68 slogan of 'enjoyment without limits', he rejigged the formula to suit himself, in several areas. So we can here see how his individual path depended on a history that it represented in exemplary fashion. We can also understand how Barthes's life could combine both continuity and change: he did not jump dramatically from one phase to the next, but worked in a more impulsive and instinctual way, following chance encounters and circumstances. His new focus meant that he could turn himself into the very space where new encounters were possible.

'Writers, Intellectuals, Professors', the text that Barthes wrote in 1971 for the special issue of *Tel Quel* devoted to his work, made this shift clear. In it, Barthes showed a twofold shift in his relation to the body. On the one hand, there was the social and professional body of the 'teacher' or 'intellectual'; on the other, the floating, separated body of the 'writer'. On the one side, the speaking body, guided by theory; on the other, the writing body in the grip of practice. Here Barthes restated his hatred of the spoken word; as we have seen, the triumph of the spoken word in 1968 had merely made this hatred more intense. The spoken word was self-dramatization and hysteria; it was also, conversely, oppression and Law. It paralysed the teacher, and also the intellectual, who was equally content merely to transcribe his or her words. On the other hand, the writer was the person who rejected the power of the spoken word, who placed it in crisis by confronting what had never been said, what was missing, what was impossible. This last word, 'impossible', expressed the shock of the encounter between writing and the real; it was taken from Bataille and was used frequently by Barthes in the texts of the early 1970s, especially in *The Pleasure of the Text*.[2] So if he was to remain a teacher, a critical intellectual, he would have to move the spoken word into regions unknown to it, regions in which uncertainty, the rejection of stereotypes and a reaction against the doxa were all the norm. By staging the imposture of the teacher in a very characteristic piece of critical fiction ('Imagine that I am a teacher', said the professor at the EPHE), who sees his mystification laid bare, exactly like the Marx Brothers disguised as Russian aviators seeing their fakes unmasked,[3] Barthes prepared his change of body. The teacher was on the side of lies and deception, the writer was on the side of truth. But for this truth to instruct the spaces usually reserved for other uses of language, we need in each and every possible circumstance to have the ethos of the seeker, the one who puts things into crisis, even if he thereby runs the risk of finding himself without a definite place: '[A]gainst all discourses (speeches, inauthentic writings, rituals, protocols, social symbolics), only the theory of writing, today, even in the form of a luxury, makes language into something *atopic*: without a place; it is this dispersion, this non-situation, which is materialistic.'[4] The idea of a politics of the body is thus proposed as counter to the political arrogance associated with the spoken word, and it leads to defining oneself as a writer. But as this process of setting oneself up as a writer is somewhat awkward and indeed paradoxical (after all, you cannot give a place to the absence of place), it is going to imply a variety of practical experiments.

The Pleasure of the Text was the manifesto for this change of place, or rather this self-affirmation as a thinking and feeling being.

This brief text, published immediately in book form, was one of Barthes's few works not to have been commissioned. It holds a key place in his career. Pleasure now became the neutral space par excellence: refusing to see the distinction between pleasure and *jouissance* as a real opposition, and blurring the lines between them, Barthes reconciled – or at least he may have felt this was what he was doing – the two contradictory postulations that had always preoccupied him. On the one side there was the Modern, violence, breaks with the past, subversion (i.e., *jouissance*); on the other, there was Classicism, comfort, the novelistic and the spread (i.e., pleasure). The advantage of the erotic vocabulary employed was that it could not be used as a label to classify texts into one or other category. It implied a subject that chose and varied his mode of approach. Thus, the reader could highlight a system of reading any text 'in accordance with *jouissance*'. In this case, he would be attentive to its edges, its gaps, its verticality, its crests. To read 'in accordance with pleasure', on the other hand, meant remaining within a comfortable practice of reading. Barthes no longer disguised the way he inclined to both sides *at once*, in the same logic of reversal that he had so astutely noted in those characters in Proust who can turn a proposition upside down while still maintaining its validity.[5] He was no longer afraid to affirm the pleasure he derived from the classics, while defending the moderns. He agreed to set himself up as an *anachronistic subject*, straddling the divide: 'Now the subject who keeps the two texts in his field and in his hands the reins of pleasure and bliss is an anachronic subject, for he simultaneously and contradictorily participates in the profound hedonism of all culture (which permeates him quietly under cover of an *art de vivre* shared by the old books) and in the destruction of that culture: he enjoys the consistency of his selfhood (that is his pleasure) and seeks its loss (that is his bliss). He is a subject split twice over, doubly perverse.'[6] The proclamation was issued loud and clear, without beating about the bush. Barthes asserted his right to belong to several different times and affirmed his perversion, considering it as both a deviation and an inversion. Hélène Cixous, to whom he sent a copy of his book in February 1973, hailed the way it had 'lifted various kinds of censorship'.[7] *The Pleasure of the Text* thus presents its propositions as the political consent to a certain form of *déclassement*: hedonism, suggests Barthes, is demoted to being something rather 'lower class' in a society that places an exaggerated value on the discourse of desire, conferring upon it a particular, epistemic dignity. Barthes defined himself as definitively atopical – a position he would claim as his own even more trenchantly in *A Lover's Discourse*. By choosing to side with pleasure, with the modest practices of a Sunday painter and an amateur pianist, he also accepted the fact that he would sometimes

be outside the languages of the present day – with all the solitude
that this attitude might entail.

The eye and the hand

From 1971 to 1975, and much less frequently thereafter, Barthes
painted. This activity was inseparable from his thoughts about
writing. Here, he was becoming ever more radical: writing could
sometimes become unreadable or illegible, not just verbally (as in
Guyotat or Sollers), but by using a language of empty signs – pure
graphic elements without any apparent meaning. The exemption
from meaning that had made such an impact on him in Japan,
together with his experiments in calligraphy, led him to extend his
(extremely pleasurable) investigations in this area. His pleasure
initially took the form of being attracted to the materials he used,
to colour and high-quality paper, 'an almost obsessive relation to
writing instruments'.[8] For example, when we see his room in the rue
Servandoni, filmed by a television director at the time of publication of *The Pleasure of the Text*, what we see around Barthes are
neither books, nor the accessories that generally denote a writer's
work, such as a pen or a typewriter, but rather saucers for mixing
paints, a great number of paintbrushes and little paint pots for
different colours. So he painted in Paris, in the morning when he
woke up, or just after his afternoon nap, when his attention was still
floating and not yet geared up to tackle intellectual questions. But
it was in Urt, in the summer or the spring, or at Christmas, that he
painted the most. Here, he was removed from meaning, on vacation from the time-consuming tasks that absorbed him in Paris.
Of the 380 drawings and paintings preserved in the Fonds Roland
Barthes at the Bibliothèque nationale, nearly three-quarters of them
are dated from those periods when he was on holiday in the South-
West, where everything – the light, the tranquillity, the weather
– combined to encourage such an activity. Gérard Genette tells how
he came to Urt with his wife for lunch one day in 1973, and Barthes
gave them one of his productions as a present. Indeed, he was very
generous with his works: it is estimated that he created some 700
pieces, about half of which are in private collections. Barthes definitely did not attach great importance to his pictorial and graphic
experiences, otherwise he would not have given out his drawings so
freely, thereby running the risk of placing his recipients in his debt.
He happily recognized the fact: 'With no illusions, but quite cheer-
fully, I play at being an artist.'[9] Nonetheless, his investigations in
this area were noteworthy and well worth dwelling on for a while.

Severo Sarduy, who wrote a 'Portrait de l'écrivain en peintre,
le matin' ('Portrait of the writer as a painter, in the morning')

remembers that it had all started in Japan: 'It was as if the empire of signs, in all its varied and mobile ideograms – neon lighting at night in the streets of Tokyo, the cartouches at the entrance to Zen monasteries, the outlines of the stone gardens where the cherry blossom glowed red in the autumn – overflowed from an opaque language and wanted to settle somewhere else, somehow else.' He had seen Barthes copying Japanese engravings: 'Reverent geishas, monks in dialogue with a cockerel, a buffalo drawing along a palanquin, lotus and other types of flower, landscapes by Hiroshige, which he livened up with a Chinese-style glossolalia, judiciously arranged in columns. A few seals too, as if stamped in lacquer. Unless they were moons . . . These Japanese copies are like the ideograms of Ezra Pound [. . .] like the upside down answer to a riddle.'[10] Later, his style freed itself from being a copy, without ever losing the obsession with illegible graphic marks. Over the nine years of Barthes's productivity – five of these years being particularly intense – there were no particular developments in his style. Apart from a few figurative experiments, little men and women reduced to a few lines and presented on the page like so many punctuation signs, or flowers evoking a love of the arabesque that was shared by Baudelaire, Barthes's endeavours were mainly abstract, a tracery of short little curves, lines and points combined in various ways.

Three aspects of Barthes's pictorial activities are worth noting. First, there is the hand that scurries along, light and joyful, pleasantly surprised to discover its liberty and the many paths it can follow. Second, his works can be very close to writing when it forgets to make sense, when it turns into a trace, remembers the productions of childhood, the scribbling. And third, he was forever in pursuit of colour, a colour that was always balanced and harmonious, if perhaps a little unadventurous. His influences are easy to see: Henri Michaux, Jackson Pollock, André Masson and Cy Twombly, even if none of his pieces is as impressive as any of their work – especially Twombly's. As the art historian Céline Flécheux puts it, only Barthes's hand seemed to be fully engaged.[11] He was not painting with his whole body, perhaps not even with his whole being. What he was seeking was not entirely to be found in these productions, which continued to be a form of exercise or undemanding leisure activity. Barthes remained an imitator, happy to bob along in the wake of the works he loved – almost all of them falling under the general rubric of abstract expressionism. And his drawings were almost all inspired by circumstance. His readers, who first discovered this activity through the cover of *Roland Barthes by Roland Barthes* in 1975, were first drawn to the caption to this image, which states the book's ultimate circumstance: 'Memory of Juan-les-Pins, summer 1974.' At the end of the book, they are told what meaning they are to give this practice, as 'the graphic sign for

nothing . . .', '. . . or the signifier without the signified' are the captions referring to two other 'scribbles'. When they do not have any
precise date, almost all these images include a reference to the date
they were made, and sometimes the place. Perhaps because we look
at them from a particular angle, as the works of a writer and not the
works of an artist (and thus not as works of art in the full sense), it
is difficult for us not to think of them in terms of translation. They
seem to be the graphic transcription of an infra-verbal sensation, or
the shorthand version of an emotion. They do not aim to be original, as they are adopting new developments that occurred earlier
in the history of art and painting: abstraction and decomposition.
They make it possible for us to enter a world – a childhood world? a
spiritual world? – without any formed language, any preconstructed
thought. So this activity, apart from being a relaxing way of fostering the free-floating state necessary to the labour of writing, was a
form of experiment, part of Barthes's more general investigations
into writing rather than the plastic arts. They are still of value –
including pictorial and graphic value.

The hand that draws is a hand that thinks in a different way,
playing on its own clumsiness and ambiguity. Barthes remarks in
Roland Barthes by Roland Barthes that his left-handedness got in
the way of his attempts to learn practical things: the everyday world
presented itself to him the wrong way round. Material life was made
quite tricky and induced the sensation of a certain marginality: 'a
modest, inconsequential exclusion, socially tolerated, marked adolescent life with a tenuous and persistent crease: you got used to it,
adapted to it, and went on . . .'[12] But the temptation of normality,
with pressure from his teachers, led to him attempting to correct his
posture as a child, to force his body to be just like everyone else's. He
drew with his right hand but instinctively coloured with his left – an
ambidextrous practice that may well have continued to be the norm
in much of his later pictorial work. When he let his hand lead him
into shapeless and unreadable figures, he was rediscovering the irregular doodles of childhood, disruptions to the system provoked by the
encounter between the particularities of his body and the constraints
imposed by the norm. The distinction Barthes draws between the slow
hand and the galloping hand, in *The Preparation of the Novel*, was
first formulated in a 1973 text with the title 'Variations sur l'écriture'
('Variations on Writing') for publication in an Italian review. 'By a
sort of move back towards the body'[13] he dwelt at length on the phenomena of 'scription', the different relations between the hand and
the words it formed. He drew on important work then being done on
this subject (some of them, such as the books by Marcel Cohen and
James Février, are still classics),[14] and he focused in particular on
the way the act of writing had been speeded up across history, from
Egyptian demotic and Sumerian cuneiform – two kinds of writing

linked to simplifications – to the introduction of ligatures that made to possible to write more rapidly. This was either to save space (the material support of writing was expensive), or to save time. Cursive writing fulfilled a function and modified culture profoundly: '[T]hat writing should race ahead!' he urges. 'Race after what? Time, speech, money, thought, bedazzlement, affect, etc. If only my hand were as quick as my tongue, my eyes, my living memory: demiurgic dream; all of literature, all of culture, all of "psychology" would be different had the hand not moved at a slower pace than the inside of our heads.'[15]

After his thoughts on the speed of writing, he turned to the aesthetics of the graphic trace and its ritual rather than functional nature (in the history of Chinese writing, for example). We are wrong to read ancient forms of writing by focusing on the question of communication or, even worse, of the index: this is a mistake into which we are led by bourgeois ideology. From Leroi-Gourhan, Barthes took the distinction between graphism and writing. Prehistoric graphism, contemporary with the first pigments, took the shape of lines and marks engraved on bone or stone, small equidistant incisions. These first kinds of writing were rhythmic rather than meaningful; they seem to have been closer to abstraction than to imitation or meaning.[16] With painting – a very graphic painting at that – Barthes traced an entire history that led back to the body and the origin. He was thereby following his own personal history: ontogenesis reflected phylogenesis. In this history, struggling with his left-handedness, he moved on from shapeless writing to the attractive and perfectly legible handwriting, now carefully and regularly shaped, of his maturity (even if he recognized three types of handwriting: one for taking notes, one for writing his texts and another for correspondence).[17] This was a twofold genesis, then, that took the form of a shift: to move from one type of writing to another, he had to change hands. The work could be defined as a *'kinetic relationship between the head and the hand'*:[18] this relation needed to be made as favourable as possible.

One of the most interesting features to observe and understand in Barthes's visual productions is the way he was working on, and reflecting on, writing. As he often remarked, it was Japan that had opened this domain, enabling him to occupy the text as in a hedonistic, fully autonomous space. If he was to find this space for his own oeuvre, he needed to free it from the laws that held it in thrall: meaning and reference. Creating an illegible form of writing represented this stage of emancipation and indeed purification. Imaginary graphisms were neither words nor drawings, but the union of the two, thanks to a new experiment with the neutral – an oscillation between two worlds that were completely separated, the legible and the visible, here brought together in the form of the writeable. There were signs, but no meaning – this is what Barthes wished to show. So he focused on types of writing that belonged to a system beyond decipherment. In 'Variations on Writing', a crucial text for understanding the main tendencies of this period in his development, he referred to the activities of amateurs – activities that lay outside any artistic intention or professional motive. One of his examples was Mirtha Dermisache, whose works had originally been produced for teaching purposes but were then exhibited and discussed in art books – though this happened only from 1974, before Barthes's essay. He also referred to the impenetrable 'writings' of André Masson and Bernard Réquichot, stripped of any meaning, any referential alibi. This emancipation was the very condition of the appearance of the text. 'Now what is interesting – indeed stupefying – is the fact that nothing, absolutely nothing, distinguishes these authentic forms of writing from those fake forms of writing: there is no difference, except the context, between what has not yet been deciphered and what can never be deciphered. It is we, our culture, our law, who decide on the referential status of a form of writing. What does this mean? That the signifier is free, sovereign. A form of writing does not need to be "legible" to be fully writing.'[19] We can hardly fail to recognize in these words, with their exaltation of the pure signifier, Barthes's own practice as an amateur of drawing. And we can hardly fail to read his remarks as a powerful reflection on handwriting, just at the time when it was about to disappear. Barthes notes in a parenthesis that 'in the United States, everything is written directly on the typewriter – missives, literary texts – without any remaining humanist precaution'.[20] Even if it was something of a myth that handwriting could convey the affective body, the fact remained that writing by hand could still capture the memory of its illegibility: this was a guarantee against the all-powerful law of meaning.

All the texts from this period bear the trace of this pictorial and graphic *imaginaire* and of its contribution to a new way of thinking about writing. *The Pleasure of the Text*, entirely written during the summer of 1972, came before the 'Variations on Writing' and the text on André Masson; it followed immediately after the first article on Réquichot's paintings. Between 1 July and 24 August, in Urt, Barthes read around in this field (mainly texts by Serge Leclair whose *Démasquer le réel* had been published the previous year, together with Freud and Nietzsche, as well as novels by Sollers and Sarduy), while also doing a great deal of painting. In *The Pleasure of the Text*, the theme of illegibility goes off in another direction, following ideas about disfiguration and abstraction, towards liberation from the shackles of the sentence. The modern effort of artists to destroy art became, itself, one of the modes of art. Barthes described three forms of this process. Either the artist moved to another medium (the writer became a film director or painter, the painter became a writer); or the artist developed a more discursive approach, reducing art to art criticism; or else the artist simply bid farewell to writing once and for all. So as not to be forced to adopt the last solution, Barthes tried out the first two, in full awareness of the limits of these subversive but always recuperated programmes, such as the avant-garde. It was essential to escape from the paradigm of subversion and find terms that were more indirectly evasive, involving an unexpected alternative (such as laughter, in Georges Bataille).

Indeed, it was the encounter between painting and writing that produced the notion of 'text' that Barthes really gave theoretical form to just then, in summer 1972 with *The Pleasure of the Text* and also with the article he was writing at the same time (in August) for the *Encyclopaedia Universalis*: 'Texte'. By defining it as a 'fabric', he refused to turn it into a veil behind which meaning was hidden. It was the interweaving of the material that he emphasized, the idea of criss-crossing threads interlinked in a potentially infinite manner. In this weave, the subject comes undone, 'like a spider dissolving in the constructive secretions of its web'.[21] The same neologism was used by Barthes to connect the theory of the text with a *hyphology* (*hyphos* meaning fabric, veil, spider's web). The painter's canvas was like the spider's web in that the same word (*la toile*) could be used in French to refer to both: this suggested that the text was akin to painting. Furthermore, what could be read on this canvas, in this web, was a form of writing, whose value lay not in what it meant, but in its ability to produce signs. This was why, instead of being recuperated by socio-professional and institutionalized castes, writing ought to be a place for that 'particular practitioner, the *amateur*, who would still be able to operate as such in a liberated society'.[22] Finally, what overrides the distinctions between the arts, or brings them together in the same practice, was abstraction, as the considerations on the unknown language expressed in *Empire of Signs* had suggested. Abstraction could also correspond to a muddle of sounds, marked both by a productive interweaving and by an element of discontinuity (the absence of the sentence). It was all connected: going back to the body and the hand led to viewing writing as a material production of signs that placed it on the same level as any other artistic practice. This liberated art could emancipate us from many constraints, such as continuity. Though Barthes's work was still couched in sentences, it was ultimately detached from any continuous, coherent argument. *The Pleasure of the Text* was, as *Michelet* had been, fragmentary in form, though it did not even resort to the subtitles that gave each section the feel of a picture. Instead of imposing a 'rational' order on the fragments, Barthes used the 'stupid', arbitrary, obvious order of the alphabet (which he also most often followed when he was classifying his index cards): this was how he proceeded in 'Variations on Writing' and in *Roland Barthes par Roland Barthes.* This was how he achieved an individual identity, surrendering to his tastes and to concrete little idiosyncrasies.

As well as being a practical artist, Barthes also produced a great number of theoretical writings on art. This was another discourse that he produced as an amateur, and this gave it a special flavour as it was not caught up in any general discourse, whether art history, art criticism or fashion. Barthes had many friends who ran galleries, or were artists or critics. Daniel Cordier shut down his gallery in 1964, but he had kept his important private collection and maintained personal relations with certain artists, including Réquichot, whom he introduced to Barthes. He also introduced him to Yvon Lambert, with whom Barthes would collaborate on many occasions in his final years. François Braunschweig and Hugues Autexier had opened their first photography gallery and shared their discoveries with Barthes when he became interested in the history of photography. In particular, he was very close to Franco Maria Ricci (Calvino had introduced the two men); Ricci had set up his publishing house in Parma in 1963, and frequently asked Barthes to write a preface for his handsome editions of Arcimboldo portraits, the alphabets of Erté, the graphic novel that Guido Crepax produced based on Pauline Réage's *The Story of O.* Thanks to the mediation of Marcelin Pleynet in particular, *Tel Quel* was also open to contemporary art, especially the work of the Supports/Surfaces group: one of its most important figures, Marc Devade,[23] also joined the editorial committee at the time of publication of issue 47, devoted to Barthes. This all meant that Barthes was becoming acquainted with an increasing number of artists, and his diary was filled with several exhibition previews, visits to galleries and commissions to write texts about artists. In 1972, which was his busiest year in this respect, he visited Mme Cartier-Bresson, Daniel Cordier (several times), André Masson (who introduced him to Paule Thévenin), the preview of the Supports/Surfaces show at the Yvon-Lambert gallery in the rue de l'Échaudé (this was the group's last exhibition before they split up) and an exhibition of the work of photographer Bruno Sauerwein. He went to the exhibition on English posters in the 1890s ('L'affiche anglaise: les années 90') at the Musée des arts décoratifs in order to write an article on it, attended the exhibition of contemporary art at the Grand Palais, visited the museums of Amsterdam in October and went to most of the many autumn previews. If the articles from this period were especially important, this was because, remaining faithful to his method as a writer of considering works of art without any preconceived method, he always shed a singular light on them, but also developed the conception of illegible writing that corresponded to his own research.

Of the forty or so articles that he wrote on the visual arts in the course of his life, just under half were on painting. The article on André Masson was to art what *The Pleasure of the Text* was to literature. In it, Barthes developed his ideas about the text, but this time starting out from the artist's ideographic works. At that time, André Masson used Chinese writing as a source of graphic dynamism. He did not use it as an ideogram that meant something, but in order to experiment on colour and line. Barthes called this Asian period in the painter's work 'textual', confirming that, for him, the oriental *imaginaire* and the theory of the text were interdependent. It was no longer a writing that communicated something, but a 'body that beats'. The primacy of gesture over word opened the way to a truth conditioned by illegibility. By producing something illegible, Masson 'detaches writing's pulsion from the image-repertoire of communication (legibility). This is what the Text desires as well. But whereas the written text must still – and ceaselessly – struggle with an apparently signifying substance (words), Masson's semiography, directly resulting from a non-signifying practice (painting), achieves from the start the utopia of the Text.'[24] The artist commits himself body and soul to a problem; he initiates a process rather than putting forward a finished product.

If we are looking for an awareness of this complete commitment of the body, Réquichot is the best example. He sheds the brightest light on all of Barthes's writings on painting. In his work we find the key themes of illegible writing, the amateur, matter and the body. But by the force of his oeuvre, and the violence of his obsessions, Réquichot becomes the very name of painting when it becomes destruction, the end of painting. A fortnight before his suicide at the age of 32 (two days before the preview of his exhibition at Daniel Cordier's gallery in 1961, he threw himself out of the window of his studio apartment in the rue de Courcelles), the painter had written seven indecipherable texts in an unknown, invented writing: this turned non-meaning into a testament. But Barthes did not dwell on these final productions, which were somewhat marginal to the rest of Réquichot's work. Daniel Cordier (who had put on Réquichot's first personal exhibition in his gallery in 1957 and put on another exhibition of his work in 1961) asked Barthes to write on the artist; Barthes was fascinated by the disturbing power that raw matter assumed in Réquichot's work, seeing it as the expression of a wild cry, a visceral language that turned everything inside out, forcing body and soul into a muddled pulp. In his 'reliquaries', Réquichot displayed rubbish (shoes, roots, snail shells, painted and folded canvases, bones picked up from the butcher's, in the company of his friend Dado, and so on) that tempted the spectator's obsessions. Réquichot was much too 'Catholic', deep down, for Barthes to share his deepest fears and longings. His work was haunted by a sense of guilt that Barthes's Protestant upbringing had sheltered him from. On the other hand, Barthes was familiar with illness, the way the mechanism of the body could easily be reduced to a few leftovers (as a relic was a reminiscence of Réquichot in his own self-portrait), the fear of death, the haunting sense of a possible transformation. And what is striking in Barthes's fine text, 'Réquichot and his body', is that we can see Barthes being led beyond himself, into regions of instinctual drive and desire, but held as far as possible at bay: suicide, the dead man talking (Barthes had already lectured on Poe's M. Valdemar in Rabat and Geneva), rubbish and faeces, all objects that could arouse a real fascination.

Taste

In his text on Réquichot, Barthes suggested that painting had two (extra-historical) origins. The first, as we have seen, was writing; the second was cookery, 'i.e. any practice which aims at transforming substance according to the complete scale of its consistencies, by various operations such as inspissation, liquefaction, granulation, lubrification, producing what in gastronomy is called the coated, the thickened, the creamy, the crisp, etc.'.[25] Réquichot displayed the digestive, animal side of man, his insides, his cavities, while for Barthes food was generally something beneficent that came from the outside. When he liked a particular author, he would pick up one of his favourite recipes or fetish foods so as to create a link between that author and himself: nectarines, or those little aromatic tarts called 'mirlitons' in Fourier, oranges in Goethe, the salad of orange with rum in Sade, the 'cheese with Chantilly cream' in Stendhal. He did not greedily imagine actually eating these foodstuffs, but he enjoyed the reality effect that their presence created, he liked their fetishistic character. This pleasure did not give rise to a realism of decipherment or interpretation, but it did mean he could pick up an 'it was so' as he could in photography: art could make present something that no longer existed – hence our attachment to art. A few years previously, Barthes had called the stubborn detail the 'effect of the real' and described it as what could not be contained within a structure – for example, Mme Aubain's barometer in Flaubert's short story 'A Simple Heart'. By now he was more pre- pared to accept the effect of adherence that this detail presupposed. And very often, what he recognized as an effect of the real, or a point of reality, was connected with his own equilibrium in space, his way of measuring himself and his relation to time. For example, if we realize that, for Barthes, the barometer was a very meaningful reference point in his everyday life, so that he immediately had it

repaired if it stopped working properly, that in certain periods he
noted in his desk diary the pressure in millibars, we will understand
why he was so disturbed by this insistent detail in Flaubert's story.
For him it was not noteworthy – unlike the piano, it did not connote
the bourgeoisie and did not have any function in the economy of
the story. On the other hand, it *was* a major element in his own life,
and so its presence seemed even stranger in a nineteenth-century
text that related a story in which it did not seem to have much of
a role to play. Likewise, what attracted Barthes's attention in Sade
was not the orange salad with rum as such, but the fact that people
ate it in 1791 as they still did in posh restaurants in the 1970s. The
effect of the real could essentially be defined as the conjunction of an
'it was so' distant in time and for another person, together with an
'it is', now and in itself. So we are a long way from the 'objectivity'
proposed in the article of 1968 on 'The Reality Effect';[26] on the other
hand, we are closer to the encounter between two subjectivities, a
surprise that Barthes was increasingly glad to meet with.

This detail about the barometer reveals something of Barthes's
special relation with Flaubert, who was not the classic you could
turn to your own uses, like Racine or Balzac, nor the modern whose
experiments you could analyse. Rather, Flaubert was a companion,
like Proust, a presence on whom he could always count. Barthes
noted this on an index card: 'The way I use Flaubert. I don't write
about him but I use him all the time.'[27] He had a fraternal relation
with him: he recognized himself in his moments of discouragement
(the 'marinade'), his way of making life inseparable from writing,
and his obstinacy. This kinship led him to bring a very concrete
material attention to bear on Flaubert's work. He took an interest
in the types of paper Flaubert used, his crossings-out, the different types of correction he carried out. (This all looked forward to
the tireless genetic research that has since been done on Flaubert's
oeuvre.)[28] By transferring the merits of poetry to prose, Flaubert
made it possible for literature to break free, once and for all, from
the shackles of rhetoric and plunge into an infinite but uncertain
movement. This recognition had profound implications for Barthes.
It explains the way that Flaubert's novel *Bouvard and Pécuchet* was
his close, constant and (here again) fraternal companion over the
last ten years of his existence. This has sometimes been read as a
sign of Barthes's ambivalent and fascinated relation to his own stupidity, but it is probably more accurate to see it as the book that in
his view was the best (because it was the most distant) example of
the programme of the neutral. For Barthes, *Bouvard and Pécuchet*
was a book forever uncertain: in it, language guaranteed nothing.
No statement could dominate any other: '[O]f all these languages,
finally, there is not one that prevails, there is no master language.'[29]
So Flaubert was closer to Barthes's views on writing and style than

any of his contemporaries. He illustrated a discordance in time that the vertigo of concomitant dates repaired, at least in fantasy. 'I was in *troisième* when Flaubert's niece died (3 February 1931, in Antibes)',[30] Barthes noted in his diary. He could not have found a better way of expressing his desire to join Flaubert.

This taste for everything that was part of material, sensual life, in particular cookery and food, was not fortuitous. It was part of Barthes's threefold relation to the body, to aesthetics and to pleasure. He was not by temperament excessive, and could keep the pleasures of the palate under control. The people who knew him personally emphasized his liking for Morgon wine and for certain types of cigar, those cigars twisted into a spiral known as Culebras that are very expensive and difficult to come across (he would buy some when he was in Geneva). He sometimes smoked much more ordinary cigars, and cigarettes, but true pleasure was to be found in rarity. He also loved champagne and the bubbly intoxication it gave him. He acknowledged that wine could give him a way of getting out of himself. 'Perhaps the "it's working", "it's kicking off" just needs a bit of wine – a drug.'[31] He viewed it the same way as did Baudelaire – as 'remembering and forgetting, joy and melancholy', allowing the subject to be 'transported outside himself': this was the opposite of Brillat-Savarin, who felt that wine was far from being a conductor of ecstasy, but instead, a suitably balanced accompaniment to a meal, the very figure of an anti-drug.[32] If we look at all the texts Barthes wrote on food and cookery, what we see is that he almost always focused on perversity rather than functionality – except that this functionality was pushed to an extreme degree of system, as in the case of Sade, detailing the food eaten by torturers and their victims in the service of pleasure. Barthes was fascinated by Japanese cookery because it drew on almost all the different physical senses at once, sight, touch and taste, and showed great precision when it came to qualities of which he was particularly fond: the aerial, the floating, the crunchy, the fragmentary, as opposed to the smothering smoothness of French ornamental cookery. For while French cuisine may not have been functional, this did not stop it connoting a bourgeois mythology that he lampooned in *Mythologies* and other texts. So he repeated his analysis of this myth in *Empire of Signs*, contrasting the cuisine-as-writing of the Japanese with the cuisine-as-ornament of the recipes provided in *Elle*. In Japan, the art of the table was the complete opposite of the way food was prepared and laid out in the West: for, in Japan, everything was done right in front of the consumer's eyes, and not in a separate place; the chopsticks which enable the eater to pick up the food are completely different from our knives and forks, which are just miniature versions of predatory weapons (harpoons, pikes and daggers). Japanese cuisine enables us to reach a second-degree naturalness: it does not remind us of food in its original, wild state (hunting, fishing, gathering), but of 'a spring, a profound vitality', its horizon or utopia. 'Whence the *living* (which does not mean natural) character of this food, which in each season seems to fulfil the poet's wish: *"Oh, to celebrate the spring by exquisite cookeries . . .".'*[33]

The way in which signs are displayed was, as ever, what interested Barthes in cookery. He drew up a particularly flavoursome inventory of this in the preface he wrote to an edition of Brillat-Savarin's *Physiology of Taste* in 1975. This text, written in the autumn of 1974, just after he had completed the manuscript of *Roland Barthes by Roland Barthes*, brought together his various ideas about 'cookery as sign' that he had sporadically been playing with since the start of his career. He used the figure of 'bathmology' that he had also tried out in his self-portrait: this was an investigation of the different levels or degrees to which the field of discourse was subjected (the second degree and the third, fourth, fifth . . .). Thus, phenomena linked to the consumption of alcohol (excitement, stupefaction, dullness) – the 'tiering' of taste. 'This is how BS decomposes the gustatory sensation *in time* (for it is not a matter of simple analysis): 1. *direct* (when the flavour is still acting on the front of the tongue); 2. *complete* (when the taste moves to the back of the mouth); 3. *reflective* (at the final moment of judgement). All the *luxury* of taste is found in this scale.'[34] It is because it develops across time, like a language, with an important dimension of memory, that this sensation deserves all the attention it gets, for the pleasure of taste and the pleasure of language mix and mingle in it. Hence the interest Barthes took in fetish words and in fetish types of food that transmitted a social and erotic code, as well as a savour, and expressed a relation to the body: 'French by fruits (as others were "by women"): a predilection for pears, cherries, raspberries; somewhat less for oranges; and none whatever for exotic fruits such as mangoes, guavas, lychee nuts.'[35] The statement shows Barthes's preference for one season over another, for summer rather than winter: he was loyal to an old-style upbringing rather than fashion and the dictates of imported goods, the transformation of something quite simple into a fetish object. Amazed that he could find cherries on the Saint-Germain market in the middle of winter, he also missed the frustrating but fulfilling sense of alternation and expectation: 'the greatest joy of all is over – that of the return. Henceforth, on the horizon, markets without seasons: the time of differences is past.'[36]

Barthes's relation with food was something that he needed to scrutinize with care. As we have seen in connection with his time in the sanatorium, he was on rather complicated terms with his body. He spent his life keeping tabs on his weight and wore himself out trying to follow draconian diets. By the end of the 1950s, he had adopted a lifestyle that meant he ate out in a restaurant almost every evening.

This was hardly conducive to a balanced diet. He compensated for this by eating only salads and grilled food at lunchtime. But his weight was rarely stable. So, once or twice a year, he would go on a diet, when he kept a rigorous tally of what he ate, counted the calories he ingested, noted the ups and downs of his weight in his desk diary, and used an appetite suppressant called Tenuate – an amphetamine which also had stimulant properties: he rather liked the buzz it gave him.[37] This meant he could lose up to 15 kilos in two months. While his average weight was around 78 kilos, he dreamed of being much lighter on his feet than that. Even though he criticized the way contemporary society imposed its diktat of slimness on everyone, he himself was obsessed by an ideally slender self. So he suffered from significant weight swings, between 68 to 89 kilos – with the added complication that he could slip very quickly from one extreme to another. When he was following a strict diet, he would restrict himself, in the evenings, to a plate of ham in the Café du Flore, avoiding fat, bread and sugar. He would often go on a diet just before heading abroad, so as to be comfortable in his skin and enjoy the pleasures he might find while on his travels, including the pleasures of the table: while abroad he revelled in the various satisfactions he could find for his senses. In China, as we have seen, it was the meals that he noted down with the greatest enjoyment. There he discovered a type of cuisine that was completely different from the Chinese restaurants he was used to frequenting, such as La Route mandarine, where he often went for an evening meal with friends, and the 'little Chinese place' in the rue Tournon, where he would have lunch with students. In China he learned that the rice is not presented until the very end of the meal; that colours play a decisive role in the composition of the dishes, as does the balance of textures, the variety of ways the food is cut up, and the subtle use of spices. He had been quite unaware of this when he drew a hasty comparison between Japanese and Chinese cuisine in *Empire of Signs*. Here again, it was all a matter of degree and he needed to find the right words to express it. Thus Barthes's liking for bathmology joined his pleasure in neologism. The sciences of scales and degrees invited him to get inside language so as to invent it and reinvent it, to be 'maniacs of the second degree'.[38] The thought of cookery often led to the kitchen of meaning. Cuisine revealed language as well as calling on its resources. It was a rejection of what was simple, of the denoted (even the simplicity of Japanese cookery, its rawness, was denoted), of innocent repetition. Like language, cuisine should demonstrate a power of decentring, unfolding meaning: '[B]ut if I take off the brake (of reason, of science, of morality), if I put the speech-act into neutral, then I open the way to an endless detachment, I abolish language's good conscience.'[39] Neologism was a way of unpacking language, of reflecting on it while subverting it. Another way of achieving this end was sometimes to give another sense to commonplace words – what Michel Deguy calls the 'neologeme':[40] not a lexical invention or reinvention, but a new way of taking a term such as '*fadeur*' ('insipidity') and stripping it of its negative connotation (an absence of savour) so that it can refer to a pacification or equalization of things.

Hearing and vision

Barthes's emphasis on pleasure, the considerable weight he gave to the category of the amateur, always included music, both as played and listened to. In the 1970s, Barthes got to know well a great musician he very much admired, André Boucourechliev, who had commissioned an article from him ('Musical practica') for a special issue on Beethoven in the review *L'Arc*, in 1970. They continued to exchange ideas, and in 1974, Boucourechliev composed an electroacoustic work based on Mallarmé's *A Tomb for Anatole*. He asked Barthes to recite the words – to be another kind of performer. That year and the following year, he gave Barthes (who had not had a teacher since childhood) several private piano lessons, and encouraged him to play more with his whole body. In his text on Beethoven, Barthes – in line with his current preoccupations – distinguished between manual, practical music on the one hand, and a more passive, sonorous music on the other: it was the latter that tended to be culturally predominant. The major shift brought about by Beethoven was the way he separated music from being played and turned it into something passively listened to: he imagined the gradual disappearance of the amateur under the influence of a bourgeois recuperation of music. But the end of an amateur practice of music meant the end of the 'grain', that form of imperfection and fuzziness that was necessary to certain works, and in his view made Schumann's work, in particular, so intimate. This was what he said when he was invited to speak on Claude Maupomé's radio programme 'Comment l'entendez-vous?' As he wrote, in an essay on Panzéra, 'The "grain" is the body in the singing voice, in the writing hand, in the performing limb.'[41] So his assessment of music was not subjective, but erotic: a matter of 'I like' or 'I don't like' that was not subject to the laws of culture. 'The *grain* of the voice is not indescribable (nothing is indescribable), but I don't think that it can be defined scientifically, because it implies a certain erotic relationship between the voice and the listener.'[42] In this way, music is a writing of the body. Indeed, Barthes often recorded himself while playing, since this was a way of hearing the materiality of the music. Later, in 'Listening' (written with Roland Havas in 1977), an article that inspired Luciano Berio with his opera *Un re in ascolto* to a libretto by Calvino, Barthes enumerated three distinct types of listening: detecting clues to what was happening; deciphering auditory signs; and the words with which the subject transformed his intimate impressions into a text. So music was like painting and books: a heartrending moment when the reader, the listener, or the viewer needed to emerge from themselves and their comfort or their pleasure in order to allow themselves to be overwhelmed by the work.

As with many other of the questions he took an interest in, Barthes was now in great demand to discuss music and his relation to it. He wrote the sleeve notes for a recording by Panzéra, and articles on singing and on Schumann; he also took part in radio and TV broadcasts. But more than with other topics, with music he was freed of any obligation to play the expert. He had played music since childhood and it was in connection with music that he developed his private and then historical convictions about the role of the amateur. So his was always an overtly private relation to music, and this was not a pose that he had to adopt versus the 'professor' or the 'intellectual' within him. During this period, he often spoke on France Musique, where he talked directly to his listeners of his tastes, his likes and dislikes. Before the broadcast on Schumann on 21 October 1979, with Claude Maupomé, he recorded with her an 'Egotistic concert' in 1977. In 1976, he had taken part in a broadcast on the romantic song, the text of which was published with original illustrations by Daniel Dezeuze, a member of the Supports/Surfaces group.[43] While he again stated that he had, all his life, been unable to talk about music, he magnificently described his active relation to music, his liking of polyphony and counterpoint, his deep satisfaction at being able to bring them out at the keyboard. Listening was never enough and in his view the appearance of the vinyl recording was a negative development, as musical culture was now becoming much more passive than before. This liberty, based on the exclusive dimension of taste, allowed him to produce a new and original way of thinking about this art, one that was not scientific but was still precise and valuable: the idea of the grain. 'What could be more indiscreet, more tasteless than building a theory on one's personal tastes?' he asked himself in his personal notes. And yet . . . Barthes was always being told – by students, friends, listeners – that he had a beautiful voice,[44] and as a gift in return offered an idea that could bring together language and music: the grain, as a way of making writing sing – not just in language, but in instrumental music too.

In his final years, it was often with friends that he went to a concert or to the opera. Indeed, he told Claude Maupomé that he was not a real opera buff, but went along at the instigation of friends he loved, and who made him share their passion, something he was happy to do thanks to the music. In 1973, he went with André Téchiné to see The Marriage of Figaro (in a production by

Strehler); with Jean-Louis Bouttes he went to see Gluck's *Orphée*; and with Roland Havas, at the Palais Garnier, he saw *One Day or Two*, John Cage's opera-ballet with Merce Cunningham. He referred to this last piece in the interview with Bianciotti: it was that year's major controversial event. In 1974, he saw Massenet's *Don Quichotte, Turandot, The Magic Flute, Werther* and *Tosca*. Up until 1977, he would share this pleasure with many of his friends, including Roland Havas (with whom he regularly played the piano), and Romaric Sulger-Büel with whom he also sang and who accompanied Barthes on a trip to Bayreuth in the summer of 1976, where they heard the whole of Wagner's *Ring Cycle*, produced by Patrice Chéreau with stage settings by Richard Peduzzi, conducted by Pierre Boulez: this was the major artistic event of that summer (Foucault went, too). With Antoine Compagnon, Barthes again saw *Rhinegold* and *The Valkyrie* in Paris; with Éric Marty, he also went to the concerts at the Athénée. The diary note cards he kept at the time record many of his reactions to music, offering both analysis and off-the-cuff opinions. The 'Fichier vert', or green folder, which contains notes he wrote with a view to his self-portrait, includes reflections on the status of the amateur: 'He is a non-hero; He (alone) is in tune with the being *there* of the signifier: "the immediately definitive nature of music". – He is not compromised in rubato (the theft of essence in order to benefit the attribute!) – he is the counter-bourgeois artist (which is quite different from being the "socialist" artist).' He also sees the ethos of the amateur as out of step with history. 'Today, there are no more amateurs', he noted in 1972, and this formula was also a frequent theme in his contributions to France Musique programmes. When his index cards turned into a private diary, from 1976 to 1977, remarks on music became more and more numerous. They coincided with moments of radio – which he listened to while working – and reflections on concerts. Here is a selection:

22 October 76 Inwardness
    This morning (22 October 76) looking out at the grey rooftops of Paris, listening to a Schubert lied by Wunderlich, emotion, beauty, vague soulfulness, dissatisfaction, lack, metaphysics, desire, etc. I tell myself: I'm ill, neurotic; and all at once, almost at the same time: but isn't that literature? Everything that gets indicated these days as a neurosis is nothing else but (past) literature.

29 April 78
    Irresistible metonymy: all music by Franck or his school makes me think of Bayonne, of the garden, that area as it was in the 30s, the Côte, Saint-Jean-de-Luz (Mme Petit?)

30 May 78
The other day, at the *Marriage of Figaro*, the whole corner of the stalls where I was sitting stank of Palmolive. Metonymy: the *Marriage* of soap.

18 July 79
Radio: composition of a Prix de Rome (or at least winner of a Médicis bursary), Philippe Hersant: not bad (as it isn't too modern). This again raises the problem of this contemporary music; radio debates; listeners full of goodwill say and confess they don't like it. They are given irrelevant answers (referring to the continuity of musical history, etc.). But what is one to say to *I don't like?* How to struggle against *I don't like?* The buried model of this blockage: the attraction of something sexually repellent.

5 August 79
Music: I like it when the performer plays in such a way that I can *distinguish* the hands (Gould) or the instruments (Toscanini).
Instinct, a truly *polyphonic* demand.

30 September 79
Yesterday afternoon, recorded the Schumann programme with Claude Maupomé. On arriving in the booth, you can sense that the technicians are in a bad mood: it's a Saturday afternoon, and the French are always in a bad mood when they have to work; they are *already* in a hurry to get home and make no attempt to disguise it. The electrical connections won't work. The woman assistant, very poorly, it appears, is grey, bloodless, remote. The sound technician, in his forties, tells me: Schumann? I can't stand him. How nice to start off in such conditions. Hence, indeed, the question: I never ask myself *for whom* I am deciding to speak, who it is I am trying to persuade. What if it were that obtuse technician? How could I get him to like Schumann? A quite different discourse.

18 December 79
Treatise on musical aesthetics
Principle of hallucination:
= I can hear with certainty, as if it were obvious, things that other people can't hear, that the *consensus* can't hear.
E.g.: Fischer-Dieskau: I can hear (and it's a repeated feature) very unpleasant zones in his voice.* He doesn't have a *beautiful* voice, etc.
* I can localize these.

The only laws, as one can see, are those of emotion and taste, but memory also plays a role. Musical listening dictates its freedom to the listener.[45] Music took Barthes back to his past. It is one of the most powerfully continuous aspects of his existence; it awoke the memory of the house in Bayonne and his aunt Alice, and also rekindled the memory of Michel Delacroix with whom he had shared his love for Panzéra. So it is easy to see why he did not have an intellectual relation with music. Hence the impression one has of how exclusive his preferences were, for Schumann and Panzéra for example; hence, too, his sadness at the way music fell out of fashion over time and was no longer in step with the present world. On 15 October 1979, he nostalgically noted the action of time: 'Collapse, degradation, winded quality of Fauré sung by Panzéra: I was propped up by this absolute value, but I recognize, as I have to, that it is no longer shared, supported. → I am the only person who loves it.' In particular, while he might abandon ideas or things in which he had a purely intellectual interest, Barthes did not like it when he no longer loved something.

This is what had happened to him with theatre. But in the 1970s, again following the tastes of some of his friends, Barthes started going to the theatre once more, in spite of the fact that he had abandoned this art. In 1973, he went to Nanterre to see *Mother Courage* again, some twenty years after he had first been dazzled by it in 1954, in a production by Antoine Vitez. In the theatre he met Bernard Dort, who, surprised to see him there, exclaimed: 'I thought you'd stopped going to the theatre!' He wrote again on Brecht in 1975, focusing on his political writings.[46] With his friends Colette Fellous and Chantal Thomas, he went to see plays in Ivry at the Théâtre de la Cité. But he could not rekindle the fervour he had once felt. He preferred the freedom that he was granted by music or the dreamy solitude of cinema, which he continued to go to very frequently. It has often been written that Barthes was less interested in cinema than in other artistic forms. It is true that he did not have the same relation to films as he did to books, pictures and photographs. The reason is that in his case, cinema was envisaged less as an artistic object than as a practice. What he was interested in was the way cinema was used, the reasons we go to see a film, the ways we behave while there – for example 'the relaxation of postures (how many members of the cinema audience slide down into their seats as if into a bed, coats or feet thrown over the row in front!)'.[47] What he particularly liked was the intermediate, dozy, day-dreamy state you are in when you come out of the cinema. There could be all sorts of reasons for going to see a film: boredom, free time, the cultural desire to track down a definite film, looking for a sexual partner. But everyone has the same sense, when they come out, of feeling a little lost and flat – the result of the way our bodies seem to be doubled while we are sitting in front of the cinema screen. So Barthes became the ethnologist of practices that were on the point of disappearing – though he could never have guessed that they would disappear so quickly. He described the Latin Quarter in which he lived as a place that offered a cinematographic refuge at every street corner, and still had porn cinemas (including the Dragon Club, a gay porn cinema which Barthes went to frequently), showing new releases as well as classics, blockbusters as well as art films. Since the 1980s, fourteen cinemas have closed in the 5th and 6th arrondissements of Paris, including the Cluny Palace, the Quintette Pathé, the Publicis Saint-Germain, the Bonaparte on the place Saint-Sulpice, and so on. Thus, when Barthes evokes 'modern eroticism', that of the big city, the 'urban dark', where 'the body's freedom is generated',[48] he is describing a world of possibilities similar to that opened up by cinema. But this leisurely way of using cinema as a place you go on the spur of the moment, because you have an hour or two to kill and need something to do (a habit which in Barthes's case went back to his teens), or to enjoy the potential pleasures of finding a sexual partner, has now almost vanished. Watching porn has become a private activity thanks to the huge number of pornographic films available on cassette and then on the Internet, so the last 'specialist' cinemas such as Le Latin on the boulevard Saint-Michel and La Scala on the boulevard de Strasbourg have also closed.

To love the cinema, its practices, its habits, to love going into a cinema, to love coming out of one – these are all exactly how the 'ordinary man of the cinema' behaves, as Jean Louis Schefer calls him in a book published the same year as *Camera Lucida* and in the same collection. This is someone who is not especially qualified to talk about films, but often goes to the cinema. Like Schefer, Barthes mentions the rays from the projector, the mythical cave, the dark room in which you are suspended in a sheaf of light – the exact opposite of the situation with photography. It all comprises a different experience of time and memory. Schefer uses similar terms to describe the temporal effacement of the world within us that occurs as we watch the film, in places where even sleepers are active, as they are transformed into images. He also dwells on the moment when we come out of the cinema: 'When you come out into the daylight, you are always surprised to see the buses driving past and movement carrying on as before. Only the rain, when you come out of the cinema, continues the film a little – it pursues or perpetuates the same kind of ceaseless hatching through which objects constantly manage to touch us.'[49]

Though Barthes had many interesting things to say about the cinema as a social habit, and in the early 1960s focused on mass communications – on cinema as a medium – he did not produce any particularly remarkable texts on individual films, with the partial exception of the work of Charlie Chaplin. He wrote eloquently about Chaplin from a political standpoint in *Mythologies* and from an ethical standpoint in *Roland Barthes by Roland Barthes*.[50] It seems that there was something in cinema, in Barthes's view, that resisted reading and thus appropriation. Something in film resisted the complete deployment of his thinking and writing. In film there is not the embodiment which gives theatre its erotic charge; there is not the distance which limits the illusion and complaisance we experience in narrative; nor is there the 'that has been' of photography, as the 'that has been' of cinema has never really taken place. The article on Pasolini's *Salò* is written at a distance and is more interesting for what it says about Sade than about the film or its director. The two texts Barthes wrote about the films of André Téchiné insist mainly on the screenplay and are nothing more than a friendly gesture of homage. The article on Téchiné's film *Les Soeurs Brontë* has only a certain biographical interest, reminding us of Barthes's sole experience as a film actor, when he shared the daily life of the film team over a few days in England at the end of summer 1978: here too, this was not a very positive experience, since it kindled in him a desperate sense of imposture. He remembered it a year later in these terms: 'Leeds Making André's film. Night of 5 to 6 September 78. Waiting, Rain, I forget my lines. Distress. 1) Novelistic in this regard: difficult night: on the moral feeling that one should never agree, even as an act of friendship, to do something you can't do. 2) Intense feeling of shame. Neurotic theme of imposture. Nightmare of the mask that will fall. Here: imposture of pretending to be an actor.'[51] It is true that Barthes seems very uncomfortable and wooden in this film. He has only two scenes (in one of them he does not even speak), and they hardly suggest he had the slightest talent as an actor. He agreed to do it out of friendship for Téchiné and for the group filming with him; he was also friends with Pascal Greggory and Isabelle Adjani. Jean-Louis Bouttes went with him, and played the part of the reader for the publishing house of Smith, Elder & Co., Mr Williams, the staunch supporter of Jane Eyre.

Ultimately, Barthes's only major piece of writing on cinema was about Eisenstein, who allowed him to postulate a contrast between the 'obvious meaning' (the sense that is communicated) and the 'obtuse meaning' (which goes beyond communication). Even here, he worked from film stills, which was yet another way of avoiding the film object as such.[52] What lies behind this reluctance to talk about cinema as such? After all, Barthes took pleasure in going to see films – and he always tended to highlight the value of pleasure. His self-portrait provides us with a reply: he voices two objections, first to the full (the fragment is called 'Saturation of the Cinema'), and second to the continuous. The constraints of representation in cinema mean that there is rarely any room for the fragment, the haiku.[53] What Barthes tried to say (though, as he acknowledged, he failed) was probably something that Schefer did manage to express very clearly: cinema images trample us underfoot, because they resemble us and force us for a while to become the real at the same time as them: 'So it is not true that they make us reflect (this is the exception – an acquired effort).'[54] Cinema envelops us – this is perhaps what Barthes call the 'saturation' of the cinema – and limits his intelligence, or at least prevents it from being freely deployed. But even if Barthes did not produce a discourse on cinema, he continued to love going to see films.

Loving loving

The thought of pleasure as set out in *The Pleasure of the Text* was the affirmation of a subject who had always made his tastes into a stimulus but no longer sought to give them the seal of science or generality, aided in this by the comfort (a relative comfort, as we shall see) of legitimacy. While his professional life was increasingly busy (he was ever more active as a teacher, in Geneva from 1971 to 1973 and later in the Paris branches of various American universities), he adorned his material life with everything to make it easier, sweeter and more enjoyable. He no longer bought his clothes exclusively from Old England, but bought suits from Hermès and shirts from Lanvin. He also developed a remarkable fondness for rings and semi-precious stones. He regularly changed the furniture and lighting in his study, and bought the best Olivetti electronic typewriters (but he found the last one he bought was too quick for him, so gave it to Antoine Compagnon). Since he felt no sense of guilt over any of his desires, he often turned their satisfaction into a principle. His relationship to money was unchanged: the more he had, the more he needed. The penury of his early years was far behind him; but he adopted his tastes and expenditure to what he had, leading a more luxurious life and proving very generous to his friends, thereby ensuring that he was preoccupied by money and worried about not having enough. 'Money creates happiness', he noted in connection with Fourier.[55] Nonetheless, now that both he and his family were financially secure, he made his daily existence more comfortable, in spite of the constraints he worked under, and the strict timetable he followed as a consequence.

The degree of comfort he allowed himself can also be gauged from his acquaintances and his leisure activities. After Morocco, he had different friends. He was close to the students attending his seminar who were themselves increasingly impressed by his aura and his intellectual freedom. His closest friends, after 1972 (with the exception of André Téchiné, with whom he often went out) were students.

The groups were not hermetically sealed from one another, but they were distinct: Barthes did not like the 'epidemic' character of friendship:[56] he liked to keep them in separate compartments. 'Friends. I always like to be alone with a friend, because the relation between several others runs the danger of hurting me more than the relation between one other and myself.'[57] In 1972, Barthes was introduced by Henri Lefebvre, whose classes he attended, to Jean-Louis Bouttes, the most enduringly significant of the people he met at that time. This relation was based on a mutual fascination: it cannot be easily described in the vocabulary of common emotions – it was what might be called a 'necessary' relationship. It was definitely a love relationship, even if it was not based on passion, sexuality or possessiveness. The young man was obstinately trying to find his own path in writing. He wrote a tormented, obscure essay with the fine title of *Le Destructeur d'intensité* (*The Destroyer of Intensity*), and was very soon giving Barthes sections of it to read. Barthes referred to it in his course on 'Le discours amoureux' and made sure it was published by Seuil in 1979, in spite of the hesitations of several of its readers. Bouttes was an assistant professor of philosophy at Nanterre, and sought to find his own voice amid the many languages of the period: structuralism, psychoanalysis (Jungian psychoanalysis)[58] and avant-garde poetry. He was a very attractive man, as we can see from the photos of the seminar, especially the one Barthes included in the iconography of his self-portrait (with its rubric '. . . among friends') where he transfigures the whole scene, making us think of Terence Stamp in Pasolini's film *Teorema*. Barthes was bowled over by this beauty, and soon found he could not do without it. He loved going out with Bouttes, and appearing at his side in public. And Bouttes often travelled with Barthes, as when they went to Tunisia together in October 1975, to Nefta, at the Sahara Palace, and then to the home of Philippe Rebeyrol in the sumptuous residence of the French Ambassador at La Marsa. Bouttes frequently went to Urt and Barthes often talked to him about what he was writing. Bouttes contributed frequently to Barthes's seminar and gave an unusual paper at the colloque de Cerisy called 'Le diamant-foudre' ('The diamond-lightning'). He was darkly dazzling, strange, sombre, unexpected. Barthes thought he had something of Des Esseintes about him, witness an anecdote noted in his card index diary: 'J.L.: in a phase where, in the restaurant, he deconstructs the menus, greatly shocking the waiters. The other evening, at Prunier's, oysters and oyster gratin, yesterday, at Le Balzar, *oeuf en gelée* and oysters, coffee ice cream and ice cream.'[59] In *Critique*, Bouttes published a very hermetic article on *Roland Barthes by Roland Barthes*.[60] 'Jean-Louis's interventions were unpredictable, with that unpredictability that only mystical timidity can allow, and Barthes, like all of us, was fascinated by those moments of pure loss when, taking the greatest risks, he managed to produce a sort of extreme poetical ceremony, on the edge of the abyss.'[61] Bouttes introduced Barthes to Youssef Baccouche; he formed a very different but equally decisive relationship with him. The two young men shared, with others, a nice apartment in the rue Nicolas-Houël, near the Gare d'Austerlitz, and this became the scene for many evenings of lively discussion that sometimes went on very late. They played games such as truth or dare, murder party, and a game invented by François Flahault, a sort of Monopoly for intellectuals that they tried out as a group. They passed round joints. They enjoyed Baccouche's generous hospitality, with fine food and plenty of drinks. Barthes went there frequently. He had a good time, he was bored, he left earlier than the others, but he liked the warm, festive and fraught company of his friends.

There were many students with whom he had intense personal relations. They included: Évelyne Bachellier, nicknamed Adé, and her brother Jean-Louis, Colette Fellous and Chantal Thomas, with whom Barthes started going to the theatre again, Renaud Camus, whom he saw in the company of William Burke, Éric Marty and Antoine Compagnon. Several of them have written very interesting accounts of the years when they were in Barthes's circle: Patrick Mauriès, Éric Marty, Yves Navarre, Renaud Camus, Nancy Huston and Colette Fellous among them. They almost all acknowledged that Barthes had played the role of an intercessor and liberator: Nancy Huston, for example, admitted that she had written her first novel, *Les Variations Goldberg*, after his death, in memory of all that Barthes had given her. Yves Navarre also recognized his debt: 'I loved him, he loved me. We told each other so. Roland never defended me, but he read me tenderly, and wrote to tell me, in a couple of words. He was my sole master in feeling. The complete opposite of a master in thinking (*maître à penser*). He told those who made fun of me in his presence that I was "the last doomed writer". And when I asked him why he said that, he replied "because you haven't been recuperated by the intellectual domain". He added: "And that's a good thing". The last time I saw him, in Saint-Germain-en-Laye, one Sunday, with anxious questions as ever, the only reply he gave me, out in the street, was that he kissed me on the mouth and bit my upper lip.'[62] Barthes was loyal and generous, he saw his friends frequently, he helped them when he could, to get published for example, or he wrote something about their work, or for them. But he did not make this support a rule of behaviour. While his presence on the jury for the Prix Médicis meant he could support books or writers that he defended (such as Tony Duvert in 1973 and Georges Perec in 1978), and his close links with Seuil authorized him to intercede for the publication of Bouttes's strange essay, he did not want to subject his affections to emotional blackmail, to the circle of duties and debts. Some of them even rebuked him for what they interpreted as his negligence towards them. One such case was Perec. As we have said, Perec attended Barthes's seminars in the 1960s, and his work, from *Things* to *I Remember* and *The Infra-Ordinary*, was highly influenced by Barthes's procedures as a semiologist, his way of demystifying the images of contemporary society while displaying a real affection for objects, lists, all the material of everyday life. Barthes had been enthusiastic about his earliest texts and had written to tell him so on several occasions: 'I believe I can sense all the novelty you expect from it: not a realism of detail, but, in the best tradition of Brecht, a realism of situation. A novel or a story about poverty inextricably bound up with the image of wealth is very beautiful, [and] very rare nowadays', he wrote to Perec in 1963.[63] And Perec acknowledged his debt. In his lecture in Warwick, in 1967, he stated that four writers had played an essential part in his writing of *Things*: Flaubert, Antelme, Nizan and Barthes. Three times, Barthes promised to express his support for Perec in writing, but he never wrote an article. Noting that Barthes had written about several artists and writers such as Sollers and Guyotat, Perec expressed his regret that Barthes had not done the same for him: 'Reading your article on Massin in a recent *Observateur* makes me regret, yet again (and I have to say it, with increasing bitterness), that you have kept your silence. The influence you have had, through your teaching and your writings, on my work and its development has been and remains such that it seems to me that my texts have no other meaning, no other importance, no other existence than those which your reading of them may provide.'[64] This was, it has to be admitted, part of the way Barthes behaved to his closest friends, and Éric Marty noted as much in his portrait: 'As for the master, he is always outside institutions, he leaves no heritage behind.'[65] On the other hand, Barthes would spontaneously write to authors in support of their work. For example, Jean-Paul Chavent remembers receiving a very warm letter from Barthes in 1976, when his first book, *C.*, was published by Éditions Toril. He lived in the provinces, far from literary circles, as a young and completely unknown author whose work was coming out with a far from famous publisher: this letter was a powerful encouragement for him.

Barthes's friendships were numerous, loyal and intense. This did not prevent serious enmities from arising. He could provoke passions that sometimes turned into real hatreds, of the kind that found expression in one case in particular, that of the so-called 'de Roux, Lapassade' affair. When Dominique de Roux's *Immédiatement* was published in 1972, Barthes learned from an article in *Le Figaro* that it referred to him in the most disobliging of terms. It contained the following story: 'One day I was with Jean Genet, Lapassade told

me, and we were talking about Roland Barthes; the way he had separated his life into two parts, the Barthes of male brothels and the
Talmudic Barthes (my description). "I said: Barthes is a man of the
salon, he's a table, an armchair . . ." "No," retorted Genet: "Barthes
is a *bergère*".'[66] Barthes took this insult very badly. He requested
that Christian Bourgois withdraw the volume. It was a tricky business, especially as Dominique de Roux had co-founded the Éditions
Bourgois and also co-directed with Christian Bourgois the '10/18'
collection. So the page had to be removed, physically. Barthes sent
all his friends out into the bookshops of the Latin Quarter to cut
out the offending page (page 187 of the first edition) with a cutter.
The same was done to all the copies in this printing – whereupon
Dominique de Roux decided to leave the company; he would never
publish with Bourgois again. He became a reporter, mainly working
in Africa. The affair actually brought Bourgois and Barthes closer.
But Barthes had been deeply wounded, and it affected his feelings
for Genet if not for Georges Lapassade, whom he had seen a lot of
in Morocco and did not like. For several days, Barthes was preoccupied with this: he consulted the lawyer Georges Kiejman, whom
he had recently met through André Téchiné, and he asked Daniel
Cordier for his advice. One might well think that he did not want
his homosexuality to be aired in public like this. But over and above
this question, which of course offended against his desire for discretion, the remarks in the book were unusually violent and bordered
on libel. However, such attacks were rare, even if Barthes's success,
his influence on several generations, aroused the resentment or the
desire for revenge of certain people (René Pommier, Michel-Antoine
Burnier and Patrick Rambaud).[67] This was the other side (one that
ultimately had little impact) of the legitimacy he had achieved.

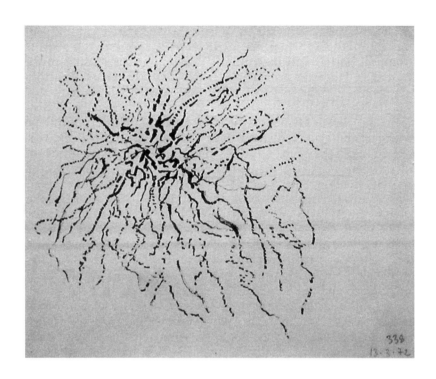

Two drawings.

Imaginary handwriting.

Barthes the calligrapher, 1978.

With Michèle Cotta, when *The Pleasure of the Text* was published.

From left to right: Roland Havas, Jean-Louis Bouttes, Roland Barthes and Youssef Baccouche.

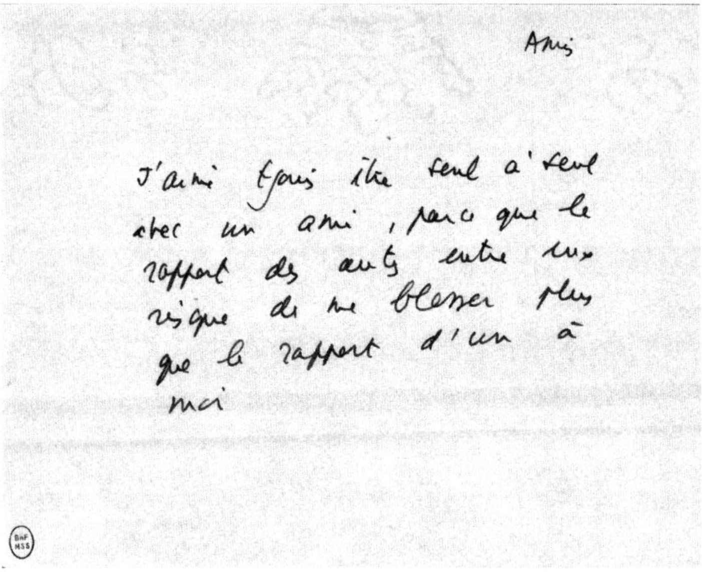

Amis

J'aime toujours être seul à seul avec un ami, parce que le rapport des amis entre eux risque de me blesser plus que le rapport d'un à moi

Grand fichier: index cards on 'Friends'.

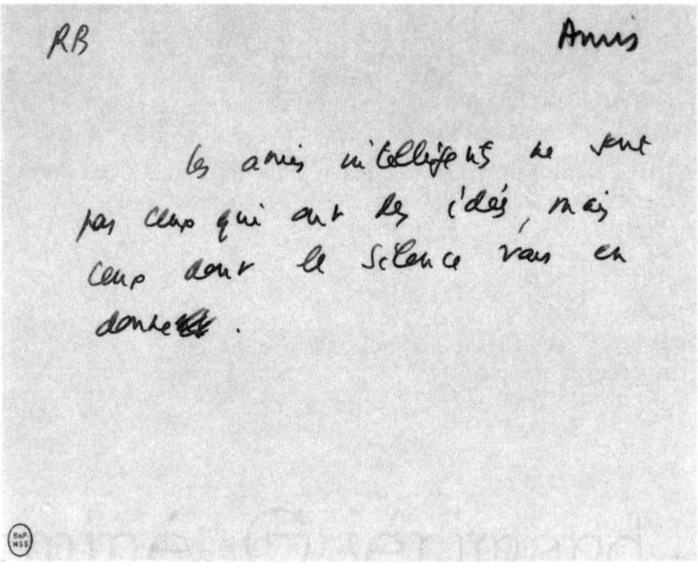

RB

Amis

Les amis intelligents ne sont pas ceux qui ont les idées, mais ceux dont le silence vous en donne.

15

Legitimacy

In the mid-1970s, Barthes was not just a recognized or fashionable thinker, but a consecrated intellectual. Consecration can be distinguished from mere recognition in that it translates fame by socially tangible elements: distinctions, privileges, money. Like other figures of his time, Barthes received these signs from several spheres at once. He was a media figure, loved by some and hated by others, always controversial. He had become one of the leading lights of the literary world, a secure presence at Éditions du Seuil, and a member of the jury for the Prix Médicis after 1973. He had found his place in the scholarly world, was constantly quoted, and asked to give lectures in universities and to address international conferences. He was also often invited abroad outside these scholarly frameworks. He was translated into English, Italian, German and Japanese. So, at the age of 60, Barthes had every reason to feel that he had been legitimated. However, as is probably the case for many people, he was not satisfied with just resting on his laurels and enjoying the benefits that he could derive from his success. There was something missing, something that impelled him to seek elsewhere while engaged ever more intensely in thinking and writing. He accepted the fact that he was in the centre – of attention, of discourse, of the institution – but he continued to feel fraudulent. We might even say that he turned this sense of not belonging into an art of living: the converse of legitimacy, a way of justifying his complaints, his boredom, his desire for something else.

The professor

By now, Barthes's reputation as a teacher was well established. In this area too, he continued to work extensively. After his time in Morocco, it was rare for him to be teaching solely at the École pratique des hautes études. In 1971–72, Barthes accepted a post as visiting professor at Geneva, and went there regularly for two days a week (Mondays and Tuesdays). There he met up with his old friends Jean Starobinski and Jean Rousset, who had been behind the invitation. He resumed his seminar on Poe's story 'The Facts in the Case of M. Valdemar' and gave a new course on *Bouvard and Pécuchet*. He made friends among the students, in particular Pierre Prentki, a brilliant man who was a devotee of Barthes's work and with whom he would stay a close friend, and Jean-Louis Bourgeois. Many of these invited him for dinner, at their homes, in Geneva and surrounding areas. He also met Bernhard Böschenstein, a specialist in Celan and Hölderlin. In addition, Barthes took this opportunity to give lectures at the polytechnic in Zurich. He enjoyed being in Switzerland and would go back just for pleasure, without obligations of any kind, to see friends and indulge in a certain *douceur de vivre*. Perhaps he also remembered his years in Leysin: in 1972, while he was in Geneva, he went back to have a look at his old haunts.

That same year, he was invited to Jean Bollack's seminar in Lille, and to Strasbourg where Jean-Luc Nancy and Philippe Lacoue-Labarthe had their research centre. He also spoke at the colloque de Cerisy on Bataille and Artaud organized by Philippe Sollers, and his paper is still remembered – his subject was Bataille, but at the same time it was a first analysis of the 'for me' based on a reading of Nietzsche: he is asking what is Bataille's text *for me*, the text I would like to have written?[1] The following year, Tom Bishop invited him to teach a course at the Paris branch of the University of New York, which he gave in tandem with his course at the École pratique des hautes études, and on the same subject ('The lexicon of the author'). As he did almost every year, in 1973 he went on a lecture tour to Italy. In 1974, with the trip to China falling in the middle of the year, he taught courses both at the Hautes études and at the State University of New York (SUNY) in Paris, and in February he lectured at several English universities, in London, Oxford and Cambridge, at the invitation of Frank Kermode. He reflected on these different exercises in transmission, and refined the protocol of his favourite kind of teaching, in small seminars. At the end of the academic year 1974, summarizing with his students at the EPHE the research they had done on the author's lexicon, he compared the way the same subject-matter could be received in two different places. With his SUNY students, he also suggested choosing words in a 'Glossary', which he then discussed in the seminar. He felt some resistance and lack of understanding on the part of American students: he explained this as the result of the fact that when foreign students spent a year in France, they expected a discussion of method or of a kind of criticism, 'not of a thought-word: there is little appeal to the body of the author, the body that writes'. The course went against what was expected, namely 'the display and demonstration of a method that was (still) deemed to be avant-garde applied to a classic author.'[2] It is easy to imagine the bafflement of the students who were expecting recipes for applying the methods of structural analysis 'made easy' to texts: what they got instead was a playful exercise conducted by Barthes, who refused to make the seminar into a place for the repetition of things that were already known, or the transmission of a well-established method, but always drove it forward, in an experimental quest.

With the posthumous publication of his courses at the Collège de France, and then of some of the courses he gave at the École pratique des hautes études, we are now in a position to see how original his teaching was. His practice of the 'seminar', in a constant dialogue with 'selected' students – from 1972, he discussed things with the audience of his restricted or small seminar and lectured alone in front of the students of the open, large seminar – meant that he could turn the pedagogic space into a veritable laboratory. Here, he could try out his books (this was true of *S/Z*, of *Roland Barthes by Roland Barthes* and *A Lover's Discourse*) that gave rise to a first oral experiment in which the spoken word was scattered and dispersed before being gathered up into a writing, and one aspect of the art of the fragment stemmed from this arrangement. 'The seminar has played a major part in my life for over fifteen years, but I also see it as having a close – albeit enigmatic – relation with writing.'[3] The courses he gave were more than just the antechambers to his books: they were their preparatory space, their 'workshop' – and the master explained that this was a rather mythological word, bearing the traces of a certain proletarian character, a populism of research. But it was still a useful word, as it evoked a 'collective place in which to work on a raw material with all the "messiness" of the labour, its fall-out etc.' The course was neither a forge nor a carpentry shop, but rather a tapestry workshop: 'We do it together without being able to see it all together, at once; we work *behind, back to front*: it is put together not in front of us, but ahead of us.'[4] So Barthes confessed to the problems and difficulties and reasons behind his work, subjecting them to collective discussion and using the exercise of his voice and his way of transmitting ideas to give them a new spin. We do not have any audio recordings of these sessions, for the very good reason that Barthes refused to allow his seminars to be recorded (though he accepted this for his lecture courses). But we can guess at his voice, we catch a sense of it in certain repetitions, in hesitations and jokes, in references to himself.

The course was also a laboratory for the teaching relationship: by giving up on the idea of the 'seminar as circus' (where he held forth in front of an increasingly large audience in a room which the École rented in the avenue Rapp), he was no longer endeavouring just to stop being professorial, but also to stop being a father – though maybe he was a mother, accompanying his students in their

'first steps' as researchers and independent thinkers. His students
were first and foremost 'friends'. In fact, there were differences: he
was on familiar '*tu*' terms with some of them but not others – even
though Barthes liked using the more formal '*vous*' as it implied a
tacit '*tu*' being held in reserve – and his own presence, his words that
everyone had come to hear, gave him a special status, a place apart.
But friendship in its very essence, as a driving force, meant that a
little utopia could be formed. The women and men who joined this
cenacle were all transformed. Patrick Mauriès later remembered the
last seminar at the EPHE, on the subject of how writers crossed out
and corrected their work. Everyone was asked to bring along work in
progress, to discuss their second thoughts and explain their changes.
'A utopia like this was difficult to sustain, and often succumbed to
the violence it contained.'[5] At a time when nobody talked about
genetic criticism, when the text was being prised away from the individuality of the author, following Barthes's own lesson, there was
something surprising about this move, which was an early harbinger
of practices of reading that are common these days. It forced all the
members in the group to look at their own writing, without falling
prey to the lure of their mirror image, and accentuating the negative. Patrick Mauriès says how intensely the premises used by the
École, with their labyrinth of staircases and corridors, the plastered
ceilings, the little rooms, remained linked to the words that were
being sought, the definition of a space which Barthes wished to turn
into a space of transference. 'The only question I am asking myself,
without having an answer, is this one: "teaching" (and its whole
transferential investment) draws in energy. Does it draw this energy
from writing? Can one teach (or be taught: as we have seen, these
are in fact the same thing) and write? Does teaching come at the cost
of writing?' This relation between teaching and writing, to which we
need to add a third term – life, biography, the self – lay at the centre
of the course. From a Nietzschean angle, Barthes defended the point
of view of subjectivity as a basis for interpretation. 'What is it for
me?' Everyone was invited to ask this question.

From the outside world, this way of teaching led to criticism that
was sometimes harsh. Barthes was rebuked for the excessively communal nature of his set-up, the way it was rather like a 'Church'
with its own 'disciples'. It was pointed out that the active listeners
risked falling into mimicry so that the whole group would end up
talking the same language. Barthes was even accused of seeking to
occupy a position of power that was all the more assured in that he
claimed to reject it. Apart from this last criticism – which is a piece
of bad faith – there was some justification for these arguments. Éric
Marty showed how friendship with Barthes was patterned on the
figures of the master and the disciple; when he refers to Jean-Louis
Bouttes, for example, he calls him the 'favourite disciple', or the one

the master loved, as in the Gospel according to Saint John. 'The Master was seated amid his disciples, and their geographical dispo- sition around him was as skilful a matter as that of the Knights of the Round Table, including even the subtle empty chair.'[6] A rela- tionship of this kind was bound to lead to imitation. When we hear the radio programme that Barthes made with six of his students, or when we read some of the interventions at the colloque de Cerisy, we are struck by the way the professor's style imbues the discourse of his pupils.[7] 'The seminar behaves like the object of an extreme complicity', said Barthes.[8] However, this occasional subjection was freely granted and everyone, as an individual, had the feeling that he or she was experiencing a rare privilege, seeing the seminar as a space that made it possible for difference to exist. 'He belonged to a tradition which, at least in France (and although we still under- value Jean Paulhan), has no name; the tradition which De Quincey, also playing on the double meaning of *sapiens*, called the "rhetori- cal" tradition and that he viewed as the alliance of intellectualism and sensuality, through a capacity for displacing boundaries.'[9] The freedom to think for yourself lay within this structure, with its room for desire and fantasy. Barthes used the image of the game of *furet*[10] as an image of the circulation of desire. Marty also relates how, before gaining a place in the restricted seminar, he had longed for this space, imagined the place he might occupy in it, and even the arrangement of the tables and the colour of the walls. 'Barthes did not speak much. He was just there. Attentive to what the students were saying. The only element of real fantasy was the presence of the two Bogdanov brothers [. . .] They formed a strange couple, apart from the rest. Barthes was fascinated by their identical beauty.'[11] Barthes was easily captivated; he allowed the other participants to be captivated by him. Many of them have preserved an indelible memory of the courses; they see them as an existential experience, a particular moment of initiation. Jérôme Peignot: 'One of the reasons for my presence at this seminar is that it was Roland Barthes has made me a writer.'[12] Colette Fellous: 'We were preparing for life, just as, a few years later, at the Collège de France, [Barthes] prepared for the novel he had never been able to write, that he thought he might perhaps write later, one day'.[13] There was an element of self-abandonment and consent in this fol- lowing of the seminar programme, requiring a subtle, free-floating attitude, open to the unpredictable; Marty gives a good impression of this self-abandonment, placing himself in the skin of the Zen disciple: 'The disciple has only one thing to do. To be there and, by the sensuality of his presence, to communicate to the master his life, something of his soul, something of his body, in exchange for which the disciple, silently and in the apparent abandonment to which the master consigns him, matures. He matures passively, drawing into himself the spiritual radiance of the master's presence, and he matures actively through the anguish he feels at not being up to that radiance.'[14] For many people, gaining a place in the seminar was like being enthroned – or at least, it replaced the ceremony of dubbing that the Visit to the Great Writer had once been deemed to confer on you. The space of the seminar, set out like a utopia, reproduced the ternary topography of Barthes's childhood home. The three spaces described at the beginning of the text that he presented to his students at the session of 8 November 1973 recall the three gardens in the Maison Lanne in Bayonne. And the text ends with the image of the 'hanging garden', bringing together 'a collectivity at peace in a world at war',[15] offering a security rather like that of childhood.

Barthes was also increasingly in demand as a thesis supervisor. He supervised doctorates and was very often invited to sit on examining juries (between fifteen and twenty per annum in the years preceding his entry into the Collège de France). Indeed, it was on one of these juries, that of his aunt Noëlle Châtelet, that Marty first met Barthes. 'Barthes had started by saying that he would have liked to write this thesis, which had caused something of a stir amid the audience. Then he had continued his patient and benevolent reading.'[16] The archives preserve most of the thesis reports that Barthes meticulously composed and that indicate how much time he spent on reading student work. He also felt duty bound to serve on examiners' juries when friends asked him to (Kristeva and Damisch at the University of Paris-7, Poulantzas and Richard at Vincennes, Lascault at Nanterre, Genette at Paris-3, and so on), and duty bound, too, to help students who had attended his seminars and whose work he had followed. He was very generous in his comments, and listened closely to what the candidates were saying. But he mainly tried to be fair, not hesitating to formulate a criticism when necessary, when a candidate confused a word with a referent, for example, or merely juxtaposed different disciplines or used puns too systematically – Barthes claimed to be impermeable to these puns even when it was a student in his own close circle who was resorting to them.

Barthes almost always began his report with a declaration of modesty, saying that he was not a specialist, emphasizing the personal, improvised nature of his considerations, leaving it to the other members of the jury to pronounce on the scientific relevance of certain projects. He spoke of the 'feeling of solidarity' or even 'complicity' that he could sometimes feel for a particular piece of work. He often noted that he would not stand in front of the work as a whole to pass judgment on it, but merely indicate a few individual points at which the work overlapped with his own interests. He liked to unveil, behind the institutional postulation of the work submitted, its 'clandestine' posture of desire and liberty. For example, discussing

Michel Chaillou's thesis on *L'Astrée*, he noted that in just one point did 'this piece of writing pick up something of the trappings of the institution – paradoxically enough, the bibliography: ample, varied, surprising'.[17] He told Raymond Carasco that his thesis, the freedom of whose montage he admired, was 'a kind of Festival'. He congratulated Chantal Thomas, who had written a thesis on Sade, for not having sought to produce results, but to write a reading: she had produced a 'very fine text, very successful as a text'. He also recognized the breadth, the responsibility and the power of the work Christian Prigent had done on Ponge. He told Lucette Finas, whose *thèse d'État* he examined as part of the jury at her viva in Aix in May 1977, that he admired the way she had overstepped structural analysis. He would later turn the remarks he made that day on the speed of reading as a modifier of meaning into an article, 'Question of Tempo'.[18] Sometimes, albeit rarely, he would express his own inclinations. For example, when Denis Viart was defending his thesis on André Gide's early work in June 1977, Barthes was there with Julia Kristeva and Hubert Damisch, and noted: 'I must in any case take into account my own relation to Gide, which is not indifferent – but it is enigmatic. So with regard to you I feel esteem and closeness, but also the hiatus of a "little difference".'

All this time-consuming and, after all, rather obscure labour shows how seriously Barthes took his job as a teacher. The wide spectrum of his centres of interest meant that he could intervene in several domains: literature, linguistics, cinema and sociology. At the University of Paris-Descartes he was even on the jury for a thesis on Chinese medicine. And he did not shy away from administrative tasks – even though he could have pleaded that he had several invitations to speak abroad so as to avoid these tasks. In 1972, Jacques Le Goff asked him if he would become a member of the bureau of the 6th section of the École pratique des hautes études. This was a period of transition in which this section was breaking away in order to become the EHESS (École des hautes études en sciences sociales); the French government had offered it a brand new building on the boulevard Raspail that had just been built by the architect Marcel Lods on the site of the former prison of Cherche-Midi. So this job was both administrative and political. Jacques Le Goff, convinced that the future of history would need it to draw closer to the social sciences as a whole, saw in the two articles that Barthes had published in *Communications*, 'Introduction to the Structural Analysis of Narratives' and 'Ancient Rhetoric, an Aide-Memoire', an analytical method applicable to a very great number of documents, including for the work of the historian. He trusted that Barthes's positively provocative side would create an image of the École as capable of shaking up the institution. So when he invited him to join a small group of five persons whose task was to imagine a future

for the section after the departure of Fernand Braudel, he was fully
aware of what he was doing, but did not think Barthes would have
time to carry out the daily paperwork. But in his homage to 'Barthes
as administrator', Le Goff described how scrupulously Barthes
acquitted himself when it came to boring or humdrum files. 'In particular, with another member of the bureau, he made it his job to
see all students who might, judging from their files, find it rather difficult to register for a doctorate.'[19] And he did so with kindness and
a great sense of fairness. Over the two years in which he was fully
involved in this work, he went abroad less frequently, was present
at almost all the Friday meetings, took part in a major meeting at
Royaumont to define a new style for the École, always expressing
his desire to simplify the statutes and make it clear that there was to
be a strong emphasis on multidisciplinarity, even if his advice was
not always followed. He attended several meetings at the Ministry,
with Jean-Pierre Soisson, who was then Secretary of State for the
Universities in Chirac's first government under Giscard d'Estaing.
The ministerial civil servants would sometimes seem flummoxed by
his language, Le Goff relates: '[S]ometimes they would gaze at him
in silence and an angel passed. More often, he would find the word
or expression that freed up the situation and created – poetically –
progress, an agreement.' Above all, Barthes had a clear vision of the
historical juncture at which the École found itself and the potential
threats hanging over it: the three risks of reproduction, marginalization and bureaucratization that would indeed become all too real in
the following years.

   If he fulfilled his tasks extremely conscientiously, Barthes did
nonetheless feel weighed down by this burdensome job. He complained to those in his circle and some of them tried to find him
a less demanding post where he would be able to devote himself
freely to his own writing. For example, Jean-Yves Pouilloux, who
with others created the department 'Science, textes et documents' at
the University of Paris-7, with a special course on Roland Barthes
himself, suggested that the latter join the team. If Barthes were to
enter this faculty, he would be freed of any administrative responsibilities. But Barthes, who was already thinking about and actively
preparing his candidacy for the Collège de France, declined. He did
however agree to give a course there the following year, on *Bouvard
and Pécuchet,* which he had started re-reading in China. Instead
of lightening his administrative load, he actually agreed to take on
extra work. If he was really to change the weighty system that his
own fame placed on his shoulders, he would probably need a more
significant sign, an even higher degree of recognition that would
liberate him once and for all from the struggle to win a name for
himself. He no doubt hoped to achieve this by canvassing for a seat
in the Collège de France.

The Collège de France

The story goes that it was Michel Foucault who was the first to suggest that Barthes try for a seat in the Collège de France, and it is true that Foucault recommended him to the other professors. Foucault also did all in his power, throughout 1975, to ensure that the campaign would be successful. However, accounts vary and a consultation of the archives suggests a rather different version of events. Didier Éribon thought it was Barthes who asked Foucault to support him, while François Wahl says he has a very precise memory of Barthes telling him: 'Michel Foucault wants me to try for the Collège.'[20] Admittedly, Foucault, elected to the Collège in 1969, to the Chair of History of the Systems of Thought, always expressed a desire to bring a breath of fresh air to the institution and introduce path-breaking new research. It was with this in mind that he encouraged Pierre Boulez to stand for election. And on the other hand, it is unlikely that Barthes would have decided to stand of his own accord. But if we examine the chronology, it is more probable that the initiative came from the historians. In fact, there were two phases in Barthes's campaign. The first opened in March 1974, when Jacques Le Goff, who doubtless wanted to thank Barthes for the help he had been giving at the École pratique des hautes études over the last two years, prepared the ground with his fellow historians at the Collège, Georges Duby and Emmanuel Le Roy Ladurie. On 5 March, they had lunch together and, in the afternoon, Barthes saw Le Roy Ladurie 'for Collège de France', as his desk diary notes. On 16 March, he met Georges Duby in his office in the place Marcellin-Berthelot and, on 20 March, Lévi-Strauss who, apparently, had no objections to his candidacy. He was relatively close to Barthes just then, as he had big plans for televising the social sciences and wanted to involve Barthes. Indeed, even before he left for China, Barthes wrote a few notes for his notice of candidacy. The discussions on the creation of a new chair were not to take place until November of the following year and it would appear that, in this preparatory phase of the campaign, Foucault was not much involved. On his return from China, in May, Barthes said he was feeling discouraged by the news from the Collège, though there was not as yet anything official. Even if he continued to see Le Goff on a regular basis, it seems that things were left hanging for a while.

A second phased opened in the spring of 1975. This was when Foucault decided to take Barthes's candidacy in hand and present him officially. On 23 April, Barthes received a letter from Le Roy Ladurie saying: 'I fully agree to your candidacy, especially now that Foucault's on your side.'[21] This note corroborates the idea that Foucault did not support Barthes at the very start, but in a second phase, when Barthes made his candidacy official. This two-phase process explains why there are contrasting stories about the events.

Things now started to accelerate. Barthes prepared his campaign with Foucault, composed the booklet that he would have to deliver to the whole body of professors, meeting with each of them individually. This booklet was titled 'Roland Barthes: Works and Projects 1975'. On his return from Urt, at the beginning of the autumn, he asked to meet the professors and started his round of visits in October and November. Foucault was lecturing in Brazil from 5 October to the eve of the elections at the end of November; Barthes became worried and phoned him several times to see how the vote was going (he drew up a table with three columns: yes, no, undecided). It has to be said that he was facing an important rival. The chair had previously been held in Greek Antiquity and occupied by the Greek specialist Louis Robert, and several classicists wanted it to stay within their discipline, even if it was the rule at the Collège that the chairs be systematically attributed to a new subject when they became free. Jacqueline de Romilly encouraged Jean Pouilloux to stand for election. He was an epigraphist, an archaeologist (he founded the French archaeological mission in Salamis, Cyprus in 1964) and a specialist on Philo of Alexandria. Several philologists fought tooth and nail for this excellent scholar to be elected, starting with the man who officially presented him, Jules Vuillemin (the philosopher who had given Foucault a post at the University of Clermont-Ferrand and then presented his chair on the 'History of the systems of thought' to the assembly of the Collège): the Indian specialist Jean Filliozat, Louis Hambis, the specialist in Mongolian civilization, André Barreau, who held the chair in the study of Buddhism, and Pierre Courcelle, who held the chair in Latin Patristics. Others, such as Emmanuel Laroche, the Hittite scholar, Marcel Bataillon the Hispanist, and the art historian André Chastel defended a third possibility, the creation of a chair in general and Romance linguistics. There were two main camps opposing one another and the campaign was hard-fought. On the one hand, there was the classical, textualist tradition, connected to the Institut de France, and somewhat right-wing; on the other, were figures who were more open to the human sciences. But Barthes was lucky enough to be able to count on a certain number of scientists thanks to Foucault's personal connections with François Jacob, but more especially because Jacques Prentki, who occupied the chair in the theoretical physics of elementary particles, spoke out vigorously to his colleagues in Barthes' support. So Barthes was sure to get a certain number of votes: scientists Pierre-Gilles de Gennes, Marcel Froissart, François Jacob, Jacques Prentki, Jacques Ruffié, Jean-Pierre Serre and Jean-Pierre Changeux were on board, as was the neuropsychiatrist Julian de Ajuriaguerra. The historians were on his side: Georges Duby, Jean Delumeau, Emmanuel Le Roy Ladurie, and Jean-Pierre Vernant. The ethnologists and anthropologists were also in the Barthes camp: Jacques Berque, André Leroi-Gourhan and Claude Lévi-Strauss. These were important supporters – but right up the end, neither Barthes nor Foucault was certain that they would be enough.

Tradition has it that the order of presentation of different chairs at the Collège is decided by lot and it first fell to Jules Vuillemin, who defended keeping a chair in epigraphy. Aware of the high stakes of the debate, he insisted on the importance of objective sciences as opposed to what might turn out to be yet another modish discourse. Then Michel Foucault presented the subject-matter that would be explored by a professor of semiology and the importance of the research that had been and might be carried out under this title. In this first round of the election, people are expected to abstain from naming the candidate under discussion and from discussing his or her work explicitly. We have the text that Foucault read out on the evening of 30 November 1975 to persuade his colleagues. His speech was almost entirely defensive: he picked up the arguments of Barthes's detractors and tried to present them with convincing counter-arguments. 'I would not be happy if I were defending a cause just because it pleases me. I wish to present a dossier. It has its positive elements. It also comes with certain question marks, and some of these strike me as significant.' Foucault first noted the force of a programme that raised the question of meaning by tackling 'the considerable example of literature', while involving the analysis of any signifying system. He then presented the path-breaking work being done. Finally, he faced up to the potential problems: was the scientific status of this work fully assured? Maybe it was just a passing fad? ('This kind of research has given rise to an inflation of pseudo-scientificity, intolerable eructations of vocabulary, a proliferation of aberrant and perverse formulations.') Foucault gave a general reply in which he referred to the disappointed and doubtless vain claim of a whole series of disciplines known as the human sciences to true scientific status, even though this had not prevented them from finding an important place within the history of culture. We need to wonder – Foucault added – whether we are not attributing too much power to so-called scientific discourse. Then, breaking with the tradition that excluded the candidate from the debate, he gave a more specific reply, speaking of 'the man who will have to carry out the highly cultivated programme that we stand for'. His whole work, and the very wide influence it had, was not simply a fad, but evidence of a fruitful enterprise. 'I will also say that the candidate in question must not be mistaken for the exaggerations that may have been committed by those close to him. Since he has had the opportunity of personally presenting to you the programme he has drawn up, I think it will have been possible to discover – and this can easily be seen from his work – and ascertain that he is a man of taste. And by "taste", I do not mean the immediate accept-ance of conformity and rules, but the perception, at once intuitive, articulate and clear, of the limit.'[22] The praise may seem a little lukewarm. But Foucault was addressing the more traditional voters who habitually saw Barthes as a provocateur, someone who would disrupt institutions. He skilfully appealed to the candidate's sense of restraint and elegance, something the professors must have noted when Barthes came to visit them, in order to reassure the commu-nity. Then it was the turn of Emmanuel Laroche to present the chair in general and Romance linguistics, and the vote took place. At 4.30 p.m., Foucault telephoned Barthes to tell him the result of the first round: twenty-three votes for his chair as against twenty-two for Jean Pouilloux's chair. That evening, Barthes went to Foucault's flat in the rue de Vaugirard to drink champagne with Duby, Le Roy Ladurie and Vernant. Jean-Louis Bouttes was also there. They discussed how the day had gone, the anxieties aroused by such a close vote: one spoilt ballot paper that was recast in a second round of voting (the first had fewer ballot papers than actual voters). The story could so easily have turned out differently.

Once the chair in semiology had been accepted in principle, the assembly of professors still had to decide on who was to fill it. This election was less risky as there was only one candidate – in spite of the almost fictitious presence of a 'second-line' candidate who had no chance of being elected, in this case Claude Brémond; by voting for the chair in semiology, the members had already agreed on who would be filling it. But for the election to be official, a second vote was still needed: it took place on 14 March 1976. Foucault gave a speech on the candidate's research, insisting on its scientific rigour (the way it used formalism as an instrument for analysing texts), and concluded with the words: 'He has not merely applied the most rigorous methods of semiology to that uncertain object, the work of literature. He has placed the literary text, the fact and institution of literature at the crossroads of a whole series of theoretical problems where the nature of language and its social operation are put to work.'[23] He also shed light on another facet of the candidate – one that he thought was important, as it showed up Barthes's differ-ence: 'Barthes belongs to the literature of these last twenty years. He has extolled it or made it possible to read it. Yes, but more than anything, what he has said about it has had an impact on it.' This time, Barthes was elected with a comfortable margin of twenty-eight votes. All the same, there were thirteen abstentions, which indicated the still intense opposition he faced. *Le Monde* officially announced his election on 11 May. He could now relish his success and tran-quilly prepare to change jobs, especially as his new position would not start until the beginning of the following year. Thus, between the start of his campaign, in March 1974, and the 'inaugural lecture' that he gave on 7 January 1977, almost three years had elapsed. The procedure had been costly, compromises had been necessary, the fears had been intense. And all of this for a result that forcefully rekindled his sense of being an imposter. On an index card dated 1 December 1975, Barthes tried to explain the indecisive nature of the vote, the effect on him of being elected by a majority of just one vote: 'That wandering, unlocatable voice (it can be anyone's voice) is the designation (the realization) of *atopia* – of my *atopia*, which makes me: *the poor representative of something for some people*: the sign (of a blockage) but a dubious sign.' The following day, his distress was even more intense since he recognized in this event a pure obsessional episode that was explicitly connected with the 'old episcopal dream of Imposture'. He, who had sought all his life long the University as something 'defined, decided, as an authority that sanctions non-imposture', saw himself – thanks to his election by one vote and the episode of the spoilt paper – on the very edge of imposture. He knew that his election had not 'gone well' and was worried there might be an appeal. 'So the contingency of the election has immediately constituted itself into an apparatus to block the enjoyment of success. And in fact, I haven't enjoyed the success. Probable that this will continue: for I'm now going to situate myself yet again under the sign of Debt, Gratitude (at having got through).'[24] The consecration had still been a trial to be endured and, once the desire for recognition had been satisfied, the worries resurfaced, perhaps even more intensely. If the Collège was indeed a place for 'consecrated heretics' as Bourdieu famously called it (though this is contradicted by over 80 per cent of the recruitments!), it was not without having to go through a degree of suffering that the authentically marginal figures found themselves at the centre.

Roland Barthes by Roland Barthes

In the middle of the decade, the consecration that Barthes had most intensely sought finally arrived: he was now recognized in the public space as a writer. When *Roland Barthes by Roland Barthes* came out in February 1975, the word appeared in almost all the reviews the book attracted. Thus, the double page spread that *Le Monde* gave to Barthes's work on 14 February (a highly significant accolade) made his new status certain three times over. There was the general article by Jacques Bersani: 'It is not literature, as an imitation of the world, that Barthes rediscovers, after his long expiatory detour through the human sciences, but writing as an act of naming. [. . .] Barthes? Yes, definitely, and in every sense, an "*écrivain de toujours*".'[25] Second, there was Robbe-Grillet's comment: 'Barthes [. . .]

is something quite different from a critic in the narrow sense of the term, but instead, definitely, a writer.' And third there was Claude Roy, saying: 'Barthes is, first and foremost, a poet.' This legitimization was all the more spectacular in that it had involved the self-affirmation of Barthes's name. Indeed, the operation carried out by *Roland Barthes by Roland Barthes* was especially declarative and subversive at the same time. Taking the collection's format literally (the titles were of the form *X by himself* or *Y by herself*) – a format that he simultaneously showed to be metaphorical – Barthes to some degree carried out the programme of madness (taking yourself for yourself) while destroying it through the system of doubling he introduced between his name and his initials, between the first-person and third-person pronouns. Twenty years after *Michelet*,[26] 'by himself' but actually written by Roland Barthes, here was Roland Barthes by himself, but written by Roland Barthes, who took himself for somebody else. The feint explains the epigraph: 'All of this . . .'. The precaution was a way of authenticating the content: if the Roland Barthes making this utterance was fictitious, the R.B. under discussion was perfectly real and it was his existence that was thus being fragmented and fragmented. It was not the person being described who was a character in a novel (so Barthes was not naively saying 'my life is a novel'), but the one making the utterance – who thereby placed his book outside the domain of autobiographical, referential writing and in that of literature instead.

With this powerful gesture, Barthes decided to consecrate his name himself, in a distanced, ironic fashion. He brought a poetical dimension of reverie into the process, turning the proper name into a sign reflecting visions, a territory, a milieu. He endeavoured to release it from what it designated: since Roland Barthes had become, in social space, the name of modern criticism, the eponym of the critic, the boldness of the move consisted in placing his patronymic in the name of the novel, on the one hand, and of the individual on the other. This displacement is made clearer by two references. The first is to the chapter in Montaigne's *Essays* which begins with the following remark: 'No matter how varied the greenstuff we put in, we include it all under the name of salad. So too here: while surveying names I am going to make up a mixed dish from a variety of items.'[27] One and the same name can become the name of all kinds of things and many ideas, anecdotes, memories and fragmentary thoughts can be subsumed under one name. Barthes does not refer to this text by name (he always said that he had not read much Montaigne), but the reference echoes in two aspects of the book: the exploration of the name and the alphabetical order. Among Montaigne's remarks in the same chapter, we also find this: 'Just as amusing as seating guests at table according to their names was the idea of the Emperor Geta who arranged his bill of fare according to the first letter of the name of each dish, serving up together those that begin with M, such as mutton, marcassin, merle, marsouin and so on.'[28] And this is the rule followed by the table (of contents, this time) in *Roland Barthes by Roland Barthes*, following a principle that he had already experimented with several times, but that was here made even more subtle, as it was twofold: the table, in which alphabetical order is sometimes concealed, is accompanied by 'Repères' that are also set out in alphabetical order like an index. He plays several games with this arrangement. The fragment named 'Alphabet', for example, appears under the letter *p*, as it takes the place of the word 'plan'; a list of 'rare, cherished words' appears in the preparatory documents excluding all the terms that begin with the letters *b* and *r*, those of his name, and with the letter *j*, the initial of '*je*' ('I'). The alphabet can be a source of euphoria in that it frees you from order and logic in favour of a meaningless, senseless list. 'This [alphabetical] order, however, can be mischievous: it sometimes produces effects of meaning; and if these effects are not desired, the alphabet must be broken up to the advantage of a superior rule: that of the breach (heterology): to keep a meaning from "taking".'[29] Thanks to this, Barthes can indulge in the free, ambulatory style – precisely the same style as the *Essays* of Montaigne, a tutelary form of interaction between life, literature and thought. Alphabetical order is also a nod to the encyclopaedia; Barthes was forever experimenting with ironic and shifting versions of the encyclopaedia, modelled on what he found in *Bouvard and Pécuchet*. The encyclopaedia of languages was also what he found so fascinating in Proust, but Flaubert's novel added the mirror of stupidity, one of the main themes of Barthes's self-portrait. The power of this stupidity was that it provided him with a remedy for stupidity itself: the copy of all languages abolishes any master language. '*Bouvard et Pécuchet* is the final farce of encyclopaedic knowledge. As the etymology suggests, forms of knowledge do indeed circulate, but *without ever stopping*. Science has lost its ballast. Nothing means anything any more: not God, nor Reason nor Progress, etc. And then, language makes its entry, and another Renaissance announces itself: there will be *encyclopaedias of language*, a whole "mathesis" (basis of knowledge) of forms, of shapes, of inflexions, of questions, threats, types of mockery, quotations and puns.'[30] Each one of these was made up of codes that could not be grasped in their entirety. Quoting them without inverted commas, in *Roland Barthes by Roland Barthes*, was a way of tackling his own 'stupidity' while demonstrating the vanity of the old protocols of knowledge. In the fragment 'The work as polygraphy', the author suggests that the work's disorder acts like a mirror, reflecting the fragmentation of the subject. 'Like the encyclopedia, the work exhausts a list of heterogeneous objects, and this list is the work's antistructure, its obscure and irrational polygraphy.'[31]

Another major reference point in his self-portrait is given by
Barthes himself in an article in the *New Critical Essays*, 'Proust
and Names'. Before the 1979 celebrated lecture at the Collège de
France, this text (dating from 1967) was already highlighting the
connection between biography and novel: '[T]he precocious desire
to write (formed as early as his lycée years) was followed by a long
period not of failures but of groping, as if the true and unique
work were being sought, abandoned, resumed, without ever being
found.'[32] Barthes was talking about Proust, but also about himself,
even in the subsequent section where he refers to a 'crossing of literature' in which the books of others fascinate and then disappoint
us . . . If the narrator discovers the possibility of writing thanks to
his memories, the author needs to make a similar discovery that
can stand in for these memories: this is the discovery of the proper
name, which can – like memories – constitute the essence of novelistic objects. 'The proper name possesses the three properties which
the narrator concedes to reminiscence: the power of essentialization
(since it designates just a single referent), the power of quotation
(since one can at will summon up all the essence enclosed within
the name simply by uttering it), and the power of exploration (since
one "unfolds" a proper name exactly as one does a memory).'[33] The
name is a sort of total sign – and here, Barthes's approach was akin
to that of Deleuze: although he did not read Deleuze's *Proust and
Signs* until after he had written his article, he was very impressed by
it and added a footnote to his Proust article in 1972. As a sign, the
name is open to exploration. It is a storehouse of novelistic possibilities (with all the history, the landscapes and images this involves)
and a hub connecting the different signs of the work. To write a
novel, then, is to invent names: the narrator of *In Search of Lost
Time* becomes the reader, the interpreter, the decoder of the names
which the author has invented: Parma, Guermantes, Combray.
Actually, one of the problems Barthes encountered when he felt
the desire to write a novel was that he was fascinated by the names
made up by others but felt unable to invent any for himself: 'I can't
invent proper names and I really think that the whole novel lies in
proper names – the novel as I read it, of course, and this indeed is
what I've already said with regard to Proust. Right now, I resist
having to invent names, and at the same time I have a very strong
desire to invent them. Maybe I'll write a novel the day I've invented
the proper names for this novel.'[34] Barthes traced this rather
mysterious fascination for onomastics back to the names of the
bourgeois families of Bayonne, 'their consonance, their pure poetic
phonetism, as well as their social and historical weight'.[35] He quotes
their names: 'Mmes Leboeuf, Barbet-Massin, Delay, Voulgres,
Poques, Léon, Froisse, de Saint-Pastou, Pichoneau, Poymiro,
Novion, Puchulu, Chantai, Lacape, Henriquet, Labrouche, de

Lasbordes, Didon, de Ligneroles, Garance.'[36] Each of these names, from childhood, from novels, illustrates the move from the signifier to *significance*, to the opening of a desire that is not so much for a person as for sounds and smells, for the remnants of something that exists no longer.

In this kaleidoscopic self-portrait, made up of fragments – images with captions and little blocks of text – Barthes shifts his name from out of the social sphere and brings it into that of fiction, turning it into a sort of pseudonym. Thus he can stage himself, in an imaginary form, in accordance with his fantasy and 'without proper names'. He explains this tactic in fragments entitled 'Myself, I' and 'The book of the Self': '"I" mobilize the image-repertoire, "you" and "he" mobilize paranoia.'[37] A distance is thus created between the 'I' and the 'me', as when he also uses 'he' to refer to 'himself'. There are several characters and they are all characters in a novel, including the R.B. used in passages where a 'he' would be ambiguous (and to which, indeed, Barthes does not want us to attach too much importance). The book works by alternating these ploys, inviting us to change our ideas of genre: 'Let the essay avow itself almost a novel: a novel without proper names.'[38] In other words, if we are to believe Barthes (and even though Robbe-Grillet had showed that it was perfectly possible to write novels without proper names), not exactly a novel.

It took a while for the shape of the book to be decided. It all started on 19 September 1972, with a lunch in the rue Jacob where the 'Écrivains de toujours' series was being discussed. Denis Roche, the editor of the series since 1970, joked that it would be a nice idea to ask a living writer to write a *real* 'X by him/herself'. Barthes immediately said that he would find it amusing to accept the challenge. He thereupon drew up a preparatory, experimental programme with two basic plans. First, in the summer of 1973, he reread all his own work to make a list of themes and notions (he indexed this, which gave him the idea of a glossary) and to choose suitable passages for an anthology (which he finally did not compile, even though this was usually part of the format requirements of the series). And in the autumn of 1973, he started to give his course on 'Le lexique de l'auteur', in which he asked his students to work from the glossary he had drawn up over the holiday period in Urt. As for his solitary work, this rested on a twofold approach: he would analyse the subject 'Roland Barthes' according to two different temporalities at once: the past (this was the function of his rereading and the composition of the 'biography' that we quoted in the first chapters, above), and the present. To grasp the present without falling back into pure subjectivity, he started a diary on 1 July, keeping it up regularly throughout the summer, before consigning it to index cards in September. By resorting to this complex, staggered approach, he was trying to avoid two main risks in the whole enterprise: infatuation and the mirror. He thus managed to cohabit pleasantly with the project, 'but with the constant and unresolved presence of a Fault: 1) talking about oneself; 2) taking it for granted that one has created an "oeuvre".'[39]

The whole of this work in progress is preserved in a separate dossier, the 'Fichier vert', which contains more than 2,000 index cards.[40] Barthes again went back to the idea of the glossary on which his doctorate on fashion had been based; but this time it was much more difficult to compile because the alphabetical entries did not refer to words, but to themes and motifs that ran through his life and work. When he started giving his course on 8 November 1973, he had already done the entries for the first letters of the alphabet (ninety-four words beginning with A: Aggression, Aimer [Love], Amaigrissement [Slimming], Anachronism, Automobile, etc.; thirty-five beginning with B (including Barthes, Bayonne, Bêtise [Stupidity], Biography and *Bouvard and Pécuchet*), and sixty-seven beginning with C (Café, Chaplin, Citation [Quotation], Code, Corps [Body], etc.). He found it very difficult to draw up these lists and, during the autumn of 1973, he was tempted to ditch the lot. But, after a discussion with Denis Roche in December 1973, he decided to make the glossary more flexible by using a system of fragments (that would include the material from several index cards). He started to write them in the spring of 1974 and gave them their final form in mid-1974 while on a long summer break at the home of his friend Daniel Cordier in Juan-les-Pins from 25 July to 16 August. At the same meeting with Roche, he abandoned the 'selected passages' approach: they were just too difficult to disentangle. He hesitated between a very simple plan: literature/teaching; or weaving the anthologies into the text; or else 'just including successful sentences, formulas, quotations (but then I'd have to reread myself yet again!)'. By freeing himself from this work, and thus the chronology of his oeuvre, Barthes could finally go for a disseminated organization.

Rereading himself proved to be a disturbing experience. He was now a reader of his own work, unable to catch his texts in the nets of his own desire. 'My books. Occasionally (when reading some dazzling contemporary work: Julia [Kristeva]) I feel so inferior ("depressed"), so reduced to non-existence, that I am forced, in order to exist just a bit, to remember that the books by me have been published, acknowledged – and so I have at least their consistency.'[41] In the same bundle of remarks that he had eliminated or marked for revision: 'Rereading. The risk of mere chatter. Rereading myself – to do this book on myself, by myself – I swing between two opposing feelings: 1) that I immediately started out saying intelligent things, interesting things, that it's all remarkable, subtle, coherent, well-expressed, etc.; in short that I'm not recognized enough, undervalued; 2) that I'm a moron, that it's full of holes, *improbable* things, etc. I note this, a commonplace feeling, because it's the situation of the tragic hero struggling with the *uncertainty* of the signs of God (the god of value, of quality, *does not speak*) – and also the Proustian situation where he discusses the way signs become reversed. – Also the feeling that I can comment very slowly, step by step, in great detail (one whole morning spent on a short page in *Degree Zero*). Any text is good for me: the *chatterbox* can hold forth.' As he explained in his course, he was scared of rereading because to write 'is to kill, to liquidate, to disinvest';[42] either it's botched (in the present) or it was good (in the past and thus impossible to do again). Furthermore, rereading involved a certain weariness; it forces us to realize how boring we are, sometimes. The index cards on his books, if reread in the right order, show a consummate art of self-critique. One rubric, entitled 'scoria', brings together the passages he now rejected, for example in *Critical Essays*: 'Écrivains and écrivants: it's bad, confused, useless – apart from the actual distinction between them.' Every book he had published was dealt with in a number of index cards, from five (for *The Eiffel Tower*) to a good score (for *Mythologies* and *Empire of Signs*). Some examples:

— *On Racine*. A book of great wisdom, of great common sense – which only a madman could declare was mad.

— *The Language of Fashion*. The strange thing is that this book was never acknowledged by linguist-semiologists. A neglected book? Censored? Why? (after all, the pure, orthodox semiologists would at least have had to *cite* it).

— *S/Z*. It seems that, right from the start of *S/Z*, the style changed into its current form: something more finely honed, more continuously successful.

— *Empire of Signs*. The 3 texts on the Haiku are so good that I can't think of anything to say about them – and I'm scared, really scared, that I'll never do anything like them again.

— *The Pleasure of the Text*. A *reactive* book. Every fragment is an *attitude towards the other*: not to apologize; the answer to all those who accuse you of contradicting yourself, etc.

— *The Pleasure of the Text* is full of interlocutors who are never named – but they slip by at the turn of a sentence. – Friendly opponents: Lévi-Strauss, Greimas, Todorov, Goldmann, etc.

Other index cards contain anecdotes or notes that might shed light on his character or life. They are often, but not always, headed by a title linking them into the glossary:

— *Subversion.* An important idea: mistrust of 'madness' (Flaubert: making holes in discourse *without making it sense-less*). A difficult attitude: you can't be against madness (all of modernity: Foucault, Deleuze, Sollers, Artaud, Bataille, etc.) – but at the same time you need to resist the demagogy of madness (Blessed are the Mad for they shall be Modern!). Behind all that: I'm scared of the mad because they're *such a bore.*

— *Fiction.* An example of Fiction: I need to get back to Paris, and come up with the idea of using my time in the train to set up a *system for saving money* (I'm spending too much) that I will put into practice in Paris.

— *Indirect.* Explain why (such a paradox) RB, though he is greedy for language, (and especially the word) has never been interested in *Poetry*. This is because he needs the *indirect*, i.e. a greedy prose (or a prosaic poetry: Baudelaire).

— *Neutral.* Could *exemption of meaning*, this theme that is so distant and persistent within me (probably ever since childhood, where I demanded a sort of right to the *neutral*) have – neurotically – the same scope as the *rejection of conflict* (*saying-no* to conflict)?

— *Fear.* Absence of the Father → paradoxically: Fear, for – you're not protected: the Mother: you're afraid on her behalf. – In the Freudian version, the discourse that you're afraid because, not having a father, you don't have an Enemy.

— *Avant-garde.* Castration. RB. My attachment to style, to the sentence, to the classic, to the fragment, etc. is homosexual (let's call it perverse). The (feminine) *chora* merely gleams like a *later.* Not to die a homosexual![43]

The fascinating genesis of *Roland Barthes by Roland Barthes*, largely revealed by Anne Herschberg Pierrot in her excellent edition of the *Lexique d'auteur*, where she reproduces the full set of abandoned fragments (but not all those preparatory index cards or all the abandoned cards), remains an open construction site, a rare example in an author who was systematically going back over his work. The experience is especially interesting because, in Barthes's effort to turn the reader into an author, his self-affirmation as a writer involves a reading, in the literal and the figural senses of the term. To turn oneself into the object of a course – since, with his students, he was not just working on texts, but also on habits, tastes, whims (he liked smoking cigars, he was an amateur piano player . . .) – meant immediately presenting oneself as something to be read. The reader and the writer, following the programme begun with *S/Z* in which the domain of reading is considerably extended, are inseparable figures. Every reader is potential writer. Every writer is first a reader.

The first course avoided several pitfalls, including that of the superior posture, of the 'critical imposter'. If Barthes had merely created a double figure out of himself, RB^1 and RB^2, the whole thing would inevitably have appeared parodic. He even says that he thought for a while that he might follow the layout of his *Michelet* and apply it to himself. So there was the fleeting temptation of self-pastiche. The false distance created by self-doubling could also have seemed really artificial. By using several pronouns, conversely, he was creating a constellation rather than a hierarchy. In this way, he avoided the danger of transforming his life into a destiny and giving it a regular or at least explicable shape. The book's slow process of maturation gave it an experimental character. By agreeing to submit his doubts to public appraisal, noting the absence of a precise image for the project, his changes of mind, taking advantage of the remarks people made to him and the transformations time imposed on his venture, Barthes was gradually creating a new object that could not be subsumed into any preconceived genre or idea.

Having finished reading and revising his manuscript at the end of summer 1974, he once again gave it to Jean-Louis Bouttes (who had attended the seminar) for a critical reading. Barthes made some major corrections in response to the criticisms of Bouttes, and dropped some fragments even though they were already finished. 'Abandoned after J.L. read through it: Metaphor, The return, the cloth, I am merely a sign (pretentious), Displacement, Reversal as production (pretentious), The double expression, Philology, The mirror, Happy (no – who's that going to interest?!), What is the use of Ancient Greece (weak), Seeing (banal), Top of the class (the risk of self-infatuation), Life as text.'[44] Anything that might seem banal, stereotypical, flattering or predestined was systematically dropped. In this way, Barthes developed a new form of autobiography, an advanced form of autofiction (the term was coined only a few years later, by Serge Doubrovsky) where different levels were mixed together: the like-a-novel, the reminiscence (the 'anamneses' whose genesis we analysed above), the essay and the analysis. The invention lay in what he called the 'biographematic', using a biographeme to conduct an argument and create a form of writing that he had been developing since *Sade, Fourier, Loyola*, as the discreet, delicately fragmented shape you may give to somebody's life. This Barthesian theme has become very widespread (and the word 'biographeme' is now in the dictionaries). Writers had long since taken on board the idea that the self is dispersed and that it is difficult to produce a chronicle of identity, but the term 'biographeme' itself came as a welcome label for the resultant shards. A biographeme is not metonymic: it is not a kind of blazon, a fragment expressing some totality of being. Nor is it an insignificant detail. It defines a taste, a value, a milieu, a desire:

'When I buy colours, it is by the mere sight of their name.'[45] And: 'In recalling the little things he had been deprived of in his child-hood, he found what he liked today: for instance, iced drinks.'[46] It draws distinctions, but in a way that is ethnographical rather than sociological. Thus Barthes came to realize, before everyone else, the consequences of the end of unifying reason for the way we think of the subject and the importance of finding new forms of narra-tive for the self. The routes taken by autofiction, by biographical narrative in contemporary literature, owe a great deal to this path-breaking text that inaugurated what can already be considered to be something of a French tradition.

The association between the biographeme and the photograph, made explicit in *Camera Lucida*, was first demonstrated in the self-portrait. The photos in the first part are not there simply as illustrations, nor just because the format of the series required it. The interplay between images and captions is another way of producing a biographeme, an open form of meaning emerging from the detail. It also encourages us to read the fragments that follow as snapshots, freed from the illusory continuity of the nar-rative, readable as so many moments in the life of a body. Barthes paid great attention to this section and its layout on the page, and worked on this aspect with Isabelle Bardet at Seuil. The genesis of the captions and the number of 'abandoned captions' – they can be consulted in *Le Lexique de l'auteur* – are proof of this. The photos, the drawings, the examples of handwriting, do not have the same function as in *Empire of Signs*, where the images still appeared as moments from a traveller's tale, even if they did not constitute pure illustrations. They are so many surfaces in which the subject is reflected for a moment or in brief flashes of light. Writing, in its movement, abolishes depth: 'The text *figures* the infinite of language: without knowledge, without rationale, without intel-ligence.'[47] And: 'Whereby I cast over the written work, over the past body and the past corpus, barely brushing against it, a kind of patchwork, a rhapsodic quilt consisting of stitched squares. Far from reaching the core of the matter, I remain on the surface, for this time it is a matter of "myself" (of the Ego); reaching the core, depth, profundity, belongs to others.'[48] If the autobiographi-cal gesture has its critical aspect, this is not because it wards off the subject that once was (as Sartre does in *Words*), but because it prevents any unification by narrative or meaning. It repeatedly diffracts and then retracts that subject, constructing it as the object of a mobile, non-totalizing encyclopaedia that is endlessly being recomposed, giving knowledge with one hand while taking it away with the other.

When it came out, the book was very well received, even though reviews were not always aware of the radical nature of Barthes's work, or at least merely reduced it to the circularity of 'by himself'. The style of the interviews with Barthes and the questions he was asked changed. He was asked many more personal questions, to which he gave patient and benevolent answers. He thus brought into the social sphere elements that had been absorbed in his writing – biographical and family details, indications about his milieu and his preferences. This re-established a sense of continuity even though Barthes told Jean-Louis Ézine in an interview for *Les Nouvelles littéraires* that he preferred the shuffling of a kaleidoscope to the idea of a unified subject. He did not want to endorse the feeling that his working life had an evolution, a meaning, but in interviews he was often drawn into marking out phases, stages, changes. One of the reasons for sometimes being tempted to divide Barthes's work into 'moments' actually comes from *Roland Barthes by Roland Barthes* itself, where there is a fragment – entitled 'Phases' – that divides his oeuvre into four 'genres' corresponding to four successive periods and different intertexts: social mythology, semiology, textuality and morality.[49] In line with the programme of the self-portrait, we should abstain from reading this passage independently and put it in the context of the rest of the book. However, people jump on it as if it were promulgating some final truth; interviews exaggerated this process, which fostered a sense of definite breaks and evolution. Barthes reinstated a sense of continuity in the spoken word: 'when I was a child', 'when I was young' . . . 1975 was the year of 'Twenty Key Words for Roland Barthes', a text that was to some degree a continuation of the glossary in *Roland Barthes by Roland Barthes*, albeit without the interplay between the persons and the fragments. The fictional aspect disappeared. This was also the year in which Barthes gave a long interview to Jacques Chancel on France Inter, 'Radioscopie', in which he talked about himself at length. But if several newspapers added confidential remarks to the confession, others, such as *Le Monde*, allowed other voices to be heard. Alain Robbe-Grillet, Pierre Barbéris, Claude Roy and Philippe Sollers were given an opportunity to say who Barthes was for them. Sollers, for example, said that he had 'grown up in Barthes's shadow', and that Barthes was the least right-wing writer of any he had had the occasion to meet. And Robbe-Grillet saw him as a great transfigurer of language. Many critics agreed that Barthes had his own style: they could do so not just because of the author's personal tone in this book, but because *Roland Barthes by Roland Barthes* began with a positive conception of style, which had previously been seen rather negatively in *Writing Degree Zero* and *Sade, Fourier, Loyola*. 'In what he writes, there are two texts. Text I is reactive, moved by indignations, fears, unspoken rejoinders, minor paranoias, defences, scenes. Text II is active, moved by pleasure. But as it is written, corrected, accommodated to the fiction of Style, Text

I becomes active too.'[50] Ellipsis, fragment, variation, rhythm: such
is style, allowing him to free himself from an immediately reactive
discourse. Style also has the qualities of the voice, whose grain it
allows to be heard in writing. The voice has the fragility of the body,
it bears its humours and its affects. It shares with photography a
way of pointing to something that 'has been'. So it is easy to see why
the seminar 'The author's lexicon' was accompanied by a workshop
on the voice, in which he played *lieder* sung by Charles Panzéra,
Fritz Wunderlich and Kathleen Ferrier. 'It is the body that sings,
in a way both dazzling and secret', a *'full-throated murmur'*.[51] This
discreet intimacy, offering a certain sense of familiarity, was doubtless what most deeply touched Barthes's correspondents, who wrote
to thank him for sending them copies of his book. Fernand Braudel
loved its 'simplicity and poetry'; Maurice Pinguet was struck by
its elegance: 'This is an elegance purified of any theatricality, any
insolence, any modishness. And it coincides with the wisdom that is
so greatly to be desired and the perfect freedom to be.' Jean-Pierre
Richard mentioned 'the book's almost boundless slipperiness' and
spoke of its 'familiarity' and 'purity', 'a note that belongs to you
alone, and where delicacy, insolence and sensuality are indissociably
combined'.[52]

But the most spectacular critical notice of the book came from
Maurice Nadeau, who gave Barthes the opportunity to disseminate
the proper name even further. 'Barthes puissance trois' ('Barthes
cubed') was published in *La Quinzaine littéraire* on 1 March 1975.
Barthes here subjected his text to the type of analysis he had
deployed in *Mythologies*, exposing the ideology underlying it and
the imagery accompanying it. At the same time, Barthes ironically
dismantled the legitimacy of his name dispersed into many different figures. 'However much he might try to pile up declarations,
interviews and articles, surrounding himself with a cloud of commentaries, like the cuttlefish with its ink, it will not work: as an
imaginary and ideological subject, miscognition (not error, but the
endless passing on of truth through language) is his fateful lot, whatever he may write on himself and whatever name he signs his work
with – even if it were the most tried and tested of pseudonyms: his
own name, his Proper Name.'[53] Barthes was now definitely keeping
his name within the realm of the imaginary. He showed that it, too,
could be a fantasy. He thus relativized the scope of any consecration. This meant that, on Jacques Chancel's radio programme, he
could say: '[G]ratifications of a social order can be intense, but they
never last very long, as you are drawn back by the responsibility of
your work, by the need to do something else, to continue, and you
are then caught up in the old doubts, anxieties and difficulties that
are the usual fabric of our lives.'[54] So he allowed his name to be
diluted into so many pseudonyms.

The colloque de Cerisy

Cerisy saw the triumph of 'R.B.', who has since enjoyed a great
critical success. What had initially been a designation 'with no
importance', borrowed from Sollers to clarify the occasionally
ambiguous meaning of 'he', assumed all the features of a myth: that
of the *written Barthes* – Barthes in his writings, the Barthes on whom
people wrote without taking his person into consideration, the
Barthes who wrote or was about to write. At the 1977 conference,
calling Barthes by his initials also signalled a certain familiarity with
him. Here too, Barthes himself was not keen on turning this into
a 'familiar code'; he might conceivably turn it into a pseudonym
like Erté, but he would write it with an 'h', as 'Herbé' (Philippe
Roger would turn this figure into a character in a 'novel'). In the
conclusions to the conference, Barthes even mentioned the feeling
of a dispossession, whether a pleasant or unpleasant feeling is difficult to say: 'Imitating the Tao, we have practised Wang-Ming,
the Abstinence of the Proper Name, as if the deeper purpose of the
conference was to teach us to let go of the name. And even when the
proper name (mine) has been uttered, this has always been, it seems
to me, through a practice of the indirect.'[55] And those speaking at
the conference were indeed asked to use Barthes and his work as
a 'pretext' to develop their own ideas: Barthes may have had the
impression of being submitted to the 'idol' of each of them. He
appreciated the indirect for himself, but he was not necessarily that
keen on being a prop or instrument for every language.

It was in 1976 that Mme Heurgon-Desjardins told Barthes that
she wished to organize a colloque de Cerisy dedicated to his work.
She had already asked him, but he had declined. Her daughter Édith
Heurgon sent Barthes a letter on 23 January 1973 saying that she
would like to organize a session on his work at Cerisy in July 1974,
to which he replied: 'I am very touched . . . but in all sincerity I do
not really feel ready for such a conference; I have the feeling (perhaps
illusory) that my work still has new phases to go through and for
now it would not offer itself up to collective commentary with sufficient richness.'[56] This time, he accepted the invitation, so as not to
construct an image of himself as the person who refused to have a
conference on his work, but also because, now, he felt that his work
had taken off enough and his legitimacy was tangible enough to act
as a pretext. However, he laid down one condition: the management
of the conference should be entrusted to one of his favourite students,
a young man he had met the previous year, Antoine Compagnon.
This decision caused some surprise. Compagnon was 26, and had
no experience of this kind of event. Probably Barthes wanted to
avoid having to 'choose' between his long-term friends, especially

as there were dissensions and rivalries between them. He did not want to favour those in the *Tel Quel* group (Sollers, Kristeva), nor those from the École pratique (Genette, Todorov, Brémond) or from Vincennes (especially Jean-Pierre Richard). A student who was as yet not known to anyone struck him as a neutral choice. It was also a choice dictated by his feelings. At that time, Compagnon was one of his major interlocutors. Barthes dined with him almost every week and talked to him at length about his work, to which, in return, his friend imparted the dynamism of his youth, his desire for literature and his own projects. 'In a conversation, it was impossible to impute an idea to one or other of us. Barthes would set out a difficulty; and we talked; all at once he would pause, open his notebook and scrawl a few words.'[57] Barthes knew he could count on someone completely dedicated to him, like a disciple – their lifestyle and their work meant that they were still very close.

This decision did however raise eyebrows. And at the conference, which took place between 22 and 29 June, several people were conspicuous by their absence. At the last moment, Sollers declined to come and Genette, Todorov and Brémond decided not to attend. Kristeva was absent, too, but for more personal reasons: she had recently become a mother and had better things to do than waste her time at conferences. The fact remains that the intermediary generation, between the ages of 35 and 45 – people who had been close to Barthes in the 1960s – was hardly represented (except by Jacques-Alain Miller, a somewhat marginal figure because of his speciality, and Hubert Damisch). However, some of those who were near contemporaries of Barthes (Jean-Pierre Richard and Alain Robbe-Grillet, both born in 1922, and François Wahl, born in 1925) and a throng of students (Françoise Gaillard, Éric Marty, Patrick Mauriès, Contado Calligaris, Évelyne Bachellier, Jean-Loup Rivière, Jean-Louis Bouttes, Frédéric Berthet, etc.) did turn up. About a hundred people registered for the event, because they liked the work or simply to meet a famous man. As always at Cerisy, the public was very varied, but everyone gathered in the double dining room and slept in the different buildings of the property, the chateau, the old farm, and the stables. Like all VIPs, Barthes was accommodated in a room in the chateau. He was accompanied, for the whole week, by a young student from Caen whom nobody else knew, and who – said Éric Marty – looked like Yann Andréa: it was indeed Yann Lemée (the future Yann Andréa), whom Barthes had met two months before. Early each morning, he would go for a coffee in the village with Compagnon: a time he could be apart from the others in a beneficent little ritual. Every evening he would phone his mother at home, who had been ill since the spring and whose health was causing him terrible worries.

Barthes was seriously worried, and threatened by the greatest dread – the death of his mother, a dread that in different ways haunted the conference. 'At the origin of everything, Fear' – the formula that he used at the start of his own paper: fear of stupidity, fear of humiliation, fear of being deprived of protection; above all, the fear at the origin, in the place of and instead of the father; and fear of conflict, the object of his paper. In spite of all this, the week went off well. Robbe-Grillet's contribution was its high point. It gave rise to a dialogue with Barthes and a confrontation with the audience that turned it into a real happening (part of the legend of that mythical era, when the big conferences in the human sciences resembled boxing rings). Robbe-Grillet very acutely noted the difficulty at the heart of Barthes's very name; he suggested this was not just a reference to the writer, but indicated a powerful presence of the body in his text: 'In short, louche, suspicious relations, or at any rate relations that are condemned by a whole tendency in modernity that even recently I still thought it was worth encouraging.'[58] Their difference of opinion in the 1960s was given a friendly airing and, quite spectacularly, Robbe-Grillet adopted the role of the critic, proclaiming the death of the author, while casting Barthes in the role of the author: 'This very intense intervention of the character in the text, the sensation that I am dealing with a body, with instincts, with things that are probably a bit unclean, means that the text tends to become a mere spokesman for this body, which is after all hateful for somebody who, like me, has taken part in this whole evacuation of the author from his text.' The roles had been swapped, but Robbe-Grillet still saw Barthes as being ahead of the game. The French New Novel had come to a dead end: if anything new could happen in the novel, it would have to come 'from somebody who would refuse to be a professional novelist'. 'With *A Lover's Discourse*', Robbe-Grillet told Barthes, 'you've taken not a step towards society, but your own step to what will, perhaps, in 20 years' time, appear as the New New New Novel of the 1980s. Who knows?'[59] There was still this idea that Barthes's intelligence made him a precursor, that there was more future in his contradictions than the authoritarian affirmations and manifestoes of modernity.

Barthes responded to everyone with a great deal of generosity and benevolence. He did not contradict anyone head-on but was able to show firmness in his disagreements. For example, he maintained, against Jacques-Alain Miller and Alain Robbe-Grillet, that his body was not in his text, but a fantasy of the body. He took care that nobody in the audience would feel excluded. He was not always very comfortable about being so much the centre of attention, the object of discourse. His desire to reduce the glare of the light being directed at him come across clearly in the allegory he invented for the occasion, with a place that would not be called Cerisy-la-Salle but Brume-sur-Mémoire or Haze-on-Memory: 'This is an idea that might have consequences for writing; writing could be the domain of the haziness of memory, and this haziness of memory, this imperfect memory that is also an imperfect amnesia, is basically the domain of thematic criticism.'[60] Haziness, indirection, secrecy, mentioned earlier at the conference in connection with Stendhal's *Armance* (where the secret is not revealed) remained kindly fairies, tempering the 'me' and the 'for me' with uncertain shadows.

The first half of 1977, from the inaugural 'Lecture' at the Collège de France in January to the publication of the *Lover's Discourse* in March and the colloque de Cerisy in June was indubitably a moment of consecration. Coming shortly before the death of Barthes's mother, it soon revealed how vain is public legitimacy when it can no longer be recognized by the person you love most. The private cataclysm immediately swept away all the symbolic benefits of distinction.

At the home of Daniel Cordier, while writing
Roland Barthes by Roland Barthes.

The seminar.
Front row, left to right: Roland Havas, Denis Ferraris, Roland Barthes,
Jean-Louis Bouttes, Christine de Buzon, Mathieu Lindon. Second
row: Jean-Loup Rivière, Patrice Guy, Sylvaine Pasquet, Évelyne
Cazade, Chantal Thomas, Youssef Baccouche, Colette Fellous, Renaud
Zuppinger, Joël Farges.

16

Barthes and Foucault

At Cerisy, Robbe-Grillet suggested that Barthes and Foucault were akin in that they were often placed in an impossible situation: 'You just have to see the glee with which society recuperates Barthes and Foucault. When Foucault, a cutting-edge, marginal figure, talks with great subtlety against sexual discourse, you have to see how *L'Express* and even *L'Observateur* publish articles: "Ah, at last, we're free of the dictatorship of sex!"'[1] When we read on the Internet or elsewhere how much the two writers are quoted on every subject, with the critical dimension of the *Mythologies* losing all its effectiveness when the texts are quoted to evoke a nostalgic exaltation of the objects discussed (the Citroën DS, red wine and steak frites), we can see how right Robbe-Grillet was to speak of 'recuperation'. The particular place occupied by these two thinkers in the shadow casts by the years 1960–70 can be explained by the way their work has been absorbed into a certain form of doxa, even if they always fought against this very doxa. They were both aware of the mechanism of this inversion, which Barthes explicitly denounced. The tetrasyllable 'Barthes and Foucault' is used to refer to an entire period, the influence of French thought, the renewal of the human sciences, a time when theory turned out 'great names' or 'great figures'. How often do we hear people these days lamenting that there are no more 'great thinkers', while failing to see that the fostering of such models does not depend solely on their own qualities but on the choice a society makes to identify with them. The fact remains that we may feel nostalgic for a period in which theorists, philosophers and writers could be turned into media stars – that is, representatives and possible objects with which to identify – even if this involved a reductive reading of their work.

The reasons for the two to be coupled together were also different. Deleuze was also often quoted, and his work used as a toolbox, though his person was less emblematic: during his lifetime he was less present on the media stage, even if he was involved (and probably more directly than Barthes) in major endeavours such as La

Borde and Vincennes. His image remained that of the singular writer, involved in a quest to construct his conceptual oeuvre. On the other hand, the activities and commitments of Foucault and Barthes were to be seen as inseparable from their intellectual production (even if the latter was also developed to a great extent in scholarly concentration and withdrawal). This goes some way to explaining the biographical constellation that has spread around them, as if understanding their lives could give us access to their thought. One plausible hypothesis is that their relation to history, expressed very differently in their work but in both cases a major question, raises the issue of their own place in history (an issue debated both by them and by others). A second hypothesis lies in the (relative) marginality conferred on them by their homosexuality: their critical intelligence led them both not to separate their desire from their objects of study and to see homosexuality not as an orientation but as a way of questioning the world. This was perhaps even truer of Barthes than of Foucault, in spite of what appearances might suggest. While, unlike Foucault, Barthes never turned his sexuality into a space for contest and combat, partly because he disliked the noisiness of confrontational language, he nonetheless pushed very far something that, at the time, might have corresponded to his critical programme: the rejection of the 'natural', of what seems self-evident, of the bourgeois order presented as spontaneous, and the liking for the fragmentary, the indirect, alternative ways of writing that resisted the orders of logic, continuity and progression. For example, in a note from his index-diary, we read: 'Homosexuality interesting only if it leads, through particular breakthroughs, through themes, to thinking the world. If it deforms, transforms itself into something else (e.g. intolerance to what seems to be self-evident).'[2] In this sense, if Foucault was more explicit in his public commitments, Barthes went furthest in exploring the critical scope of this issue. Foucault denounced the omnipotence of the order of discourse, but he did so while remaining within its laws of continuity and logical argument – laws which Barthes (and herein lies, perhaps, his freedom as a writer) endeavoured to subvert.

Parallel lives

Homosexuality played a major part in the friendship between the two men. At its most intense, their relationship saw them going out in the evenings to places where they could go cruising; they went on pleasure trips to Morocco, and attended bouts of all-in wrestling, whose popular figures had become gay icons of the day. Of course, they had a great deal in common intellectually, but their literary and theoretical discussions acted more as a supplement than as the main reason for their closeness. They had been introduced by Robert Mauzi, at the time a student at the Fondation Thiers where Foucault had recently been a boarder. This was back in 1955; since the previous year, Foucault had been a lector at the University of Uppsala in Sweden, a post he had obtained thanks to Georges Dumézil. He wanted to invite Barthes to give a lecture at the Maison de France, where he organized such events while mainly teaching courses at the university. He came back regularly to France and it was on one of these occasions that he met Barthes, at the end of the year. Foucault had published his first book, *Mental Illness and Personality*, while teaching psychology at the École normale supérieure in 1954. He was much less influential than Barthes at this time, but in many ways their paths were similar: Barthes was well acquainted with the network of French academics abroad; the time he had lost while in the sanatorium placed him at the same point in his career as Foucault, and they were both writing a thesis. Barthes was ten or so years older than Foucault, and thus better known, but he was not that much ahead in terms of a formal career. He accepted Foucault's invitation and went to Sweden for a first visit in the spring of 1956. With his great zest for life, and his beige Jaguar, Foucault transformed this stay into something intensely pleasurable, though few traces of it remain. What did Barthes talk about? Perhaps theatre, his main subject of interest at the time, and Foucault also ran a theatre club with students in Uppsala. But he probably also talked about myth, as he had just finished writing 'Myth Today'.

Foucault had done all the right things: École normale supérieure, *agrégation* in philosophy, the Fondation Thiers, and he had all the signs of legitimacy that Barthes lacked. He also had a powerful, authoritarian father, and much of his initial trajectory had been directed against this father. These differences between Foucault and Barthes partly explain their diverging relations to the law: their behaviour was often poles apart. In research, Foucault felt driven to pursue his work with fierce devotion, while Barthes just drifted with his desires. Foucault never relaxed, while Barthes could sometimes do so, in Urt or in a Paris café. Foucault adopted radical tactics (his suicide attempts, the direct political commitments of the 1970s), while Barthes was afraid of conflict and frontal opposition. The former was unacquainted with fear, while the latter was imbued with it. However, they were alike in three ways. First, they were both drawn to literature: this was probably more clearly stated by Barthes, but in the form of a projection, a fantasy (as with Foucault – Didier Éribon claims that in the early 1960s, it was Blanchot who represented Foucault's dream figure). Second, they both found France a hidebound country, with its immutable institutions and its dead languages, and so they were both very tempted by other countries, escaping for long and significant periods abroad. And third, they were both aware of belonging to a sexual minority, and interiorized their feelings about this in different ways: Foucault had been a pupil at a diocesan school and was filled with guilt, while Barthes had been brought up a Protestant and was imbued with a sense of secrecy; this led them to an aloofness and an exacerbated sense of the margin, with individual strategies to find some new centre.

In 1960, Foucault returned to France after his stays in Uppsala, Warsaw and Hamburg, and took up a post at the University of Clermont-Ferrand. This marked the start of the most intense phase of their friendship. From the autumn of 1960 to the summer of 1963, they saw a great deal of each other, almost every evening in November–December 1960, and two or three times a week thereafter. They formed a gang with Robert Mauzi and Louis Lepage and frequented the homosexual bars in the quartier Saint-Germain: the Fiacre in the rue du Cherche-Midi, the Speakeasy, in the rue des Canettes, and, very often, the Flore, where the first floor was traditionally a gay haunt. They sometimes went to a night club, to Cherry Lane or the Boîte à chansons, or the cabarets that had just opened in Montmartre. Barthes would often see Foucault alone, and they discussed their research and what they were reading. Foucault introduced Barthes to Jean Beaufret and Louis Althusser;[3] Barthes introduced Foucault to literary circles. In 1963, together with Michel Deguy, they both joined the editorial committee of the review *Critique*, which Jean Piel had taken over after the death of Bataille in 1962;[4] Foucault wrote about literature, including Bataille – he contributed an essay on Bataille (as did Barthes and Sollers) in the 1963 special issue. This was also the period in which he was writing his book on Roussel (reviewed in *Critique* by Robbe-Grillet in December 1963). Foucault often called by at the apartment in the rue Servandoni and met Henriette Barthes; Barthes, on his way to Urt, stopped off in Vendeuvre near Poitiers to meet Anne Foucault in the 'Piroir', the family house where Foucault spent almost every August. In summer 1963 they stayed in Marrakesh (at the Hotel Mamounia) and, in July, they were in Tangiers. After their return from this trip to Morocco, their relationship waned. They may have quarrelled over a boy. The story goes that Foucault, having now decided to live with Daniel Defert in an apartment in the rue Monge, wanted to keep his other friends at a distance. And it is likely that the change in his lifestyle led to them drifting apart. Some people go a bit further and claim that Defert did not like Barthes. In his *Une Vie politique*, Defert does not explicitly admit this, but he does mention his hesitations about Barthes, whom he had met the previous year in the Fiacre with Jean-Paul Aron; he did not much like the way Mauzi and Barthes behaved to young men: 'They wanted both to seduce and were afraid of being manipulated.' Suddenly finding himself dragged into the group's routines ('dinner in Saint-Germain, then part of the night in the Fiacre'), that evening left him with a very unpleasant memory: 'There was something exaggerated about the way the differences in age and social status were always being highlighted, especially by Barthes. Years later, I told Foucault how much I'd hated that first evening – which had almost been our last.'[5] Barthes had taken the liberty of addressing Defert as '*tu*' right from the start, and Defert had interpreted this as a way of treating him as a gigolo. It is very likely that Defert's unease about Barthes led Foucault to distance himself from the latter.

According to Philippe Sollers, Barthes perceived this distance as a real break-up. However, we should not read too much into this episode: after all, every relationship has its ups and downs. Foucault was completely immersed in his research,[6] and circumstances did not favour their meeting very often. In 1966, Foucault went to teach in Morocco, where Defert was a *coopérant*; he stayed there until 1968. In 1969, it was Barthes's turn to go to Morocco. But a letter Foucault sent Barthes in February 1970, after reading *S/Z*, shows that there was still a certain warmth in their relationship: 'I've just read you in one sitting: it's magnificent – the first real piece of textual analysis that I've ever read.'[7] They had hitherto been tracing parallel paths, but these crossed over after 1968. Barthes went to North Africa just as Foucault was returning to France. Above all, Barthes was moving away from the political just as Foucault was becoming intensely politically committed. They were no longer in that period of open indecision that could take their work wherever they wished even though they did not quite know where. Each of them continued to work in fields where he felt most at home and was most recognized: history and philosophy for Foucault, literature and writing for Barthes. In a radio interview with Jacques Chancel, Foucault put it thus: 'The area I am investigating, probably that of non-literature, is so different from his that now, I think, our paths have really diverged, or are not exactly on the same level.'[8] It is striking to see how Foucault refers to his own area in negative terms, as 'non-literature', emphasizing the renunciation of what he had once desired. This was yet another way of paying homage to Barthes. Their social paths crossed again in 1975 when Barthes was standing for election to the Collège de France; Foucault had been teaching there since 1970 and we have seen how he supported Barthes. They both died in the Pitié-Salpêtrière Hospital, Barthes in March 1980, Foucault in June 1984, and their friends gathered at the morgue and in the same courtyard of the amphitheatre to pay homage to them. After this, some went to the family home – Urt for Barthes and Vendeuvre-du-Poitou for Foucault.

An accompaniment

One of the bedrocks of their relation was the way each respected the other's work. Barthes was highly impressed by Foucault's intelligence and his apparently inexhaustible capacity for work. Foucault learned a great deal from Barthes's critical abilities and his ways of reading texts. In some remarks he made in 1982, he linked the names of Barthes and Blanchot, and endeavoured to explain the force of their relation to the book. 'To read a book, to talk about a book, was an exercise in which they to some extent indulged for themselves, for their own benefit, to transform themselves. To talk well about a book they did not like or to try and talk with enough distance about a book that they liked a little bit too much – all this effort meant that from writing to writing, from book to book, from the work to the article, something was transmitted. What Blanchot and Barthes introduced into French thought was considerable.'[9] Foucault realized that the force of their critical dynamism had been that it dehierarchized reading and writing and thus overcame institutional separations. The political dimension of this liberation lay in the way thought was deployed in a single movement, extending from one activity to another irrespective of distinctions. There were not writers on one side and readers on the other, as if we were talking about rich and poor, men and women, the dominant and the dominated. This movement of blurring the boundaries aimed to overthrow all fixed designations, to think in terms of difference rather than essences or categories. For his part, Barthes immediately saw Foucault's originality as consisting in two areas. First, he set up *another*, relativist historical discourse that led to a continual rereading of the sources, something that had already fascinated him in Febvre. In his article on Foucault's *Madness and Civilization,* based on his doctorate (written in Uppsala and defended in front of Georges Canguilhem and Daneil Lagache) and published in 1961, Barthes set him within that tradition: 'How Lucien Febvre would have enjoyed this audacious book, since it restores to history a fragment of "nature" and transforms into a phenomenon of civilization what we hitherto took for a medical phenomenon: madness.'[10] And second, Barthes recognized that Foucault had shaken up knowledge by seeing it no longer as 'that calm, proud, reassuring, reconciling act which Balzac opposed to the will which burns',[11] but as a disquiet created by the movement between madness and reason. Barthes saw this as an epistemological earthquake that had changed the very way he thought and he would, over the next few years, often refer to the 'vertigo' introduced by Foucault when he started to talk about 'the couple constituted by reason and madness' and their slippery contents.[12]

Foucault was very pleased at this gesture of recognition, all the more so as Barthes reprinted the article originally published in *Critique* in his *Critical Essays* of 1964. This text saw Foucault as forming a link between two advance posts of modern science: linguistics and ethnology. Barthes compared Foucault's approach with Mauss's and the 'ethnological gaze' applied to one's own society was what he himself had attempted in *Mythologies*; and he himself wished to occupy a similar, mobile place in the disciplines. The other work by Foucault that Barthes analysed in depth was *Birth of the Clinic: An Archaeology of Medical Perception*, first published in 1963. The common point here was the sign, and the book showed how boundlessly dynamic a sign could be. Barthes saw this book as falling fully within the programme of semiology, as the signifier of illness led to a signified that, on being named, changed back into being a signifier. Thus, Foucault had found a way of posing the problem of the language of the clinic – and the role of language in the birth of the clinic – which coincided with his own research. Barthes noted in particular the distinction between symptom and sign, the symptom being the fact of illness and the substance of the signifier and the sign subsuming this symptom into a description. Thus, the clinic as a space means the problem of language can be posed as a real question: 'For if is the semiological nature of the field of diseases – and this is Foucault's hypothesis – corresponds to a certain history, then the predominance of the notion of the sign, the *culture* of the notion of the sign, would correspond to a certain ideological phase of our civilization.'[13] Here we can see Barthes's constant concern with metalanguage, always caught up in the critique it brings to bear. We can also see him looking forward to the end of a certain historical moment: with the benefit of hindsight, we can see the connections it makes between knowledge, politics and ideology.

The first volume of *History of Sexuality*, *The Will to Knowledge*, was published in 1976 and *A Lover's Discourse* in 1977. In his book, Foucault makes a remarkable volte-face: power is not what forbids, but rather an injunction to speak. This came from Barthes, especially *Sade, Fourier, Loyola*: 'Social censorship is not where you prevent someone from speaking, but where you force them to speak.'[14] Barthes drew a connection between the two works published simultaneously: at a time when sexual liberation was triumphing, love, he claimed, had been left on the sidelines of contemporary philosophies. 'Was it time to make a few adjustments? This is what Foucault did, too.'[15] However, Didier Éribon relates that some eye-witnesses had heard Foucault mocking *A Lover's Discourse*, which he considered to be a load of immodest rubbish. All the same, once Barthes had joined the Collège de France, the two men resumed something of their old closeness, and regularly met up to dine and work together.

For example, they took part in a seminar on musical analysis with Pierre Boulez, Gilles Deleuze and members of IRCAM in February 1978; and they met very frequently at the Collège itself. In March 1980, Foucault visited Barthes in hospital several times. It was he who gave a brief memorial speech to the assembly of the Collège in April 1980, one that gave witness of his great affection. Before referring to Barthes's friendship for the administrator Alain Horeau, for the members of the administration and for his colleagues as a whole, Foucault gave voice with some emotion to his own intense friendship: 'A few years ago, when I proposed that you make him one of your number, the originality and significance of a body of work that had been pursued for over twenty years and made him a renowned figure meant that I did not need to refer to my friendship for him in order to support my request. I did not have to forget it. I could keep it one side. The work was there. This work is now alone. It will continue to speak; others will make it speak and will speak about it. So allow me, this afternoon, to make room for friendship alone. Friendship which, with death (which it hates), should at least have this much in common: neither of them need say very much.'[16] Foucault was here responding almost word for word to the homage Barthes had paid him in *Lecture*: 'As for the present, allow me to exempt from the discretion and silence incumbent upon friendship the affection, intellectual solidarity, and gratitude which bind me to Michel Foucault, for it is he who kindly undertook to present this chair and its occupant to the Assembly of Professors.'[17] It is moving to compare these two expressions of gratitude today, establishing a link between friendship and silence – moving because, irrespective of the little disagreements or moments of distance between them, essentially the result of circumstances, the bond between the two men was tangible and historic. Their names are not only uttered together because they belong to the same moment in an adventure of thought, but because they constructed that moment together, in mutual recognition and friendship.

Two styles

Their difference, and their sporadic differences of opinion, lay less in theoretical divergences than in ways of being. Those who knew Barthes and Foucault, together or separately, noted their contrasting styles. Maurice Pinguet, for example, was very close to them in Japan (he even sought to get both of them over there for a long stay), though he knew Foucault from his days at the École normale supérieure; he described the notable differences between them. While Barthes paid a great deal of attention to his appearance and to the context in which he lived his life, and had a profound love of music, Foucault showed 'a large degree of indifference to clothes, food, the décor of life. He claimed to like music, but he was not dreamy enough (being more sensitive than sentimental) to need it'.[18] In these juxtaposed reminiscences, Maurice Pinguet passes no judgement, positive or negative. He merely sketches portraits in which we can discreetly perceive their stylistic contrasts. From the 1970s onwards, these differences deepened; while Foucault demonstrated exuberance and generosity in all he did, in his coming out as a homosexual, in his commitment to prison reform, in the affirmation of the positions he took, Barthes presented himself more than ever in his singularity and his rejection of hysteria. His benevolence was perceived by all, but it did not have the same energy as Foucault's generosity. It could appear, to those who did not see the fictional dimension of the posture, as a withdrawal into his 'self'. It is not always easy for other people to see the difference between 'living in accordance with literature', as Barthes put it in 'Fragments pour H.', and living in accordance with the norms that generally regulate our relations with others.

Mathieu Lindon, who met Barthes when he was 18, at a dinner at his father's, says that everyone who knew both Foucault and Barthes preferred Foucault – he was more unbridled, more generous, more amusing. Lindon's narrative of the different episodes of his relation with Foucault largely coincides with the impressions of Daniel Defert and, in particular, Hervé Guibert, who says that Barthes asked him to sleep with him in return for a preface.[19] As Barthes wrote to him subsequently, 'I found myself alone in the apartment, stuck with the image of a bastard who has failed to get what he wanted.'[20] Barthes's letters to Guibert evoke a complicated but quite gentle relationship. Guibert's rather one-sided account does not report what happened altogether accurately. In March 1977, Barthes had promised to write a preface for a text by Guibert with the title *La Mort propaganda no. 0*. It is possible that, playfully, Barthes had suggested the 'contract' referred to in *S/Z* in connection with the epilogue to *Sarrasine*, namely a text in exchange for a night of love. But it was mainly his anxiety about his mother's illness and the relative apathy that resulted from this that seems to have been behind this defection. Mathieu Lindon tells this story: 'He was expecting an act of more than just words from me, and when I was reluctant, I was immediately expelled from that world, unable to attend the seminar ever again, which struck me as at once deserved and gross. It was as if I had suddenly ceased to exist.'[21] These episodes need to be seen within their contexts and their communities. Barthes had his group of friends, centred on Jean-Louis Bouttes and Youssef Baccouche, but also André Téchiné, François-Marie Banier, Renaud Camus, his seminar students, Frédéric Berthet, Éric Marty and Antoine Compagnon. Foucault had his group of friends, including Daniel Defert, of course, but also Mathieu Lindon and Hervé Guibert. It is to be expected that the stories should differ. But sometimes the groups overlapped. This happened when Foucault organized some rather special evenings to which he invited several from his circles of friends. One of these evenings took place on 28 October 1979, around a Japanese male dancer who danced naked for the guests. Lindon saw Barthes for the first time after their quarrel. He saw this encounter – Barthes's stupefaction on seeing him at Foucault's, 'saved', as he put it, 'from the dustbins of homosexuality' – as a revenge; but in so doing he constructs the rivalry between them. He acknowledges the fact: 'Michel, to whom I had never mentioned this, cannot have suspected that we knew each other.'[22]

The difference in style between Barthes and Foucault is also evident in the way they spoke and wrote. Their inaugural lectures and their seminars at the Collège de France have often been compared and contrasted. This is an interesting parallel: in Barthes's inaugural lecture, while setting out his own course, he also brings his discourse into a direct dialogue with Foucault's lecture, 'The Order of Discourse', delivered in 1970 and published in 1971. Like Foucault, Barthes raised the question of the relations between the spoken language and power. Foucault listed the ways in which 'in every society the production of discourse is at once controlled, selected, organized and redistributed by a certain number of procedures whose role is to ward off its powers and dangers, to gain mastery over its chance events, to evade its ponderous, formidable materiality'.[23] According to Foucault, discourse is always a violence exercised against things, especially as it is generally a discourse in thrall to a certain doctrine. Barthes picks up these three themes, the spoken word, power and violence, and links them to the problem of having to maintain a discourse (the subject of the seminar he gave at the Collège between January and June). 'Since, as I have tried to suggest, this teaching has as its object discourse taken in the inevitability of power, method can really bear only on the means of loosening, baffling, or at the very least, of lightening this power.'[24] These words are an almost literal repetition of the definition of teaching that Foucault gave in his inaugural lecture: 'a distribution and an appropriation of discourse with its forms of power and knowledge.'[25] The oppression that this gesture presupposes is highlighted in Barthes's own lecture: 'To speak, and, with even greater reason, to utter a discourse is not, as is too often repeated, to communicate; it is to subjugate.'[26]

Although the research the two men were to pursue, set out as a programme in their lectures, was quite different, they had a similar position: their relation to discourse, to the theatricality of the spoken word, was uneasy. But Barthes went much further than Foucault in

extending the field of action of violence to language as a whole:
'But language – the performance of a language system – is neither
reactionary nor progressive; it is quite simply fascist; for fascism
does not prevent speech, it compels speech.'[27] This statement –
'over-the-top, exaggerated, scandalous, almost crazy',[28] could not
be understood as it is literally untenable. On the linguistic level it
is meaningless – you cannot confuse the register of the language
with the register of the spoken word or discourse. On the logical
level it radically reduces speaking subjects to language itself. On the
ideological level it picks up a fashionable presumption, treating any
manoeuvre of authority as 'fascist'. The remark shocked everyone
right from the start and has since given rise to many attempts to
explain it. For some, it is a symptom of stupidity; for others, a
provocation. Barthes's words have also been read as an attempt to
go one better on Foucault,[29] a form of reply to Foucault's more or
less explicit reservations about his own work. For example, in 'What
Is an Author?', Foucault speaks of the 'empty statement that the
author has disappeared', a direct attack on Barthes's 'The Death of
the Author', or in 'The Order of Discourse' when he says the emancipation of literature from the field of discourse in the name of the
'intransitive character which [the writer] gives to his discourse', an
obvious allusion to 'Authors and Writers'. It may be that Barthes,
who carefully read Foucault's lecture before writing his own, was
trying to answer back here: the point concerned the salutary difference of literature as writing, which resists discourse, even if this
requires playing tricks with language. That he should do so in an
aphoristic, assertive way was typical – he would always begin by
affirming something before qualifying it. What is more surprising is
that he was here succumbing to a stereotype of the age, when he was
usually so quick to demystify them. The provocation was doubtless
deliberate. And it did not crop up in his lecture spontaneously – it
shows the violence of which Barthes was sometimes capable: the two
rough drafts include these words. To say 'language is fascist', in the
way one said 'CRS, SS', could be a way of illustrating the truth of
the statement in its very form: language is fascist, and the proof lies
in the fact that my discourse is fascist in saying so.

   In other respects, Barthes was simply extending to language a
remark that he had long been making about the spoken word, its
arrogance, its will to mastery, its authoritarian character. So the
phrase is not so surprising if we bear in mind the contrast between
speech and writing that ran through Barthes's texts. The radical
nature of the formulation was in line with the radical nature of the
response one can bring to language, namely, according to Blanchot,
silence: either mystical singularity, described by Kierkegaard to
describe Abraham's sacrifice as 'an action unparalleled, void of
speech, even interior speech, performed against the generality, the

gregariousness, the morality of language'; or else 'the Nietzschean "yes to life", which is a kind of exultant shock administered to the servility of speech, to what Deleuze calls its reactive guise'.[30] Compared to these sublime gestures, which presuppose a belief that Barthes did not possess, literature appears as the sole place where a language outside power can gain a hearing. And it is here that Barthes replies to Foucault: 'The forces of freedom which are in literature depend not on the writer's civil person, nor on his political commitment – for he is, after all, only a man among others – nor do they even depend on the doctrinal content of his work, but rather on the labour of displacement he brings to bear upon the language.'[31] He takes up a notion that has been so crucial since *Writing Degree Zero*, the 'responsibility of form', to set out the scope of this 'loosening of power'. The *Lecture*, which began by hailing the Collège de France as a place 'outside the bounds of power',[32] thus ends with this programme of literature as a renunciation of all the servilities of language. If we bear in mind that all the courses that Foucault was giving at that time – 'Society must be defended' in 1976, 'Security, territory, population' in 1978, 'Birth of biopolitics' in 1979) – were concerned with power, it is clear that, on the essentials at least, the elements of a dialogue existed.

Letting go of power was also the basis for a form of teaching leading to research, to a quest, and not to knowledge or a fixed language. As opposed to the theatrical character of the lecture delivered from on high (also denounced by Foucault in *The Order of Discourse*), what is needed is a form of the spoken word that registers its own disquiet,[33] that preserves its transitory, uncertain status, aware of itself and of the unease that had afflicted the academic system since May 1968. Hence the way that both Foucault and Barthes resisted the 'high society' aspect of the lectures at the Collège de France where the microphones often failed to work and some of the audience were forced to listen without being able to see, turning the teachers into performing animals. Hence the reluctance that both thinkers expressed when it came to publishing their courses. Foucault left a note in his will saying 'No posthumous publication' and Barthes did not want his course on 'The neutral' published: 'I think that part of a life's activity should always be set aside for the Ephemeral: what happens only once and vanishes, it's the necessary share of the Rejected Monument.'[34] In spite of these attempts to stop the courses being published, they have in fact come out: so we need to read them with the awareness that they are tentative in nature (even if both Barthes and Foucault prepared them with great care, in Barthes's case often during his time in Urt in the preceding summer); we need to hear the repetitions and corrections, the tone and grain of the voice. Reading the courses or listening to the recordings also brings out the differences of style.

Foucault spoke in a lively, sometimes staccato way; Barthes spoke slowly, in a voice that was at once clear and deep. In particular, Foucault based his discourse on the retrospective gesture, on the archaeological method, going over the things he had already said, correcting or accentuating his ideas as he engaged in new readings and new dialogues. Barthes's teaching, conversely, was entirely forward-looking, based on a fiction or a fantasy. The disquiet occasioned by going back over something is not the same as the disquiet of desire. The former deepens what is already there, and is still concerned with producing knowledge; the latter goes beyond the given, and endeavours to displace knowledge through the 'for me'. These two distinct forms of disquiet find an expression in the way the two wrote their books, rejecting systems in very different ways. Foucault undermined them by deconstructing them; Barthes renounced them by scattering them in fragments. What brings them together is the analysis (explicit in Foucault, implicit in Barthes) of the importance of the process of subjectivation.

Inaugural lecture at the Collège de France, room 8.

First draft of the inaugural lecture (page 1).

17

Heartbreak

Being strangers is inevitable and necessary, except when evening falls.

Barthes, *How to Live Together*

1977

Like 1955 and 1966, the year 1977, which began with the inaugural lecture on 7 January, and 'ended' with the death of Henriette Barthes on 25 October, was a pivotal year in Barthes's life. The greatest consecration was followed by the most radical and heartbreaking catastrophe, after which nothing could be the same. It was also the year when *A Lover's Discourse* was published – a time when Barthes gained considerable fame, thanks to this book in which another kind of distress was staged, namely the heartbreak imposed on the subject by the passion of love.

The presence of Barthes's mother in the front row of room 8 where the many guests had assembled to listen to his inaugural lecture (while the courses are open to all, inaugural lectures at the Collège de France are invitation-only events), is a good symbol of that year: a presence became an absence, a plenitude became a lack. Without naming his mother, Barthes paid her an indirect homage, stating that the sole law was that of desire and abandonment to the mother. 'I should therefore like the speaking and the listening that will be interwoven here to resemble the comings and goings of a child playing beside his mother, leaving her, returning to bring her a pebble, a piece of wool, and thereby tracing around a calm centre a whole locus of play within which the pebble, the wool come to matter less than the enthusiastic giving of them.'[1] Barthes described a space constructed by affects, an alternative to the place where classes are given, which is often a place of mastery. But he also expressed the fear of separation: the bit of wool is reminiscent of the game with the reel played by Freud's grandson, the *fort-da* the child uses to bring back to him what had been separated. He also referred to a text by Winnicott, quoted several times in *A Lover's Discourse* and an important reference point for Barthes throughout that period.[2] The reference to psychoanalysis was less an explanation than a demonstration of the plenitude of that affective space where the gift in all its forms is possible. In the first draft of his lecture, Barthes had added: 'I sincerely believe that at the origin of all teaching we must locate an affect.' He replaced the term 'affect' by 'fantasy' in the final version,[3] probably so as to disguise his feelings and project his desire towards the future. This leaves a piece of word-painting that might belong to the genre 'tranquil scene', depicting a child playing peacefully at its mother's feet.

The inaugural lecture had a great impact. *Le Monde* reported it two days later, presenting extracts from Barthes's lecture and commenting on the ambience: 'The audience may have confirmed the worldly tradition of inaugural lectures, but rather gave the lie to the lecturer, who said that the Collège de France is "outside power" and writers, no longer the "guardians of superior values", cannot "strut around" any more.'[4] Robbe-Grillet, Nadeau, Klossowski, Sollers, Kristeva, Boulez, Téchiné, Cordier, most of the students from the seminar: all Barthes's close friends were there, and most of the professors from the Collège. That evening, Barthes's friends gathered for a party in the rue Nicolas-Houël, at the home of Youssef Baccouche.[5] In spite of the feeling of imposture to which Barthes was still prone, and his sensitivity to the criticisms of his audacious claim that 'language is fascist', Barthes appreciated this solemn and yet friendly moment of recognition.

A few days later, on 12 January, he gave his first class on the theme proposed the previous year: 'How to live together'. His course took place in room 6, every Wednesday at 11 a.m. for 13 weeks. Following the custom of the Collège, he also gave a seminar on the same day, with the title 'To give a discourse' and where, in line with what he had said in the inaugural lecture, he explored the different types of arrogance to be found in language. He invited several people to speak: François Flahault, Jacques-Alain Miller, Louis Marin and others. In the course, he focused on more peaceable modes of sociability, examples of resistance to the intimidations of society, of organizations and languages. In his private life too, he experienced restricted collectivities, friendly communities where people gathered together in a certain place. The apartment where Jean-Louis Bouttes, Youssef Baccouche and Paul Le Jéloux lived performed this reassuring role. An intimate and festive circle also formed around André Téchiné, where people could get together and enjoy their evenings in company. But that year the pleasure was short-lived; Henriette Barthes, already feeling tired over the winter, fell ill in the spring, just as *A Lover's Discourse* was being published. On the evening of 28 March, the very day when Barthes had presented copies to Éric Marty, Alain Robbe-Grillet and Jean-Louis Bouttes, she felt so poorly she had to take to her bed. Her state worsened in April to the extent that Barthes and his brother arranged for home care to be laid on by the Salpêtrière Hospital. Even as the book was being well received and Barthes was giving many interviews and broadcasts, he was at his mother's side as often as possible; he cut down his social activities and went out much less in the evenings. On 29 April, he appeared on the TV programme 'Apostrophes', where Bernard Pivot interviewed him for the first time (alongside Françoise Sagan and Anne Golon, the author of *Angélique, marquise des anges*) on the theme of love; Barthes seemed attentive and benevolent, but was still very concerned for his mother. That evening, he contrasted romantic love (passionate and painful) with maternal love (powerful and serene). Over the next few weeks, he continued to travel: to Aix for Lucette Finas's thesis viva on 7 May, and to Rome on 20 May (for a conference on music where he talked about Panzéra's voice) – but he kept these trips as short as possible, staying in Rome for just a night. Caught up between worries over his mother and the media frenzy around his book, he was constantly preoccupied. Henriette Barthes's state gradually improved. On 13 June, home care was no longer necessary. She was still weak, but the danger had passed.

Love

In order to understand the origin and motivations of *A Lover's Discourse*, which was Barthes's biggest success in his lifetime (70,000 copies were sold the year it came out), we need to go back a few years to when its author was starting his seminar at the EPHE on 'The lover's discourse'. We also need to examine the developments in his private life at that time, which played a significant part in the genesis of the book. They are not of merely anecdotal importance: Barthes had for some years endeavoured to graft writing onto his affects, the obsessional repetition of the same themes. Since he had fostered the system of restricted seminars, especially the year he focused his course on 'the author's lexicon', a little society had been set up in which desire circulated (between teacher and students, between different students). Taking the lover's discourse as the topic for his course was obviously a way of playing on this state of affairs, emphasizing it, bringing new configurations into being. After disclosing some of his habits and his tastes in the sessions preparatory to his self-portrait, Barthes could go further this time, to the most private level, displaying the moments when the subject is no longer scattered, elusive, diffuse, but completely constituted by his passion.

This led to the establishment of a space with unclear boundaries, a close mixture of the pedagogic relation, literary experimentation and love life, the most auto-fictitious space imaginable. This comprised Barthes's real political invention in this period, and it corresponded to the lure of communities and the time of sexual liberation. A new place for collective life could be set up, as against the existing organizations: in this new space, different types of language could be analysed and liberated. The book on the lover's discourse bears the trace of this singular experiment. Texts from a bibliographical corpus are interwoven with bits of conversations Barthes had with one or another friend, designated in the margins by their initials. But this anonymity was entirely relative, as the list of acknowledgements at the end gives the full names of these privi-leged interlocutors who were all (apart from François Wahl, Severo Sarduy and Philippe Sollers) students attending the seminar. The archive of the book's genesis is even more telling (and we do not have everything, as some of the documents are still private): just after delivering the final manuscript of *Roland Barthes by Roland Barthes*, for example, Barthes started keeping a notebook-diary in which he noted and organized the narrative of his love life: he recorded the successive episodes, on a day-by-day basis, and linked them to the type of discourse and commentary that could be drawn from them (every double page of the notebook is divided into four columns, bearing the 'date', 'event', 'figure' and 'emblem' of each episode). For example, this very individual type of diary began on 20 September 1974 (it was quickly to be transformed into a working document for Barthes, with a chronology and an index), and in the 'narrative' column we find the remarks: 'Waiting for R.H. to phone, in Urt'; in the 'figure' column the word 'dependency' and in the 'emblem' column the words 'I daren't go out in case . . .'. In the published book, the figure entitled 'Dependency' uses the two main elements in the note: having to wait for a telephone call is a supreme form of subjection and the holidays are a factor aggravating desire and impatience.[6]

Since the academic year 1973–74, another 'little group' of favour-ite students had formed around Barthes, in addition to his friendship for Jean-Louis Bouttes and his group from the seminar. This second group consisted of Évelyne Cazade, Roland Havas and Patrice Guy. They lived together in an apartment in the rue George-Sand, in the sixteenth arrondissement of Paris, and very close but complicated bonds united them. Initially, although Barthes saw Roland Havas alone – they played piano and went to concerts together – he had friendly relations with the entire group, and these intensified in the period of his trip to China: on the day before his departure, he spent the evening with the three of them, and the day he came back, on 5 May, he went to see them in the rue George-Sand and mentioned

them in his travel diaries. He was apparently a little in love with the
two boys, but it was mainly his passion for Havas that gradually grew
and asserted itself. Havas was a medical intern, preparing to special-
ize in psychiatry. This young man, who was a devotee of music,
completely fascinated Barthes, and this may have stemmed partly
from his Romanian origins – he had spent the first fifteen years of
his life in Romania, and this meeting sharpened Barthes's nostalgia
for the very close friendships that he had enjoyed there in 1948–49,
a nostalgia that was still keen despite the time that had elapsed and
the fact that he was a whole generation older than Havas. In the
summer of 1974, as Barthes was completing his self-portrait at the
home of Daniel Cordier, and spending several evenings at the Hotel
Belles Rives in Golf-Juan, at the home of Casimir Estène,[7] Havas
joined him for a few days before going to stay with Évelyne Cazade
in Marseille – with something of a sigh of relief, as Barthes had been
putting huge pressure on him. He never concealed from Barthes the
nature of the relationship he had had with Cazade since 1971 (she
later became his wife). But a certain ambivalence, the fear of hurting
him, the surprise that an intellectual of his age and fame could be
so smitten with him may have led him to behave in such a way that
Barthes might hope for success.

In the course of the following year, Barthes fell deeply in love and
suffered greatly. It was in this context that he started his notebook
diary with the figures of the lover's discourse (which he called the
'R Text' or 'Novel for R') and decided to dedicate a seminar to this
subject. They travelled together, to Switzerland at the end of 1974,
to Geneva and Zurich where they attended a performance of *Tosca*,
and Venice in August 1975. Barthes was not seeking a relationship
as a couple, or even an exclusive bond – in any case, he had a great
many lovers himself – but the nature of his feelings and the reserve
kept by Havas, who was not very talkative, exacerbated the sense of
being trapped in his own passion: he was jealous, desperate, impatient. The quarrels and separations were frequent. Havas often tried
to free himself from a relationship that had become a real prison,
but found this difficult. He himself acknowledged that he could do
so only after the publication of *A Lover's Discourse*. As with Robert
David in the years at the sanatorium, when his effusive feelings were
so intense that he felt on the edge of madness, Barthes – yet again
in love with a man who could not respond to his love – expressed
his despair by pouring out his passion in endless letters, hundreds
of pages of them, to his friend. These letters might be published one
day: they will shed great light on Barthes's personality, reserved
but capable of a demonstrative exuberance in this kind of circumstance. His desk diary indicates that he could spend whole days
writing letters to Roland Havas: on 6 February 1975, 1 April, 14
May – 'long letter to RH (about last night's little quarrel: sociability

of writing)' – and, from 11 to 19 July, he wrote another three long letters. This led him to transform his course on 'the lover's discourse' and turn it into a book. From then onwards, he used the figures and the ideas that his story inspired in him to compose this text, drawing both on the seminar and the 'R Text'. These details shed light on the moment of the course – the session of 10 April 1975 – on 'The Roland Text'. It was theorized both as a pre-text and as an individual, methodological text (going beyond subjectivity) whose value lay in placing the canonical text (*Werther*, or the 'W Text') on the same level as its lived version, which was also subjected to philological analysis.

The unhappy love story of this period and the heartbreak it entailed led Barthes to undergo an analysis with Jacques Lacan. He had several motivations for doing so. Julia Kristeva's journey to China had led her to move away from the political to the psychoanalytical; she had been following Barthes's seminars for a long time and she encouraged him to go into analysis (and François Wahl had long been urging him to do so). His conversations with Roland Havas were often about psychoanalysis, which Havas intended to practise. Apart from reading Lacan's *Écrits* when they came out in 1966, he also read Lacan's seminar I (*Freud's papers on technique*) and seminar XI (*The Four Fundamental Concepts of Psychoanalysis*) – the two seminars that had been published to date. His studies then led him to focus in a more systematic way than hitherto on the discourse of psychoanalysis: he also read Winnicott and Serge Leclair, Theodor Reik and the review *Ornicar*, all of which duly make their appearance in the bibliography of the *Lover's Discourse*. The psychoanalyst Hubert Ricard also gave him access to notes he had taken at Lacan's seminar on the small object, the relation between the idea ego and the ego ideal, and on love.[8] This document, part of the preparatory dossier on his seminar course, was used several times during his course.

Barthes's first consultation with Lacan took place on 29 June 1975; the second, a few days before he composed the long letter to Roland Havas (a fact that is probably not unconnected) on 3 July; the third and last on 15 September, followed by another letter to Havas, on psychoanalysis. Lacon received him in his apartment at 5 rue de Lille, at a time when he was overwhelmed by patients. 'Between 1970 and 1980 he [i.e. Lacan] saw an average of ten patients an hour on an average of about twenty working days a month: i.e., the equivalent of eight hours of analysis a day for ten months, most of the year.'[9] We do not know whether Barthes experienced the 'degree zero' version of the session, which made Lacan notorious at the time; probably not: the fact that their paths had already crossed and could still do so,[10] the importance of Barthes in the human sciences, and the acquaintances they shared, probably forced Lacan to listen. What we do know, via (for example) Julia Kristeva, is that the encounter was not very conclusive: 'An old fool with an old fogey' Barthes supposedly said after the sessions.

This was not the first time that, while writing a book, Barthes sought an accompaniment in psychoanalysis – which immediately raised a certain resistance in him. *S/Z* had been written in this 'undecided' relation to psychoanalysis, as he called it at the time. However much he would mock the 'psychoanalytical vulgate', he often resorted to it, starting with the way he defined 'fantasy'. Around 1975, with his single (failed) experience of treatment, and his wider reading, Barthes became involved in a more direct dialogue with psychoanalysis as a language. He sought to understand the way psychoanalysis handled the discourse of love, over and above the discourse on sexuality. In particular, he contrasted his own discourse with the set of contemporary languages that had made the language on romantic love, on passionate love, so out of kilter with the times. 'The lover's discourse is today *of an extreme solitude*', he wrote in the short preface to *A Lover's Discourse*; 'it is completely forsaken by the surrounding languages: ignored, disparaged, or derided by them, severed not only from authority but also from the mechanisms of authority (sciences, techniques, arts).'[11] Barthes's provocative gesture here lay in becoming the spokesperson for this solitary discourse, even expressing it in the first person, behind an 'I' that is not his own, of course (it is a simulation, a fiction if you will, a power of affirmation) but behind which one cannot fail to see him too. Here again he was choosing the margin, atopia: he was appropriating the most advanced of current thought (Lacan, Deleuze) while at the same time staging a certain distance. Barthes acknowledged that some psychoanalytical descriptions of being in love had their own validity, but he demurred from the idea that romantic love was an illness of which you needed to be cured. 'So my relation with psychoanalysis in this book is very ambiguous; it's a relation that, as ever, uses psychoanalytical descriptions and notions, but uses them rather as if they were the elements of a fiction that is not necessarily credible.'[12] And yet the texts of that period are imbued with psychoanalysis, especially Lacanian terminology: 'On Leaving the Cinema', which also dates from 1975, sees the state of someone coming out of a cinema as a kind of hypnosis, but also refers to two major Lacanian concepts: the trio of 'RSI' ('Real, Symbolic, Imaginary') and the mirror stage. 'The Real knows only distances, the Symbolic knows only masks; the image alone (the image-repertoire) is *close*, only the image is "*true*" (can produce the essence of truth).'[13] In the same period, he wrote a review of Christian Metz's book introducing psychoanalysis into cinema, for the review *Ça*. Also in 1975, together with Roland Havas, he wrote 'Listening', the third part of which was dedicated to listening in psychoanalysis and the way in which free-floating attention, a listening that circulates and permutates, has modified the way we think about listening as an intentional, directed act of audition.[14] So Barthes's relation with Havas goes a great way to explaining the way his own discourse was suffused with Lacanian vocabulary in the years 1974–77, as well as his wider reading in this area and a greater rigour in the use of concepts. But Barthes refused to stick strictly to psychoanalysis. As was his habit, he appropriated certain ideas and turned them into themes for his own writing. One example is the notion of 'decoy', which he used in S/Z and in 'On Leaving the Cinema', referring to its definition in psychoanalysis and then returning it purely and simply to its everyday meaning as illusion. Then there was 'obscene', in A Lover's Discourse: the first occurrence is accompanied by a reference to Lacan; Barthes then used the word in the sense of unseemly: 'no Bataille will give a style (écriture) to that obscenity'.[15] By isolating a term or a schematic representation, Barthes was deliberately deforming it. From 1977 onwards, he saw himself as fully occupying the register of the Imaginary, which he first used in a Lacanian sense, later changing its meaning by going back to Sartre's use of it in The Psychology of Imagination.

Thus the psychoanalytical corpus on which he drew in A Lover's Discourse was doubled by another, that of classical philosophy on one hand (Plato, Leibniz, Nietzsche) and mysticism on the other, including Ruysbroeck, whom he quoted in the translation by Ernest Hello (the same translation that had been read by Valéry and Gide), and St John of the Cross. The mystics' vocabulary occupied a major place here: 'annulment', 'askesis', 'laetitia', the language of fire and flame, 'to be unknown', 'to be engulfed', 'to be ravished' 'union'. It came as a complement to the language of romanticism, taken mainly from Werther; he to some extent desexualized it, by seeing it outside the relation between a man and woman staged by Goethe; and he gave it its full mystical scope, in other words (Barthes here relieved it of its theological meaning), its element of unpredictability. 'One must turn to the mystics for a good formulation of what can cause the subject to deviate in this way', he wrote in his self-portrait.[16] Ecstasy was simultaneously a loss and an excess; it surpasses and increases the possibilities that had been glimpsed by desire.

However, compared with the seminar, the 1977 book is more focused on the heartbreak of romantic love than on happiness and fulfilment. Barthes distinguishes between two types of love: a happy, fulfilled love, found by the mystics in God (its secular equivalent may reside in maternal love); and romantic, passionate love. While Barthes set out, between the lines, a few ideas about maternal love (for example, the way it can put up with injustices committed by the loved one, for example, its constantly gratifying character), he devoted his discussion as a whole to the second sort of love. The book stages a subject ('I') who loves, and an object ('he') who is loved. The response of the loved one to the love offered him by the subject who loves clearly does not correspond to the latter's expectations, and *cannot* do so. The feelings that the latter then expresses are very violent: despair, exclusion, ridicule, impatience, irritability, imperiousness. The lover is anxious, jealous, sacrificed, mourning, stupid. As he cannot tolerate being cut off from the loved one in absence, he feels perpetually wounded, lost. While knowing that he will never find fulfilment, he still hopes for it and does his utmost to reach a state of fusion. His madness consists in the fact that he cannot emerge from his state, but is forced to remain trapped within himself: 'For a hundred years, (literary) madness has been thought to consist in Rimbaud's "Je est un autre": madness is an experience of depersonalization. For me as an amorous subject, it is quite the contrary: it is becoming a subject, being unable to keep myself from doing so, which drives me mad. I am not someone else: that is what I realize with horror.'[17]

Only the novel had hitherto described the disturbing and painful nature of romantic love. Barthes's originality lay in writing a treatise about it, a fragmentary and reflexive essay. This form gave the book its lyricism, though this did not abolish the philosophical dimension of the 'I' that was deployed. The book's new feature is the way it combines the different methods Barthes had so far drawn on: structural analysis (the couple of the lover and the loved constitutes an overall structure, and the lover's discourse is delivered as a set of structures), semiology (as Deleuze had noted in Proust, love turns everything into a sign), and adding the dimensions of the imaginary (projecting your fantasy into writing). The project was a form of knowledge, even if, in order to produce it, Barthes had not gone through the programme of the positive sciences. In particular, it is not a succumbing to the subjectivity of narcissistic self-absorption, even if some have said or thought this. While the author does bring his personal experience into play, this is only while placing it at a distance and insofar as it can help the structures to be displayed. Many autobiographical details can be noted in the text – the buffet at the Lausanne railway station, the little box given as a present, the obsession with the telephone, the love letter, the flowers received anonymously. But they are taken up into the methodical and combinatorial writing of the treatise, and become the kind of details that could belong to anyone, the common points at which an adventure can be shared. In Barthes's work, *A Lover's Discourse* is in no way a denial. In it, he uses simulation and variation, which had always been his way of approaching, as subtly as possible, the difference in things, as distinct from their essence. For example, how can one express contact? 'A squeeze of the hand – enormous documentation – a tiny gesture within the palm, a knee which doesn't move away, an arm extended, as if quite naturally, along the back of a sofa and against which the other's head gradually comes to rest – this is paradisiac realm of subtle and clandestine signs: a kind of festival not of the senses but of meaning.'[18] Meaning does not always give itself as a whole, a plenitude: it lies in the gradual unfolding of signs. Drawing on his own life, his experience, what he had garnered from books and from various of his friends, added a phenomenological dimension to the semiological analysis. So Barthes proposes a reflection on love that had no recent precedent, showing that it was not a subject to be treated with contempt but could be an object of thought.

His readers recognized this. They acclaimed the book, recognizing certain situations in it but also noting that Barthes kept them at a distance. The general nature of the book lay in the way it reminded each reader of an experience that belonged to all: its force, different from the generalization of conceptual argumentation, lay in the fragmentary writing and the minute description of various aspects of love. The private reception of the book was quite different. Barthes's friends had never heard him talking about himself so openly. In the 'I' of the book, they could only see the man they knew personally. A long letter from Évelyne Bachellier suggests how taken aback she was: 'In the seminar, you did not say "I", or only very rarely.'[19] The imaginary of pain was exposed so nakedly in the book that she could not help connecting it with the suffering of Barthes, a suffering that she thought was terrible. For Philippe Sollers, who had read the book before it came out, this exposure was exactly what gave *A Lover's Discourse* its force: it was 'an extraordinary book that cannot be read without discomfort and emotion; a scandalous book, as you wanted it to be, vis-à-vis everything that now acts as the institution or academy of scandal . . . You definitely have a genius for going against the flow, my dear Roland.'[20] Philippe Rebeyrol, his long-standing friend, wrote at length about the violent impact the book had on him: 'The system of fragments gives it a density that is at times difficult to tolerate, if I read it slowly, then after 15 pages I feel sick, it's too rich. Homosexuality hems me in. A dangerous theme for heterosexuals, especially if they have an ambiguous vocation. Just as difficult as to talk about psychoanalysis for those who haven't been analysed and yet every evening roll into anamnesis. Reading your book, I have the feeling of being introduced into a half-closed society, it's an initiation. Even if love is unique and eternal.' And he ended his letter by saying: 'It was you that it all applied to: another Roland, known and unknown, a hidden face that revealed itself as more brilliant and suffering than one had supposed.'[21] But the most striking letter probably came from Georges Perros, who wrote: 'I have an absolute memory, as one says, an "ear" for, our meetings, our conversations. This is not entirely painless, of course. [. . .] For there was that drop of being in love, I'm sure of it. What can be more erotic than friendship. I have known, and suffered, its torments.'[22] By this date, Perros had lost the ability to talk: he had lost his vocal cords to cancer of the larynx, which killed him a few months later, on 24 January 1978. His letter to Barthes is both painful and disturbing.

The two points mentioned, one by Sollers (the scandal) and the other by Rebeyrol and, in his way, Perros (homosexuality) were probably not made evident when the book was published (they are even less so these days), and yet they constitute the most fundamental and pioneering aspect of the book. Barthes insisted at length on the fact that his book was untimely: romantic love was not a worthy object for the scholarly discourse of the time. It was consigned to novels from the past, to soap operas, to women's magazines. So the book's first achievement was to raise it to the status of an object of knowledge. The second was even more noteworthy: Barthes freed love from the discourse on sexuality (which itself was definitely one of the contemporary languages), and above all he freed it from the difference between the sexes. He reactivated the pensive force of romantic love in the space of homosexuality where difference was contingent, not basic, and this created a crack. 'It is difficult for homosexuality to be created as meaning, as intelligible.' Hence the fact that it can be expressed through the discontinuous and the heartbreaking disposition of romantic love, prior to its bourgeois recuperation.

If Barthes took care to use pronouns in a sufficiently detached way for his description of love to be a discourse with which everyone, male or female, could identify (even we can still detect traces of the author's personal situation here and there),[23] this is because certain structures of the lover's discourse transcend the question of sexual difference. But the force of the book also stems from the fact that it concerns homosexuality and the potential link between this and romantic love, while it is most usually dealt with in the language of sexuality (even in Proust).

The 1977 course continued the interlacing of personal life and reflection upon it by focusing not on the love relation (whose ultimate aim is the fusion of two people), but on 'living together'. Barthes, whose social life was made up of little circles, of distinct 'gangs', wished to analyse the politico-social or utopian horizon that such circles could permit. Again, the purpose was to undermine the orders that he loathed: first, the heterosexual couple, which society turns into a separatist rule (when he chanced upon a wedding group in the church of Saint-Sulpice, it was, as it were, 'the very *being* of exclusion with which he had been bludgeoned'),[24] the *sistemati*, the 'pigeonholed', those who had been tidied away (swept up into the same habitable comfort as structure, but separated from desire);[25] and second, the family as the instrument of reproduction of bourgeois law. Faced with these two rejected systems of relations, Barthes set up two completely different situations: living together in small groups (which can include the 'family without familialism' formed with his mother and his brother, or certain 'successful' families)[26] and living alone. These situations may appear contradictory, but this is not so: each one is the dream horizon of the other. The model for living together is the sanatorium of *The Magic Mountain*, much more utopian than that described in the 'Sketch for a Sanatorium Society' that he wrote shortly after his return from Leysin where the circle was complicit with a 'big family' or a triumphant feudalism. In *How to Live Together*, Barthes presented it as a society in which everyone could follow his or her own rhythm – it would be completely idyllic if death did not lurk there. Idiorhythmia meant one could stave off both the excess of self-protection (solitude, the rejection of the group, eremitism) and the excess of integration one finds in large-scale communities that are always structured by an architecture of power (and here power always involves dysrhythmia, heterorhythmia). It would be a 'median, utopian, Edenic, idyllic form'; this is why it remains very eccentric, very marginal.

The fantasy behind these ideas was the idiorhythmia of coenobitic monasteries: the monks are both isolated and linked within the structure; each of them has his own rhythm without this harming the community. In concrete terms, the dream place was Mount Athos, which Barthes himself never visited but which François Wahl told him about; he had also read descriptions of it in Jacques Lacarrière's *L'Été grec*, published in 1976: '[T]he Mediterranean, the terrace, the mountain (in the fantasy, we erase: in this case, the dirtiness, the faith). Basically, it's a landscape. I can picture myself there, standing on the edge of a terrace, the sea in the distance, the white roughcast, with two rooms to myself and the same number for a few friends, not far away.'[27] This is another example of the dream of the Mediterranean house glimpsed in Morocco; and the same method, set out in principle in the inaugural lecture, where you work under the impulse of a desire that shapes reality as it will. Here, the significant mystical corpus, which extends the readings of the previous years, is read without taking the signified into account – a rich irony, since God is to some extent the absolute signified, the signifier of nothing but himself. Together with monasticism, the literary corpus allowed Barthes to explore the contrasting spaces of living together: Gide's *Judge Not* illustrates the bedroom, the cell; *The Life and Adventures of Robinson Crusoe* deals with the lair; the *Lausiac History*, by Palladius of Galatia, with its anecdotes on the monks of Egypt, Palestine and Syria, is set in the desert; Thomas Mann's *The Magic Mountain* has the sanatorium-hotel as its setting; and finally

Zola's *Pot-Bouille* takes place largely in the apartment block, the bourgeois form of living together. Barthes's suggestions are interesting: as literature generally appears as a reservoir of models for constructing the self, we often neglect the way that it also indicates ways in which we can live together. This is partly because of the reader's solitary situation; but in a seminar, readings are shared, and so there is a better opportunity to explore other models, as in all novels there are 'bits and pieces of material pertaining to Living-Together'.[28]

Most of these models are riven by contradiction and thus lead to an aporia. If he takes the sanatorium as an example, for example (and in his course Barthes waxed particularly lyrical about his personal experience there), this is a collective whose ultimate end is death – an absolute solitude that affects some of the residents. Hence, as we have seen, Barthes connected it with the category of the heartbreaking: 'Function of the group (of Living-Together): statistical representation of the risk of death; the chances of your neighbour dying, bearing in mind that your neighbour could be you. This is no longer the indirect, it's the implicit.'[29] The aporias stem mainly from the ambiguity in the notions of autarchy and closure, which are sometimes positive and sometimes negative in Barthes. In an article on *Notre-Dame de Paris*, Quasimodo embodies a very positive form of closure,[30] especially because he replaces the balcony or hanging garden with the cave or lair; we find similar examples in the texts on Jules Verne and in *How to Live Together*. But autarchy can also be a withdrawal, a triumph of the bourgeois space that is 'on every side, where not the slightest shadow can offer a way out, an escape, a place where one can tremble or dream';[31] the triumph of consumer society lies in the way that the most valuable thing that money gives you is a self-sufficient world. (The very example of negative closure, though it is also compared to a ship or a belly, is the Folies-Bergères, on which Barthes wrote the second of his mythologies in 1953.)[32]

The utopia of a living together based on the respect for the idiosyncracies of each person seems doomed. The only utopia can be found in collective life, one that is subject to regulations in which idiosyncracies are sacrificed. 'This would probably be the most significant problem of Living-Together: how to identify and regulate that critical distance, on either side of which a crisis occurs.'[33] The problem is even more acute these days, continues Barthes, because 'what's most precious, our ultimate possession, is space'. So the utopia that needs to be invented would be one in which *room was given*. But the problem of 'how' to achieve this leads, at every phase of the argument, to an impasse. So we need to let ourselves be carried along by this open negativity (it might be melancholy), with its concepts that are never closed, never definitive, that boundlessly extend the territory of writing, where everything always needs to be gone over again, like life, like each day. Writing can grant temporary forms of consolation, and knowledge then hovers tremulously over experience. 'The community arms itself with courage to confront the night (think of a very isolated bit of countryside, without light, where nightfall really represents the threat of darkness). → Living-Together: only perhaps to confront together the sadness of evening. Being strangers is inevitable and necessary, except when evening falls.'[34]

To arm oneself with courage to confront the night: uttered at the end of the session of 27 April 1977, as Henriette Barthes was seriously ill, these words express a great sorrow. The course of 1977 was suffused with Barthes's terrible fear of losing his mother: the spectre of death, glimpsed in the sanatorium, the repetition of the metaphors of the belly and the ship signifying maternal protection, the image of the shroud that recalls his childhood memory of his mother and himself wrapped up together in a curtain to chase away a bat . . . One can sense that Barthes felt haunted.

Death

The second great break in the life of Roland Barthes, after the sanatorium, was also an encounter with death. But this second encounter was more direct and less general. When the event of his mother's death, so greatly feared, actually happened, it did not make any difference that he had always dreaded it and to some extent prepared himself for it, it was still heartbreaking. How could he live without her?

She suffered throughout the summer in Urt. Dr Lepoivre had to be summoned regularly, as she kept having falls and choking. Michel Salzedo, whose wife Rachel had needed to undergo a delicate operation in August, was not able to visit as often as usual. Barthes read Meister Eckhart, Dionysius the Areopagite and Swedenborg for his course on 'The neutral', but he barely did any work. He tended the garden a bit, and planted tomatoes, but spent almost all his time with his mother. On 26 August, they both flew back to Paris; Jean-Louis Bouttes brought the car back in the train. Henriette Barthes now weighed only 43 kilos. Barthes met up with a few friends (Renaud Camus, Pascal Greggory, Antoine Compagnon, Michel Cressole and others). He tried to do some reading for his course, but still found it difficult to work. The only text he wrote at this time was one to accompany photos by Daniel Boudinet and his landscapes, so peaceful that they are heartbreaking. A bend in the road took Barthes back to his childhood; an orchard made him think of a non-repressive culture; a white horse reminded him of joy. 'The photos of D.B. are very musical. They have a soothing effect, produce a sort of subtle and never violent catharsis: your body can breathe more easily.'[35]

Any respite was short-lived. Henriette Barthes's state became more worrying every day. Every time she tried to swallow something, she succumbed to choking fits and found it so hard to get her breath that she preferred not to eat at all. Barthes bought her only the things she liked the best, and sometimes managed to get her to swallow a little sole and raspberries. It was decided to arrange another session of home treatment for her; from 5 October, a nurse came to see her twice a day. On 23 October, her condition worsened so much that Barthes could now hardly sleep. She had to be given injections to calm her down. Friends came by to help out with material tasks (shopping, the chemist's); Barthes did not leave her bedside. He gave her massages, held her hand, changed her sheets with his brother. The hours followed on their ineluctable course: all he could do was stay with her and note, in a neutral and matt way, what happened:

24 October: a good night until 4 a.m., but I often get up to check on her. She is short of breath after 4 a.m., she wants me to stay with her, holds my hand. At one time, says to me in whisper, over and over: 'My Roland, my Roland.' – I can't bear it.

Maman can't sleep. She talks to Michel. It's difficult to follow what she's saying. 'I want to sleep.' Blétry visits. JL visits. Went to bed early.

25 October: very calm night, almost motionless. Taking Dolosal, breathing steadily. At 7 a.m. she starts wheezing, doesn't feel well and can't express herself. For me, a disturbed night, I kept waking. Migraine.

Maman a bit restless, wheezing, groaning, unconscious. At one moment recognizes me, touches my arm, tries to smile, eyes unconscious. 'Stay there'. movement on my arm, more conscious. 'You're uncomfortable' (because I'm fanning her on the stool, you're uncomfortable).

Doctor's visit. Injection.

Afternoon: maman sleeps, motionless. Breathing calm. Gradually her head falls to one side, her face changes. I call Michel. Last breaths. She passes away gently without waking again at 3.30 p.m.

His mother was dead. She was 84. Just after 3 p.m. Barthes interpreted this as a symbol. A parenthetical remark in a session of *The Preparation of the Novel* notes this: 'Half-past three in the afternoon (the time of my mother's death; – as if I'd always known it would happen then – the time of Christ's death).'[36] This is the catastrophic moment of mourning, which is still protective insofar as it is an event and involves rituals. Barthes straightaway called his friends so that they could come and pay her a final homage, and perform a vigil over the body, as was the custom: Jean-Louis Bouttes, Youssef Baccouche, Violette Morin, Éric Marty, Philippe Sollers – they all came. Éric Marty remembers: 'Once I was in the room where she lay, where her body was resting, as I didn't know what to do, I knelt as if to say a prayer, which didn't seem to surprise him. Then, we went into his room. And he started to cry. I realized from the endless ringing of the doorbell that, all day long, people would come, friends, and the scene I had just experienced would repeat itself until nightfall.'[37] The funeral took place on 28 October in the cemetery of Urt, in the presence of many of the locals. Jean-Louis Bouttes accompanied Barthes [from Paris] in the funeral car. They stopped for lunch in a roadside cafe in Sorigny near Tours. Michel Salzedo came by train with his wife Rachel. A Protestant priest from Bayonne was present. He had known Henriette Barthes for a long time and spoke movingly about her. Barthes returned to Paris by train the next evening. 'On his return, we were waiting for him at the station with Youssef and there was a sort of funeral meal that same evening for him. Deep down, Youssef, through his culture, through the Arabic tradition, was closer to him at this time than all the rest of us. We had become strangers to the world of death, and this was a lack in us.'[38]

One of the first things that Barthes noted after his mother's death was something she had said: 'She would say with relief: the night is finally over (she suffered during the night, alone, a cruel business).'[39] For him, another form of night was starting. Alone, in the second storey apartment, he was surrounded by her absence, on the edge of the void. Nothing made sense any more, not even the 'never again', since one day he would no longer be there to think or say this. His mother's death forced him to confront the most painful loss, cut him off from the person he loved the most and who, he knew, had loved him deeply. She turned his own death into something real: 'henceforth and forever I am my own mother', he noted on 4 November;[40] this was a way of displacing the fusion he had experienced with her and at the same time to absorb the possibility of his own death.

The *Mourning Diary*

As soon as his mother passed away, Barthes stopped organizing his days in the way he had been doing. For a whole year, he no longer noted in his desk diary the different activities or encounters that divided up his daily life. On separate index cards, he noted his grief.

His life was now made up of mourning. The 1978 desk diary was empty until 25 October, on which date Barthes decided to resume it, 'the anniversary of the death of Mam – to note my work'. He did so after going to Urt for the day to visit his mother's tomb. In the year leading up to this, he noted nothing apart from things relevant to her death and his grief. The notes he took in the year 1977–78 (they would eventually form the *Mourning Diary*) all bear the mark of the incomplete, the unfinished. Their fragmentary aspect say that something was happening that was not yet finished and that neither writing nor formal considerations even attempted to complete. This was a particularly poignant feature at the moment of his loss, as it corresponded very closely to the formless nature of grief. But his notes were also an art of the present where we read the inscription of a moment, and a first transformation of the event, however minimal, into memory. We can detect in them a contingency that the sentence has not yet tried to efface. We read the nuance, the division of nature, the individual trait – a reality effect similar to the one captured by photography.

The *Mourning Diary* can be read as the quest for something that cannot be found, something incomplete (like the name of '*mam.*' that Barthes now used to refer in writing to his mother).[41] It is so overwhelming for the reader not simply because of its object, or its subject, however moving these may be, but because these notes *could not* become a book without their object, and their subject, passing away, disappearing in turn. 'Liquidate without interruption what prevents me, separates me from writing the text about maman: the active departure of Suffering: accession of Suffering to the Active position.'[42] The intensity of the present was all the stronger in that the moment could not be written into duration: its true nature was to be discontinuous. The book's truth lies in the way it reflects, and reflects on, a time out of joint, a present that is no longer, a present cut off. It is the present of the mother, when he thinks of her now: 'In the sentence "She's no longer suffering," to what, to whom does "she" refer? What does that present tense mean?';[43] it is also the present of the son who is absolutely terrified by the chaotic, discontinuous nature of grief. Separation affects the very pain that it creates. By undoing the entire bond, death deprives of all continuity, including that of sadness. It is absolutely private and true for everyone. Grief is neither a duration nor a wave, but a radical break.

In this act of private writing, this introspective gesture, Barthes seeks to understand what is becoming of him now that she is gone. In the index card diary, other remarks complement the *Mourning Diary*: 'My mother made me an adult, not a child. Now she is gone, I'm a child again. A child without a Mother, without a guide, without a Value. The specificity of *mam.* was that she made me an adult – without suppressing a sort of powerful mothering (powerful?

the proof is that, when she died, I didn't have any problems of a practical kind: I could "get by").[44] He had not just lost his mother, he had also lost his child (hence his emotion when he rediscovered the photo of his mother as a young girl).[45] His mother was not 'in the order of things' because the love between them had created a sort of family bloc without genealogy, where each of them could occupy every place: 'November 19. [Status confusion]. For months, I have been her mother. It is as if I had lost my daughter (a greater grief than that? It had never occurred to me.)'[46] This is the reason for the impotence of psychoanalytical discourse, and the rebellion against the idea of a work or rhythm of mourning: time could perhaps soothe a 'natural' loss but it can do nothing against the amplitude of a multiple pain. For his mother was also to some extent his wife. He formed a couple with her. He often compared her with Madeleine, André Gide's wife, and by writing about her he might have hoped to do something akin to what Gide did for Madeleine in *Et nunc manet in te*. He ponders the connection between the first night of mourning and the wedding night. On 27 October 1977, the second index card in the *Mourning Diary* bears this short imaginary dialogue: '"You have never known a Woman's body!" – "I have known the body of my mother, sick and then dying".'[47] It is difficult not to read in these phrases an anticipatory response to Duras's remarks: 'I can't view Roland Barthes as a great writer: something always limited him, as if he had lacked the most ancient experience in life, the sexual knowledge of a woman.'[48] Barthes countered the stupidity of common sense or provocation by describing a face-to-face love that was so complete that it could see everything and say everything, even the most difficult thing of all: the integrity of the body and its degradation. Here, there was no need for transgression to gain access to the mother's body. As Éric Marty emphasizes in an eloquent text on the *Mourning Diary*, Barthes offered a discourse that was quite different from that of Genet or Bataille, a 'full light' that was 'in this sense more provocative than any transgressive scenario'.[49]

Barthes was angered by the word 'mourning', which implied a fake distance. He preferred the word 'grief', which better expressed his emotion and the sensation of being torn away from something. He was angered by all the people who clumsily tried to console him by reducing his experience to something commonplace and general. He frequently insisted on the difference between grief and mourning: the former cannot be subjected to continuous time, and thus to change, any more than to a generalizing discourse or a form (a book, a sentence). 'Explained to AC, in a monologue, how my distress is chaotic, erratic, whereby it resists the accepted – and psychoanalytic – notion of a mourning subject to time, becoming dialectical wearing out, "adapting".'[50] Grief had not swept away everything all at once; but, along with this, it does not get eroded.

Only Proust, whom Marty quoted to him, and whose correspondence and chronicles he read in the Bibliothèque nationale, had the
power to put his finger on just what he was feeling. As Proust wrote
to André Beaunier: 'If such a thought did not continually lacerate
me, I would find in memory, in survival, in the perfect communion
in which we lived an unknown sweetness.'[51]

The 330 index cards that comprise the *Mourning Diary* endeavour to describe in minute detail the gestures, rhythms and thoughts
of someone who has just lost the person he loves most. They form
a sort of short manual of the daily life of mourning, which is also
true of the evocation of behaviour that he shares with all those in
mourning. Among these 'practices of grief', one thing we note is a
hypersensibility to his milieu, to everything he hears, which always
brings him back to his loss; an obsession with tidying, as if he had to
put everything in good order so as to prepare for his own departure;
thoughts of suicide, quickly dismissed as self-inflicted death, would
make it impossible for his grief to survive, and is seen as an act of
betrayal; he catches himself adopting some of her gestures, her little
moments of forgetfulness; in the street, he notices expressions that
were hers, glimpses silhouettes in which he thinks he recognizes her.
From this almost clinical analysis of his daily behaviour, he develops a set of ideas about mourning that can be read as an alternative
to psychoanalytic discourse which involves a 'work' over a period of
time. Sensitive to the palpitations of grief from the time he travelled
in the funeral procession to Urt, perturbed by the 'blank' moments,
the very temporary moments of 'forgetting', he expresses the idea
of a 'mourning in layers – a kind of sclerosis',[52] resulting from the
cracks and cracklings (the verb 'to crack' appears several times in
Barthes's notes). A central term he uses to express his experience
is that of 'wavering'. This appears in the *Diary* (12 May 1978): 'I
waver – in the dark – between the observation (but is it entirely
accurate?) that I'm unhappy only by moments, by jerks and surges,
sporadically, even if such spasms are close together – and the conviction that deep down, in actual fact, I am continually, all the
time, unhappy since maman's death.'[53] For this alternating state,
which corresponded very closely to the heartbreak of death, Barthes
tried to produce a first theorization in his classes on 'The neutral':
always being on both sides at once, hesitation and indecision can be
a discourse or a screen, but they mainly point to the existence of a
'vibrated' time where everything is played out as alternation rather
than continuity. He again used the term in 1978, in connection with
Sollers, and explained how society resists the absence of a fixed,
posed image.[54] Likewise, common discourse wants mourning to go
through stages, levels, after which it gradually loses its intensity and
stabilizes. Barthes did not believe in a logic of mourning. Quite the
opposite: the thought of the profoundly chaotic nature of mourning

complements and completes a lifetime's thinking about the neutral: '[A]lternation, like a "desperate" tactic in the part of the subject in the subject's relation to death, a "wishing-to-live" that has, however, become decanted of all vitality.'[55]

The feeling that what he is living through is out of step with the common discourses of consolation lead him to try and external-ize his grief as much as possible. He would sometimes weep in the presence of friends, but most often he succumbed to tears when he returned home, when he heard a waitress say 'here you go' with the same inflexions that his mother's voice had had, or listening to Gérard Souzay (whom he had not much liked in previous years) singing 'J'ai dans le coeur une tristesse affreuse'. Barthes felt that he could experience his pain only inside himself, and share it really with nobody apart from his brother and sometimes his sister-in-law, who, he sometimes thought, resembled his mother in her attitudes. 'My grief has not been hysterical, scarcely visible to others (perhaps because the notion of "theatralizing" my mother's death would have been intolerable).'[56] This note, from 18 May 1978, flies in the face of what most eye witnesses felt: for Barthes's close friends, his mother's death was a catastrophic event, transforming his whole being and the way he behaved. His way of expressing it was cer-tainly not 'hysterical', and yet everyone could see it. And the work as we have it today also suggests that this reserve was far from being the whole story: Barthes referred in public to his mother's death, in front of the large audience at the Collège de France on 18 February 1978: 'In my life, as some people know, a grave event has happened, a loss.' All the texts written after 25 October 1977 bear the mark of his pain, in one form or another. But what Barthes did not display was the irreducibility of his grief, the way it consumed him. 'What still bothers me now', writes Éric Marty, 'is that, at the end, I was so little aware of the melancholy decline. I saw nothing of it.'[57] Barthes called this melancholy 'acedia' in the *Mourning Diary*: a form of indifference to everything, a form of spiritual malady in which the loss of the loved person is accompanied by the pain of no longer loving and no longer oneself; the 'hard-heartedness' that characterizes the exit of love from life.[58]

He tried to give an appearance of normality to his life. His obses-sion with rhythms helped him, gave him a framework. He was even amazed to see that some habits continued imperturbably, as in his sexual and social life. He travelled (to Tunisia, staying with Philippe Rebeyrol from 19 to 27 November 1977, then to Morocco in February 1978, in the spring of that year and again in July), but he soon wanted to come back home: 'Disappointment of various places and trips. Not really comfortable anywhere. Very soon, this cry: *I want to go back!* (but where? since she is no longer anywhere, who was once *where I could go back*).'[59] He attended the first night of Le Palace nightclub, opened by his friend Fabrice Emaer on 1 March 1978. The description of the club he wrote for *Vogue hommes* the following month gives an idea of the distance with which he viewed everything: 'Solitary, or at least a little aloof, I can "dream". In this humanized space, I can suddenly exclaim: "How strange this all is!".' In the haze that sometimes covered the track, the dancers looked like dancing puppets standing out from the sumptuous décor designed by Gérard Garouste. Everything looked to him as if were behind the glass of an aquarium, as Proust had described the stalls in the Opéra through the astonished eyes of a child.

Barthes's mother never made a negative 'remark' to him. She never imposed on him. She was kindly, elegant (Barthes evokes the 'rice powder' that fascinated him when he was a child, he remembered her perfume, Éric Marty recalled the beauty of her eyes, the same colour as Barthes's, and her voice that never seemed to grow old), gentle, without hysteria: she was the good enough mother as described by Winnicott, providing for everything but leaving room for the child to desire something outside of her. 'Writing is the part of me that is out of the mother's reach', Barthes noted in his diary on 22 January 1980.[60] This emancipation was all the more free and fine in that it did not create any sense of guilt. The son was sure of her love, and of the love he bore her, even in the trials of the dream: 'Dreamed of maman again. She was telling me – O cruelty! – that I didn't really love her. But I took it calmly, because I was so sure it wasn't true.'[61] The transcription of this dream helps us understand the form of this love: tranquil, total but not domineering.

The death of Henriette Barthes sharpened his desire to write: he needed to keep her alive, to create a memory for her. The obsession with leaving a monument to her is found in all the notes from that period; this would be less an enduring stele than an act of gratitude and recognition. While Barthes felt no desire for his own posthumous fame, he 'cannot endure that this should be the case for maman (perhaps because she has not written and her memory depends entirely on me).'[62] An equivalence was created between the mother and literature: in them there was a shared nobility, worth devoting your life to. So Barthes's last two years were those in which writing became a vow, in the religious sense of the term: a commitment, a promise, the intense desire (and doubtless the last fantasy) to complete a work of art that would be this monument.

Barthes and Rebeyrol in Tunis.

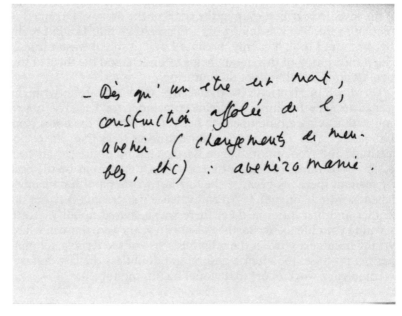

Index card from the *Mourning Diary*.

Henriette Barthes.

Henriette Barthes
with Jean-Louis
Bouttes and Paul
Le Jéloux in Urt.

– J'ajoute : une réflexion sur le Neutre : pour moi : un façon de cher-
cher – d'une façon ~~libre~~ libre – mon propre style
ou présence aux luttes de mon temps.

③ → Procédure : de préparation, d'exposition.

ⓐ La Bibliothèque. — ① Topique. — Pour préparer ce cours : j'ai "promené"
le mot "Neutre", en tant qu'il a pour référent, un affect en moi, un
affect obstiné (à vrai dire depuis le D℥) le long d'un certain nombre de
lectures : = la procédure de la Topique : grille de la Topique n'est pas
on balade un "Sujet". → Noter que le procédé "engagé" en use : prenez un
si archaïque qu'il paraît : tous le disons "engagé" avec n'importe quel
mot-mana : aujourd'hui : "Pouvoir" couplé le (Verdgloire) "Pouvoir
autre mot et parler : "Pouvoir et Intransient" cependant : j'espère (j'
et Sexualité" +Pouvoir et Nature Morte" etc — ce croie) que ma Topique n'a pas aussi maniaque : car j'ai promené le Neutre non pas le long d'une grille de mots : mais d'un
réseau de lectures . cad d'une bibliothèque. Cette bibliothèque : et
ni raisonnée (je n'ai pas suivi un programme bibliographique
l'Intertexte qui vais et distribué) ni exhaustive : Biblio thèque un
livre : encore maintenant (je) vais lire un livre nouveau dont certains
passages peuvent cristalliser autour de la notion de Neutre : comme
une sourcellerie fantaisiste : je lis, la baguette se lève : il y a
du Neutre là dessous → et par là-même, la notion de Neutre s'
e'tend, s'infléchit, se modifie ② Donc, quelle bibliothèque? — Celle de
et se me modifie — ma maison de vacances, cad : loin-temps où la perte de rigueur mé-
thodologique en compensée par l'intensité et la jouissance de la lecture
libre — Définir cette bibliothèque, expliquer son origine, serait entrer
dans la biographie, l'histoire familiale : Bibliothèque d'un sujet :
= une identité forte, complète, un "portrait" (cf. la pharmacopée) → je
dirai seulement, en gros : classique (litt et philosophie) + une mo-
dernité "humanité" qui s'arrête à la guerre de 40 + un apport latéral venant de hasard voyageurs de ma propre vie et concerté : 2 remarques
1. — La donnée (ou le donné) de réflexion est arbitraire : bibliothèque qui
me vient d'un ailleurs (familial) : énormes carences "typiques" : par ex : rien sur
la neutralisation husserlienne (je laisse cette carence en l'état) ; mais bien
plus : dans cette bibliothèque, j'ai opéré les choix très arbitraires de lecture :
j'ai assumé de ne pas contrarier ce que j'appellerai une esthétique du
travail (valeur value par la science) : des livres, dont la pensée et la forme
sont "inesthétiques" : j'ai toujours envie que le matériel soit "racé" : par
ex : en ψ, je retiens de lire du Freud ou du Lacan, mais Karel Horney ou
Reich, ça tombe hors de ma sensibilité de lecture et donc de travail : je ne "cristallise pas" (mot amoureux) — 2. Cette bibliothèque : d'auteurs morts → Cela peut sonner funèbre, passéiste (≠ Dona : s'
intéresser au présent, laisser les morts enterrer les morts etc) — je ne le
prends pas ainsi : a) Distance critique, créatrice : pour m'intéresser vivement
à mon contemporain, je puis avoir besoin du détour par la mort (l'Histoire)
exemple de Michelet : absolument présent à son siècle mais travaillant sur
la "vie" des Morts : je fais penser les Morts en moi : les vivants m'embou-
rent, m'empêguent, me prennent justement dans un système d'écho —
plus ou moins conscient mais seuls les Morts sont des objets créateurs
(seul vivant qui m'ait donné la sensation que je créais : Brecht)

The Neutral: page 1.

καιρός

Huit Heures Vingt du matin . Par
hasard, de mon bureau, je regarde
~~[crossed out]~~ le ciel ; très en haut ,
une moitié de lune très pâlie ,
aux contours légers dans le bleu
lisse du ciel . Or un menu
⟶

776

fragment de nuage, une floculation
légère , petite comme une voiture d'
enfant, passe doucement devant et
s'en va . Théâtre .

Grand fichier: index card from 10 October 1979.

18

'Vita Nova'

15 April 1978

A few months after Henriette Barthes's death, just after finishing his class at the Collège de France, Barthes went to Morocco to stay with Alain Benchaya in Casablanca. This was his second journey since the beginning of 1978. In February, he had given a seminar on reading at the universities of Rabat and Fez. In April, he was on holiday with friends. On Saturday 15 April the weather was fine, and they all decided to go together to the Cascade, a restaurant in a small valley on the Rabat road, between Tit-Mellil and Ain-Harrouda. They travelled in two cars. In spite of the loveliness of the place, the warm welcome given by M. and Mme Manfrenni, and the little lake with its waterfall, Barthes felt the same boredom that had continually prevented him, since his mother's death, from enjoying the present. On his return, alone in his friend's apartment, he was depressed and restless. At this moment an idea came to him, that of a '"literary" conversion – it's those two very old words that occur to me: to enter into literature, into writing; *to write*, as if I'd never written before: to do only that'.[1] This attempt at a retrospective narrative, as presented to the audience at the Collège de France, does not say everything. The illumination, which Barthes compared with that experienced by the narrator at the end of *Finding Time Again*, is not just that of wanting-to-write or literature as the total horizon of a life. It comes from the encounter between a work to come and a content: the novel to be written has to be a response to the absolute nature of maternal love. So it is envisaged as an act of love, producing a monument to that love. In the notes on his mother that comprise the *Mourning Diary*, Barthes pondered at length on the nature of this benevolence, this infinite kindness. It dumbfounds him each time he remembers the last words she spoke to him: In its abbreviated form, 'My R., my R.', the memory – 'the abstract and infernal crux of pain' – reappears three times in the *Mourning*

Diary. Each time, the grief that submerges him is connected with the form of love known as pity; it is this that he wants to write a book about. On one occasion, he hears someone mention 'my novel' (*'mon roman'*) and he immediately links this quasi-homophone to 'my Roland' (*'mon Roland'*), forever linking his mother's last words to what will henceforth keep him alive, his novel. And he adds, parenthetically: 'I am writing my course and manage to write *My Novel*. And then I think with a certain laceration of one of maman's last utterances: *Mon Roland, Mon Roland!* I feel like crying.'[2] And Barthes adds: 'No doubt I will be unwell, until I write something *having to do with her* (*Photo*, or something else).'

What documents do we have that will help us understand the nature and aim of this project, which intensely preoccupied Barthes for the last two years of his life? The published elements appear in the last course at the Collège de France, 'The preparation of the novel', and in the transcription of the successive plans he envisaged in the summer of 1979 for his future work, published as an appendix to the *Oeuvres complètes*. The unpublished archives contain much more material. First, under the title of the 'Grand fichier', there are 1,064 index cards, which we know he wanted to include in the work. They correspond to what he calls 'fragments' in the plans and he regularly spent time classifying them into bundles so as to place them in his composition. He indexed them by theme: homosexuality, mourning, music, leisure . . . Some of these index cards are reflections on the work in progress, and in this case they are labelled 'VN', i.e. 'Vita Nova': 'By "novel" I mean a monumental work, a summa, even novelistic (!), of the kind R[echerche du] T[emps] P[erdu][3] or G[uerre] & P[aix],[4] not a little work (even though the minor can be an adult genre, cf. Borges): at once a cosmogony, an initiatory work, a summa of wisdom.'[5] Then there are the unpublished diaries, from 1974 and 1977, both written in Urt, certain travel diaries (apart from those which were used for *Incidents* that Barthes had already finalized in 1969, and regularly got his friends to read, asking them whether he should publish it).[6] If *Incidents* was a book ready for publication, this was not the case for other posthumous works such as 'Soirées de Paris' or the *Mourning Diary* that would probably have been included in the 'Vita Nova'. Barthes relates that Sollers, very intrigued by the description of the 'wretched failure' of one of his Parisian evenings published in *Tel Quel* in the spring of 1979, suggested that he continue the descriptive enterprise he had begun with this piece, and relate his nocturnal wanderings, what he did and what happened to him evening by evening. '24 August 79. Letter from Sollers who likes the diary extract (Deliberation). What if I tried to relate my evenings in this way? In a "subtly" flat way, without underlining their meaning? Would not a true portrait of this period emerge?' Barthes embarked on this work that very same day and noted down his wanderings from 24 August to 17 September 1979. Under the title 'Vain evenings', he turned them into an important element in his project, like a pendant to the consistency of true love, the mother's love. Published after *Incidents* under the title 'Soirées de Paris' (not the title that Barthes gave them), these texts lose much of their force, which lay precisely in a reflection on this vanity in the context of the broader and more ambitious project of the novel.

The unfinished state or failure of this novelistic work should not be interpreted. For what these unpublished writings allow us to read is a thinking of the fabrication of the work that goes far beyond the question of the book to be written or the novel to come. Barthes had before (or behind) him an impressive number of unpublished fragments, mostly indexed and classified, lying between private life, observation and reflection, and wondered whether he could make a work out of them. He had already composed his previous works (*Roland Barthes by Roland Barthes*, *A Lover's Discourse*) based on this classification by variable geometry of a certain number of existing index cards, and produced strange hypertextual objects that looked forward to new modes for the display and organization of data and information that would be made available by the Internet. With the 'Vita Nova' project, he gave an even more fascinating extension to this idea, revealing his acute awareness of the way a book could pass over into something else, which he called, for want of a better word, the 'album' in *The Preparation of the Novel*. The album did not produce the totality (or the work of art) through continuity or succession, but by disposition, stratification and various manoeuvres of recomposition. He did not abandon the novel because of his dislike of the continuous, the smooth sheet, but rather because he changed paradigm. No longer was the volume, the book as object, a form-meaning able to express, these days, a relation to the knowledge circulating in the world and the connection between works of art, literature and life. Behind this enterprise there lay, of course, the dossier of notes and sketches assembled by Mallarmé for his 'Book', whose dispersed and fragmentary character was the complete opposite of the pure book that Mallarmé himself dreamed of; but ahead there also lay this combinatorial possibility to which, barely ten years later, the World Wide Web would give shape.

Barthes noted the gradual disappearance of the book, which had lost any sacred character. It was no longer the object of any special attention; it was no longer protected; bibliophilia was now an obsession indulged in by just a few eccentrics; there were no longer many book binders ('a profession that enabled my mother to support us as best she could during my adolescent years'[7]). The secularization of the book as object relieved it of its mythical character that had made of it an origin, a guide or a reflection (and only stupidity could still allow anyone to believe in that – *Bouvard and Pécuchet*, for instance, still retained an absolute idea of the book); it led to the antagonistic form of the album. This was characterized by its heterogeneity, its circumstance and its disorder: 'A *page of an album* can be moved or added at random.' Its composition was rhapsodic, dictated by variation and mutability. 'There are great creators on the side of the album: Schumann, for example.' This form was not evidence of a lesser or more minor kind of thinking; but it did represent a different world: 'Album: perhaps the representation of the world as *inessential*.'[8] We need to weigh up this incidental remark, linking it to the contemporary spread of the hypertext: things and ideas are now decentred, dispersed, infinitized; they can no longer be conceived as essences, but as multiple, permutable and exchangeable items. The appeal of the rhapsodic expresses a certain truth of the world, namely its profound disorganization: whether we break the universe into pieces (Nietzsche) or multiply the way in which it is organized, 'in any case, the whole will make a disorganization' (John Cage).[9]

When it came to the form he needed to give to the 'Vita Nova', rhapsodic composition also involved a certain machinery of writing (and Barthes had been practising this for a long time, working on and from his index cards), but one that would produce a complete work this time, aiming at nothing less than a new art of memory. The project involved sewing together scattered fragments, as Proust had done in his novel: 'The Rhapsodic, the tacked together (Proust: the Work as made by a Dressmaker) → the Rhapsodic distances the Object, magnifies the Tendency, the *Writing*.'[10] Here again we see the emphasis on writing as a movement that resists reification and all the intimidations of language. It is not surprising that Barthes should have sought a form that would foster this infinite process. The form lay, not in the fragment as such, but in the organization or arrangement that could be made from the fragments. He underlined this on an unpublished index card from 16 July 1979: 'I can clearly see this much (I think): my "notes" (Diary) as such, are not enough (I incline towards them but in fact they're a failure). What's needed is another turn of the screw, a "key", which will turn these Notes-Diary into the mere notes of work that will be constructed and written *continuously*: basically, to write notes, the *index cards*: to classify them, turn them into bundles, and as I usually do, *compose* by taking one bundle after another.'[11] The plans published in the appendix of the *Oeuvres complètes* indicate the obsessive character of this preoccupation: he needs to conceive at once 'the fragment, the diary, the novel' or 'the already done: the Essay, the Fragment, the Diary, the Novel, [the Comic?], Nostalgia'.[12]

Barthes took two main models for this work to come: the *Pensées* of Pascal and the romantic novel according to Novalis, which brings together all literary forms in the mode of the *poikilos*, a Greek word meaning the changing, the many-hued, the brightly coloured. '*Art of the Novel.* Shouldn't the novel include all kinds of styles, variously linked to and animated by the common spirit? The art of the novel excludes all continuity. The novel should be an edifice that is built anew in each of its eras. Each little fragment should be something cut out – something circumscribed – a whole worth something in itself.'[13] 'Vita Nova' could thus link the account of an intellectual quest, the story of Barthes's evenings, pseudo-dialogues that would stage the language of politics, and the outlines of a great work. Indeed, Pascal's *Pensées* are such an outline: fragments or bits and pieces of an 'Apology' for something[14] –Barthes often used the term 'Apology' instead of 'Vita Nova' to refer to his project. Another reference gradually appears to refer to this difficult form: the 'stromata', a term that Chateaubriand had taken from Clement of Alexandria (who gave this title to the third volume in his trilogy) to designate his own writing, made up of disparate elements. In Ancient Greek, the term *stromata* refers to a colourful fabric, with a mixed texture; from this, it came to designate, in literature, a composite collection made of varied subjects, in a mixture of styles and genres. Chateaubriand always associated this term with couture, weaving, embroidery:[15] thanks to this word, Barthes could connect Proustian couture, the romantic *poikilos* and the multicoloured weave of thoughts, and link them with his own conception of the text as a hyphology, a fabric and spider's web. On 31 August, in Urt, he referred to this 'new project of stromata (in Chateaubriand). Tapestry, book made of fragments. Call it Stromata for myself.' So Barthes invested his practices in existing literary forms but did not settle on any one; he could not get beyond copying, like Bouvard and Pécuchet, or returning to the school exercises of childhood, and to dictation, mentioned twice over in *Roland Barthes by Roland Barthes*:[16] 'To end with, all that would be left would be: to copy, to settle down once more to copying.'[17] The index card diary of 1979 bears the trace of these procrastinations and a certain discouragement; Barthes could not work out how to get beyond this preparatory stage:

> 10 July 1979: Project of the novel being written.
> Level 0: absolute secrecy: the real work that I want to write, laying bear its scaffolding, its equipment, its special effects = the work as it will be published.
> Level 1: the equipment (apparatus and departure) of the work: Vita Nova, the story of what is To Be Done;
> Level 2: the projected fiction (which will not be written);
> What separates level 0 and level 1:
> 0: I know that the novel is impossible and that I won't write it;
> 1: people think the novel will be written, I seek with courage and hope to write it;

But level 0 may in its turn become a trick and thus be fiction-
alized and so turn into level 1, so displacing the others by one
notch.

14 July. Sovereign Good of the Novel: glimpsed face to
face in April (in Casa), but finally I am separated from it – by
mourning, grief, depression – acedia.

18 July. I realize it's impossible to write – and, as it happens,
simply to embark on – a novel. This means, alas: Impossibility
of creating the Other.
    Closed circle: I had conceived the Novel as an act of love
(Casablanca, 15 April 78): I see now that I am unable to
perform this act of love – with my fragment-notes, reduced
to my egotism, my impotence to imagine, to love the Other,
reduced to the egotistic figure of Montaigne-Valéry.

30 November. Work (VN). All of this, all of this book always
means: we don't understand death.
    Option / My problem is this:
    15 April 1978, I wanted to conceive a great work *defined* by
the break in my life, intended to make up for it but without any
relation to this period of transformation in terms of content;
    Gradually the Transformation has become the very object of
the book (Vita Nova); so all I have in front of me, to work on,
is a *dated*, limited, *immediate* material (my notes from these last
few months).[18]

These remarks reveal a certain form of helpless disarray: Barthes
felt abandoned by his project and especially by the strength which
the conversion of 15 April 1978 had given him. They also tell us
something about the project he had envisaged: a work of love, an act
of love. Here too, the models he called on for the content (different
from those that would help him with the form) enable us to detect an
idea that was initially very confident, but which gradually became
more uncertain as time went by. Barthes's references make it clearer
what he understood by 'love'. *War and Peace* and *In Search of Lost
Time* (and, to a lesser degree, *The Divine Comedy* and Rousseau's *La
Nouvelle Héloïse*) were his models. It is easy to understand why he
chose Proust, who had accompanied his life and work from the start.
Dante was there for the idea of a guide secretly leading him through
the work (with the mother as Beatrice). The presence of *La Nouvelle
Héloïse*, less commonly referred to by Barthes than Rousseau's
Reveries of a Solitary Walker, can be explained in at least two ways.
First, it is a novel about 'pity', the form of love whose shape he
is seeking to grasp in 'Vita Nova'. And second, Rousseau's novel

perhaps proves that a Calvinist novel is possible. This is confirmed by a note he made on 13 July 1979. Barthes ponders his resistance to the novel, to untruth. 'Can this be linked to a sort of infusion of Calvinist morality? Are there any Calvinist novelists? (Rousseau, *Héloïse*?) And do I really have a bedrock of Calvinist morality? In any case, this is not through the catechism, but through the indefinable morality of mam. (an "air", a "habitus").'[19] Precisely by seeking to describe his mother's ethical sense, he comes close to the work and philosophical thinking of Rousseau.

Barthes was convinced that all great novels were novels of love. The revelation of 15 April 1978 had laid on him the injunction to produce the missing novel, the novel of maternal love. In so doing, he was aware that he was still resorting to an untimely language, as with *A Lover's Discourse*; but since nostalgia was an affect that concerned this particular subject with the all-encompassing and compassionate love of the mother, being out of step with the times actually became a part of his subject. And this coincided with his conviction that the novel as he dreamt it, something monumental and definitive, was nowadays impossible, and itself pointed to a nostalgic desire. So it was 'under the cover of describing this nostalgia that the present-day world will be described'.[20] The decision he made on 15 April 1978 was a decision to write 'a great work of Love to join the great literary models (*War and Peace*)'. He said this in a different way at the beginning of his course: the novel had no meaning unless it could give voice to 'those one loves', do justice to those one has known and loved, bear witness on their behalf, immortalize them. Or, in the lecture he gave on 19 October: 'I expect from the Novel a kind of transcendence of egotism, insofar as to say whom one loves is to testify that they have not lived (and frequently suffered) "for nothing".'[21]

The idea of bearing witness was crucial. It explains the sort of mystique of the novel that Barthes was drawn to just then, to the surprise of both his friends and his audience. 'What changed in Barthes with the death of his mother was the strange pressure, the strange imperative to write a novel.'[22] Those in Barthes's circle were uneasy, thinking that he would never get past the preparatory stages: 'We didn't understand what he was after. One day, François-Marie Banier, whom Youssef, by various worldly ploys, had inveigled into coming to his evening gatherings, said of Barthes: "He'll never be able to tell a story . . .".'[23] Gérard Genette, who was astonished to see Barthes proclaiming *urbi et orbi* that he was going to write a novel, remembers telling him: 'You're really not superstitious!', to which Barthes merely replied: '"I'm confident", which confirmed his intent.'[24] Even today, critics and old friends doubt the extent to which Barthes was committed to the form of the novel. Antoine Compagnon sees it rather as a belated investment in poetry, which he had hitherto kept at bay and rediscovered in the captive presence of the haiku.[25] Some prefer to see it as a pure object of speculation; and others see it as evidence of his liking for the novelistic, manifest in his most personal writings as the only acceptable part of the novel that could be taken from the genre. However, an attentive reading of all the documents relating to the 'Vita Nova' project makes it possible to venture a contrary opinion. Admittedly, the gigantic novel, the novel he dreamt of, one that would be different from all other novels, was a fantasy: after all, he chose as models not just any novels, but two out of the countless host: *In Search of Lost Time* and *War and Peace*. But as we have seen, each of Barthes's works placed a fantasy at the origin, so this point should not lead to a suspicion of unfeasibility – quite the opposite. If he chose these two novels, it was not to equal their form or their greatness (and he was not actually fascinated by *War and Peace* on this level),[26] but because they were the only novels to have described the incandescence of the spiritual love expressed at the moment of death and constituting the truth of its subject. In Tolstoy, it is the last words that Prince Nikolai says to his daughter Maria before dying: he says that the absolute love he bears her is the only good that can fight against death. In Proust, it is the death of the grandmother, and especially the grief, veneration and piety that her daughter (the narrator's mother) displays in the moments leading up to it, that draw Barthes's attention: her humility as she feels unworthy to touch the most precious thing she knows, her face bending over her mother's, the last words she says to her ('No, dear Mama, we won't let you suffer like this, we'll find something to help you, just be patient for a moment').[27] All of this reminds Barthes of his own mourning, while at the same time being the promise of a transfiguration. The comparison between these two scenes forcefully highlights the nature of the project, which concerns precisely 'pity' as the response to the most complete love. 'Locate with precision the "topical" frisson: it is *War and Peace*, and more precisely Tolstoyan "pity". But there is also a Proustian pity. So do not lose this.'[28]

The force of 'Vita Nova' lay in this radical consent to pathos, to the moment of intense emotion, which gave Barthes's project its magnificent ambition. It was this that enables us to understand a whole set of diverse materials in the book: his friends, his vain evenings, his clandestine loves, his difficulties in getting things done, his endless repetitions, his 'sensation of shame, of "posing", of guignol', the 'rambles' ('cinema, streets with gigolos, locating the saunas, probably with the possibility of some sexual pleasure on the horizon – but also with quite an intense activity of observation and laziness'), the incidents, the Moroccan boy displaying the very essence of *charity*[29] . . . As against the common opinion which rejects compassion and extols a literature 'without pathos',[30]

Barthes reaffirms the force of the emotion aroused by suffering. Thanks to pity, the non-meaning which tragedy holds up against the meaning given to evil and violence can be sustained; it allows us to hear the irreducible cry of the mourning voice. If the modern novel can still have a truth and a function, it needs to remember the tragic principle of compassion. Barthes recognizes the truth of this pathos as a force of reading and as an absolute necessity of literature: 'One must acknowledge that the work to be written [. . .] actively represents, *without saying so*, a sentiment of which I was sure but which I now have great difficulty naming, for I cannot emerge from a circle of worn-out words, dubious by dint of having been used without rigor. What I can say, what I cannot help but say, is that this sentiment which must animate the work has something to do with love; what then – kindness? generosity? charity? Perhaps, simply because Rousseau has given it the dignity of a "philosopheme", pity (or compassion).'[31] He really became fully aware of this from his mother's last words. He noted this again on 26 August 1979, connecting the event to the revelation of the meaning of the word 'rosebud' in Orson Welles' film: 'At the end, discovery, the eruption of the buried secret – like the child's sleigh in *Citizen Kane*: Mam. saying to me "My R., my R.".'

So there is nothing exaggerated in thinking that Barthes would have finally found the form for these many scattered raw materials (index cards, desk diaries, old or ongoing private diaries, current notes, narratives to come, the planned discussion of homosexuality) if death had not brought his work and his reflection to an end. The work would certainly not have corresponded to the current definition of the novel as narration and the unfolding of a plot, but the history of forms tells us that the word 'novel' has been used to designate the most diverse objects. In spite of the moments of inevitable discouragement to which the desk diary bears witness,[32] he had 'confidence', as he had told Genette, and the pensive and emotional weight of his ideas about pathos and love incline us to share that confidence. Four unpublished pages dated 10 December 1979 seem to confirm this intuition. Under the title 'Apology' – the mark of the work's Pascalian roots – he lists the advantages to drawing on these notes, seeing the whole project as essentially based on the incident, the jotting, and turning himself into his own material. 'Conceive a two-part discourse: the note and what goes beyond it, the source of its value; a veritable self-critique, but as a way of going beyond and discovering, not value, but a way of posing it.' It remains to be seen whether or not these fragments can be given a meaning. But their textual interest is undeniable: 'The note is written without teleology. Only retrospectively does it become the material for a commentary.'[33] The account of Barthes's loss and then of the *vita nova* might lead to the neutral display of the fragments, and an explanation of them might come afterwards. Written a month before Barthes's accident, this plan clearly indicates the tenacity with which Barthes worked on his project and envisaged its publication.

New life?

The theme of the *vita nova*, associated with Dante and in the middle of the path of life, is frequently found in Barthes's career. It was already evident in his teenage letters and was repeated at regular stages of his life. In 1978, he was aware that the time left for him to live was long past the middle of his own life, but he noted that this point was not actually an arithmetical fact (Dante experienced it at the age of 35, and had twenty-one years still left to live), but a threshold, a levelling, a shock that would allow him to define 'that mutation, that transformation of the landscape which I have called the "middle of life"'.[34] As for Proust in 1905, the mother's death marked this 'middle of life', after which nothing could be the same because he now had to face the certainty of his own death. So he needed to use what life remained, his last life, as fully as possible, and emerge from the melancholy into which his loss had plunged him. '"*Vita Nova*," Michelet said, marrying at 51 a girl of 20 and preparing to write new books of natural history; [. . .] for the subject who writes, who has chosen to write, there can be no "new life," it seems to me, except in the discovery of a new practice of writing.'[35]

Apart from the projected novel which Barthes was now engaged on, his everyday life changed little under the effect of this revelation and this choice of a 'last life'. In spite of the void left by the death of his mother, he continued to live in the second-floor apartment in the rue Servandoni, using his 'bedroom' on the top floor less frequently than before, as it had become more difficult for him to climb the stairs. But his usual distractions, his travels and evenings out, no longer had the same savour. From November 1977 to June 1978, he went to North Africa three times, returning to Morocco, which he had rather neglected over the last few years. As we have seen, each time he went now, he was seized by the 'desire to go home'. From 5 to 12 November, he accepted the invitation of Tom Bishop and Richard Howard to give a lecture and two seminars at New York University: he was given the welcome that befitted the prestigious person he had become. He travelled first class. At the airport, a limousine was waiting for him and he flew back in Concorde. In New York, he gave his famous lecture on Proust and on his own desire to write a novel – the same lecture he had given at the Collège de France two months earlier. On 21 November, a big cocktail party was organized at Seuil to celebrate the twenty-five years he had been active with the company. Here too, he was feted and honoured, surrounded by close friends. But he was still a little distant. At Le Seuil, it was the presence of Rachel Salzedo, his brother's wife, that struck him; on that day, she had the same dignity and discretion as his mother. Genette remembers Barthes's stay in New York (Genette himself was travelling there for a longer stay): 'We were not in the same cabin and on one occasion I went over to talk to him. He was fast asleep, his head thrown back, his mouth open and, for a moment, I saw him looking as dead as the mummy in *Plain-Chant*, without its golden mask.'[36]

Barthes's sexual frenzy after his mother's death had often been commented on, with sadness or even malice. The publication of the 'Soirées de Paris' has intensified this tendency, but we should not give it much credence. Barthes had always sought immediate satisfactions; he frequented saunas, porn cinemas and gay clubs. This was not anything new in his behaviour, and it did not indicate that he was particularly unhappy. As well as the more or less regular lovers whom he saw in his various little gangs of friends, he always liked seeing gigolos; he found eye contact, and sometimes an exchange of words, could already be erotic. If he regularly spent his nights at Le Palace nightclub, this was not because he suddenly felt the need to try and forget his grief by immersing himself in his pleasures, but because he had always done so; he had known Emaer for more than three decades, and he called him 'Fabrice' while Emaer called him 'my philosopher'.[37] Only the places he frequented changed, because the night also changed quickly. These were regular habits of his; the fact that he was growing old may have made them a little more pathetic, but that is all. Age limited the classic form of cruising, as Barthes had realized for quite a while: 'All that an old man (or growing old) has left is to cruise for gigolos (luckily, this has its charm, its simplicity).'[38] It was also a historical phenomenon. Today, now that sexuality is both privatized and puritanized, these everyday practices can appear excessive or deviant. The AIDS virus had yet to be discovered; it was almost the rule for homosexuals to have multiple partners. One need only read some of the authors who were Barthes's contemporaries to discover how common such activity was at the time: Tony Duvert, Hervé Guibert, Renaud Camus – he was personally acquainted with them all, and had sometimes been seduced by them or fallen briefly in love with them.

He had been thinking for some time of writing something about homosexuality. He wanted to do so without arrogance and without essentializing identities. The idea of 'I'm a this' or 'He's a that' filled him with horror; the strength of this topic, in his view, was that it was not a matter of knowledge. He did not want either the militancy extolled by Guy Hocquenghem (whom he met at the home of Youssef and Jean-Louis) and the Homosexual Revolutionary Action Front, nor the tranquil coming out of Dominique Fernandez – even though Barthes had fought for him to win the Prix Médicis in 1974. Writing on homosexuality was not just a matter of explaining one's own sexual preferences, but of expressing the difference and marginality that homosexuality could draw on to think in a different way. However, when he did choose to discuss it publicly, it was by writing a preface to Renaud Camus's *Tricks*, a book whose sexual and indeed pornographic tendency can hardly be ignored. Renaud Camus and Barthes were close friends. But while Camus's recent bizarre utterances go completely against everything Barthes stood for in his convictions and his writings, it needs to be acknowledged that he has often written very well about Barthes. His *Journal de travers* refers to Barthes frequently, always tenderly, and with a real fascination for his intelligence. Camus attended Barthes's seminar right up to the end, and took part in the ritual dinners that were organized almost every Saturday. He invited Barthes to parties, and introduced him to Andy Warhol. Barthes dedicated to him, to William Burke and to Yvon Lambert the article he wrote on Cy Twombly in 1979 ('To Yvon, to Renaud and to William'). And he admittedly did him a friendly favour by writing a preface to his novel, which ensured that it would attract notice. But the gesture had other implications too. By noting the difference between social, stereotypical and 'pinning-down' discourse, on the one hand, and literary discourse, on the other, with the latter being able to say things 'simply', to display their being-there and subtly diffuse their meaning, Barthes was using this opportunity to restate what had been, forever and on every subject, his own place, the site from which he was speaking. Once he had made this clear, he could also talk about himself: 'But what I like best of all in *Tricks* are the preparations: the cruising, the alert, the signals, the approach, the conversation, the departure for the bedroom, the household order (or disorder) of the place.'[39] This moment, where the scene leaves the register of critical discourse and becomes a novel, a space of possibility and play, was also what he preferred in life, what made him go out in the evenings, for a surprise, a new face, an exchange of glances, a hint of complicity, and sometimes nothing at all.

Barthes continued to move in the same circles. Youssef Baccouche became a sort of organizer of his pleasures, arranging his evenings, seeking to keep him entertained, taking him to a big dinner in honour of Rudolf Nureyev one evening at Le Palace, and with Maurice Béjart a few months later. And he often took Barthes to the Monsieur Boeuf restaurant, where Barthes sometimes encountered Aragon – in his diary notes, he paints a striking portrait of this writer. 'Aragon, very old, almost every evening at the Restaurant Boeuf, sometimes alone: he dozes off, staggers around over the cleared table or burns a candle. Yesterday evening I was again heartbroken at the spectacle of old age, impressed by

the *absent-mindedness* of the guy, it was almost like madness (in
the aggressively modernized dining hall, superficial and sensual-
ist), almost an *innocence*, for sometimes the old man, raising his
head while keeping his eyes closed, had a very moving expression
of *child-like beatitude* (though he's a rather malicious person and
has seen everything, said everything).'[40] He also often went out with
François-Marie Banier, to parties, to Le Palace or to the Bains. He
saw Philippe Mezescaze, Hervé Guibert, Jean-Paul Manganaro,
Romaric Sulger-Büel, Frédéric Berthet, Jean-Noël Pancrazi, and
Jacques Damade. He had affairs with many of them, not all. He
went to the parties thrown by André Téchiné in his new apartment
in the rue de la Tournelle. Here he met the actors with whom he had
filmed *Les Soeurs Brontë*. In July 1979, he went to Cabourg for the
opening of a seaside branch of Le Palace. Apparently he was bar-
racked by two boys (this was his Pasolini side); luckily, he was with
Robert Mauzi, who dragged him away. With other friends, he spent
his evenings more quietly. He regularly met Claude Maupomé, a
producer at France Musique; he formed a close friendship with her
at this time (this was one of the few new female friends of his own
generation that he made). He listened to music with Éric Marty
– they both took out a subscription to the 'Musical Mondays' at
the Athénée, 'a formula which allows me to go to concerts under
simple, calm conditions'.[41] He also saw Antoine Compagnon: he
would usually meet Marty and Compagnon alone, at the Flore, the
Bonaparte or the concert, in another form of sociability. With all
these people, Barthes was extremely generous. He loved paying for a
meal, buying flowers for them and presenting them with small gifts.
But in spite of all this, he gave his friends the impression of always
being rather bored and lonely.

Barthes also felt that he was growing old, and this caused him
distress. Age aggravated his difference and his marginality. The difficulty of growing old is expressed in many texts, especially in the
way he increasingly tackles the question of differences in age and the
relations between different societies and different ages. In the course
on 'The lover's discourse', he focused on ill-defined figures: the
aged child or *puer senex*, the childish old man or *senex puerilis*, who
creates havoc. He liked these indistinguishable and reversible figures
who in their own ways fought against the differences imposed
on them, with the difference in age here including the difference
between the sexes. But society faced him with other images. 'The
"old man" is the attributed to someone by a "young man" who, on
this basis, sees himself as "young". This impulse triggers a certain
racism: I exclude myself from an exclusion that I impose and that is
how, in my turn, I exclude and thus consist.'[42] Though he wrote, in
Le Nouvel Observateur, 'old age stirs me more than childhood',[43] he
did not like the degradations of the body, his increasing weariness.

He continued to go on diets and even joined a gym. But he was 63 and did not exactly look any younger. A woman who talked to him in 1979 described him as a 'grey-haired man with a discreet demeanour'.[44] He had never thought of himself as very attractive, but now his body, which he enveloped in big overcoats, tired him. This all explains the feeling that many people had, looking back, that he had succumbed to melancholy, a sense of abandonment, a presentiment of the end. The 'non-will-to-possess' mentioned at the end of *A Lover's Discourse*, the sense of standing back evoked in his classes, was compounded by a more negative expression of renunciation. In autumn 1978, the secretariat of the Collège de France forwarded to him some protests from students who thought his classes were disappointing and banal. He was dismayed and wondered whether to retire from teaching. He had the – partly justified – feeling that a generation was trying to push him out. This negative impression may also explain his attitude at the time of the polemics around the *nouveaux philosophes* in 1977: he did not want to support them explicitly, especially as his friend Gilles Deleuze was hostile to them; but nor did he wish to be relegated entirely to the limbo of the past. He wrote a personal letter to Bernard-Henry Lévy who, a few months later, did a long, and very fine, interview with him for *Le Nouvel Observateur*,[45] expressing interest in his work. Lévy took the liberty of publishing part of this letter in *Les Nouvelles littéraires* on 26 May 1977. Barthes criticized Lévy for his negative attitude (which he said was mistaken) towards the philosophy of Deleuze, but he acknowledged the validity of some of his ideas, especially those relating to the crisis in historical transcendence. 'Might there not be a sort of agreement between the optimistic ideology of historical "progress" and the instrumentalist conception of language? And conversely, might there not be the same relation between any critical distancing of history and the subversion of intellectual language by its writing?'[46] Barthes thus drew a comparison between Lévy's *Barbarie à visage humain* and his own ethic of writing, which was one way of expressing his support. The publication of this letter – something that Barthes had not wished for – made Deleuze very angry: he summoned Barthes to a sort of friendly tribunal to explain himself. Barthes was too much in demand, and sometimes torn by incompatible friendships; he rarely hesitated about the right way to behave, but he sometimes could not decide how to cope with paradoxical situations or conflicting demands. He found it increasingly difficult to be constantly dependent on the good will of others. 'I don't refuse to receive requests (I probably need people to make them of me) but what I can't stand is that they are addressed to me at the good pleasure of, and for the convenience of, the person making the request, without paying attention to my own time: a telephone call that cuts me off while I'm talking, a request for an article that interrupts a piece of work. I would like to divide, rigorously and almost insanely, my time into weeks for myself and weeks for others.'[47]

When he spoke of his novel in terms of 'liquidations', as happened frequently, Barthes confirmed his desire to finish something if not to finish with it. On one of his index cards he glued some lines from an interview given by Fellini in *Libération*, 18 July 1979: 'I haven't travelled much, I haven't read a great deal, I'm not a revolutionary manning the barricades. I film *en solde*. I liquidate my stocks.' Barthes too viewed his recycling activities somewhat askance; perhaps his art of memory was just a pure egotistical rambling? In his darker times, he was tempted to give up. Barthes felt he was wandering, as if his whole life were assuming the form of the unrealizable; vain evenings, scattered fragments, discouragement – the 'marinade', as he had long since called it, taking the word from Flaubert to refer to his occasional depressions: '[W]hen the depths of agony are plumbed, Flaubert throws himself on his sofa: this is his "marinade", an ambiguous situation in fact, for the sign of failure is also the site of fantasy, whence the work will gradually resume, giving Flaubert a new substance which he can erase anew.'[48] The marinade was linked with solitude, grief, the intermediary state between abandonment and a new zest: but it was now not just a temporary discouragement as he had once experienced it, but a continual state of mind that cast a shadow over his whole life.

Clarity

'A photograph [. . .] is *clear evidence* of what was there.'[49]

However, there was some light at the end of Barthes's life. For a work that had always been based on fantasy, it is admittedly significant that death should catch him before he could construct his monument, when his work, though extensive, was all in bits and pieces. But *Camera Lucida*, which is the book of the mother, carries out part of the project by enshrining her memory for ever in a book. In an ingenuous way, almost without noticing it, Barthes in fact carried out the musical score of his work with two powerful gestures that completed it while giving it a meaning and a future. The first was the course on 'The neutral', given while still traumatized by his loss, which sets out and names the path his ideas had taken ever since *Writing Degree Zero*; the second was the composition and publication of his book on photography, which gave a magnificent shape, filled with resonances, to the interwoven threads of private life and reflection.

His trip to Greece, from 7 to 18 June 1979, was imbued with this great clarity. Barthes had just finished writing *Camera Lucida* (dated 15 April to 3 June 1979), and the ideas on light that he developed in it were reflected by the intensity of the Mediterranean. The index cards of the travel diary draw on the terminology he had dreamt up for photography: the *studium* was the interest he brought to languages, the ethno-sociographic strata as he called them; the *punctum* refers to the register of emotions and surprise. One example was the Orthodox baptism he accidentally encountered on 11 June, going into a church in Piraeus: he was struck by the noise, the bustle, the absence of any meditative atmosphere, the sense of a festivity, the shapeless chanting. Many incidents added life to the scene (the naked baby girl howled when she was dipped into the font, the holy oil was contained in an ouzo bottle, the Orthodox priest pulled up his sleeves and donned an apron like a cook to perform the immersion). It was a perfectly ordinary scene, and beautiful in this very ordinariness, without sublimation, without any particular devoutness either. Barthes returned frequently to the lively impressions this moment had awoken in him. In Salonica, he observed ladies embroidering in the public gardens while gossiping, men alone at the tables, cigarettes, lighters and sunglasses placed in front of them, and children darting between the tables. He liked the open air tavernas, the fruit, the heart, the fresh water, the *bougatsa* of cinnamon eaten in the port. There was also a marvellous encounter with young Lefteris, which was made part of the 'Vita Nova' project as the pure figure of the 'radiance of the encounter'.

This clarity which, fortunately, shone out from the dark periods, giving them their moments of discovery and happiness, was also a clarity that Barthes seems to have sought to turn upon himself, in finishing his projects, in explaining his thought – a procedure that his interlocutors found intriguing. 'From where did the singular clarity of Barthes come? From where did it come *to him*, since he too had to receive it? Without simplifying anything, without doing violence to either the fold or the reserve, it always *emanated* from a certain point that yet was not a point, remaining invisible in its own way.'[50] This dimension of clarification appears explicitly in the course on 'The neutral' in 1978. Here, Barthes deploys the power and career of the notion that, having been a theoretical proposition (the neutral as 'zero degree') became a veritable ethic (against arrogance), leading to an aesthetic (of the jotting, the incident). Although he was, like any white western male, trapped in the rigidity of binarisms and the oppositional paradigms of rationality, his fantasy had always consisted in envisaging forces capable of outplaying them. In writing, in ways of reading, and also in forms of moral behaviour, he had found ways of doing or saying things that would prevent meaning from being caught in categories, language in the definitive, Being in stable identities. In grammar: neither masculine nor feminine; neither active nor passive. In politics: not to decide between two conflicting parties . . . The neutral was mainly a utopia, and it defines Barthes at the deepest level; it was a way of dealing with language,[51] the body, the gesture so as to deprive them of their authoritarianism of essence and fixed definitions. Hence his predilection for thresholds, vestibules, the in-between, all those intermediary places where you are not really anywhere, through which you pass without stopping. There are, of course, negative images of the neutral, both on the political level and on the ethical level; but if we decide to turn it into a utopia, we will highlight the movement by which it destabilizes everything, refuses all that is done-and-dusted, given, obvious. The moral values promoted by the neutral, such as benevolence, delicacy and gentleness, may sometimes be mocked as effeminate, and yet they are the values that are embodied, without authority, by the maternal feminine as Barthes receives and conceives it. It is also the principle of respect for the singular pleasure extolled by Sade in a letter to his wife, quoted in *Sade, Fourier, Loyola*: the enjoyment of all that is small, trivial, marginal, through which individualities express their truth, in other words in their fragile moments. 'I will happily call the non-violent refusal of reduction, the evasion of generality by means of inventive, unexpected, non-paradigmatizable forms of behaviour, the elegant and discreet flight from dogmatism, in short the principle of delicacy – in the final analysis, I will happily call this: gentleness.'[52] Unlike in Blanchot, the neutral in Barthes is neither the negative, nor the unspeakable, nor the night. Its positive force lies in the way it reduces intimidations of every kind: arrogance, totality, virility, the definitive judgement. It attenuates without abolishing, calms without lulling completely to sleep, renders expression more subtle and less vain. Herein resides its strange power of clarification. Instead of displaying thought in the harsh light of an illusory intelligibility, the neutral makes it glitter for a while as it scatters it in fragments, creating gaps and pauses, times and places that elude meaning.

The light at the heart of *Camera Lucida* is of the same nature. It is not the intense clarity of the Mediterranean sun nor the luminous explanation, the full and entire understanding of events and deeds, but a muted light, as it were, more mysterious, more neutral (that is, more mobile), because it emanates not from life but from death. Two circumstances triggered this revelation – in the optical as well as the spiritual sense of the term – of photography. The first was a commission: in 1978, Gallimard asked Jean Narboni to start a collection that they would issue together with *Les Cahiers du cinéma* on the arts of the image. The idea was not to ask specialists to contribute, but rather thinkers who would discuss this area using their intelligence, their competence and their tastes as amateurs. Narboni,

who knew Barthes through Christian Metz, as well as through his
articles on press photography and art photography (Boudinet,
Bernard Faucon, Wilhelm van Gloeden), made the first friendly
overtures. Barthes was delighted, as he was not being asked for a
theoretical discourse; he would not have to immerse himself in writings on photography or delve into its history, even though, in New
York, he had seen his friend Susan Sontag and she had encouraged
him to read her essay on photography; he very much liked it and
immediately suggested that Christian Bourgois publish a translation.[53] His remarks could follow his desires. Like many people in
mourning, he was at that time sorting through and contemplating
old photographs, and it was this which provided the second trigger
for *Camera Lucida*. In December 1978, he had gone to a photographer in the Belleville district of Paris to ask him to restore some
very old, damaged photos of his mother. When Jean Narboni set
him thinking about this subject again in March 1979, he placed the
photo of his mother as a little girl on his desk in front of him and
knew that he had something to discover in this quest; something
both very intimate and very general, which would give meaning to
his project. He immediately bought a few books on photography
at the La Hune bookshop and Delpire (in particular the special *Le
Nouvel Observateur* issues on photography published by the latter),
asked Daniel Boudinet for advice, went to a certain number of
galleries and, back in Urt in April, embarked on the writing of an
essay that would soon take the form of an investigation, with clues,
gradual progress and revelation.

Up until then, while Barthes had taken an interest in photography as a sign, he had always mistrusted its analogical capacity, its
realist dimension. He viewed the photo (especially the fashion or
press photo) from something of a distance, either simply analysing
it or maintaining a certain emotional reserve (witness, for all its pertinence, his article on Boudinet). The discovery of his mother in the
winter garden of the house where she was born in Chennevières-sur-
Marne turned things completely upside down: here too, we could
speak of a 'conversion', as for the revelation of 15 April 1978. On 13
June 1978, coming across this photo, he wept. On 29 December 1978,
after receiving the reproduction he had asked for from Belleville,
Barthes wrote: 'This image enters into conflict with all the ignoble
little combats of my life. The image is really a measure, a judge
(I understand now how a photo can be sanctified, how it can guide
→ it's not the *identity* that is recalled, it's, within that identity, a rare
expression, a "virtue").'[54] The terms employed explicitly connect the
project on love with the astonishment produced by this image. With
it, Barthes was effectively carrying out an experiment that changed
his relation to photography and led him to experience his mourning
in a new way. This discovery shifted his thoughts from a reflection

on the meaning of images, on the one hand, to a reflection on the being of photography – it's 'that's it', it's 'such', as language clumsily puts it when trying to indicate the assumption of the referent that photography can perform. 'The Photograph belongs to that class of laminated objects whose two leaves cannot be separated without destroying them both: the windowpane and the landscape, and why not: Good and Evil, desire and its object: dualities we can conceive but not perceive (I didn't yet know that this stubbornness of the Referent in always being there would produce the essence I was looking for).'[55]

Camera Lucida stages the experience of this reversal. The first part makes its way through the impressions and emotions triggered by certain photographs chosen by Barthes. It sets out the famous distinction between the *studium* (culture, the subject of the photo) and the *punctum* (the emotion – which is defined in quite divergent ways in this part of the book, sometimes as an incident, the pain of mourning, sometimes as the expansive power of the fantasy, as pathos and neutrality). This survey of celebrated, 'public' photos shows how desire functions but says nothing about the nature of photography. Indeed, it sidelines a whole swathe of reflection about photography: the *operator*, the photographer himself, his intention and his work, are virtually ignored. The photo exists solely for the *spectator* who looks at it and this fulfils the fantasy expressed in the 'shock photos' he describes in *Mythologies*: that the images be given exclusively to those who look at them.[56] 'I would have to descend deeper into myself to find the evidence of Photography, that thing which is seen by anyone looking at a photograph and which distinguishes it in his eyes from any other image.'[57] The image of his mother as a little girl, next to her brother Philippe Binger, on a little bridge of the greenhouse that acted as a Winter Garden in the Bingers' fine residence at Chennevières, produces a revelation akin to that of involuntary memory in Proust. It does not simply restore the past, but the truth of that past in the force of its presence, instantly. So the photo is not an image of Henriette Barthes when she was little, but of his mother, now *his* 'little girl', the daughter of Barthes himself as an ageing man. 'Ultimately I experienced her, strong as she had been, my inner law, as my feminine child. Which was my way of resolving Death.'[58] To express the particular nature of this presence that outplays chronology and the usual ordering of times and tenses, Barthes shifts his point of view, passing from the stereotype of the darkroom to the image of the camera lucida. He no longer speaks in mechanical or physical terms, but in chemical terms, emphasizing the action of light on certain substances.[59] The encounter with the loved person that photography enables does not abolish death; it brings a comfort akin to spectral presences for those who believe in spirits. The revelation (in the chemical sense) does nonetheless produce a resurrection (in the religious sense), which authorizes a real contact with the dead person. 'The photograph of the dead person, as Sontag says, will touch me like the delayed rays of a star. A sort of umbilical cord links the body of the photographed thing to my gaze: light, though impalpable, is here a carnal medium, a skin I share with anyone who has been photographed.'[60] The relation is similar to that between Odysseus and his mother in the kingdom of the dead. And it points to a truth of death that is not just one of disappearance. The caption that Barthes adds to the portrait of Lewis Payne by Alexander Gardner reads, 'He is dead and he is going to die', so that death is expressed both in the past and the future. The magic lies in the ordeal represented by that reality, which Bataille calls the Impossible: the rending impact of death, both wounding and blinding. Having experienced this revelation, Barthes can, at the end of his book, bring together his reflection on photography and the conversion leading to the *vita nova*. This convergence is focused around the word 'pity', which unites the *punctum* of photography with maternal love. 'I collected in a last thought the images which had "pricked" me (since this is the action of the *punctum*), like that of the black woman with the gold necklace and the strapped pumps. In each of them, inescapably, I passed beyond the unreality of the thing represented, I entered crazily into the spectacle, into the image, taking into my arms what is dead, what is going to die, as Nietzsche did when, as Podach tells us, on 3 January 1889, he threw himself in tears on the neck of a beaten horse: gone mad for Pity's sake.'[61]

The end

Barthes signed the press copies of *Camera Lucida* on 13 February 1980. He gave copies to a few close friends; he was anxious about how the book would be received. The second part of his book was much more intimate than *Roland Barthes by Roland Barthes* and the *Lover's Discourse*. He did not use the science of degrees that had always been his manner and that acted as a shield. He was annoyed that some of his contemporaries commented on his choice of photographs, saying that they would not have made the same selection, that they would not have chosen that particular photo by Mapplethorpe. Luckily, other readers were less crass. Éric Marty told him that it was his most modern book, the one that reconciled modernity and death. Julia Kristeva was fascinated by the clarity of an argument that saw photography as being based on '"extreme love" and the vision that your mother bequeathed to you'.[62] Marthe Robert, in a letter written on 22 February and probably one of the last that he read before his accident, told him of the 'mixture of

sorrow and strange solace' that his book continued to immerse her
in: she herself had lost her mother a few months earlier and was also
seeking the image that would contain all others.[63]

In spite of the dormant period that precedes the publication of
a book, his schedule barely changed. He dined with Sollers one
evening, with Wahl and Sarduy the next. He heard the pianist Jean-
Philippe Collard at the Athénée with Éric Marty; he played the
piano at the Trillings's, who had invited Boucourechliev, he dined
with François Braunschweig at the Tiburce, went to Le Palace with
Youssef Baccouche and Pascal Bonitzer, and in the afternoon went
to the Bains Pereire or the Bains Odessa. He went on a diet. He
started the paper on Antonioni he was due to deliver in Bologna,
took part at a thesis defence in Nanterre with Jean-François
Lyotard and gave interviews on the things that made the French
nostalgic, and on photography. On 10 February, Michel and Rachel
Salzedo went to Israel to stay with Rachel's family at their home
near the border with Lebanon. Barthes had felt very close to them
since the death of his mother. He celebrated Jewish holidays with
them, and attended the circumcision of the baby boy of Rachel's
sister in Créteil in December 1979. The previous year, they had all
three gone on a pilgrimage to Bedous; the two brothers were filled
with emotion as they recalled the year they had spent there in 1934,
at the start of the illness that had put an end to Barthes's childhood.
He gave his two classes at the Collège every Saturday morning,
and then had lunch with his friends from the seminar in the rue de
Tournon. Ever since the course had been shifted from Wednesdays
to Saturdays, the problems with the lights, the microphones and the
electric connections that were in those days common at the Collège
de France had grown worse, as the technician was often away. In
fact, this was probably the reason why, on 25 February 1980, after
the lunch with François Mitterrand, he decided to go and check the
technical installations for the session on Proust and photography:
he wanted to show some photos by Nadar and, as the whole class
would be based on his commentary on them, he wanted to avoid any
unpleasant surprises.

On 22 February, he revised the notes for his class, and filled out
his tax form. That afternoon, a television crew came to his home
to record a TF1 broadcast on photography. He went to a reception at the Centre Daniel-Douady, where he met, as always, old
friends from the sanatorium: but that day he found the atmosphere
was so depressing that he left straightaway. He had a drink with
Claude Maupomé, then had dinner with Claude Jeantet in a restaurant near the Collège de France. On Saturday 23 February, he
taught his eleventh class of the year and had lunch with his group
in the Chinese restaurant. He went for a walk in Montmartre in the
afternoon. He had dinner at the home of Youssef Baccouche and

dropped into a party organized by François Flahault. On Sunday, he went to the market in the morning, spent part of the day reading theses and then went to Orly Airport to meet Michel Salzedo who was just back from Tel Aviv. He took him to Bofinger's and a few friends joined them. On Monday 25 February, he got up late. He typed the text on Stendhal before going to the lunch in the rue des Blancs-Manteaux. That afternoon, he was knocked down by a van in the rue des Écoles.

It was a 'cold, yellow' day he had noted in his desk diary before leaving. He survived for another month. He received visits, but he could no longer relate to anyone. He did nothing, wrote nothing. He died on 26 March 1980, at 1.40 p.m., in the Pitié-Salpêtrière Hospital.

Vita Nova   22 VIII 79

Méditation · Bilan
Morale sans espoir d'application

Ⓘ
9ᵇ

Rendre dialectique :
plus dialectique et déifiant
schéma trop décepty

Prologue   — Deuil
                — le problème vital de l'Agir (pertinence de ce qui suit ;
                  que faire ? Comment faire ?)

I.   L'acédie amoureuse
        — Suite de RH
        — quête relisitaire

II   Que les "plaisirs" sont insusceptibles de force
        — la Musique   } la Drague
        — Abandon de la peinture
        — Dérisions : le Tricot, le kobolo

III Le Monde comme objet contradictoire de spectacle et indif-
     férence. Examen et Typologie des Discours
     le "réel" ? Le Militant. la mauvaise foi

IV   La décision du 15 Avril 1978. La littérature comme substitut,
     rejoindre d'amour

V   Imagination d'une V.N
              Régimes

VI   Littérature : il ne s'agit que d'une initiation ? Déceptes,
     impuissance ?
        — le Déjà fait : l'Essai. le Journal. Le Roman
        — le Fragment. le Journal
        — le Complexe
        — la Nostalgie

VII L'Oisiveté pure : le "rien faire philosophique" (le Neutre,
     le Tao/ le Tas.
        — les Amis (Fantasme de ne s'occuper que d'eux)
        — le Retour aux places antérieures. Continuer. Pas de VN

Épilogue :   La Rencontre

10 XII 79

Reprenant
mes notes - Journal
(début jusque vers 1978)

INCIDENTS
APOLOGIE

Types de notes
qqf de Journal
Nb de Notes Journal

— Mythologies
— Cénesthésiques
— Observations

le Martinet
Temps à Urt
Bêtes choses vues
Incidents

✳ Apol : il faut tout de même une pertinence :
une valeur (Pascal = Religion) ?

— Observations morales   par S/les Français

Apol   — les Français / La Bêtise ?
             — les Femmes

la plupart de mes observations sont discutables, récusa-
bles — au bénéfice, précisément d'une plus grande
intelligence, générosité
→ concevoir un discours à 2 volets : la note
et son dépassement, d'où surgit la valeur
véritable auto-critique, mais comme dépassement
et découverte non de la valeur mais d'une
manière de la poser. 27 Déc 69 la Carrière du Floro
↳ Je me fais moi-même mon propre matériel, mes
citations.

↳ INCIDENTS

Je reviens (peut-être parce que premières fiches 1969 ?) à la
ti vieille idée des INCIDENTS. Cela, à une autre tour de
la spirale :

✛ 1) Auto-commentaire Aufheben
   2) Classement par liasses (cf Pascal)
   3) Apologie d'une valeur (et non plus simple dé-
      mystification)
   4) Soin systémie de la forme (aussi ferme et intelli-
      gent que du Pascal)

'Apology': one manuscript page.

25

RTP
III 886

Valéry

ma mère

Camera Lucida: manuscript.

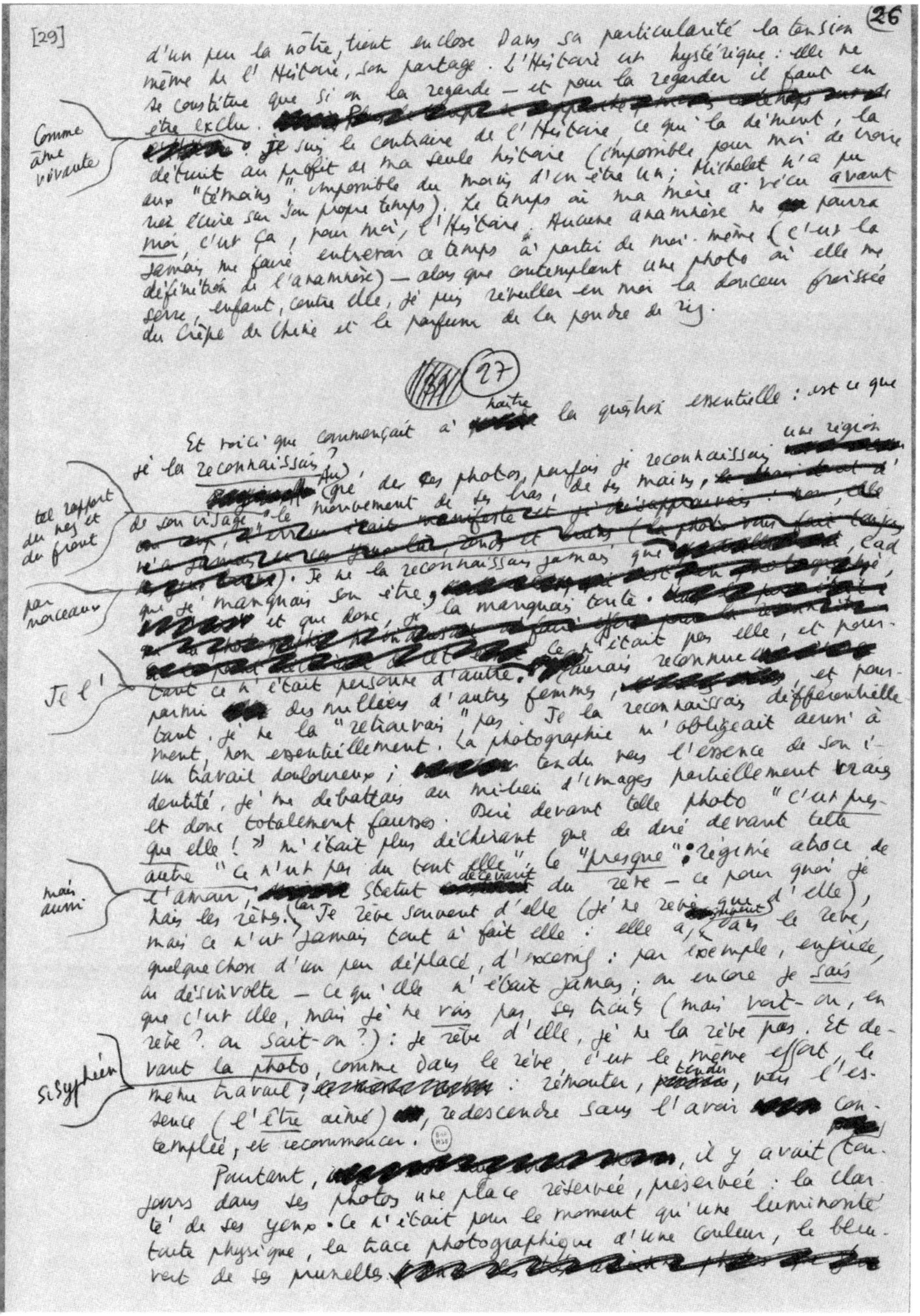
[29] 26

d'un peu la nôtre, tient enclose dans sa particularité la tension même de l'Histoire, son partage. L'Histoire est hystérique : elle ne se constitue que si on la regarde — et pour la regarder il faut en être exclu. Je suis le contraire de l'Histoire, ce qui la dément, la détruit au profit de ma seule histoire (impossible pour moi de croire aux "témoins" ; impossible du moins d'en être un ; Michelet n'a pu rien écrire sur son propre temps). Le temps où ma mère a vécu avant moi, c'est ça, pour moi, l'Histoire. Aucune anamnèse ne pourra jamais me faire entrevoir ce temps à partir de moi-même (c'est la définition de l'anamnèse) — alors que contemplant une photo où elle me serre, enfant, contre elle, je puis réveiller en moi la douceur froissée du crêpe de Chine et le parfum de la poudre de riz.

Comme âme vivante

27

Et voici que commençait à naître la question essentielle : est-ce que je la reconnaissais ?

Au gré de ces photos, parfois je reconnaissais une région de son visage, le mouvement de ses bras, de ses mains. Je ne la reconnaissais jamais que par morceaux, c'est-à-dire que je manquais son être, et que donc, je la manquais toute. Ce n'était pas elle, et pourtant ce n'était personne d'autre. J'aurais reconnue parmi des milliers d'autres femmes, et pourtant je ne la "retrouvais" pas. Je la reconnaissais différentiellement, non essentiellement. La photographie m'obligeait ainsi à un travail douloureux ; tendu vers l'essence de son identité, je me débattais au milieu d'images partiellement vraies et donc totalement fausses. Dire devant telle photo "c'est presque elle !" m'était plus déchirant que de dire devant telle autre "ce n'est pas du tout elle". Le "presque" : régime atroce de l'amour, statut décevant du rêve — c'est pourquoi je hais les rêves. Car je rêve souvent d'elle (je ne rêve que d'elle), mais ce n'est jamais tout à fait elle : elle a, dans le rêve, quelque chose d'un peu déplacé, d'excessif : par exemple, enjouée, ou désinvolte — ce qu'elle n'était jamais ; ou encore je sais que c'est elle, mais je ne vois pas ses traits (mais voit-on, en rêve ? ou sait-on ?) : je rêve d'elle, je ne la rêve pas. Et devant la photo, comme dans le rêve, c'est le même effort, le même travail : remonter, tendu, vers l'essence (l'être aimé), redescendre sans l'avoir contemplée, et recommencer.

Pourtant, il y avait toujours dans ses photos une place réservée, préservée : la clarté de ses yeux. Ce n'était pour le moment qu'une luminosité toute physique, la trace photographique d'une couleur, le bleu-vert de ses prunelles.

tel rapport du nez et du front

par morceaux

Je l'

mais aussi

sisyphéen

Camera Lucida: manuscript.

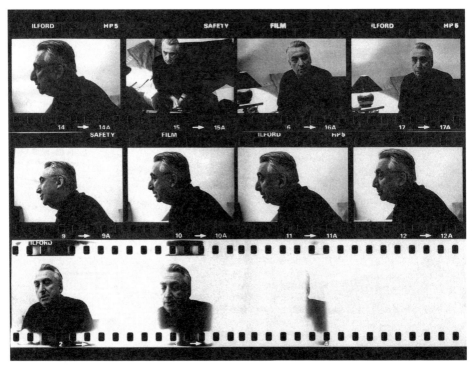

Photo series by Michel Delaborde, carried out fifty days before Barthes's death, for the review *Culture et communication*.

Barthes's office in Urt.

FEVRIER

25 LUNDI S. Roméo 56-310

m

levé tard — *Froid*
jaune

← *Préparation*
Thèse Blanchard,
(BnF MSS) *(dérangé)*

9me Semaine

Desk diary, 25 February 1980.

Notes

Prologue: The death of Roland Barthes

1 'One Always Fails in Speaking of What One Loves', in Barthes, *The Rustle of Language*, translated by Richard Howard (Oxford: Basil Blackwell, 1986), pp. 296–305 (p. 305).

2 In Sollers's view, François Wahl and his colleagues at Éditions du Seuil did not want to tell the truth about Barthes's condition because the connection that journalists would inevitably have made between the luncheon with Mitterrand that Barthes had just left and his accident might have overshadowed the forthcoming electoral campaign. Interview with the present author, 3 September 2013.

3 Philippe Sollers, *Women*, translated by Barbara Bray (London: Quartet, 1991), p. 123.

4 Sollers, *Women*, p. 116.

5 Éric Marty, *Roland Barthes, le métier d'écrire* (Paris: Seuil, Fiction & Cie, 2006), p. 102.

6 Mathieu Lindon, *Ce qu'aimer veut dire* (Paris: POL, 2011), p. 242.

7 Julia Kristeva, *The Samurai*, translated by Barbara Bray (New York: Columbia University Press, 1992), pp. 302–303. It is very moving to read in parallel today the overlapping accounts of Barthes's death in Sollers's *Women* and in this novel by Kristeva. The pseudonyms are not identical, but Werth and Bréhal are tangibly two images of one and the same man, the products of the affection and personalities of the authors composing them. The image is more ambiguous in Sollers, more endearing and fragile in Kristeva.

8 Denis Roche, 'Lettre à Roland Barthes sur la disparition des lucioles', in *La Disparition des lucioles: réflexions sur l'acte photographique* (Paris: Éditions de l'Étoile, 1982), p. 157.

9 BNF, NAF 28630, 'Grand fichier', 26 September 1979. In the homage he paid Barthes in June 1981 under the title 'Lezione di crepusculo' ('Lesson of twilight'), Franco Fortini described what he saw as the amazing connections between Barthes and Pasolini. See Franco Fortini, *Insistenze* (Milan: Garzanti, 1985).

10 Dominique Noguez, 'Roland Barthes à Bologne en janvier 1980 (extraits de journal)', unpublished work kindly communicated by Noguez.

11 Barthes, 'One Always Fails in Speaking of What One Loves', p. 296.
12 Roche, *La Disparition des lucioles*, p. 164; my emphasis.
13 Italo Calvino, 'In Memory of Barthes', in *Collection of Sand. Essays*, translated by Martin L. McLaughlin (London: Penguin Books, 2013), pp. 71–76 (p. 73).
14 Michel Chodkiewicz, the editor of the reviews *La Recherche* and *L'Histoire*: an Arabic specialist who converted to Islam, he was professor at the École des hautes etudes, where he taught Sufism and Muslim mysticism. At Éditions du Seuil, he edited the 'Microcosme' series. He had a reputation for being an extremely demanding reader and an energetic entrepreneur. See Jean Lacouture, *Paul Flamand, éditeur. La grande aventure des Éditions du Seuil* (Paris: Les Arènes, 2010).
15 Marty, *Roland Barthes, le métier d'écrire*, p. 105.
16 Susan Sontag, 'Remembering Barthes', *The New York Review of Books*, 15 May 1980, reprinted in Sontag, *Under the Sign of Saturn* (New York: Farrar Straus Giroux, 1980), pp. 169–177 (pp. 176–177).
17 Jean Roudaut, 'Roland Barthes', in *La Nouvelle Revue française*, no. 329, June 1980, pp. 103–105 (p. 105). The date at the end of the article is 28 February 1980. This means that Roudaut wrote this article a few days after the accident and a month before Barthes's actual death.
18 Michel-Antoine Burnier and Patrick Rambaud, *Le Roland-Barthes sans peine* (Paris: Balland, 1978).
19 Jacques Derrida, 'The Deaths of Roland Barthes', in *Psyche: Inventions of the Other*, edited by Peggy Kamuf and Elizabeth Rottenberg, vol. 1 (Stanford, CA: Stanford University Press, 2007), pp. 264–298 (p. 264).
20 Derrida, "The Deaths of Roland Barthes', pp. 282–283.
21 *Roland Barthes by Roland Barthes*, translated by Richard Howard (London: Macmillan, 1977), p. 59.
22 Barthes, *The Preparation of the Novel: Lecture Courses and Seminars at the Collège de France (1978–1979 and 1979–1980)*, translated by Kate Briggs (New York: Columbia University Press, 2010), p. 298.
23 *OC* V, pp. 634–635: English translation 'Day by Day with Roland Barthes', in *On Signs*, edited by Marshall Blonsky (Baltimore, MD: Johns Hopkins University Press, 1985), pp. 98–117 (pp. 103–104) (translation slightly modified).
24 'Textual analysis of a Tale by Edgar Allan Poe', in *The Semiotic Challenge*, translated by Richard Howard (Oxford: Blackwell, 1988), pp. 261–293 (p. 285).
25 Barthes referred to this in Strasbourg in 1972, at a meeting of the Groupe de recherches sur les théories du signe, as well as the text by Philippe Lacoue-Labarthe and Jean-Luc Nancy (*OC* IV, p. 141); he also drew a connection between the nightmare of death which speaks and the paintings of Bernard Réquichot in 'Réquichot and His Body', in *The Responsibility of Forms: Critical Essays on Music, Art, and Representation*, translated by Richard Howard (New York: Hill and Wang, 1985), pp. 207–236 (p. 210) and *The Pleasure of the Text*, translated by Richard Miller (Oxford: Blackwell, 1990), p. 43.
26 Barthes, 'Chateaubriand: *Life of Rancé*', in *New Critical Essays*, translated by Richard Howard (New York: Hill & Wang, 1980), pp. 41–54 (p. 43).

27 BNF, NAF 28630, 'Délibération', Urt diary, 13 July 1977.
28 'Longtemps, je me suis couché de bonne heure ...', lecture at the Collège de France, 19 October 1978 (*OC* V, p. 468); English translation (under the same title) in *The Rustle of Language*, pp. 277–290 (p. 287).
29 Julia Kristeva, 'La Voix de Barthes', in *Communications*, no. 36, 1982, pp. 119–123 (p. 119).
30 Michel Schneider, *Morts imaginaires* (Paris: Grasset, 2003), p. 17.
31 Barthes, *Michelet*, translated by Richard Howard (Berkeley: University of California Press, 1992), pp. 84–85.

Introduction

1 André Gide, *Journals*, vol. 4 (1939–49), translated by Justin O'Brien (Chicago: University of Illinois Press, 2000), p. 117.
2 BNF, NAF 28630, 'Délibération', Friday, 22 July 1977. Urt diary, mostly unpublished; extracts were published in *Tel Quel* in 1979 (*OC* V, pp. 668–681), and in English translation as 'Deliberation', in *A Barthes Reader*, edited by Susan Sontag (London: Cape, 1982), pp. 479–495 (p. 480).
3 BNF, NAF 28630, 'Grand fichier', 21 September 1979.
4 Michel Foucault, 'Radioscopie', interview with Jacques Chancel, France Inter, 10 March 1975 (my emphasis).
5 Barthes, 'Responses. Interview with *Tel Quel*', translated by Vérène Grieshaber, in *The Tel Quel Reader*, edited by Patrick ffrench and Roland-François Lack (London: Routledge, 1998), pp. 249–268 (p. 249).
6 Pierre Bourdieu, 'The Biographical Illusion', in *Identity: A Reader*, edited by Jessica Evans, Paul du Gay and Peter Redman (London: Sage, 2000), pp. 299–305. What Bourdieu's article denounces is the idea of a historicity of the subject marked by a linear continuum: 'To speak of "life history" implies the not insignificant presupposition that life is a history' (p. 299).
7 Barthes, *Sade, Fourier, Loyola*, translated by Richard Miller (London: Cape, 1977), p. 9.
8 Barthes, *Sade, Fourier, Loyola*, p. 9.
9 Barthes, *Le Lexique de l'auteur. Séminaire à l'École pratique des hautes études, 1973–1974*, edited by Anne Herschberg Pierrot (Paris: Seuil, 2010), p. 183.
10 On the objection in principle to any biography of Barthes in France, see Diana Knight, 'L'homme-roman, ou Barthes et la biographie taboue', in *French Studies Bulletin*, no. 90, Spring 2004, pp. 13–17.
11 Barthes, *Michelet*, translated by Richard Howard (Berkeley: University of California Press, 1992), p. 3.
12 'I like certain biographical features which, in a writer's life, delight me as much as certain photographs; I have called these features "biographemes"; Photography has the same relation to History that the biographeme has to biography' (Barthes, *Camera Lucida: Reflections on Photography*, translated by Richard Howard (London: Vintage, 1993), p. 30).

13 'Longtemps, je me suis couché de bonne heure . . .', in Barthes, *The Rustle of Language*, translated by Richard Howard (Oxford: Basil Blackwell, 1986), pp. 277–290 (p. 283).

14 Louis-Jean Calvet, *Roland Barthes: A Biography*, translated by Sarah Wykes (Cambridge: Polity, 1994). The original French text has also been translated into German (Suhrkamp, 1993).

15 'Life as a text: this will become commonplace (it is so already) unless we specify: it is a text to be *produced*, not to be *deciphered*. – Already said at least twice; in 1942: "It is not 'Edouard's Journal' that resembles Gide's; on the contrary, many entries in Gide's *Journal* have the autonomy of 'Edouard's Journal'" ['On Gide and His Journal', first published (in French) in 1942]; and, in 1966: Proust's work does not reflect his life; it is his life that is the text of his oeuvre ["Les vies parallèles", 1966]).' (Barthes, *Le Lexique de l'auteur*, p. 324).

16 Marie Gil, *Roland Barthes. Au lieu de la vie* (Paris: Flammarion, 2012), p. 23.

17 Gil, *Roland Barthes*, p. 18.

18 Patrick Mauriès, *Roland Barthes* (Paris: Le Promeneur, 1992).

19 Éric Marty, *Roland Barthes. Le métier d'écrire* (Paris: Seuil, 2006).

20 Tzvetan Todorov, *Duties and Delights: The Life of a Go-Between; Interviews by Catherine Portevin*, translated by Gila Walker (Longford: Seagull, 2008); Antoine Compagnon, *Une Question de discipline: entretiens avec Jean-Baptiste Amadieu* (Paris: Flammarion, 2013); Gérard Genette, *Bardadrac* (Paris: Seuil, Fiction & Cie, 2006); Mathieu Lindon, *Ce qu'aimer veut dire* (Paris: POL, 2011).

21 Colette Fellous, *La Préparation de la vie* (Paris: Gallimard, 2014), pp. 44–45.

22 See Nathalie Piégay-Gros, 'Roland Barthes, personage de roman', in *Empreintes de Roland Barthes*, edited by Daniel Bougnoux (Nantes: Cécile Defaut; Paris: INA, 2009), pp. 185–202.

23 Hervé Algalarrondo, *Les Derniers Jours de Roland Barthes* (Paris: Stock, 2006); Christian Gury, *Les Premiers Jours de Roland Barthes, précédé de Barthes en Arcadie* (Paris: Non Lieu, 2012); Jean Esponde, *Roland Barthes, un été (Urt 1978)* (Bordeaux: Confluences, 2009).

24 Bernard Comment, *Roland Barthes, vers le neutre* (Paris: Christian Bourgois, 1991).

25 It was confirmed by the publication of Barthes's *The Neutral: Lecture Course at the Collège de France, 1977–1978*, translated by Rosalind E. Krauss and Denis Hollier; edited by Thomas Clerc under the direction of Éric Marty (New York: Columbia University Press, 2005), and by Thomas Clerc's fine article 'Roland le neutre', in *Revue des sciences humaines*, no. 268(4), 2002, pp. 41–53.

26 Jacques Derrida, 'Otobiographies: The Teaching of Nietzsche and the Politics of the Proper Name', in *The Ear of the Other: Otobiography, Transference, Translation: Texts and Discussions with Jacques Derrida*, edited by Christie McDonald, translated by Peggy Kamuf (Lincoln: University of Nebraska Press, 1988), pp. 1–38.

27 These desk diaries are now kept in the Roland Barthes archive in the Manuscripts Department of the Bibliothèque nationale de France (dépôt 2013). After being kept and evaluated for a long time at the

IMEC (Institut Mémoires de l'édition contemporaine, at the Abbaye d'Ardenne near Caen), the archives were deposited at the BNF in 2011, in accordance with Michel Salzedo's wishes.
28 'Longtemps, je me suis couché de bonne heure . . .', p. 286.

Chapter 1 Setting off

1 *Le Lexique de l'auteur. Séminaire à l'École pratique des hautes études, 1973–1974*, edited by Anne Herschberg Pierrot (Paris: Seuil, 2010), pp. 249–257.
2 *Roland Barthes by Roland Barthes*, translated by Richard Howard (Berkeley: University of California Press, 1994), pp. 107–110.
3 In French schools, the classes are counted backwards: in primary schools, they go from the first year (*dixième* or 'tenth') to the last (*septième*) and, in secondary schools, from the first year (*sixième*) to the penultimate (*première*) and the last (*terminale*), at which point pupils may sit the baccalaureate, which can cover subjects from both the arts and the sciences. (Trans. note.)
4 BNF, NAF 28630, 'Biographie'. In bold, the memories that were rewritten to provide the anamneses in *Roland Barthes by Roland Barthes*. The rest of this text will be found at the start of my chapters 2 and 3 (below).
5 Claude Simon, *Le Tramway* (Paris: Minuit, 2001), p. 14.
6 Barthes, 'Responses. Interview with *Tel Quel*', translated by Vérène Grieshaber, in *The Tel Quel Reader*, edited by Patrick ffrench and Roland-François Lack (London and New York: Routledge, 1998), pp. 249–268 (p. 250).
7 *Roland Barthes by Roland Barthes*, p. 50.
8 'Responses', p. 250.
9 'Responses', p. 249.
10 'Responses', p. 250.
11 'The Light of the Sud-Ouest', in *Incidents*, translated by Richard Howard (Berkeley: University of California Press, 1992), pp. 3–11 (p. 8).
12 'Responses', p. 249.
13 On this subject, see Christophe Bouneau, 'Chemins de fer et développement régional en France de 1852 à 1937: la contribution de la Compagnie du Midi', in *Histoire, économie et société*, 9th year, no. 1, 'Les transports', 1990, pp. 95–112.
14 On this subject, see Séverine Pacteau de Luze, 'Protestants et juifs de Bordeaux. Deux minorités, un même parcours', http://ha32.org/spip/IMG/pdf/Protestants-Juifs_Bx_web.pdf, accessed 30 July 2013.
15 'Responses', p. 250. See also the filmed interview with Jean Thibaudeau for the 'Archives du XXe siècle'.
16 *Roland Barthes by Roland Barthes*, n.p.
17 Marcel Proust, *The Way by Swann's*, translated by Lydia Davis (London: Penguin, 2003), p. 55.
18 Louis-Jean Calvet, *Roland Barthes: A Biography*, translated by Sarah Wykes (Cambridge: Polity, 1994), p. 8.
19 Calvet, *Roland Barthes: A Biography*.

20 Paul Chack, *Sur les Bancs de Flandre* (Éditions de France, 1927), reprinted in *La Grande Guerre des écrivains, d'Apollinaire à Zweig*, edited by Antoine Compagnon (Paris: Gallimard, 'Folio classique', 2014), pp. 303–311 (pp. 307–308). Paul Chack, after commanding the torpedo ship the *Massue* between 1915 and 1917, enjoyed a successful career in the Navy, and after the war published many books (reviews, short stories and novels) on war and naval combat.
21 Chack, *Sur les Bancs de Flandre*, p. 310.
22 *Roland Barthes by Roland Barthes*, pp. 44–45.
23 Françoise Gaillard, 'Barthes juge de Roland', in *Communications*, no. 36, 1982, pp. 75–83 (p. 78).
24 *Roland Barthes by Roland Barthes*, p. 63.
25 *Roland Barthes by Roland Barthes*, p. 126.
26 *Roland Barthes by Roland Barthes*, n.p.
27 Barthes, *The Preparation of the Novel: Lecture Courses and Seminars at the Collège de France (1978–1979 and 1979–1980)*, translated by Kate Briggs (New York and Chichester: Columbia University Press, 2010), p. 365.
28 'An Interview with Jacques Chancel (*Radioscopie*)', in Barthes, *'Simply a Particular Contemporary': Interviews, 1970–1979*, translated by Chris Turner (London: Seagull Books, 2015), pp. 45–81 (p. 68).
29 *Roland Barthes by Roland Barthes*, p. 45.
30 BNF, NAF 28630, 'Grand fichier', 9 March 1978.
31 Georges Perec, *W, or, The Memory of Childhood*, translated by David Bellos (London: Collins Harvill, 1988), pp. 25–26.
32 Perec, *W, or, The Memory of Childhood*, p. 29.
33 'Responses', p. 249.
34 *Roland Barthes by Roland Barthes*, n.p.
35 Interview with Julia Kristeva, 25 September 2013.
36 Antoine Compagnon, ed., *Prétexte: Roland Barthes* (Paris: Christian Bourgois, Actes du Colloque de Cerisy-la-Salle, 2003), p. 333.
37 Or a wave of the sea – French '*vague*' can mean both. (Trans. note.)
38 *Roland Barthes by Roland Barthes*, pp. 121–122.
39 *Roland Barthes by Roland Barthes*, p. 63.
40 *Roland Barthes by Roland Barthes*, p. 86.
41 *Roland Barthes by Roland Barthes*, p. 46.
42 *Roland Barthes by Roland Barthes*, p. 164.
43 'Responses', pp. 249–250 (translation slightly modified).
44 'Rasch', in *The Responsibility of Forms: Critical Essays on Music, Art, and Representation*, translated by Richard Howard (New York: Hill and Wang, 1985), pp. 299–312 (p. 311).
45 *Roland Barthes by Roland Barthes*, p. 115.
46 *Camera Lucida: Reflections on Photography*, translated by Richard Howard (London: Vintage, 1993), p. 72.
47 Captain [Louis-Gustave] Binger, *Du Niger au golfe de Guinée par le pays de Kong et de Mossi (1887–1889), a work containing a general map, several detailed sketches and one hundred and seventy-six engravings on wood after drawings by Riou*, 2 vols (Paris: Hachette, 1892), vol. 1, p. 1.
48 Binger, *Du Niger au golfe de Guinée*, p. 27.

49 Claude Auboin, *Au Temps des colonies. Binger explorateur de l'Afrique occidentale* (Nice: Bénévent, 2008). This work, which redounds to the praises of colonial conquest, uses some of this photographic collection. Claude Auboin does not make any link between this illustrious administrator and his grandson Roland Barthes. He does, however, mention the marriage of Binger's daughter: 'On 11 February, at the town hall of Saint-Médard-de-Mussidan, his daughter Henriette Barthes married Louis Barthes, captain of an ocean-going ship, the son of Léon Joseph Barthes, inspector general of the Chemins de fer du Midi, now retired, and of Marie Berthe de Lapalut his wife, both living in Bayonne. The ceremony was celebrated in the absence of his mother, Noémie Lepet, who had given her consent in an authentic document signed in the presence of her notary in Paris (notarial certificate of Maître Salle, notary in Paris)' (p. 245). Saint-Médard-de-Mussidan, in Dordogne, was where the father had bought a farmstead in 1910 and where he settled with his second wife, his daughter and his three sons.
50 The Africanist Yves Person, author of a doctoral thesis on Samori (*Samori. Une révolution dyula*, Mémoires de l'Institut fundamental d'Afrique noire, no. 80, Dakar, IFAN, 3 vols, 1968, 1970, 1975) devotes a whole chapter to Binger (vol. III, Part 5, chap. 2b: 'The reign of Binger'). For an overview of this history of French opposition to the Malinke conqueror Samori, see 'Samori, construction et chute d'un empire', in *Les Africains* (Paris: Éd. Jeune Afrique, 1977), vol. I, pp. 249–286.
51 He was the author of an 'African' novel of adventures published in 1904, *Le Serment de l'explorateur* (*The Explorer's Vow*), published by Tallandier. More interesting are his memoirs, written in collaboration with his son Jacques and published two years after his death. See Jacques Binger, René Bouvier and Pierre Deloncle (eds), *Louis-Gustave Binger, une vie d'explorateur. Souvenirs extraits des Carnets de route* (Fernand Sorlot, 1938).
52 See Alain-Michel Boyer, 'Binger à la croisée des arts', in *L'Afrique en noir et blanc, du fleuve Niger au golfe de Guinée (1887–1892). Louis Binger explorateur*, Musée d'art et d'histoire Louis-Selencq de L'Isle-Adam (Paris: Somogy éditions d'art, 2009), pp. 75–88.
53 'Bichon and the Blacks', in *Eiffel Tower and Other Mythologies*, translated by Richard Howard (Berkeley: University of California Press, 1997), pp. 35–38.
54 'Bichon and the Blacks', p. 35. The illustrated edition of *Mythologies* by Jacqueline Guittard (Paris: Seuil, 2010) reprints the article from *Paris-Match* with its illustrations and its edifying captions, pp. 82–91 (p. 82).
55 'Bichon and the Blacks', p. 38.
56 'The *Nautilus* and the Drunken Boat', in *Mythologies*, selected and translated by Annette Lavers (London: Jonathan Cape, 1972), pp. 65–67 (pp. 66–67).
57 'The *Nautilus* and the Drunken Boat', p. 65.
58 BNF, NAF 28630, 'Notes des cours de Maroc' ('Notes on classes given in Morocco'). Barthes takes up the main threads here in 'Where to Begin?', in *New Critical Essays*, pp. 79–90.

59 Binger met Jules Verne in 1889. Michel Verne, the novelist's son, used the writings of Louis-Gustave Binger when completing *L'Étonnante Aventure de la mission Barsac*, the novel that his father left unfinished at his death. See the study by Edmond Bernus, 'De L.-G. Binger à Jules Verne', *Journal des africanistes*, vol. 67, no. 2, 1997, pp. 172–182. Thanks to Marie Gil for pointing this out to me; she has produced a precise hermeneutical analysis of the relations between the role played by Verne in Barthes's *imaginaire* and the figure of his grandfather in her *Roland Barthes*, pp. 51–57.

60 See Christophe Prochasson, 'Sur l'environnement intellectuel de Georges Sorel (1899–1911)', in *Cahiers Georges Sorel*, vol. 3, no. 1, 1985, p. 35.

61 'Lectures de l'enfance', in *H. Histoire*, 5 June 1980 (interview recorded on 31 January 1980) (*OC* V, p. 247).

62 Michel Jarrety, *Paul Valéry* (Paris: Fayard, 2008), p. 550.

63 The index to Barthes's *Oeuvres completes* includes no fewer than sixty references to Valéry, very evenly spaced out over the years.

64 *The Neutral: Lecture Course at the Collège de France, 1977–1978*, translated by Rosalind E. Krauss and Denis Hollier; edited by Thomas Clerc under the direction of Éric Marty (New York and Chichester: Columbia University Press, 2005), p. 97.

65 'Lectures de l'enfance' (*OC* V, p. 949).

66 'Saussure, le signe, la démocratie', *Le Discours social*, April 1973 (*OC* IV, p. 332).

67 'He hasn't been accepted into modernity and this is a pity as he does after all says things that are important, in my view, and very insightful ... In any case there is a category of subjects, including myself, who think in words, who have a kind of word-thought, and personally this is what I think I'm doing' (interview with Abdallah Bensmaïn, *L'Opinion*, Rabat, 6 February 1978; *OC* V, p. 536).

68 'The wisdom of art', in *The Responsibility of Forms*, pp. 177–194.

69 *Le Lexique de l'auteur*, p. 318.

Chapter 2 'Gochokissime'

1 Source: Marie and Raymond Chabaud, *Les Rues de Bayonne* (Biarritz: Atlantica, 2010), p. 100. The library of the Marquis de Paulmy is currently held in the name of, and on the site of, the Bibliothèque de l'Arsenal. There is still no rue Roland-Barthes in Bayonne, which the authors of this book regret, even if there is a chemin des Barthes – the Gascon term refers to the land subject to flooding that extends along watercourses, and by extension any swampy ground.

2 *Roland Barthes by Roland Barthes*, translated by Richard Howard (Berkeley and Los Angeles: University of California Press, 1994), n.p.

3 The ramparts of Bayonne were included in the Supplementary Inventory of Historical Monuments on 6 November 1929. Some members of the city council were furious: 'Mere common sense requires the Administrators of the City of Bayonne not to sacrifice the needs of modern life to the exaggerated preoccupations of a few archaeologists

. . . .' Quoted in Monique Larran and Raymond Chabaud, *Il y a 100 ans, Bayonne* (Anglet: Éd. Lavielle, 1997), p. 57.

4 *A Lover's Discourse: Fragments*, translated by Richard Howard (London: Vintage, 2002), p. 216.

5 *Roland Barthes by Roland Barthes*, n.p.

6 *OC* IV, p. 898.

7 BNF, NAF 28630, 'Grand fichier', 1 May 1978.

8 BNF, NAF 28630, 'Grand fichier', 1 May 1978.

9 *Mourning Diary: October 26 1977 – September 15 1979*, edited by Nathalie Léger; translated by Richard Howard (New York: Hill and Wang, 2010), p. 251.

10 Barthes, *Sade, Fourier, Loyola*, translated by Richard Miller (London: Cape, 1977), p. 154.

11 'Responses. Interview with *Tel Quel*', translated by Vérène Grieshaber, in *The Tel Quel Reader*, edited by Patrick ffrench and Roland-François Lack (London: Routledge, 1998), pp. 249–268 (p. 250).

12 Pascal Quignard, *Leçons de solfège et de piano* (Paris: Arléa, 2013), p. 21.

13 'Piano-souvenir', *OC* V, p. 898. This text was first published in *Panorama de la musique*, March–April 1980, under the title 'Piano-Mémoire'.

14 'Piano-souvenir' (*OC* V, p. 899).

15 BNF, NAF 28630, 'Grand fichier', 14 October 1979.

16 This idea is developed in connection with the mother, in Barthes, *Camera Lucida: Reflections on Photography*, translated by Richard Howard (London: Vintage, 1993).

17 See the chapter on Barthes in François Noudelmann, *The Philosopher's Touch: Sartre, Nietzsche and Barthes at the piano*, translated by Brian J. Reilly (New York: Columbia University Press, 2012), p. 105.

18 See Suzanne Tucoo-Chala, ed., *Le Protestantisme à Bayonne. Cent cinquantenaire du temple de Bayonne, 29 juin 1997* (Pau: Centre d'étude du protestantisme béarnaise, 1998).

19 Source: R. Ferret, *Un Évangéliste: Louis Bertrand* (Mission populaire évangélique de France, 1948).

20 It was to this hostel that Henriette Barthes's clothes and other belongings were given after her death. See *Mourning Diary*, p. 138.

21 'Question de tempo', *Gramma*, 1977 (*OC* V, pp. 335–339; p. 338).

22 'The Light of the Sud-Ouest', in *Incidents*, translated by Richard Howard (Berkeley: University of California Press, 1992), pp. 3–11 (p. 6).

23 Claude Maupomé, *Comment l'entendez-vous, Roland Barthes?*, France Musique, October 1979.

24 'The Light of the Sud-Ouest', p. 5.

25 *Mourning Diary*, p. 238.

26 *A Lover's Discourse*, pp. 14–15.

27 Index card for 16 June 1978; reproduced in *Mourning Diary*, pp. 254–255.

28 Sources: *Les Juifs de Bayonne, 1492–1992*, exhibition at the city library of Bayonne, Musée basque, 1992; Henry Léon, *Histoire des Juifs de Bayonne* (Marseille: Laffitte Reprints, 1976 [1893]).

29 See Louis-Jean Calvet, *Roland Barthes: A Biography*, translated by Sarah Wykes (Cambridge: Polity, 1994), p. 226.

30 Interview with Bernard-Henri Lévy, *Le Nouvel Observateur*, 10 January 1977 (*OC* V, p. 371): English translation as 'Of What Use Is an Intellectual?' in *The Grain of the Voice: Interviews 1962–1980*, translated by Linda Coverdale (Evanston, IL: Northwestern University Press, 2009), pp. 258–280 (p. 266).

31 They would see each other regularly until André Salzedo died on 26 April 1956.

32 *Dictionnaire des racines des langues européennes. Grec, latin, ancien français, français, espagnol, italien, anglais, allemande* (Paris: Larousse, 1940, 1949, 1994).

33 'Of What Use Is an Intellectual?', p. 259.

34 *In Grèce*, 122 photographs by Antoine Bon, with an introduction by Fernand Chapouthier (Paris: Éd. Paul Hartmann, 1932); Guy de Pourtalès, *Nietzsche en Italie* (Paris: Grasset, 1929). The latter work, dedicated to Paul Valéry, is really rather insignificant: it contrasts the intellectual and the Christian in the chapter on the death of the gods. 'For the former, all happiness is in oneself or from oneself, all ecstasy, all life.' Any excitable teenager is likely to relish this kind of thing!

35 BNF, NAF 28630, 'Grand fichier', July 1979.

Chapter 3   His whole life ahead of him

1 Anamneses that were not used in *Roland Barthes by Roland Barthes*. Published by Anne Herschberg Pierrot in *Genesis*, no. 19, 2002, p. 46.

2 A competitive nationwide exam taken in *première/terminale*: a good result is a mark of great prestige. (Trans. note.)

3 Letter to Philippe Rebeyrol, 7 April 1933. Fonds Philippe Rebeyrol, IMEC.

4 Letter to Philippe Rebeyrol, 7 April 1933.

5 'Premier texte', *L'Arc*, 1st quarter 1974 (*OC* IV, p. 497).

6 Jules Lemaître, *En Marge des vieux livres, contes*, Librairie générale d'imprimerie et de librairie, 1905. This work offers six pastiches 'on the margins' of the *Odyssey*, the *Iliad*, the *Zend Avesta*, the Gospels and *The Golden Legend*.

7 Barthes, 'Premier texte' (*OC* IV, p. 497).

8 Letter to Philippe Rebeyrol, 14 April 1933.

9 On 17 January 1934, he sent Philippe, on music paper, his very first musical composition, a divertimento in F major, 'a literally very rare copy, entirely hand-copied by the author, for his friend Philippe Rebeyrol'.

10 Roughly equivalent to the Lord Chancellor in the UK. (Trans. note.)

11 BNF, NAF 28630, 'Grand fichier', 1 August 1979.

12 Barthes, *Mourning Diary: October 26 1977 – September 15 1979*, edited by Nathalie Léger, translated by Richard Howard (New York: Hill and Wang, 2010), p. 125.

13 Letter to Philippe Rebeyrol, 1 January 1934.

14 Letter to Philippe Rebeyrol, 5 October 1935.

15 Letter to Philippe Rebeyrol, 9 August 1934.

16 Roland Barthes, 'Loving Schumann', in *The Responsibility of Forms: Critical Essays on Music, Art, and Representation*, translated by

Richard Howard (New York: Hill and Wang, 1985), pp. 295–297 (p. 294), originally in French as the preface to Marcel Beaufils, *La Musique pour piano de Schumann* (Phoebus, 1979; *OC* V, p. 722).

17 'Loving Schumann', p. 294.

18 *Camera Lucida: Reflections on Photography*, translated by Richard Howard (London: Vintage, 1993), p. 70. See also the fine analysis of 'Rasch' (*The Responsibility of Forms*, pp. 299–312) in Christian Doumet's essay 'Barthes au piano', in *Empreintes de Roland Barthes*, edited by Daniel Bougnoux (Nantes: Éd. Cécile Defaut, Paris, INA, 2009), pp. 21–34.

19 François Noudelman, *The Philosopher's Touch. Sartre, Nietzsche, and Barthes at the Piano*, translated by Brian J. Reilly (New York: Columbia University Press, 2012), p. 115.

20 Extracts from letters to Philippe Rebeyrol.

Chapter 4   Barthes and Gide

1 See, for example, the accounts of such visits given by Julien Green, Maurice Sachs, Klaus Mann, Lucien Combelle, and Jean Genet . . . And this is leaving aside for the moment the role he played as a director of conscience, an adviser for homosexuals who felt obliged to hide, and whom his words liberated. See also Olivier Nora, 'La Visite au grand écrivain', in *Les lieux de mémoire* (Paris: Gallimard, 'Quarto', 1997), vol. 2, pp. 2131–2155.

2 Albert Camus, 'Rencontres avec André Gide', *La Nouvelle Revue française*, 'Hommage à André Gide', November 1951, pp. 223–228 (p. 225).

3 'Gide, favourable to the Soviet Union and then hostile towards it, and also adopting a position on colonialism, was one of the last to play the role of the intellectual who is still at the same time a writer.' Barthes recognized Malraux and Aragon as having played a similar role, but later denounced the ever greater importance attributed to the intellectual, the teacher, at the expense of the writer. Barthes, 'La crise du désir', interview of 31 January 1980 for the review *H. Histoire* published on 5 June 1980 (*OC* V, p. 941): English translation 'The Crisis of Desire', in *The Grain of the Voice: Interviews 1962–1980*, translated by Linda Coverdale (Evanston, IL: Northwestern University Press, 2009), pp. 361–366.

4 Barthes, 'On Gide and His Journal', translated by Richard Howard, in *A Roland Barthes Reader*, edited by Susan Sontag (London: Vintage, 1993), pp. 3–17.

5 'On Gide and His Journal', p. 4.

6 'On Gide and His Journal', p. 8.

7 'On Gide and His Journal', p. 17.

8 *Writing Degree Zero*, translated by Annette Lavers and Colin Smith (London: Cape, 1967), pp. 12, 74.

9 'Jean Cayrol et ses romans', *Esprit*, March 1952 (*OC* V, p. 159).

10 *Roland Barthes by Roland Barthes*, translated by Richard Howard (London: Macmillan, 1977), pp. 99, 145.

11 Jean Duvignaud, 'Barthes', *La Nouvelle Revue française*, no. 269, 1975, pp. 93–95 (p. 95).
12 Interviews with Normand Biron in 1975 and 1977, for Radio Canada. Transcribed in the special issue of the *Revue d'esthétique*, 'Sartre/Barthes', 4th quarter, 1981 (*OC* V, p. 420).
13 According to Philippe Roger, it seems that when Barthes uses the term *Abgrund*, as he does in several other texts, he is mainly referring to Meister Eckhart, of whose work he owned the translation by Maurice de Gandillac: *Abgrund* corresponds to the 'Deity', the 'Desert', 'the unfathomable abyss that cannot be reached by any reasoning, by any distinction'. See Philippe Roger's enthralling discussion of this notion in *Roland Barthes, roman* (Paris: Grasset, 1986, Le Livre de poche), pp. 396–401.
14 *Roland Barthes by Roland Barthes*, p. 99.
15 Susan Sontag, 'Writing Itself: On Roland Barthes', in *A Roland Barthes Reader*, pp. vii–xxxvi (p. vii).
16 André Gide, *Conseils au jeune ecrivain; de l'influence en littérature*, edited by Dominique Noguez and Jérôme Vérain, 2nd edn (Paris: Proverbe, 1993), p. 27.
17 Sontag, 'Writing Itself', p. xviii.
18 *Writing Degree Zero*, p. 12.
19 Emily S. Apter, 'Le Mythe du "degré zero"', *Critique*, no. 473, 1986, pp. 967–972 (p. 969).
20 Frank Lestringant, *Gide l'inquiéteur* (Paris: Flammarion, 2012), vol. 2, p. 830.
21 'Of What Use Is an Intellectual?', in *The Grain of the Voice*, pp. 258–280 (p. 261).
22 André Gide, *Notes sur Chopin* (Paris: L'Arche, 1949), p. 18.
23 Gide, *Notes sur Chopin*, p. 34.
24 'Loving Schumann', in *The Responsibility of Forms: Critical Essays on Music, Art, and Representation*, translated by Richard Howard (New York: Hill and Wang, 1985), pp. 295–297 (p. 295).
25 BNF, NAF 28630, 'Grand fichier'. In his note, Barthes indicates that he is referring to Bach's Fourth Partita.
26 'Loving Schumann', p. 298.
27 'Of What Use Is an Intellectual?', p. 261.
28 André Gide, *If It Die*, translated by Dorothy Bussy (New York: Vintage, 2001), p. 252.
29 François Mauriac, answer to a survey in the review *Les Marges*, on homosexuality in literature, March–April 1926, quoted in Daniel Durosay, 'Gide homosexual: l'acrobate', in *Littératures contemporaines*, no. 7, 'André Gide' (Paris: Klincksieck, 1999), pp. 55–85 (p. 55).
30 Barthes, 'Une Idée de recherche', in *Paragone*, October 1971 (*OC* III, p. 920): English translation: 'An Idea of Research', in *The Rustle of Language*, translated by Richard Howard (Oxford: Basil Blackwell, 1986), pp. 271–276 (p. 274).
31 'Une Idée de recherche'.
32 Letter to Philippe Rebeyrol, 2 August 1942. Fonds Philippe Rebeyrol, IMEC.
33 Barthes, *Le Discours amoureux: séminaire à l'École pratique des*

hautes études, 1974–1976, edited by Claude Coste (Paris: Seuil, 2007), p. 445.

34 Barthes, *Incidents*, translated by Richard Howard (Berkeley: University of California Press, 1992), p. 36.

35 BNF, NAF 28630, 'Grand fichier', 19 November 1979.

36 Under this name, anthropologists gather all the ways in which people resort to writing in line with the demands of private life and social existence. See Daniel Fabre, ed., *Écritures ordinaires* (Paris: POL/BPI, 1993).

37 *Roland Barthes by Roland Barthes*, p. 95.

38 Éric Marty, *L'Écriture du jour. Le "Journal" d'André Gide* (Paris: Seuil, 1985), p. 160.

39 Éric Marty, 'L'écriture journalière d'André Gide', in *Poétique*, no. 48, 1981.

40 'I've never kept a journal – or rather, I've never known if I should keep one. Sometimes I begin, and then, right away, I leave off – and yet, later on, I begin again', as he puts it in 'Deliberation', in *A Barthes Reader*, edited by Susan Sontag (London: Cape, 1982), pp. 479–495 (p. 480).

41 Marty, *L'Écriture du jour*, p. 218.

42 'Deliberation', p. 480; 'Délibération', in BNF, NAF 28630. See also Franz Kafka, *The Diaries of Franz Kafka, 1910–1923*, edited by Max Brod, translated by Joseph Kresh et al. (London: Minerva, 1992), entries for 2 October 1911 and 27 September 1911 respectively (pp. 60, 55).

43 'Deliberation', p. 495.

44 'Lectures de l'enfance', in *H. Histoire*, 5 June 1980 (interview of 31 January 1980) (*OC* V, p. 949).

45 'On Gide and His Journal', p. 5.

Chapter 5   His whole life behind him

1 Daniel Cordier, *Alias Caracalla* (Paris: Gallimard, 2009). 'And so, here are, day by day, three years of that singular life that for me began on 17 June 1940, with my rejection of Pétain's speech and my embarkation on the *Léopold II*, at Bayonne. I was nineteen.' Thus Daniel Cordier presents his memories of the war years in which he was the secretary of Jean Moulin and a Compagnon de la Libération. Barthes met him in 1964, at the major exhibition in the Galerie Daniel Cordier, 'Pour prendre congé' ('To take my leave'). This was the start of a rewarding friendship, intensified by their shared origins in the South-West, by their sexual orientations, and also by their common admiration for Réquichot. Daniel Cordier did not come out as a homosexual until 2009, when *Alias Caracalla* was published.

2 'Lettre au sujet du Groupe de théâtre antique', in *L'Arche*, 1962 (*OC* II, p. 25).

3 Jacques Veil, typescript, private archive. Sylvie Patron wrote an article on the first years of the Groupe: 'Le Groupe de théâtre antique de la Sorbonne', in *Les Cahiers de la Comédie-Française*, no. 23, 1997, pp. 48–53.

4 Veil, typescript.

5 Veil, typescript.

6 Quoted in Veil, typescript.

7 As regards the rest of the cast, Marie Dienesch played the queen, Pierre Henry the messenger, and Henri Grall played Xerxes.

8 Maurice Blanchot, *The Infinite Conversation*, translated and with a foreword by Susan Hanson (Minneapolis: University of Minnesota Press, 1993), p. 361.

9 Barthes, 'Témoignage sur le théâtre', in *Esprit*, May 1965 (*OC* II, p. 711).

10 Barthes, *On Racine*, translated by Richard Howard (New York: Performing Arts Journal Publications, 1983), p. 148 (translation slightly modified).

11 *Roland Barthes by Roland Barthes*, translated by Richard Howard (London: Macmillan, 1977), n.p.

12 Barthes, 'La musique, la voix, la langue', first published as 'La musica, la voce, il linguaggio', in *Nuova rivista musicale italiana*, 1978 [1977]; English translation as 'Music, Voice, Language', in *The Responsibility of Forms: Critical Essays on Music, Art, and Representation*, translated by Richard Howard (New York: Hill and Wang, 1985), pp. 278–285 (p. 283). See also, in *Mythologies*, 'L'Art vocal bourgeois' ('Bourgeois Vocal Art'), in which Gérard Souzay embodies excessive expressivity where Barthes rejects intention. Here, bourgeois art is characterized as that which 'over-indicates intention', for fear that intention might not be grasped: such an art 'emphasizes the word by making its phonetic aspect stand out too much'.

13 'Témoignage sur le théâtre'.

14 *Roland Barthes by Roland Barthes*, p. 177.

15 The expressions used to describe 'the diseases of theatre costume' are similar to those condemning the articulation of singers or the expressivity of the actors in the Comédie-Française. 'The costume must always keep its value as a pure function, it must neither smother nor swell the play; it must avoid substituting independent values for the signification of the staged action. Hence it is when the costume becomes an end in itself that it becomes condemnable': *Théâtre populaire*, 1955; English translation as 'The Diseases of Costume' in *Critical Essays*, translated by Richard Howard (Evanston, IL: Northwestern University Press, 1972), pp. 41–50 (p. 42).

16 'Of What Use Is an Intellectual?', in *The Grain of the Voice: Interviews 1962–1980*, translated by Linda Coverdale (Evanston, IL: Northwestern University Press, 2009), pp. 258–280 (pp. 278–279).

17 Persida Asllani, *Roland Barthes: questions* (Paris: Manucius, 'Le Marteau sans maître', 2009), pp. 19, 181). The first question comes from the text 'Culture et tragédie', published in *Les Cahiers de l'étudiant* in 1942 (*OC* I, p. 29), where Barthes discusses the great tragic centuries: the fifth century BC in Athens, the Elizabethan period, and the seventeenth century in France.

18 *Le Lexique de l'auteur*, p. 289. The fragment is dated 7 July [1974].

19 BNF, NAF 28630, 'Grand fichier', 1 August 1979.

20 Letter to Philippe Rebeyrol, 19 August 1937. Fonds Philippe Rebeyrol, IMEC.

21 As 'En Grèce' puts it: 'At Delos, we thought we were approaching an outlying rock, it was the island itself': *Existences*, July 1944 (*OC* I, p. 68).

22 'En Grèce', p. 69.

23 'The *Blue Guide*', in *Mythologies*, selected and translated by Annette Lavers (London: Jonathan Cape, 1972), pp. 74–77 (p. 74).

24 'En Grèce', p. 68.

25 Jean-Pierre Richard, *Roland Barthes, dernier paysage* (Lagrasse: Verdier, 2006), back cover.

26 *Empire of Signs*, translated by Richard Howard (New York: Hill & Wang, 1982), pp. 24–25.

27 'Réquichot and His Body', in *The Responsibility of Forms*, pp. 207–236 (p. 217).

28 '"Prendre" et "tourner"' ('"To catch" and "to turn"'), in *Le Lexique de l'auteur. Séminaire à l'École pratique des hautes études, 1973–1974*, edited by Anne Herschberg Pierrot (Paris: Seuil, 2010), p. 286.

29 'Ornamental Cookery', in *Mythologies*, pp. 78–80 (p. 78).

30 Barthes, *How to Live Together: Novelistic Simulations of Some Everyday Spaces. Notes for a Lecture Course at the Collège de France (1976–1977)*, translated by Kate Briggs, edited by Claude Coste (New York: Columbia University Press, 2013), p. 6.

31 Letter to Philippe Rebeyrol, Good Friday [April] 1939.

32 *L'Abécédaire de Gilles Deleuze*, conversations with Claire Parnet, directed by Pierre-André Boutang, 'A comme animal' ('A is for animal'), 'L comme littérature' ('L is for literature'), DVD Éd. Montparnasse, 2004.

33 Letter to Philippe Rebeyrol, 7 March 1940.

34 Letter to Philippe Rebeyrol, 27 November 1939. He writes 'circumstances' instead of 'consequences' – in the circumstances, this may appear a highly revealing slip of the pen.

35 Cayroux's report, 11 December 1939. BNF, NAF 28630, 'Documents administratifs'.

36 A similar expression, 'On coming out of the cinema' is the title of an article published in *Communications* in 1975, in which Barthes describes the hyper-perceptive state of anyone who has placed himself in a state of quasi-hypnosis in a cinema, staring at the screen.

37 Letter to Philippe Rebeyrol, 7 March 1940.

38 Letter to Philippe Rebeyrol, October 1940.

39 His thesis for the diploma of higher studies, 'Évocation et incantation dans la tragédie grecque' ('Evocation and incantation in Greek tragedy') was deposited with the collection of Roland Barthes's manuscripts at the BNF, 1st deposit (1997–98).

40 François (Fanch) Abgrall, *Et moi aussi, j'ai eu vingt ans!*, preface by Roland Dorgelès (Carhaix: Éd. Armorica, 1935). The book was republished in 2000 by the Éditions Terre de Brume.

41 Thomas Mann, *The Magic Mountain: A Novel*, translated by John E. Woods (New York: A. Knopf, 1995), pp. 58–59.

42 A law passed in 1929 had imposed severe restrictions on former TB patients hoping for careers in the state's administrative departments by fixing obligatory periods of leave for them. Article 23 of the order of 19 October 1946 on the civil service opened this to TB patients who

had recovered. See Pierre Guillaume, *Du Désespoir au salut. Les tuberculeux aux XIXe et XXe siècles* (Paris: Aubier, 1986), p. 279.
43 The statistics show that the decline in mortality became really noticeable only after 1945. The war and the Occupation were factors that aggravated the death rate from tuberculosis. These details are taken from an article by Dr Malthète and Dr Boulanger, 'La tuberculose en France depuis 1938', in *Journal de la Société statistique de Paris*, vol. 87, 1946, pp. 243–268. The illness affected a considerable number of students. The figures provided at the Liberation by Dr Douady show that nearly 8% of the students examined were ill (BDIC 4th delta 1183/7/12).
44 Letter to Philippe Rebeyrol, 6 November 1942.
45 'Remember this private game with Michel Delacroix (cf. perhaps inimitable life, as in Jules Romains) where we would take people we knew, endow them with a set of signs (a way of talking that we could ape, for example) and project them into imaginary (comic) scenes of dialogue, either among themselves or with historical personages (Hitler, etc.)' (BNF, NAF 28630, 'Grand fichier', June 1979).
46 Isabelle Grellet and Caroline Kruse, *Histoires de la tuberculose. Les fièvres de l'âme, 1800–1940* (Paris: Ramsay, 1983), p. 16. The two authors were Barthes's students at the EPHE.
47 He wrote to Veil's parents and his sister Hélène on 5 July 1944: 'I will never forget him, as you mourn him; I always spoke of him as a very beautiful soul, who had all the virtues of his superiority, and whose acute divination of the Good and the Just was always instantly accompanied by a total commitment of his person to the cause he had chosen; his death makes him even greater' (letter to M. and Mme Veil, 5 July 1944, private collection).
48 Marcel Proust, *The Way by Swann's*, translated by Lydia Davis (London: Penguin, 2003), p. 65.
49 Benoîte Groult, *Les Trois Quarts du temps* (Paris: Grasset, 1983), p. 175.
50 Jean Rousselot, *Le Luxe des pauvres* (Paris: Albin Michel, 1956), p. 151.
51 Serge Doubrovsky, *Un Homme de passage* (Paris: Grasset, 2011), p. 194.

Chapter 6   New vistas

1 'Interview [with Laurent Dispot]', in *Playboy*, March 1980 (*OC* V, p. 938).
2 *Roland Barthes by Roland Barthes*, translated by Richard Howard (London: Macmillan, 1977), n.p.
3 Interview in *Playboy* (*OC* V, p. 938). In his text on Brillat-Savarin, Barthes returned to the veritable 'ascesis' constituted by going on a diet. 'Reading Brillat-Savarin', in *The Rustle of Language*, translated by Richard Howard (Oxford: Basil Blackwell, 1986), pp. 250–270.
4 M. Béraud, *Essai sur la psychologie des tuberculeux*, Thesis in medicine, Lyon, 1902, quoted in Pierre Guillaume, *Du Désespoir au salut. Les tuberculeux aux XIXe et XXe siècles* (Paris: Aubier, 1986), p. 262.
5 *Roland Barthes by Roland Barthes*, n.p.

6 'I truly like measuring my temperature four times a day, because it makes you notice what one minute, or even seven, actually means – especially since the seven days of a week hang so dreadfully heavy on your hands here': Thomas Mann, *The Magic Mountain: A Novel*, translated by John E. Woods (New York: A. Knopf, 1995), p. 74.

7 Barthes, 'Michelet, l'histoire et la mort', in *Esprit*, April 1951 (*OC* I, p. 109).

8 Antoine Compagnon, 'L'entêtement d'écrire', in *Critique*, August–September 1982, special issue on Roland Barthes, p. 676.

9 *The Pleasure of the Text*, translated by Richard Miller (Oxford: Blackwell, 1990), pp. 16–17.

10 'Encore le corps', television interview with Teri Wehn Damisch, 13 October 1978; transcribed in *Critique*, 1982 (*OC* V, p. 561).

11 *Roland Barthes by Roland Barthes*, p. 60, quoting *The Pleasure of the Text*, p. 16 (the translations vary slightly between the two texts).

12 Barthes, 'The Grain of the Voice', in *Image – Music – Text*, edited and translated by Stephen Heath (London: Fontana, 1977), pp. 179–189 (p. 183); originally published in French in *Musique en jeu*, November 1972 (*OC* IV, p. 151). The text is yet another opportunity for celebrating Panzéra's performance against Fischer-Dieskau's: 'With FD, I seem only to hear the lungs, never the tongue, the glottis, the teeth, the mucous membranes, the nose. All of Panzéra's art, on the contrary, was in the letters, not in the bellows (simple technical feature: you never heard him *breathe* but only divide up the phrase' ('The Grain of the Voice', p. 183).

13 'Inaugural Lecture, Collège de France', in *A Barthes Reader*, edited by Susan Sontag (London: Cape, 1982), pp. 457–478 (p. 477).

14 *Le Lexique de l'auteur. Séminaire à l'École pratique des hautes études, 1973–1974*, edited by Anne Herschberg Pierrot (Paris: Seuil, 2010), p. 306.

15 Barthes, *How to Live Together: Novelistic Simulations of Some Everyday Spaces. Notes for a Lecture Course at the Collège de France (1976–1977)*, translated by Kate Briggs, edited by Claude Coste (New York: Columbia University Press, 2013), session of 9 February 1977, p. 45.

16 *How to Live Together*, p. 16.

17 Letter to Philippe Rebeyrol, 26 March 1942. Fonds Philippe Rebeyrol, IMEC. It is echoed by this remark in *How to Live Together*: '(after years in the sanatorium, Hans Castorp comes to a standstill (*le point mort*): he no longer has any investment in illness, death itself): he's "on the verge of suicide" [. . .] a dull hopelessness' (pp. 21–22).

18 Letter to Robert David, 28 September 1945. BNF, NAF 28630, private collection.

19 'Deliberation', in *A Barthes Reader*, pp. 479–495 (p. 493).

20 Letter to Philippe Rebeyrol, 26 March 1942.

21 Max Blecher, *Aventures dans l'irréalité immédiate*, translated by Marianne Sora and Maurice Nadeau (Paris: Denoel, 1972), p. 33; English translation Max Blecher, *Adventures in Immediate Irreality*, translated by Michael Henry Heim (New York: New Directions Publishing Corporation, 2015).

22 *How to Live Together*, session of 16 February 1977, p. 54.
23 This is highlighted by Barthes in the example of the bedroom of Abbé Faujas in Zola's *The Conquest of Plassans*: 'There was not a single paper on the table, not an article of any kind on the chest of drawers, not a garment hanging against the walls: the wood was bare, the marble was bare, the walls were bare' (*How to Live Together*, p. 53).
24 Letter to Robert David, 24 November 1945.
25 'Responses. Interview with *Tel Quel*', translated by Vérène Grieshaber, in *The Tel Quel Reader*, edited by Patrick ffrench and Roland-François Lack (London: Routledge, 1998), pp. 249–268 (p. 252).
26 Letter to Robert David, 19 January 1946 (Barthes's emphasis).
27 *Roland Barthes by Roland Barthes*, n.p.
28 Guillaume, *Du Désespoir au salut*, p. 264.
29 André Lepeuple, his room-mate in Saint-Hilaire, relates that 'on the first evening, when it was time to go to bed, Barthes's getting undressed was an absorbing spectacle. He appeared dressed not in the classic pyjamas of everyone else but in a huge white shirt with long sleeves, the collar and sleeves embroidered with red thread, ending in the two swathes of a long tail [. . .] I decided to myself that he was stating his indifference to convention, which struck me as both eccentric and likeable': André Lepeuple, 'Chambre 18. Témoignage', in *Revue des sciences humaines*, no. 268/4, 2002, pp. 143–150 (p. 144).
30 Overfeeding was part of the mythology of sanatoria. When Kafka was thinking of entering one in 1924, he was afraid of the terrible way he would be forced to eat certain things. *The Magic Mountain* is literally stuffed with descriptions of sumptuous meals, so copious as to be almost disgusting.
31 Letter to Mme Rebeyrol, Philippe's mother, 23 January 1944. Fonds Philippe Rebeyrol, IMEC.
32 *How to Live Together*, session of 30 March 1977, p. 110.
33 Letter to Philippe Rebeyrol, 22 May 1942.
34 'Entretien avec Jacques Chancel', interview 17 February 1975, first published in *Radioscopies* (Paris: Laffont, 1976; *OC* IV, p. 900); English translation 'An Interview with Jacques Chancel (Radioscopie)', in *Simply a Particular Contemporary. Interviews, 1970–79*, translated by Chris Turner (London: Seagull, 2015), pp. 45–81 (p. 70).
35 The correspondence with Georges Canetti indicates that, before he met David, Barthes had been immersed in a passionate love for another young man.
36 Letter to Robert David, 5 December 1944.
37 Letter to Robert David, 8 December 1944.
38 Letter to Robert David, 10 December 1944.
39 Letter to Robert David, November 1945.
40 Quoted in Guillaume, *Du Désespoir au salut*, p. 294.
41 Letter to Philippe Rebeyrol, 12 July 1945.
42 Letter to Robert David, 15 February 1946.
43 Letter to Georges Canetti, 23 April 1944. Private collection.
44 Lepeuple, 'Chambre 18', p. 147.
45 Letter to Philippe Rebeyrol, 4 April 1942.
46 Letter to Georges Canetti, 23 April 1944.

47 Letter to Robert David, 26 September 1945.

48 *Michelet*, translated by Richard Howard (Berkeley: University of California Press, 1992), p. 17.

49 The review has been entirely digitized by the Conservatoire des mémoires étudiantes: http://www.cme.u.fr.

50 'Note de la rédaction', in *Existences*, May 1942, p. 4.

51 Paul Hertzog, 'Un traitement de la tuberculose pulmonaire par l'immobilisation absolue et le silence', in *Existences*, July 1942, pp. 56–57.

52 'Culture et tragédie', in *Cahiers de l'étudiant*, 'Essais sur la culture'. First republished by Philippe Roger in *Le Monde*, 4 April 1986 (*OC* I, p. 32).

53 'The germ of the fragment comes to you anywhere [. . .]; then you take out your notebook, to jot down not a "thought" but something like a strike, what would once have been called a "turn"': *Roland Barthes by Roland Barthes*, p. 94.

54 Barthes, 'A propos du numéro special de *Confluences* sur les problèmes du roman', in *Existences*, nos 21–24, July–August 1943 (*OC* I, p. 43).

55 See François-Bernard Michel, 'Roland Barthes: de *La Montagne magique* à *La Chambre claire* – le corps: un lieu fantasmatique', in *Le Souffle coupé. Respirer et écrire* (Paris: Gallimard, 1984), pp. 165–178. This book, written by a lung specialist, examines the link between lung illnesses (tuberculosis, asthma) and writers and includes chapters not only on Barthes but also on Queneau, Valéry, Proust, Gide, Laforgue and Camus.

56 'On Gide and His Journal', translated by Richard Howard, in *A Roland Barthes Reader*, edited by Susan Sontag (London: Vintage, 1993), p. 17.

57 'Réflexion sur le style de *L'Étranger*', in *Existences*, July 1944 (*OC* I, p. 78). [*Bérénice* is a play by Racine noted for its minimal plot and spare but lyrical language – Trans. note.]

58 'Réflexion sur le style de *L'Étranger*', p. 75.

59 On 7 September 1972, a minor earthquake that he felt in Urt rekindled Barthes's memories of this first one.

60 Letter to Robert David, 2 January 1946.

61 Letter to Philippe Rebeyrol, September 1945.

62 Letter to Robert David, January 1945.

63 Letter to Robert David, 1 November 1945.

64 'Esquisse d'une société sanatoriale', unpublished essay reprinted in *R/B, Roland Barthes*, catalogue of the exhibition in the Centre Pompidou, edited by Marianne Alphant and Nathalie Léger, 2002, pp. 170–177 (p. 174).

Chapter 7   Sorties

1 'Responses. Interview with *Tel Quel*', translated by Vérène Grieshaber, in *The Tel Quel Reader*, edited by Patrick ffrench and Roland-François Lack (London: Routledge, 1998), pp. 249–268 (p. 252).

2 'Responses'.

3 Philippe Roger, 'Barthes dans les années Marx', in *Communications*, no. 63, 1996, pp. 39–65 (p. 41).

4 Letter to Philippe Rebeyrol, late July 1946. Fonds Philippe Rebeyrol, IMEC.

5 Letter to Robert David, 19 January 1946. BNF, NAF 28630, private collection.

6 '"Scandale" du marxisme', in *Combat*, 21 June 1951 (*OC* I, p. 125).

7 'Brissaud, worried by the way I'm running after odd jobs, has asked me very seriously on two occasions to ask you in detail what my living and working conditions would be like there' (letter to Philippe Rebeyrol, 2 November 1946).

8 Letter to Philippe Rebeyrol, 10 February 1942.

9 In an account published in *La Quinzaine littéraire* in 2003, she described that hostile world where life was at stake and where 'exchanges of ideas, discussions at those rare moments of freedom that could be grabbed from a tight set of regulations with their implacable schedules enabled people to overcome the boredom and, for a while, get away from it all' (Jacqueline Fournié, 'Notre ami Roland', *La Quinzaine littéraire*, no. 844, 2002, p. 30).

10 See Maurice Nadeau, *Grâces leur soient rendues* (Paris: Albin Michel, 1990), p. 314. In this book, Nadeau confuses two memories: the time he met Barthes, which was actually June 1947 (a letter to Rebeyrol of 20 June 1947 confirms this, even if Nadeau says it was July), and the time Barthes sent his first articles. In a personal interview with him, when I pointed out the inconsistency in these dates (the meeting and the publication of the first articles were at almost exactly the same time), he told me that the first article must have been sent earlier. In 'Responses', Barthes dated to about 1946 the article on blank writing and the commitment of form and to 1947 the commissioning of the articles that were eventually published in *Combat*.

11 'Faut-il tuer la grammaire?', *Combat*, 26 September 1947; republished under the title 'Responsabilité de la grammaire' (*OC* I, pp. 96–98). Between 1947 and 1952, Barthes published six reviews in *Combat*: in 1950, on *La Loi des révolutions* (*The Law of Revolutions*) by André Joussain, *Marcel Rivière éditeur* (*Marcel Rivière the publisher*) by Benoît Hepner, and *Lazare parmi nous* (*Lazarus among us*) by Jean Cayrol; in 1951, *Description du marxisme* (*Description of marxisme*) by Roger Caillois, *Race et civilisation* (*Race and civilization*) by Michel Leiris, and *Phénoménologie et matérialisme dialectique* (*Phenomenology and dialectical materialism*) by Tran Duc Thao, as well as an account of 'the dispute between Egyptologists'.

12 'Réponses' (*OC* III, p. 1027).

13 Yves-Marc Ajchenbaum, *À la vie, à la mort. Histoire du journal 'Combat', 1941–1974* (Paris: Le Monde Éditions, 1994), p. 197; republished as *'Combat', 1941–1974. Une utopie de la Résistance, une aventure de presse* (Paris: Gallimard, 'Folio Histoire', 2013).

14 On the publication of his first book, Barthes said: 'As the subject of a combat or what I felt was such, namely the demonstration of the political and historical commitment of literary language, I was sure of myself, but as the subject who had produced an object offered publicly to the gaze of others, I felt somewhat ashamed' ('Responses', p. 253).

15 *Combat*, 1 August 1947.

16 Maurice Nadeau, 'Roland Barthes: *Le Degré zéro de l'écriture*', in *Les Lettres nouvelles*, June 1953; reprinted in *Serviteur! Un itinéraire critique à travers livres et auteurs depuis 1945* (Paris: Albin Michel, 2002), pp. 195–203 (p. 203).

17 *Roland Barthes by Roland Barthes*, translated by Richard Howard (London: Macmillan, 1977), p. 94.

18 Nadeau abandoned his books page in 1951 when Henri Smadja became the sole editor in chief of *Combat* (a post he would keep until he died, and the paper folded in 1974), bringing in Louis Pauwels, so that the paper swung perceptibly to the right. Claude Bourdet invited Nadeau to pursue his activities in *L'Observateur*, and put him in charge of its literary supplement; Nadeau agreed, and asked Barthes to write for it just after the latter had come back from Alexandria.

19 Nadeau, *Grâces leur soient rendues*, p. 322.

20 Maurice Nadeau, 'Barthes puissance trois', in *La Quinzaine littéraire*, no. 205, 1 March 1975. The lead was not reproduced in *OC* IV, p. 775.

21 Nadeau, *Grâces leur soient rendues*, p. 318.

22 'Où/ou va la littérature?', dialogue with Maurice Nadeau in the radio programme 'Dialogues' with Roger Pillaudin, France Culture, 13 March 1974 (*OC* IV, pp. 547–563). First published in *Écrire . . . pourquoi? pour qui?* (Grenoble: Presses universitaires de Grenoble, 1974); then as a separate booklet with the title *Sur la littérature* (*On Literature*) (Grenoble: Presses universitaires de Grenoble, 1980).

23 Maurice Nadeau, 'Roland Barthes. Un souvenir de Montmorency', in *La Quinzaine littéraire*, no. 323, 16 April 1980.

24 Letter to Philippe Rebeyrol, 26 April 1947.

25 Barthes, *The Preparation of the Novel: Lecture Courses and Seminars at the Collège de France (1978–1979 and 1979–1980)*, translated by Kate Briggs (New York and Chichester: Columbia University Press, 2010), p. 231.

26 BNF, NAF 28630, box 7, 'Documents administratifs'.

27 See the photo of the official document in *Roland Barthes by Roland Barthes*. Archives of the French Ministry of Foreign Affairs, Nantes. File on 'Bucharest'.

28 After closing in 1949, the Institut reopened in 1970 as the Bibliothèque française. In 1989, bilateral agreements between Romania and France gave it back its status as the Institut français of Bucharest.

29 André Godin, *Une Passion roumaine. Histoire de l'Institut français des hautes études en Roumanie (1924–1948)* (Paris: L'Harmattan, 1998), p. 186. This book is one of our sources of information on this period. See also the article by Micaela Ghiţescu on Barthes's time in Romania, 'Roland Barthes in România', *România literară*, no. 48, 2000, www.romlit.ro/jos. Thanks also to Alexandru Matei for the information he provided me with on this period.

30 'Nouvelles de l'Institut', report addressed to Philippe Rebeyrol in February or March 1949. Fonds Philippe Rebeyrol, IMEC.

31 Letter from Henriette Barthes to Robert David, 21 March 1948.

32 '[. . .] Arrived at your place around 11, couldn't find anyone there and went away so angery [sic] that I thought of leaving Bucharest

straightaway, without even seeing you again. And all this because it was so nice outside, and I'd been so looking forward to the walk we had planned! . . . Unfortunately, I'd asked a certain young man if I could introduce him to you this evening, and since I don't want to break my promise to him (I've done so several times already), here I am obliged to pay for your ingratitude by the greatest benefit: to deliver into your hands a very attractive boy, a bit thick-set, noisy and whimsical, but apart from that really likable and above all devilishly nice for all those who wish him well . . . Furthermore, I'd be grateful if you would take good care not to increase my displeasure by being over-attentive to that particular gentleman, whom I am bringing along more to keep an eye on you in my absence than to keep you entertained. Farewell, until this evening . . .' (letter from Petre Sirin to Roland Barthes, 3 February 1949, private collection).

33 Petre Sirin, *Castele în Spania. Cronică de familie (1949–1959)* (Bucharest: Humanitas, 2013). Much of this chronicle concerns his affair with the violinist and musicologist Mihai Rădulescu, arrested for indecent behaviour in 1959 and for his involvement in the dissident group Noica-Pillat: he committed suicide while in prison. Petre Sirin depicts Barthes under the name of Amphytrio in an unpublished *roman à clé* preserved in his archives. (See Alexandru Matei, 'Barthes en Roumanie, 1947–1949. L'enfer de l'Histoire et le purgatoire de l'amour', forthcoming).

34 Letter to Robert David, 7 May 1948.

35 Letter to Robert David, 7 January 1946.

36 A search through the archives of the Securitate, where every citizen can nowadays consult his or her dossier (at the CNSAS, the Consiliul Naţional pentru Studierea Arhivelor Securităţii or National Council for Studying the Securitate Archives) reveals nothing under the entries 'Barthes' or 'Roland Barthes'. Admittedly, several archives were destroyed by fire in 1990.

37 Annie Guénard, *La Présence culturelle française en Europe centrale et orientale avant et après la Seconde Guerre mondiale (1936–1940; 1944–1949)*, a PhD thesis in history, with the thesis director René Girault, Université de Paris I, 1994, quoted by Godin, *Une Passion roumaine*, p. 201.

38 'La politisation de la science en Roumanie' ('The politicization of science in Romania'), a document of 21 July 1949, Archives de l'Institut français de Bucarest. Part of this analysis would be repeated almost word for word in the chapter of *Writing Degree Zero* devoted to 'Political modes of writing' (pp. 19–28).

39 Letter to Philippe Rebeyrol, 18 June 1949.

40 Letter to Philippe Rebeyrol, 18 June 1949.

41 Jean-Claude Chevalier, 'Barthes et Greimas à Alexandrie, 1949–1950', preceded by 'Barthes à Bucarest, 1947–1948', in *Documents pour l'histoire du français langue étrangère ou seconde*, no. 27, December 2001, pp. 115–126. Archives of the French Ministry for Foreign Affairs. Dossier 'Relations culturelles, 1949–1959', no. 435.

42 Letter to Philippe Rebeyrol, 3 January 1950.

43 Letter to Philippe Rebeyrol, 3 January 1950.

44 Charles Singevin, *Essai sur l'un* (Paris: Seuil, L'Ordre philosophique,

1969); *Dramaturgie de l'esprit* (Dordrecht, Boston and London: Kluwer, 1988).

45 Chevalier, 'Barthes et Greimas à Alexandrie', p. 116.

46 See Georges Matoré, *La Méthode en lexicologie* (Paris: Librairie Marcel Didier, 1950).

47 Michel Arrivé notes that the itinerary that led Greimas from Suassure to Hjelmslev coincided exactly with that of Barthes, in 'Souvenirs scientifiques et autres sur A. J. Greimas', *Nouveaux actes sémiotiques*, no. 25, 1993, 'Hommages à A. J. Greimas', Limoges, PULIM, 1993, pp. 13–23 (p. 18). In the closing interview at the colloque de Cerisy devoted to Greimas, however, the latter said of Hjelmslev: 'I don't know if it was Barthes who told me it was important, or whether it was me who told Barthes' (Michel Arrivé and Jean-Claude Coquet, *Sémiotique en jeu. À partir et autour de l'oeuvre d'A. J. Greimas* (Paris and Amsterdam: Hadès and Benjamin, 1987), p. 303).

48 A. J. Greimas, 'L'actualité du saussurisme', in *Le Français modern*, no. 3, 1956, p. 193.

49 A. J. Greimas, 'Roland Barthes: une biographie à construire', in *Bulletin du Groupe de recherches sémio-linguistiques*, no. 13, March 1990.

50 Jean-Claude Chevalier and Pierre Encrevé, *Combat pour la linguistique, de Martinet à Kristeva. Essai de dramaturgie épistémologique* (Lyon: ENS Éditions, 2006), p. 334.

51 Greimas, in an interview with Jean-Claude Chevalier and Pierre Encrevé, republished in Chevalier, 'Barthes et Greimas', p. 124.

52 Chevalier, 'Barthes et Greimas', p. 125.

53 Letter to Philippe Rebeyrol, 1 April 1950.

54 Letter to Philippe Rebyrol, [April] 1952.

55 *L'Espace humain* was first published by Éditions La Colombe in 1953, and republished by Nizet in 1976.

56 Matoré, *La Méthode en lexicologie*, p. XIII.

57 Letter to Philippe Rebeyrol, 3 November 1952.

58 BNF, NAF 28630, 'Boxes of index cards', 2nd box, 'Index-glossary'.

59 Dossier on scholarly and administrative career, mission of national archives at the CNRS, Gif-sur-Yvette, quoted in Jacqueline Guittard, 'Hygiène du roman. *Le Degré zero de l'écriture* sous influence', in *Romanesques*, no. 6, 2014, pp. 19–32 (p. 21); this article studies the impact of these lexicographical studies on the first of Barthes's published books.

60 Letter to Philippe Rebeyrol, 20 April 1952.

61 The first letter from Cayrol to Barthes indicates that he was writing 'on the recommendation of [my] friend Albert Béguin'.

62 Letter reproduced in Philippe Forest, *Histoire de Tel Quel, 1960–1982* (Paris: Seuil, Fiction & Cie, 1995), p. 18.

63 There are many sources for the history of Éditions du Seuil. See especially: Anna Boschetti, 'Légitimité littéraire et stratégies éditoriales', in Roger Chartier and Henri-Jean Martin (eds), *Histoire de l'édition française. Le livre concurrence, 1900–1950* (Paris: Fayard, Cercle de la librairie, 1986), pp. 510–551; Hervé Serry, *Les Éditions du Seuil, 70 ans d'histoires* (Paris: Seuil, 2008); Jean Lacouture, *Paul Flamand éditeur.*

La grande aventure des Éditions du Seuil (Paris: Les Arènes, 2010); and André Parinaud, '"Le Seuil", le plus jeune des "grands", nous explique comment on deviant éditeur', in *Arts*, no. 594, November 1956, 21–2.

64 Letter from Raymond Queneau, 8 February 1952, private collection. 'From the purely publishing point of view, there is little chance of us publishing such a short work here. [. . .] None of this should stop you publishing the unpublished part in the T[emps] M[odernes].' When he was writing *Roland Barthes by Roland Barthes*, Barthes made index cards for all his books, and one of his notes referred to this episode: 'Degree zero: The second part of DZ much better, much more successful than the first (it was, I think, the original part). (Wasn't that the part that was turned down by Gallimard?)' See BNF, NAF 28630, 'Fichier vert 1'.

65 Letter from Albert Béguin, 2 October 1950. Private collection. 'Monsieur, I would very much like to get in touch with you and, if possible, persuade you to write for *Esprit*. Your article last year, on the degree zero, had made a great impression on me, and I decided I would like to meet you. Forgive me for having waited until today to express this wish, and to ask you if you would like to write for us. Yours ever, Albert Béguin.' The subsequent correspondence continued to express Béguin's admiration for Barthes, one that he expressed article after article, book after book, never skimping on his compliments.

66 'Un prolongement de la littérature de l'absurde', in *Combat*, 21 September 1950 (*OC* I, p. 105).

67 'Michelet, l'Histoire et la mort', in *Esprit*, April 1951 (*OC* I, p. 123).

68 Lucien Febvre, *Michelet, créateur de l'Histoire de France*, edited by Brigitte Mazon and Yann Potin (Paris: Vuibert, 2014). The course from the previous year, part of which Barthes might have attended, is published as *Michelet, la Renaissance*, edited by Paule Braudel (Paris: Fayard, 1992).

69 Lucien Febvre, 'Michelet pas mort', in *Combat*, 24–25 April 1954, p. 1. In the rest of the article, Febvre heaped praise on Barthes's book. He even pointed out that the publication of Michelet's *Journal* would confirm some of Barthes's powerful intuitions.

70 'Jean Cayrol et ses romans', in *Esprit*, March 1952 (*OC* I, p. 157). The article focuses on Cayrol's two first stories, brought together under the title *Je Vivrai l'amour des autres* and *Le Feu qui prend*.

71 See the article by Bernard Comment, 'Prétextes de Roland Barthes', in *Magazine littéraire*, no. 314, October 1993, pp. 59–63, showing how Barthes appropriated texts by Cayrol, Camus and Robbe-Grillet.

72 *Writing Degree Zero*, translated by Annette Lavers and Colin Smith (London: Cape, 1967), p. 3, and BNF, NAF 28630, 'Le degré zero de l'écriture. Manuscrits'.

Chapter 8   Barthes and Sartre

1 *How to Live Together: Novelistic Simulations of Some Everyday Spaces. Notes for a Lecture Course at the Collège de France (1976–1977)*,

translated by Kate Briggs, edited by Claude Coste (New York: Columbia University Press, 2013), p. 6.

2 'La dernière des solitudes', interview with Normand Biron, in *Revue d'esthétique, Sartre/Barthes*, p. 114 (reprinted in *OC* V, p. 419).

3 *Roland Barthes by Roland Barthes*, translated by Richard Howard (London: Macmillan, 1977), p. 76.

4 See also 'Twenty Key Words for Roland Barthes', in *The Grain of the Voice: Interviews 1962–1980*, translated by Linda Coverdale (Evanston, IL: Northwestern University Press, 2009), pp. 205–232, where Barthes says: 'When I began to write, after the war, Sartre was the avant-garde. The encounter with Sartre was very important to me. I have always been, not fascinated, the word is absurd, but changed, carried away, almost set on fire by his writing as an essayist. He truly created a new language of the essay, which impressed me very much' (p. 213).

5 Marielle Macé, 'Barthes-Sartre, comme un roman', a lecture given on 17 January 2003 at the conference on 'Barthes et la traversée des signes' ('Barthes and the voyage through signs'), Centre Georges Pompidou. Thanks to the author for allowing me to read this piece.

6 Mikel Dufrenne, 'Présentation', in *Revue d'esthétique*, special issue 'Sartre/Barthes', 1991, p. 5.

7 Susan Sontag, 'Writing Itself: On Roland Barthes', in *A Roland Barthes Reader*, edited by Susan Sontag (London: Vintage, 1993), pp. vii–xxxvi (p. xxi).

8 BNF, NAF 28630, 'Mythologies'.

9 Jean-Paul Sartre, *What is Literature?*, translated by Bernard Frechtman (London: Methuen & Co., 1950), pp. 22–23.

10 *Writing Degree Zero*, translated by Annette Lavers and Colin Smith (London: Cape, 1967), p. 15.

11 The neutral and the degree zero are more or less the same in Brøndal. The degree zero is a term that contrasts with the negative and the positive (which designate any kind of opposite) and is defined by the non-application of the relation (the zero term of morphology or degree zero of phonology). For example, the degree zero is the indicative as an a-modal form (neither subjunctive, nor imperative) or the third person (neither the first person nor the second). See Claude Zilberberg, 'Relation et rationalité. Actualité de Brøndal', in *Langages*, 22nd year, no. 86, 1987, pp. 59–77. Barthes did not quote Brøndal by name in *Writing Degree Zero*. He did so later, in *Elements of Semiology*, translated by Annette Lavers and Colin Smith (New York: Hill and Wang, 1977).

12 'Tragédie et hauteur' (*OC* I, p. 976).

13 'The Eiffel Tower', in *The Eiffel Tower and Other Mythologies*, translated by Richard Howard (Berkeley: University of California Press, 1997), p. 7.

14 *On Racine*, translated by Richard Howard (New York: Hill & Wang, 1964).

15 'École', in 'Fragments inédits du *Roland Barthes par Roland Barthes*', in *Le Lexique de l'auteur. Séminaire à l'École pratique des hautes études, 1973–1974*, edited by Anne Herschberg Pierrot (Paris: Seuil, 2010), p. 277.

16 *Writing Degree Zero*, p. 87.

17 This is the view of Jean-Claude Milner: 'Sartre had stopped on the edge of language, Barthes bore the spear of intelligence flushing out its prey in the materiality of words and phrases; he dared to maintain that literature, as an ideological form, implies decisions about writing – and, conversely, that every decision about writing involves an ideology': Milner, *Le Périple structural* (Paris: Verdier Poche, 2002), p. 161.

18 *Writing Degree Zero*, pp. 9, 87.

19 *Roland Barthes by Roland Barthes*, p. 106.

20 *Writing Degree Zero*, p. 26.

21 *Writing Degree Zero*, p. 28.

22 *Writing Degree Zero*, p. 71.

23 J. B. Pontalis, 'Roland Barthes, *Le Degré zero de l'écriture*', in *Les Temps modernes*, November 1953, pp. 934–938.

24 This manifesto, signed by 121 intellectuals and published in September 1960, protested against the French government's use of torture in the Algerian War and called for recognition of the Algerians' right to independence. (Trans. note.)

25 *Roland Barthes by Roland Barthes*, p. 45.

26 Jean-Paul Sartre, *Words*, translated by Irene Clephane (London: Penguin, 2000), p. 19.

27 *Words*, p. 15.

28 *Words*, p. 19.

29 *Roland Barthes by Roland Barthes*, n.p.

30 'Final stasis of this lineage: my body. The line ends in a being *pour rien*' (*Words*, p. 22).

31 Jean-Pierre Martin, *Éloge de l'apostat. Essai sur la* vita nova (Paris: Seuil, Fiction & Cie, 2010), p. 103. He is quoting from Jean-Paul Sartre, *War Diaries: Notebooks from a Phoney War November 1939 – March 1940*, translated by Quintin Hoare (London: Verso, 1984).

32 Antoine Compagnon, 'Lequel est le vrai?', in *Magazine littéraire*, no. 314, October 1993, pp. 26–28.

33 'Roland Barthes was a fluid thinker [. . .] slippery as an eel [. . .] his shifts are not simply the result of chance, nor do they come from a weakness in judgement or character flaw': Alain Robbe-Grillet, *Ghosts in the Mirror*, translated by Jo Levy (London: John Calder, 1988), pp. 51–53.

34 Robbe-Grillet, *Ghosts in the Mirror*, pp. 51–53 (translation modified).

35 Martin, *Éloge de l'apostat*, p. 183. The expression 'theoretical superego', or, more exactly, 'weakening of the theoretical superego', appears in Barthes, *The Preparation of the Novel: Lecture Courses and Seminars at the Collègege de France (1978–1979 and 1979–1980)*, translated by Kate Briggs (New York: Columbia University Press, 2010), p. 206.

36 'Twenty Key Words for Roland Barthes', in *The Grain of the Voice*, pp. 205–232 (p. 231).

37 On this, see *The Preparation of the Novel*, in which Barthes refers to the disappearance of the great forms of literary leadership, a transformation brought about by Sartre who endeavoured to bring about the myth's self-destruction.

38 'Barthes often taught us that knowledge arises from the practice of

writing and not from an abstract diagram whose applications we would then try out' (Umberto Eco, 'La maîtrise de Barthes', *Magazine littéraire*, no. 314, 1993, p. 42).

39 *Roland Barthes by Roland Barthes*, p. 106.

40 *Roland Barthes by Roland Barthes*, n.p.

41 Jean-Paul Sartre, 'Explication de *L'Étranger*', in *Cahiers du Sud*, February 1943; reprinted in *Situations I* (Paris: Gallimard, 1947), p. 93.

42 'The empire of signs is prose': Sartre, *What is Literature?*, p. 11.

43 'À propos de Sartre et de l'existentialisme', an interview with Ellis Donda and Ruggero Guarini for RAI Due, recorded at the Collège de France on 15 February 1980; transcribed and published in *L'Espresso*, 27 April 1980; translated and published in the *Magazine littéraire*, no. 314, October 1993, pp. 51–53 (p. 52). This interview was not included in the *Oeuvres complètes*.

44 'À propos de Sartre et de l'existentialisme'.

45 This seminar, announced orally, did not in fact take place (probably because Barthes did not give a seminar in 1978).

46 *Camera Lucida: Reflections on Photography*, translated by Richard Howard (London: Vintage, 1993), p. 21.

47 'Inaugural Lecture, Collège de France', in *A Barthes Reader*, edited by Susan Sontag (London: Cape, 1982), pp. 457–478 (p. 463). See also 'Literature as mathesis' in *Roland Barthes by Roland Barthes*, pp. 118–119.

48 'Inaugural Lecture', p. 464.

49 Marcel Proust, *The Way by Swann's*, translated by Lydia Davis (London: Penguin, 2003), p. 391.

50 Jean-Paul Sartre, *The Psychology of Imagination*, translated by Bernard Frechtman (London: Methuen, 1972), p. 66.

51 *Roland Barthes by Roland Barthes*, p. 161.

52 Sartre, *Nausea*, translated by Robert Baldick (Penguin: 2000), p. 17.

53 *The Preparation of the Novel*, p. 38.

54 'Vers le Neutre' ('Towards the Neutral') announces Bernard Comment in the title of his book: the preposition is important (*Roland Barthes, vers le neutre* (Paris: Christian Bourgois, 1991).

55 *Criticism and Truth*, translated and edited by Katrine Pilcher Keuneman (London: Continuum, 2007), p. 24.

56 'Barthes en bouffées de langage', interview with Claude Bonnefoy, in *Les Nouvelles littéraires*, 21 April 1977 (*OC* V, p. 395).

Chapter 9   Scenes

1 *Roland Barthes by Roland Barthes*, translated by Richard Howard (London: Macmillan, 1977), p. 159.

2 Barthes never quotes this book, even though some of his analyses, especially on rhetoric, overlap with Paulhan's. In a hostile article on Claudel, Barthes acknowledged Paulhan's lucidity about the 'etymological proofs' that Claudel gave of religious faith ('L'Arlésienne du catholicisme'; *OC* I, p. 283); but, as we shall see, Paulhan was more of an enemy for Barthes in the 1950s.

3 *How to Live Together: Novelistic Simulations of some Everyday Spaces. Notes for a Lecture Course at the Collège de France (1976–1977)*, translated by Kate Briggs, edited by Claude Coste (New York: Columbia University Press, 2013), pp. 154–169.

4 *A Lover's Discourse: Fragments*, translated by Richard Howard (London: Vintage, 2002), p. 208.

5 Éric Marty, 'Présentation' (*OC* I, p. 17).

6 *Prétexte: Roland Barthes*, Actes du Colloque de Cerisy-la-Salle, 22–29 June 1977, edited by Antoine Compagnon (Paris: Christian Bourgois, 2003), p. 408.

7 BNF, NAF 28630, 'Fichier vert 1: Livres, morceaux choisis'.

8 *Michelet*, translated by Richard Howard (Berkeley: University of California Press, 1992), p. 201.

9 Letter from Gaston Bachelard, 8 April 1954. Private collection. He goes on to express his wish to read Michelet's *Journal,* which he hopes has not been redacted – he wants all of Michelet's 'moods' to be observable: 'Then we will need to use your tables, your snapshots, your nourishing information, in order to read with benefit the private remarks of a great Living Presence.'

10 Letter from Starobinski, 18 July 1954. Private collection.

11 *Roland Barthes by Roland Barthes*, p. 125.

12 Éric Marty uses the term 'predation' to characterize Barthes's method in *Michelet* ('Présentation', p. 17).

13 Letter to Robert David, 20 December 1945. BNF, NAF 28630, private collection.

14 Letter to Robert David, 26 December 1945. Barthes's emphasis.

15 Letter to Robert David, 24 November 1945: 'You must try and find me a photo-portrait (a photo, not a painting) of Michelet. There is one, I know, I've seen it. You might find it in a shop in the Rue des Écoles opposite the Sorbonne, there's another shop in the Rue de Seine, on the left as you go towards the Seine, in the stretch between the boulevard Saint-Germain to the Rue de Buci.' – Letter to Robert David, 14 December 1945: 'This morning I received the fine photograph of Michelet. How can I ever thank you? [. . .] The photo perplexes me and disturbs the brilliant – but unverifiable – improvisations I had already made on the demoniac first portrait. I can't manage to make any comments on the second portrait, even though it makes a vivid impression on me. The Kindness of a face is always difficult to describe, I've already felt as much with regard to you.'

16 *Michelet*, p. 20. Here, Barthes seems to give an alimentary meaning to the verb 'to graze'. In his seminar at the Collège de France in 1977, 'Tenir un discours' ('Holding a discourse'), he adds a mechanical sense to this same verb (in French '*brouter*)': 'to cut in a jerky way, when speaking of certain tools, to act in fits and starts, when speaking of a brake, a clutch, a machine'.

17 Milner, *Le Périple structural* (Paris: Verdier Poche, 2002), p. 162. See also Marielle Macé, 'Barthes et l'assertion', in *Revue des sciences humaines*, no. 268, 4/2002, pp. 151–162.

18 BNF, NAF 28630, 'Michelet'.

19 *Michelet*, p. 3.

20 Bernard Dort, 'Vers une critique "totalitaire"', in *Critique*, X, no. 88, 1954, pp. 725–732.

21 Albert Béguin, 'Pré-critique', in *Esprit*, no. 215, 1954, pp. 1013–1019 (p. 1013).

22 Febvre, 'Michelet pas mort', in *Combat*, 24–25 April 1954.

23 Letter to Philippe Rebeyrol, October 1953. Fonds Philippe Rebeyrol, IMEC.

24 'Entretien sur les *Essais critiques*', with Guy Le Clec'h, in *Le Figaro littéraire*, 16–22 April 1964 (*OC* II, p. 621).

25 *Roland Barthes by Roland Barthes*, n.p.

26 *The Preparation of the Novel: Lecture Courses and Seminars at the Collège de France (1978–1979 and 1979–1980)*, translated by Kate Briggs (New York: Columbia University Press, 2010), session of 19 January 1980, p. 218.

27 Letter to Philippe Rebeyrol, 10 December 1953.

28 *Roland Barthes by Roland Barthes*, n.p.

29 Emmanuel Lemieux, *Edgar Morin, l'indiscipliné* (Paris: Seuil, 2009), p. 251.

30 Violette Morin and Joseph Majault, *Un Mythe moderne, l'érotisme* (Brussels: Casterman, 1965).

31 When she died in 2003, an issue of *Humoresques*, 'Hommage à Violette Morin', no. 20, June 2004, brought together some of her unpublished texts on this subject.

32 This text was included in the *Critical Essays*, translated by Richard Howard (Evanston, IL: Northwestern University Press, pp. 37–41. Barthes's name disappeared from the committee after issue no. 6 (February 1958).

33 Later, Edgar Morin would say this was the reason why Barthes left: he 'did not share this experience and this culture and was not very comfortable at our meetings': Edgar Morin, 'Une tribune de discussion', in *Rue Descartes*, no. 18, 'Kostas Axelos et la question du monde' (Paris: PUF/Collège international de philosophie, 1997), p. 122.

34 Gil Delannoi, '*Arguments*, 1956–1962, ou la parenthèse de l'ouverture', in *Revue française de science politique*, 34th year, no. 1, 1984, pp. 127–145 (p. 141). On this subject, see also the issue of *Rue Descartes* devoted to Kostas Axelos (see n. 33).

35 Georges Friedmann (1902–62) had been trained as a philosopher, worked in the Centre de documentation sociale at the École normale supérieure at the beginning of the 1930s, and focused on labour and social relations. He was a Marxist and went to study these questions in the USSR, publishing two works of a comparative nature on the economic situation in that country; he was lucid about the difficulties, and this brought him into conflict with the French Communist Party. He returned to France to join the Resistance during the war, and after the Liberation he found the position he deserved thanks to the publication of his thesis on automation, *Le Machinisme industriel*. He was appointed head of the Centre d'études sociologiques at the CNRS and organized a considerable amount of research in the field of the sociology of labour and also in other areas of technological culture, such as the media and communication. His main works, all

528 Notes to pp. 203–209

published by the Éditions Gallimard, include: *Le Travail en miettes.*
Spécialisation et loisirs (1956; English translation: *The Anatomy of*
Work; The Implications of Specialization, translated by Wyatt Rawson
(London: Heinemann, 1961)), *Signal d'une troisième voie?* (1961), and
Fin du peuple juif? (1965; English translation: *The End of the Jewish*
People?, translated by Eric Mosbacher (London: Hutchinson, 1967)).
In 1961, Barthes published in *Annales* a note on the Centre d'études
des communications de masse, indicating and defending its existence.
36 This report authorized Jean Stoedzel, at the time Director of the
Centre d'études sociologiques, to entrust Barthes with a day's discussion of 'the sociology of the spectacle and its audience'. AN, 'Archives
de la direction centrale du CNRS', 197803015, box 10.
37 Violette Morin, 'À Georges Friedmann', in *Communications*, no. 28,
1978, pp. 1–4 (p. 2).
38 Letter to Philippe Rebeyrol, spring 1954. The name 'Milhaud' (spelled
'Millaud' in his tentative 'Biography', quoted at the beginning of
chapter 3 above) refers to their teacher at Louis-le-Grand.
39 Jean-Claude Chevalier and Pierre Encrevé, *Combat pour la linguis-*
tique, de Martinet à Kristeva. Essai de dramaturgie épistémologique
(Lyon: ENS Éditions, 2006), p. 336.
40 Letter from Jean Paulhan, 20 December 1953. Private collection.
41 Letter to Marcel Arland, 4 September 1954. The words I have put in
italics are crossed out in the draft and replaced by 'before any other
satisfaction; and for this, the support of the CNRS is necessary to me,
I cannot feel really free until I have done all I can to obtain it'. Private
collection.
42 *Roland Barthes by Roland Barthes*, p. 177.
43 'Le théâtre populaire d'aujourd'hui', in *Théâtre de France*, 1954 (*OC* I,
pp. 529–533).
44 Brigitte Jaques-Wajeman, 'Retour à Barthes', in *Empreintes de Roland*
Barthes, edited by Daniel Bougnoux (Nantes: Éd. Cécile Defaut and
Paris: INA, 2009), pp. 97–107 (p. 105).
45 Morvan Lebesque was the drama critic of *Carrefour* and a journalist
on *Le Canard enchaîné*. He was also President of the Association des
amis du théâtre populaire. Guy Dumur wrote drama criticism for *La*
Table ronde and in *Médecine de France*. He had been an actor and had
several novels to his name.
46 Jean Duvignaud, '*Théâtre populaire*: histoire d'une revue', in *Magazine*
littéraire, no. 314, 1993, pp. 63–64.
47 Marco Consolini, *Théâtre populaire, 1953–1964. Histoire d'une revue*
engagée, translated by Karin Wackers-Espinosa (Paris: Éditions de
l'IMEC, 1998).
48 Letter to Robert Voisin, 18 July 1953. Archives de l'Arche.
49 'L'Arlésienne du catholicisme' (*OC* I, p. 285).
50 Barthes, 'Éditorial', in *Théâtre populaire*, no. 5, January–
February 1955, p. 4.
51 'Fin de *Richard II*', in *Les Lettre nouvelles*, March 1954 (*OC* I, p. 471).
52 *OC* IV, p. 868.
53 'Responses. Interview with *Tel Quel*', translated by Vérène Grieshaber,

in *The Tel Quel Reader*, edited by Patrick ffrench and Roland-François Lack (London: Routledge, 1998), pp. 249–268 (p. 255).

54 Consolini, '*Théâtre populaire, 1953–1964*, p. 34.

55 'La rencontre est aussi un combat', in *Rendez-vous des théâtres du monde*, April 1957 (*OC* I, p. 877).

56 Morvan Lebesque, 'Ionesco "démystificateur"', in *Carrefour*, 22 February 1956.

57 Roland Barthes' 'Éditorial' [unsigned], in *Théâtre populaire*, no. 9, September–October 1954, pp. 1–2.

58 Michel Vinaver, interview with Marco Consolini, in Consolini, '*Théâtre populaire'*, *1953–1964*, p. 72.

59 Consolini, interview with Pierre Trotignon, in Consolini, '*Théâtre populaire'*, *1953–1964*, pp. 170–171, note 1.

60 Published by Seuil (Pierres Vives) in 1960.

61 Published by Seuil in 1971.

62 Chantal Meyer-Plan05, *Bernard Dort: un intellectuel singulier* (Paris: Seuil, 2000).

63 'For me he was someone very important insofar as, precisely, he was around the years . . . between 1955 and 1965, at a time when he was alone too . . . he was certainly the one who helped us most to shake off a certain form of academic knowledge that was non-knowledge' (Michel Foucault, *Radioscopie*, interview with Jacques Chancel, France Inter, 10 March 1975). On the relations between Barthes and Foucault, see the chapter below devoted to this topic.

64 Vinaver's remarks on this demonstrate a great deal in common with Barthes's arguments on the force of Brecht's theatre. It would certainly be interesting to study this dialogue in detail. See Michel Vinaver, *Écrits sur le théâtre* (Lausanne: Aire, 1982).

65 'À propos des *Coréens*', in *Théâtre populaire*, March 1957 (*OC* I, p. 888). Barthes wrote two further articles in this play: one of them, the most striking, was published only in 1978 in a volume edited by Michel Vinaver; the other came out in *France Observateur* on 1 November 1956 (*OC* I, pp. 887–888).

66 Letter to Michel Vinaver, n.d. Michel Vinaver archives.

67 'La fête du cordonnier', in *Théâtre populaire*, 2nd quarter, 1959 (*OC* I, p. 987).

68 Letter from Michel Vinaver, 15 October 1970. The term 'recognition' recurs in Vinaver almost every time he writes to Barthes about his books: 'I'm reading your work and it's simultaneously a recognition and a surprise' (letter from Michel Vinaver, 21 November 1961; BNF, NAF 28630).

69 Philippe Roger, 'Barthes dans les années Marx', in *Communications*, no. 63, 1996, pp. 39–65.

70 'Tragédie et hauteur' (*OC* I, p. 974).

71 'Pour une définition du théâtre populaire' (*OC* I, p. 515).

72 'Le théâtre populaire d'aujourd'hui' (*OC* I, p. 530).

73 'Une tragédienne sans public' (*OC* I, p. 494).

74 'Comment s'en passer' (*OC* I, p. 517).

75 'Sept photos modèles de *Mère Courage*' (*OC* I, p. 997).

76 Geneviève Serreau, 'Croisés et hérétiques', in *L'Arc*, no. 55, 'Brecht', 1973, pp. 70–72.
77 '*L'Étranger*, roman solaire', in *Club*, April 1954 (*OC* I, p. 480). On the polemic between Sartre and Camus that led to the split between them, see *Les Temps modernes*, May and August 1952.
78 '*La Peste*. Annales d'une épidémie ou roman de la solitude?', in *Club*, February 1955 (*OC* I, pp. 544–545).
79 Letter from Albert Camus, 13 January 1955. Private collection.
80 Jean-Paul Sartre, *What is Literature?*, translated by Bernard Frechtman (London: Methuen & Co., 1950), p. 135 (translation modified).
81 'Réponse de Roland Barthes à Albert Camus', in *Club*, April 1955 (*OC* I, pp. 573–574).
82 Jean Guérin, 'Mythologies', in *La Nouvelle NRF*, June 1955, pp. 1118–1119.
83 'Suis-je marxiste?', in *La Nouvelle NRF*, June 1955, pp. 1118–1119 (*OC* I, p. 596). Under the title 'M. Barthes se met en colère', Guérin responded to Barthes's reply: 'M. Barthes enjoys the favours of bourgeois society which, unless I am mistaken, subsidizes him. It is highly likely that, in 15 years, he will be the French Minister for Education. He will not be a bad minister. But let us hope he does not come to persecute us. This would be in dubious taste' (*La Nouvelle NRF*, October 1955, pp. 802–804).
84 On 28 May 1952, demonstrations against the Korean War taking as their pretext the visit of General Ridgway led to the arrest and jailing of Jacques Duclos, the then acting Secretary General of the French Communist Party: some pigeons and a rifle were found in his car (he had just been hunting); the birds were seen as carrier pigeons meant to send coded messages to Moscow. The episode is known as the 'carrier-pigeon affair'.
85 *OC* I, p. 565.
86 'Jean Cayrol, *L'Espace d'une nuit*', in *Esprit*, July 1954 (*OC* I, p. 506).
87 'Cottage industry' in *The Eiffel Tower and Other Mythologies*, translated by Richard Howard (Berkeley: University of California Press, 1997), p. 148.
88 'Sur le régime du général de Gaulle', reply to a questionnaire addressed by Maurice Blanchot, André Breton, Dionys Mascolo and Jean Schuster to ninety-nine writers, in *14 juillet*, 18 June 1959 (*OC* I, p. 986).
89 *Mythologies*, illustrated edition, edited by Jacqueline Guittard (Paris: Seuil, 2010).
90 *OC* I, p. 721.
91 *OC* I, p. 823.
92 *OC* I, p. 675.
93 *OC* I, p. 854.
94 'La vedette: enquêtes d'audience?', in *Communications*, no. 2, 1963 (*OC* II, p. 228).
95 'The cover of *Mythologies* showed a car, a Citroën DS, and this is what drew me to it' (Antoine Compagnon, *Une Question de discipline. Entretiens avec Jean-Baptiste Amadieu* (Paris: Flammarion, 2013), p. 73).
96 BNF, NAF 28630, 'Mythologies. [Copie pour impression].'

97 BNF, NAF 28630, 'Fichier vert'.
98 Barthes mentioned this first stay in America in his intervention at
the colloque de Cerisy (*Prétexte: Roland Barthes*, edited by Antoine
Compagnon (Cerisy: 1977), p. 460). See also Richard Howard,
'Remembering Roland Barthes', in *The Nation* (20 November 1982):
'Mutual friends brought us together in 1957 [*sic*]. He came to my door
in the summer of that year, disconcerted by his classes at Middlebury
(teaching students unaccustomed to a visitor with no English to
speak of) and bearing, by way of introduction, a fresh-printed copy
of *Mythologies*. (*Michelet* and *Writing Degree Zero* had already been
published in France, but he was not yet known in America – not even
in most French departments. Middlebury was enterprising)', reprinted
in Steven Ungar and Betty R. McGraw (eds), *Signs in Culture: Roland
Barthes Today* (Iowa, Idaho: University of Idaho Press, 1989), p. 32.
Howard is mistaken about the date of Barthes's first American trip.
Postcards sent to Georges Poulot (Georges Perros) in July 1958 confirm
the date of this stay in Middlebury in 1958; in particular there was a
card sent from Vermont: 'New York, what an admirable city! In a few
hours I felt at home; 12 million men all to oneself, and freedom.'

Chapter 10   Structures

1 'Voies nouvelles de la critique littéraire en France', in *Politica*,
Belgrade, May 1959 (*OC* I, pp. 977–980).
2 Letter to Philippe Rebeyrol, 2 April 1956. Fonds Philippe Rebeyrol,
IMEC.
3 Letter to Jean-Paul Sartre, 7 December 1955. Private collection.
4 In 1979, he told Pierre Boncenne that he was 'very strongly tempted
these days to write a long, continuous work, something non-fragmen-
tary': 'Roland Barthes on Roland Barthes', in *The Grain of the Voice:
Interviews 1962–1980*, translated by Linda Coverdale (Evanston, IL:
Northwestern University Press, 2009), pp. 321–337 (p. 329). And he
added that this temptation was so strong that he was basing the whole
of his course on this question.
5 'Responses: interview with *Tel Quel*', translated by Vérène Grieshaber,
in *The Tel Quel Reader*, edited by Patrick ffrench and Roland-François
Lack (London: Routledge, 1998), pp. 249–268 (p. 257).
6 BNF, NAF 28630. 'Mythologies'. For example, 'myth is a type of
speech' is provided with a reference to Valéry before being presented
as Barthes's own definition.
7 According to Louis-Jean Calvet, *Roland Barthes, un regard politique
sur le signe* (Paris: Payot, 1973).
8 *Mythologies*, selected and translated by Annette Lavers (London:
Jonathan Cape, 1972), p. 111.
9 *Mythologies*, p. 159.
10 'A great rhetorician of erotic figures', in *The Grain of the Voice*,
pp. 252–257, p. 257.
11 'Cinéma droit et gauche', in *Les Lettres nouvelles*, 11 March 1959 (*OC*
I, pp. 943–945).

12 Hence the title of his article 'Le problème de la signification au cinéma', in *Revue internationale de filmologie*, January–June 1960 (*OC* I, pp. 1039–1046).

13 Barthes, *New Critical Essays*, translated by Richard Howard (New York: Hill & Wang, 1980), pp. 23–40 (p. 33).

14 'Langage et vêtement', in *Critique*, no. 142, March 1959 (*OC* I, p. 949). On the way, Barthes's ideas left their mark on Michel de Certeau; see Michael Sheringham, *Everyday Life: Theories and Practices from Surrealism to the Present* (Oxford: Oxford University Press, 2009).

15 According to Rémi Hess, *Henri Lefebvre et l'aventure du siècle* (Paris: Métailié, 1988), p. 321.

16 Maurice Blanchot, *The Infinite Conversation*, translated by Susan Hanson (Minneapolis: University of Minnesota Press, 1993), section on 'Everyday Speech', pp. 238–245 (pp. 238, 239–240).

17 Georges Perec, *Species of Spaces and other Pieces*, translated and edited by John Sturrock (London: Penguin, 1999), p. 203.

18 *Mythologies*, p. 11. And the mythologist's connection with the world is 'of the order of sarcasm' (p. 158).

19 *The Language of Fashion*, translated by Andy Stafford, edited by Andy Stafford and Michael Carter (London: Bloomsbury, 2013), p. 37.

20 *Système de la mode* (*OC* II, p. 1132).

21 *Système de la mode* (*OC* II, p. 1190).

22 *Mythologies*, p. 159.

23 *Système de la mode* (*OC* II, p. 1192).

24 See Jacques Revel and Nathan Wachtel (eds), *Une École pour les sciences sociales. De la VIe section à l'École des hautes études en sciences sociales* (Paris: Le Cerf, 1996), pp. 11–12.

25 *Criticism and Truth*, translated and edited by Katrine Pilcher Keuneman (London: Continuum, 2007), p. 27.

26 'De Gaulle, les Français et la littérature', in *France Observateur*, 12 November 1959 (*OC* I, p. 996).

27 Maurice Blanchot, *Pour l'amitié* (Paris: Fourbis, 1996), p. 20.

28 This was the main Algerian party agitating for independence from France. (Trans. note.)

29 See for example *Le Lexique de l'auteur. Séminaire à l'École pratique des hautes études, 1973–1974*, edited by Anne Herschberg Pierrot (Paris: Seuil, 2010), with its fragment (which was not ultimately used) of the self-portrait entitled 'The intellectual and his *imaginaire*': 'There is always in the revolutionary intellectual the whiff of a *role*: he is the one who thinks he is Lenin or Mao, decides to found a Party, to enlighten the masses, etc. And yet he is never anything other than a being of language, though these great examples give him the illusion that it is possible, by natural metonymy, to slip from language to action (his power)' (p. 313). And: 'Wherever the *Doxa* presents a type of behaviour, it turns this into an *attitude*; it transforms the action into a gesture. If only it were to leave this gesture with its aesthetic mendacity fully visible – but the *Doxa naturalizes* everything that it touches, and is glued down in its own discourse; heroism is an excrescence of nature, not a *difference* of desire.'

30 'Textes préparatoires, lignes, définitions de la *Revue internationale*', in *Lignes*, no. 11, 1990, p. 179. This issue brings together the documents composed in the period when attempts were being made to create the review in 1961, and various exchanges of letters between the different members in 1961–65. See also the account in Christophe Bident, *Maurice Blanchot, partenaire invisible* (Seyssel: Champ Vallon, 1998), pp. 403–417.

31 His anti-Gaullism remained intransigent until the end of his life. This is proved by a significant detail: while his desk diaries contain no mention of external events, for 27 April 1969 there is this note: 'no in referendum', which may refer to his own vote as well as to the general result; and for 10 November 1979 there is the entry: 'Death of de Gaulle'. BNF, NAF 28630, 'Agendas'.

32 Letter from Blanchot, 28 September [1962]. Private collection.

33 Letter from Blanchot to Uwe Johnson, 1 February 1968, in *Lignes*, no. 11, 1990, p. 270.

34 Letter from Vittorini to Blanchot, 1 March 1963, in *Lignes*, no. 11, 1990, p. 280.

35 'The translator will be, to some extent, the real writer of the review.' Citing the example of Hölderlin, Blanchot presented translation as a form of literary activity. 'The translator is the secret master of the difference of languages, not to abolish this difference, but to use it, so as to awaken, in his own language, by the changes he brings about within it, the presence of those differences that are found in the original work' ('Textes préparatoires, lignes, définitions de la *Revue internationale*', in *Lignes*, no. 11, 1990, p. 187).

36 'Trois fragments' (*OC* II, pp. 559–562). These texts appeared in Italian translation. A final fragment, with the title 'Une société sans roman?' was accidentally left out: it is published in *OC* II, p. 563.

37 'Vie et mort des revues', interview with Maria-Teresa Padova (1979), in *Scarabée international*, Spring 1982 (*OC* V, p. 779).

38 This text was sent by Blanchot to Barthes on 11 May 1967, together with a letter in which he asked him for his opinion on the initiative and that he ended with the words 'Would you sign this text?' BNF, NAF 28630.

39 Unpublished letter to Maurice Blanchot, 22 May 1967, published by Éric Marty in *Cités*, special issue, 'Voyages inédits dans la pensée contemporaine', edited by Yves-Charles Zarka (Paris: PUF, 2010), pp. 459–460.

40 Interview with Jean-Claude Milner, 9 August 2009.

41 *OC* II, pp. 253–254.

42 *Elements of Semiology*, translated by Annette Lavers and Colin Smith (New York: Hill and Wang, 1977), p. 63.

43 'Inventaire des systèmes de signification contemporains' (*OC* II, p. 613).

44 'Rhetoric of the image', in *The Responsibility of Forms: Critical Essays on Music, Art, and Representation*, translated by Richard Howard (New York: Hill and Wang, 1985), pp. 21–40.

45 *Elements of Semiology*, p. 41.

46 *Elements of Semiology*, pp. 90–91.

47 'The Structuralist Activity', in *Critical Essays*, translated by Richard Howard (Evanston, IL: Northwestern University Press, pp. 213–220), pp. 214–215.

48 Jacques-Alain Miller, 'Pseudo-Barthes', in *Prétexte: Roland Barthes*, Collque de Cerisy, 22–29 June 1977, edited by Antoine Compagnon (Paris: Christian Bourgois, 2003), pp. 227–228.

49 Interview with Jean-Claude Milner, 9 August 2009.

50 'L'École', in 'Fragments inédits du *Roland Barthes par Roland Barthes*', *Le Lexique de l'auteur*, pp. 276–277.

51 'Responses', p. 261.

52 See Anna Boschetti, *Ismes. Du réalisme au postmodernisme* (Paris: CNRS Éditions, 2014).

53 English translation: *Structuralism*, translated and edited by Chaninah Maschler (London: Routledge and Kegan Paul, 1971).

54 English translation: *Homo academicus*, translated by Peter Collier (Cambridge: Polity, 1988).

55 English translation: *Resistances of Psychoanalysis*, translated by Peggy Kamuf, Pascale-Anne Brault, and Michael Naas (Stanford, CA: Stanford University Press, 1998).

56 'Twenty key words for Roland Barthes', in *The Grain of the Voice*, pp. 205–232 (p. 212).

57 François Dosse, *History of Structuralism*, translated by Deborah Glassman (Minneapolis: University of Minnesota Press, 1997), vol. 2: *The Sign Sets, 1967–Present*, p. 281.

58 Card from Lévi-Strauss, 13 January 1960. BNF, NAF 28630.

59 'I read [Vladimir] Propp in English, though I don't remember precisely when': 'Answers', in Barthes, *'Simply a Particular Contemporary'. Interviews, 1970–79*, translated and edited by Chris Tuner (London: Seagull Books, 2015), p. 23.

60 François Dosse, *History of Structuralism*, translated by Deborah Glassman (Minneapolis: University of Minnesota Press, 1997), vol. 1: *The Rising Sign. 1945–1966*, p. 216.

61 'Answers', p. 25.

62 Marcel Hénaff, *Claude Lévi-Strauss and the Making of Structural Anthropology*, translated by Mary Baker (Minneapolis: University of Minnesota Press, 1998), p. 15.

63 *Roland Barthes by Roland Barthes*, translated by Richard Howard (London: Macmillan, 1977), p. 166.

64 Vincent Debaene, *Far Afield: French Anthropology between Science and Literature*, translated by Justin Izzo (Chicago: University of Chicago Press, 2014), p. 302.

65 On these conflicts, see Boschetti, *Ismes*, pp. 258–264.

66 Claude Lévi-Strauss and Didier Eribon, *Conversations with Claude Lévi-Strauss*, translated by Paula Wissing (Chicago: University of Chicago Press, 1991), p. 73.

67 'Sociology and socio-logic. Apropos of two recent works by Claude Lévi-Strauss', in *The Semiotic Challenge*, translated by Richard Howard (Oxford: Basil Blackwell, 1988), pp. 160–172.

68 'Sociology and socio-logic', p. 170.

69 Preface to the catalogue to the exhibition 'L'Affiche anglaise: les années 1890', at the Musée des arts décoratifs, 1972 (*OC* IV, p. 186).

70 Lévi-Strauss, *Structural Anthropology*, vol. 2, translated by Monique Layton (Harmondsworth: Penguin, 1978), p. 275.

71 Letter from Lévi-Strauss, 18 March 1966. BNF, NAF 28630, 'Critique et vérité'.

72 'From Science to Literature', in *The Rustle of Language*, translated by Richard Howard (Oxford: Basil Blackwell, 1986), pp. 3–10 (pp. 4, 5).

73 'From Science to Literature', p. 7.

74 BNF, NAF 28630, box 1, 'Agenda 1963'. The *agenda* (desk diary) for 1964 also has, for 27 April, the entry 'Fashion ended!'

75 *The Language of Fashion*, p. 24.

76 'On *The Fashion System* and the structural analysis of narratives', in *the Grain of the Voice*, pp. 43–55 (p. 51).

77 'On *The Fashion System*', p. 52.

78 Letter from Lévi-Strauss, 31 March 1970, published in *Claude Lévi-Strauss* (Paris: Gallimard, 'Idées', 1979), pp. 495–497.

79 Lévi-Strauss and Éribon, *Conversations with Claude Lévi-Strauss*, p. 73.

80 Letter from Lévi-Strauss, 5 April 1970. BNF, NAF 28630, '*L'Empire des Signes*'.

81 *Mourning Diary: October 26 1977 – September 15 1979*, edited by Nathalie Léger; translated by Richard Howard (New York: Hill and Wang, 2010), p. 255.

82 Diary for 1973 (unpublished).

83 'The light of the Sud-Ouest', in *Incidents*, translated by Richard Howard (Berkeley, CA: University of California Press, 1992), pp. 3–11 (p. 3).

84 Letter to Philippe Rebeyrol, July 1961.

85 'The Light of the Sud-Ouest', p. 6.

86 'Inédits du *Roland Barthes par Roland Barthes*', in *Le Lexique de l'auteur*, pp. 260–261.

87 *Roland Barthes by Roland Barthes*, p. 46. See also the photos of Barthes at his desk and their captions on p. 38: 'This space is the same everywhere, patiently adapted to the pleasure of painting, writing, sorting.'

88 *Roland Barthes by Roland Barthes*, n.p.

89 *Roland Barthes by Roland Barthes*, p. 81.

90 *Roland Barthes by Roland Barthes*, n.p.

91 'The Light of the Sud-Ouest', p. 5.

92 Emmanuel Planes, 'Les beaux étés de Barthes à Urt', *Sud-Ouest*, 21 July 2011.

93 BNF, NAF 28630, 'Grand fichier', 6 August 1978.

94 Elias Canetti, *The Voices of Marrakesh: A Record of a Visit*, translated by J. A. Underwood (London: Penguin, 2012), p. 17.

95 *Empire of Signs*, translated by Richard Howard (New York: Hill & Wang, 1982), p. 6.

96 'The Rustle of Language', in *The Rustle of Language*, pp. 76–79 (p. 79).

97 Letter to Philippe Rebeyrol, 25 March 1979.

98 *Roland Barthes by Roland Barthes*, p. 179.

Chapter 11   Literature

1 'Authors and Writers', in *Critical Essays*, translated by Richard Howard (Evanston, IL: Northwestern University Press, 1972), pp. 143–150 (p. 144). ['Authors' here translates '*écrivains*' and 'writers' is '*écrivants*'. (Trans. note.)]
2 'Authors and Writers', p. 149.
3 'Oeuvres de masse et explication de texte', in *Communications*, no. 2, March 1963 (*OC*, II, p. 201).
4 See 'Conversation on a Scientific Poem', in *The Grain of the Voice: Interviews 1962–1980*, translated by Linda Coverdale (Evanston, IL: Northwestern University Press, 2009), pp. 63–67 (p. 67; translation modified).
5 Gérard Genette, 'Enquête sur la critique', *Tel Quel*, no. 14, 1963, p. 70.
6 'Literature and Signification', in *Critical Essays*, pp. 261–279 (p. 276).
7 'Kafka's Answer', in *Critical Essays*, pp. 133–138.
8 'What is Criticism?' in *Critical Essays*, pp. 255–260 (p. 255).
9 Barthes's relation with Fortini did not survive the Algerian War: following the repression of 17 October 1961, Fortini accused Barthes of not acting as an intellectual. Barthes replied rather heatedly, and their exchange of ideas dried up. See Roland Barthes and Franco Fortini, 'Lettere scelte 1956–1961', in the periodical *L'ospite ingrato*, 1999, pp. 243–266.
10 Barthes had met Georges Perros in 1952. Perros had recently abandoned his career as a member of the Comédie-Française and divided his time between readings for Vilar's TNP and a column in the *Nouvelle NRF*. When he settled in Douarnenez in 1959, he and Barthes stayed in touch by letter and tried to meet up every time Perros stayed in Paris.
11 'F.B.', in *The Rustle of Language*, translated by Richard Howard (Oxford: Basil Blackwell, 1986), pp. 223–232 (p. 223 n.).
12 'F.B.'
13 'F.B.', p. 225. A very similar definition of the 'incident' can be found in the preface to Pierre Loti's *Aziyadé*, in *New Critical Essays*, translated by Richard Howard (New York: Hill & Wang, 1980), pp. 105–121, and in *Empire of Signs*, translated by Richard Howard (New York: Hill & Wang, 1982).
14 'F.B.', p. 231.
15 For the history of this gallery and biographical information, see: Harry Lunn, 'François Braunschweig & Hugues Autexier. (Photography's Lost Generation)', in *American Photo*, vol. 4, no. 2, March–April 1993, p. 71. François Braunschweig died of AIDS in 1986 and Hugues Autexier committed suicide six weeks later.
16 'Cayrol and Erasure', in *The Rustle of Language*, pp. 181–190 (pp. 182–183).
17 Maurice Blanchot, 'Inspirations méditerranéennes', in *Journal des débats*, 30 September 1941, p. 3. Quoted in Marielle Macé, *Le Temps de l'essai* (Paris: Belin, p. 212).
18 Maurice Blanchot, *The Book to Come*, translated by Charlotte Mandel (Stanford, CA: Stanford University Press, 2003), pp. 205–209.

19 *Writing Degree Zero*, translated by Annette Lavers and Colin Smith (London: Cape, 1967), p. 76.

20 'There is no Robbe-Grillet school', in *Critical Essays*, pp. 91–96 (p. 91).

21 'Literature and signification', in *Critical Essays*, p. 272 (translation slightly modified).

22 'On *The Fashion System* and the Structural Analysis of Narratives', in *The Grain of the Voice*, pp. 43–55 (p. 51).

23 'Listening', in *The Responsibility of Forms: Critical Essays on Music, Art, and Representation*, translated by Richard Howard (New York: Hill and Wang, 1985), pp. 245–260 (p. 256).

24 *Camera Lucida: Reflections on Photography*, translated by Richard Howard (London: Vintage, 1993), p. 106.

25 'I didn't know Paulhan or Blanchot or Lukács': 'Answers', in *'Simply a Particular Contemporary'. Interviews, 1970–79*, translated and edited by Chris Turner (London: Seagull, 2015), pp. 1–44 (p. 12).

26 Éric Marty, 'Maurice Blanchot, Roland Barthes, le neutre en question', in *Cahier de l'Herne 'Maurice Blanchot'*, L'Herne, 2014, p. 346.

27 Maurice Blanchot, 'The Search for Point Zero', in *The Book to Come*, translated by Charlotte Mandell (Stanford, CA: Stanford University Press, 2003), pp. 202–209 and 'La grande tromperie (à propos de *Mythologies*)', in *La Nouvelle NRF*, June 1957 (this essay was not reprinted as part of a volume).

28 'On Reading', in *The Rustle of Language*, pp. 33–43 (p. 41; translation modified), and 'Relations between Fiction and Criticism according to Roger Laporte', in *'A Very Fine Gift' and Other Writings on Theory'*, translated by Chris Turner (Chicago: Seagull Books), pp. 185–189.

29 *A Lover's Discourse: fragments*, translated by Richard Howard (London: Vintage, 2002), p. 116. As Éric Marty emphasizes in the article mentioned above, the expression 'conversation (long ago)' highlights the temporal distance in which the reference is inscribed.

30 *The Neutral: Lecture Course at the Collège de France, 1977–1978*, translated by Rosalind E. Krauss and Denis Hollier, edited by Thomas Clerc under the direction of Éric Marty (New York: Columbia University Press, 2005), p. 17. The reference is to Maurice Blanchot, *The Infinite Conversation*, translation and foreword by Susan Hanson (Minneapolis: University of Minnesota Press, 1993), p. 77.

31 *The Neutral*, p. 21.

32 'Objective Literature', in *Critical Essays*, pp. 13–24 (p. 13; translation slightly modified).

33 'Literal Literature', in *Critical Essays*, pp. 51–58 (p. 53).

34 'There Is No Robbe-Grillet School', p. 95 (translation modified).

35 Alain Robbe-Grillet, *Why I Love Barthes* (Cambridge: Polity, 2011).

36 Barthes kept the very many letters that Michel Butor sent him from the United States when, in 1960, he took up a post at the University of Bryn Mawr in Pennsylvania. In them, Butor describes problems of a highly practical nature, his teaching, and his difficulties in working. The correspondence also contains several drawings and pastel pictures. Butor's artistic activities may have encouraged Barthes in his own, which he undertook on a regular basis only at the beginning of the 1970s.

37 'Literature and Discontinuity', in *Critical Essays*, pp. 171–184 (p.

182). A few years later, Michel Butor published a very fine essay on Barthes, 'La fascinatrice', in *Les Cahiers du Cinéma*, no. 4, 1968, reprinted in *Repertoire IV* (in *Oeuvres completes de Michel Butor*, edited by Mireille Calle-Gruber (Paris: La Différence, 2006), pp. 391–413).

38 Letter from Alain Robbe-Grillet to Philippe Sollers, 10 January 1965 (Sollers archives), quoted by Philippe Forest in *Histoire de Tel Quel, 1960–1982* (Paris: Seuil, 'Fiction & Cie', 1995), p. 176.

39 'Entretien sur les *Essais critiques*', with Guy Le Clec'h, *Le Figaro littéraire*, 16–22 April 1964 (*OC* II, p. 620).

40 *Critical Essays*, p. xii.

41 *Critical Essays*, p. xxi.

42 BNF, NAF 28630, 'Fichier vert 1: Livres, morceaux choisis'.

43 'About Stupidity . . .', in *Roland Barthes by Roland Barthes*, translated by Richard Howard (London: Macmillan, 1977), p. 51. On this topic, see Claude Coste, *Bêtise de Barthes* (Paris: Hourvari, 2011).

44 Letter from Barthes to Jean-Edern Hallier (Hallier archives), quoted by Forest, *Histoire de Tel Quel*, p. 195.

45 'Plaisir aux classiques', in *Existences*, 1944 (*OC* I, p. 59).

46 'La Bruyère', in *Critical Essays*, pp. 221–238 (p. 225).

47 'On behalf of the "New Criticism," Roland Barthes replies to Raymond Picard', in *The Grain of the Voice*, pp. 38–42 (p. 38).

48 *On Racine*, translated by Richard Howard (New York: Performing Arts Journal Publications, 1983), p. ix.

49 'La Bruyère', p. 223.

50 *On Racine*, p. x.

51 'Note sur André Gide et son *Journal*' (*OC* I, p. 36).

52 'Chateaubriand: *Life of Rancé*', in *New Critical Essays*, pp. 41–54 (p. 41).

53 *On Racine*, p. 8.

54 Racine, *Théâtre* (Paris: Club français du livre, 1960).

55 Louis Althusser, *Lettres à Franca (1961–1973)* (Paris: Stock/IMEC, 1998), p. 412.

56 Raymond Picard, 'M. Barthes et la "critique universitaire"', in *Le Monde*, 14 March 1964. The article criticizes the author of *Mythologies* for forging or yielding to a 'mythology' of academia that is said to be entirely dominated by a monotonous, rather coarse 'biographical criticism'.

57 Raymond Picard, 'Racine et la nouvelle critique', in *Revue des sciences humaines*, no. 117, January–March 1965, pp. 29–49.

58 *On Racine*, p. vii.

59 Tzvetan Todorov, *Devoirs et délices: une vie de passeur: entretiens avec Catherine Portevin* (Paris: Seuil, 'Points', 2002), p. 72.

60 Quoted by François Dosse in *History of Structuralism*, translated by Deborah Glassman (Minneapolis: University of Minnesota Press, 1997), vol. 1, p. 195.

61 Pierre Bourdieu, *Homo academicus*, translated by Peter Collier (Cambridge: Polity, 1990), pp. 115–118.

62 Raymond Picard, *Les Prestiges* (Paris: Gallimard, 1947).

63 Raymond Picard, *Nouvelle Critique or nouvelle imposture?* (Paris:

Pauvert, 'Libertés', 1965). The series 'Libertés' was edited by Jean-François Revel.

64 Picard, *Nouvelle Critique*, p. 36.
65 *Criticism and Truth*, translated and edited by Katrine Pilcher Keuneman (London: Continuum, 2007), p. 20, n. 17.
66 Philippe Sollers, 'Picard, cheval de Bataille', in *Tel Quel*, no. 24, 1965, p. 92. Jean-François Revel replied to Sollers's article in 'J'ai cherché à ouvrir une discussion', in *La Quinzaine littéraire*, 15 April 1966.
67 'Si ce n'est toi . . .', in *Le Nouvel Observateur*, 10–16 November 1965 (*OC* II, p. 720). Barthes didn't know how right he was. René Pommier would devoted his thesis and indeed his whole life to demolishing *On Racine* and its author, over more than a thousand pages! See René Pommier, *Le 'Sur Racine' de Roland Barthes* (CDU and SEDES, 1988).
68 Agenda 1966. BNF, NAF 28630.
69 *Criticism and Truth*, p. 24.
70 Claude Coste, *Bêtise de Barthes* (Paris: Hourvari, 2011), p. 132.
71 The person involved was Olivier de Meslon: Barthes had been deeply in love with him between 1956 and 1961. We do not know whether Barthes's letters have been preserved. What we do know, however, from the desk diary for 1961, is that he spent two days in December writing de Meslon a very long letter, after the latter had decided to separate from Barthes. In a letter to Jean Cayrol written in April 1957, Barthes said that he had been to Bordeaux for two days 'with a friend, Olivier de Meslon, whom you met one day on the terrace of the Café des Deux Magots; he's from that part of the world' (Fonds Jean Cayrol, IMEC).
72 Letter from Michel Butor, 17 March 1966; letter from Louis-René Des Forêts, 17 March 1966; letter from Jacques Lacan, 12 April 1966; letter from J.M.G. Le Clézio, 19 April 1966; letter from Gilles Deleuze, 6 May 1966; letter from Jean Starobinski, 16 May 1966. BNF, NAF 28630.
73 BNF, NAF 28630, 'Séminaire sur la rhétorique'. He added, to emphasize his point: 'Rhet: made by man, *the person who wishes to speak, the person who wishes to write, and this has always touched me.*'
74 See 'L'ancienne rhétorique', in *Communications*, no. 16, 1970 (*OC* III, p. 528).
75 Julia Kristeva, interview with the author, 25 September 2013. Marthe Robert's paper on this occasion evidently left a deep impression. In *Bardadrac*, Gérard Genette notes with an amused sense of distance that there was a rumour going round at the time that Barthes and Kristeva were having an affair.
76 Jean Starobinski, 'Le texte dans le texte', and Ferdinand de Saussure, 'Extraits inédits des cahiers d'anagrammes', in *Tel Quel*, no. 37, spring 1969.
77 *S/Z*, translated by Richard Miller (Oxford: Blackwell, 1990), p. 14.
78 Translated as 'Kristeva's *Semeiotike*', in *The Rustle of Language*, pp. 168–171.
79 'Kristeva's *Semeiotike*', p. 168.
80 'Kristeva's *Semeiotike*', pp. 170–171.
81 The conference proceedings would be published a few years later, with a title that highlights the theoretical revolution that the conference

had represented: Richard Macksey and Eugenio Donato (eds), *The Structuralist Controversy. The Languages of Criticism and the Sciences of Man* (Baltimore: Johns Hopkins University Press, 1970, 1972). The Ford Foundation also financed the Maison des sciences de l'homme which was home to the EHESS, in whose creation Barthes would play something of a part in the 1970s, as we shall see.

82 See the account given by Élisabeth Roudinesco of this conference in her *Jacques Lacan & Co. A History of Psychoanalysis in France, 1925–1985*, translated by Jeffrey Mehlman (Free Association, 1990), pp. 407–417. She says that Lacan thought Barthes's paper was excellent (p. 409).

83 Interview with the author, 9 July 2012.

84 Jacques Derrida, *Of Grammatology*, translated by Gayatri Chakravorty Spivak (Baltimore, MD: Johns Hopkins University Press, 1998), p. 83.

85 Umberto Eco, 'La maîtrise de Barthes', a paper delivered at the conference on Roland Barthes (Reggio Emilia, 13–14 April 1984), translated (into French) by Myriem Bouhazer, *Magazine littéraire*, no. 314, 'Roland Barthes', 1993, p. 43. At that time (1966) we should remember, Barthes had already give in to the friendly insistence of Maurice Nadeau and published this article in a volume together with *Writing Degree Zero*, which was brought out by Denoël in 1965.

86 Maurice Pinguet, *La Mort volontaire au Japon* (Paris: Gallimard, 1984).

87 Pinguet, *Le Texte Japon*, rare and unpublished works edited by Michaël Ferrier (Paris: Seuil, 'Réflexion', 2009), p. 39.

88 Letter to Maurice Pinguet, 9 June 1966. Fonds Maurice Pinguet, IMEC.

89 Letter to Maurice Pinguet, 20 June 1966.

90 'Why I Love Benveniste', in *The Rustle of Language*, pp. 162–167 (pp. 163–164).

91 Italo Calvino, 'In memoria di Roland Barthes', in *Saggi 1945–1985* (Milan: Mondadori, 1995), vol. 1, p. 481.

92 See Umberto Eco and Isabella Pezzini, 'La sémiologie des *Mythologies*', in *Communications*, no. 36, 1982, pp. 19–42.

93 Cesare Segre, review of Roland Barthes: *Saggi critici* (Turin: Einaudi, 1966), in *Strumenti critici*, no. 1, October 1966, pp. 89–91. See also Cesare Segre and Maria Corti (eds), *I metodi attuali della critica in Italia* (Turin: Edizioni RAI, 1970).

94 Georges Péninou, *Intelligence de la publicité* (Paris: Robert Laffont, 1972).

95 Roland Barthes, 'L'image publicitaire de l'automobile: analyse sémiologique', 30 pp. + annexes, 1966, unpublished. See Jacques Durand, 'Georges Péninou (1926–2001), l'un des créateurs de la sémiologie publicitaire', in *Hermès*, no. 32–33, 2002/1, pp. 581–588.

96 'Semiology and Cinema', in *The Grain of the Voice*, pp. 30–37 (p. 34).

97 'My dear Jean, I'm catching the train in a minute but I can't resist telling you that we (François B. and I) were *bowled over* by your film; what force, what beauty, what mystery and also what clarity; it's heart-breaking and yet I came out of it with the courage to live; it's

ambiguous and yet uncompromising; we are so very glad to be *for* it
. . .' (letter to Jean Cayrol, 1965. Fonds Jean Cayrol, IMEC).
98 Michel Brault, in *Le Cinéma est ce qu'on veut en faire*, dir. Pina
   Sherman, 1993.
99 'La civilisation de l'image', in *Communications*, no. 2, 1964 (*OC* II,
   p. 565). [*Fumetti* – Italian – are comic strips. (Trans. note.)]
100 See *The Eiffel Tower and Other Mythologies*, translated by Richard
   Howard (Berkeley and London: University of California Press, 1997),
   p. 12; see also 'Semiology and Urbanism' (*The Eiffel Tower and Other
   Mythologies*, p. 193), where Barthes praises Victor Hugo for conceiv-
   ing the cathedral as a kind of writing in *Notre-Dame de Paris*; and see
   above all his great text on Hugo's novel, 'La cathédrale des romans',
   which analyses the ideas of height and panorama in a way similar to
   The Eiffel Tower (*OC* I, pp. 873–876). 'A model of intelligent geography': Barthes's admiring description of Hugo's description of the
   towers of the cathedral could be applied to himself as well.
101 *The Eiffel Tower*, p. 3.
102 *The Eiffel Tower*, p. 7 (translation modified).

Chapter 12   Events

1 Eugen Herrigel, *Zen in the Art of Archery*, translated by R. F. C. Hull;
   foreword by D. T. Suzuki (London: Arkana, 1985); Georges Braque,
   Le Tir à l'arc (Paris: Louis Bonder, 1960); Alan Watts, *The way of
   Zen* (London: Arkana, 1999); D. T. Suzuki, *Essays in Zen Buddhism*
   (London: Souvenir, 2010).
2 'Masculin, féminin, neutre', in *Échanges et communications. Mélanges
   offerts à Claude Lévi-Strauss* (Paris: Mouton, 1970) (*OC* V, pp. 1027–
   1043). The text was written in 1967 and comprised a first outline of
   what was to become *S/Z*.
3 'The Exercises is somehow machine-like, in the cybernetic sense of the
   term: a raw "case" is fed in, which is the material of election; it should
   give back not, of course, an automatic response, but a coded and
   thereby "acceptable" (in the sense this word can have in linguistics)
   request': *Sade, Fourier, Loyola*, translated by Richard Miller (London:
   Cape, 1977), p. 57. The text on Loyola was first published in 1969 in
   issue 38 of *Tel Quel* with the title 'Comment parler à Dieu?'
4 Seminar of 21 November 1968, *'Sarrasine' de Balzac: séminaires à
   l'École pratique des hautes études, 1967–1968, 1968–1969*, edited by
   Claude Coste and Andy Stafford (Paris: Seuil, 2011), p. 325.
5 One of the texts in *A Lover's Discourse*, with the title 'Sobria ebrietas',
   is entirely devoted to this notion of what the translator renders as the
   'non-will-to-possess': see *A Lover's Discourse: Fragments*, translated
   by Richard Howard (London: Vintage, 2002), pp. 232–234.
6 'The Death of the Author', in *The Rustle of Language*, translated
   by Richard Howard (Oxford: Basil Blackwell, 1986), pp. 49–55 (p.
   49). The text was initially published in English ('The Death of the
   Author', *Aspen Magazine*, nos. 5–6, Autumn–Winter 1967) alongside several minimalist works. This, the sole double issue of the

avant-garde magazine edited by Phyllis Johnson also contains texts by
Susan Sontag and recordings by John Cage, William Burroughs and
Samuel Beckett. The text was commissioned from Barthes by Brian
O'Doherty, an artist and art critic who had been introduced to Barthes
by Susan Sontag.

7 Barthes, *'Sarrasine' de Balzac*, p. 66.
8 *'Sarrasine' de Balzac*, p. 138.
9 Julia Kristeva, *Semeiotike* (Paris: Seuil, 1969), p. 85.
10 Michel Foucault, 'What Is an Author?', in *Essential Works of Michel
   Foucault 1954–1984*, vol. 2, *Aesthetics, Method and Epistemology*, edited
   by James D. Faubion (New York: Free Press, 1999), pp. 205–222.
11 Balzac's novella tells the following story: In eighteenth-century Italy,
   a sculptor, Sarrasine, falls madly in love with the singer Zambinella.
   When, after a certain number or twists and turns in the tale that
   are meant to maintain his illusions, he discovers that this apparently female singer is in fact a castrato, he wants to kill her, and is
   himself murdered on the orders of Cardinal Cicognara, the singer's
   protector.
12 Barthes referred to the example of the sixth patriarch who succeeded
   the fifth patriarch because he did not understand Buddhism but merely
   the Way: see *The Neutral: Lecture Course at the Collège de France,
   1977–1978*, translated by Rosalind E. Krauss and Denis Hollier, edited
   by Thomas Clerc and Eric Marty (New York: Columbia University
   Press, 2005), p. 28.
13 *'Sarrasine' de Balzac*, p. 334. It is interesting to note how Barthes and
   Lacan thought alike on this issue, even if they did not use the same
   teaching techniques in their respective seminars. The first page of Book
   I of Lacan's *Seminar* demonstrates this kinship: 'The master breaks the
   silence with anything – with a sarcastic remark, with a kick-start. That
   is how a Buddhist master conducts his search for meaning, according
   to the technique of *zen*. It beseeches students to find out for themselves the answer to their own questions. The master does not teach
   ex cathedra a readymade science; he supplies an answer when the students are on the verge of finding it' (Jacques Lacan, *Freud's Papers on
   Technique, 1953–1954*, edited by Jacques-Alain Miller, translated by
   John Forrester (Cambridge: Cambridge University Press, 1988), p. 1).
14 André Malraux questioned the managerial capacities of Henri Langlois
   and decided to relieve him of his duties as administrative director of the
   Cinémathèque; this decision was condemned by Daniel Cohn-Bendit
   and, in the National Assembly, François Mitterrand. This was the
   start of the 'Langlois Affair', in which many leading personalities from
   artistic and intellectual circles in France and abroad were involved.
15 'Leçon d'écriture' (*OC* III, pp. 33–34).
16 *Sade, Fourier, Loyola*, p. 95.
17 Letter to Maurice Pinguet, 9 June 1968. Fonds Maurice Pinguet,
   IMEC.
18 Gérard Bonnot, 'Université', in *L'Express*, exceptional supplement II,
   'L'affrontement', 2 June 1968, pp. 12–13.
19 'Une lettre de M. Roland Barthes', in *L'Express*, 17–23 June 1968, p.
   32. Barthes's letter was followed by one from 'M. Lucien Goldmann';

although Goldmann had been feted by the article as a teacher open to the reforms, he also corrected a certain number of mistakes.

20 Barthes, 'La vaccine de l'avant-garde' (*OC* I, p. 565).
21 *'Sarrasine' de Balzac*, p. 320.
22 'Writing the Event', in *The Rustle of Language*, pp. 149–154 (p. 154).
23 'Structuralisme et sémiologie', conversation with Pierre Daix, in *Les Lettres françaises*, 31 July 1968 (*OC* III, p. 82).
24 'Writing the Event', p. 154. Another text, this time written in 1969, stated very clearly the problem of a cultural critique cut off from its political argument: this was a reflection of the hippy movement, a movement that, while it quite justifiably criticized the wild excesses of consumer society and a civilization of the well-off, also came up against the problem of real poverty which it did not tackle politically even if it appropriated its codes through *'disguise*, a lower form of cultural narcissism': see 'A Case of Cultural Criticism', in *The Language of Fashion*, translated by Andy Stafford, edited by Andy Stafford and Michael Carter (London: Bloomsbury, 2013), pp. 104–107 (p. 107). Barthes provided a trenchant analysis, which ended with the quest for another response to modern life, one that was doubtless difficult to imagine: 'Could we conceive of a political critique of culture which is an active form of criticism and no longer a simply analytical or intellectual one, which would operate beyond the ideological conditioning by mass communications [. . .]? The political critique and the cultural critique don't seem to be able to coincide' ('A Case of Cultural Criticism', p. 107).
25 Michel Deguy, *Choses de la poésie et affaires culturelles* (Paris: Hachette, 1986).
26 *'Sarrasine' de Balzac*, p. 317.
27 See also 'Writing the Event', pp. 149–154 (pp. 150–151).
28 'The insistence with which it was repeated, on either side, that, whatever happens, *afterwards* can no longer be like *before* doubtless translates, negatively, the fear (or the hope) that in fact *afterwards* would become *before*: the event being speech, it can, mythically, cross itself out' ('Writing the event', p. 150n.).
29 'Structuralisme et sémiologie' (*OC* III, p. 79).
30 'Structuralisme et sémiologie', pp. 82–83.
31 'La vie des hommes infâmes', in *Cahiers du chemin*, January 1977, p. 12.
32 We should also mention Nathalie Sarraute's novel *Do You Hear Them?*, translated by Maria Jolas (London: Calder and Boyars, 1975).
33 *Sade, Fourier, Loyola*, p. 126.
34 *Sade, Fourier, Loyola*, p. 85.
35 *Sade, Fourier, Loyola*, pp. 8–9.
36 'Voyage autour de Roland Barthes', interview with Gilles Lapouge, in *La Quinzaine littéraire*, 1–15 December 1971 (*OC* III, p. 1046).
37 See 'From Work to Text', in *The Rustle of Language*, pp. 56–64: 'The Text, on the other hand, is read without the Father's inscription' (p. 61), for life is produced by an 'I' of paper.
38 *Sade, Fourier, Loyola*, p. 15.
39 *Sade, Fourier, Loyola*, p. 77.

40 'Khatibi and I are interested in the same things: images, signs, traces, letters, marks. And thus, because he displaces these forms as I see them, because he lures me far from myself, in his own territory, and yet as it were at the far end of my own self Khatibi teaches me something new, shakes up what I know' ('What I Owe to Khatibi', 1979; *OC* V, p. 666).

41 '*D'un soleil réticent* de Zaghloul Morsy', in *Le Nouvel Observateur*, 17 June 1969 (*OC* III, p. 103).

42 From 1967, Morsy followed a diplomatic career, in New York, Paris and, after 1972, with UNESCO. He produced not only poetry but also a significant body of work on the sciences of education. He played a role in the creation of the review *Souffles*, in 1966, which was then taken over by his former students, Abdellatif Laâbi and Tahar Ben Jelloun, as well as Mohammed Khaïr-Eddine, who gave it a strongly militant feel in the years 1969–72.

43 'Reflections on a Manual', in *The Rustle of Language*, pp. 22–28.

44 'Style and Its Image', in *The Rustle of Language*, pp. 90–99 (pp. 97–98).

45 'The Sequences of Actions', in *The Semiotic Challenge*, translated by Richard Howard (Oxford: Basil Blackwell, 1988), pp. 136–148.

46 These two words are in English in Barthes's text. (Trans. note.)

47 'One Always Fails in Speaking of What One Loves', in *The Rustle of Language*, pp. 296–305 (p. 299).

48 Preface to Pierre Loti's *Aziyadé*, in *New Critical Essays*, translated by Richard Howard (New York: Hill & Wang, 1980), pp. 105–121 (p. 116).

49 Loti did indeed buy a house in Hendaye where he kept his mistress, Juana Cruz-Guainza: this was the maison Bachar-Etchea, in the rue des Pêcheurs (Barthes would see it when he happened to be in Hendaye), but he almost never lived in it; instead, he soon settled Juana in a house in the suburbs of Rochefort.

50 Preface to *Aziyadé*, p. 118.

51 Letter from Louis Althusser to Roland Barthes, 4 October 1972. Private collection.

52 Mohammed El-Ayadi, 'Les mouvements de la jeunesse au Maroc. L'émergence d'une nouvelle intelligentsia politique dans les années soixante et soixante-dix', in Didier Le Saout and Marguerite Rollinde (eds), *Émeutes et mouvements sociaux au Maghreb* (Paris: Karthala, 1999), pp. 201–230 (p. 221).

53 *Incidents*, translated by Richard Howard (Berkeley, Los Angeles and Oxford: University of California Press, 1992), p. 34.

54 *Camera Lucida: Reflections on Photography*, translated by Richard Howard (London: Vintage, 1993), p. 27.

55 *Incidents*, p. 39.

56 'Digressions', in *The Grain of the Voice*, pp. 113–127 (pp. 121–122).

57 Claude Gérald Palazzoli, *Le Maroc politique. De l'indépendance à 1973* (Paris: Sindbad, 1974).

58 See Ridha Boulaâbi, 'Barthes et l'Orient: lecture d'*Incidents*', in Ridha Boulaâbi, Claude Coste and Mohamed Lehdahda (eds), *Roland Barthes au Maroc* (Meknès: Publications de l'Université Moulay-Ismaïl, 2013), pp. 35–51 (p. 46).

59 Claude Coste, 'Notes de cours pour le Maroc', in Boulaâbi et al. (eds), *Roland Barthes au Maroc*, pp. 9–22 (p. 18). See also Jacques Berque, Jean-Paul Charnay et al., *L'Ambivalence dans la culture arabe* (Paris: Anthropos, 1968).

60 'Digressions', p. 124.

61 Notes from a course on polysemy, quoted in Coste, 'Notes de cours pour le Maroc', p. 19.

62 *Roland Barthes by Roland Barthes*, translated by Richard Howard (London: Macmillan, 1977), p. 111.

63 *Incidents*, p. 29 (translation modified).

64 *Incidents*, p. 19.

65 Alain Benchaya, who was acknowledged at the beginning of *Roland Barthes by Roland Barthes*, took the photograph of palm trees on the road to Tafraout reproduced in the iconographic section of the book.

66 François Wahl, 'Ouf!', in Marianne Alphant and Nathalie Léger (eds), *R/B, Roland Barthes*, catalogue of the exhibition at the Centre Pompidou, 2002, p. 108.

67 *Incidents*, p. 39. Wahl confirmed this biographical detail: 'It was here, in this spot caught between a suffocating mass of colours and odours and the disaster of a field of human ruins, that, on the terrace of the hotel, Sunday after Sunday, Roland Barthes read Lacan's *Écrits*' ('Ouf!', p. 108).

68 *Camera Lucida*, p. 38. The photo, reproduced on p. 39, has the rubric: 'I want to live there.'

69 *How to Live Together: Novelistic Simulations of some Everyday Spaces. Notes for a Lecture Course at the Collège de France (1976–1977)*, translated by Kate Briggs, edited by Claude Coste (New York: Columbia University Press, 2013), p. 7. In a 1979 text on Cy Twombly, Barthes compared the painter's canvases to 'big Mediterranean rooms, warm and luminous, with their elements lost in them (*rari*), rooms the mind seeks to populate': 'The Wisdom of Art', in *The Responsibility of Forms: Critical Essays on Music, Art, and Representation*, translated by Richard Howard (New York: Hill and Wang, 1985), pp. 177–194 (p. 183).

70 *Camera Lucida*, p. 40.

71 'Writers, Intellectuals, Teachers', in *The Rustle of Language*, pp. 309–331 (p. 331). In his course on 'The neutral', Barthes came back to this lazy, friendly, silent benevolence created by hashish: he contrasted it with the harder-edged, indifferent benevolence of the Tao (on hashish, see, e.g., *The Neutral*, p. 29).

72 Desk diary, 7 March 1970: 'To El Jadida with Jean-Pierre to buy myself a Djellaba.'

73 The text of *Empire of Signs* was finished on 16 November 1968, but Barthes spent a good deal of 1969 doing research for the illustrations. The composition of *S/Z* lasted until 22 July 1969, when he handed the manuscript over to François Wahl.

74 *S/Z*, translated by Richard Miller (Oxford: Blackwell, 1990), p. 129.

75 *Empire of Signs*, translated by Richard Howard (New York: Hill & Wang, 1982), p. 12.

76 *'Sarrasine' de Balzac*, p. 176.

77 *Empire of Signs*, p. 4.

78 'Digressions', p. 135.
79 'Digressions'.
80 *S/Z*, p. 11.
81 Jacques Derrida, *De la Grammatologie* (Paris: Minuit, 1967), p. 367.
82 *S/Z*, p. 151.
83 *S/Z*, pp. 41-42.
84 Letter from Paule Thévenin, 1 May 1970. Fonds Roland Barthes, 'S/Z'.
85 Letter from François Wahl, 4 August 1969; letter from Philippe Sollers, 15 August 1969; letter from Jacques Derrida, 22 March 1970; letter from Gilles Deleuze, 24 April 1970; letter from Jacqueline Risset, 17 April 1970; letter from Michel Leiris, 10 July 1970. BNF, NAF 28630, 'S/Z'.
86 Jean Reboul, 'Sarrasine ou la castration personnifiée', in *Cahiers pour l'analyse*, March–April 1967 (quoted in *S/Z*, p. 16).
87 Pierre Citron, in *Le Monde des livres*, 9 May 1970; this article was published at the same time as a more positive review by Raymond Jean. See also Pierre Barbéris, 'À propos de *S/Z* de Roland Barthes. Deux pas an avant, un pas en arrière?', in *L'Année balzacienne*, 1971, pp. 111–123.
88 'Digressions', p. 139.
89 See Élisabeth Roudinesco, *Jacques Lacan*, translated by Barbara Bray (Cambridge: Polity, 1997), p. 354.
90 *Empire of Signs*, pp. 28 and 29.
91 This absence of centre is verified in languages other than verbal language, for example cooking: 'no Japanese dish is endowed with a center (the alimentary center implied in the West by the rite which consists of arranging the meal, of surrounding or covering the article of food); here everything is the ornament of another ornament' (*Empire of Signs*, p. 22). In the notes to *Sollers Writer*, Barthes suggested a new and essential set of ideas in connection with the possibility of building up a relation between the subject and utterance that would involve a process of decentring – something that takes the subject out of its mother tongue.
92 Maurice Pinguet says as much: 'Barthes noted his ideas and shaped his sentences on little isolated and permutable index cards': *Le Texte Japon*, rare and unpublished works edited by Michaël Ferrier (Paris: Seuil, 'Réflexion', 2009), p. 25.
93 'At the Floating Market in Bangkok, each vendor sits in a tiny motionless canoe' (*Empire of Signs*, p. 15).
94 For example: 'In pachinko, no sex (in Japan – in that country I am calling Japan – sexuality is in sex, not elsewhere; in the United States, it is the contrary; sex is everywhere, except in sexuality)' (*Empire of Signs*, pp. 28–29). And, on stationery: 'That [sc. the stationery] of the United States is abundant, precise, ingenious [. . .]. The object of the Japanese stationery store is that ideographic writing which to our eyes seems to derive from painting, whereas quite simply it is painting's inspiration' (*Empire of Signs*, pp. 85–86). The same type of comparison is found in the correspondence with Maurice Pinguet written from Baltimore just before Barthes's third visit to Japan, which, as we have said, Barthes flew to directly from the United

States in December 1967: 'My stay here is productive – of *boredom*, and boredom can also, fortunately, be narrated. [...] it's a country without any sense of pleasure or the unexpected (at least on my scale); true, there is a host of things to discover and observe and I make the most of these, but once you've done this, judgement intervenes, and for me it irresistibly takes the form of a comparison with Japan: the same technical furrow, but in the art of living, the two poles: everything, in this evaluation, turns out to the profit of Japan. To compare an American bar with a Japanese bar is a (gloomy) hell versus heaven! At the moment, my mother and my brother are with me, which is a great joy; they will be leaving around 25 November; then I have a lecture tour for three weeks.' On this tour, which took him to the West Coast, Barthes wrote to say he felt better in California, 'which reconciles me a bit to the United States (climate, mixture and kindness of the people – and a lot of Asians!') (letters to Maurice Pinguet, 10 November and 2 December 1967, Fonds Maurice Pinguet, IMEC).

95 Letter to Maurice Pinguet, 8 April 1967. Barthes wrote this letter straight after he had got back from his second trip.

96 Letter to Maurice Pinguet, 28 August 1967.

97 Letter to Maurice Pinguet, 15 January 1968.

98 *Empire of Signs*, pp. 23 and 37.

99 Nicolas Bouvier stayed in Japan in 1964 and 1965 and published a book with the title *Japon* (Lausanne: Éditions Rencontres, 1967) which Barthes possessed.

100 *Empire of Signs*, p. 41.

101 *Empire of Signs*, p. 90.

102 *S/Z*, pp. 106–107, where the implications of the letter Z in Balzac's name are discussed.

103 *Sade, Fourier, Loyola*, p. 173.

104 'Erté, or À la lettre', in *The Responsibility of Forms*, 103–128 (p. 128).

105 *S/Z*, p. 201.

106 'Masculin, féminin, neutre' (*OC* V, p. 1042).

Chapter 13   Barthes and Sollers

1 With the turn to Maoist doctrines in 1971 (in the issue devoted to Barthes, in fact), the review put forward a chronology of its recent history that returned to the 'silence' of summer 1968 and justified it in these terms: 'The analysis is that the Soviet intervention is being exploited by the Right and, specifically, by the opponents of *Tel Quel* (i.e. those who oppose *Tel Quel* as regards its specific work, for reactionary reasons specific to the field of our practice). The combat that takes precedence over the others is that of the consolidation of the group and the review. Silence. "Narrow" position' ('Chronologie', in *Tel Quel*, no. 47, 1971, pp. 142–143).

2 For a detailed account of these intense antagonisms, see Philippe Forest, *Histoire de Tel Quel, 1960–1982* (Paris: Seuil, 1995), pp. 342–360. On Barthes's own position, see Claude Bremond and Thomas Pavel, *De Barthes à Balzac. Fictions d'un critique, critiques d'une fiction* (Paris: Albin Michel, 1998), pp. 17–27.

3 'Lettre à Philippe Sollers', 25 October 1970. Fonds des Éditions du Seuil, IMEC. This letter was published by Éric Marty in the annexes of Barthes's *Oeuvres completes* (*OC* V, p. 1044), my emphasis.

4 'Roland Barthes, tel quel', interview given by Philippe Sollers to Jérôme-Alexandre Nielsberg, in *Contrepoint*, 2 December 2002 (available online). In *Médium* (Paris: Gallimard, 2014), Sollers returned to the reason for his distance from the rest of France: 'In my case, in the South-West protected by a whole number of filters, the Ocean, wine, the islands, a whole series of casual slow-downs. A Girondin who believes in France? You won't find such a thing' (p. 41). See Barthes, 'The Light of the Sud-Ouest', in *Incidents*, translated by Richard Howard (Berkeley: University of California Press, 1992), pp. 3–9.

5 The two questionnaires were published in *Critical Essays*, translated by Richard Howard (Evanston, IL: Northwestern University Press, 1972) as 'Literature today' (pp. 151–162) and, coming as the volume's conclusion, 'Literature and Signification' (pp. 261–279).

6 This was the only text to which Barthes gave three different destinies.

7 'Drama, Poem, Novel', in *Sollers Writer*, translated by Philip Thody (London: The Athlone Press, 1987), pp. 39–68 (p. 59).

8 'Drama, Poem, Novel', p. 56.

9 'Over Your Shoulder', in *Sollers Writer*, pp. 75–92 (p. 85).

10 'Soirées de Paris', in *Incidents*, pp. 51–73 (p. 58).

11 'Deliberation', in *The Rustle of Language*, translated by Richard Howard (Oxford: Basil Blackwell, 1986), pp. 359–373.

12 *Sollers Writer*, pp. 91–92.

13 This 'dialogue' was inserted by Barthes into his column in *Le Nouvel Observateur* no. 739, 6 January 1979, reprinted in *Sollers Writer*, p. 37.

14 Letter from Philippe Sollers to Michel Chodkiewicz, 10 January 1979. Archives du Seuil, IMEC, 'dossier Sollers'.

15 *Art Press*, no. 44, January 1981, p. 10, 11.

16 Philippe Sollers, *Un vrai roman. Mémoires* (Paris: Plon, 2007), p. 111.

17 Philippe Sollers, *Femmes* (Paris: Gallimard, 1983), p. 133.

18 Forest, *Histoire de Tel Quel*, p. 196.

19 Renaud Camus, 'Biographèmes', in *La Règle du jeu*, no. 1, May 1990, p. 60. In comparison with his relation to Sollers, Barthes's feelings for Wahl seemed to comprise an 'almost fearful affection, which actually seemed curiously filial, even though Wahl was much younger than he was'.

20 Éric Marty, *Roland Barthes, le métier d'écrire* (Paris: Seuil, 'Fiction & Cie', 2006), p. 94.

21 This issue also included the transcription of 'Answers', the interview with Jean Thibaudeau, and a very detailed bibliography; it began with Barthes's own article 'Writers, Intellectuals, Teachers'.

22 Philippe Sollers, 'R.B.', in *Tel Quel*, no. 47, autumn 1971, p. 19.

23 'R.B.', p. 21.

24 'The origin of this expression, the fact that I am sometimes called R.B., is not at all an esoteric expression, it was first used by Sollers in a text in issue 47 of *Tel Quel* – not a private origin, but a literary origin'; discussion following the intervention of Evelyne Bachellier, in *Prétexte: Roland Barthes*, proceedings of the colloque de Cerisy-la-Salle, 22–29 June 1977, edited by Antoine Compagnon (Paris: Christian Bourgois, 2003), p. 165.

25 It is Kristeva who tells a similar story, in *The Samurai*, translated by Barbara Bray (New York: Columbia University Press, 1992), p. 25.

26 BNF, NAF 28630, 'Agendas 1976–1979', 1979.

27 BNF, NAF 28630, 'Grand fichier', envelope 5/6.

28 Sollers, *Un vrai roman*, p. 102.

29 *Travels in China*, edited by Anne Herschberg Pierrot, translated by Andrew Brown (Cambridge: Polity, 2012), p. 195.

30 BNF, NAF 28630, 'Grand fichier', 24 August 1979.

31 Barthes, 'Critique et autocritique', interview with André Bourin, in *Les Nouvelles littéraires*, 3 March 1970 (*OC* III, p. 645).

32 'What Becomes of the Signifier', in *The Rustle of Language*, pp. 236–237 (p. 236).

33 'Positions du Mouvement de juin 71', in *Tel Quel*, no. 47, Autumn 1971, p. 136.

34 A text justifying the actions of the commandos was signed by Philippe Sollers, Marcelin Pleynet, Jacques Henric, Guy Scarpetta, Jean-Louis Houdebine and others – the very great majority of them members of *Tel Quel* or closely associated with it.

35 When the hostages were seized, Michel and Rachel Salzedo were actually in Israel.

36 Her expulsion became effective only at the end of the 1970s.

37 Maria-Antonietta Macciocchi, *De la Chine*, translated by Louis Bonalumi, Gérard Hug, Micheline Pouteau and Gilbert Taïeb (Paris: Seuil, 1971), p. 503.

38 *De la Chine*, p. 117.

39 Élisabeth Roudinesco, *Jacques Lacan & Co. A History of Psychoanalysis in France, 1925–1985*, translated by Jeffrey Mehlman (London: Free Association, 1990), p. 545.

40 Sollers, 'Pourquoi j'ai été chinois?', interview with Shuhsi Kao, in *Tel Quel*, no. 88, 1981, p. 12.

41 Sollers, 'Le supplice chinois de Roland Barthes. Sur les *Carnets du voyage en Chine*', in *Le Nouvel Observateur*, 29 January 2009.

42 'Reading through my notes to make an index, I realize that if I were to publish them as they are, it would be exactly a piece of Antonioni. But what else can I do?' (*Travels in China*, p. 195). Barthes referred to Antonioni's film in 'The Rustle of Language' (*The Rustle of Language*, pp. 76–79 (pp. 78–79); the essay was first written in 1974.

43 *Travels in China*, p. 47.

44 *Travels in China*, p. 102.

45 *Travels in China*, p. 143.

46 *Travels in China*, p. 155.

47 *Travels in China*, p. 115.

48 'One of the great features of this journey will have been: my almost daily bad migraines: fatigue, absence of siesta, food, or more subtly: big change in routine, or even: more serious resistances: *revulsions?*' (*Travels in China*, p. 97).

49 *Travels in China*, p. 17.

50 *Travels in China*, p. 103.

51 Barthes took the term from cybernetics and used it to refer to a block of stereotypes. As he wrote in 'Alors, la Chine?', 'Every discourse

seems to advance along a trail of commonplaces ("topoi" and clichés) analogous to those sub-programmes that cybernetics calls "bricks'" (*OC* IV, p. 518). He gave the same definition as that provided by Mandelbrot in *Logique, langage et théorie de l'information*: "'Bricks" or "subroutines" are "bits of pre-coded calculation used as bricks in the construction of any code' (*OC* II, p. 984).

52   *Travels in China*, p. 100.

53   *Le Lexique de l'auteur. Séminaire à l'École pratique des hautes études, 1973–1974*, edited by Anne Herschberg Pierrot (Paris: Seuil, 2010), session of 8 May 1974, p. 234.

54   *Travels in China*, p. 173.

55   *Travels in China*, pp. 85–86.

56   *Travels in China*, p. 42. As Anne Herschberg Pierrot, the editor of Barthes's *Travels in China*, notes, the adjective 'grassy' comes from the calligraphic style known as 'grass script', which corresponds to cursive.

57   Marcelin Pleynet, *Le Voyage en Chine. Chroniques du journal ordinaire, 14 avril–3 mai 1974* (extracts) (Paris: Marciana, 2012), p. 140.

58   *Travels in China*, p. 122.

59   *Travels in China*, p. 57.

60   Pleynet, *Le Voyage en Chine*, pp. 54, 46, 39.

61   François Wahl, 'Ouf!', in *R/B, Roland Barthes*, edited by Marianne Alphant and Nathalie Léger; catalogue of the exhibition at the Centre Pompidou, 2002, p. 107.

62   'Ouf!', p. 108.

63   Simon Leys described the discourse to which Barthes aspired, 'neither assertive, nor negative, nor neutral', as 'a tiny trickle of lukewarm water': 'Notule en marge d'une réédition barthienne', in *Images brisées* (Paris: Robert Laffont, 1976), p. 180.

64   François Wahl, 'La Chine sans utopie', in *Le Monde*, 15–19 June 1974.

65   Philippe Sollers, 'Réponse à François Wahl', in *Tel Quel*, no. 59, autumn 1974, p. 8.

66   See Christophe Bourseiller, *Les Maoïstes. La folle histoire des gardes rouges français* (Paris: Plon, 1996).

67   'Alors, la Chine?' (*OC* IV, p. 517).

68   Barthes, *Le Lexique de l'auteur*, p. 245. Barthes's article referred to the gradual acquiescing of the soldier to the Korean world he was discovering, a position that Barthes called 'assent' as opposed to choice or conversion. '*Aujourd'hui ou Les Coréens*', in *France Observateur*, 1 November 1956 (OC I, p. 666). See also 'Assent, Not Choice', in *Roland Barthes by Roland Barthes*, translated by Richard Howard (London: Macmillan, 1977), p. 48.

69   Introduction to Bernard Minoret and Danielle Vezolles, *La Fuite en Chine*, based on *René Leys*, by Victor Segalen (Paris: Christian Bourgois, 1970) (*OC* III, p. 608).

Chapter 14   The body

1   *The Pleasure of the Text*, translated by Richard Miller (Oxford: Blackwell, 1990), pp. 11–13.

2 *The Pleasure of the Text*, p. 5.
3 In the film *A Night at the Opera*, a work that Barthes thought was an allegory for many textual problems. 'Writers, Intellectuals, Teachers', in *The Rustle of Language*, translated by Richard Howard (Oxford: Basil Blackwell, 1986), pp. 309–331 (p. 313).
4 'Writers, Intellectuals, Teachers', pp. 329–330.
5 It is enantiology (the discourse of opposites) that, in his view, is essential to Proustian inversion: see 'An Idea of Research', in *The Rustle of Language*, pp. 271–276. This text was written two years before *The Pleasure of the Text*.
6 *The Pleasure of the Text*, p. 14.
7 Hélène Cixous, card from Montreal, March 1973. BNF, NAF 28630, 'Le Plaisir du texte'.
8 The title of an interview in *The Grain of the Voice: Interviews 1962–1980*, translated by Linda Coverdale (Evanston, IL: Northwestern University Press, 2009), pp. 177–182.
9 'Le degré zero du coloriage', in *Les Nouvelles littéraires*, 30 March 1978 (*OC* V, p. 453).
10 Severo Sarduy, 'Portrait de l'écrivain en peintre, le matin', in *La Règle du jeu*, no. 1, 1990, p. 73.
11 *Les Dessins de Roland Barthes* (BNF, NAF 28630), cycle of 'Les trésors du patrimoine écrit', a video presenting the holdings, with commentaries by Guillaume Fau, Marie-Odile Germain and Céline Flécheux, Connaissance des arts/Institut national du patrimoine.
12 'Left-handed', in *Roland Barthes by Roland Barthes*, translated by Richard Howard (London: Macmillan, 1977), p. 98.
13 'Variations sur l'écriture' (*OC* IV, p. 267).
14 Marcel Cohen, *La Grande Invention de l'écriture et son evolution*, 3 vols (Paris: Klincksieck, 1953–58); James Février, *Histoire de l'écriture* (Paris: Payot, 1959).
15 *The Preparation of the Novel: Lecture Courses and Seminars at the Collège de France (1978–1979 and 1979–1980)*, translated by Kate Briggs (New York: Columbia University Press, 2010), p. 264.
16 'Variations sur l'écriture', p. 280. The book to which Barthes was here referring was André Leroi-Gourhan, *Le Geste et la parole* (Paris: Albin Michel, 1964).
17 For anyone who has spent time reading his manuscripts, Barthes's writing did indeed register variations in speed, meaning that we can see it was produced in different circumstances, but it remained remarkably uniform – and legible.
18 *The Preparation of the Novel*, p. 265.
19 'Variations sur l'écriture', p. 284.
20 'Variations sur l'écriture', p. 294.
21 *The Pleasure of the Text*, p. 64; 'Texte (théorie du)' (*OC* IV, p. 452). It was the same definition that was given in each of these pieces, with minor variations.
22 'Texte (théorie du)', p. 456.
23 The work of Marc Devade (1943–83) included several collaborations with *Tel Quel*. Some of his paintings were based on the first words of *Paradis* by Sollers; others conducted a dialogue with Dante and Joyce.

He also published poems in *Tel Quel*, and Pleynet and Sollers wrote important articles on him.

24 'Masson's semiography', in *The Responsibility of Forms: Critical Essays on Music, Art, and Representation*, translated by Richard Howard (New York: Hill and Wang, 1985), pp. 153–156 (p. 156).

25 'Réquichot and his body', in *The Responsibility of Forms*, pp. 207–236 (p. 213).

26 'The Reality Effect' in *The Rustle of Language*, pp. 141–148.

27 BNF, NAF 28630, 'Grand fichier', box 5, 'Linguistique, St Simon, Brecht, Zavriev'. These words echo *The Pleasure of the Text*, where Barthes writes 'Proust is what comes to me' and notes the kinship between the ways he approaches the two writers: 'Elsewhere, but in the same way, in Flaubert, it is the blossoming apple trees of Normandy which I read according to Proust' (p. 36).

28 'Flaubert and the sentence', in *New Critical Essays*, translated by Richard Howard (New York: Hill & Wang, 1980), pp. 69–78.

29 'The crisis of truth', in *The Grain of the Voice*, pp. 246–252 (p. 247).

30 BNF, NAF 28630, 'Grand fichier', 6 October 1979.

31 BNF, NAF 28630, 'Grand fichier', 2 August 1979.

32 'Reading Brillat-Savarin', in *On Signs*, edited by Marshall Blonsky (Oxford: Blackwell, 1985), pp. 61–75 (pp. 63–64).

33 *Empire of Signs*, translated by Richard Howard (New York: Hill & Wang, 1982), p. 12.

34 'Reading Brillat-Savarin', p. 61.

35 'French', in *Roland Barthes by Roland Barthes*, p. 96.

36 'Day by Day with Roland Barthes', in *On Signs*, pp. 98–117 (p. 101).

37 In July 1979, on an index card: 'Sometimes take Tenuate to make it easier to work: it makes things flow, I can even be bold, euphoric at having defeated sterility. But as the effect wears off and I read a bit of what I've written, I'm shocked at how dull it is. The drug doesn't act on intelligence but on my awareness of it' (BNF, NAF 28630, 'Grand fichier').

38 'The Second Degree and the Others', in *Roland Barthes by Roland Barthes*, p. 66.

39 'The Second Degree and the Others'.

40 Michel Deguy, 'Le démon de la néologie', in *R/B, Roland Barthes*, edited by Marianne Alphant and Nathalie Léger; catalogue of the exhibition at the Centre Pompidou, 2002, pp. 86–90.

41 'The grain of the voice', in *The Responsibility of Forms*, pp. 267–277.

42 'The Phantoms of the Opera', in *The Grain of the Voice*, pp. 183–187 (p. 184).

43 This fine piece on the romantic song was published in a limited edition of 220 copies, as a special issue of the review *Gramma* in January 1977. The text was read out on a programme broadcast by France Culture on 12 March 1976. See 'The Romantic Song', in *The Responsibility of Form*, pp. 286–292.

44 Althusser, Kristeva and Pinguet (among others) expressed their fascination for his voice. See Althusser, *Lettres à Franca (1961–1973)* (Paris: Stock/IMEC, 1998,), p. 364; Kristeva, 'La voix de Barthes', in *Communications*, no. 36, 1982, p. 119; Pinguet, *Le Texte Japon*,

rare and unpublished works edited by Michaël Ferrier (Paris: Seuil, 'Réflexion', 2009), p. 31.

45 Sollers realized this; he wrote in a 1973 letter to Barthes to thank him for an article on Sollers's *H* in which Barthes evoked the 'swing' of writing. Sollers said 'that the "reader" would occupy a place evidently equal to that of the Jazz listener, an almost sacred place, dictated and emancipatory, a *contagious* complement'.

46 'Brecht and Discourse: A Contribution to the Study of Discursivity', in *The Rustle of Language*, pp. 212–222.

47 'Leaving the Movie Theater', in *The Rustle of Language*, pp. 345–349 (p. 346).

48 'Leaving the Movie Theater', p. 346.

49 Jean Louis Schefer, *L'Homme ordinaire du cinéma* (Paris: Éd. des Cahiers du cinema, 'Petite bibliothèque des cahiers du cinéma', 1997 [1980]), p. 111.

50 See 'The Poor and the Proletariat' in *Mythologies*, selected and translated by Annette Lavers (London: Jonathan Cape, 1972), pp. 38–39 and 'Chaplin' in *Roland Barthes by Roland Barthes*, pp. 54–55 (the substance of the latter was repeated in the text on Saul Steinberg, *OC* IV, p. 952).

51 BNF, NAF 28630, 'Grand fichier', 5 September 1979.

52 'The Third Meaning. Research Notes on Some Eisenstein Stills', in *The Responsibility of Forms*, pp. 41–62.

53 *Roland Barthes by Roland Barthes*, pp. 54–55.

54 Schefer, *L'Homme*, p. 112.

55 *Sade, Fourier, Loyola*, translated by Richard Miller (London: Cape, 1977), p. 85.

56 The fragment 'The Informer', in *A Lover's Discourse: Fragments*, translated by Richard Howard (London: Vintage, 2002), pp. 138–139, stages a comic transposition of the constellation formed by two clans which meet.

57 'Fichier vert 6: 'Éliminé et/ou à revoir (suite et fin).'

58 He published *Jung, la puissance de l'illusion* (Paris: Seuil, 1990).

59 BNF, NAF 28630, 'Grand fichier', 3 January 1975.

60 Jean-Louis Bouttes, 'Faux comme la vérité', in *Critique*, no. 341, October 1975, pp. 1024–1052.

61 Éric Marty, *Roland Barthes, le métier d'écrire* (Paris: Seuil, 2006), p. 53.

62 Yves Navarre, *Biographie, roman* (Paris: Flammarion, 1981), p. 53.

63 Letter to Georges Perec from the end of 1963, quoted in David Bellos, *Georges Perec: A Life in Words*, revised edition (London: Harvill Press, 1999), p. 298.

64 Letter from Georges Perec, 15 June 1970. BNF, NAF 28630. This regret did not stop Perec re-stating, in November 1981, after Barthes's death and just a few months before his own: 'My real master is Roland Barthes': Georges Perec, *Entretiens et conferences*, edited by Dominique Bertelli and Mireille Ribière (Paris: Éditions Joseph K., 2003), vol. 2, p. 328.

65 Marty, *Roland Barthes, le métier d'écrire*, p. 74.

66 Dominique de Roux, *Immédiatement* (Paris: La Table ronde, 'La Petite

Vermillon', 1995), p. 189. The book was first published by Bourgois in 1972 and the first, uncensored edition by L'âge d'homme in 1980.

67 See René Pommier, *Assez décodé!* (Paris: Roblot, 1978); Michel-Antoine Burnier and Patrick Rambaud, *Le Roland Barthes sans peine (parodie)* (Paris: Balland, 1978).

Chapter 15   Legitimacy

1 The text can be found as 'Outcomes of the Text', in *The Rustle of Language*, translated by Richard Howard (Oxford: Basil Blackwell, 1986), pp. 238–249.

2 *Le Lexique de l'auteur, Séminaire à l'École pratique des hautes études, 1973–1974*, edited by Anne Herschberg Pierrot (Paris: Seuil, 2010), session of 30 May 1974, 'Le Glossaire: quelques remarques finales', pp. 217–219.

3 *Prétexte: Roland Barthes*, proceedings of the colloque de Cerisy, 22–29 June 1977, edited by Antoine Compagnon (Paris: Christian Bourgois, 2003), p. 116.

4 *Le Lexique de l'auteur*, p. 66.

5 Patrick Mauriès, 'Fragments d'une vie', in *Critique*, nos. 423–424, August-September 1982, p. 753.

6 Éric Marty, *Roland Barthes, le métier d'écrire* (Paris: Seuil, Fiction & Cie, 2006), p. 24.

7 'L'invité du lundi'; 'Les après-midi de France Culture' (1976). Those taking part in the seminar were: Évelyne Bachellier, Jean-Louis Bachellier, Jean-Louis Bouttes, Antoine Compagnon, Roland Havas and Romaric Sulger-Büel.

8 *Prétexte: Rolland Barthes*, p. 115.

9 Mauriès, 'Fragments d'une vie', p . 755.

10 A game rather similar to Pass the Slipper. (Trans. note.)

11 Marty, *Roland Barthes, le métier d'écrire*, p. 37.

12 *Prétexte: Roland Barthes*, p. 118.

13 Colette Fellous, *La Préparation de la vie* (Paris: Gallimard, 2014), p. 43.

14 Marty, *Roland Barthes, le métier d'écrire*, p. 41.

15 'To the Seminar', in *The Rustle of Language*, pp. 332–342 (p. 341).

16 'To the Seminar', p. 30.

17 This report, like the rest of the information in this paragraph, is drawn from the archives: 'Reports on thesis viva examinations', BRT2 A10 04.

18 *Gramma*, no. 7, 1977 (*OC* V, pp. 335–339). Barthes's text would be reprinted as the preface to Finas's *Bruit d'Iris* (Paris: Flammarion, 1978).

19 Jacques Le Goff, 'Barthes administrateur', in *Communications*, no. 36, 1982, p. 46.

20 See Didier Éribon's account in *Michel Foucault et ses contemporains* (Paris: Fayard, 1994), pp. 217–229.

21 BNF, NAF 28630, 'Formulaires, lettres administratives et comptes rendus', folder on 'Collège de France'.

22 'Rapport de Michel Foucault pour proposer la création d'une chaire de

sémiologie littéraire', meeting at the Collège de France, 30 November 1975. Unpublished document.

23 'Rapport de Michel Foucault pour la présentation des candidats à la chaire intitulée sémiologie littéraire', unpublished text quoted in Éribon, *Michel Foucault et ses contemporains*, p. 229.

24 BNF, NAF 28630, 'Grand fichier', 1 and 2 December 1975.

25 The series published by Éditions du Seuil in which *Roland Barthes by Roland Barthes* appeared is called 'Les Écrivains de toujours', a (very) slightly less grand claim than the English equivalent 'Writers of all time'. (Trans. note.)

26 The French original, part of the same series, bore the title *Michelet par lui-même* (*Michelet, by himself*). (Trans. note.)

27 Montaigne, *Essays*, translated by M. A. Screech (London: Allen Lane, 1991), p. 308.

28 Montaigne, *Essays*.

29 *Roland Barthes by Roland Barthes*, translated by Richard Howard (London: Macmillan, 1977), p. 148. Barthes plays many games with the alphabet.

30 'Situation', in *Sollers Writer*, translated by Philip Thody (London: The Athlone Press, 1987), pp. 93–95 (p. 93).

31 *Roland Barthes by Roland Barthes*, p. 148.

32 'Proust and Names', in *New Critical Essays*, translated by Richard Howard (New York: Hill & Wang, 1980), pp. 55–68 (p. 57), first published in *To Honour Roman Jakobson* (The Hague: Mouton, 1967).

33 'Proust and Names', p. 58, translation modified.

34 *Prétexte: Roland Barthes*, p. 281.

35 'Twenty Key Words for Roland Barthes', in *The Grain of the Voice: Interviews 1962–1980*, translated by Linda Coverdale (Evanston, IL: Northwestern University Press, 2009), pp. 205–232 (p. 215).

36 *Roland Barthes by Roland Barthes*, p. 51.

37 *Roland Barthes by Roland Barthes*, pp. 168, 119.

38 *Roland Barthes by Roland Barthes*, p. 120.

39 *Le Lexique de l'auteur*, p. 91.

40 Here is the description of the 'Fichier vert', which derives its name from the fact that the titles of the rubrics are written in green ink. BNF, NAF 28630: 'Fichier vert 1: Books, selected passages', 363 index cards; 'Fichier vert 2: Fragments completed', 501 cards; 'Fichier vert 3: Fragments completed (continued)', 300 cards; 'Fichier vert 4: Cards not used', 325 cards; 'Fichier vert 5: Discarded and/or for revision', 300 cards; 'Fichier vert 6: Discarded and/or for revision (continued to end), 300 cards. There is also a *fichier* on photography and a *fichier* entitled 'Notes without a date', some 200 cards that are 'incidents' and notes drawn from the Urt diary in the summer of 1973 or the 'harvest diary' kept by Barthes throughout the time he was writing the book, in Paris, from autumn 1973 to spring 1974.

41 BNF, NAF 28630, 'Fichier vert 5'.

42 *Le Lexique de l'auteur*, p. 101.

43 All these index cards are taken from the 'Fichier vert 5' and the 'Ficher vert 6'.

44 BNF, NAF 28630, 'Fichier vert'. These fragments are published in the annexes of the *Lexique d'auteur*.
45 *Roland Barthes by Roland Barthes*, p. 129.
46 *Roland Barthes by Roland Barthes*, p. 96.
47 *Roland Barthes by Roland Barthes*, p. 119.
48 *Roland Barthes by Roland Barthes*, p. 142.
49 *Roland Barthes by Roland Barthes*, p. 145.
50 *Roland Barthes by Roland Barthes*, p 43.
51 *Le Lexique de l'auteur*, p. 381.
52 BNF, NAF 28630. '*Roland Barthes par Roland Barthes*'.
53 'Barthes puissance trois', in *La Quinzaine littéraire*, 1 March 1975 (*OC* IV, p. 777).
54 Interview with Jacques Chancel, 'Radioscopie', France Inter, 17 February 1975 (*OC* IV, p. 899).
55 'Conclusions', in *Prétexte: Roland Barthes*, p. 487 (*OC* V, p. 520).
56 Letter to Édith Heurgon, January 1973. BNF, NAF 28630. 'Exploitation de l'oeuvre.'
57 Antoine Compagnon, *Une Question de discipline*, conversations with Jean-Baptise Amadieu (Paris: Flammarion, 2013), p. 78.
58 *Prétexte: Roland Barthes*, p. 274.
59 *Prétexte: Roland Barthes*, p. 283.
60 *Prétexte: Roland Barthes*, pp. 278–279.

Chapter 16   Barthes and Foucault

1 Antoine Compagnon, ed., *Prétexte: Roland Barthes* (Paris: Christian Bourgois, Actes du Colloque de Cerisy-la-Salle, 2003), p. 298.
2 BNF, NAF 28630, 'Grand fichier', 31 July 1979.
3 In Althusser's *Lettres à Franca (1961–1973)* (Paris: Stock/IMEC, 1998), we read of two dinners at which Foucault, Barthes and Althusser were all present on 6 October and 12 November 1962 (Stock/IMEC, 1998), pp. 229, 284.
4 Barthes, Deguy and Foucault were the sole members of the editorial committee until 1965 when they were joined by Pierre Charpentrat. Derrida joined them in 1967, Roger Errera in 1968 and Michel Serres in 1969. Foucault officially left the committee in 1977, but he had not published an article in the review since 1970.
5 Daniel Defert, *Une Vie politique, conversations with Philippe Artières and Éric Favereau* (Paris: Seuil, 2014), p. 32.
6 In the 'Chronology' of Foucault's life that he provides at the beginning of the latter's *Dits et écrits*, Defert notes soberly, under 'October 1963': 'Intense work breaks the rhythm of the nightly dinners with Roland Barthes in Saint-Germain-des-Prés. Their relationship wanes': Michel Foucault, *Dits et écrits* (Paris: Gallimard, 1994, vol. 1), p. 25.
7 Letter from Michel Foucault, 28 February 1970. Fonds Roland Barthes, BNF, NAF 28630, 'S/Z'.
8 Michel Foucault, 'Radioscopie', interview with Jacques Chancel, France Inter, 10 March 1975.

9 Michel Foucault, 'Pour en finir avec les mensonges', in *Le Nouvel Observateur*, 21 June 1985, pp. 76–77.
10 'Taking sides', in *Critical Essays*, translated by Richard Howard (Evanston, IL: Northwestern University Press, 1972), pp. 163–170 (p. 164).
11 'Taking sides', p. 168.
12 'Taking sides', p. 168. See also 'I don't believe in influences', in *The Grain of the Voice: Interviews 1962–1980*, translated by Linda Coverdale (Evanston, IL: Northwestern University Press, 2009), pp. 25–29, and 'Mass Culture, High Culture' in '*A Very Fine Gift' and Other Writings on Theory: Essays and Interviews*, translated by Chris Turner (London: Seagull Books, 2015), pp. 45–51 (p. 45).
13 'Semiology and Medicine', in *The Semiotic Challenge*, translated by Richard Howard (Oxford: Blackwell, 1988), pp. 202–213 (p. 212).
14 *Sade, Fourier, Loyola*, translated by Richard Miller (London: Cape, 1977), p. 126 (translation modified). On this, see Éric Marty, *Pourquoi le XXe siècle a-t-il pris Sade au sérieux?* (Paris: Seuil, 'Fiction & Cie', 2011), p. 164.
15 'Barthes sur scène', in *L'Express*, 17 April 1978 (OC V, p. 545).
16 Michel Foucault, 'Voici, en bien peu de temps . . .', in *Annuaire du Collège de France*, 1980, pp. 61–62.
17 'Inaugural Lecture, Collège de France', in *A Barthes Reader*, edited by Susan Sontag (London: Cape, 1982), pp. 457–478 (p. 458).
18 Maurice Pinguet, *Le Texte Japon* (Paris: Seuil, 2009), p. 47.
19 Hervé Guibert, interview with Didier Éribon, in *Le Nouvel Observateur*, 18–24 July 1991.
20 'Fragments pour H.', letter to Hervé Guibert, 10 December 1977, in *L'Autre Journal*, 19 March 1986 (OC, p. 1006).
21 Mathieu Lindon, *Ce qu'aimer veut dire* (Paris: POL, 2011), p. 240.
22 *Ce qu'aimer veut dire*, p. 241.
23 Michel Foucault, *L'Ordre du discours* (Paris: Gallimard, 1971), p. 47. See also the English translation: 'Foucault, "The Order of Discourse"', translated by Ian McLeod, in *Untying the Text: A Post-Structuralist Reader*, edited by Robert Young (London: Routledge and Kegan Paul, 1981), pp. 51–76 (p. 52).
24 Barthes, 'Inaugural Lecture', p. 476.
25 Foucault, *L'Ordre du discours*, p. 47.
26 'Inaugural Lecture', p. 460.
27 'Inaugural Lecture', p. 461.
28 Éric Marty, 'Présentation' (OC V, p. 15).
29 This is the view of Jean-Marc Mandosio, 'Naissance d'un stéréotype: "la langue est fasciste" (Roland Barthes)', in *NRF*, no. 589, April 2009, p. 91. For a detailed discussion of Barthes's statement, see Hélène Merlin, *La Langue est-elle fasciste? Langue, pouvoir, enseignement* (Paris: Seuil, 2003).
30 'Inaugural Lecture', p. 462.
31 'Inaugural Lecture'.
32 'Inaugural Lecture', p. 458.
33 *Une Parole inquiète* (An unquiet speech) is the title of Guillaume

Bellon's study comparing the courses given by Barthes and Foucault
at the Collège de France (Grenoble: Ellug, 2012).
34 *The Preparation of the Novel: Lecture Courses and Seminars at the
Collège de France (1978–1979 and 1979–1980)*, translated by Kate
Briggs (New York: Columbia University Press, 2010), p. 7.

Chapter 17   Heartbreak

1 'Inaugural Lecture, Collège de France', in *A Barthes Reader*, edited
by Susan Sontag (London: Cape, 1982), pp. 476–477 (translation
modified).
2 'I explained to the mother that her son dreaded the separation he was
attempting to deny by pulling on the string, just as we deny our separation from a friend by resorting to the telephone' (D. W. Winnicott,
Playing and Reality, quoted in *A Lover's Discourse: fragments*, translated by Richard Howard (London: Vintage, 2002), p. 115).
3 'Inaugural Lecture', p. 477.
4 'Portrait du sémiologue en artiste', in *Le Monde*, 9–10 January 1977.
5 Witness a note addressed to Frédéric Berthet: 'Frédéric, after the
lecture, try and come to a nice little gathering at a friend's house,
Youssef Baccouche, 7 rue Nicolas Hoël [*sic*], lift A3, 8th on left – from
8 pm' (private archive).
6 *A Lover's Discourse*, pp. 82–83.
7 Estène was at this time the grand master of gay festivities and the
whole Riviera jet set. He has described part of this unbridled and brilliant existence in a *roman à clef* that he published as *L'Écart* under the
pseudonym of Rémi Santerre.
8 Nine manuscript pages by Hubert Ricard on Lacan, BNF, NAF
28630, 'Fragments d'un discours amoureux'.
9 Élisabeth Roudinesco, *Jacques Lacan*, translated by Barbara Bray
(Cambridge: Polity, 1997), p. 397.
10 They met at the restaurant La Calèche before Barthes left for China;
and they also attended the same private screening of Oshima's *Empire
of the Senses* on 13 February 1976.
11 *A Lover's Discourse*, p. 2.
12 Interview with Jacques Henric, in *Art Press*, May 1977 (*OC* V, p. 403).
13 'Leaving the Movie Theater', in *The Rustle of Language*, translated
by Richard Howard (Oxford: Basil Blackwell, 1986), pp. 345–349
(p. 348).
14 'To Learn and to Teach', in *The Rustle of Language*, pp. 176–178;
'Listening', in *The Responsibility of Forms: Critical Essays on Music,
Art, and Representation*, translated by Richard Howard (New York:
Hill and Wang, 1985), pp. 245–260. This latter essay, originally an
article in the *Encyclopédie Einaudi*, was written in collaboration with
Roland Havas in 1975.
15 *A Lover's Discourse*, p. 178.
16 'Paradox as pleasure', in *Roland Barthes by Roland Barthes*, translated
by Richard Howard (London: Macmillan, 1977), p. 112.
17 *A Lover's Discourse*, p. 121.

18 *A Lover's Discourse*, p. 67.
19 Letter from Évelyne Bachellier, [April] 1977. BNF, NAF 28630, 'Fragments d'un discours amoureux'.
20 Letter from Philoppe Sollers, 18 December 1976. BNF, NAF 28630, 'Fragments d'un discours amoureux'.
21 Letter from Philippe Rebeyrol, 1 May 1977. Fonds Philippe Rebeyrol, IMEC.
22 Letter from Georges Poulot [Georges Perros], April 1977. BNF, NAF 28630, 'Fragments d'un discours amoureux'.
23 The French pronoun '*il*' sometimes designates the loved object of whatever sex ('*objet*' is masculine), but sometimes refers to a masculine character.
24 *Roland Barthes by Roland Barthes*, p. 86.
25 *A Lover's Discourse*, pp. 45-7.
26 In his course, Barthes makes a parenthetical remark: 'There would not be any families at all if some of them were not successful!' *How to Live Together: Novelistic Simulations of some Everyday Spaces. Notes for a Lecture Course at the Collège de France (1976–1977)*, translated by Kate Briggs, edited by Claude Coste (New York: Columbia University Press, 2013), p. 11; translation modified.
27 *How to Live Together*, p. 12.
28 *How to Live Together*, p. 13.
29 *How to Live Together*, p. 45.
30 'La cathédrale des romans', in *Bulletin de la Guilde du livre*, March 1957 (*OC* I, pp. 873–876).
31 'Avignon, l'hiver', in *France Observateur* (*OC* I, p. 473).
32 'Folies-Bergère', in *Esprit*, February 1953 [not included in *Mythologies*] (*OC* I, pp. 234–244).
33 *How to Live Together*, p. 131.
34 *How to Live Together*, p. 129; translation modified.
35 'Sur des photographies de Daniel Boudinet', in *Créatis*, 1977 (*OC* V, p. 327).
36 *The Preparation of the Novel: Lecture Courses and Seminars at the Collègege de France (1978–1979 and 1979–1980)*, translated by Kate Briggs (New York: Columbia University Press, 2010), p. 41. The recording of the course indicates that Barthes did not make this remark aloud.
37 Éric Marty, *Roland Barthes, le métier d'écrire* (Paris: Seuil, 'Fiction & Cie', 2006), p. 64.
38 Marty, *Roland Barthes, le métier d'écrire*, p. 65.
39 *Mourning Diary: October 26, 1977 – September 15, 1979*, edited by Nathalie Léger; translated by Richard Howard (New York: Hill and Wang, 2010), p. 5.
40 *Mourning Diary*, p. 36.
41 The apocope, the dropping of the last syllable *–an*, became general in the notes he made at this time, though it had been much less systematic previously, when Barthes wrote '*maman*' as often as '*mam.*' But we should avoid fetishizing this '*mam.*', even though some critics have done so ever since the publication of the *Mourning Diary*. Of course, the abbreviation does intimate incompleteness and separation; but it

is also part of the common system of abbreviations in the index card diary (M. for Michel, R. for Roland, JLB for Jean-Louis Bouttes, etc.). In particular, Barthes did not call his mother '*mam.*' but '*maman*'.

42 *Mourning Diary*, p. 204.

43 *Mourning Diary*, p. 15.

44 BNF, NAF 28630, 'Grand fichier', 22 August 1978.

45 In *Thrène* by Boucourechliev, which he recorded in 1974, Barthes spoke some phrases from *Pour un tombeau d'Anatole*, by Mallarmé, on the death of his child.

46 *Mourning Diary*, p. 56.

47 *Mourning Diary*, p. 4.

48 Marguerite Duras, *La Passion suspendue, entretiens avec Leopoldina Pallotta della Torre*, translated from the Italian by René de Ceccatty (Paris: Seuil, 2013), p. 141. There are similar remarks in *Practicalities*: 'A writer who has never known women, has never touched a woman's body [. . .] and yet thinks he's been involved in literature, is mistaken'; such a man cannot be 'an intellectual leader' (Marguerite Duras, *Practicalities: Marguerite Duras speaks to Jérôme Beaujour*, translated by Barbara Bray (London: Flamingo, 1991), p. 36). After Barthes's death, and after her own encounter with Yann Andréa, Duras could say some very harsh things. In a text that is simultaneously unfair and startling, she refers to his 'falseness': 'You mentioned Roland Barthes. I reminded you how I felt about him. I said I would give all of Roland Barthes' books for my tea roads in the Burmese forests, the red sun, and the dead children of the beggar women along the Ganges. You already knew this. I also said that I could never bring myself to read him, that for me Roland Barthes was false writing and that falseness was what had killed him' (Marguerite Duras, *Yann Andréa Steiner*, translated by Barbara Bray, new edition (London: Sceptre, 1995), p. 19). She warned Yann Andréa against the fascination that Barthes had or might once have had for him. She was probably aware of the brief relationship Barthes and Steiner had in 1977.

49 Éric Marty, *Roland Barthes, la literature et le droit à la mort* (Paris: Seuil, 2010), p. 33.

50 *Mourning Diary*, p. 71.

51 Quoted in *Mourning Diary*, p. 170.

52 *Mourning Diary*, p. 28.

53 *Mourning Diary*, p. 124.

54 *Le Neutre: notes de cours au Collège de France, 1977–1978*, edited by Thomas Clerc (Paris: Seuil/IMEC, 2002), pp. 170–176; *Sollers écrivain* (*OC* V, pp. 619–620).

55 *Le Neutre*, pp. 174, 39–40.

56 *Mourning Diary*, p. 128.

57 Marty, *Barthes, le métier d'écrire*, p. 74.

58 'Horrible figure of mourning: acedia, hard-heartedness: irritability, impotence to love. Anguished because I don't know how to restore generosity to my life – or love. How to love?' (*Mourning Diary*, p. 178).

59 *Mourning Diary*, p. 176; see also the variations on this same theme, pp. 190, 193.

60 BNF, NAF 28630, 'Grand fichier'.
61 *Mourning Diary*, 18 July 1978, p. 161.
62 *Mourning Diary*, 29 March 1979, p. 234.

Chapter 18 'Vita Nova'

1 *The Preparation of the Novel: Lecture Courses and Seminars at the Collège de France (1978–1979 and 1979–1980)*, translated by Kate Briggs (New York: Columbia University Press, 2010), p. 8.
2 *Mourning Diary: October 26, 1977 – September 15, 1979*, edited by Nathalie Léger; translated by Richard Howard (New York: Hill and Wang, 2010), p. 216.
3 Proust's *In Search of Lost Time*. (Trans. note.)
4 Tolstoy's *War and Peace*. (Trans. note.)
5 BNF, NAF 28630, 'Grand fichier', 20 July 1979.
6 Antoine Compagnon relates this episode in *Une Question de discipline*, saying that he himself discouraged publication; Éric Marty, in *Roland Barthes, le métier d'écrire* (Paris: Seuil, 'Fiction & Cie', 2006), says that he gave Barthes a positive response after reading the work; Renaud Camus, Jean-Louis Bouttes, François Wahl and many friends read it but Barthes finally decided against publication.
7 *The Preparation of the Novel*, p. 179.
8 *The Preparation of the Novel*, p. 186.
9 Barthes refers to Cage's words in *For the Birds* in *The Preparation of the Novel*, p. 653, n. 2.
10 *The Preparation of the Novel*, p. 144.
11 BNF, NAF 28630, 'Grand fichier'.
12 'Transcription de Vita Nova' (*OC* V, pp. 1010, 1008).
13 *The Preparation of the Novel*, pp. 143–4.
14 The notes assembled after Pascal's death under the title of *Pensées* (*Thoughts*) were destined to comprise an 'Apology for the Christian Religion'. The relation between the index cards and Barthes's diary notes on the one hand and the 'Vita Nova' on the other is similar to that between Pascal's 'Thoughts' and his 'Apology'.
15 Barthes's attention to this term may have been drawn by the recent publication, at that time, of the *Theories of the Symbol* by Tzvetan Todorov, which mentions the intertextual theory of Clement of Alexandria. When Barthes re-read Chateaubriand's *Memoirs from Beyond the Grave*, at the beginning of September 1979 (he refers to it several times in the course of the 'Soirées de Paris'), it was doubtless in response to this suggestion. One of Barthes's last interviews confirms this: in December 1979, he told Jean-Paul Enthoven that he had started to read the *Memoirs from Beyond the Grave* properly a few months earlier, and was 'astounded'; 'For a Chateaubriand of Paper', in *The Grain of the Voice: Interviews 1962–1980*, translated by Linda Coverdale (Evanston, IL: Northwestern University Press, 2009), pp. 346–350 (p. 346). See also Agnès Verlet, *Les Vanités de Chateaubriand* (Paris: Droz, 2001), pp. 81–92.

16 *Roland Barthes by Roland Barthes*, translated by Richard Howard (London: Macmillan, 1977), p. 45, p. 105.

17 BNF, NAF 28630, 'Grand fichier', 21 July 1979.

18 BNF, NAF 28630, 'Grand fichier', 10, 14, 18 July 1979; 30 November 1979.

19 BNF, NAF 28630, 'Grand fichier', 13 July 1979.

20 BNF, NAF 28630, 'Grand fichier', 10, 14, 18 July 1979; 30 November 1979.

21 'Longtemps, je me suis couché de bonne heure . . .', in *The Rustle of Language*, translated by Richard Howard (Oxford: Basil Blackwell, 1986), pp. 277–290 (p. 288).

22 Marty, *Roland Barthes, le métier d'écrire*, p. 65.

23 Marty, *Roland Barthes, le métier d'écrire*, p. 66.

24 Gérard Genette, *Bardadrac* (Paris: Seuil, 2006), p. 386.

25 Antoine Compagnon, *Les Antimodernes, de Joseph de Maistre à Rolande Barthes* (Paris: Gallimard, pp. 436–440).

26 His desk diary dated 8 August 1977 notes: 'Finished [reading] *War and Peace* before the end. All of a sudden I'd had enough.' In *The Preparation of the Novel*, Barthes admitted that he preferred Tolstoy's *Notebooks* to his novels (p. 208).

27 Marcel Proust, *The Guermantes Way*, translated by Mark Treharne (London: Allen Lane, 2002), p. 659.

28 BNF, NAF 28630, 'Grand fichier', 14 July 1978.

29 *Incidents*, translated by Richard Howard (Berkeley, Los Angeles and Oxford: University of California Press, 1992), p. 34.

30 Flaubert's *Dictionary of Received Ideas* places it as one of the stereotypes of literary criticism: 'PATHOS: Lambast it, rise in rebellion, declare haughtily that real literature has no room for it. Congratulate an author for having been able, in his novel, to avoid the reefs of pathos. Write: it is a fine, serious book. Add immediately: but without pathos.'

31 'Longtemps, je me suis couché de bonne heure . . .', p. 288.

32 For example: 'I'm giving up the idea of the novel' (12 July 1979); 'It's going better. I'm refloating the idea of the Vita Nova' (19 July); 'Can't make any progress with Vita Nova' (21 July); 'Perhaps the real beginning of work X (Vita Nova); integration of the index cards on various projects into this single project' (17 August), etc.

33 BNF, NAF 28630, 'Incidents', folder 3, 'Apologie'.

34 'Longtemps, je me suis couché de bonne heure . . .', p. 285.

35 'Longtemps, je me suis couché de bonne heure . . .', p. 286. See also the first session of the course on *The Preparation of the Novel*, pp. 3–8.

36 Genette, *Bardadrac*, p. 386.

37 See the homage Barthes paid him in a note on Le Palace published in *Le Quotiden de Paris*, 31 December 1979 (*OC* V, p. 773): 'Fabrice is an artist because he has the intelligence of what he does: intelligence, or, ultimately, the art of thinking of others.'

38 BNF, NAF 28630, 'Grand fichier', 23 November 1975.

39 'Preface to Renaud Camus's Tricks', in *The Rustle of Language*, pp. 291–295 (p. 293).

40 BNF, NAF 28630, 'Grand fichier', 7 May 1978.

41 Barthes, 'How to Spend a Week in Paris: 8–14 October 1979', in

On Signs, edited by Marshall Blonsky (Oxford: Blackwell, 1985), pp. 118–121 (p. 118).

42 '*Puer senilis, senex puerilis*' (extracts from the course on 'The lover's discourse', *NDLR*, November 1978 (*OC* V, pp. 481–483).

43 *OC* V, p. 636.

44 'Rencontre avec Roland Barthes', conversation with Nadine Dormoy Savage, in *The French Review*, February 1979 (*OC* V, p. 735).

45 'Of what use is an intellectual?' in *The Grain of the Voice*, pp. 258–280.

46 Letter to Bernard-Henry Lévy, in *Les Nouvelles littéraires*, 26 May 1977 (*OC* V, p. 315).

47 BNF, NAF 28630, 'Grand fichier', 'Linguistique, St Simon, Brecht, Zavriev', 2 January 1980.

48 'Flaubert and the Sentence', in *New Critical Essays*, translated by Richard Howard (New York: Hill & Wang, 1980), pp. 69–78 (p. 70). The noun 'marinade' is not found in Flaubert, but we encounter the verb 'mariner' in a letter to Ernest Chevalier on 12 August 1846: 'I work, I read, I do a bit of Greek, I ruminate on Virgil or Horace, I wallow on a green morocco sofa that I recently had made for me. Destined to marinade on the spot, I have my bowl decorated the way I like and I live in it like a day-dreaming oyster' (Gustave Flaubert, *Correspondance*, edited by Jean Bruneau (Paris: Gallimard, Pléiade, 1973, vol. I, p. 293).

49 'From Taste to Ecstasy', in *The Grain of the Voice*, pp. 351–352 (p. 352).

50 Jacques Derrida, 'The deaths of Roland Barthes', in *Psyche*, vol. 1, pp. 264–298 (p. 265).

51 See this fascinating note in the index card diary: '12 November 1979: On this, my birthday, I have made the same mistake ten times over while writing: in adjectives and past participles, I've put myself in the feminine: *je suis déso*lée, *etc.*'.

52 *The Neutral: Lecture Course at the Collège de France, 1977–1978*, translated by Rosalind E. Krauss and Denis Hollier; edited by Thomas Clerc under the direction of Éric Marty (New York and Chichester: Columbia University Press, 2005), p. 66.

53 Her book, *Susan Sontag on Photography* (London: Allen Lane, 1978), did indeed come out in a French translation published by Bourgois in 1982.

54 *Mourning Diary: October 26 1977 – September 15, 1979*, edited by Nathalie Léger; translated by Richard Howard (New York: Hill and Wang, 2010), p. 220.

55 *Camera Lucida: Reflections on Photography*, translated by Richard Howard (London: Vintage, 1993), p. 6.

56 The absence of emotion he felt at the exhibition of 'Photos-chocs' at the Galerie d'Orsay stemmed from the fact that the photographer and his intentions were too intrusive in the photograph: 'The photographer has stood in for us too generously in the formation of his subject'; 'Photos-chocs', in *Mythologies* (*OC* I, p. 752).

57 *Camera Lucida*, p. 60.

58 *Camera Lucida*, p. 72.

59 'So there seems to be, in *Camera Lucida*, a "chemical fiction" as it

were, balancing the painful, absolute sense of death by the belief or
(very beautiful) hope of a possible resurrection, there, in the rebound
of the photo'; Bernard Comment, *Roland Barthes, vers le neutre*
(Paris: Christian Bourgois, 1999), p. 127. In December 1979, Barthes
took part in Lucien Clergue's thesis defence in photography at the
University of Aix-Marseille: the laboratory in which the viva took
place belonged to the department of chemistry.

60 *Camera Lucida*, pp. 80–81; translation modified.
61 *Camera Lucida*, pp. 116–117.
62 Letter from Julia Kristeva, 16 February 1980. BNF, NAF 28630.
63 Letter from Marthe Robert, 22 February 1980. Private collection.

Image credits

Index